Birds of Europe

TEXT BY LARS SVENSSON
AND PETER J. GRANT

ILLUSTRATIONS BY KILLIAN MULLARNEY
AND DAN ZETTERSTRÖM

Translated by David Christie

Princeton University Press
Princeton, New Jersey

Published in North America by Princeton University Press,
41 William Street, Princeton, New Jersey 08540

In the United Kingdom, published by
HarperCollins*Publishers* Ltd
77–85 Fulham Palace Road
London
W6 8JB

Originally published in 1999 in Swedish, *Fågelguiden. Europas och
Medelhavsområdets fåglar i fält*, by Bonniers, Stockholm

Translation and English adaptation David A. Christie & Lars Svensson

Copyright © 1999 Lars Svensson (text and maps), Peter J. Grant (text),
Killian Mullarney and Dan Zetterström (illustrations)

3 5 7 9 8 6 4 2

Library of Congress Catalog Card Number 99-067747

ISBN 0-691-05053-8
ISBN 0-691-05054-6 (pbk.)

The plates on pp. 363 and 365 are painted by Larry McQueen

Reproduction: Colorgrafic, Milano
Printing: Printer, Trento
Printed in Italy 2004.

Princeton Field Guides

Rooted in field experience and scientific study, Princeton's guides to animals and plants are the
authority for professional scientists and amateur naturalists alike. **Princeton Field Guides** present
this information in a compact format carefully designed for easy use in the field. The guides illustrate
every species in color and provide detailed information on identification, distribution, and biology.

Coral Reef Fishes, by Ewald Lieske and Robert Myers
Birds of Kenya and Northern Tanzania: Field Guide Edition, by Dale A. Zimmerman,
  Donald A. Turner, and David J. Pearson
Birds of India, Pakistan, Nepal, Bangladesh, Bhutan, Sri Lanka, and the Maldives, by
  Richard Grimmett, Carol Inskipp, and Tim Inskipp
Birds of Australia, by Ken Simpson and Nicolas Day
Birds of Europe, by Killian Mullarney, Lars Svensson, Dan Zetterström, and Peter J. Grant

Princeton University Press
http://pup.princeton.edu

Contents

The making of a book

Books come about in different ways, some easily and others slowly. This one took a long, long time and much labour to complete. Some of the background to this should be outlined.

An old dream to create 'the perfect field guide' was revived one August day in 1982 in Skanör in south Sweden when meeting Peter J. Grant and Killian Mullarney. Peter was then already an established and respected ornithologist, Killian a young new bird artist of unusual talent. After some time I managed to persuade them both to join with me and set about producing a new field guide to the birds of Europe and adjacent areas. Two publishers, Bonniers in Sweden and Collins in England, supported our efforts from the start.

The road to completion has been enjoyable and inspiring but also hard and laborious, and we have suffered some tragic losses. Peter Grant's untimely death in 1990 was a severe blow. Killian and I lost a dear friend, and the book project a key participant. At the time of his death, Peter had written drafts of the text only for loons, grebes, seabirds, waders and gulls, but he made a significant and lasting contribution in the planning stage and through the long and stimulating discussions the three of us had about how best to arrange and design the book. My own at times casual approach benefited from Peter's exactitude and striving for consistency and logic. Killian and I are happy to have brought the project finally to its completion and are especially pleased that it also carries his name.

It became apparent after some time that the task of painting all the plates was too great for one artist alone, and we were very pleased when in 1991 Dan Zetterström, one of the foremost bird artists in the world, agreed to join the team. His participation was crucial, giving the project a new lease of life at a time when it was most needed.

Apart from Peter, we also lost two publishers who had supported us in spite of the trying and costly delays on our part. Crispin Fisher at Collins drew up the first agreements and participated in the early meetings when the book was planned. He died in 1989, held in grateful memory.

Ebbe Carlsson, publisher of the then Bonnier Fakta, gave us his support in our time-consuming struggle for perfection. At a critical point, with Collins withdrawing from financing the project, and even facing a possible closure, Ebbe came like an angel to the rescue. Bonniers went in as sole publishers, and new resources were provided. Ebbe Carlsson died in 1992. Killian, Dan and I remember him with warmth and deep gratitude.

What originally was expected to take three or four years to complete has taken more than fifteen—a substantial part of our adult life!

L.S.

Preface

This book is intended to facilitate the identification of birds througout Europe, from the Urals to the Atlantic and from Scandinavia to the Middle East.

It has been prepared with close collaboration between authors and artists. Thus, the authors have commented on the plates, from initial design and sketch to finished painting, and the artists have critically read the draft text pages and proposed additions based on their personal observations. It has been a most fruitful teamwork with the aim to achieve the best possible aid to bird identification in the field. Nonetheless, authors have of course written the text and artists painted the plates, and they take full responsibility for their own respective domain.

The project took a long time to complete. Knowledge of birds in our part of the World grows quickly, and new discoveries and findings are published all the time, not least on how best to separate similar species. We wanted our book to reflect all these advances. However, most of our knowledge is self-taught, and such learning takes time. We have visited most of the countries within the treated region, and with the odd exception we have managed to see and study all breeding species and also a majority of the regular or rare visitors described in the book.

Right from the start, we decided to limit the book to 400 pages, because we believe that, not much above that size, a book becomes cumbersome to carry in one's pocket or hand luggage. Still, we wanted to include not only all the bird species found in Europe but also those in North Africa and much of the Middle East. And plates and text were to deal not only with essentials but also with variations in age and sex, with variants and geographical variation. Range maps should be right next to the species account and plate for quick and easy reference. To squeeze all this into 400 pages required the type size to be small and the bird images on the plates not so large as in some other books. We are aware of the potential inconveniences this may cause to some, but still think that the advantage of having a wealth of information in a small package is greater.

We have also set out to arrange text and plates in a pedagogic way. Ideally, both beginners and more experienced birdwatchers should be able to use the book. For instance, for as many species as possible we have tried to include, apart from the main pictures, small-scale illustrations showing typical habitat and what the birds look like when far away and when seen in poor light, in other words how you so often see birds in real life. We have also added pointers and brief captions on the plates in order to promote active reading when looking at the plates and, to some extent, bridge the difference between written descriptions and pictures.

Killian Mullarney and Dan Zetterström account each for about half of the plates in the book. Who painted which is indicated with initials at the bottom of each plate. The artwork in the introduction and in the vagrants section has been done by Dan Zetterström. The American artist Larry McQueen was commissioned to paint the American passerines on pp. 362–365 to ensure best possible quality.

The text puts emphasis on identification, dealing mainly with appearance and voice. Virtually all plumages are described which can be separated in the field (i.e. without examination in the hand); in addition, some characteristic subspecies are dealt with, too. Whenever space permits, behaviour and general biology are hinted at: for instance, breeding biology and migratory habits are often useful clues when encountering an unfamiliar bird. *Italics* indicate that a certain character described in the text is particularly significant.

The vocal renderings have been given rather ample space; many people are helped—not denying the general difficulties of the method—by the comparison of a heard call with a written description to see if this further supports any visual impression. And not all birds are at all so easily seen.

Acknowledgements

Many have helped us during the many years of work; without unselfish friends we could not have produced the book. We cannot list them all, but a few must be mentioned.

All three of us have in one way or another received help and good advice from Per Alström, Dick Forsman, Lars Jonsson, Hannu Jännes, Urban Olsson and Hadoram Shirihai. A hearty thanks to them all.

Paul Doherty, Dave McAdams, Anthony McGeehan and Colm Moore assisted K.M. with good advice and picture references. Bill Zetterström and Göran Ekström helped D.Z. in a corresponding way. We are very grateful for this.

L.S. wishes to give credit to Håkan Delin, who indirectly has contributed much to the quality of the text through his deep knowledge and sound judgement, which have rubbed off during countless discussions over the years on mutual excursions and expeditions. Thanks also to David A. Christie, who provided useful comments on the text, and to Carl Edelstam for valuable advice.

Krister Mild, Richard Ranft and Olga Veprintseva gave advice and help regarding calls and recordings. Krister Mild helped in other ways, too.

David Noakes obligingly sent his unique collection of wingspan measurements taken from live and freshly killed birds. Similar measurements have also been provided by Anders Hansson and Peter Mortensen, taxidermists at the Naturhistoriska Riksmuseet, Stockholm.

Göran Frisk at the Naturhistoriska Riksmuseet, Stockholm, and Peter Colston, formerly at the British Museum (Nat. Hist.), Tring, assisted in connection with the study of skins. Mark Beaman is thanked for fruitful discussions about taxonomy and nomenclature. Ante Strand helped with sought-after or overlooked references.

Last but not least, we thank our severely tried relatives and friends, as well as our publishers, for patience and support.

Lars Svensson, Killian Mullarney, Dan Zetterström
September 1998

Introduction

This book treats all bird species which breed or regularly occur in Europe, North Africa north of 30°N, and Israel, Palestine, Jordan, Lebanon, Syria, Turkey, Armenia and Azerbaijan, that is in a large part of the Middle East. Also included are the Canary Islands, Madeira and the Sinai peninsula. (Excluded are the Azores, the Cape Verde Islands, Iraq and Iran.) Europe is bordered in the east by the ridge of the Ural mountains, the Ural river and the Caspian Sea.

722 species are described, of which 57 are occasional visitors. Another 23 species or variants are treated which are either probable escapes from captivity or were originally introduced to the area and which now breed in a feral state without further introductions. An additional 103 very rare stragglers from other continents are listed.

Taxonomy and names

When planning this book, the taxonomy was based on the widely used *List of Recent Holarctic Bird Species* (Voous 1977). In the course of writing, new concepts of splitting a few species have been adopted, and a few genera have been enlarged while others have been split. The end result corresponds closely with the taxonomy and nomenclature in *Palearctic Birds* (Beaman 1994).

The scientific name of a species is written in Latin (or in latinized form) and consists of two words, the generic name (written with an initial capital letter) and the species epithet (all lower-case letters); these two words constitute the species name. It is recommended that the scientific species names, and the subspecific and generic names as well, are written with a different typeface, i.e. usually with *italics*. The scientific name of e.g. the White Wagtail thus is *Motacilla alba*.

To indicate geographical variation within a species, distinct populations—so-called subspecies or races—are designated with a third word, a subspecies epithet (e.g. Pied Wagtail *Motacilla alba yarrellii* of NW Europe, as opposed to *Motacilla alba alba* of the rest of Europe).

In a very few cases we have put a species epithet within brackets followed by a subspecies epithet, e.g. *Phylloscopus* (*trochiloides*) *nitidus*. This indicates that the 'entity' in question is on the border between subspecies and species and in our opinion cannot on present knowledge be confidently classified in either category. Also, the evolution of life forms in nature is slow, nearly continuous, and it is to be expected that certain forms at a given moment are borderline cases.

With few exceptions, the English names follow those in *Palearctic Birds* (Beaman 1994). A way of showing both these English names adapted for international use (i.e. with added modifiers for a large number of common species) and the shorter names for everyday use is introduced: at the head of each species entry, bold face is used for the ordinary names and normal type within brackets for the extra modifiers; '(Western) **Jackdaw**' serves as an example. Only two new names are proposed, Persian Wheatear and Hill Sparrow.

Although the sequence closely follows Voous and Beaman (see above), we have made a few minor adjustments within genera and, at times, families. The sole purpose of these is to bring together those species which show the greatest resemblance and thereby to facilitate comparisons.

Abundancy symbols

For easy assessment of whether a certain species occurs commonly in Great Britain and Ireland, or whether it is merely a rare vagrant to the isles, abundancy symbols are given to the right of the species name. If you have seen a flock of unknown birds in your garden, it might be a waste of time to read in depth about species which do not even occur in the region. The symbols are explained below.

Status in Great Britain and Ireland

r**B**	Resident breeding species.
m**B**	Migratory breeding species.
r+m**B**	Breeder; some are residents, others migratory.
r(m)**B**	Breeding species; mainly resident but a minority are migrants.

To these a qualifier is attached:

1	Very abundant	(estimated > 1 million pairs)
2	Abundant	(estimated > 100,000 pairs)
3	Fairly abundant	(estimated > 10,000 pairs)
4	Scarce or local	(estimated > 100 pairs)
5	Rare	(estimated ≤ 100 pairs)

W	Winter visitor (common; many immigrants).
P	Passage visitor (common).

Here, too, a qualifier may be added (cf. above under breeding); if so, estimates refer to number of birds, not pairs.

V	Vagrant.

To this, again a qualifier is attached:

*	Annual vagrant in some numbers.
**	Only one or a few records a year, or in most.
***	Only one or a very few records per decade. ('Three-star rarity.')
[**V**]	No record considered a result of genuine and unassisted vagrancy, or all records thought to involve escapes from captivity; records which are open to question for other reasons.
—	No record in Great Britain or Ireland.

Distribution maps

Besides the abundancy symbols, distribution maps are included for most species and should help establish quickly whether it is reasonable or not to expect a certain species at a

Breeding range, abandoned in winter.

Present all year around, including when breeding.

Range where the species can be seen on migration.

Winter range.

Main migration direction (not necessarily exact route).

certain site and a given season. Although it was necessary to make the maps small, they should still give a useful summary of the normal occurrence. Unlike in many other books, the maps also show where the birds usually occur during autumn and spring migrations, so far as this is known.

An effort has been made to present as up-to-date and clear maps as possible. All national checklists and atlas surveys covering the treated area have been consulted. It should be noted that, at the time when the maps for this book were prepared, modern mapping of the bird fauna had not been published for such important areas as Spain, Greece, Turkey (non-passerines), Jordan, Algeria, Morocco and for most of the states which were earlier a part of the Soviet Union.

Size of birds

Each species account opens with the size of the bird, expressed as the length in centimetres from tip of bill to tip of tail measured in the stretched bird (L). For most species which are often seen in flight the wingspan is added (WS).

To indicate the normal size variation within any one species, a size range is always given instead of a single average figure. Many birdwatchers are unaware of the magnitude of this normal size variation, and it is all too easy then to arrive at the wrong conclusion if an identification is based too heavily on a size evaluation.

The length measurements have been taken largely from series of well-prepared skins and in some cases from freshly killed or live birds. (Hardly any have been obtained from the current larger handbooks.)

The wingspans are meant to indicate the largest possible extents which the birds themselves can achieve in flight. (Slightly larger values can be reached if, on a live bird, the wings are stretched tightly by pulling the primaries, but such artificial measurements have been avoided.) Quite a few measurements in the current literature are misleading. Those presented in this book are based to a large extent on original measurements taken on live birds. They have been supplemented by measurements on skins and photographs.

Terminology and symbols

In order to make the book easily accessible to a large public interested in birds and natural history, the specialist jargon has been kept to a minimum. A few technical terms, however, are very useful to know and use, such as the precise terms for different plumages and ages, and these are explained below. It should be noted that most of the terms relating to feather tracts and body parts, the topography of the bird, are also explained separately on the inside of the covers.

PLUMAGES AND AGES

juvenile (*juv.*) – young, fledged bird wearing its first set of true feathers (the juvenile plumage), but which has not yet moulted any of these feathers.

post-juvenile – all plumages or ages following the juvenile.

young – imprecise term usually referring to juvenile and/or 1st-winter without distinguishing between these two.

immature (*imm.*) – a bird wearing any plumage other than adult, generally corresponding to the word 'young'.

1st-autumn – bird in its first autumn, 2–5 months old. The term refers to the age, not a particular plumage.

1st-winter (*1st-w.*) – age category usually referring to the plumage following that of the juvenile, usually gained through a partial (in some species complete) moult in late summer/autumn of 1st calendar-year, and worn until next moult in the spring of 2nd calendar-year.

1st-summer (*1st-s.*) – age category usually referring to the plumage worn at the approximate age of one year and attained in late winter/spring through partial (in some species complete) moult from 1st-winter plumage, or through abrasion of this plumage; worn until next moult, usually in late summer/autumn in the same year, when replaced by 2nd-winter plumage.

2nd-winter (*2nd-w.*) – age category usually referring to the plumage following 1st-summer, usually gained through a complete (in some species partial) moult in late summer/autumn of 2nd calendar-year, and worn until next moult in the spring of 3rd calendar-year.

2nd-summer (*2nd-s.*) – age category usually referring to the plumage worn at the approximate age of two years. It follows the 2nd-winter plumage and is worn until next moult; see also under 1st-summer.

subadult (*subad.*) – nearly adult, not quite in definitive plumage; imprecise term, often used when exact age is difficult to establish, e.g. among larger gulls or raptors.

adult (*ad.*) – old, mature bird in definitive plumage. Some species have the same appearance in both summer and winter; others have separate plumages, *adult summer* (*ad.s.*) and *adult winter* (*ad. w.*).

breeding plumage – usually more colourful set of feathers gained by many birds, primarily males, through abrasion or in a spring moult (autumn moult for ducks).

non-breeding plumage – usually equivalent to adult winter plumage, a more cryptic plumage appearing among species with seasonal plumage changes; the term is often used when this plumage is acquired early, even in summer.

eclipse plumage – cryptic, female-like plumage attained by male ducks in summer while moulting the flight-feathers and becoming flightless, and thus needing camouflage. (Cf. *breeding plumage*.)

1st-year, 2nd-year, etc. – age category referring to the entire first, second, etc. year of life, from summer to summer.

calendar-year (*cal.-year*) – a bird is in its 1st calendar-year from hatching until 31 Dec of the same year, in its 2nd calendar-year from 1 Jan until next 31 Dec, etc.

GENERAL TERMINOLOGY

albinism – innate lack of pigment, usually in the feathers, leading to partly or completely white plumage.

alula – a group of feathers attached at the digital bone, near the wing-bend on upper forewing. (Syn.: *bastard wing*.)

'arm' – the same as *inner wing*, the part of the wing inside the wing-bend (incl. secondaries and accordant coverts).

axillaries – the feathers covering the armpit.

carpal – the 'wrist', often referred to as the *wing-bend*.

carpal bar – usually dark bar along the leading edge of the inner wing, from the carpal and inwards.

cere – bare skin on the base of upper mandible and around nostrils in some groups, e.g. raptors.

eye-stripe – usually contrasting *dark* stripe *through* the eye from near bill-base and backwards to the ear tract.

Fenno-Scandia – Norway, Sweden, Finland and the Kola Peninsula.

'fingers' – the spread tips of the outermost long primaries on broad-winged, soaring birds, e.g. eagles, storks, cranes.

flight-feathers – the long quills on the wing (primaries, secondaries and tertials).

foot projection – the part of the feet (incl. any part of the *tarsus*) which extends beyond the tail-tip in flight.

forewing – usually the upperwing-coverts (or at least the foremost of these) on the 'arm' of a spread wing.

gape – naked skin at the corner of the mouth.

habitat – natural environment preferred by a certain species.

'hand' – the same as *outer wing*, the part of the wing outside the wing-bend (incl. primaries, alula, primary coverts).

hover – hold position in the air by quick wing movements.

hybrid – a cross between two different species.

inner wing – see *'arm'*.

'jizz' – the shape and movements of a bird, its 'personality'. (Jargon possibly derived from UK military parlance: GISS, General Impression of Size and Shape.)

leucism – innate pigment deficiency leading to pale, washed-out colours of the plumage.

lore – area between eye and base of upper mandible.

malar stripe – narrow stripe, often dark, along the side of the throat, below the moustachial stripe (if present).

mantle – tract of feathers covering the fore-part of the back.

melanism – innate surplus of dark pigment (notably melanin) causing the plumage to become darker than normal, at times even black.

midwing-panel – area on inner upperwing, often on median and longest lesser coverts, of contrasting colour (lighter on e.g. harriers and petrels, darker on young small gulls).

'mirror' – term used to describe a small white (or light) patch just inside the tip of longest primaries (on gulls).

morph – variant of certain appearance within a species and which is not geographically defined (cf. *subspecies*). The same as formerly often used *phase*.

moult – a natural process of renewal of the plumage, whereby the old feathers are shed and new ones grown.

moustachial stripe – usually narrow stripe, often dark, running from near base of the lower mandible and along the lower edge of the cheek. (Cf. *malar stripe*.)

nominate subspecies – within a species the subspecies first to have been named and which therefore, according to the rules of Zoological Nomenclature, is given the same subspecific epithet as the specific, e.g. *Motacilla alba alba*.

orbital ring – eye-ring of bare, unfeathered skin.

outer wing – see *'hand'*.

Palearctic – ('Old Arctic') the zoogeographical or 'natural' region comprising Europe, North Africa south to the Sahara, often the entire Arabian Peninsula, and Asia south to Pakistan, the Himalayas and central China.

panel – term often used in ornithology to describe an elongated patch of contrasting colour (cf. *wing-panel*).

pelagic – referring to the open sea.

primaries – the quills growing on the 'hand'.

primary patch – pale patch at the base of the primaries, on upperwing or underwing, e.g. on raptors and skuas.

primary projection – the part of the primaries which on the folded wing extends beyond the tip of the tertials.

secondaries – the quills growing on the 'arm', or ulna.

species (sp.) – important entity in taxonomy which in brief is a group of natural populations whose members can interbreed freely but which are reproductively isolated from members of other such groups (i.e. other species).

speculum – distinctive, glossy patch on upper secondaries, often on ducks.

submoustachial stripe – a usually light stripe between dark moustachial stripe and dark malar stripe.

subspecies (ssp.) – morphologically (colour, size) on average discernibly different, geographically defined population within a species. The use of quotation marks around a subspecies name indicates that the form is either subtle, or questionable or invalid (e.g. '*omissus*'). (Syn.: *race*.)

supercilium – usually contrasting light stripe above the eye from near forehead and backwards along side of crown.

taiga – predominantly coniferous, northerly (boreal), wide and largely continuous forest zone in northern Europe.

tail-streamers – elongated outer or central tail-feathers.

tarsus – short for tarsometatarsus, the fusion of the metatarsal bones, in everyday speech the 'leg' of the bird.

tertials – the innermost wing-feathers, usually with somewhat different shape and pattern, serving as cover (protection) for the folded wing. On larger birds tertials are attached to humerus (inner arm), on smaller birds to ulna (and thus are not 'true tertials' but inner secondaries).

tibia – the lower leg, on birds colloquially named 'thigh'.

variety (var.) – a variant form within a population (cf. *morph*); also, a domestic breed of constant appearance.

'window' – referring to paler and more translucent inner primaries, e.g. on some raptors and young gulls.

wing-bar – contrastingly coloured, often lighter bars on the wing, often formed by white tips of wing-coverts.

wing-bend – the same as the carpal, the joint between 'hand' and 'arm' of the wing.

wing-panel – imprecise term referring to contrastingly coloured oblong area on the wing.

wing projection – the part of the wings which extends beyond the tail-tip when the bird is perched.

wingspan (WS) – distance from wing-tip to wing-tip.

SYMBOLS AND SIGNS

♂, ♂♂	male, males
♀, ♀♀	female, females
>	more than, larger than
<	less than, smaller than
±	more or less, to a varying degree

Voice and transcriptions

Owing to lack of space, and in order to achieve simplicity and clarity, especially with beginners in mind, only the common and distinct calls are described. Many subtle variations of the normal contact- and alarm-calls are excluded.

Although rendering bird voices in writing inevitably is inexact and personal, a serious effort has been made to convey what is typical for each call by trying to select the letters and style of writing which are most apt. We know by experience that it can be very helpful to read a fitting rendition, particularly after just having heard a certain call. We do not share the opinion that written voice transcriptions are so subjective that they have little value at all.

Whenever you hear an unfamiliar bird voice, do not be afraid to note down what it first brings to mind, be it another bird or something quite unrelated; more than likely this first impression is exactly what you will be reminded of next time you hear it. Your own impressions will thus be important additions to the voice descriptions offered in the book.

Transcriptions of calls are indicated by quotation marks. Syllables in **bold** face are more stressed than the others. Very explosive or fierce calls end with an exclamation mark.

The choice of consonants is meant to show whether the sounds are hard or soft: 'tic' is sharper overall than 'gip', 'kick' has a harder opening than 'bick'. 'z' indicates a sharper and more 'electric', fizzing tone than 'ts'.

The vowels are selected in an attempt to hint somewhat at the relative pitch, although this is not so easy in English. To the common English vowels is added German 'ü' (as in Lübeck or the French word 'mur', pronounced between 'sue' and 'sync') since there is often a need for it. The call 'too-ü' has a rising pitch whereas 'dee-u' is downslurred.

Double vowels denote a longer sound than single: 'viit' is more drawn out than 'vit'. When a vowel at the end of a call is followed by an 'h', as in 'tüh', it is drawn out but somewhat fading at the end, or sounds 'breathed out'.

The way of writing suggests how rapidly the syllables are delivered. 'ki... ki... ki...' is very slow, 'ki, ki, ki,...' denotes a composed rhythm, 'ki ki ki...' is a little quicker, whereas 'ki-ki-ki-...' is rapid like a shuttle, and 'kikikiki...' is very fast (shivering). Even faster is 'kr'r'r'r'r'...', indicating a vibrant, rolling sound. Now and then a strict application of these guidelines has had to give way to legibility.

The plates

To help beginners, in particular, to find their way when looking at the plates with their wealth of small images, we have aimed at: (1) similar scale for all main images which are not obvious 'distant views'; (2) constant posture and location on the plate of adult males, adult females, juveniles, etc. (summer males always at lower far right, juveniles at far left, etc.); (3) addition of vignettes and tiny 'distant views' showing characteristic habitat, posture and behaviour, and how each species will appear at long range and in poor light (i.e. as they are so often seen!); and (4) addition of pointers and brief captions highlighting particularly useful clues, which will make the plates easier to 'read'. Fine rules have been inserted between the species in order further to facilitate a quick survey among the many images on the plates.

It should be pointed out that, although great care has been

A Lapwing in bright sunshine (left)—rather as it is shown on the plate on p. 137—and huddled up in dull weather (right)—a totally different creature.

taken to choose typical postures and plumages for the birds portrayed, odd birds which you see live in nature will nevertheless look different from the images on the plates. Some have an abraded or stained plumage, others are in poor condition and adopt uncharacteristic postures, while others again are in good shape but have a posture which is rather odd and which could not be fitted in on the plate. The light, too, can cause all colours to be subdued or the pattern to be less contrasting. It is best therefore to view the illustrations as a guide but not to expect every single detail of posture and plumage to match the bird you have in front of you.

Moult and abrasion of plumage

As soon as a feather is fully grown it becomes a dead part. Sunshine and abrasion bleach and wear the feathers gradually, and in the end their function as a means to achieve flight and to serve as waterproofing or heat regulation is impaired. Unlike fur and nails, feathers are not continuously renewed. Instead, they are replaced in a usually annual process which is called moult.

Another reason for moult, especially of feathers on head and body, is the signalling function which colours and patterns in the plumage of many species have, important in the social life of the bird; different signals may be required at different seasons.

It is disadvantageous to moult heavily during migration (the flight capacity is then often impaired) and, for many species, also while breeding (both breeding and feather growth require much energy). Therefore, most species moult in concentrated periods between these two stages.

The time after the breeding season but before the autumn migration is utilized by many species for a complete moult. Others, especially those wintering in the tropics, undergo their annual complete moult in the winter quarters.

A Herring Gull in autumn approaching the end of the annual complete moult: only the outermost primaries are still growing (making the bird appear confusingly pale-winged, with much of the black on wing-tips still concealed!).

Many of those moulting completely in late summer also have a partial moult in early spring in which some body-feathers and wing-coverts are replaced (but no flight-feathers). And the long-distance migrants with the complete moult in winter often renew some body-feathers either before the autumn migration or prior to the spring migration.

Very large birds which are dependent on undiminished powers of flight and which often soar, e.g. large raptors, storks and pelicans, replace their flight-feathers slowly during a large part of the year. Since a new quill grows only by 5–10 mm a day, each quill requires up to two months for renewal (the longest primaries of large eagles and pelicans even 2½ months). With 10–11 primaries and 15–22 secondaries in each wing of these large species, a complete replacement of the flight-feathers requires 3–4 *years* in order not to hamper the ability to fly.

Ducks and geese shed all their flight-feathers simultaneously. This is done in summer, usually after breeding or near its end. They are flightless for 3–7 weeks (the larger the species is, the longer the time) but survive by keeping in cover in marshes or out of the way on the open sea.

Many ducks have rather peculiar and complex moult strategies. The breeding plumage of the males is often acquired in late autumn, since ducks usually mate in winter. In the summer, when the males of other birds are at their most handsome, male ducks instead change to a female-like so-called eclipse plumage so as to be better camouflaged when the moult renders them temporarily flightless.

The Crane is unique among the landbirds in shedding all flight-feathers simultaneously in summer, like the ducks. The moult takes place apparently only every second year, or at even longer intervals. The moulting bird keeps well hidden on wide, sparsely forested bogs or in reedbeds until capable of flying again, in time for the autumn migration.

As is evident from the examples, the variations in moult are considerable, and almost every species has its own strategy for renewal of the feathers. To master all these variations requires specialist knowledge, but the fundamentals are easy to learn. And they are useful to know since they enable you to age the birds you see closely and sufficiently well, even with

The difference in wear and shape of the tail-feathers between winter adult and young Common Redpolls. Note rounder tips and more fresh edges on the adult.

Adult winter   **1st-winter**

species in which the different age-groups have similar plumages. Correct ageing is often supporting evidence—at times even a prerequisite—for reliable identification.

It is even more common that a means of reliably ageing a bird allows you to sex it as well. In many species the plumages of adult females and young males are very similar (e.g. Horned Lark, some members of the thrush family, starlings, numerous finches and buntings), but if the age is established these two categories can usually be separated.

When young birds become fledged they have fresh wing- and tail-feathers, whereas adults have abraded feathers, these having been grown six months to almost a full year earlier. Soon thereafter, however, the adults of many species start to moult their wing- and tail-feathers in a complete moult, and after a short time the scene is reversed: from about late summer *the wings and tail of adults are fresher than those of young birds*. Since the quality of the juvenile plumage is somewhat inferior and hence is more susceptible to bleaching and abrasion than later plumages, the difference becomes more obvious through autumn and winter.

Juveniles of many species also have body-feathers a little looser in structure and duller, and the *wing- and tail-feathers and some coverts are often slightly paler and less glossy and are narrower and more pointed*, whereas adults have *slightly darker, glossier and broader feathers with more rounded tips*.

In species with a slower renewal of flight-feathers, e.g. large raptors, juveniles can often be told by having *all wing- and tail-feathers uniformly fresh* (or worn), whereas older birds may be recognized by *slight unevenness in the length, darkness and degree of abrasion among the wing-feathers*.

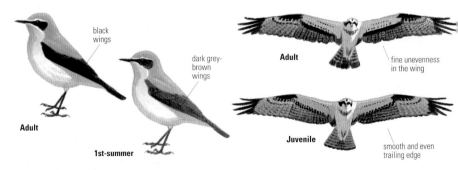

black wings

dark grey-brown wings

Adult

fine unevenness in the wing

Adult

1st-summer

Juvenile

smooth and even trailing edge

Two male Wheatears in spring. The left-hand one has black wings without light edges and is at least two years old. The one on the right has dark grey-brown wings (the juvenile feathers) with traces of light edges, and is thus one year old.

Two Ospreys in autumn. The upper bird has slightly uneven trailing edge of wing, and the flight-feathers are not quite homogeneous; it is adult. The lower bird has uniformly fresh and evenly long flight-feathers finely tipped white; it is juvenile.

In a few species the juveniles, too, have a complete moult in late summer and early autumn, renewing wings and tail at the age of only a few months, e.g. larks, Moustached Warbler, Bearded Reedling, Long-tailed Tit, starlings, sparrows, and Corn Bunting. After this post-juvenile moult there is *no way of separating adults and young birds* of these species.

How birds are identified

One of the thrills of becoming a birdwatcher is the joy of discovery. Therefore you do not want everything on a plate. The perplexities and mistakes experienced as a beginner can be frustrating, but generally only spur you to new efforts. Still, a few general pieces of advice may be appropriate. Bird identification in the field is difficult enough as it is.

The first question to be asked when suspecting that a Black-winged Kite just flew over the local heath or a Citril Finch alighted in the garden: *Is it reasonable?* Is this species supposed to occur in Britain or Ireland, and at this season? Look for a commoner species (e.g. male Hen Harrier and Greenfinch in these examples) if both abundancy symbol and range map argue against the suspected rarity!

Is the habitat the right one? There is at least something in the species accounts hinting at the typical environment in which each species thrives. If it does not fit, try other alternatives.

Does the observed behaviour match the description? In many accounts (but not all) there is an indication of characteristic flight and movements, degree of shyness, mating or feeding behaviour, etc. It is of course reassuring if the observed habits match those described under the suspected species.

If everything you have observed matches the selected description so far, now is the time to examine the appearance of the bird more critically. First establish: *What size is it?* If the size is correctly assessed now, much trouble is saved later. Therefore a lot of work has been put in to ensure that accurate measurements of size are given in the book.

It may seem a trivial and easy matter to some to assess size correctly when attempting to identify an unknown bird. But experience shows that both beginners and well-practised birders often make mistakes. And once you have misjudged the size of a bird it is all too easy stubbornly to follow up the wrong clue. 'Oh, yes, it *looked* like a Red-backed Shrike all right, only this bird was considerably bigger!'

Prejudices about the size of birds can lead you astray. Frequent practice in the field helps, especially if combined with careful study of the sizes given in the book.

against the light   with the light

Whether the light is against or with the observer will affect the impression of the shape of a bird. Seen against the light, this Greenshank appears slimmer ('the light eats the edges') than it does in flat light from behind the observer.

The contrast between bird and background affects the size impression. The dark Arctic Skua appears larger against a light, calm sea than against a dark and stormy one, while the opposite is true for the pale Kittiwake.

A source of error which birdwatchers are likely to encounter is the optical size-illusion occurring when a flock of birds is studied through a telescope with powerful magnification. Since the telescope contracts the field of vision so much, the birds farther away *appear* larger than the conspecific birds in the foreground, being in fact of equal size.

The contrast between bird and background also affects the size impression. As a rule, *strong contrast makes a bird look bigger whereas slight contrast makes it look smaller.* A dark bird against a dark sea appears smaller than a white one even if they are equal in size. And a light bird does not look so impressive against a light background as a black one would.

After having tried to assess the size of the bird, a number of important questions follow: *Is the bill small or big, wedge-shaped or thin? If long and slender, is it longer than the length of the head? What is the shape of the body? Has it got long or short neck and tail? Are the legs strikingly long and thin or just 'average'?* Consider such questions on location while observing the bird, not back at home when memory starts to fade and you are unable to check uncertain details further. Ideally, you should take some notes and make a sketch while still with the bird. Even a very rough sketch is usually very helpful later when studying the book or consulting friends.

Now look at colours and patterns and ask yourself similar questions to those regarding the shape: *What are the main colours above and below? Are there any bright and colourful patches? What colours are the legs, eye and bill? Are there any light wing-bars or a supercilium above the eye? Is there any noteworthy pattern on throat, breast, back or crown? Is the rump concolorous with the back or perhaps contrastingly white? Does the tail have white sides or other pattern?*

When examining the plumage of a bird, remember that *the weather and type of light affect the appearance of the colours.* In sunshine at noon the colours of the upperparts certainly look bright, but finer nuances might be subdued or lost and the underparts are in darkest shadow. In overcast but bright weather the contrasts decrease, but on the other hand finer shades are more apparent. On dark and gloomy days, both the true colours and the patterns are difficult to see.

Finally, keep in mind that *the voice is an important clue.* To distinguish between the many similar species in such families as waders, larks, pipits and warblers, it is very helpful to compare what you hear with the voice descriptions in the book while still in the field. You can also try to memorize or note down your own version of the calls you have heard and compare these notes with recordings at home.

LOONS (DIVERS) *Gaviidae*

Four species, all rather large. Loons, also known as divers, usually swim low (like cormorants, unlike ducks), but float higher when resting or preening. Long body and neck. Feet placed far back, making movements on land ungainly. Differ from cormorants in silhouette, shape of bill and in being 'tailless', from grebes in larger size and thicker neck, from mergansers in bill shape and longer neck.

To catch food (mainly fish), they dive with smooth, neat 'bow' (not leaping, as cormorants often do), often remaining submerged for a minute or more, covering sometimes long distances underwater. Dives often preceded by reconnaissance from surface with head submerged for long periods ('snorkelling').

Breed mainly at pools and lakes in woodland or on tundra. Nest a shallow cup close to the water. Require stable water-level by the nest. Winter along coasts or in bays, sometimes on lakes, at times in larger, loosely scattered gatherings, more often seen singly or in small parties. Migrate (Apr–Jun and Sep–Nov) mostly over sea, singly or in small parties (rarely larger flocks), birds within flocks widely spaced, never in dense formation (like ducks or cormorants). Often fly high when wind is light, or in tail-winds, with continuous beats of long narrow wings, and on direct course.

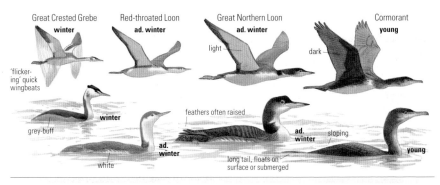

Great Crested Grebe — winter — 'flickering' quick wingbeats — grey-buff — white

Red-throated Loon — ad. winter — winter — ad. winter

Great Northern Loon — ad. winter — light — feathers often raised — long tail, floats on surface or submerged

Cormorant — young — dark — ad. winter — sloping — young

IDENTIFICATION OF LOONS

Identification easy when in distinctive and strikingly beautiful adult summer plumages. Immature and adult winter plumages less distinctive, but swimming birds can generally be identified, given reasonably close views. Look carefully for the full range of differences before making a firm diagnosis: these mainly involve size; bill shape and bill colour; precise pattern and extent of light and dark areas on head and neck (often easier to discern at long range than size and bill shape); and pattern of fine markings—if any—on upperparts.

Identification of flying birds much more tricky: requires much practice in making rather difficult assessments of size; structure (esp. thickness of neck, 'hunchbackedness', and foot projection); and depth and speed of wingbeats (variable according to wind speed and relative wind direction). At closer ranges, look also for the diagnostic differences in colour, shape and size of the bill, and in the pattern and extent of light and dark on head and neck. Odd flying loons at a distance must be left unidentified even by experienced observers. Flying loons are illustrated on p.14.

Red-throated Loon *Gavia stellata* rB4 / W3

L 55–67 cm (excl. feet *c.* 7), WS 91–110 cm. Commonest loon in most regions. Breeds on often small and fishless pools on tundra or on forest bogs, commuting to larger lakes or coast for food.

IDENTIFICATION Smallest loon, but only slightly smaller than Black-throated. Bill uptilted with straight culmen, usually held *pointing slightly upwards*. Forehead flat, and inclination to have angled hindcrown. Usually noticeably flat-chested (useful esp. at long range; Black-throated has prominent chest). In flight, look for *slimmer neck*; also, *more 'sagging' neck* giving hunchbacked impression; bill often pointing slightly upwards even in flight; usually *modest foot projection*, making wings set behind centre (but a few have feet projecting more, as on Black-throated); generally somewhat *faster and deeper wingbeats* than Black-throated in comparable winds; and rather common *habit of moving head* as if 'calibrating vision' (Black-throated does this only infrequently). – Adult summer: Rufous neck patch is dark, and can look black at a distance, so (pale) grey throat and plain upperparts best long-range marks. – Adult winter: In profile, *more than half of neck is white* (50/50 on Black-throated), visible in flight too, and, seen from behind, some white visible on sides of neck (Black-throated usually entirely dark-necked from rear), and a little white surrounds eye (esp. in front); whole upperparts finely speckled with white. Flanks show as a complete pale band (mottled) above waterline (if any pale visible), usually not as a conspicuous white patch at rear. – Juvenile (often retained to midwinter, partly to first spring): As adult winter, except white areas on head and *neck have fine, dusky streaking* (often extensive), not pure white, and upperparts have duller, greyer speckling. – 1st-summer: Summer plumage only partial. Often twin dark stripes on foreneck in transition.

VOICE Flight-call loud and monotonous (somewhat goose-like) cackling, 'kah kah kah...'. Song is far-carrying duet of ♂'s loud, 'grinding' 'oo **rroo**-uh, oo **rroo**-uh, oo **rroo**-uh,...' and ♀'s stronger, higher-pitched '**arro**-**arro**-arro-...'. Also a drawn-out, wailing 'eeaaooh'. Some calls resemble barking of a fox. Silent in winter.

RED-THROATED LOON

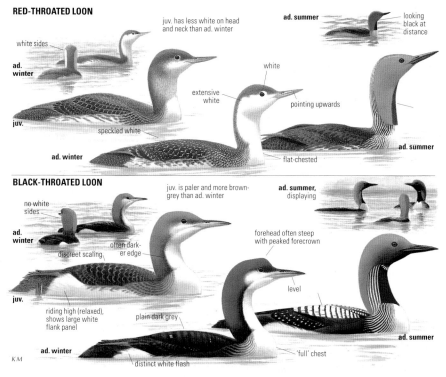

juv. has less white on head and neck than ad. winter

white sides

ad. winter

juv.

speckled white

ad. winter

extensive white

white

pointing upwards

flat-chested

ad. summer

looking black at distance

ad. summer

BLACK-THROATED LOON

juv. is paler and more brown-grey than ad. winter

no white sides

ad. winter

discreet scaling

often dark-er edge

juv.

riding high (relaxed), shows large white flank panel

plain dark grey

ad. winter

distinct white flash

ad. summer, displaying

forehead often steep with peaked forecrown

level

'full' chest

ad. summer

KM

Black-throated Loon *Gavia arctica*   r**B**4 / **W**4

L 63–75 cm (excl. feet *c*.10), WS 100–122 (127) cm. Unlike Red-throated, breeds on clear, fish-holding freshwater lakes (or sea-bays without tide). Often gregarious in winter.

IDENTIFICATION Appears somewhat larger than Mallard, though shape slimmer. (A few large individuals same size as smallest Great Northern.) Dagger-shaped bill with slightly curved culmen, slimmer than Great Northern's; *carried horizontally* (or nearly; Red-throated's more clearly upwards). Forehead often steep, hindcrown smoothly rounded. *Thick neck* (same-thickness head and neck), and has prominent chest at waterline (Red-throated more flat-chested). In flight, compared with Red-throated, *neck slightly thicker and carried straighter* (less 'sagging'), as is bill; feet always large and obvious, *projecting prominently*, making wings set close to centre; slightly slower and shallower wingbeats on average than Red-throated in comparable winds (but dependent on individual size; small birds more like Red-throated, large more like Great Northern). – Adult summer: Velvety pale grey crown and hindneck, black foreneck and throat, and a pattern of *distinct white patches on upperbody*. – Adult winter: In profile, *at least half of neck dark*, visible in flight too, and border between grey hindneck and white foreneck usually *highlighted by swarthy line*. Generally no white around eye (but beware juv. Red-

throated, which can show reduced white). Swimming bird often *shows distinctive, isolated white patch on rearmost flanks*. Upperparts plain dark grey. Bill (pale) grey with blackish tip. – Juvenile (often retained to midwinter, partly to first spring): As adult winter, except pale feather fringes on upperparts form neat, fine *scaly pattern*; upperparts slightly paler and browner; tip of bill less blackish. – 1st-summer: Summer plumage only partial.

VOICE Hard, croaking 'knarr-knorr' and drawn-out gull-like wailing '**aaah**-oh' are heard from territory, often at night. Song is loud, desolate but evocative, rhythmic whistling 'cloo**ee**-co-cloo**ee**-co-cloo**ee**-co-clo**ee**', each 'cloo**ee**' a strongly rising whistle. When display-diving, sometimes a fierce, abruptly cut-off 'co**eet**!'. Generally silent in flight (only rarely subdued 'karr-arr-arr'). Silent in winter.

Red-throated Loon   Black-throated Loon

Great Northern Loon *Gavia immer* **P / W**4

L 73–88 cm (excl. feet *c.* 13), WS 122–148 cm. Breeds on large, deep lakes and bays in woodland, and on tundra. About 300 pairs in Iceland. Main range in North America.

IDENTIFICATION Large and strongly built, much as a Cormorant. (With size variation, smallest match large Black-throated Loons, largest may equal Yellow-billeds.) When swimming, note *heavy, horizontally held bill*, large head, and on most rather thick neck; *forehead steep*, and can be raised to create small *crest-like 'bump'* making *crown appear concave*. When floating high, pale (mottled) flanks often show as complete light band above waterline (as on Red-throated). In flight: thick neck held straight out; *large well-protruding feet*, often with spread toes adding to large size; comparatively slow wingbeats with 'elastic' outer wing sometimes characteristic (but still not a great difference from the flight of large individuals of Black-throated); and *greater bulk* and *bill size* at times obvious. – Adult summer: *All-black head* and *white-chequered upperparts* and white-striped patch on side of neck. – Adult winter: First establish that bill is carried *horizontally* (or at most insignificantly upwards), and is bluish *grey-white with dark tip and culmen*. Then check pattern of dark and light on head and neck: prominent *pale eye-ring*, rather *distinct demarcation between dark hindneck and white foreneck*, and *blackish half-collar on lower side of neck* emphasized by *white indentation* above it. Contrast between darker hindneck and paler upperbody. Lacks juvenile's scaly upperparts, and retains some inconspicuous white-spotted lesser wing-coverts from summer. – Juvenile: As adult winter, except that rather broad, pale fringes on upperparts form prominent, *neat scaly pattern* (at long range giving paler appearance to upperparts than on juv. Black-throated); wing-coverts lack fine white spots; and pale eye-ring less obvious. – 1st-summer: Remains in fully juvenile-like plumage. – 2nd-winter: As adult winter, but upperparts often slightly darker, and has paler, not so blackish bill-tip;

lacks white-spotted lesser wing-coverts.

VOICE Frequently heard (incl. as 'atmosphere' in films) is anxiety/contact-call, a repeated high-pitched eerie laughter which often opens with a lower note, 'ho-yeyeyeyeya'. The song is a wailing with structure reminiscent of Black-throated Loon, 'aaoooh... **wee** we-a **wee** we-a **wee** we-a'. Also a monosyllabic, moaning, drawn-out call.

Yellow-billed Loon *Gavia adamsii* **V**∗∗

L 77–90 cm (excl. feet *c.* 14), WS 135–150 cm. Breeds on arctic coasts of Russia, wintering in small numbers along coasts of N Norway and rarely in North Sea and Baltic.

IDENTIFICATION Largest loon, on average slightly larger than Great Northern. Bill usually held pointing clearly upwards, and practically straight culmen (exceptions insignificant) and marked upward angle of gonys add to *distinctive uptilted look*. *Bill-tip and outer part of culmen invariably pale*. Neck thick (same-thickness head and neck). Against dark background, pale colour of bill makes it look large, but at long range or against pale background not always so massive-looking. In flight, slightly larger size than Great Northern makes 'weight' and slower wingbeats more obvious in comparison with Black-throated. – Adult summer: *Bill yellowish-white* or ivory-coloured (all black on Great Northern, but can gleam pale in strong light, or rarely have extensive whitish tip in summer). White markings on neck and upperparts larger and fewer than on Great Northern. – Adult winter: Bill less yellowish and often with dark shade at base (esp. along culmen, at times to 2/3 of length). *Head and hindneck paler grey-brown*, and light throat/foreneck more tinged brownish than on Great Northern (which is more contrasting greyish-black and white); also *more pale around eye and on side of hindneck*, behind ear. (In late winter, a few much-faded Great Northerns may approach, but never quite match, Yellow-billed's paleness.) The more extensively retained summer wing-coverts have larger and

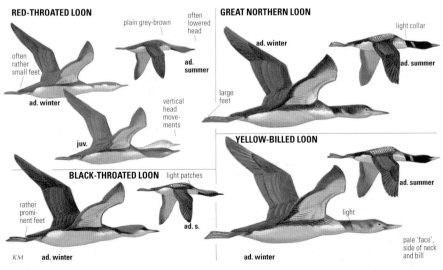

RED-THROATED LOON   plain grey-brown   often lowered head   often rather small feet   ad. winter   ad. summer   vertical head movements   juv.

GREAT NORTHERN LOON   light collar   ad. winter   ad. summer   large feet

YELLOW-BILLED LOON   ad. summer   ad. winter   light   pale 'face', side of neck and bill

BLACK-THROATED LOON   light patches   rather prominent feet   ad. s.

KM   ad. winter

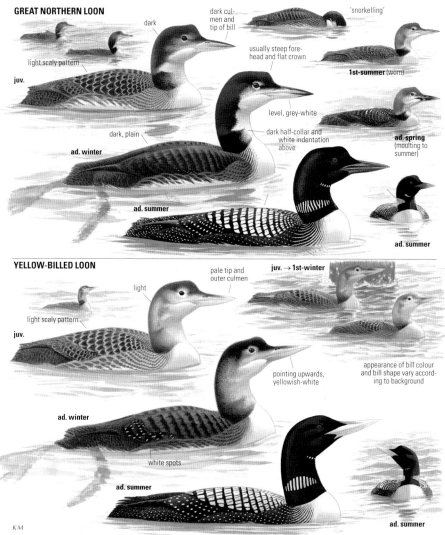

GREAT NORTHERN LOON

dark culmen and tip of bill

'snorkelling'

dark

light scaly pattern

usually steep forehead and flat crown

1st-summer (worn)

juv.

level, grey-white

dark, plain

dark half-collar and white indentation above

ad. spring
(moulting to summer)

ad. winter

ad. summer

ad. summer

YELLOW-BILLED LOON

pale tip and outer culmen

juv. → 1st-winter

light

light scaly pattern

juv.

appearance of bill colour and bill shape vary according to background

ad. winter

pointing upwards, yellowish-white

white spots

ad. summer

ad. summer

K M

therefore more easily seen white spots than those of Great Northern Loon. – Juvenile: Upperparts have *neat, scaly pattern*. Pale overall impression. Less typical bill shape than in later stages. – 1st-summer: Remains in fully juvenile-like plumage. – 2nd-winter: Upperparts appear all dark. No white-spotted wing-coverts. – 2nd-summer: Mixture of adult and juvenile. Scattered 'sugar lumps' on upperparts, and head and neck (incl. foreneck) largely uniformly sooty-grey (lacking white markings of adult).

VOICE Similar to that of Great Northern Loon.

Great Northern Loon   Yellow-billed Loon

GREBES *Podicipedidae*

Aquatic birds, highly specialized and accomplished divers (counterpart to the loons in shallow, well-vegetated lakes and shallow sea-bays). Streamlined body with feet placed far back to facilitate fast diving. Move awkwardly on land. Toes lobed (feet thus lacking the complete webbing of loons and wildfowl). Flight almost invariably close over water, appears laborious, wings small. Food small fish, aquatic insects, plants, etc. Build a floating nest of plant material. Five breeding species and an American vagrant.

Horned Grebe (Slavonian Grebe)
Podiceps auritus   m**B**5 / **W**4

L 31–38 cm, WS 46–55 cm. Breeds on shallow, well-vegetated lakes; accepts small ponds with little open water so long as they do not dry up in summer; also on clear, open ponds in uplands in N Fenno-Scandia. Winters on coastal waters, lakes, reservoirs, mainly at W European coasts.

IDENTIFICATION Rather small, about as large as a Teal. Longish neck, *flat crown peaking at rear*, flat-topped head when viewed head-on, and longish body give shape like miniature Great Crested rather than Little Grebe. 'Powder puff' rear end not usually so prominent as on Black-necked. *Bill straight and rather short*, often with *pale tip*. In flight, shows *small white shoulder patch* and *white speculum confined to secondaries*. Flight somewhat auk-like, path veering; migrants have habit of raising head high (at times feet too) in flight for a brief moment or longer. – Adult summer: Unmistakable, but in transition to or from summer plumage dark on ear-coverts can give pattern like winter Black-necked; at distance, reddish foreneck can look black. – Adult winter: Sharply contrasting black-and-white pattern on head; neat black cap sharply demarcated from white cheeks, with rather *straight division from bill through eye* (no prominent dusky downward bulge on ear-coverts) and only *slight if any 'hook-back' at nape*; head-on, cap appears as *forward-tilted 'black beret'*; from rear, *very thin dark line down upper hindneck* termed 'wrap-around' white cheeks; dusky band across upper foreneck sometimes extensive (as on Black-necked); at close range, *whitish spot on lores*. – Juvenile: Like adult winter, but with dusky band across cheek, slightly browner above, and with more extensive pale on bill-base. Caution: some individuals less well marked, and distance or bright light can give Black-necked more contrasting black-and-white head pattern than usual.

VOICE Commonest call a rather feeble but far-carrying, trembling or rattling 'hii-arrr', falling in pitch. Display-call is a squealing, *pulsating* trill, each wave of rapid, giggling notes turning into whinnying ones which descend and end with a nasal drawn-out note. Mainly silent in winter.

Black-necked Grebe *Podiceps nigricollis*   m**B**5 / **W**4

L 28–34 cm. Breeds, usually in small colonies, on shallow ponds and lakes with much emergent vegetation, frequently associated with Black-headed Gulls or Black Terns; prefers access to rather large patches of open water. Winters on coastal waters, lakes, reservoirs in W and S Europe.

IDENTIFICATION Slightly smaller than Horned Grebe, and more elegant with *thinner neck*. Dumpy body and usually prominent 'powder-puff' rear end give shape recalling Little Grebe; *steep forehead*, with *crown rounded* or *peaking over eye*; bill rather tiny, uptilted to sharp point (shape obvious only at close range). In flight, white on secondaries *extends to inner primaries*, and *lacks white shoulder patch*. – Adult summer: Unmistakable; note especially *drooping, thin fan of yellowish-white cheek feathers*. – Adult winter: Head pattern *less sharply contrasting black and white* than Horned (but beware distance or bright light) because of *grey downward bulge on rear ear-coverts; prominent whitish 'hook-back' up* sides of nape. Caution: juvenile Little Grebe can show similar head pattern, but coloration dark brown/buff (not black/grey/white); also eye black, and different bill shape.

VOICE Territorial call easiest to recognize, a rising, somewhat strained, repeated 'pü-**iii**(ch)' . More unobtrusive, short whistling 'wit'. In display, and territorial encounters, a fast, vibrant, rather low, hard trill. Silent in winter.

Little Grebe *Tachybaptus ruficollis*   r**B**3

L 23–29 cm. Breeds in vegetated margins of often small inland waters (ponds, even ditches). Shy, keeps in cover of reeds and sedges for long periods. Winters on often less vegetated lakes, reservoirs, sheltered coasts of W Europe.

IDENTIFICATION *Smallest grebe* (can be mistaken for duckling!), with shortish neck, *very dumpy body*, and *prominent 'powder-puff' rear end*; tiny straight bill. *Lacks white on wing.* – Adult summer: *Chestnut cheeks and foreneck*, with *prominent pale yellow fleshy gape*. – Adult winter: General coloration *brown and buff*, lacking black, grey and white contrasts of Horned and Black-necked; foreneck and cheek sandy-buff. – Juvenile: Like adult winter, but with short dark stripes behind and below eye, and bill-base yellowish-flesh; plumage very faded sandy-buff by first winter.

VOICE Varying high-pitched calls, e.g. 'bee-eep' and 'bit, bit bit', accelerating into a far-carrying, rattling, high-pitched trill, often drawn-out and in chorus, 'bibibibi-bibibi...'; somewhat like call of ♀ Cuckoo. Silent in winter.

Pied-billed Grebe *Podilymbus podiceps*   **V**∗∗

L 31–38 cm. Rare vagrant from America; often stays long.

IDENTIFICATION Shape and plumage like a large, stocky, heavily built adult winter Little Grebe (and could thus easily be overlooked at distance or if size not obvious), but *bill very thick and heavy*. – Adult summer: Bill is whitish *with a thick black vertical band; thin white eye-ring* and *black chin*. – Winter: Bill whitish or yellowish, at most with hint of band; no black chin.

VOICE Silent in winter.

Horned Grebe   Black-necked Grebe   Little Grebe

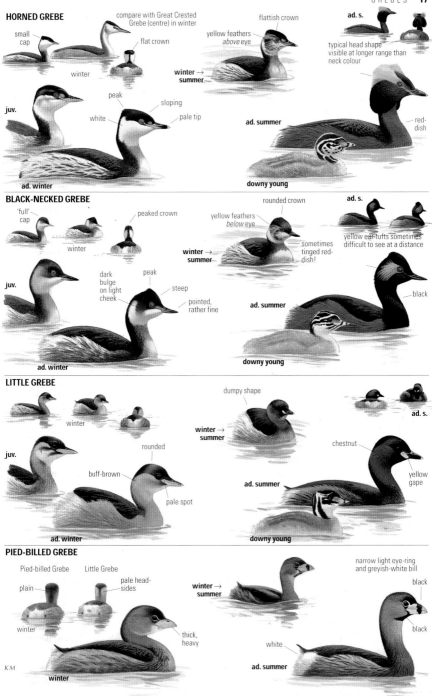

HORNED GREBE

small cap

flat crown

compare with Great Crested Grebe (centre) in winter

winter

flattish crown

yellow feathers *above* eye

ad. s.

typical head shape visible at longer range than neck colour

winter → summer

juv.

peak

sloping

white

pale tip

ad. summer

red-dish

ad. winter

downy young

BLACK-NECKED GREBE

'full' cap

winter

peaked crown

rounded crown

yellow feathers *below* eye

sometimes tinged red-dish!

ad. s.

yellow ear-tufts sometimes difficult to see at a distance

juv.

dark bulge on light cheek

peak

steep

pointed, rather fine

winter → summer

ad. summer

black

ad. winter

downy young

LITTLE GREBE

winter

dumpy shape

winter → summer

ad. s.

juv.

rounded

buff-brown

pale spot

chestnut

yellow gape

ad. summer

ad. winter

downy young

PIED-BILLED GREBE

Pied-billed Grebe

Little Grebe

plain

pale head-sides

winter

winter → summer

narrow light eye-ring and greyish-white bill

black

black

winter

thick, heavy

white

ad. summer

KM

Great Crested Grebe *Podiceps cristatus* rB4 / W3

L 46–51 cm, WS 59–73 cm. Breeds commonly on reeded larger waters. In winter, offshore or on lakes, reservoirs, mostly in W Europe. Not shy, spends much time openly on unvegetated waters. Nest a large mound of reed stems.

IDENTIFICATION *Largest* and most familiar grebe in most of Europe. Shape distinctive: long low body and *long slender neck* either held erect or (when inactive) lowered with head resting in mid-back; *bill* long, slim and *more extensively pale* than other grebes. In flight, exceptionally *long skinny outline* with flickering wingbeats, slightly stern-heavy, and blackish upcurled feet projecting; *white secondaries and shoulder patch prominent.* – Adult summer: Unmistakable; *head plumes* held compressed when alert, or raised, fanned and vigorously shaken in head-to-head courtship displays which climax in 'penguin dance' in which pair-members raise whole body upright, breast to breast. Bill reddish-pink. –Winter: Head, foreneck and flanks more extensively white than on other grebes, with *white above eye* and *black loral line from eye to bill.* – Juvenile: Striped cheeks; bill pale pink. –1st-summer: Head plumes are incomplete or lacking.

VOICE Highly vocal, giving *loud, far-carrying calls.* During display (incl. on spring nights) has very strong, *rolling* 'crrra-ahrr', slowly repeated; hard, moaning, nasal sounds; and shorter 'krro'; also series of hard 'vrek-vrek-vrek-...' during head-shaking phase of display. Young beg with persistent, clear, whistling 'pli(e), pli(e), pli(e),...', somewhat like distant Oystercatcher.

Red-necked Grebe *Podiceps grisegena* W4

L 40–46 cm. Breeds on reeded waters, often smaller and more vegetated than for Great Crested. Winters on coasts, occasionally lakes, reservoirs, in W and S Europe. Mostly shy and retiring habits, reluctant to expose itself much.

IDENTIFICATION Slightly smaller than Great Crested, with *shorter, stockier neck* and often *small 'powder-puff' rear end* (shape thus between Great Crested and Horned); bill slightly shorter, more wedge-shaped and held slightly down, often giving *subtle drooping effect* unlike Great Crested. In flight, less skinny than Great Crested, with shorter, dark neck and less prominent white on shoulder. Unlike Great Crested (but like smaller grebes), *dives usually with pronounced jump clear of water.* – Adult summer: Unmistakable; courtship display as Great Crested. Small *clear-cut yellow patch at base of bill.* –Winter: *Head pattern without sharp black and white contrast* as on Great Crested and Horned; whitish or pale buff throat and light 'hook-back' behind ear-coverts contrast diffusely against *dusky ear-coverts* and *extensively grey upper foreneck*; breast often whitest part. A hint of the yellow patch at bill-base visible when close. – Juvenile: Like winter, but cheeks and ear-coverts whitish with thin dark stripes, and *upper foreneck and neck-sides reddish-brown*; *yellow bill-base* not clear-cut, and is more extensive than on adult.

VOICE Noisy when breeding. Display-calls include loud, repeated, grating 'cherk, cherk, cherk...' and drawn-out, wailing and mournful 'aaoouuh', which can turn into pig-like squeals (recalling Water Rail but much louder and longer, and more baleful tone). Silent in winter.

Great Crested Grebe   Red-necked Grebe

WATCHING SEABIRDS

Special trips and tactics are usually necessary for seeing the truly oceanic species such as shearwaters and petrels (pp. 20–25) and coastal or island cliff-nesting seabirds such as Fulmar (p. 20), Gannet (p. 26) or the auks (pp. 194–197).

Seabird colonies. Breeding-season visits to nesting cliffs or islands undoubtedly provide the best views. The mass of birds, the variety of species, the spectacular urgent activity, the noise—and the smell!—at a large seabird colony provide one of the most exciting birdwatching experiences. Colonies on mainland sea-cliffs are the most easily accessible, but many major seabird islands are served by 'seabird special' boat trips. Before any visit, it is necessary to find out about sites, visiting hours, boat times, etc.

Ferries and 'pelagics'. Commercial ferry routes can provide sometimes excellent opportunities for seeing seabirds. Some routes are better than others, and these are well known to seabird enthusiasts; appropriate enquiries are necessary to discover which they are. On a large boat, a *sheltered* spot on an open *upper* deck near the *front* is usually the best position. Special 'pelagic' boat trips for birdwatchers, which go far out into the ocean, are more commonly organized in N America than in Europe, but like some oceanic liner crossings they provide the best chances for seeing shearwaters and petrels in their offshore feeding areas. Otherwise, these species come close inshore only when driven by severe storms, and they come in to their nesting sites only at night.

Seawatching. For most birdwatchers, this is the most usual and most convenient way to look for seabirds. It involves often long periods of looking out to sea from a coastal head-

in overcast weather   in afternoon sun

Note how different light can create dramatically different impressions of the same species (above, Manx Shearwater).

GREAT CRESTED GREBE

winter

rapid 'white-flicker-ing' wingbeats

courtship

resting and preening birds

large feet

white

extremely rakish build

ad. s.

white

pale

white

compare with Red-throated Loon (right)

juv.

winter

ad.-s.

RED-NECKED GREBE

winter

rather compact, thick neck

ad. s.

Red-necked in spring (centre) flanked by two Horned Grebes (that on the left is moulting from winter to summer plumage)

compare with winter Great Crested (right)

more inclined to 'spring-dive' than Great Crested

compare with Horned Grebe (right)

dark with yellow base

red-brown

dark

juv.

winter

ad. s.

K M

land which projects out into regular seabird migration routes. Fresh or strong onshore winds are usually required to bring the birds in close, and particular sites are better at different times of year: again, enquiries of local birdwatchers are necessary to find out the sites, and the best times of year and weather conditions.

Seawatching, however, is a somewhat acquired taste. This is because the birds are often distant, just 'dots on the horizon', with identification based on silhouette and flight action, requiring a good deal of experience and identification skill. For the beginner, seawatching can be a daunting experience, but the following hints may help.

• At least initially, it is essential to seawatch with an experienced birdwatcher who can point out the distinctive silhouettes and flight actions of various groups or species.

• Having located passing seabirds with binoculars, a good telescope is essential to get closer views: a telescope with 20× to 30× magnification is ideal, and wide-angle oculars are naturally to be preferred.

• Long periods on a windswept headland can become uncomfortable, so always dress warm and choose a sheltered position so that binoculars and telescope can be held steady out of the wind. A comfortable sitting position is best, with telescope on tripod positioned ready for instant use. A con-

ventional ball-and-socket joint is almost useless for following moving targets; make sure you are equipped with a fluid-head joint designed for film cameras.

• Giving accurate directions is important so that others can quickly locate any potentially interesting passing seabird. Agreeing particular reference points (buoys, ships, offshore rocks, etc.) and deciding what is 'straight out' is a good idea at the beginning of any seawatch. Directions to a particular bird should always include *direction from the observers* (the usual method is to use the observers as the centre of an imaginary clockface, with '12 o'clock' being straight out), whether it is *flying left or right*, whether it is *flying above or below the horizon*, an approximation of *distance*, and *when it is passing one of the previously agreed reference points*:'Skua at 2 o'clock, flying left, just below horizon, middle distance... approaching the red buoy and passing it 3...2...1...Now!' is obviously better than the frustratingly vague directions so often heard on seawatches! Using a binocular field of view, although varying somewhat according to makes, as an approximate unit of distance can also be useful, e.g.:'Half a field above the horizon' or 'Two fields left of the yacht'. Once the basics have been learned, a good seawatch can provide very exciting birdwatching, and a convenient chance of seeing seabirds from remote places.

SHEARWATERS, PETRELS et al. *Procellariiformes*
A group of highly pelagic birds: albatrosses (*Diomedeidae*; see p. 26), fulmars, shearwaters and petrels (*Procellariidae*), and storm-petrels (*Hydrobatidae*). The larger species have long, narrow wings and can glide for hours over the sea with hardly a wingbeat; they use a special switchback flight, exploiting the wind-speed difference in the wave troughs compared with higher up. The smallest species, storm-petrels, are shorter-winged and use more wing action in flight. Straight bill with hooked tip and tube-shaped nostrils; nasal glands secrete the seawater's salt. Take food from the sea (fish, crustaceans, plankton, molluscs). Breed on rocky remote islands and coasts, visiting nests (on cliff-ledge or in burrow) mostly at night.

(Northern) **Fulmar** *Fulmarus glacialis* rB2
L 43–52 cm, WS 101–117 cm. Breeds in loose colonies on ledges on steep coastal cliffs or in burrows on inaccessible slopes, but locally also in exposed sites on buildings along N Atlantic coasts. Diurnal at nest site (unlike relatives). Chick spits oily gastric juice at intruders. Versatile forager (takes crustaceans, fish offal, whale flesh), and large gatherings may be seen far from colonies.
   IDENTIFICATION Looks like a small, compact Herring Gull, but flight and shape differ clearly, even at long range when plumage details (such as lack of both black-and-white pattern at wing-tip and white trailing edge) not visible. *Glides* over sea or back and forth along breeding precipice *on stiff, straight wings*, now and then giving a series of *stiff, shallow, quite rapid wingbeats*. Floats high when swimming, and needs a pattering run-up in order to take off. Has *short, thick neck* and *large head*. Bill short and deep, lead-grey and yellowish. Wings are more bluntly rounded at tip than on large gulls. Commonest plumages are *pale medium grey above* (base of 'hand' with diffuse pale patch) and *white below*; head white with small dark spot at corner of eye. Occurs in various morphs (not well differentiated), from light grey above and white below to fairly dark grey above and somewhat paler grey below; dark birds ('Blue Fulmar') commonest in far north.
   VOICE Series of throaty, guttural cackling notes, varying in speed, often accelerating and with increasing power in duet between the sexes; heard mostly at colonies.

Cory's Shearwater *Calonectris diomedea* P4
L 45–56 cm, WS 112–126 cm. Breeds colonially in burrows on rocky islands and precipitous coasts in Mediterranean and E Atlantic S of 40°. Small loose flocks often seen foraging, visible from land. Almost all winter in S Atlantic (odd ones remain S of Sicily). Some dispersal

into N Atlantic Jul–Oct, regularly north to S Ireland.
   IDENTIFICATION Roughly size of Lesser Black-backed Gull, and characterized by *long, flexible wings* which at all times are held slightly or distinctly *bowed*. Flies with *long glides* close above the water (even in calm conditions!), relieved by 3–4 (rarely 6–7) *relaxed, flexible beats* of the bowed wings; wing-tips look somewhat blunt, and 'hand' is *angled backwards*. Brownish-grey above ('hand' somewhat darker), with diffusely paler uppertail-coverts (normally seen only at close range), whitish below (no dark marks on axillaries or belly) with characteristic *dirty grey side of breast, neck and head. Bill pale pinkish-yellow* with dark near tip; in good light, pale bill can be seen at long range.
   VOICE At dusk and dawn noisy at colonies, giving both crow-like and frog-like hard, dry rolling sounds and strained, nasal or whining notes (voice most like Kittiwake's) with harder ending, roughly 'gaooh-ak'.

Great Shearwater *Puffinus gravis* P4
L 43–51 cm, WS 105–122 cm. Breeds on islands in S Atlantic, wintering (during European summer) at sea east of N America. On southward migration takes a more easterly route and found regularly in W Europe, mainly Aug–Oct; rarer in North Sea. Often attracted to vessels.
   IDENTIFICATION Despite its name, a shade smaller than Cory's Shearwater, which it somewhat resembles; has e.g. *white uppertail-coverts*. Distinguished by *stiffer and more rapid wingbeats* (reminiscent more of Fulmar and Manx Shearwater); clearly *contrasting dark* (sooty-brown) *cap*, accentuated by *conspicuous whitish neck-side; discrete dark mark at side of breast*; dark bars and spots in armpit and on inner part of underwing; diffuse *dark patch on central belly* ('oil stain'; but often hard to see) and dusky (not white) undertail-coverts; *black bill*; and somewhat more pointed wing-tip.

Fea's Petrel *Pterodroma feae* V?
L 33–36 cm, WS 86–94 cm. Breeds late summer and *autumn* in small colonies in burrows in Madeira (Bugio) and Cape Verdes. Very few in number, threatened. Visits nest at night, forages by day at sea. Probably this species which has occurred in W Europe.
   IDENTIFICATION First impression may be of a small Cory's or Great Shearwater, but *underwing almost entirely blackish*. Upperparts grey with dark W-pattern (obviousness depending on light and range). *Uppertail uniformly pale grey*. Sides of breast washed grey (but lacks complete dark breast-band of similar-looking rare straggler, Soft-plumaged Petrel; p.386). Fast flight. Fea's and Zino's Petrels are thought to be near-inseparable in the field; Fea's is *larger* than Zino's and has *slightly heavier bill*.
   VOICE Drawn-out mournful sounds, sometimes terminating with a hiccup, at night at colonies.

Zino's Petrel *Pterodroma madeira* V?
L 32–34 cm, WS 80–86 cm. Nests late spring–summer in Madeira (main island), in inaccessible rock crevices on inland mountains (1650 m). Highly threatened (only *c.* 50 pairs known). Visits nest at night, forages by day at sea.
   IDENTIFICATION Very like Fea's Petrel (which see).

Fulmar   Cory's Shearwater

FULMAR

floating on updraught

long glides on stiff wings

(dark)

smoky

pale primary patch

thick neck

nests on cliff-ledges

(dark)

gull-like on water, but note thickset build and short, stout bill

(light)

(light)   (intermediate)   (dark)

darker lores and bill-band on dark morphs

CORY'S SHEARWATER

Fulmar   Cory's

short   white

diffuse dark border

generally unmarked

clean white

variable white

pale, yellowish

flight action seems more relaxed, at times almost lethargic, compared with Fulmar and Great Shearwater

GREAT SHEARWATER

dark markings

dark 'shoulder' mark

Great Shearwater

Gannet, 2nd-w.

beware: young Gannets can be superficially similar

looks oil-stained

dirty-looking belly and vent area most obvious when banking

sharp division

dark

obvious white

light collar visible at long range

Great   Cory's

FEA'S PETREL

clearly two-coloured upperwing

almost all dark

ZINO'S PETREL

dark   slightly paler

long, pale, pointed

short, heavy bill

somewhat thinner bill

KM

Little Shearwater *Puffinus assimilis*   **V****

L 25–30 cm, WS 58–67 cm. Breeds in smallish colonies in spring on Atlantic islands (race *baroli*; Azores, Madeira, Canaries). Only rarely seen N of breeding areas.

IDENTIFICATION A small version of the Manx Shearwater (latter common in N Atlantic), and similarly very dark above and white below. Besides *smaller* size, differs as follows: *shorter, broader wings* with more rounded tip; often appears to have *narrower dark border to underwing*; proportionately *more slender bill* and *more rounded head*, which is often *held high* and sometimes raised in flight; upperwing more two-toned with a *diffuse pale area on inner wing* (greater coverts often white-tipped); *white of cheeks extends upwards to enclose dark eye* and accentuates dark of neck-sides. In comparable winds, flight is more flapping with *quicker wingbeats* in *longer series* than in Manx (but comparison with auk still far-fetched). Occasionally hangs in wind above sea surface with wings raised and feet dangling, snatching food.

VOICE On dark, moonless nights, usually after nightfall, high-pitched laughing, rhythmic series with emphasis on second note heard from colonies,'ka-**ki**-kukukur-kaa'.

Manx Shearwater *Puffinus puffinus*   m**B**2

L 30–35 cm, WS 71–83 cm. Breeds colonially on islands and coastal cliffs in N Atlantic; huge numbers Britain & Ireland. Gregarious. Nest usually in burrow, visited at night. Numerous on passage, especially in autumn. Does not normally follow ships.

IDENTIFICATION Medium-large shearwater, *uniformly sooty-black above and white below*. Head dark to below eye, and dark of upperparts extends onto breast-sides. Note *uniformly dark wings above* (without paler secondaries) and *white undertail-coverts*. Sexes and ages similar in plumage. Typical shearwater flight, in calmer weather low over water with series of rapid, shallow *beats of stiff, straight wings*, relieved by long *glides with slightly downturned, rigid wings*; in strong wind almost exclusively gliding flight, one moment shearing over the sea surface in the wave troughs and the next sweeping up (sometimes to many metres) and veering down again.

VOICE At colonies on dark nights, raucous, coughing calls, four-syllabled 'chi-ki gah-ach' and the like, the latter notes hoarser, more drawn out and deeper.

Mediterranean Shearwater *Puffinus yelkouan*   **P**4

L 34–39 cm, WS 78–90 cm. Breeds on coastal cliffs and islands in Mediterranean, where also winters. Scarce visitor to N Atlantic in late summer and autumn. Closely related to Manx Shearwater.

IDENTIFICATION Somewhat bigger than Manx (but noticeably smaller than Sooty), slightly heavier in build, often seems slightly longer-necked, more pot-bellied and shorter-tailed (with projecting toes). Western race *mauretanicus* (Balearics) is brown above and *dirty brownish-white below*, but usually *somewhat paler on breast and belly*. Majority have *dusky undertail-coverts and armpit*. Eastern race *yelkouan* (Italy, Aegean Sea) is a shade darker above and cleaner white below, very similar to Manx and probably not safely distinguished away from normal range.

VOICE As Manx, but more drawling and with a drawn-out, stressed falsetto note, repeated 'a**ii**-ah eech'.

Sooty Shearwater *Puffinus griseus*   **P**3

L 40–50 cm, WS 95–110 cm. Breeds in southern hemisphere but spends 'winter' in northern; when southward passage begins many are in W European waters and are then seen in association with storms, mainly Aug–Oct; regular (incl. flocks) off British & Irish coasts.

IDENTIFICATION A medium-sized, dark shearwater with long pointed wings. Flight powerful and direct, the *pointed, narrow wings slightly bowed and with the 'hand' somewhat backswept* in strong wind. In poor light looks *all black*, but in good conditions looks more chocolate-brown with *paler, almost silvery-looking underwing pattern* (of variable prominence). Can be confused with darkest Mediterranean Shearwater, the only other shearwater likely to turn up in our waters that does not have white belly, but that species is smaller and shorter-winged, often appears more pot-bellied and is not so athletic a flyer as Sooty. Dark-morph skua employing shearwater flight, and juvenile Gannet, can recall Sooty Shearwater.

Bulwer's Petrel *Bulweria bulwerii*   **V*****

L 25–29 cm, WS 67–73 cm. Breeds colonially on islands in E Atlantic, in our region mainly in Madeira but also a few in Canaries (off Lanzarote), Jun–Oct. Nests among boulders or in cliff cavity, often near sea. Visits colonies at night. Forages alone; does not flock.

IDENTIFICATION A moderately big, largely all-dark, graceful petrel with long, narrow wings and long tail. The only feature in the otherwise uniformly dark brown plumage is paler diagonal wing-covert panels above. Dark plumage may suggest Sooty Shearwater when size difference not obvious, but Bulwer's has longer tail, all-dark underwing, and flight action is quite different, with looser, deeper wingbeats. Often glides on downturned wings.

VOICE Silent at sea and when returning to colonies at dusk. At night, hollow, hoarse yapping sounds heard from nest burrows, 'hroo hroo hroo...' (like steam-engine).

Little Shearwater   Manx Shearwater   Mediterranean Shearwater   Sooty Shearwater

LITTLE SHEARWATER

sometimes raises head high in flight

slender

pale side of head

dark border narrow

wings shorter and blunter than on Manx

at close range narrow light tips

dark eye stands out

white 'face', cute, rounded head

arched wings

subtle silvery-grey area

MANX SHEARWATER

banking flight

some have a little dark on 'armpits'

slightly flexed wings

dark extends below eye

all dark; often shows brownish cast in sunlight

MEDITERRANEAN SHEARWATER

short tail, toes project slightly

some dark markings

more brownish than Manx

a few are darker below

(typical)

Mediterranean (dark)

pot-bellied

SOOTY

trim shape

yelkouan (E Mediterranean)

SOOTY SHEARWATER

looks almost black at distance but more brown in good light

long, narrow and pointed wings

more uniform head and underparts than Mediterranean Shearwater

silvery

head and body always all dark

wings swept back in strong wind

PARASITIC SKUA

Sooty

skuas, too, practise banking flight in strong winds

pale

long

a young Gannet is twice the size

BULWER'S PETREL

rounded, full tail may show momentarily

diffuse pale carpal bar

wings often arched

long tail, usually folded and narrow

plain underwing

heavy bill

very long wings

KM

(European) **Storm-petrel** *Hydrobates pelagicus* m**B**2/**P**
L 15–16 cm, WS 37–41 cm. Breeds on inaccessible rocky islands and coasts in N Atlantic and W Mediterranean; especially abundant W Ireland, NW Scotland and Faroes. Nests quite near water in burrow or among rocks. Passage migrants sometimes more numerous in autumn storms.

IDENTIFICATION The *smallest* storm-petrel in European waters, barely the size of a House Martin (which, with its dark upperparts and snow-white rump, it can momentarily recall), and with *more fluttering and 'busier' flight* than its relatives. Commonest confusion is with Leach's Storm-petrel, but flight action of that species usually clearly indicates its larger size; *lacks obvious covert band on upperwing* (though a narrow whitish bar is shown by juveniles) but has *diagnostic broad white band on underwing*; *broader and uniformly white rump patch extends far onto sides*.

VOICE From nest burrow at night gives a purring sound with interposed grunts (like stomach-rumbling).

Wilson's Storm-petrel *Oceanites oceanicus* **V**∗∗
L 16–18½ cm, WS 38–42 cm. Southern-hemisphere breeder, visiting N Atlantic Jun–Oct (Nov) (e.g. Biscay, waters SW of Britain & Ireland, off NW Africa); seldom seen from land. Like Storm-petrel, often follows ships.

IDENTIFICATION Closest to Storm-petrel, being *all dark with broad white rump* and *square-cut tail*. Differs in being somewhat bigger, with more *obvious pale covert band on upperwing, plain underwings*, and *longer legs* (project slightly beyond tail in flight). *Broader*-winged than Storm-petrel, *wings mostly held straight*, with less obvious carpal. Capable of extraordinarily sustained glides on almost flat wings.

Leach's Storm-petrel *Oceanodroma leucorhoa* m**B**4 / **P**
L 18–21 cm, WS 43–48 cm. Breeds northernmost N Atlantic; nests in cavities on rocky coasts. Winters S Atlantic. Sometimes large numbers on autumn passage in association with autumn storms. Does not follow ships.

IDENTIFICATION A fairly large and long-winged storm-petrel, considerably larger than Storm-petrel. Note *rather long, somewhat V-shaped white rump patch with hint of central divide* (visible only at very close range), *prominent pale covert band* on upperwing (often more obvious than white rump!), *dark underwings* and *more pointed and proportionately longer wings*. Forked shape of tail visible only from certain angles, but sides often raised to give rather ragged shape in profile. In strong wind flight quite powerful: glides on slightly bowed, *angled wings* (carpals pressed forward to give 'headless' silhouette), gives a few *powerful wingbeats*, veers off, pulls up, hangs in air etc.

VOICE From burrow at night gives strange rattling cooing, now and then interrupted by a falsetto 'wuee-cha' and ending with spirited 'chu-chatte**ri**cha chu-chitte**ri**!'.

Madeiran Storm-petrel *Oceanodroma castro* **V**∗∗∗
L 19–21 cm, WS 43–46 cm. Breeds on islands on rocky coasts, incl. off Portugal and Madeira (and probably Azores). Elusive; pelagic by day, not seen in flocks off (usually small) colonies; does not follow ships. Nests both late summer and late autumn, in burrows or rock crevices.

IDENTIFICATION *Dark with white rump* and thus difficult to separate from several relatives. In almost all respects much more like Leach's Storm-petrel than Wilson's or European, but following differences most useful: *less prominent covert band on upperwing*; *negligible fork in tail*; *white rump patch seems more wide than long* (usually the reverse on Leach's) and on many the white extends prominently onto the sides of rump. At close range *bill noticeably heavy*. Thorough familiarity with storm-petrels a prerequisite to judging subtle wing-shape and flight-action differences: Madeiran's wing often seems to have less pronounced angle at carpal (but much more 'arm' than Wilson's), and typical flight incorporates tight twists and short glides on direct switchback course.

VOICE From burrow at night gives cooing 'kr'r'r'r' and squeaky 'chi**wee**' ('rubbing finger on windowpane').

Swinhoe's Storm-petrel *Oceanodroma monorhis* **V**∗∗∗
L 18–21 cm, WS 45–48 cm. This species, with main breeding distribution in E Asia, has, surprisingly, been recorded several times in N Atlantic and trapped, e.g., at Selvagens N of Canaries and on rocky coast of NE England, in Norway, France, Spain, Portugal, Italy and Israel. 1st N Atlantic record in 1983, but species is probably overlooked owing to its nocturnal habits and similarity to Leach's Storm-petrel (same size, same wing pattern, forked tail). Differs from Leach's in having *rump dark*, like back, and *primary shafts pale at base*.

White-faced Storm-petrel *Pelagodroma marina* —
L 19–21 cm, WS 41–44 cm. Breeds (very numerous) on Selvagens N of Canaries, visiting burrows at night. Rarely seen at sea. Follows whale and dolphin schools.

IDENTIFICATION The region's only storm-petrel with *white underparts*. Shape most similar to Wilson's Storm-petrel, but looks bigger, with even longer legs, longer bill and *large butterfly-like wings*. Dark 'mask' surrounded by white, and grey of mantle extends prominently onto side of breast. Sails low over sea on stiffly outstretched wings (recalling flyingfish!) and uses its long legs to 'kick off' from the surface. Possibly confusable with winter-plumaged phalaropes (latter pelagic), but this would require great imagination.

VOICE Stifled slowly repeated 'koo, koo, koo, …', sometimes with squeaky falsetto 'kyi' notes interspersed, heard from nest.

Storm-petrel Leach's Storm-petrel Madeiran Storm-petrel

STORM-PETREL

smallest storm-petrel

broad white band

square or round-ended **juv.**

rather angled wings

plain, faded brownish wing-coverts in summer

white reaches far down on side

(worn)

juv.

typical flight views

thin wing-bar on fresh juv. (Oct)

WILSON'S STORM-PETREL

shorter 'arm' than Storm-petrel and Leach's

bronzy sheen, lacks white band

square or round-ended

smoothly curved leading edge, no angle

short pale panel

toes project

primary moult almost complete (late summer)

white nearly encircles tail

typical flight views

long glides on flat wings

from some angles tail appears notched!

projecting toes difficult to discern

long legs

LEACH'S STORM-PETREL

strong contrast on upperwing

long pale panel

hint of central divide

'face' often greyish

reduced white on side

forked

typical flight views

long, arched wings, forked tail

in direct comparison with Storm-petrel, Leach's appears much bigger

MADEIRAN STORM-PETREL

somewhat less contrast on upperwing than Leach's

inconspicuous pale panel

heavy bill

white often extensive on side

slightly indented

slightly shorter wings than Leach's

square or slightly notched

width of rump patch greater than length

LEACH'S STORM-PETREL (to compare)

forked

length of rump patch greater than width

SWINHOE'S STORM-PETREL

beware: some Leach's show very little white on rump!

forked

wing shape as Leach's

dark

light shafts (difficult to see in the field)

BULWER'S PETREL (to compare)

long, narrow

WHITE-FACED STORM-PETREL

sails on stiffly outstretched, flat wings (cf. phalaropes, p. 152)

very long legs

long-winged, wings broad-centred

typical flight views

appears to 'bounce' from side to side over surface

paddle-shaped wings

KM

GANNETS *Sulidae*

Large seabirds with long, pointed wings and long, pointed tail, plus straight, pointed bill. Dive for fish, often spectacularly, from a height. Sexes alike. Two species.

(Northern) **Gannet** *Morus bassanus* r+m**B**2

L 85–97 cm, WS 170–192 cm. Breeds colonially along steep rocky coasts and on inaccessible rocky islands in N Atlantic, with largest concentration in W Scotland (St Kilda). Pelagic and mobile outside breeding season: some reach W Africa, others W Mediterranean, many remain in breeding area. Numerous along W European coast in autumn. Nest of seaweed, on cliff-ledge or steep slope.

IDENTIFICATION With its *considerable size*, its *long, narrow wings* and its characteristic flight with *quite fast, shallow and uniform wingbeats interspersed with short glides*, generally easy to identify even at distance. In very windy conditions inclined to bank and shear like a shearwater and, especially in the case of immatures, may be mistaken for one of the large shearwater species, but Gannet is much bigger and has *more projecting, wedge-shaped tail* and *longer head/neck*. Makes stunning steep, diagonal dives for fish from height of 10–40 m, wings thrown back just prior to striking water. – Adult: *White*, with head tinged yellow-buff, and *black wing-tips* . – 4th-winter: As adult, but central tail-feathers and odd scattered secondaries are usually black. – 3rd-winter: Most tail-feathers and secondaries black, but scattered white ones intermixed. Head and body largely as adult. – 2nd-winter: Underparts and head largely white, as are uppertail-coverts and usually some lesser upperwing-coverts. Often some dark on crown and partial 'collar' (at distance may recall Great Shearwater). – Juvenile: Plumage wholly grey-brown but for whitish uppertail-coverts. At close range, entire plumage seen to be finely speckled white, giving beautiful silvery sheen to head and back in good light. – Note that individual variation leads to deviations from the above-described plumage development.

VOICE Loud, grating sounds at colonies.

Brown Booby *Sula leucogaster* —

L 65–75 cm, WS 135–150 cm. Breeds in tropical coastal waters, including islands in Red Sea; seen regularly in e.g. Gulf of Aqaba (Eilat). *Smaller* than Gannet, with somewhat *more rounded tail. All dark brown above*. Below, brown with *white secondary coverts* and *sharply defined white belly*. (Immature has pale brown-grey belly.) *Pale bill* and *pale facial skin* contrast with otherwise dark head. (Bill-base bluish in breeding season.) Dives steeply like Gannet, but also at oddly shallow angles. Often rests on buoys.

Black-browed Albatross *Diomedea melanophris* **V**∗∗

L 80–95 cm, WS 200–235 cm. S Atlantic species. The only albatross likely to be seen in the N Atlantic, where very rare summer and autumn visitor. Single birds have over-summered in Gannet colonies in Scotland. Wingspan as Mute Swan's. *Underwing white with broad black frame* (broadest at front). *Dark, short eye-stripe. Bill yellow* with orange at tip. Immature has grey bill and *narrow grey neck-collar*, as well as dusky underwing.

PELICANS *Pelecanidae*

Very big waterbirds with huge bill equipped with elastic skin pouch on lower mandible, with which fish are captured. Skilled soaring birds which, unlike storks and large raptors, *circle in orderly flocks with large parts of the flock in synchronized motion*, not a swarm of individualists. Sexes alike. Two species; both have declined greatly and are in need of protection. Breed at sheltered, shallow, fish-rich waters. Nest a pile of plant material on ground.

White Pelican *Pelecanus onocrotalus* [**V**]

L 140–175 cm (neck extended), WS 245–295 cm. Rare and local breeder at coastal swamps and shallow inland lakes. Migrates overland to winter in NE Africa.

IDENTIFICATION Adult has *white plumage* with, in breeding season, *faint yellow-pink tinge*; usually looks pure white at distance. *Throat sac greyish-yellow* (brighter yellow when breeding). *Feet yellow-pink* (more reddish when breeding). *Iris dark* (red), *framed by flesh-coloured bare skin* (orange when breeding). In flight, *black flight-feathers below* contrast strongly with white wing-coverts (thus same pattern as White Stork, but different soaring behaviour; see intro above). – Juvenile: Rather *dark brown-grey on upperparts*; dirty white below. Throat sac yellowish, *orbital skin and legs pink*. In flight resembles Dalmatian Pelican, but has *somewhat darker remiges below* and *greater contrast between remiges and paler central panel*.

VOICE Colonies produce a buzzing hum of stifled mumbling and various unarticulated grunting sounds.

Dalmatian Pelican *Pelecanus crispus* —

L 160–180 cm (neck extended), WS 270–320 cm. Very rare and local breeder at shallow lakes and swamps; also accepts smaller inland waters. Short-distance migrant.

IDENTIFICATION Like White Pelican but averages *slightly bigger*. Standing adult differs in *curly nape-feathers, grey feet, grey-tinged* white plumage (but as White Pelican with yellowish breast patch), *pale iris* with *very small area of pale surrounding skin*, plus *reddish throat sac* when breeding. In flight nearly *all-pale underwing* (grey-white, *whiter central band*), *with only wing-tips dark*. – Juvenile: Pale brown-grey above and dirty white below, *slightly paler and greyer* than juv. White; has *grey feet* and *greyish-white orbital skin*. (Throat sac yellowish.)

VOICE Poorly known. As White Pelican's but higher.

Gannet   White Pelican   Dalmatian Pelican

GANNET

4th-w.

4th-w
(variation)

2nd-winter
(Aug–Sep)

juv.

ad. summer

3rd-w.
(Aug–Sep)

juv.

ad. winter

BROWN BOOBY

juv.

brownish

ad.

colour of bill and
facial skin varia-
ble, sometimes
more blue-grey
than shown

at long range
can be confused
with young
Cormorant
(below left)

ad.

juv.

BLACK-BROWED ALBATROSS

Gan-
net

jizz reminiscent of a
giant, long-winged
Fulmar

light

clearly heavier
and more long-
winged than
Gannet

wide
black
edge

collar

narrow
black
edge

1st-s.

grey

pointed

swimming with
imm. (3rd-s.) Gannet (left)

ad.

WHITE PELICAN

juv.

pinkish

black

rather dark
brown-grey

ad. winter

pink
skin

juv.

DALMATIAN PELICAN

juv.

grey

light

pale
grey-
ish

ad. winter

throat sac
reddish
when
breed-
ing

juv.

KM

ad. summer

ad. summer

CORMORANTS *Phalacrocoracidae*
Medium-sized to large aquatic, mainly dark-plumaged birds. Body elongated, neck and tail long, latter much rounded. Bill strong, straight with hooked tip. All four toes webbed. Swim with body low and bill raised. Dive, often with leap from surface, for food, mainly fish. Frequently fly far between fishing waters and breeding sites or roosts. After dives, often perch on rocks or elevated sites with wings spread to dry in 'prehistoric' fashion. Breed colonially.

(Great) **Cormorant** *Phalacrocorax carbo*　　r**B3** / **P** / **W**
L 77–94 cm, WS 121–149 cm. Breeds on cliff-ledges along sea coasts (ssp. *carbo*, Atlantic; *maroccanus*, Morocco) or in trees at lakes or coasts, at times in reedbeds or on ground (*sinensis*; E and S Europe, presumably all breeders in Baltic). Northern birds migratory, British disperse locally. Roosts on sandbanks, rocks or take-net poles etc., often in large, dense flocks. Nest of seaweed, reed, twigs. Tree-nesting birds eventually kill their nest-trees by their droppings. Numbers have increased recently.
　IDENTIFICATION Large with long, thick neck. *Head profile rather wedge-shaped and angular*, bill strong (though at times confusingly thin on some juvs.). In flight superficially goose-like (similar size and wingbeat rate, neck outstretched, often flying at some height, incl. over land, generally in formation when in flock), but told by incidence of *brief glides breaking active flight*, by slightly shallower wingbeats, *longer tail*, *kinked neck*, and less orderly flock formation; also bill and tail held rather high. Single birds often fly low over the water (cf. Shag). Swims with body low and bill pointing up, and at long range could be confused with Yellow-billed Loon, but note *angular hindcrown*, *more erect neck* and *more strongly inclined bill*, and habit of frequently *leaping into dive*, and of usually diving without prior surveillance with head submerged in water, so typical of loons. – Adult: Black with bluish and some green gloss (amount of green not sufficient for picking out ssp. *sinensis*), wings tinged bronze and scaled black. *Bare skin at base of lower mandible yellow, surrounded by white* area. A white thigh patch is worn in early breeding season only (often lost as early as Jun). Crown and hindneck with varying amount of white feathers, on average more on old birds and in ssp. *sinensis* (but overlap considerable); much of these white feathers lost during summer. In winter less glossy, and white on cheeks and throat becomes duller and less clear-cut. – Juvenile: Dark brown above, underparts with varying amount of white, generally on centre of throat, breast and belly. 1st-year birds can look very white beneath, or have *patchy breast and belly with contrast between pure white and dark streaks*. – Immature: Gradually darker and more glossy

over two-year period until adult plumage attained. – Variation: In Morocco, adults have some white on foreneck and upper breast (ssp. *maroccanus*), or have all-white breast and upper belly contrasting with solidly dark lower belly (southern race *lucidus* or extreme variation of *maroccanus*?).
　VOICE Various deep, guttural calls at colony.

(European) **Shag** *Phalacrocorax aristotelis*　　r**B3**
L 68–78 cm, WS 95–110 cm. Breeds in loose colonies on coastal cliffs. Nest, in crevice, small cave or under large boulder, a heap of vegetation.
　IDENTIFICATION Somewhat smaller and slimmer than Cormorant, with *thinner neck*, *smaller, more rounded head* (*forehead steep, crown rounded*) and *thinner bill*. Differs in flight in *neck being straighter, outer wing slightly more blunt, wings appearing attached 'astern of midships'*, flightpath lower (usually close to water), wingbeats somewhat more elastic and fast without interspersed brief glides. Dives with more pronounced leap clear of water. Almost invariably seen on sea or perched on rocks, piers, etc. – Adult breeding: Black with green gloss, wings tinged purplish, scaled black. *Gape prominently yellow, contrasting with dark surround* including bill (Atlantic race; Mediterranean ssp. *desmarestii* has paler, more yellowish bill, reducing contrast). During early breeding has *upcurved, black crest on forecrown*, subsequently lost. – Adult non-breeding: Slightly duller, less glossy. Chin pale. *Bill yellowish*. – Juvenile: Dark brown above, pale brown below, chin whitish (ssp. *desmarestii* usually entirely or extensively off-white below). Small and thin-billed Cormorants in paler plumage told by: patchy dark and white breast, *not so uniform and pale brown* as Shag; bill off-white or pale horn, not *yellowish* as Shag; feet dark, not *pale* (webs flesh-coloured) as Shag; also, note *different head shape and face pattern*. Pale tips to upperwing-coverts form *pale wing-panel* in flight (Cormorant usually all dark, but pale imm. may have a hint). – Immature: Gradually darker and more glossy over two years until adult plumage attained.
　VOICE Various clicking and grunting calls at colony.

Pygmy Cormorant *Phalacrocorax pygmeus*　　—
L 45–55 cm, WS 75–90 cm. Breeds colonially at freshwater lakes and coastal deltas with rich vegetation. Swims in dense parties, perches on branches or climbs on reed stems. Nest of twigs and grass, in low, dense trees, or in reedbeds.
　IDENTIFICATION Rather *small*, about Coot-sized. *Tail very long; bill proportionately short and thick* ('baby-faced'); *neck* appears short too, but *can be stretched when swimming*. Blackish with dark green and bronzy gloss. – Adult breeding: Head, neck and underparts have small white feather tufts, subsequently lost in summer. – Adult non-breeding: Whitish chin and paler, brown-tinged chest. Has no white spots on head, neck or body. – Juvenile: Duller and browner; slightly streaked pattern on head and breast.
　VOICE Little known. Silent away from nesting sites. Croaking and grunting calls at colony.

Cormorant　　　　　　Shag　　　　　　　　Pygmy Cormorant

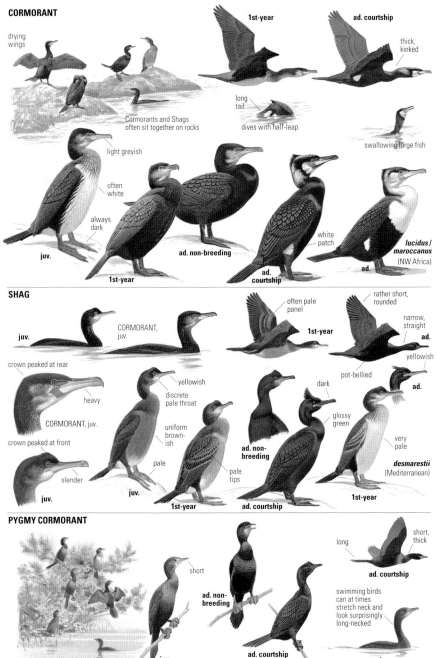

CORMORANT

drying wings

Cormorants and Shags often sit together on rocks

1st-year

ad. courtship

thick, kinked

long tail

dives with half-leap

swallowing large fish

light greyish

often white

always dark

juv.

1st-year

ad. non-breeding

ad. courtship

white patch

lucidus / maroccanus (NW Africa)

ad.

SHAG

juv.

CORMORANT, juv.

often pale panel

1st-year

rather short, rounded

narrow, straight

ad.

yellowish

pot-bellied

dark

ad.

crown peaked at rear

heavy

CORMORANT, juv.

crown peaked at front

slender

juv.

yellowish

discrete pale throat

uniform brownish

pale

juv.

pale tips

1st-year

ad. non-breeding

ad. courtship

glossy green

very pale

desmarestii (Mediterranean)

1st-year

PYGMY CORMORANT

short

ad. non-breeding

juv.

ad. courtship

long

short, thick

ad. courtship

swimming birds can at times stretch neck and look surprisingly long-necked

juv.

KM

HERONS, STORKS and IBISES *Ciconiiformes*

A group of large or medium-sized wading birds with long legs, neck and bill. Toes not webbed. Included are bitterns, egrets and herons (*Ardeidae*), which retract their long necks in flight, storks (*Ciconiidae*), which hold their necks outstretched in flight and which often soar high up, and ibises and spoonbills (*Threskiornithidae*), which have characteristic bill shapes but otherwise most resemble the storks.

(Great) **Bittern** *Botaurus stellaris* r**B**5 / **W**4

L 69–81 cm, WS 100–130 cm. Breeds only in extensive *Phragmites* reedbeds. Retreats from ice, but is hardy, returns early. Food mainly fish, frogs, insects. Polygamous. Nest a platform of dead reeds at water-level in reedbed.

IDENTIFICATION *Large buff-brown heron*; slightly smaller than Grey Heron, but shape much more *compact and stocky*, with *thicker neck* (usually hunched into shoulders), loose throat feathering, and shorter legs. Flies rather infrequently, mainly in spring and early autumn. In flight, note *broad wings*, *quicker wingbeats* than Grey Heron, *'thick' front end* and trailing feet; *at distance looks all ginger-brown* (broad wings and brown colour recalling buzzard or owl) with only *slightly paler wing-coverts than darker* (barred) *flight-feathers*. Rarely seen on ground (stays hidden in reedbed), and presence mostly revealed by *distinctive voice*; when alarmed in reedbed, adopts camouflage posture with bill pointing up ('bitterning posture'). – Juvenile: Like adult, but crown and shorter moustachial stripe browner (not black).

VOICE Flight-call a single or repeated, deep and hoarse 'graoh', somewhat recalling fox or large gull. Song of ♂ (so-called 'booming') is peculiar, far-carrying (up to 5 km on calm nights), very low, foghorn-like, exhaled, breathy 'whump', usually repeated 3–5 times with 2½-sec. intervals; when close, quieter inhalation also audible, 'uh-**whump**', and brief series of subdued, short opening notes.

American Bittern *Botaurus lentiginosus* V***

L 59–70 cm, WS 95–115 cm. Breeds in N America; very rare vagrant in W Europe, mostly in Oct–Nov. Smaller than Bittern, with thinner bill; *size and flight action may recall Night Heron*. Plumage Bittern-like except *flight-feathers plain blackish* (not barred), and *upperwing-coverts much paler*; *crown brown* (not blackish); *black moustachial stripe thicker* (though narrow and less black on juv.); and loose feathering of *foreneck more prominently striped with brown*.

Little Bittern *Ixobrychus minutus* V**

L 33–38 cm, WS 49–58 cm. Breeds in extensive or small reedbeds, overgrown reedy ponds, ditches. Summer visitor (mostly Apr–Oct); winters in Africa. Rare vagrant in Britain

& Ireland. Food fish, frogs, insects. Nest a platform of reeds often raised above water-level in reedbeds or bushes.

IDENTIFICATION Very small heron, *smaller than a Moorhen*. Secretive, but not infrequently comes to feed at edges of reedbeds etc.; often retreats by climbing and running like a crake rather than flying. In flight, quick jerky wingbeats distinctive, and *creamy wing patches unmistakable* on adults, less clear-cut on juveniles. – Adult ♂: Crown and upperparts *black*; wing patch buff-white, neat, contrasting. – Adult ♀: Black parts of ♂ are *brown*; wing patch buff-brown, unstreaked but less contrasting. – Juvenile: Like dull ♀ with *streaked* neck, upperparts and wing patch.

VOICE Flight-call an abrupt, nasal 'kwekwekwe'; also shorter 'kwer' or 'kerack'. Song, mostly at night but at all hours, monotonous, continuous series of a low and muffled croaking (still far-carrying) 'hogh', repeated every 2½ sec.

(Black-crowned) **Night Heron**
Nycticorax nycticorax V*

L 58–65 cm, WS 90–100 cm. Breeds colonially at marshes, ponds and riversides. Summer visitor (mainly Mar–Oct); winters in Africa. Rare visitor to mainly S Britain & Ireland, (esp. Apr–Jun). Food fish, frogs, insects. Active mainly at night, roosting communally in trees during daylight. Nests in trees, sometimes reedbeds; nest is platform of sticks.

IDENTIFICATION Short-billed, very *stocky*, medium-sized heron. In flight, has *compact, stumpy-ended outline* (feet not much noticeable) with *slightly raised body and drooping bill*, and stiff wingbeats. Most often seen at dawn or dusk, flying to and from roosts, but not always strictly nocturnal, and daytime sightings not infrequent. – Adult: Unmistakable in good views, but in flight often looks *all grey* (black back often difficult to see). Legs dull pinkish-yellow, reddish when breeding. – Juvenile/1st-winter: *Brown and buff* with *prominent white spotting* (gradually lost). – 2nd-winter: Like adult but crown and back faded grey-brown, not black.

VOICE Noisy at colonies; various raucous croaking notes. Flight-call a coarse, nasal, rather frog-like croak, 'quark'.

Mangrove Heron (Striated Heron, Green Heron)
Butorides striatus V***

L 40–47 cm, WS 60–73 cm. In W Palearctic, breeds only in S Sinai (ssp. *brevipes*) in mangroves; rare visitor N to Eilat, S Israel. The only records in Europe (Britain), and on Azores, in Oct–Nov, were N American race (*virescens*), by some regarded as a separate species.

IDENTIFICATION A small and dark, *long-billed* heron, slim-necked when alert, *thickset* when relaxed. – Adult: *Dark slate-grey, silvery-grey or brownish-grey above* (often just looks 'dark' at distance), with *wing-feathers neatly fringed buff-white* or rufous. *Sides of head, neck and breast varying from buff-grey to deep rufous*. – Juvenile: Brownish, with white spots/streaks on wings and bold stripes on neck. Cf. juv. Night Heron (which is larger, and shorter-billed).

VOICE A sharp 'skyek' call when flushed.

Bittern

Little Bittern

Night Heron

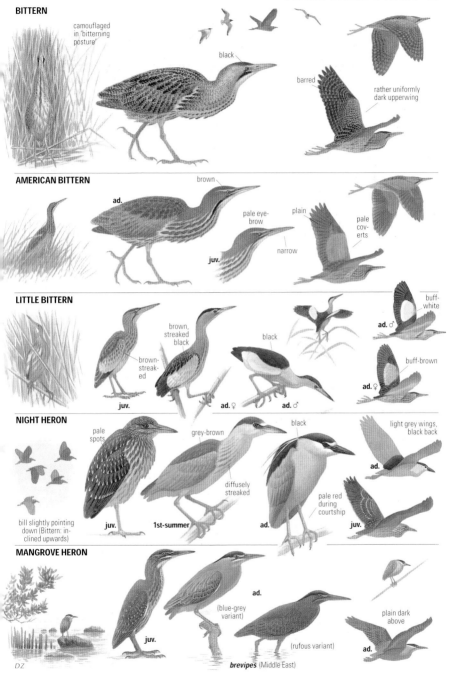

BITTERN

camouflaged in 'bitterning posture'

black

barred

rather uniformly dark upperwing

AMERICAN BITTERN

brown

ad.

pale eye-brow

plain

pale coverts

juv.

narrow

LITTLE BITTERN

brown, streaked black

black

brown-streaked

buff-white

ad. ♂

buff-brown

ad. ♀

juv.

ad. ♀

ad. ♂

NIGHT HERON

pale spots

grey-brown

black

light grey wings, black back

ad.

diffusely streaked

pale red during courtship

bill slightly pointing down (Bittern: inclined upwards)

juv.

1st-summer

ad.

juv.

MANGROVE HERON

ad.

juv.

(blue-grey variant)

plain dark above

(rufous variant)

ad.

DZ

brevipes (Middle East)

Cattle Egret *Bubulcus ibis*   **V****

L 45–52 cm, WS 82–95 cm. Nests colonially in trees and bushes by lakes and rivers, but forages in *often dry habitats*, among grazing cattle, on fields and grassland, but certainly also in wet marshes. Short-distance migrant. Range expanding. Eats insects; grasshopper specialist.

IDENTIFICATION Quite *small, white* heron with *compact body, short bill* and fairly short neck often held retracted. *Rounded head with well-feathered chin* ('undershot jaw'). Bill and legs generally greyish-yellow; pinky-orange when breeding, when also has *orange tone to crown, breast and mantle*. Active and mobile, makes short dashes. Flies with fast wingbeats in small disorderly flocks and lines.

VOICE In flight may give monosyllabic, quite soft croaks, 'kre'and'ehg'. Commonest call otherwise a gruff 'rick-**reck**'. Hoarse buzz heard from colonies.

Squacco Heron *Ardeola ralloides*   **V****

L 40–49 cm, WS 71–86 cm. Breeds in small colonies at shallow marshy lakes, ponds and rivers with reeds, bushes and lines of trees. Outside breeding season mostly solitary or in small groups. Summer visitor, winters Africa. Rare vagrant Britain. Food insects, small fish, amphibians.

IDENTIFICATION Quite small, *buffy-brown heron with white wings*; startling 'quick-change number' when light brown bird takes off and in flight looks almost all white! – Adult summer: Elongated nape-feathers. Back pale ochre with faint violet shimmer. Head and neck-sides almost unstreaked yellowish buff-white. Bill bluish with black tip, legs yellowish-pink (briefly coral-red during courtship). – Adult winter/immature: Lacks ornate nape-feathers, head- and neck-sides extensively streaked, upperparts duller, darker grey-brown. Bill yellowish with darker culmen/tip, legs greenish.

VOICE Often gives a hoarse, croaking'kaahk', quite like ♀ Mallard. Pounding, nasal'kak kak kak...'and more thick 'ah ah ah...' heard from colonies.

Little Egret *Egretta garzetta*   **W**4 / **P**4

L 55–65 cm, WS 88–106 cm. Nests colonially in dense trees and bushes at shallow marshy lakes, rivers and coastal lagoons. Mostly migratory in Europe; winters Africa, Middle East, some S Spain and NW Europe. Takes fish, frogs, insects, snails etc. from shallow lakes, fish ponds, flooded fields and so on, often in small groups.

IDENTIFICATION Medium-sized white heron, closer in size to Cattle Egret than to Great Egret, but *slim and elegant*. *Black legs with sharply contrasting bright yellow toes*, unlike any other W Palearctic white heron (but see similar Reef Egret, and rare vagrant Snowy Egret, p. 378). In

flight, *legs moderately projecting*, wings look near centrally placed (Great Egret very long-legged, wings 'fixed well forward'). *Bill black*; lores blue-grey for greater part of year, reddish during courtship period. In nuptial plumage delicate plumes formed by *two elongated nape-feathers*.

VOICE Mostly silent away from colonies. On rising, sometimes a Rook-like, hoarse yell, 'aaah'. Greeting call a loud 'da-**wah**'. At colonies several hoarse hard calls and a typically gargling 'gulla-gulla-gulla-...'.

(Western) Reef Egret *Egretta gularis*   —

L 55–68 cm, WS 88–112 cm. In region treated here breeds only in S Sinai, otherwise locally along Red Sea coasts (race *schistacea*); regular in small numbers at Eilat and Suez. Very rare vagrant Morocco from breeding sites mainly in Senegal (race *gularis*). Coastal habits; rests on shores, buoys, jetties, fishing poles etc. Fish-eater.

IDENTIFICATION Two morphs, *white* and *dark grey*. Close relative of Little Egret, and white morph very like latter; same size and shape, except that *bill is usually a touch longer*, often deeper-based but through rest of its length narrower and almost always *slightly curved* (hint of sabre shape). Bill colour variable, usually *yellowish* with darker culmen. *Legs greenish grey-black to halfway or more down tarsus, rest of tarsus and toes dull yellow*; legs can be more extensively greyish-yellow. Immature white morph often has scattered dark remiges.

Great Egret *Egretta alba*   **V****

L 85–100 cm, WS 145–170 cm. Breeds in colonies at large, shallow swampy lakes, preferably with reeds and some bushes and trees. Partial migrant, winters in Mediterranean region or Africa. Rare but annual vagrant in Britain. Feeds (on fish, aquatic insects) in flood meadows and along rivers, but also in somewhat drier terrain.

IDENTIFICATION A *very big all-white heron*. Almost the size of Grey Heron but a shade more elegant, with longer legs and neck. Needs to be told primarily from Little Egret and white-morph Reef Egret. (Cattle Egret also white, but is smaller and podgier and often has distinct ochre elements in plumage, so hardly confusable). Differs from Little Egret in: *slower, more dignified wingbeats*; proportionately *longer legs, which project a very long way past tail in flight*; *yellowish tibia* ('thigh') *and in part tarsus; yellowish bill except in breeding season*; *lacks nape plumes*; larger size. Told from white-morph Reef Egret by e.g. larger size, longer legs, plus straight dagger-shaped bill (not long and narrow with hint of sabre shape).

VOICE Silent except at colonies. Calls include a thick, rolling, almost ricocheting 'kr'r'r'rah', dry and wooden.

Cattle Egret   Squacco Heron   Little Egret   Great Egret

CATTLE EGRET

short yellow bill (on juv. black)

court-ship

non-breeding

summer

SQUACCO HERON

much whiter in flight than standing

imm. / ad. winter

ad. summer

LITTLE EGRET

non-breeding

blue-grey

straight, all dark

courtship

summer

bill longish, slightly decurved, strong base

usually partly yellow or orange

courtship

summer

REEF EGRET

imm. (light)

(dark)

yellowish

legs black

toes yellow

legs not clean black

non-breeding

schistacea (Asia, E Africa)

often all black during courtship

GREAT EGRET

in winter with Grey Heron (right)

tibia becomes reddish during courtship

long aigrettes

summer

non-breeding

long

dark

CATTLE

yellow

LITTLE

GREAT

KM

Grey Heron *Ardea cinerea* rB2

L 84–102 cm (neck extended), WS 155–175 cm. Breeds in colonies, or sometimes solitarily, in woodland with tall trees beside lakes and brackish sea-bays. Waits patiently, stock-still, for prey (mostly fish) on lakeshores and riversides; rests on one leg in shallow water, often at edge of reeds. Hardy, just retreats from ice in N, but some migrate to W Europe. Nest a flat basket of sticks in tree crown.

IDENTIFICATION Very *big*, strongly built heron, mostly *medium grey above* and greyish-white below. Distinguished from Crane by *retracted neck* in flight, and often when standing. *Bill straight, powerful*, greyish-yellow (orangey when breeding), legs greyish-yellow or grey. Flies with *slow, somewhat irregular beats*, all the time with *wings strongly bowed*, often high up. Upperwings bicoloured, grey with black remiges and primary coverts; also *two paler patches at carpal*, well visible in front view. (For differences from Purple Heron, see latter.) – Adult: *Forehead, crown-centre and head-sides white*; *crown-sides and nape black*; long, narrow black nape plume (seldom visible); *neck-sides pale greyish-white* with black-streaked white central band. – Juvenile/1st-winter: *Forehead and crown grey*; nape greyish-black with short plume; *head-sides and neck-sides medium grey*, as back; neck-centre buffish.

VOICE Commonest call, often heard at dusk from birds flying to roost, a loud, harsh and croaking 'kah-**ahrk**, which often has a sing-song, echoing quality. At colonies gives knocking and croaking series.

Purple Heron *Ardea purpurea* V*

L 70–90 cm (neck extended), WS 110-145 cm. Breeds in colonies at extensive, shallow swampy lakes with reedbeds. Forages in shallow water in gaps among reeds and along rivers, or more in open in wet meadows. Summer visitor (mostly Apr–Oct), wintering in tropical Africa. Feeds on fish, frogs, insects. Nests in reeds (often Europe) or trees.

IDENTIFICATION Big, *lanky* heron, usually *quite dark-looking* in the field. Main confusion risk is Grey Heron. Note the following differences: *longer, more uniformly narrow bill* ('bayonet' rather than 'dagger'); *narrower head* (merges more into bill); *wings* in front view *slightly bent at carpal*, and *hint of jerkiness in wingbeats*; somewhat *narrower neck*, which in flight often forms *more angular 'neck keel'*; *longer toes*, sometimes held *more splayed and disarranged*; slightly smaller size. – Adult: Head-sides and *neck-sides reddish-brown*, neck with distinct, thin black border. *Back dark grey*, wing-coverts uniform dark grey with *purple-brown cast* (most marked on ♂). – Juvenile/1st-winter: Head- and neck-sides, *back and upperwings ochre-brown*, upperparts mottled (feather centres

dark, fringes ochre), dark margins along neck-side indistinct. – 1st-summer: Neck and back almost as adult, but *wings still variegated brown* (juv. feathers, now worn).

VOICE In flight a gruff, monosyllabic 'krrek', like Grey Heron's but shorter, straighter (not faintly disyllabic as Grey Heron's) and 'deader', less resonant.

White Stork *Ciconia ciconia* P5

L 95–110 cm, WS 180–218 cm. Breeds in open farmland with access to swampy riversides, marshes and floodlands. Stronghold in E Europe, declining in NW (overhead cables and draining probably main causes). Nests, often in small colonies, in stick nest (readily accepts specially erected carriage wheels and platforms) on house roofs, church towers, telephone poles; thus not shy, is approachable. Summer visitor, winters in tropical Africa. Notable passage at Bosporus and Gibraltar end Aug, return in Apr. Food frogs, insects, also snakes, young birds etc.

IDENTIFICATION *Very big*, with *long neck* and *long legs*. *Black and white* with *red bill* and *red legs* (imm. has duller red bill with slightly darker tip; close views needed). Unmistakable when seen on the ground (slow, dignified walk); in flight at distance could be confused with White Pelican, but *holds neck straight out*, has *projecting legs* and *soars in much more disordered fashion*, not with contingents well synchronized like the pelicans. (Cranes can also look almost black and white in strong light, but their legs project farther and the neck is a bit longer.)

VOICE Virtually silent, but compensates for this by loud bill-clapping, especially when partners meet at nest.

Black Stork *Ciconia nigra* V**

L 90–105 cm, WS 173–205 cm. Breeds in vast, swampy forests, mostly in aged mixed coniferous forest interspersed with rivers and marshes. Nest of sticks high in tree crown. Shy and withdrawn at nest site. Summer visitor, winters in Africa; migrates a month later than White Stork, returns in May. Food mainly amphibians, insects.

IDENTIFICATION Barely smaller than White Stork, which it resembles in shape. At close range, easily told from White by *black head, neck, breast and back with metallic green or violet gloss*. In flight at distance the differences can be more difficult to see than expected; note that underwing has only *white triangles on axillaries*. – Adult: Bill and legs red. – Juvenile: Bill and legs *grey-green*.

VOICE Seldom heard owing to discreet nesting habits and shy behaviour. At nest gives rasping series, 'shi-luu shi-luu shi-luu...', with first syllable hoarse, second clear. Said also to have a buzzard-like mewing 'piu'. Bill-clapping quiet and rarely used.

Grey Heron   Purple Heron   White Stork   Black Stork

GREY HERON

patiently waiting for prey

toes medium-long, kept folded

ad.

'neck keel' rounded

dark crown

strong, dagger-shaped

white forehead

juv.   2nd-winter   ad.

PURPLE HERON

'jerky' flight on rakish wings

toes long, often spread

ad.

'neck keel' often angular

bill often pointing upwards

juv.

striped 'face'

long and narrow

narrow

juv.   ad.

WHITE STORK

breeds near man, often nesting on buildings

white

dark tip

juv.   ad.

BLACK STORK

in strong light, upperparts can appear as pale as on White Stork

black

shy, nests in deep forests

violet and green metallic gloss

grey-green

dull greenish-black

grey-green   juv.   red   ad.

DZ

Glossy Ibis *Plegadis falcinellus*   **V*****
L 55–65 cm, WS 88–105 cm. Breeds colonially at shallow, well-vegetated marshes; nests in trees (often with herons) or reeds. Most migrate in winter to Africa, returning in Apr. Gregarious; feeds (on insects, frogs) in small groups in wet marsh, wading in shallow water.

    IDENTIFICATION *Dark. Legs and neck quite long,* curlew-like *downcurved bill.* Plumage *dark purple-brown, with green gloss* on wings. Superficially like Bald Ibis, but has longer legs and neck, and in flight, when *feet project past tail-tip,* shows *longer, narrower neck,* and *curlew-like wing-beats* are more mechanical, with *frequently interspersed short glides* (so distant head-on silhouette like Pygmy Cormorant, another dark bird that may be seen in flocks in same habitat). Often flies in lines, flock's *flightpath a little undulating.* – Adult breeding: Head and neck dark. Lores blue with narrow white border. – Adult summer/winter: As breeding, but head/neck somewhat duller brown and dotted with white. Lores all dark. – Juvenile/1st-winter: As adult non-breeding, but still duller brown on head and neck and paler brown below.

    VOICE Not vocal. Hoarse grunting 'grru' sometimes heard. Grunting and croaking sounds at breeding site.

(Northern) Bald Ibis *Geronticus eremita*   **—**
L 70–80 cm, WS 120–135 cm. One of the region's most threatened species; extinct since 1989 in Turkey (only free-flying captive-bred birds left) and merely remnants in Morocco. Breeds colonially in barren terrain, e.g. rocky semi-desert, with proximity to running water. Nests on ledge or in cavity in cliff face. Migrant, but winter quarters poorly known. Food insects and small animals, captured on dry ground, fields and at edges of rivers.

    IDENTIFICATION Large, *black*, rather *short-legged* but *long-winged* and long-tailed; *downcurved bill.* Black plumage has metallic green and purple-brown gloss. *Bill red. Head 'bald', skin red. Nape-feathers elongated, droop* like unkempt hair. Wing shape characterized by rather short 'arm' and *long, quite narrow 'hand'. Feet do not project past tail* in flight (cf. Glossy Ibis). *Wingbeats shallow* but notably *powerful and flexible,* and not necessarily relieved by short glides as in Glossy Ibis on longer flights (though gliding not uncommon; wings then held slightly bowed).

    VOICE Silent away from colonies. At latter, calls include short, guttural 'hrump' and hoarse, high 'hyoh'.

(Eurasian) Spoonbill *Platalea leucorodia*   **P**5
L 80–93 cm, WS 120–135 cm. Breeds in colonies (sparse, local) in large reed swamps with some bushes and trees. Nests in trees or reeds, normally not mixed with other species. Requires access to sheltered shallow open water; also salt ponds. Food molluscs, crustaceans, small fish.

    IDENTIFICATION Unmistakable at close range, with *long bill with spatula-shaped tip.* At distance can be confused only with one of the white egrets owing to its size and *all-white plumage.* Note *bushy nuchal crest* ('Indian chief' style) and typical foraging behaviour: bill is held lowered in the water and *head is swung from side to side* while the bird wades forwards. *Flies with neck extended* (like storks, unlike herons), *wingbeats quite fast* (quicker than those of the large egrets) interspersed with glides. – Adult breeding: Bushy crest (longer on ♂), ochre breast patch (as on pelicans), all-white primaries, black bill with yellow tip. – Adult summer/winter: As breeding, but lacks crest and ochre breast patch. – Juvenile/1st-winter: As adult non-breeding, but *black tips to outer primaries* and with initially pinkish legs and bill which gradually darken.

    VOICE Silent.

FLAMINGOS *Phoenicopteriformes*
Big wading birds inhabiting shallow salt or brackish water. Extremely long neck and long legs. Hefty downward-bent bill. Colonial; do not breed every year. Food small aquatic animals, plankton. Nest a pile of mud.

(Greater) Flamingo *Phoenicopterus ruber*   **[V**]**
L 120–145 cm, WS 140–170 cm. European race *roseus* breeds in a few but big colonies on low islands and banks on extensive, open, shallow, muddy beaches or at salt lakes, sea-bays etc. Sensitive to disturbance.

    IDENTIFICATION Unmistakable. White with pinky tone, red wing-coverts and black flight-feathers. Note that the bill is mostly light red with *only extreme tip black* and that the *legs are entirely pink* (without blazing red 'knees'), also that plumage is *more white than pink* (American race *ruber,* an occasional escape from European bird collections, has bright pink-red plumage). Often seen in large, tightly packed flocks (like whitish-pink strip on the horizon). In flight the *red on the wings is conspicuous,* and neck and legs are held fully extended (neck drooping a little). – Juvenile: Grey-brown and whitish, lacking red.

    VOICE Loud cackles, somewhat recalling Greylag and Bean Geese; trumpeting notes as well as deeper grunts.

Chilean Flamingo *Phoenicopterus chilensis*   **[V**]**
S American species kept in several bird collections in Britain and Europe, and free-flying individuals may be met with. Somewhat *smaller* than Flamingo, has *over half of bill black,* has *buff-grey legs with contrasting red 'knees'* and toes, and has often *pinker-toned* plumage.

Glossy Ibis   Bald Ibis   Spoonbill   Flamingo

GLOSSY IBIS

wetland species

juv.

ad. winter

ad. summer

project far

long and narrow

flight in disordered flocks or undulating lines

BALD IBIS

nests on cliff-ledge or in shallow cave

juv.

ad.

soars frequently (unlike Glossy Ibis)

flight powerful and flexible

feet not projecting

compact

mostly desert-dwelling

SPOONBILL

light

juv.

Spoonbill   Great Egret

resting birds; note posture and carriage

ad. breeding

juv.

black tips

extended neck (on white egrets retracted)

ad.

FLAMINGO

juv.

ad.

ad.

grey

red 'knees'

CHILEAN FLAMINGO

extensive black

very long

feeding flock

DZ

SWANS *Cygnus*
Very large, white waterfowl with long neck used for feeding in shallow waters. Heavily built, and laborious take-off requires running and strong flapping with wings. Gait clumsy, waddling. Food plants, mainly submerged. Nest on ground or on mound of vegetation in marsh or lake or on shore. Monogamous, pair for life. Gregarious in winter.

Mute Swan *Cygnus olor*   **rB3**
L 140–160 cm (body *c.* 80), WS 200–240 cm. Breeds on freshwater lakes, generally with reedbeds, and along coasts. Hardy, requires only open water in winter. Nest a large mound of reed stems etc., or, on coasts, a heap of seaweed. Not shy, and can act aggressively. ♂♂ have territorial fights with wing-splashing rushes and long 'slides' on the water.
IDENTIFICATION *Huge*. Plumage *white*. Neck very long, head small. Tail comparatively long and pointed (useful to know when a swan is upending). *Bill orange-red with prominent black knob* on forehead, black nostrils, cutting edges and nail. *Neck held* either fairly straight (much like Whooper) or, more typically, *smoothly bent in S-shape* when swimming. Threat posture with *wings raised like sails and head lowered* over back diagnostic. Sexes similar (♂ larger; bill-knob of ♂ larger, especially when breeding; colour of bill deeper orange on ♂). Difficult to separate from Whooper in flight at distance; at times, however, head looks more abruptly 'cut off' in front. – Juvenile: Grey-brown with pink tinge; bill first dark grey, then pinkish-grey, without knob. Separated from juvenile Whooper by *darker and browner plumage*. White plumage attained in 1st summer or 2nd autumn. A rare variety is born pure white ('Polish Swan').
VOICE Despite name, has some distinctive calls. Most commonly heard is an explosive, snorting or rumbling 'heeorr!'. Lone swimming birds seeking contact sometimes give rather loud, somewhat gull-like 'ga-oh'. Young and immatures have rather weak, piping 'büi-büi-büi-...'. Aggressive call a 'mean', snake-like hissing. *A loud singing or throbbing sound with each wingbeat in flight* is diagnostic.

Whooper Swan *Cygnus cygnus*   **W4 / (mB5)**
L 140–160 cm (body *c.* 75), WS 205–235 cm. Breeds on tundra pools and small lakes with sheltering vegetation, on damp bogs and in marshes, typically in remote areas in far north, but has spread south recently (linked with less shy, more confiding habits). Migrates to open waters in NW Europe. Hardy, closely following retreat of ice in spring.
IDENTIFICATION *Huge*. Plumage *white*, but many in spring and summer have *head and neck stained brown* (rarely seen in Mute). Neck long, upper part generally held straight when swimming. Best told from Mute and Bewick's by *long, wedge-*

shaped bill, largely yellow* with black tip, yellow forming pointed wedge, reaching in front of nostril. – Juvenile: *Grey* (tinged brownish), clearly *less brown and slightly paler than juvenile Mute*; very similar to juvenile Bewick's but (in British Isles) often slightly paler. *Bill pattern of adult discernible* (black of adult is pink, yellow is off-white).
VOICE Highly vocal. *Calls loud and bugling* in quality, similar to those of Bewick's Swan but usually louder, slightly lower-pitched on average, *notes more straight*, not with such a marked diphthong, and notes often *given in groups of three or four*, 'kloo-kloo-kloo', instead of one or two as most often in Bewick's. *Insignificant, slight hissing sound from wing-beats*, unlike musical throb of Mute.

Bewick's Swan (Tundra Swan)
Cygnus columbianus   **W4**
L 115–127 cm (body *c.* 60), WS 170–195 cm. Breeds on far NE tundras by the Arctic Ocean, winters in NW Europe.
IDENTIFICATION Very large. A smaller version of Whooper Swan, with *proportionately slightly shorter neck, bigger head and more compact body and bill*; these differences often difficult to appreciate when observing single birds. Safest separation by pattern of bill, Bewick's having *slightly less yellow than black* (ssp. *bewickii*, Europe), the *yellow generally a square or rounded patch* (diagnostic), rarely more wedge-shaped (recalling Whooper, but yellow not reaching in front of nostril, and black around gape more solid). Also, with experience, voice is good clue (see below). – Variation: Very rarely N American vagrants (ssp. *columbianus*, 'Whistling Swan') occur, distinguished by practically all-black bill (only a tiny yellow patch in front of eye). – Juvenile: Greyish (often a shade darker than Whooper). *Bill pattern of adult discernible* (black of adult is pink, yellow is off-white).
VOICE Vocal. Calls similar to those of Whooper Swan but *less bugling, more yapping or honking*, and on average *higher-pitched* (large overlap; flight-call rather deep) and softly 'bent' (diphthong impression). Also, notes not repeated in threes or fours, usually in twos, or given singly.

Snow Goose *Anser caerulescens*   **V∗∗**
L 65–75 cm, WS 133–156 cm. Breeds in extreme NE Siberia (Wrangel Is) and N America. Genuine vagrant to Europe or, more often, escape from captivity.
IDENTIFICATION Of Pink-footed Goose size. Two morphs. – Adult: *Bill and feet reddish*. White morph *white with black primaries*; dark morph ('Blue Goose') has only *head, upper neck and tip of tail white*, rest is various shades of *grey*, palest on upper forewing and on tail-coverts. – Juvenile: *Bare parts dark grey*. Plumage pale greyish with whitish uppertail and darker flight-feathers (white morph) or rather uniform dark grey (dark morph). – Can be confused with smaller Ross's Goose *A. rossii* (p. 389), but apart from smaller size that has much smaller bill.
VOICE Has rather peculiar, soft, cackling notes with an upward-inflected diphthong, 'koeek'. Alarm a deep cackling 'angk-ak-ak-ak'.

Mute Swan

Whooper Swan

Bewick's Swan

MUTE SWAN

1st-y.

1st-y.

strong contrasts
Mute

subdued pattern
Whooper / Bewick's

juv.

1st-winter (Feb)

orange-red

long tail

ad.

WHOOPER SWAN

pair on breeding pool

juv.

juv.

1st-winter (Feb)

Icelandic 1st-winter birds acquire a whiter look more rapidly than birds from Fenno-Scandia or Russia

characteristic profile, longer and straighter than Bewick's

yellow projects to below nostril

ad.

BEWICK'S SWAN

resting on field

juv. can look surprisingly long-billed

solid black

juv.

juv.

1st-winter (Feb)

shorter neck than on Whooper often apparent

amount of yellow varies somewhat

columbianus
(N America)

less yellow on bill than on Whooper

ad.

SNOW GOOSE

ad. Snow Goose among Greenland White-fronts

ad.

1st-winter

ad.
('Blue Goose')

ad.

KM

GEESE *Anser, Branta*

Large, heavily built wildfowl, largely specialized on grazing, therefore have strong and fairly long feet centred under body to facilitate walking. Medium-long neck and strong, conical bill with saw-toothed edges of upper mandible. Gregarious, especially during migration and on winter grounds. Shy and wary, but can become remarkably confiding in areas where there is no shooting; in particular, juveniles from arctic breeding sites can be fearless in autumn. Migratory, following traditional pathways, travelling in family parties or large flocks, in flight forming V or undulating, bent line. – Two genera of geese occur, 'grey' (*Anser*) and 'black' (*Branta*). Food vegetable matter. Nest on ground, lined with down. Monogamous, pair for life. Both parents tend the young. Adults moult all flight-feathers simultaneously and become flightless for *c*. 3–4 weeks in summer, usually coinciding with young being unfledged.

IDENTIFYING 'GREY' GEESE

Although, in theory, separating the five species of 'grey' *Anser* geese in the field should present little problem, practice is different. Geese are normally shy birds which do not tolerate close approach, and all too often the interesting individuals are partly hidden by other geese in dense flocks, or by vegetation, or will have their legs stained by mud, or they simply lie down to rest before bill and leg colours are established. Even at moderate range, and against the light, bill and leg colours become surprisingly difficult to assess properly. The orange-red of Bean Goose, e.g., often appears dull tomato-red at a distance or in overcast weather, and can sometimes even give a pinkish-red impression. Light conditions can be critical when it comes to goose identification.

Size variation is a potential pitfall. ♂♂ are larger than ♀♀, adults larger than juveniles. The extremes may confuse the unwary if they occur in mixed flocks, their size alone implying that they should belong to different species.

Most problems are caused by the trio *Bean Goose, Pink-footed Goose* and *young White-fronted Goose*. With Bean, it is essential to realize amount of variation in bill (shape, pattern), size and proportions due to geographical variation within wide breeding range; at least two rather distinct races of Bean Goose, and possibly some rare varieties, involved. Young—and even some adult—Pink-footed Geese do not always 'look typical', and angle of light and previous experience are both important for correct identification. Some young White-fronted Geese have not only dark nail but also some dark smudges at the base of the bill and on culmen, and thus resemble Bean Goose at first glance.

Finally, it is important to age geese correctly, the basis for reliable identifications. The ageing of 'grey' geese is similar for all species, and involves assessment of degree of neat grooves on the neck ('water-combing' effect), the width and shape at the tips of certain feathers, and the amount of distinct white tips to some of these; the colour of the nail on the bill is a further supportive character in most species. (Cf. the figures at lower left.)

(Greater) White-fronted Goose *Anser albifrons* **W**3

L 64–78 cm, WS 130–160 cm. Breeds on tundra in far northeast (ssp. *albifrons*), migrating to winter in W, C and SE Europe; birds breeding in Greenland (ssp. *flavirostris*; a separate species according to some) winter largely in Ireland and SW Scotland.

IDENTIFICATION Medium-sized, rather short-necked and compact. Legs orange-red. Adult has *prominent white blaze surrounding base of bill* and *black transverse markings on belly*, confusable only with Lesser White-fronted Goose, but is *larger* (marginal overlap!); *lacks prominent yellow orbital ring* (indistinct, narrow ring on some only); has *heavier bill*; *white blaze does not normally extend to forecrown, is fairly straight in side view* (blaze reaches forecrown on Lesser White-fronted, and outline is angled in side view). Ssp. *flavirostris* (see above) is slightly larger, longer-necked and heavier-billed, darker-plumaged (notably breast), with bill orange-yellow (pink restricted to tip), not reddish-pink with just a little yellow at base. – Juvenile: Lacks white blaze and dark belly markings, bill dull pinkish with *dark nail*. Confusable at distance with Bean Goose, but told by *darker grey feathering around base of bill and on forehead*, giving contrast to paler cheek; also, *pale feather edges on upperparts less prominent*, and *base of lower mandible not solidly black* as on Bean Goose.

VOICE Compared with Bean and Greylag Geese, calls are more high-pitched and musical or laughing in quality, not so nasal and raw. Usual call is disyllabic (sometimes tri-), 'kyü-yü' (or 'kyu-yu-yu'). Some calls are deeper, more like those of the larger species.

Lesser White-fronted Goose *Anser erythropus* **V**∗∗

L 56–66 cm, WS 115–135 cm. Breeds on marshes and bogs in boreal mountains, generally in willow and birch zone. Has declined, now very rare in Europe. Reintroduction in Fenno-Scandia, (colour-ringed) young programmed to migrate towards southwest in winter (where biocide levels and shooting pressure estimated to be more favourable), having Barnacle Geese as foster parents.

IDENTIFICATION Slightly smaller than similar White-fronted (which see), but marginal overlap. Best told by *promi-*

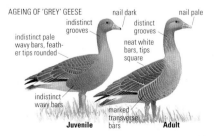

AGEING OF 'GREY' GEESE

nail dark — nail pale

indistinct grooves — distinct grooves

indistinct pale wavy bars, feather tips rounded — neat white bars, tips square

indistinct wavy bars — marked transverse bars

Juvenile — **Adult**

White-fronted Goose — Lesser White-fronted Goose

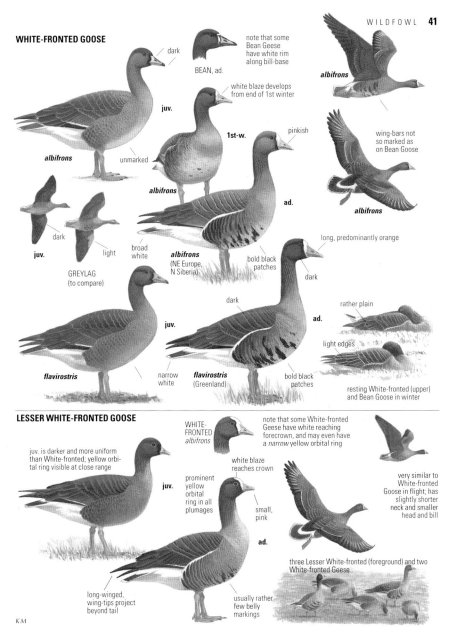

WHITE-FRONTED GOOSE

note that some Bean Geese have white rim along bill-base

BEAN, ad.

albifrons

juv.

white blaze develops from end of 1st winter

1st-w.

pinkish

wing-bars not so marked as on Bean Goose

albifrons

albifrons

unmarked

albifrons

ad.

albifrons

juv.

dark

light

broad white

GREYLAG (to compare)

albifrons (NE Europe, N Siberia)

bold black patches

dark

long, predominantly orange

dark

rather plain

light edges

juv.

ad.

flavirostris

narrow white

flavirostris (Greenland)

bold black patches

resting White-fronted (upper) and Bean Goose in winter

LESSER WHITE-FRONTED GOOSE

WHITE-FRONTED *albifrons*

note that some White-fronted Geese have white reaching forecrown, and may even have a *narrow* yellow orbital ring

juv. is darker and more uniform than White-fronted; yellow orbital ring visible at close range

white blaze reaches crown

juv.

prominent yellow orbital ring in all plumages

small, pink

ad.

very similar to White-fronted Goose in flight; has slightly shorter neck and smaller head and bill

three Lesser White-fronted (foreground) and two White-fronted Geese

long-winged, wing-tips project beyond tail

usually rather few belly markings

KM

nent yellow orbital ring (also on juv.); white blaze reaching forecrown, white area angled in side view; bill small ('cute-looking'), always pink; plumage rather dark, but black belly markings fewer. Wings narrow, flight agile, wingbeats fast. Feet orange-red. – Juvenile: Resembles juvenile

White-fronted, but is on average smaller and darker overall, and nail is usually pale. Still, often inseparable but for presence of *yellow orbital ring*.

VOICE Similar to calls of White-fronted Goose, but even more high-pitched and yelping in character.

Bean Goose *Anser fabalis*   **W**4

L 69–88 cm, WS 140–174 cm. Breeds on bogs, marshes and pools in remote taiga (ssp. *fabalis*) or on wet tundra (ssp. *rossicus*), both wintering in W and C Europe. Migrants passing S Fenno-Scandia 2nd half Apr and Sep/Oct. Huge roosting and wintering flocks at favoured places in S Sweden and N Continental Europe; scarce in Britain. Shy and wary.

IDENTIFICATION *Medium-large to large*, rather *dark*, long-winged. Distinct white edges to dark tertials and upper-wing-coverts. Head and neck rather dark. Differs from Greylag and Pink-footed in *orange* (or dull red) legs, not pink; also, *in flight upperwing rather dark*, not strikingly pale, and *underwing all dark* (cf. Greylag). Sometimes difficult to separate from Pink-footed, especially at a distance, when orange of bill and legs often looks indeterminably dull red; *back just as dark as flank area* (paler on Pink-footed) helpful, as is narrower white terminal tail-band of Bean. Many have narrow white rim at base of bill; those with most can resemble White-fronted Goose (which see). – Ecologically differentiated subspecies *fabalis* and *rossicus* differ slightly but distinctly. Ssp. *fabalis* about as large as Greylag but has *narrower neck, smaller head, slimmer bill and body*; *bill* is usually *long*, and base not too deep; amount of orange (or dull red) variable, some with dark restricted to base of lower mandible, tip and a little on culmen, others with a lot of dark at base of bill resembling *rossicus* and Pink-footed. Ssp. *rossicus* is slightly *smaller*, has *shorter neck, darker head and neck* which contrast more markedly with paler body than in *fabalis*, all characters which make it more similar to Pink-footed; bill is short, deep-based and triangular, *pale* (reddish) *patch almost invariably small*, and base of lower mandible is deeper and more curved. In large flocks of N Europe some birds appear to be intermediates.

VOICE Commonest call is a deep, nasal, trumpeting, disyllabic or trisyllabic, jolting 'ung-unk' or 'yak-ak-ak', at slightly varying pitch when heard from flocks. With practice discernibly deeper in pitch than Pink-footed (otherwise similar).

Pink-footed Goose *Anser brachyrhynchus*   **W**2

L 64–76 cm, WS 137–161 cm. Closely related to Bean Goose. Breeds on arctic tundra and mountainsides in Greenland, Iceland and Svalbard, winters NW Europe. Nests on the ground, at times on rocks.

IDENTIFICATION Slightly smaller and more compact than taiga Bean Goose (*fabalis*), about equal in size and proportions to tundra Bean (*rossicus*). *Legs pink* (diagnostic), but surprisingly difficult to determine at some distance or in poor light. *Bill* rather *short and triangular*, typically mostly *black with only a pink band across outer part* (some have a

little more pink). Head rounded, *neck rather short. Head* (and upper neck) *dark* brown-grey, *contrasting with pale* (lower) *neck and body*. A very few have a thin white rim at base of bill (just like many Bean and some Greylag). Lower neck and body pale brown-grey, upperparts often with a 'frosty' blue-grey cast, breast with pinkish-buff suffusion. *Flank area darkest part of body, darker than back. In flight, upperwing and back very pale*, distinctly lighter than on Bean and White-fronted. (Greylag has even lighter forewing, but on the other hand darker back.) Also useful to know that Pink-footed has a *wider white trailing edge to tail* than Bean. – Juvenile: For ageing, see p. 40. Resembles adult, but at least some birds are less distinctive, being a little darker and browner, with less contrast between head and body, and lacking blue-grey cast above; leg colour duller and less clean pink than on adult.

VOICE Common calls similar in structure to those of Bean Goose but slightly higher-pitched on average, often discernibly so with experience. Differ from calls of White-fronted Goose in lower pitch and lack of laughing quality. Softer 'wink-wink' also heard.

Greylag Goose *Anser anser*   r**B**4 / **W**3

L 74–84 cm, WS 149–168 cm. Breeds in variety of habitats, mainly wetlands, from shallow lakes with reedbeds and freshwater marshes to islets in larger lakes, coasts (even brackish water), heather, rocky slopes, etc. British breeders mainly resident, most others migratory. Increasing in numbers in Europe. Only grey goose to be seen in large numbers in summer in Europe.

IDENTIFICATION *Large*, equalled in size only by largest taiga Bean Goose (which see), but *bulkier*, with *thicker neck, larger head* and *heavier bill*, latter being *all pinkish-orange or pink*. Legs dull pinkish. Wings broad, flight heavy. Plumage rather *plain brown-grey* without strong contrasts, *head and neck* typically *rather pale*. A few have insignificant thin white rim at base of bill, and many have some dark marks on belly. In flight, *upper forewing strikingly pale ash-grey*, contrasting sharply with darker rear parts of wing and with darker back. *Underwing* characteristic, too, otherwise dark wing *having pale grey leading edge* distinctly set off, thus two-coloured, unique among European geese. Greylags flying away from observer can be recognized by size and *pale grey rump*, contrasting with dark brown tertials and back. – Variation: Western birds (ssp. *anser*, most of Europe) comparatively darker, smaller and with more orange tinge to bill; eastern (ssp. *rubrirostris*, Russia, Asia) paler, larger and have pinkish bill; E European breeders appear to be intermediates.

VOICE Loud, raw, nasal cackling calls, most characteristic trisyllabic with first higher-pitched (falsetto-like), drawn out (almost disyllabic) and more stressed than following two, 'ki**yaaa**-ga-ga'. Commonly also deep, raw 'ank-ang-ang' (thus somewhat more like Bean Goose). Repertoire varied: some calls are deep, others shrill, all being similar to those of domestic goose.

Bean Goose   Pink-footed Goose   Greylag Goose

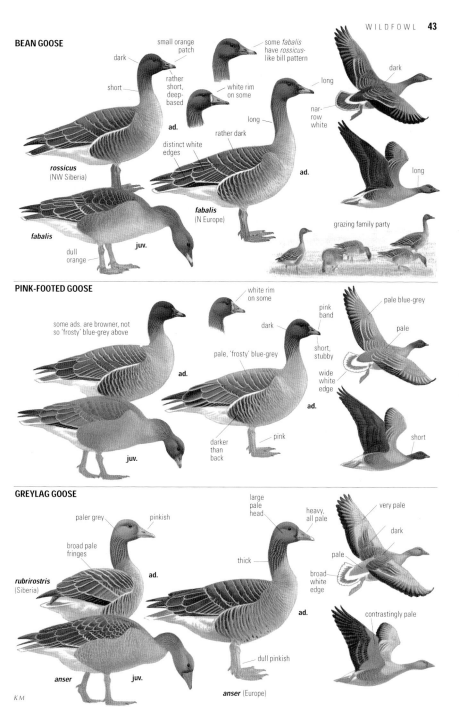

BEAN GOOSE

small orange patch

dark

rather short, deep-based

short

some *fabalis* have *rossicus*-like bill pattern

white rim on some

long

narrow white

dark

ad.

long

rather dark

distinct white edges

long

rossicus (NW Siberia)

fabalis (N Europe)

ad.

long

fabalis

juv.

dull orange

grazing family party

PINK-FOOTED GOOSE

white rim on some

pink band

pale blue-grey

some ads. are browner, not so 'frosty' blue-grey above

dark

pale

short, stubby

pale, 'frosty' blue-grey

ad.

wide white edge

ad.

darker than back

pink

short

juv.

GREYLAG GOOSE

large pale head

heavy, all pale

very pale

paler grey

pinkish

dark

broad pale fringes

thick

pale

rubrirostris (Siberia)

ad.

broad white edge

ad.

dull pinkish

contrastingly pale

anser

juv.

anser (Europe)

KM

Canada Goose *Branta canadensis* r**B**3

L 90–100 cm, WS 160–175 (European birds, mainly of nominate ssp.). Breeds on lakes and marshes, along rivers and seashores. Introduced American species; in many areas half-tame or at least not shy. Northern birds migratory.

IDENTIFICATION *Large, with very long neck. Black neck and head* with *white patch on head* separates from all except Barnacle Goose, but is much larger, longer-necked, and *breast is pale*, not black; *body brownish*, paler below (Barnacle black, dark grey and white); *the white on head forms 'throat-strap'* (more white on face on Barnacle). Wings long, wingbeats rather slow. – Adult: Buff-white tips on upperparts and flanks form neat bars; head/neck glossy black; 'throat-strap' pure white. – Juvenile: Pale bars on upperparts and flanks less even and well marked; head/neck duller brown-black; white 'throat-strap' tinged pale brown.

VOICE Vocal. Most characteristic call loud, disyllabic, nasal 'awr-**lüt**', second syllable higher-pitched. Variety of other deep, nasal, honking calls, often repeated.

Barnacle Goose *Branta leucopsis* **W**3

L 58–70 cm, WS 120–142 cm. Breeds colonially, mainly on arctic islands and coasts, preferring rocky coasts and steep slopes to flat tundra. Also, since mid 1970s, on low grassy islands and shores in the Baltic. Migratory, main movements in Oct–early Nov and Apr–May.

IDENTIFICATION Medium-sized, fairly compact, with *thickset, short neck, rounded head* and *small black bill*. Neck and breast black, *head mostly white*, underparts silvery-white, upperparts grey and barred black and white. In flight, white head surprisingly difficult to see at a distance; *strong contrast between black breast and whitish belly* better character to separate from Brent Goose ssp. *bernicla*; slightly *paler upperwing* sometimes useful clue, too. Wings slightly longer than on Brent, and wingbeat rate roughly as White-fronted, slightly slower than Brent. Flock formation often irregular U-shaped line (like Brent). – Juvenile: Very similar to adult, differing mainly in *less well-marked dark barring on flanks*, and not such solidly black neck and breast; pale tips on upperparts less clean white than on adult, and black and grey more diffuse. Whitish 'face' on average less tinged yellow than on adult; amount of dark marks around eye varies, however, and is unreliable age character.

VOICE Vocal. Basically only one call, a shrill, monosyllabic bark, 'kaw', at slightly varying pitch when heard in chorus from flocks.

Brent Goose *Branta bernicla* **W**2

L 55–62 cm, WS 105–117 cm. Breeds on arctic islands and coasts, preferring low tundra near sea coasts. Migratory,

main movements late Sep–Oct and late May, largely keeping to traditional routes; often concentrated passage in spring. Habits duck-like, often resting on open sea (dense flocks) and feeding in shallow waters, upending to reach main food of eel-grass; also grazes on mudflats and grassy fields.

IDENTIFICATION Somewhat smaller than Barnacle Goose, *slimmer-bodied* with slightly longer neck, *smaller head* and *narrower wings*. Darkish with *bright white stern. Small white crescent on side of upper neck* visible at close range. In flight appears slim and elegant, with pointed wings swept back a little; wingbeats slower than Eider but somewhat quicker than Barnacle Goose. Migrating flocks often very large (esp. in spring), flock formation disorderly U-shaped lines or muddle of lines. – Variation: Ssp. *bernicla* (Russia, W Siberia, migrates through Baltic to NW Europe) has dusky *dark grey belly* and slightly paler flanks and dark grey upperparts; ssp. *hrota* (Svalbard, Greenland, passing Iceland and Norway to winter Denmark, England and Ireland) has much *paler underparts*, pale grey-white with rather *clear contrast against black breast*, and buff-tinged upperparts; ssp. *nigricans*, 'Black Brant' (E Siberia, Alaska, NW Canada, rare vagrant), has strong contrast between whitish flanks and very dark belly, and the white crescents on neck are large and widest on foreneck (often merging at front). – Adult: Upperparts *plain* dark brown-grey. – Juvenile: *Upperwing-coverts tipped off-white*, giving barred appearance; white neck-crescents lacking at first, developed (late Sep) Oct–Dec. In all three races, juveniles have darker flanks (uniform with belly) than adults, making subspecific identification difficult or even impossible. – 1st-winter: Keeps white bars on upperparts. From Oct, paler flanks of ssp. *hrota* develop, facilitating separation from *bernicla*.

VOICE Call a gargling, guttural 'r'rot' or 'rhut', at slightly varying pitch from flocks.

Red-breasted Goose *Branta ruficollis* **V**⁎⁎

L 54–60 cm, WS 110–125 cm. Breeds in small colonies on arctic tundra near coasts or along river mouths, often together with birds of prey (e.g. large falcon) as protection. Migratory. A very few accompany congeners to W Europe.

IDENTIFICATION A trifle smaller than Brent Goose. *Neck thick, bill very small.* Plumage striking, *deep chestnut-red, black and white*, unmistakable at close range, but at a distance surprisingly dull-looking; then appears *dark* with *broad white flank-stripe*. – Adult: Only *two* (distinct) *white bars* (tips to wing-coverts) *on closed wing.* Red *cheek patch large, leaving narrow white border*. – Juvenile: *4–5 narrow white bars on closed wing.* (Dull) red *cheek patch small* (virtually absent on some), *leaving broad white border*.

VOICE A shrill, high-pitched 'ki-kwi' or 'kik-yik'.

Canada Goose

Barnacle Goose

Brent Goose

Red-breasted Goose

CANADA GOOSE

small form
('Lesser Canada')

pale breast

ad.

ad.

juv.

BARNACLE GOOSE

light grey

some are
tinged yel-
low on head

black breast

diffuse
pattern

strong
contrast

neatly
barred

juv.

ad.

ad.

BRENT GOOSE

hrota
1st-winter

bernicla
ad.

white bars

hrota
(Svalbard,
Greenland)

hrota
juv.

white

broad
neck
patch

dark

plain
grey

grey-black

ad.

hrota
1st-winter

hrota

bernicla

bernicla
1st-winter

dark

nigricans
(N America)
ad.

bernicla
(Russia)
ad.

bernicla ad.

RED-BREASTED GOOSE

surprisingly inconspi-
cuous in flock
of Barnacles

migrating with
Brent Geese

narrow, indistinct
bars

two prominent
white bars

wide white flank-stripe

fat-necked

juv.

ad.

ad.

KM

(Common) Shelduck *Tadorna tadorna* rB3

L 55–65 cm, WS 100–120 cm. Breeds along seashores, at larger lakes and rivers, preferring open, unvegetated areas. Feeds on shallow water, grassy shores and arable fields, latter sometimes far from water. Migratory in N and E. Nests in burrow, rarely in tree-hole or under building.

IDENTIFICATION Medium-sized, goose-like duck with boldly patterned plumage. Body plump, neck, head and legs rather long. Wings long and rather pointed, arched in normal flight, wingbeats deep when accelerating. *White* with *dark green head*, *red bill*, a *broad chestnut belt across breast*, and black scapulars, flight-feathers, tip of tail and stripe on belly. – Adult ♂: *Bright red bill* with *prominent knob*, especially when breeding. Larger size apparent when pair seen together. – Adult ♀: Bill often *duller* with *small knob*. Chestnut and black marks on chest/belly narrower and less neat. – Juvenile: Forehead, 'face', chin, throat and foreneck white, crown and hindneck brown-grey. No chestnut chest-band or black stripe on belly. – 1st-summer: Like adult, but distinguished in flight by *white trailing edge of wing*.

VOICE Vocal. In spring, ♂ utters high, whizzing whistle, 'sliss-sliss-sliss-...', often in flight when pursuing ♀. Also a repeated disyllabic 'piu-pu'. ♀ has a strong, straight, somewhat nasal, whinnying 'gagagagagaga...', often in flight. Also a disyllabic, growling 'a-ank', used as alarm, and raucous rolling 'grah grah...'.

Ruddy Shelduck *Tadorna ferruginea* V***

L 58–70 cm, WS 110–135 cm. Breeds in variety of inland habitats: shores of lakes, saltmarshes, rivers, in hills and even on mountainsides, at times far from nearest water. Nests in hole in cliff, bank, tree or ruin. Largely migratory. Often seen flying at considerable height. W European records mainly involve escapes from captivity, but influxes of wild birds sometimes occur (e.g. 1994).

IDENTIFICATION Roughly the same size as Shelduck (marginally larger), and similar proportions, with fairly long neck and legs, long and rather narrow wings. *Body bright orange-brown, head paler* cinnamon-buff or creamy-white, especially pale on forehead and 'face'. Rump, tail and flight-feathers black, partly with greenish gloss. *Forewing* (upper and under) *pure white.* Bill black. – Adult ♂: Narrow *black neck-collar*. Slightly darker orange-brown on mantle and breast. – Adult ♀: No neck-collar. Tendency to have more clearly set-off white 'face-mask'. – Juvenile: Resembles ♀, but has grey wash on white of forewing.

VOICE Typical is strongly nasal, honking quality. In flight, loud trumpeting 'ang' and disyllabic 'ah-üng' (latter recalling Canada Goose, and—more valid considering range—distant donkey). Hollow, rolling 'ahrrrr' also heard.

Egyptian Goose *Alopochen aegyptiacus* rB4

L 63–73 cm. African species. Feral resident population in S England (introduced 18th century). Found in parkland with rivers, lakes and marshes.

IDENTIFICATION Somewhat larger than Ruddy Shelduck, with which it can be confused at long range, especially in flight (both being *pale brown with large white wing-panels*); stocky build, less orange-buff tinge on body, *dark eye-surround*, and, at closer range, *dull pink-red bill* with dark outline separate it. *Long-legged*, legs being dull pinkish-red. Dark brown breast patch. Sexes similar. Rather extensive individual variation. – Juvenile: Duller, lacking dark brown patch on breast and around eye, crown being dull brown, not whitish.

Bar-headed Goose *Anser indicus* —

L 68–78 cm. Central Asian high-altitude species, but escaped feral birds may appear in Europe.

IDENTIFICATION Bean Goose-sized and *very pale* grey (in flight largely whitish-looking). At close range shows distinctive *white head with two black cross-bars*. Hindneck dark grey. Outer parts of flight-feathers dark. Bill and legs yellow, bill comparatively small.

PERCHING DUCKS *Cairinini*

Medium-small, compact ducks with small bill, freely perching in trees. Habits otherwise similar to those of dabbling ducks (p. 48). Nest in tree-hole. Two species introduced.

Mandarin Duck *Aix galericulata* rB4

L 41–49 cm, WS 65–75 cm. Breeds in E Asia, feral population established in Britain 20th century. Found on lakes and rivers, prefers shores with overhanging willows, reedbeds and other sheltering vegetation.

IDENTIFICATION Medium-small and compact, long tail, large head. Sexes markedly different. – Adult ♂: Striking appearance and unmistakable: red bill; *wide whitish band from bill above eye to end of fluffy crest*; orange, 'combed' whiskers; large *orange 'sails'* at rear of back. – Adult ♀: Dull olive-grey with *white spectacles* and *narrow line back towards nape*; white narrow line inside base of bill, and white chin and throat; secondaries have green speculum and white tips. Flanks boldly spotted pale. – Juvenile: Like ♀ but duller and browner, with more indistinct head markings.

VOICE Rather silent. ♂ has a short upward-inflected 'pfruib'. Alarm shrill whistling 'uib', on taking wing. ♀ has low, clucking notes.

Wood Duck *Aix sponsa* [V***]

L 43–51 cm. American species, kept in some wildfowl collections in Europe, and escapes occasionally seen. Genuine vagrants reported from Iceland.

IDENTIFICATION Slightly larger than closely related Mandarin Duck. – Adult ♂: Unmistakable: *head and upperparts metallic blue and green, head with fine white lines*; chin and upper throat white, sides of neck and breast dark rufous, speckled white. – Adult ♀ (and eclipse ♂): Much more similar to Mandarin; told by having *more white surrounding eye*; *darker head without pale striation on sides of cheeks*; *different outline of base of bill*; dark nail; *finer pale spotting on flanks*.

Shelduck   Ruddy Shelduck

SHELDUCK

bill-knob

ad. ♂

white trailing edge on young

juv.

juv.

ad. ♂

RUDDY SHELDUCK

ad. summer ♂

♂ loses black neck-ring in winter

juv.

ad. ♀

juv.

ad.

EGYPTIAN GOOSE

dark eye-surround

sexes similar

long, dull red

ad.

BAR-HEADED GOOSE

lacks cross-bars

juv.

ad.

very pale plumage

ad.

MANDARIN DUCK

eye-ring and eye-stripe narrow and neat

white streak

pale nail

paler and somewhat greyer than ♀ Wood Duck

ad. ♀

rounded spots

ad. ♂

WOOD DUCK

eye-ring and eye-stripe wide and slightly uneven

dark nail

ad. ♀

rather thin spots

ad. ♂

KM

DABBLING DUCKS *Anatini*

Surface-feeding small to large-sized ducks of lakes, rivers and shallow water, often upending. Take off from water readily and without prior running. Sexes markedly dissimilar in most. ♂♂ adopt ♀-like, cryptic so-called eclipse plumage in summer during simultaneous moult of flight-feathers, making adults flightless for 3–4 weeks.

Mallard *Anas platyrhynchos*   **rB2 / P+W2**

L 50–60 cm, WS 81–95 cm. Most familiar duck, and ancestor of domestic duck. Breeds in parks, by canals in towns, on eutrophic lakes, woodland marshes, seashores; accepts very small waters (tiny pools, ditches, etc.). Resident in much of Europe except in N and E, where it retreats from the ice in winter. Wide range of nest sites: under bush, tree-hole, artificial nest-basket, near or on buildings.

IDENTIFICATION Large, with stocky build. Head and bill large, tail short. In flight, looks *heavy, wings rather blunt-tipped and broad*, especially at base, wingbeats moderately quick. Legs orange. Often told by size, shape, and *dark blue speculum very prominently bordered white*. – Adult ♂ breeding: *Head metallic green, narrow white neck-collar*, breast purplish-brown, rest of body largely pale grey, stern black, central tail-feathers upcurled; the *bill is uniform dull yellow*. – Adult ♀: Streaked brown, crown and eye-stripe darker, leaving pale supercilium; *bill orange, with blackish culmen* irregularly invading sides of bill at centre (cf. Gadwall); outer tail-feathers dusky buff-white; in flight, note *dark belly* and whitish underwing-coverts. – Adult ♂ eclipse: Like ♀, but *bill uniform yellow, breast tinged rufous* and less well marked; head slightly more contrasting. – Juvenile: Very similar to adult ♀.

VOICE Vocal. ♂ has soft, nasal, low 'rhaeb', often repeated when alert on water. Gives a short whistle, 'piu', when courting ♀. Quacking of ♀ loud, a series of hoarse notes, the first one or two being stressed, the following dying off, 'quaek-quaek-quak-quak-quah-qua-...'; in anxiety, can give prolonged slower series of hard quacks at even pitch.

Gadwall *Anas strepera*   **rB4 / W4**

L 46–56 cm, WS 78–90 cm. Breeds on variety of fresh (and rarely brackish) waters, mostly on eutrophic lakes or bays with reedbeds and wooded islets. Local breeder in Britain, partly introduced, increasing.

IDENTIFICATION Slightly smaller than Mallard, and of *slimmer build* with *narrower wings* and body. In flight, note *whitish belly* (Mallard pale brownish). Main feature is *small white speculum*, but note that this is prominent only on adult ♂ ('lump of sugar'), and practically non-existent on juvenile ♀. – Adult ♂ breeding: Head medium brown; *stern*

black (but tail pale brown), rest of *body grey, finely vermiculated*, boldest on breast; *long scapulars pale grey-buff*; *bill grey-black*. In flight, *prominent white speculum, and black and chestnut on upperwing*. – Adult ♀: Resembles Mallard, but has *whitish belly, small white speculum*, different bill pattern with *orange even stripe along cutting edges*, and *darker brown-grey tail-feathers*. – Adult ♂ eclipse: As ♂ but retains adult ♂ wing; bill with some orange, recalling ♀. – Juvenile: As adult ♀ but body colour brighter buff, contrasting with greyer head.

VOICE ♂ has a low, short, croaking 'ahrk', and high-pitched whistled 'pee' in courtship. ♀ has quacking call like Mallard, but often somewhat harder and more mechanical.

(Northern) **Pintail** *Anas acuta*   **r+mB5 / W3**

L 51–62 cm (excl. elongated tail-feathers of ♂ c. 10), WS 79–87 cm. Breeds on lakes in lowland and steppe, also mountain and tundra pools. Local breeder in Britain. Partly migratory.

IDENTIFICATION Nearly Mallard-sized but *much more slim and elegant*. Wings long, narrow and pointed; *tail long and pointed*, on ♂ markedly so; neck long and narrow; head small; a greyhound among ducks! Flight fast, outer wings swept back a little, long neck and tail obvious. – Adult ♂ breeding: Unmistakable, with long central tail-feathers (cf. Long-tailed Duck); head and upper neck brown, *breast and lower neck white, extending as narrow stripe into brown of head* on each side. Speculum blackish-green, bordered white at rear and pale rufous at front. – Adult ♀: Like a slim Mallard, scalloped and mottled brown, but: *slim bill dark grey; head almost uniformly brownish, contrasting with rather grey body with more coarse, patchy marks*; and speculum dark brown, at front thinly (hardly visible) but *at rear prominently bordered white* (visible at a mile!). Belly pale brownish-white. – Adult ♂ eclipse: As adult ♀ but retains upperwing of adult ♂, and scapulars are longer and greyer. – Juvenile: As adult ♀ but less neatly scalloped on body, more diffusely spotted and barred. White trailing edge of secondaries less broad, speculum duller brown, tinged greenish on ♂♂.

VOICE ♂ has a short, clear whistle, 'krrü', recalling Teal but lower-pitched; at close range a simultaneous whizzing 'wee-weey' can be heard. During courtship, ♀ has a deep crowing 'cr-r-r-rah', almost like a quarrelling Carrion Crow. Quacking of ♀ intermediate between Mallard and Teal.

(American) **Black Duck** *Anas rubripes*   **V****

L 53–61 cm. American species; genuine vagrants believed to have reached Europe, but many records probably escapes.

IDENTIFICATION Mallard-sized, and plumage much as very dark ♀ Mallard (beware of melanistic such!). Sexes and ages similar. Head pale brown-grey, contrasting with *very dark* brown-grey and almost unmarked body. *Tail dark; wing speculum bluish-purple* (or turquoise), *bordered narrowly and indistinctly off-white* at rear. Bill *yellowish* on both sexes, ♀ with only a hint of darker culmen.

Mallard   Gadwall   Pintail

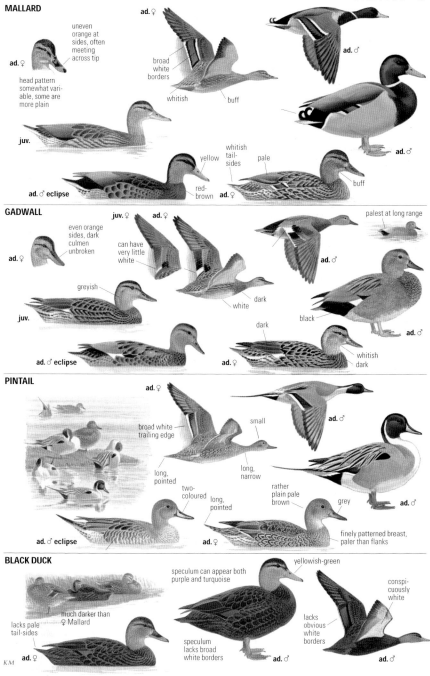

MALLARD

ad. ♀

uneven orange at sides, often meeting across tip

ad. ♀

broad white borders

head pattern somewhat variable, some are more plain

whitish

buff

ad. ♂

juv.

ad. ♂

yellow

whitish tail-sides

pale

ad. ♂ eclipse

red-brown

ad. ♀

buff

GADWALL

juv. ♀

ad. ♀

palest at long range

even orange sides, dark culmen unbroken

ad. ♀

can have very little white

ad. ♂

greyish

dark

juv.

white

black

ad. ♂

dark

ad. ♂ eclipse

ad. ♀

whitish dark

PINTAIL

ad. ♀

broad white trailing edge

small

ad. ♂

long, pointed

long, narrow

rather plain pale brown

grey

two-coloured

long, pointed

ad. ♂ eclipse

ad. ♀

finely patterned breast, paler than flanks

ad. ♂

BLACK DUCK

speculum can appear both purple and turquoise

yellowish-green

conspicuously white

much darker than ♀ Mallard

lacks obvious white borders

lacks pale tail-sides

speculum lacks broad white borders

ad. ♂

ad. ♂

ad. ♀

KM

(Northern) **Shoveler** *Anas clypeata*   m(r)**B**4 / **W**3
L 44–52 cm, WS 73–82 cm. Breeds on shallow eutrophic lakes with rich vegetation, or marshes with sufficient open water. Largely migratory. Although fairly common and widespread, usually seen in pairs or smaller parties only.

IDENTIFICATION Medium-large duck with short neck but *strikingly long and broad bill*, giving *front-heavy* look both when swimming and in flight. Wings rather evenly broad, but appearing slightly narrower than on Mallard. – Adult ♂ breeding: Unmistakable; *head green* (appearing black at distance), *breast white, belly and flanks vividly chestnut*. Upper forewing pale blue, speculum green, bordered white at front. – Adult ♀: Resembles Mallard except for *huge bill*, and *belly dark brown, contrasting with white underwings*; speculum dull green-grey *without white trailing edge* (white bar at front only, being narrower towards body), and upper forewing dull pale grey. – Adult ♂ eclipse: As adult ♀, but especially flanks and belly more rufous-tinged, head darker, and pale blue upper forewing retained. – Juvenile: As adult ♀, but crown and hindneck darker, and belly slightly paler.

VOICE Most often heard is disyllabic, nasal knocking call of ♂ when flushed, 'took-took...took-took...' (sometimes monosyllabic). ♀ has a similar call but wheezy or muffled, 'kerr-aesh'; also, a short, hoarse quacking, falling in strength and pitch, like a coarse-voiced ♀ Teal.

(Eurasian) **Wigeon** *Anas penelope*   r(m)**B**4 / **W**2
L 42–50 cm, WS 71–85 cm. Breeds on boreal forest lakes and marshes, tundra pools, also on temperate shallow fresh waters. Migratory in N, wintering largely in marine habitats, also lakes and reservoirs. Gregarious except when nesting. Vegetarian; often grazes on arable fields in winter.

IDENTIFICATION Medium-sized, *short-necked*, with *rounded, comparatively large head*, *small bill* and *pointed tail*. In flight, these characters apparent as well as *narrow neck*, *pointed wings*, and outer wing generally swept back. Flight fast. In all plumages, note *distinct white belly patch*. Axillaries and underwing-coverts dusky pale grey (cf. American Wigeon). – Adult ♂ breeding: Unmistakable; *head and neck chestnut, forehead and crown creamy-yellow*, breast greyish-pink, rest of body grey with white and black stern. In flight, *large white patch on upper forewing* striking, speculum green. – Adult ♀: Rather dull rufous-brown or greyish (some variation, with inclination towards two morphs) with variable diffuse mottling and blotching (some are rather plain), best recognized by: *rather dark plumage; shape; small, pale blue-grey bill with black tip*; and *contrasting white belly*. Speculum dull, dark; innermost secondaries usually edged pale, forming narrow whitish patch (recalling 1st-year ♀ Gadwall). – Adult ♂ eclipse: Resembles adult ♀ but *retains white upper*

forewing, and plumage *more rufous-tinged*. – Juvenile: As adult ♀, but white underparts often faintly mottled, and speculum still duller. – 1st-year ♂: As adult ♂ breeding, but *upper forewing is chiefly grey-brown*, not largely pure white.

VOICE ♂ has characteristic *loud whistling glissando note*, often preceded by low, brief note (and ending with subdued dry trill), 'wu, **wee**-oo(rr)'; at a distance only '**wee**-oo' audible. Also more subdued, conversational 'wip... wee... wip-wü', etc., somewhat recalling ♂ Tufted Duck. In autumn, and at times at other seasons as well, coarse, snorting'rrah','ra-**kaah**' and variants are heard. Flight-call of ♀ is a repeated growling, 'karr karr karr...', recalling Great Crested Grebe in tone.

American Wigeon *Anas americana*   **V***
L 48–56 cm. American species; rare straggler to Europe. About 10–20 records annually in Britain.

IDENTIFICATION Roughly of same size as Wigeon; shape much the same, with rounded head and pointed tail, but on average head appears a fraction larger with steeper forehead and fuller nape. – Adult ♂ breeding: *Forehead and centre of crown white, broad stripe over eye and to nape dark green* (looking blackish at distance); rest of head freckled grey and white; both breast and flanks pinkish-brown. – All other plumages: Very similar to Wigeon and at times difficult to distinguish. Note: On average *greyer head and neck* with much more *marked contrast with rufous-brown breast. Axillaries and median underwing-coverts white* (axillaries at the most with faint dusky shafts and indistinct subterminal bars on some), whereas these are pale greyish with brownish-grey shafts and patterning on most Wigeons (may *appear* whitish on Wigeon in strong light, though, and a few *do have* paler underwing). Paler forehead and darker mottling around eye give impression of *dark eye patch* at distance (only a hint of this on some Wigeons). White bases to greater upperwing-coverts on adult ♀ give *pale bar along midwing*.

Marbled Duck *Marmaronetta angustirostris*   —
L 39–42 cm, WS 63–70 cm. Breeds rarely and locally (declining; now probably < 200 pairs left in Spain) in lowland, shallow, well-vegetated fresh waters. Lives much as a dabbling duck, but also shows some affinities to the pochards (smaller diving ducks), to which it is sometimes referred.

IDENTIFICATION Rather small and slim with long wings and tail and *slender dark bill* (recalling ♀ Pintail), head appearing fairly large and oblong owing to crest-like feathers at nape. *Plumage pale sandy-brown*, diffusely blotched off-white; *eye-surround dusky*. In flight, *wings look pale without marked pattern* (does not have a speculum), but *secondaries palest*, and leading edge shows two pale spots in carpal area when seen head-on, much as on Grey Heron. Sexes and ages similar, ♂♂ tending to have more crest and blacker bill, juvs. having more diffuse and buff-white blotches.

VOICE Usually silent. During courtship, a high-pitched and squeaky whistle, 'vee-veeh', is given by ♂.

Shoveler   Wigeon   Marbled Duck

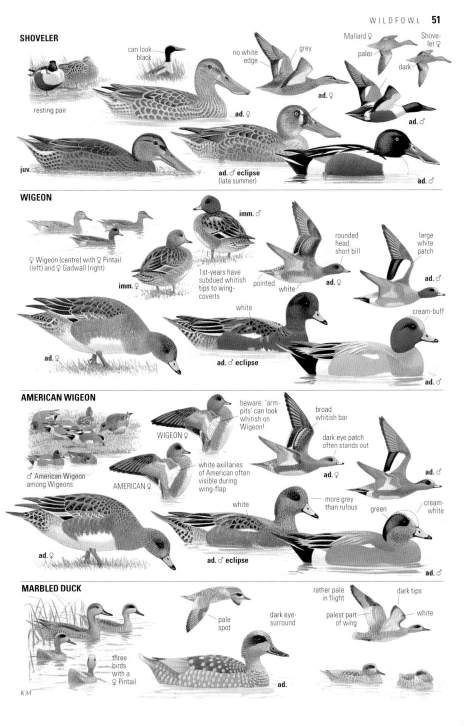

SHOVELER

can look black

no white edge

grey

Mallard ♀

paler

Shoveler ♀

dark

ad. ♀

ad. ♂

resting pair

ad. ♀

juv.

ad. ♂ eclipse
(late summer)

ad. ♂

WIGEON

imm. ♂

rounded head, short bill

large white patch

♀ Wigeon (centre) with ♀ Pintail (left) and ♀ Gadwall (right)

1st-years have subdued whitish tips to wing-coverts

imm. ♀

pointed

white

ad. ♀

ad. ♂

ad. ♀

white

ad. ♂ eclipse

cream-buff

ad. ♂

AMERICAN WIGEON

beware: 'arm-pits' can look whitish on Wigeon!

WIGEON ♀

broad whitish bar

dark eye patch often stands out

ad. ♀

ad. ♂

♂ American Wigeon among Wigeons

AMERICAN ♀

white axillaries of American often visible during wing-flap

more grey than rufous

green

cream-white

ad. ♀

white

ad. ♂ eclipse

ad. ♂

MARBLED DUCK

rather pale in flight

dark tips

palest part of wing

white

pale spot

dark eye-surround

three birds with a ♀ Pintail

ad.

KM

(Common) Teal *Anas crecca* r(m)**B**4 / **W**2

L 34–38 cm, WS 53–59 cm. Breeds on variety of fresh and brackish waters, preferring lakes and ponds (even quite small ones) in forests, pools in taiga bogs or mountain willows, also along rivers and shallow, well-vegetated sea-shores, and on eutrophic lakes if near forests, where nest is placed. A common bird, forming large flocks on coastal bays or shallow lakes outside breeding season. Birds from N Europe winter in Britain, but also in Holland, France, etc.

IDENTIFICATION *Smallest* duck, appearing almost wader-like in flight, with *narrow, pointed wings, short neck, fast and agile flight* and *dense flock formation*; takes off from water easily and rises steeply, will twist and turn readily in flight. At distance in flight, appears *dark with short, broad white bar along centre of upperwing* (both sexes). Speculum glossy green. – Adult ♂ breeding: Head chestnut with green sides, green colour thinly bordered yellow. *Sides of undertail pale yellow, bordered black*, visible even at distance. Horizontal white line along grey body. – Variation: N American ssp. *carolinensis* (rare vagrant) lacks most of thin yellow lines on sides of head, and has *vertical* white line on side of breast (not horizontal along body). – Adult ♀: Brown, streaked and mottled dark. Swimming bird resembles Garganey, but note: *small size; small bill*, often a little *orange at base*; moderately dark eye-stripe and *lack of dark stripe over cheeks* make head look fairly plain; a *pale patch or streak along base of tail-side*; chin/throat not so clean and pale buff-white. In flight told by wing pattern; belly diffusely paler at centre; underwing has whitish centre and dark leading and trailing edges. – Eclipse ♂ and juvenile very similar to adult ♀, juveniles generally slightly darker (also on belly), and flanks more 'striped' dark (adult ♀ has more delicate scaly pattern).

VOICE Vocal. ♂ has a clear, ringing whistle, 'treel', confusable only with Pintail's, but is higher-pitched. ♀ quacks feeble, high-pitched with a nasal voice, first note higher, following descending, 'peeht pat pat'; also a hard, fast 'krek-ekekek' when pursuit by ♂ is causing stress.

Garganey *Anas querquedula* m**B**5

L 37–41 cm, WS 59–67 cm. Breeds on shallow, eutrophic fresh waters in lowland and steppe habitats. Nests in tussock on lakeside meadow. Summer visitor (mainly Apr–Sep); strictly migratory, wintering in Africa. Never seen in large flocks in northern part of range (though often in southern).

IDENTIFICATION Slightly larger than Teal, with longer and straighter bill, and on average slightly longer tail. In flight, *wings are slightly paler* (especially outer wing). *Only rarely* upends, prefers to skim surface ('dabble') or dip head (Teal frequently upends). – Adult ♂ breeding: Head purple-brown ('dark' at distance) with *white crescent over eye to side*

of nape; breast dark brown, flanks pale grey; scapulars black and white, pointed. In flight, *pale, dull blue-grey upper forewing* and *sharp contrast between white belly and dark breast*. – Adult ♀: Resembles Teal, but told by slightly *larger size; longer, straighter all-grey bill* (no orange at the base); hint of *darker stripe across cheeks* and of *pale loral patch* at base of bill, making *head look more striped*; lack of pale patch at base of tail-side. Further, ♀ Garganeys (and imm./eclipse ♂♂) often have quite *clean, pale creamy chin/throat* compared with ♀-type Teals. In flight, *grey-brown forewing* much as on Teal, but slightly paler outer wing, and lacks broad white midwing-bar (has narrow ♀ only), and has *broad white trailing edge to secondaries* in ♂ Pintail fashion. – Adult ♂ eclipse: Like adult ♀, but retains adult ♂ wing with *pale blue-grey forewing*. – Juvenile: Like adult ♀, but belly is less pale, and white trailing edge to secondaries is narrower.

VOICE ♂ has characteristic display-call, a dry, wooden rattle, swaying a little in pitch, 'prrerrorrer', like running a fingernail across a comb. ♀ rather silent; has nasal 'ga, ga-ga, ga...', and a feeble, short, high-pitched quacking.

Blue-winged Teal *Anas discors* **V**∗

L 37–41 cm. American species. 5–15 records annually in British Isles (may involve escapes among genuine vagrants).

IDENTIFICATION Breeding ♂ distinctive (but beware that eclipse ♂ Shoveler often has white half-moon bordering base of bill). ♀-type plumages resemble Garganey, Teal and, especially, Cinnamon Teal (American species, sometimes kept in European wildfowl collections and may escape from these; cf. p. 390). Note *prominent pale loral spot* but *lack of dark horizontal, diffuse streak from bill across cheek*; chin and belly pale, finely mottled brown (but not white); green-ish or dull yellow feet; *bright pale blue upper forewing*, almost as blue as on adult ♂; *lack of white trailing edge to secondaries*; no pale patch at base of tail-side.

Baikal Teal *Anas formosa* [**V**∗∗∗]

L 39–43 cm. N and E Siberian species. Declining. Very rarely seen in Europe, and arguably doubtful whether any record involves a genuine straggler.

IDENTIFICATION Breeding ♂ unmistakable, with *striking head pattern; white vertical narrow line at side of breast*. Adult ♀ and juveniles brownish and streaked like other teals, and wing and head patterns recall both ♀ Teal (often has a pale patch at base of tail-side) and ♀ Garganey (well-patterned head; rather similar wing pattern). Slightly larger and longer-tailed than Teal; bill thin and all grey; *speculum is bordered pale rufous in front*, not whitish, and *white rear border always broader*. – Adult ♀: Head pattern distinctive, with small but *very prominent and circular white loral spot* (enhanced by dark surround); *dark eye-stripe only behind eye*; on many, *a whitish bar* or wedge runs from the white throat *vertically up across the cheek* towards eye; and sometimes there is *a dusky kidney-shaped mark on the upper cheek*. – Adult ♂ eclipse: Like adult ♀, but plumage much richer rufous. – Juvenile: Slightly duller brown-grey than adult ♀. Most similar to Teal, but usually told by more prominent pale loral spot with darker surround (not so conspicuous as on adult ♀, still usually more prominent than on any Teal), all-grey bill, and lack of white midwing-bar.

Teal Garganey

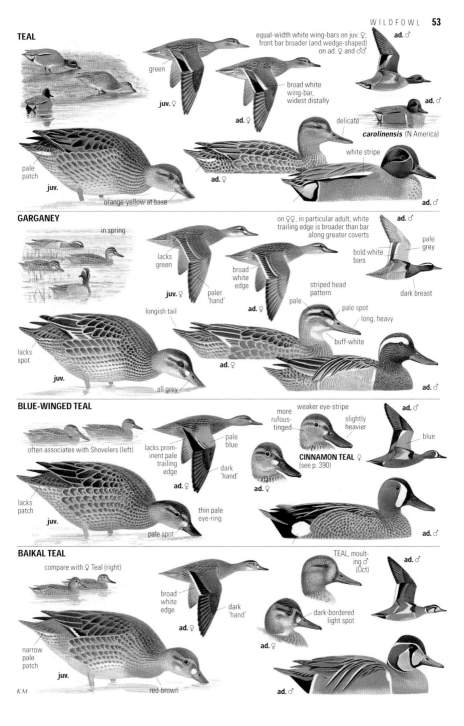

TEAL

green

juv. ♀

equal-width white wing-bars on juv. ♀;
front bar broader (and wedge-shaped)
on ad. ♀ and ♂♂

ad. ♂

broad white
wing-bar,
widest distally

ad. ♀

delicate

carolinensis (N America)

white stripe

pale
patch

juv.

orange-yellow at base

ad. ♀

ad. ♂

GARGANEY

in spring

lacks
green

juv. ♀

paler
'hand'

broad
white
edge

ad. ♀

on ♀♀, in particular adult, white
trailing edge is broader than bar
along greater coverts

ad. ♂

pale
grey

bold white
bars

dark breast

striped head
pattern

pale

pale spot

long, heavy

buff-white

longish tail

lacks
spot

juv.

all grey

ad. ♀

ad. ♂

BLUE-WINGED TEAL

often associates with Shovelers (left)

lacks prom-
inent pale
trailing edge

pale
blue

dark
'hand'

ad. ♀

more
rufous-
tinged

weaker eye-stripe

slightly
heavier

CINNAMON TEAL ♀
(see p. 390)

ad. ♂

blue

ad. ♀

lacks
patch

juv.

thin pale
eye-ring

pale spot

ad. ♂

BAIKAL TEAL

compare with ♀ Teal (right)

broad
white
edge

dark
'hand'

ad. ♀

TEAL, moult-
ing ♂
(Oct)

ad. ♂

dark-bordered
light spot

ad. ♀

narrow
pale
patch

juv.

red-brown

ad. ♂

KM

DIVING DUCKS *Aythya, Somateria* et al.
is a rather loosely applied group name which designates all species, fairly small to large, which feed mainly by diving, only rarely practising upending. Vegetarian or omnivorous. Body rather heavy, wings somewhat shorter (and in some cases blunter) than on dabbling ducks, hence take off from water generally only after prior running on surface. One group ('pochards') found mainly on shallow, eutrophic lakes, another (eiders, scoters, sawbills) in primarily marine habitats. Nest on ground, near water, a scrape lined with down. ♀ alone tends young. Moult as in dabbling ducks (p. 48). Beware of confusing hybrids, though rare, occurring particularly among 'pochards' (p. 58).

(Common) Pochard *Aythya ferina*   r(m)**B4** / **W3**
L 42–49 cm, WS 67–75 cm. Breeds on eutrophic lakes and marshes with sufficient open water (depth > 1 m). Birds in N and E Europe winter in W and S, ♂♂ often already moving in summer. Gregarious. ♂♂ appear more numerous than ♀♀. Often dives for food, but also practises upending and dabbling for food from surface. Nests in vegetation near water.

IDENTIFICATION Medium-sized, short-tailed (rear end sloping down on swimming bird) with long neck and *long bill with concave culmen* running without step into *sloping forehead*, giving fairly distinctive profile with *smoothly peaked crown*. In all plumages, wings have *indistinct greyish wing-bars*. – Adult ♂ breeding: *Head bright chestnut; bill blackish with pale grey band across outer part; eye reddish; breast black* with gloss; *flanks and back pale ash-grey*, appearing whitish in strong light; *stern black*. In flight, medium grey upperwing-coverts and pale grey wing-bar give the bird a rather washed-out, pale appearance. – Adult ♀: Along with ♀ Wigeon, most nondescript duck: grey-brown, flanks and back tinged greyish, breast, crown and neck darker and tinged brownish. Diffuse pale and dark head marks, along with head/bill profile, often best clue: diffuse pale loral patch, eye-ring and line behind eye, and diffuse dark patch below eye which reaches lower base of bill; bill with a narrow, dull pale band across outer part (winter), or appearing all dark (summer). *Eye* rufous-*brown*. – Adult ♂ eclipse: Differs from breeding in having breast and stern dark brown-grey, and head duller rufous. Eye remains reddish. – Juvenile: Similar to adult ♀; typically more uniform above, and lacks pale line behind eye. Eye yellowish-olive.

VOICE Rather silent. Display-call of ♂ a characteristic wheezing abruptly cut off by a nasal, short note, 'aaa**ooo**-chaa(e)', like a ricocheting bullet; also, and more commonly heard, 3–4 short, sharp whistles, 'ki ki ki ki', during courtship. ♀ has loud, repeated purring 'brre-ah' (slightly downslurred), often in flight.

Red-crested Pochard *Netta rufina*   **V**∗ / (r**B5**)
L 53–57 cm, WS 85–90 cm. Breeds on fairly large, reed-fringed eutrophic lowland lakes and sea-bays, also on larger lagoons and saline marshes. Migratory only in north. Regular vagrant, especially in autumn and winter, to Britain, 10–50 records annually, and a few breed. Habits much as for dabbling ducks, upending and dabbling for food in shallow, richly vegetated waters. Vegetarian.

IDENTIFICATION Rather *large*, with long, bulky body and *large, rounded head*. In all plumages, *very conspicuous, broad white wing-bars*. – Adult ♂ breeding: Rusty-orange head (palest on crown, but impression may vary depending on angle of light) and *striking coral-red bill*; breast, stern and centre of belly black, *flanks white*; swimming bird typically shows *white narrow patch at side of mantle*; upperparts plain brown. In flight, broad white wing-bars and peculiar *white oval flank patches lined with black* distinctive. Immediately told from ♂ Pochard by red bill and darker, brown back. – Adult ♀: General appearance like a large, pale ♀ Common Scoter, with off-white sides of head and foreneck and dark brown forehead, crown and hindneck; body plain brown, often diffusely patchy on flanks; *bill dark grey with pink near tip*. Eye brown. – Adult ♂ eclipse: Like adult ♀ but *bill all red*. – Juvenile: Like adult ♀ but *bill all dark*.

VOICE Rather silent. ♂ has a loud, often repeated 'baeht', and a 'stifled sneeze'. ♀ pursued by ♂ utters hard 'wrah-wrah-wrah-...' (likened to distant barking dog), and subdued 'rerr-rerr' during courtship on the water.

Ferruginous Duck *Aythya nyroca*   **V**∗
L 38–42 cm, WS 60–67 cm. Breeds in same habitats as Pochard; less gregarious (and scarcer!); also appears more shy. Rare visitor in Britain autumn–spring.

IDENTIFICATION Medium-small, rather short-bodied, with *long bill* and neck, and characteristically high forehead and *peaked crown*. In flight, very striking, *broad, pure white wing-bars running to tip of wing*. On all but some juveniles, *white undertail and (separated) white belly patch* are obvious. Beware of some ♀♀ Tufted Ducks with white on undertail (though less pure and extensive). – Adult ♂ breeding: Whole plumage *deep chestnut* (tinged purplish), darkest on back and palest on flanks, except for *white undertail and belly*; narrow black neck-collar (rarely seen). *Eye white*. – Adult ♀: Dark brown with reddish tinge on head. *Pure white undertail. Eye dark.* Note *head/bill profile*, which separates from Tufted Duck, as do *longer and broader white wing-bars* in flight. – Adult ♂ eclipse: Like adult ♀, but tinged more obviously reddish, and retains *white eye*. – Juvenile: Resembles adult ♀ with dark eye, but main colour more dull brown, and both belly and undertail have less pure and extensive white patches (thus resembles Tufted Duck less).

VOICE Rather silent. ♀ has a purring flight-call with characteristic *dry ring*, snoring 'errr errr errr errr...'. ♂ has Tufted Duck-like '**wee**-whew' during courtship and also hard, nasal staccatonotes, 'chk-chk-chk-...'.

Pochard   Red-crested Pochard   Ferruginous Duck

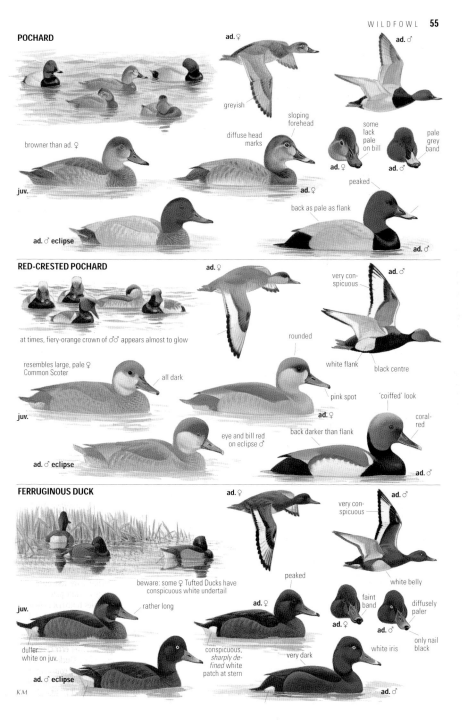

POCHARD

ad. ♀

ad. ♂

greyish

sloping forehead

diffuse head marks

some lack pale on bill

pale grey band

ad. ♀

ad. ♂

browner than ad. ♀

juv.

ad. ♀

peaked

back as pale as flank

ad. ♂ eclipse

ad. ♂

RED-CRESTED POCHARD

ad. ♀

ad. ♂

very conspicuous

at times, fiery-orange crown of ♂♂ appears almost to glow

rounded

resembles large, pale ♀ Common Scoter

all dark

white flank

black centre

juv.

pink spot

'coiffed' look

eye and bill red on eclipse ♂

ad. ♀

back darker than flank

coral-red

ad. ♂ eclipse

ad. ♂

FERRUGINOUS DUCK

ad. ♀

ad. ♂

very conspicuous

beware: some ♀ Tufted Ducks have conspicuous white undertail

peaked

white belly

juv.

rather long

ad. ♀

faint band

diffusely paler

ad. ♀

ad. ♂

duller white on juv.

conspicuous, *sharply defined* white patch at stern

very dark

white iris

only nail black

ad. ♂ eclipse

ad. ♂

KM

(Greater) **Scaup** *Aythya marila*   **W**3–4 / (r**B**5)

L 42–51 cm, WS 71–80 cm. Breeds in marine habitats (fjords, archipelagos) on salt or brackish water, or on freshwater lakes and pools in mountains (birch and willow zones) and tundra. Migratory. Wintering birds gregarious, diving for molluscs on open sea, or are seen along coasts and in bays.

IDENTIFICATION Medium-sized with rather large, rounded head, and sloping end of body when swimming. ♂ distinctive. Other plumages similar to Tufted Duck, with similar *white wing-bar*, but note: *no hint of crest* on hindcrown; *head shape more elongated and profile smoothly rounded*; body longer; and less black on tip of bill (mainly *just nail black*; Tufted has whole tip black). Beware of confusing hybrids (cf. p. 58), and the possibility of a rare vagrant Lesser Scaup *A. affinis* (N America; p. 379). – Adult ♂ breeding: Head black with *green gloss*, eye yellow; breast and stern black; flanks white, *back greyish-white* (fine vermiculation apparent only at closer range). Bill pale grey with small, fan-shaped black nail patch. In flight, light back usually obvious, as are white wing-bars; upper fore-edge of wing vermiculated, appearing medium grey (darker than back but not black as on Tufted). – Adult ♀: Dull brown with pale brown-grey flanks and slightly darker back, latter with some greyish vermiculation (visible at close range only), and striking *broad white band surrounding base of bill* (Tufted may have some white at bill-base though usually less, and only rarely extending clearly over culmen). In late spring/summer, a *prominent pale patch on ear-coverts* on most. – Adult ♂ eclipse: Rather similar to breeding, but with brown cast on head, breast and back, and often a little white around bill-base. – Juvenile: Resembles adult ♀, but less white at bill-base, slightly darker bill with indistinct darker nail area, and paler flanks. Young ♂ attains most of adult plumage by end of 1st winter (Feb–Apr), but not fully until 2nd winter.

VOICE ♂ mostly silent. During display a chorus of low whistles, 'wü-wüp wü-wo wüpüwee...', recalling Tufted Duck but lower-pitched; now and then more typical falling 'püooh' (voice reminiscent of Eider). Growling call of ♀ like Tufted Duck's but is deeper, more drawn out and voice raucous, 'krrah krrah krrah...'.

Tufted Duck *Aythya fuligula*   r**B**4 / **W**3

L 40–47 cm, WS 65–72 cm. Versatile in choice of breeding habitat, therefore common: open, clear, oligotrophic lakes in forested areas; densely vegetated, eutrophic lowland lakes and marshes; along seashores; on tundra pools; slow-flowing rivers; reservoirs; park lakes; etc. Mainly migratory. Gregarious when not breeding, forming large, dense flocks.

IDENTIFICATION Small, short-bodied, with narrow neck and rather *large head with crest* (long and drooping on

breeding ♂, only a shorter tuft in other plumages) at hindcrown. Head 'unevenly rounded' with *high forehead and flattish crown*; *bill short but broad, pale blue-grey with most of tip 'dipped' in black*. In flight, *white wing-bars* prominent (as on Scaup). – Adult ♂ breeding: Swimming bird distinctive, has *black plumage with sharply defined rectangular white flanks* and *long drooping crest*. Eye yellow. – Adult ♀: Brownish with paler flanks diffusely blotched darker on most. Resembles Scaup, especially when showing white at bill-base, but told by *smaller size, hint of crest, different head shape, darker brown, especially above*, and *more black at tip of bill*. A few have some white on undertail, especially in autumn, recalling Ferruginous Duck, but told by different head shape, hint of crest, and *shorter and less prominent white wing-bars*. Eye usually deep yellow. – Adult ♂ eclipse: Crest short, flanks dull brown, black parts of breeding plumage tinged brown. – Juvenile: Like adult ♀, but a little paler brown on head with a little buff feathering at bill-base. Eye brown. Young ♂ attains most of adult plumage in 1st winter (Dec–Mar), but fully only in 2nd winter.

VOICE Display-call of ♂ a nervously quick, 'bubbly' or even giggly series of accelerating notes on slightly falling pitch (also in flight at night), 'wip wee-weewüwüp' ('Turkey in falsetto'). ♀ has growling call typical of *Aythya* ♀♀, 'krr krr krr...', slightly faster and higher-pitched, and each segment shorter, than in Pochard; higher-pitched than Scaup.

Ring-necked Duck *Aythya collaris*   **V**∗

L 37–46 cm. American species. Certainly at times genuine vagrant in Europe (annually in Britain & Ireland), but many are likely escapes from wildfowl collections. Birds tend to reappear at same sites in several consecutive years.

IDENTIFICATION Small, short-bodied, head rather large and of distinctive shape: *forehead very high and steep, crown peaked at hindcrown*, and hint of rounded crest at hindcrown creating *small indentation between crown and nape*. Bill of adults slate-grey with wide black tip and white subterminal band, thus *is three-coloured*; breeding ♂ also has narrow white band at base, and nostrils encircled white. *Tail* rather *longer* than on Tufted Duck, and often *conspicuously raised*. In flight, very similar to Tufted but told by *grey wing-bar*, not white. Beware of confusing hybrids (cf. p. 58), and mainly ♂ Tufted Ducks. – Adult ♂ breeding: Plumage like Tufted, but *flanks pure white only at front, forming vertical 'spur'*, and diffusely along upper edge, *otherwise grey*; also, *upper edge of flank panel more markedly S-curved* than on Tufted. Indistinct purplish-brown neck-collar (often hidden). – Adult ♀: Best told by head shape and bill pattern (though latter less clear than on ♂, esp. in early autumn, thin white band along bill-base missing); plumage recalls ♀ Pochard more than Tufted, having *pale throat, diffuse pale patch bordering bill-base, pale eye-ring* and, often, a *pale line behind eye*. Eye dark. – Adult ♂ eclipse: Resembles adult ♀ with some pale feathering bordering bill, and lack of distinctive white band at bill-base, but *retains yellow eye*, and head *lacks pale eye-ring and line behind eye*; also, head and breast darker, blackish-brown. – Juvenile: Very similar to adult ♀, but possibly distinguished by *almost all-dark bill*, pale subterminal band developing during 1st autumn. Young ♂ attains adult plumage as early as (late) 1st winter.

Scaup   Tufted Duck

SCAUP

winter flock

1st-winter ♂

ad. ♀

1st-winter ♀

ad. ♀

1st-winter ♂

ad. ♂

ad. ♀

ad. ♂

whitish back

juv. often has less white above bill than ad. ♀

subtle greyish vermiculations

much white

pale cheek patch

rounded head

body browner than ad. ♀

ad. ♀ winter

small black nail

ad. ♀ summer

faintly tinged green

pale

juv.

ad. ♂ eclipse

ad. ♂

TUFTED DUCK

ad. ♀

ad. ♂

black back

some show extensive white like Scaup (but note bill pattern)

sometimes white undertail

hint of tuft

♀

invariably tufted

duller brown than ad. ♀

ad. ♀ winter

uniform dark brown

hint of pale band

broad black tip

juv.

ad. ♂ eclipse

ad. ♂

RING-NECKED DUCK

compare with ♀ Pochard (upper):

grey

dark

ad. ♀

ad. ♂

grey

♂ Ring-necked (2nd from right) asleep among Tufted Ducks

pale band faint or lacking

head shape distinctive in all plumages

1st-winter ♂

peaked hind-crown

ad. ♂

white bands

juv.

ad. ♀

prominent tail

light grey

white 'spur'

ad. ♂

ad. ♂ eclipse

KM

WILDFOWL HYBRIDS

Although wild birds do not normally mate with birds other than representatives of their own species, exceptions do occur. Generally, a cross between two different species is most likely to occur in areas where one of the two is much less common than the other; interspecific barriers may break down if a bird in breeding season cannot easily find a mate of its own kind, and reasonably similar ones are at hand.

In our part of the world, hybrids appear to be more common among wildfowl and game-birds than in other groups. There may be genetic reasons, as yet unexplored, for this situation; but it may be no more than an impression.

Firstly, birds of both groups are handled in thousands by hunters, who will report on oddities which they happen to bag. Secondly, the impression may be partly due to the widespread keeping of wildfowl in parks; in these artificial conditions, where birds of some species are singles or, at least, in a minority among congeners, and where perhaps the normal sexual activity during courtship cannot take place to a full extent owing to pinioned wings or lack of space, hybrids become more frequent. In many wildfowl parks, locally hatched birds are allowed to fly freely, which means that we are likely to see a few of these hybrids later on at natural sites. Another likely reason for the apparent frequency of wildfowl and game-bird hybrids is that they are fairly obvious and easy to observe. Hybrids among warblers and chats may be just as common, but who would notice it?

A rather puzzling fact is that, among wildfowl, hybrids seem to occur more commonly among geese and members of the 'pochards', genus *Aythya*, than among dabbling ducks. The reason for this is not clear.

Below, some of the most frequent and confusing hybrids of 'pochards' are described. Emphasis is put on males, not because they are more common but because they are easier to detect for the average birdwatcher. Hybrid females are notoriously difficult to spot and designate correctly, a task for the expert. In the majority of cases, a fair guess can be made as to which are the two parent species of a certain hybrid. To say which was the male and which was the female is usually much more difficult.

When studying a hybrid duck, always pay close attention to: *pattern, size and shape of bill*; *iris colour*; *shape of head seen in profile*; and presence or not of *fine vermiculation* on grey or grey-brown parts.

HYBRID

Pochard ♂ × Tufted Duck ♀

This hybrid has Pochard ♂ and Tufted Duck ♀ as parents. It can be deceptively similar to a Tufted Duck ♂ moulting out of eclipse plumage (which you would see in late autumn), but note *darkish eye*; *very short 'stand-off' crest* like some

Tufted Duck × Ring-necked Duck

This hybrid has some characters intermediate between the parent species but is often very similar to Ring-necked Duck and at a casual glance could be mistaken for one. Clues to its mixed parentage are usually the presence of a tiny crest (not just a peaked hindcrown), and both the white band at the

Scaup × Tufted Duck

This hybrid between Scaup and Tufted Duck looks superficially like a Scaup ♂, with head glossed predominantly green, but close attention to detail will reveal: *darker grey*

CONFUSION SPECIES

Tufted Duck ♂ eclipse

adult ♀ Tufted Ducks; and *not entirely black upperparts*, being *very finely vermiculated* on some (visible at closest range only); the *flanks are rather darker towards belly*, sometimes *finely vermiculated*.

Ring-necked Duck ♂

base of the bill and the white 'spur' at the fore-edge of the flank (characters typical of a Ring-necked Duck) being reduced in extent or lacking altogether. Note that this hybrid often has a wholly or partly white wing-bar, unlike a true Ring-necked Duck.

Scaup ♂

back and scapulars than genuine Scaup, *vermiculation often being finer and more diffuse*; also, *more black on tip of bill* (Scaup has only the nail black); many 'Scaup ♂ type' hybrids

KM

have a *firm, pointed crest* (like the one shown here, at bottom of p. 58), giving a characteristically peaked or angled crown never seen on Scaup (but those without any hint of crest can

look markedly Scaup-like, with rounded head); other hybrids have a *shorter bill with broader tip*, just like Tufted Duck.

Tufted Duck ♂ × Pochard ♀

A now well-known hybrid is that between Tufted Duck ♂ and Pochard ♀. Surprisingly, this cross frequently produces offspring which resemble a third species, the Lesser Scaup of N America (cf. p. 379), a rare vagrant to Europe. The head is tinged purplish-brown and the crown is peaked, rather like on that species. Important field marks which separate from Lesser Scaup are: *rather dark grey back with very fine, indis-*

Lesser Scaup ♂

tinct vermiculation (Lesser Scaup has white back with rather coarse dark vermiculation, still giving a fairly light back, and vermiculation readily visible even at some distance); *tip of bill much more extensively black*, and *base of bill usually dusky grey* (on Lesser Scaup whole bill pale grey, with only nail black). Check wing-bar, too, *white only on secondaries* on true Lesser Scaup.

Pochard × Ferruginous Duck?

This hybrid is more rarely encountered than the others and is liable to be mistaken for a Redhead *Aythya americana*, a N American species (to date only one record in Europe; cf. p. 387). One such hybrid was seen in Malmö in S Sweden in the 1960s, originally identified as the first record ever of Redhead in Europe (yellow eye, rather rounded head), but the record was later withdrawn as the bird was obviously just

Redhead ♂

a hybrid. Certainly Pochard is one of its parents; the other parent species is more uncertain, but Ferruginous Duck seems the most likely. Points to note which reveal that it is not a genuine Redhead are: *bill pattern of Pochard ♂*, with both much black at tip and dark grey base (Redhead has pale grey bill with tip 'dipped in black' and a subterminal whitish band); *medium-dark grey back* (Redhead light grey).

Pochard × Ferruginous Duck

Another tricky but much more Ferruginous-like hybrid can result from the same crossing as above. It closely resembles Ferruginous Duck, but usually shows a combination of two or more of the following differences: *red or yellow eye* (instead of white as on ♂ Ferruginous Duck); *breast contrastingly*

Ferruginous Duck ♂

darker than flanks (more uniformly chestnut on Ferruginous Duck); *fine vermiculation on back and flanks* visible at close range (never any vermiculation on Ferruginous Duck); *undertail not purely and extensively white*; *tip of bill with much black* (only the nail black on Ferruginous Duck).

Scaup × Tufted Duck

This ♀ hybrid between Scaup and Tufted Duck is most similar to a ♀ Scaup, but note the following distinguishing points: much white feathering at the base of the bill (indicating Scaup), yet *extensive black at the tip of the bill* (indicating Tufted Duck); no hint of a crest on the rounded head (indi-

Scaup ♀   KM

cating Scaup), yet *noticeably dark back, clearly darker than the flanks* (indicating Tufted Duck). Other ♀ hybrids between these two parent species can have a hint of a crest, a more Scaup-like paler back or reduced black on the bill, and some will be very difficult to recognize as hybrids.

(Common) Eider *Somateria mollissima* rB3

L 60–70 cm, WS 95–105 cm. Marine in habits. Breeds commonly along coasts and in archipelagos on salt and brackish waters. Visits fresh water occasionally. Large flocks of immatures and other non-breeders common sight along coasts. Dive for crustaceans and molluscs (primarily sea mussels) at moderate depth. Nests close to water, often openly, ♀ sits tight. Nest lined with (celebrated) down.

IDENTIFICATION Large, *heavily built*, with fairly *short neck*, large head with *long, wedge-shaped bill*. In flight gives heavy impression (possible to confuse with geese at horizon range), *wings broad* and comparatively short, wingbeats fairly slow, *head held rather low*. Flock formation often rather disorderly, *loose clusters or irregular, long lines*. – Adult ♂ breeding: *Largely white, with black belly*, sides and stern, white rounded 'thigh patch', white tertials; *head white* with black crown; sides of nape pale green. – Adult ♀: Brown, barred dark; dark speculum bordered white. – Adult ♂ eclipse (late Jun–Sep): *Very dark, unbarred; upperwing-coverts and long, curved tertials white* (if not moulted; generally in Aug); some white bases to feathers of mantle and upper scapulars sometimes show. – Juvenile: Like adult ♀, but *dark speculum usually not bordered white*, and *head and upperparts more uniform*; juvenile ♂ has *dark head with pale stripe over eye* (like 1st-summer eclipse ♂); *tertials rather short and not strongly curved*. – 1st-year ♂: Juvenile plumage moulted from late autumn, when some white feathers appear on breast, mantle and back, then scapulars and flanks. – 2nd-year ♂: Like adult ♂, but in breeding plumage *upperwing-coverts and tertials not pure white*, shape of latter less curved.

VOICE Vocal during breeding season. ♂ has characteristic cooing display-call during communal courtship, a far-carrying, deep 'a-**ooh**-e' (at long range may recall distant Eagle Owl). ♀ has incessant chuckling 'gak-ak-ak-ak-...', like distant throbbing of vessel engine.

King Eider *Somateria spectabilis* V*

L 55–63 cm, WS 87–100 cm. Breeds in Arctic on tundra pools and, less commonly, along sheltered, shallow seashores, wintering along sea coasts. Habits much as for Eider, and single birds often seen with Eiders. Rare winter visitor in Britain, occurring especially in N.

IDENTIFICATION Slightly *smaller and more compact* than Eider, body and bill shorter. – Adult ♂ breeding: Unmistakable; *prominent orange knob at base of bill; coral-red bill*; crown and (well-rounded) nape blue with purplish tinge; lower neck and breast salmon-pink; mantle white (as on Eider) but *back and scapulars black* (Eider: white), *scapulars with triangular erect 'sails'*. In flight, white patches on forewing. – Adult ♀: Distinguished from Eider by *shorter, darker*

bill, with *bulging feathering above culmen reaching farther down on bill than feathering at sides*; plumage more *warm reddish-brown*, and *dark marks more open, U-shaped* and have dark central spot, especially on mantle and flanks; size slightly smaller; often rather pale cheeks and area around bill-base, dark gape contrasting (and has 'happy-looking' expression). – Adult ♂ eclipse: Resembles imm. ♂ (since knob shrinks) but keeps *white forewing patches*. Bill pale red. General impression is dark, but often shows traces of white on side of breast. – Juvenile: Like ♀, but more similar to Eider in colour (colder brown, not so rusty) and pattern (more simple barring, less U-shaped 'scallops'). Told by size, shape of bill, and feathering at base of bill. – 1st-summer ♂: Like Eider, but *bill shorter and pink* (not dull yellowish-grey), and *back never has any white* (only mantle).

VOICE Rather less vocal than Eider. ♂ has a deep, vibrating cooing in spring, 'hroo, roo roo-e', falling slightly in pitch at the end; flock calls can recall cooing Black Grouse. Clucking of ♀ similar to that of ♀ Eider.

Steller's Eider *Polysticta stelleri* V***

L 42–48 cm, WS 68–77 cm. Breeds on arctic tundra, winters along seashores in N. Prefers shallow coastal waters, especially with inflowing fresh water from creeks, swimming right up to shoreline, upending among boulders and seaweed; also good diver, but rarely seen far out from land.

IDENTIFICATION Medium-small. Differs from other diving ducks in having shape and some habits more like a dabbling duck; body elongated, tail long, *bill oblong, not so wedge-shaped*; shape of head characteristic, *crown flat, forehead and nape rather angled*; wings rather long and narrow, permitting easy take-off from sea. Flight rapid and light. – Adult ♂ breeding: *White* with *orange-buff sides*, darkening to chestnut on belly (and black on centre of lower belly); chin, eye-surround, collar and back of neck, mantle, back and stern black, *scapulars and tertials black and white* giving striped effect; rounded tuft on rear crown, and loral patch, green; a black spot on side of breast visible at waterline level on swimming bird; bill lead-grey; in flight, *forewing is white*. – Adult ♀: Dark brown; *speculum blue, distinctly bordered white* in Mallard fashion; tertials dark, almost invariably *with pale tips*, shape well curved. – Adult ♂ eclipse: Like ♀ but readily separated in flight by white forewing. – Juvenile/1st-winter: Juvenile like adult ♀, but *speculum dull brown*, insignificantly bordered off-white; *tertials dull brown and short*, shape less curved. Often a rather obvious *pale eye-ring and pale line behind eye* (more so than on adult ♀). ♂ has *chin, forehead and nape patch dark*, darker than on ♀; from late winter, sex positively revealed by the first white feathers appearing on head. – 2nd-summer ♂: Similar to adult ♂, but is distinguished by a varying amount of dark feathers lingering on head and upperwing-coverts.

VOICE Rather silent. Raucous quacking 'gah gaah geeah'. Wing noise a fine whistling (slightly more obvious than Mallard's).

Eider   King Eider   Steller's Eider

EIDER

ad. ♀
ad. ♂

white borders
pale tip
ad. ♀
barred

juv.

diffuse pattern

ad. ♂ eclipse

1st-summer ♂

variable depending on moult stage

ad. ♂

KING EIDER

a 1st-summer ♂ Eider (far right) together with King Eiders

ad. ♂

ad. ♀
compact

ad. ♂
black shoulders

ad. ♀
1st-s. ♂   1st-s. ♂

less red-brown than ad. ♀, 'paler-faced' and has narrower pale wing-bars

dark bill and 'happy-look-ing' gape

dark nail

even at long range, darker salmon-pink breast of ♂ King Eider compared with ♂ Eider is visible

ad. ♀
U-shaped bars

juv.

buff-pink

ad. ♂ eclipse

'sails'

1st-summer ♂

variable depending on moult stage

ad. ♂

STELLER'S EIDER

ad. ♀
ad. ♂

forms tight flocks, ♂♂ appear mostly white

Eider is con-siderably larger

long tertials

long   short, dull brown tertials

ad. ♀

long tertials

juv.

thin white borders

broad white borders (often concealed by flank-feathers)

1st-summer ♂

ad. ♂ eclipse

ad. ♂

K M

Common Scoter *Melanitta nigra* m(r)**B**5 / **W**3

L 44–54 cm, WS 70–84 cm. Breeds near lakes and rivers in boreal forests (upper coniferous, birch/willow) and close to tundra waters. Migratory, spring migration largely on broad front over land at night, autumn migration diurnal along coasts and over sea. Gregarious, can form very large flocks. Most ♂♂ return S as early as late summer.

IDENTIFICATION Medium-sized, plump-bodied. Bill fairly small, ♂ with knob at base. Longish tail often exposed when swimming. All-dark plumage *without white in wing*. Dives usually with small leap, *wings kept folded tight to body* (cf. p. 64). Wing-flapping punctuated with quick downward thrust of head. Resting *flocks usually very dense*, more so than with Velvet Scoter, and frequently larger. – Adult ♂: Whole plumage *black*. In flight *primaries are contrastingly paler*, thus wings two-toned, especially in strong light. *Centre of bill* (culmen) *yellow*, sometimes visible at longer range in good light, especially viewed head-on. – Adult ♀: *Sooty-brown with paler cheeks* and dark brown forehead and crown; superficially recalling a swimming ♀ or juvenile Red-crested Pochard, though smaller and darker-bodied, invariably with all-dark bill, and habitat usually different. (A few birds have centre of cheek mottled brown, creating a hint of the 'two-pale-spots pattern' typical of Surf Scoter, which see.) – Juvenile: Like adult ♀ but *belly paler*, brownish-white instead of medium brown-grey; plumage somewhat browner, less grey. (Moulting 1st-winter ♂♂ can also show hint of two pale spots on cheeks just as some ♀♀.) Young ♂♂ attain adult plumage largely in 1st winter but retain pale belly (can look strikingly white in flight!), and by spring wings noticeably faded, brownish. – Variation: NE Siberian and American (ssp. *americana*, 'Black Scoter') ♂♂ are distinctive, having a large, swollen orange-yellow area on the bill and lacking the black knob at the base; ♀♀ appear inseparable in the field. A few winter records in W Europe.

VOICE ♂ has soft piping 'pjü', regularly repeated about once per second; heard during display, but most often during spring nights (late Apr/early May) over land in N Europe from NE-bound flocks. Also drawn-out 'pü-ih' and other short, repeated calls during courtship. ♀ has a repeated 'karrr', similar to many other ♀ diving ducks. Wingbeats produce fine whistling noise.

Velvet Scoter *Melanitta fusca* **W**4

L 51–58 cm, WS 79–97 cm. Breeds along coasts on salt or brackish waters (such as the Baltic Sea coasts), and on fresh waters of mountain and tundra; often found on large lakes and rivers in boreal coniferous forests. Breeds late, often a month later than Eider. Migratory, movements usually along coasts. Nests on ground, usually not far from water.

IDENTIFICATION Medium-large, stocky, rather long-bodied with *thick lower neck* (though upper neck can look thin when neck is stretched). *Wedge-shaped bill* rather heavy. *All-dark plumage* with *white secondaries* makes it distinctive in flight even at long range; wings rather broad, but appearing narrower when seen against the sky owing to the white secondaries. White in wing often, but not always, visible as a narrow patch on swimming birds as well. Resting flocks rarely so large and dense as those of Common Scoter. Dives without leap, *wings semi-open* (cf. p. 64). Wing-flaps with head held up and bill raised, showing white secondaries. – Adult ♂: Whole plumage *black* except for the white secondaries, and tiny white mark under eye (difficult to see except at close range). *Bill has pale orange-yellow band along sides*, readily visible at a distance. – Adult ♀: Sooty-brown with white secondaries; belly only slightly paler, brown-grey. Head pattern variable: on breeding birds usually *a rather large diffuse pale loral patch*, generally also *a smaller but rather distinct pale patch on ear-coverts*; a few look darker with very diffuse patches only; during later stages of breeding, wear and bleaching can cause sides of head to appear much paler. – Juvenile: Like adult ♀ but *belly much paler* (esp. juv. ♀), being off-white, and *facial patches generally more distinct*.

VOICE During courtship 'morning flights' by pair in spring, ♀ has slightly hoarse, vibrating 'braa-ah... braa-ah... braa-ah...'. Apart from this, rather silent. ♂ has an insignificant, low, nasal call during courtship, 'aah-er'.

Surf Scoter *Melanitta perspicillata* **V**∗

L 45–56 cm. American species, rare vagrant in Europe, mainly ♂♂ recorded (♀♀ probably easily overlooked) in autumn, winter or spring. In Britain & Ireland, a few recorded annually.

IDENTIFICATION Only a trifle larger than Common Scoter, appearing of same size; clearly somewhat smaller than Velvet Scoter. As two congeners, largely all-dark plumage; *no white in wing*. *Bill large and triangular*, making head look heavy. Feathering at base of culmen extends forward horizontally (cf. Common Scoter). *Crown in profile flatter* than on Common Scoter. Swimming birds often have *tail prominently cocked*. Dives with little leap forward and *wings half-open* (p. 64). Wing-flaps with rigid (not drooping) neck. – Adult ♂: *Black*, with *large white patch at nape* (rarely partially lost in summer–early autumn) and *smaller white patch on forehead*. Bill, swollen at base, appearing *bright yellow-orange* at distance; if seen close, bill has white base and black rounded patch at base of bill-side (appearing as extension of feathering). *Eye white*. – Adult ♀: Sooty-brown, as ♀ Velvet Scoter with *two pale patches on side of head* (variable, can be indistinct or missing), but additionally often has *small white patch on nape*. Note heavy triangular bill with straight or even slightly convex culmen (Velvet has slightly concave culmen), and dark feathering extending horizontally over base of culmen. Eye usually dark, but sometimes paler (brownish-white). – Juvenile: Like adult ♀, but *belly whitish* (not pale brown) and cheeks and throat usually paler; never pale patch on nape; eye dark. Young ♂♂ acquire most of adult pattern in 1st winter, but white patch on forehead and full size and colours of bill not developed until 2nd winter.

Common Scoter   Velvet Scoter

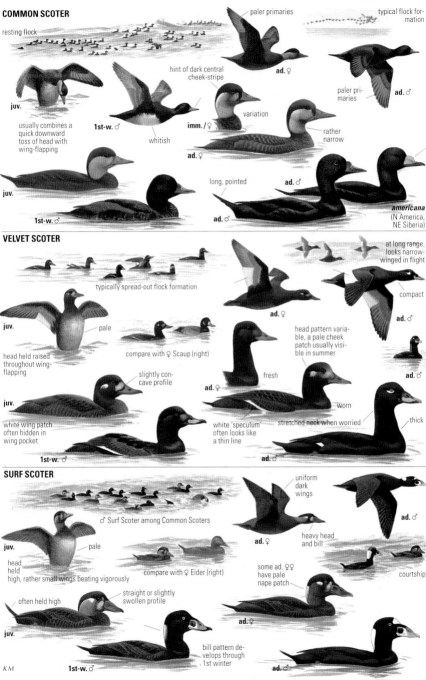

COMMON SCOTER

resting flock

paler primaries

typical flock formation

ad. ♀

juv.

hint of dark central cheek-stripe

paler primaries

ad. ♂

usually combines a quick downward toss of head with wing-flapping

1st-w. ♂

whitish

variation

imm. / ♀

rather narrow

juv.

ad. ♀

long, pointed

ad. ♀

ad. ♂

1st-w. ♂

ad. ♂

americana
(N America, NE Siberia)

VELVET SCOTER

typically spread-out flock formation

at long range, looks narrow-winged in flight

juv.

pale

ad. ♀

compact

ad. ♂

head held raised throughout wing-flapping

compare with ♀ Scaup (right)

head pattern variable, a pale cheek patch usually visible in summer

ad. ♂

slightly concave profile

fresh

juv.

ad. ♀

worn

white wing patch often hidden in wing pocket

stretched neck when worried

thick

1st-w. ♂

white 'speculum' often looks like a thin line

ad. ♂

SURF SCOTER

uniform dark wings

♂ Surf Scoter among Common Scoters

ad. ♀

ad. ♂

juv.

pale

heavy head and bill

head held high, rather small wings beating vigorously

compare with ♀ Eider (right)

some ad. ♀♀ have pale nape patch

courtship

juv.

often held high

straight or slightly swollen profile

ad. ♀

ad. ♂

KM

1st-w. ♂

bill pattern develops through 1st winter

ad. ♂

Long-tailed Duck *Clangula hyemalis* **W**3

L 39–47 cm (excl. elongated tail-feathers of ♂ 10–15), WS 65–82 cm. Breeds commonly in the Arctic on tundra pools and marshes, also along sea coasts (local in the Baltic) and on still-standing mountain waters. Gregarious. Winters at sea, often in large, dense flocks, mainly off coasts; then restless and active, taking off and flying agilely, low over the water, in short pursuit-flights, constantly changing direction, landing with splash; dives for molluscs and other animal food. Spring migration through Baltic spectacular; main exodus from Gulf of Finland to tundras in NE on late-May evenings with tail-wind, involving over 100,000 birds on peak days. Complex moult produces at least three different-looking plumages annually; most scapulars and feathers of sides of head and neck are moulted three times a year, breast, upper mantle and rest of head and neck twice, and rest of plumage once a year.

IDENTIFICATION Rather small, brown, black and white duck. Head rounded, *bill small* and stubby, *central tail-feathers of ♂ elongated to thin line* (Pintail ♂ only other duck with same feature). Wings rather narrow and pointed, all dark, *wingbeats fast and elastic, mainly below horizontal*, adding to peculiar, almost bat-like impression, and *wings slightly swept back*. Plumages and moults complex. – Adult ♂ spring/summer (from late Apr): Largely *brown-black with grey-white flanks, white stern* and *white patch at side of head*; scapulars blackish, edged rufous-yellow. Summer moult to full eclipse during later stages of breeding changes little in appearance (new scapulars shorter and duller). Bill has pink band across centre in spring, is often all black in summer. – Adult ♂ autumn (from Sep): Becomes much whiter; upper mantle, *most of scapulars, neck and head white*, sides of lower head/upper neck with dark patch. Bill acquires pink band again. – Adult ♂ winter (from late Oct): As in autumn, but forehead and sides of head pale grey-brown, not white, and

patch on side of head/upper neck black (with chestnut lower rim), not mottled brown-grey. – Adult ♀ summer (May– Aug): Like adult ♂ but *lacking elongated tail-feathers*, and colours *duller*; also, pale patch on side of head narrower and less sharply set off, and invariably a *light collar around neck*. – Adult ♀ autumn / winter (Aug–Feb): Main difference from summer is *head*, which is *off-white with blackish crown and patch at lower cheek/upper neck*; scapulars are longer and edged more brightly rufous-buff (or even partly whitish). – Juvenile: Like adult ♀ autumn, but with less dark and distinct patch at lower cheek/upper neck, and with shorter and blunter tertials and scapulars.

VOICE Vocal. ♂ has characteristic, far-carrying, nasal yodelling, 'ow **ow**-owde**lee**, ow-owde**lee**', used both in display and during migration; chorus from flocks becomes pleasing song like distant bagpipes; also drawn-out wailing short version, 'a-**gluu**-ah', as if with falsetto 'skid' in the middle. Both sexes have nasal, low 'gak', often heard from migrating flocks.

Harlequin Duck *Histrionicus histrionicus* **V*****

L 38–45 cm, WS 63–70 cm. Breeds on fast-flowing streams in arctic tundra, within region only in Iceland, where sedentary; Icelandic population does not exceed 3000 pairs. Winters on rough waters along coasts. Accidentals outside range very rare, and not all believed to be genuine. In Britain fewer than ten records since 1950. Gregarious, though parties generally rather small. Swims energetically, even into strong currents. Dives from surface, from perch or directly from wing, not avoiding rough parts of streams.

IDENTIFICATION Rather small diving duck; *bill small, forehead high and head rounded, neck thick, tail pointed*. In all plumages *dark, with conspicuous white marks on sides of head*. Swims high, often with bobbing head. Flight rapid, *wings all dark*. – Adult ♂ breeding: *Dark blue-grey* (blue

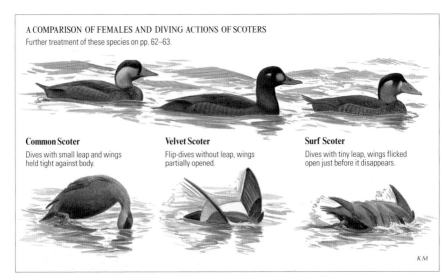

A COMPARISON OF FEMALES AND DIVING ACTIONS OF SCOTERS
Further treatment of these species on pp. 62–63.

Common Scoter
Dives with small leap and wings held tight against body.

Velvet Scoter
Flip-dives without leap, wings partially opened.

Surf Scoter
Dives with tiny leap, wings flicked open just before it disappears.

KM

LONG-TAILED DUCK

flock in winter

flock in summer

ad. ♂ winter

all-dark wings

ad. ♂ summer

white rump-sides

♀ **winter**

♀ **summer**

♀ **summer**

♀ **winter**

juv.

white eye-surround

pink patch

pale brown eye-surround

♂ **summer**

elongated tail

♂ late autumn

♂ winter / spring

HARLEQUIN DUCK

all dark

ad. ♂

♀

distinctive head pattern

small

♀

ad. ♂

ad. ♂

K M

Long-tailed Duck

Harlequin Duck

colour surprisingly difficult to see at a distance, looking almost black) with *chestnut flanks* and blackish belly and stern, attractively *marked white* (white outlined black) *on head, neck, side of breast, and back.* – Adult ♀: Head and neck dark grey; body sooty-brown except belly, which is dusky white mottled with grey; *large whitish patch between bill and ear-coverts, whitish spot above lores, and small white patch on ear-coverts* combine to form distinctive face pattern. – Adult ♂ eclipse: Dull, dark, rather similar to ♀, but with some traces of breeding pattern (some white on scapulars often visible, white line on side of breast indicated, a little chestnut remaining on flanks). – Juvenile: Very similar to adult ♀, only slightly browner, less greyish, and secondaries duller, lacking purplish-brown metallic gloss of adult ♀.

VOICE Rather silent. Fine nasal, piping 'vee-ah vee-ah...' and 'vee' heard from displaying ♂♂.

(Common) **Goldeneye** *Bucephala clangula*   r**B**5 / **W**3
L 40–48 cm, WS 62–77 cm. Breeds in forested areas by lakes, mainly clear, oligotrophic, and by slow-flowing rivers and in archipelagos; less commonly at open coasts. Mainly migratory, hardy, returning early to breeding sites. Less gregarious than most other diving ducks, often seen in pairs or smaller groups. Shy. Food animal. Courtship display in early spring by ♂ includes tossing head back on to back and then stretching neck up with bill pointing upwards, at times also splashing water with feet. Nests in tree-hole (old Black Woodpecker nest) or box.

IDENTIFICATION Medium-sized, *compact* duck with *large, rounded head* like a knob on fairly short neck; *crown slightly peaked and shape of head triangular*. Bill rather small and triangular. *Speculum white*, rest of underwing appearing blackish; much *white on upper forewing* on adults. Flight rapid but appearing laborious, wings beating fast. For separation from similar Barrow's Goldeneye, see that species. – Adult ♂ breeding: Head black with green gloss; *large white rounded loral spot*; eye yellow; *breast and flanks gleaming white*; stern and much of upperparts black; *narrow black scapular lines* hanging down over white flanks. – Adult ♀: *Head brown; eye pale yellow; collar* and belly *white*, breast and flanks ash-grey; bill dark with a yellowish band across the outer part when breeding, usually all dark at other seasons. – Adult ♂ eclipse: Like adult ♀ but retains wing pattern, with extensive white on upper forewing. – Juvenile: Like adult ♀ but head duller and greyer brown, and lacks white collar. Juvenile ♂ has wing pattern similar to adult ♀, juvenile ♀ has less white (narrow white bar on greater coverts, no pale patch on medians).

VOICE Display-call of ♂ a squeezed double-note, 'bee-**beeech**', usually accompanied by a low, dry, Garganey-like rattle, 'drrudrrir'. ♀ has loud purring or grating call, often in flight, 'brra, brra,...', very like Tufted Duck but perhaps slightly softer and slower. Most often heard and characteristic sound is *loud, musical whistling produced by wing-beats*, especially strong from ♂♂ in winter and spring (but almost absent in case of juveniles).

Barrow's Goldeneye *Bucephala islandica*   **V**∗∗∗
L 42–53 cm, WS 67–82 cm. Breeds in Iceland, Greenland and N America on tundra pools and lakes. Resident or moving to open waters. Nests in tree-hole if available or on ground in scrub.

IDENTIFICATION Somewhat *larger* than Goldeneye, which it resembles. Apart from size, head profile differs slightly but clearly, *head appearing longer* and *less triangular, forehead being higher, crown flatter* (indistinct peak well to front) and nape well rounded. Breeding ♂ has purple gloss on head

(imm. ♂ Goldeneye can be confusingly dull dark brown-black), and *white crescent on lores reaches above eye* (never so on moulting imm. ♂ Goldeneyes, which can have a partly crescent-shaped loral spot); *black of upperparts more extensive* and *reaching far down on sides of breast; scapulars have white encircled as narrow 'windows'*. – Adult ♀ and juvenile very similar to Goldeneye, but note somewhat different shape of head, and generally *more extensive yellow on bill in breeding season*.

VOICE Display-call of ♂ weak, grunting, short notes in staccato, 'wa wa-wa...'. ♀ has similar call to Goldeneye but deeper and more coarse, 'krrah krrah...'. Wing noise of ♂ similar to Goldeneye, but possibly lower-pitched.

SAWBILLS
Diving ducks of variable size, from large to rather small. Bill has small hook at tip and tooth-like lamellae along cutting edges, enabling better grip of main prey, fish. Three species, of which larger two (p. 68) similar and have elongated body and rather long neck. The third, the Smew, is smaller and more compact. Expert divers, and pursue prey very agilely; at times fish communally. Frequent various habitats, both freshwater and marine. Nest usually in hole or cavity, sometimes on ground under cover.

Smew *Mergellus albellus*   **W**4–5
L 38–44 cm, WS 56–69 cm. Breeds in northern boreal forests by clear lakes or calm rivers. Rather scarce. Migratory. Shy and restless, pairs or small parties on wintering grounds inclined to make aerial excursions, spreading out rather than keeping together (though small and medium-sized flocks can be seen at the most favoured localities), feeding close to reedbeds in shallow waters. Nests in tree-hole (old nest of Black Woodpecker) or box.

IDENTIFICATION Small, rather compact sawbill, more similar to the *Bucephala* species (and indeed occasionally interbreeds with Goldeneye). – Adult ♂ breeding: Distinctive, being *largely white*, with neat black patterning; head white with black loral 'mask' from bill backwards around eye; black line or patch at side of nape. In flight, appears surprisingly *pied black and white*. Two *large oval white patches* are visible *on upper forewing*. – Adult ♀: Dull brown-grey with *white cheeks and dark chestnut-brown forehead and crown; lores blackish*, becoming more brownish during breeding. Wing pattern similar to that of ♂, but white more restricted. – Adult ♂ eclipse (Jul–early Nov): Like adult ♀ summer (with brownish lores), but retains more extensive white wing patch, and is blacker, not so greyish, on back. – Juvenile: Very similar to adult ♀, but belly a little less whitish, more mottled grey, and loral area brown at least in 1st autumn, and sometimes longer.

VOICE Mostly silent. Display-call of ♂ low and rarely heard, a deep, accelerating, frog-like croaking ending with a hiccup, 'gr-r-r-rrr-**chic**'. ♀ has a hoarse 'krrr'.

Goleneye   Barrow's Goldeneye   Smew

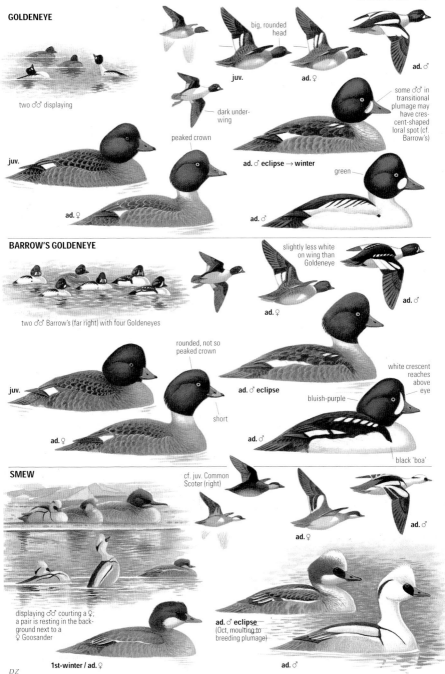

GOLDENEYE

two ♂♂ displaying

juv.

big, rounded head

juv.

ad. ♂

dark under-wing

peaked crown

ad. ♀

some ♂♂ in transitional plumage may have crescent-shaped loral spot (cf. Barrow's)

ad. ♂ eclipse → winter

green

ad. ♀

ad. ♂

BARROW'S GOLDENEYE

two ♂♂ Barrow's (far right) with four Goldeneyes

slightly less white on wing than Goldeneye

ad. ♀

ad. ♂

rounded, not so peaked crown

juv.

ad. ♂ eclipse

white crescent reaches above eye

bluish-purple

ad. ♀

short

ad. ♂

black 'boa'

SMEW

cf. juv. Common Scoter (right)

ad. ♀

ad. ♂

displaying ♂♂ courting a ♀; a pair is resting in the background next to a ♀ Goosander

ad. ♂ eclipse (Oct, moulting to breeding plumage)

1st-winter / ad. ♀

ad. ♂

DZ

Goosander *Mergus merganser*   r**B**4 / (**W**4)

L 58–68 cm, WS 78–94 cm. Breeds on lakes and slow rivers in forested areas, requiring fairly deep, clear, fish-holding waters and mature trees with holes for nesting. Nests also in nestbox, under or in house, in crevice, etc. Gregarious except when breeding; can form very large flocks (tens of thousands recorded) when ♂♂ gather to moult in late summer, or for communal fishing on favourite lakes in late autumn. Expert diver. Hardy, in winter many retreat only from ice.

IDENTIFICATION Large, *long-bodied*, streamlined, with *long, narrow, red bill ending in small hook*. Head appears rather large owing to *full crest* at hindcrown and nape. Neck long, but swimming birds often retract most of it, looking short-necked. In flight, silhouette with long, *outstretched neck* and rather *shallow, fast wingbeats with straight wings* and direct flight at times recall loons and grebes more than other ducks. – Adult ♂ breeding: Largely *white* (tinged salmon-pink in winter–early spring), with *black head/upper neck glossed green* (green cast visible at closer range or in good light only); crest mane-like, 'combed with grease', giving *odd bulge shape to nape*. Back largely black. In flight, *very large white 'boxes' on inner wing*. – Adult ♀: *Head dark red-brown* except *clearly demarcated white throat patch*; crest looser than on ♂, 'hair combed dry', often forming two tufts, one at hindcrown, one at nape; *sharp division between brown upper neck and whitish lower foreneck*; body greyish. In flight, white squares formed by secondaries and greater coverts (on some, *indistinct, thin* dark line across tips of all or a few outer greater coverts). For distinction from similar ♀ Red-breasted Merganser, see latter. – Adult ♂ eclipse: Like adult ♀, but retains extensive white on upperwing. – Juvenile: Like adult ♀, but bill duller red, crest shorter, throat less clean white, has pale loral line, and iris paler. 1st-winter ♂ has more extensive white on inner wing than ♀.

VOICE Display-call of ♂ is a pleasant, deep, hard, muffled ringing 'krroo-krraa', not loud, yet rather far-carrying. ♀ has a hard 'pra, pra-pra...' when courted. In flight, a louder, repeated 'prrah, prrah, prrah...', and a conversational, fast chuckling '**chak**erak-ak-ak-ak'.

Red-breasted Merganser *Mergus serrator*   r**B**4 / **W**3

L 52–58 cm, WS 67–82 cm. Breeds along coasts, in archipelagos and at clear inland waters both in taiga and in mountains and on tundra. Gregarious, even in breeding season, but rarely forms very large flocks (as Goosander habitually does). Nests on ground among sheltering vegetation.

IDENTIFICATION Medium-large, slimmer than Goosander but otherwise very similar. *Bill is narrower, especially at base*, and crest is more brush-like and shaggy (on ♂ almost 'punk'), giving a slightly *small-headed* appearance; neck

also narrower. – Adult ♂ breeding: Head black, glossed green; *white collar* above *black-streaked rufous-brown breast*; *black area with large white spots at side of breast* is distinctive. Most of upperparts black, flanks grey. In flight, large white patch on inner wing, but not so extensive as on Goosander. – Adult ♀: Resembles ♀ Goosander. For separation, note the following: *lack of sharp division between brown head and off-white lower neck*; *pale throat patch diffusely set off*; *bill thin at base*; *crest shorter and 'spikier'*; *head more cinnamon-brown*, not so dark red; more '*striped' face*, with pale lores and dark lines above and below; *back darker and tinged brown*, and *flanks less clean grey*; in flight, *head and neck appear slimmer*, *white square on inner wing invariably divided by obvious black line*; *upper forewing dark brown-grey*, darker and less clean grey than on Goosander. – Adult ♂ eclipse: Like adult ♀, but retains extensive white on wing. – Juvenile: Like adult ♀, but bill duller red, and crest shorter. – 1st-summer ♂: Attains most of adult ♂ plumage except for head and neck, *head being tinged brownish, neck largely lacking the white collar*; white on wing not so extensive as on adult ♂.

VOICE Display-call of ♂ weak and not often heard, rhythmic, one hiccup and a sneeze well spaced, '**chi**ka ... pit**chee**'. Call of ♀ repeated hard, grating 'prrak prrak prrak...'.

White-headed Duck *Oxyura leucocephala*   —

L 43–48 cm (incl. tail 8–10). Breeds on shallow, richly vegetated eutrophic lakes. Local and rare. Mainly resident. Reluctant to fly, prefers to swim for cover.

IDENTIFICATION Small, but somewhat larger than Ruddy Duck, with proportionately somewhat larger head, immediately told by *large bill with swollen culmen* basally. – ♂: In spring characteristic, with *huge, pale blue bill*, pale brown body and largely *pure white head*; narrow blackish crown-stripe, and variably black on nape, neck and around eye (black eye patch usually isolated on white side of head). *No white on undertail-coverts*. In winter duller. – ♀: Dull brown plumage, similar to Ruddy Duck, but note *distinctive bill shape*, larger size, and more *well-marked dark cheek-stripe*.

VOICE Mainly silent.

Ruddy Duck *Oxyura jamaicensis*   r**B**4

L 35–43 cm (incl. tail 6–8). American species, introduced in Britain and spreading to W Europe. Has hybridized with White-headed Duck in Spain (this posing a serious conservation problem). Breeds on shallow, eutrophic lakes.

IDENTIFICATION Small and compact, with *large head, strong bill*, rounded body and *long, stiff tail*, often cocked. – ♂: In spring, *body largely deep chestnut*, crown (down to eye) and hindneck black, *cheeks*, chin *and undertail-coverts white*. Bill pale blue. In winter, bill is grey and body dull brown, but white cheeks retained. – ♀: Like ♂ winter, but head dull dark brown and off-white and has a *diffuse* (strength variable) *dark horizontal stripe across cheeks*.

VOICE Mainly silent. Displaying ♂ produces varying tapping sounds by beating its bill against the chest.

Goosander

Red-breasted Merganser

White-headed Duck

GOOSANDER

communal fishing flock in Nov

flanks diffusely pale grey

pale grey

all white

white

ad. ♀

pale 'face' markings

large white wing patch

head shape (crest!) changes with mood

thick base

juv.

full crest

white chin

sharp border

ad. ♂♀

ad. ♂ eclipse

ad. ♂

RED-BREASTED MERGANSER

courtship display

flanks rather dark grey

black line

rather dark

dark

ad. ♀

ad. ♂

crest at times erect

thin base

large white wing patch

ad. ♂ eclipse

crest usually short, untidy

diffuse border

ad. ♂♀

ad. ♂

WHITE-HEADED DUCK

ad. ♂

swollen profile

♀ / juv.

ad. ♂ winter

1st-summer ♂ (dark-headed variant)

ad. ♂ summer

RUDDY DUCK

ad. ♂

concave profile

ad. ♀

juv.

ad. ♂ winter

ad. ♂ summer

DZ

BIRDS OF PREY *Accipitriformes*

45 diurnal species of varying size and shape, belonging to three different families. All are mainly carnivorous, with hooked bill and strong feet. Most of the species catch and kill their prey, except for the vultures.

Accipitridae: hawks, buzzards, eagles, kites, vultures and harriers. Largest family, 32 species. Broad, 'fingered' wings suitable for soaring and gliding.

Pandionidae: only one species, the Osprey. Specialized on catching fish after hovering over water and diving in feet-first. Feet and talons very strong.

Falconidae: falcons. 12 species of fast, skilful flyers with pointed wings. Capable of catching their prey in the air, at times after long, dashing dive.

IDENTIFICATION OF BIRDS OF PREY

This group is very difficult to master in the field owing to generally long-range or brief sightings, variation in plumages, similarities in flight silhouette between related species, infrequency of calls, and the rareness of most species offering few opportunities to practise. Do not hope for or pretend reliable identification of all birds of prey in the field—*ever*. But with sensible practice you can come a long way.

Visit any major *raptor migration site* in the area (Eilat, Bosporus, Gibraltar, Falsterbo, etc.) and start out on a trip with an *experienced leader*. Memorize the appearance of *key species* like Common Buzzard, Sparrowhawk, Marsh Harrier and Black Kite at various angles and in various lights.

Follow all the birds which have come quite close, and which have been positively identified, in your *telescope* (essential for raptor studies) as they disappear, for *as far as you can possibly see them*. This working 'backwards from the answer' is the best way to learn on your own how the various birds of prey look when they are far away and are seen under less favourable conditions—unfortunately the most common situation in raptor studies. *Observe actively* by asking yourself questions while you look at the bird.

The telescope is an essential piece of equipment, as already mentioned. But just as important is to fix it on a *stable tripod* (lightweight or budget tripods do not provide a steady view, as they shake when you move the telescope or in a wind) equipped with a high-quality *movable head-joint* (designed for film-cameras; a ball-and-socket joint is less suitable). This enables you to study *flying* raptors, which is what it is all about for 95% of the time. And, for raptor studies, it is

Lesser Spotted Eagle

The whiteness of clouds 'burns out' colours and details of the plumage. Wait until the bird comes out against the blue sky, or a very dark cloud, which provides a better view.

generally more comfortable to have an *angled* eye-piece than a conventional straight telescope, although this is a matter of taste.

Optical and *size illusions* frequently occur when observing birds of prey, especially at long range. It is easy to misjudge the size of a soaring eagle: its slow-motion-like action and dark colour against the bright sky tend to make it appear larger than it is. And experience shows that the size of raptors is misjudged even when other birds are present for comparison. Few birdwatchers realize how *extensive* the *normal size variation* is within one single species. Study the wing-span ranges in this book; they are carefully calculated from skins, photographs and live birds, and demonstrate the large overlap between various species. Still, they give a useful hint on the relative sizes, which cannot be disregarded.

Mode of flight provides a clue to identification, but it is essential to realize that to some extent it *varies* within a species *in relation to size*: the largest birds have slower wing-beats and movements than the smallest.

Plumage variation is also extensive, especially in buzzards and some eagles, but it pays to learn the full range of these variations. Unlike size and proportions, a positively seen plumage detail is far less susceptible to influence from illusions or the observer's subjectivity.

The whiteness of clouds 'burns out' much of the colours of birds flying in front of them. Hang on to a confusing bird until it comes out *against the blue sky, or against a dark cloud*, which will reveal more of its plumage.

An *understanding of moult*, finally, is essential for the correct identification, and especially ageing, of raptors. See pp. 9–10 for some general guidelines.

juvenile   adult

Spotted Eagle

A slight difference in general shape between adults and juveniles can be observed in many raptor species in flight. Adults have more evenly broad wings with broader wing-tip and shorter tail, whereas juveniles have wings with more S-curved rear edge, narrower 'hand' and slightly longer tail.

1st centre

2nd centre

White-tailed Eagle

Active moult of flight-feathers gives a clue to ageing (and is often important for reliable identification). This White-tailed Eagle in summer may look like a juvenile, but the moult pattern conclusively shows it to be at least in its 2nd summer, with two active moult centres among the primaries.

LAMMERGEIER

patrols mountainsides with wings slightly arched down

the shadow sometimes easier to spot than the bird itself against light mountainside

long and pointed wing

very dark

long, wedge-shaped

soaring young have untypically compact, almost eagle-like silhouette **juv.**

apart from flesh, readily eats bone marrow by swallowing and digesting bones

dark

pale mantle

some are slightly whiter

juv.

juv.

ad.

ad.

juv.

ad.

DZ

VULTURES *Gypaetus, Neophron, Gyps* et al.

Five species. Mostly very large and broad-winged raptors, scavengers which soar and glide to find carrion or prey remnants. Wing muscles rather weak in relation to body weight and wing-surface area, thus dependent on thermals, and generally not active in the morning hours. Often seen in parties. Many species have an unfeathered head, and some have a long neck which is withdrawn in flight in heron fashion. Claws comparatively short.

Lammergeier *Gypaetus barbatus* —

L 105–125 cm, WS 235–275 cm. Very rare and local resident in high mountains; declining, only c. 500 pairs left within region. Confined to most inaccessible, steep cliffs but patrols slopes and valleys too. Food meat from freshly killed animals and secondarily carrion, incl. bone marrow; has habit of dropping bones from height on to rock to break them into pieces, which are swallowed. Takes tortoises in talons and drops them from height on to rocks to open shell. Pair-bonds last for life. Huge nest in a cave or deep crevice.

IDENTIFICATION Huge and *long-winged*. Flight silhouette characteristic, with uniquely *narrow and pointed wings* (for such a large raptor) and *long, wedge-shaped tail, clearly longer than width of wing* (silhouette approached only by Egyptian Vulture, which is half the size, shorter-tailed and blunter-winged). Soars and glides on generally flattish

wings, only slightly arched down, but at times lowers primaries more when gliding. Patrols mountainsides endlessly on motionless wings, flight giving slow-motion impression (owing to large size and generally long range). In strong light, when upperparts look pale and merge with mountainside, often best spotted by dark shadow moving over the ground. – Adult: Underbody light, whitish with a varying degree of buffish-yellow or often rather deep rufous-buff tinge (acquired through sand-bathing!), contrasting with dark underwing. In good light lesser and median underwing-coverts are darkest, being jet-black. Upperparts lead-grey with pale feather shafts. – Juvenile: Body dull grey with contrasting dark grey head, neck and upper breast ('Hooded Crow pattern'). Upperparts not uniformly dark with lighter shafts (as on adult) but are variegated; mantle, rump and some wing-coverts light. Also, silhouette is different, with *shorter tail, broader wing and more blunt wing-tip*. – Immature: Adult pattern is attained in *c.* 5 years, subadults keeping the dark head rather long.

VOICE Usually silent; during aerial display at breeding site, utters shrill, loud whistling notes or a trill.

Lammergeier

(Eurasian) **Griffon Vulture** *Gyps fulvus* **V***

L 95–110 cm, WS 230–265 cm. Rare, mainly resident in mountains of Mediterranean area, Turkey, Caucasus. Accidental in N Europe. Declining, but still *c.* 10,000 pairs within region. Favours open, dry valleys or plateaux, which are patrolled for carrion. Soars and glides frequently, often appearing in loose flocks, keeping to ridges and peaks of mountains. Nests on cliff-ledge or in cave on steep mountainside, often in loose colonies of 10–20 pairs.

IDENTIFICATION Huge, clearly bigger than most large eagles. At a distance, size apparent mostly by *slow-motion-like movements* in the air. *Broad wings* with *very long 'fingers'* (outer, long primaries deeply emarginated and notched); a tendency to have *bulging secondaries* and *indented inner primaries* (Black Vulture has more evenly broad wings). *Tail short*, generally well rounded (a hint of wedge-shape on many). Head not very striking in flight as neck is folded back and colour is pale (little contrast against the sky). *Tips of secondaries rounded*, do not give distinct saw-tooth appearance as on Black and Lappet-faced Vultures. Flight heavy, wingbeats very slow and rather deep, a few at a time relieved by gliding. Head-on silhouette characteristic *when soaring, wings held in shallow V* like Golden Eagle (a few exceptions noted, soaring with flatter wings). When gliding, adopts flatter or more arched wing posture. When soaring, now and then takes a single, deep, 'embracing' wingbeat, peculiar to the large vultures (but usually not practised by eagles). Basically *two-coloured* (dark flight- and tail-feathers, paler wing-coverts and body), obvious in most conditions, but beware birds seen against strong light, which for a long time can look all dark. – Adult: Most easily distinguished by broad *pale buff tips to upperwing-coverts*; rather dark, *medium brown lesser underwing-coverts traversed by one or two narrow light bands*; medium brown, not so light underbody; whitish (not pale brown) ruff, visible at closer range. Bill yellowish, 'face' often swarthy. – Juvenile: *Upper greater coverts lack pale tips*; underwing-coverts cream-coloured, somewhat *lighter than on adult and more uniform*; underbody lighter than on adult; ruff buff-brown. Bill grey, 'face' often pale. – Immature: Adult plumage attained in 5–6 years, but differences between age-groups are slight.

VOICE Somewhat more vocal than other vultures. A variety of hissing and hoarse grunting notes, mainly at gatherings by carrion or at roosts.

(Eurasian) **Black Vulture** *Aegypius monachus* —

L 100–115 cm, WS 250–285 cm. Very rare, until recently having declined markedly (in Europe 1000+ pairs remain, most of them in Spain). Breeds both in arid, wild mountains and in vast lowland forests with hills or rocky outcrops.

Food mainly carrion. Nest almost invariably in tree, a huge eyrie of branches and twigs.

IDENTIFICATION Huge, on average somewhat larger than Griffon Vulture. As with Griffon, size of distant soaring bird apparent mostly by *slow-motion-like movements*. *Wings broad* with *very long 'fingers'*. The flight silhouette is more eagle-like than in Griffon owing to more *evenly broad wings*, more apparent head (due mainly to dark colour) and *all-dark plumage*. Tips of secondaries pointed, giving *saw-toothed trailing edge*. Confusion with an eagle prevented by the smaller head in comparison with the huge wings; also, the outer wings are more *deeply 'fingered'*, and the outermost two primaries flex upwards more prominently than on eagles. When soaring, now and then takes a single, deep, 'embracing' wingbeat (cf. Griffon; virtually never seen from eagles). *Tail short* as on Griffon Vulture, rounded or slightly wedge-shaped. Active flight heavy, wingbeats deep and slow. Head-on silhouette when soaring significantly different from Griffon in that *inner wings* invariably are *held flat, with primaries slightly lowered*. Unlike other large, broad-winged vultures, glides in to land *without dangling legs*; instead, often holds tail up. Colour of feet variable: bluish grey-white, pale pinkish, pale yellowish. – Adult: *Underwing-coverts not uniformly dark* but show some paler grey-brown on lesser and median (generally forming one or two diffuse bands). Also, *ruff and head are pale brownish*, not blackish as on juvenile. – Juvenile: *Underwing-coverts uniformly black*, darker than the flight-feathers. Head and ruff, too, are blackish, not lighter brown as on adult. The adult plumage is acquired over a period of *c.* 6 years.

VOICE Usually silent.

Lappet-faced Vulture *Torgos tracheliotus* —

L 98–112 cm, WS 250–280 cm. Used to breed in S Israel, now extinct. Extremely rare straggler within region. Breeds in mountains or deserts. Food mainly carrion. Nest in tree or, less commonly, on cliff-ledge, a huge eyrie of branches.

IDENTIFICATION Huge, in size close to Black Vulture. Flight silhouette most like Black Vulture, with *saw-toothed trailing edge*, although *secondaries bulge a little*, almost as much as on Griffon, and *tail is proportionately shorter* than on both. *Wings broad*, outer wings *very deeply 'fingered'*. Head-on silhouette when soaring flattish. Best separated by plumage characters: *head is light, ruff is dark, dark breast* of adult is *striped and mottled whitish*, with some white also along flanks. Upperwing-coverts and back are brownish, contrasting somewhat against darker flight- and tail-feathers (though less than on Griffon). – Adult: Underbody striped dark and pale. *Underwing-coverts black, with one pale band near leading edge* and sometimes additional indistinct rows of white spots (spots more obvious in N Africa than in Middle East). – Juvenile: Underbody and underwing-coverts rather uniform dark. – Immature: Adult plumage acquired in 6–7 years. Intermediate stages difficult to separate in the field.

VOICE Usually silent.

Griffon Vulture

Black Vulture

Lappet-faced Vulture

GRIFFON VULTURE

soars and glides on slightly raised wings (form shallow V)

glid- ing

long 'fingers'

wings appear pointed from certain angles

juv.

often broad pale lines

ad.

coverts paler than flight- feathers

bill yellowish

bill grey

pale brown

white

buff-brown

juv.

outer primaries flex upwards prominently

insignificant pale tips on greater coverts

bulging 'arm'

buff- brown

nar- rower 'hand'

juv.

ad.

greater coverts promi- nently tipped pale

BLACK VULTURE

soars and glides on flat wings, often with outer wing slightly lowered

gliding

pale feet

ad.

coverts darker than flight- feathers

black

black

black

pale brown

pale

juv.

black

black

gives very dark impression

brown-black

Black Vulture often holds tail up before landing

juv.

ad.

relatively evenly broad, rear edge saw-toothed

Griffon often holds legs dan- gling before landing

ad.

LAPPET-FACED VULTURE

soars and glides on flat wings, often with outer wing slightly lowered

gliding

pale vent

ad.

narrow pale line

juv.

pale

juv.

juv.

striped black

ad.

perched in acacia

broad wings, bulging 'arm', rear edge saw- toothed

ad.

DZ

Egyptian Vulture *Neophron percnopterus*   **V***

L 55–65 cm, WS 155–170 cm. Rare summer visitor mainly to mountains in Mediterranean area, more common only in Spain/NW Africa and Turkey; winters in Africa. Declining. Food carrion, offal at refuse dumps, etc. Nests on cliffs.

IDENTIFICATION Medium-large. Flight silhouette characteristic, with *wedge-shaped tail* (slightly shorter than width of wing) and *small head with narrow, long bill*; wings comparatively broad and well 'fingered'. Head-on silhouette fairly flat when soaring; more arched when gliding, with primaries lowered. Flight with rather slow and deep wingbeats. Peculiar white centres of flight-feathers on upperparts unique. – Adult: Body, head, tail, lesser and median wing-coverts white; head, neck, breast and mantle with a varying degree of yellowish- or grey-brown tinge. Strong contrast on underside between white parts and black flight-feathers. Yellow cere and bare skin on head show up at some distance. – Juvenile: *Dark brown, with strongly contrasting ochrous-buff* (bleaching to whitish) *broad tips* to tail-feathers, upperwing-coverts and feathers of mantle, rump, scapulars and lower belly/vent. With wear, this plumage becomes more dull brown, lacking in contrast. There is some variation, too: some juveniles have less prominent light tips and look more uniform brown than others. – Immature: Plumage less distinctly patterned, more dull brown, with pale or whitish feathers first appearing in 2nd summer on upper mantle, rump/lower back, belly and wing-coverts. Adult pattern gradually acquired over *c.* 5 years.

VOICE Usually silent.

White-tailed Eagle *Haliaeetus albicilla*   r**B**5

L 76–92 cm, WS 190–240 cm. Breeds along sea coasts and by larger lakes or rivers. Rare (except locally in Norway). Reintroduced in Scotland. Adults mainly resident except in far N, juveniles more migratory. Food fish, also waterbirds, carrion, offal. Nest huge, in crown of old tree or (along Atlantic coasts) on cliff-ledge; re-used if pair is undisturbed.

IDENTIFICATION Very large, with *long, broad wings*, outer wings well 'fingered'. *Fairly short, bluntly wedge-shaped tail* and *long neck* and *heavy bill* combine to give characteristic flight silhouette. Head-on, wings flat/somewhat arched ('arm'raised, 'hand'lowered). Active flight with *long* series of relaxed, rather shallow wingbeats, now and then relieved by short glide (cf. Golden Eagle); characteristic is sudden slight rise or descent of flightpath. Can soar for long periods at supreme height. – Adult: Brown, with *paler, yellowish-brown head and neck*. Some upperwing-coverts and feathers of mantle and scapulars irregularly tipped pale yellowish, creating 'untidy', scalloped effect. *Bill yellow. Tail pure white*, or white with brown mottling at base and tip. – Juvenile:

Whole plumage uniformly fresh/worn. Compared with adult, outer secondaries longer, creating bulging outline, and tail longer and less graduated. Head, neck and body dark brown, breast, belly, back and upperwing rufous-brown with extensive blackish tips, lesser coverts being darkest. (Darkness variable, some appearing blackish, others rather pale brown.) Underwing dark, with diffuse *light patch on axillaries* and *narrow light band on median coverts*. Tail-feathers largely dark with light centres, can appear all dark when folded (even in flight!) but quite pale when spread in good light. Bill dark. *Lores whitish*, forming a rather conspicuous light patch. – 1st-immature (1st–2nd summer): Plumage not uniformly fresh/worn (owing to protracted moult). Rufous-brown colours bleached, and some white-based feathers on breast and mantle. 'Trousers' all dark. Bill slightly paler grey. – 2nd-immature (2nd–3rd summer): Variable, but consistently more uniformly dark. Breast, mantle and wings become more brown. Some still blotched white on back and breast. Bill greyish-yellow. – 3rd-immature (3rd–5th summer): Markedly different from preceding immatures in greater similarity to adult, though still showing scattered whitish feathers, and head/neck still rather grey-brown. Bill pale yellow, eye pale brown.

VOICE Generally silent outside breeding season. Main call, especially in vicinity of nest, a loud series of shrill, cackling yaps, reminiscent of spring call of Black Woodpecker, ♂ higher-pitched than ♀, 'klee klee klee klee ...'. Alarm lower-pitched, hard knocking 'klek', a few slowly repeated.

Osprey *Pandion haliaetus*   m**B**5(4?)

L 52–60 cm, WS 152–167 cm. Summer visitor (Mar–) Apr–Sep; winters in Africa. In Britain, very rare breeder (*c.* 100 pairs, in Scotland). Breeds on clear freshwater lakes, also on coasts at brackish water, in Mediterranean at salt. Food fish, caught after dive. Nests in very top of pine tree.

IDENTIFICATION Medium-large, long-winged, ventrally pale raptor with unique flight silhouette, *wings being narrow with long 'hand'*, having only four 'fingers', *tail short* and square-cut. *Wings angled, carpals held forward when gliding*, wings in head-on silhouette distinctly *bowed* and at times recalls Great Black-backed Gull. Hovers (wingbeats heavy) over water and dives feet-first for fish. Upperparts grey-brown, *underparts white*, underwing with blackish marks. – Adult: Upperparts uniformly grey-brown, no white feather tips. Crown white. Greater coverts below all blackish; secondaries dark, barring usually indistinct. Eye yellow. ♂ has on average less prominent brown breast-band than ♀. – Juvenile: Feathers of upperparts tipped whitish. Crown white with dark streaks. Greater coverts below white, barred dark; secondaries pale but coarsely barred dark. Eye orange.

VOICE During aerial display (undulating flight high up, feet dangling), whistles mournfully 'u-**eelp** u-**eelp** u-**eelp**...'. The alarm, often given in flight, a hoarse but still sharp 'kew-kew-kew-kew-...'. Contact-call is a short, loud and 'sudden' whistle, 'pyep!'.

Egyptian Vulture   White-tailed Eagle   Osprey

EGYPTIAN VULTURE

at times feeding on refuse dumps

juv.

ad.

juv.

variation

juv.

subad.

ad.

typical silhouette with wedge-shaped tail

juv.

subad.

wedge-shaped

ad.

narrow bill

WHITE-TAILED EAGLE

attended by Hooded Crows on spring ice

head often darkest

pale bill-base

long, heavy, dark

variation

juv.

juv.

3rd-winter

pursued by Common Gulls

ad.

pale mantle

3rd-winter

juv.

long 'fingers'

narrow light band

light 'armpit'

predominantly dark but can appear light against the sky

juv.

subad.

white, wedge-shaped

ad.

yellow yellowish-brown

ad.

OSPREY

light-tipped

uniformly brown

juv.

ad.

juv.

ad.

finely cross-barred

greater coverts cross-barred

darker trailing band

dark band

juv.

ad.

hovers and dives for fish

head-on silhouette

DZ

EAGLES *Aquila, Circaetus, Hieraaetus* et al.
Common name for large, broad-winged, powerful diurnal birds of prey with strong bill and sharp talons; however, the group is not clearly defined and includes species of different size which are not all closely related. Sexes alike in plumage, but the female is generally larger. Adult plumage attained only after several years. (One species, the White-tailed Eagle, is treated on the preceding spread.)

Golden Eagle *Aquila chrysaetos* rB4

L 80–93 cm, WS 190–225 cm. Breeds in mountains and vast upland forests, sometimes also in more restricted lowland forests. In southern part of range resident; in N more migratory, especially young birds. Food mammals (hare, rabbit, squirrel, rodents, even young fox), gamebirds, carrion. Versatile hunter, soaring high up looking for prey, or flies low attempting to surprise game in Goshawk fashion. Will also sit in treetops for long periods on the lookout. Nest huge, in old tree or on cliff-ledge; re-used if pair is undisturbed.

IDENTIFICATION Very large, long-winged eagle with typically *long tail*, about as long as width of wing. Silhouette typical also in wings being slightly narrower at base and inner 'hand', producing *S-curved rear edge*, most pronounced on young birds. Flight powerful, often 6–7 rather deep, slow wingbeats relieved by glide of 1–2 sec., then further short series of beats, etc.; flightpath usually straight. Head-on silhouette when soaring, and often when gliding, typical, with *wings raised in shallow V*; at times also glides on flatter or somewhat arched wings. Common to all plumages is rather dark brown colour with yellowish-brown or light rufous-brown (due to variation, not age criterion) nape-shawl. – Adult: Flight- and tail-feathers basally grey with 3–5 broad, coarse, dark cross-bars, widely tipped blackish. *Upper* median and inner greater *wing-coverts* bleached and worn, *forming irregular pale panel* (varying in prominence). Often paler rufous breast patch and median underwing-coverts. – Juvenile: *Large pure white areas on central wing* (primaries and outer secondaries white-based) *and inner tail*. Rarely, amount of white in wing restricted to small patch (and thus no age criterion). Upperwing-coverts uniformly dark brown, *no pale panel*. Rear edge of wing S-curved, all wing-feathers uniformly fresh/worn. – 1st-immature (1st–2nd summer): Similar to juvenile but has pale panel on upperwing, and plumage not uniformly fresh/worn. – 2nd-immature (3rd–5th summer): Like 1st-immature, but a varying number of adult-type flight-feathers, grey and barred, among juvenile-type. White on base of tail kept longest, sometimes still when wings appear adult.

VOICE Rather silent. A thin, fluty whistle, 'klüh...', sometimes in flight. Eaglets and ♀ beg with disyllabic 'pee-chulp'.

(Eastern) **Imperial Eagle** *Aquila heliaca* —
L 70–83 cm, WS 175–205 cm. Rare and local breeder in E and SE Europe in forests on steppe or open plains, also in upland forests. Food mammals, birds. Nests in tree.

IDENTIFICATION Very large. Most similar to Golden Eagle, but *tail shorter*, about ³/₄ or ⁴/₅ of width of wing, and wings on average more evenly broad. Head-on silhouette often differs, too, *wings held flattish*, but can also be slightly raised (almost as on Golden). Often soars with tail folded. *Tail is more square and has sharper corners* than on Steppe Eagle. –Adult: Very dark, brown-black, with pale golden nape-shawl, paler than on Golden Eagle. Generally *no pale panel on wing-coverts above*, but at times an indistinct one. Flight-feathers grey, diffusely barred, *underwing-coverts contrastingly black*. *Inner tail paler* and more densely barred than on Golden, outer with *broad black band at tip* (at long range, two-coloured tail can recall pattern of young Golden). *White patches on shoulders* (sometimes small and difficult to see). – Juvenile: Body and wing-coverts sand-coloured, breast, mantle and coverts coarsely streaked cold brown; typically has *contrast between streaked* (at distance: dark) *breast and mantle, and unmarked pale belly and lower back*, respectively. Flight- and tail-feathers and upper greater coverts blackish, widely tipped whitish; *inner three primaries typically contrastingly paler*, visible on both surfaces. *Pale primary patch insignificant*, giving slightly different upperwing pattern compared with immature Steppe Eagle and the two spotted eagles. (Exceptionally shows hint of light mid-wing-band below, recalling young Steppe Eagle, but rest of characters should be conclusive.) – 1st-immature: Similar to juvenile but, owing to moult, plumage is not uniformly worn. Pale trailing edges of wings and tail somewhat less conspicuous. – 2nd-immature (from c. 3rd summer): Gradually, dark feathers grow, commencing on throat, upper-body and lesser coverts; can look quite *pied* in intermediate stages. Adult plumage attained from c. 5 years of age.

VOICE Fairly vocal. Calls deeper than Golden Eagle's. Commonly, a quick series of harsh barking notes, 'owk-owk-owk-...', often during dives in aerial display.

Spanish Imperial Eagle *Aquila adalberti* —

L 72–85 cm, WS 180–210 cm. Closely related to Imperial Eagle (treated as conspecific by some). Very rare breeder in C and SW Spain (c. 150 pairs). Nests in tree.

IDENTIFICATION Very similar to similarly sized Imperial Eagle, differing in following ways: Adult has pure *white leading edge of wing above and below*, and usually *larger white shoulder patches* (located further forward, often appearing as extensions of the white upper leading edge of wing). *Flight-feathers* on average *darker, less barred*. *Inner tail is paler* grey, appearing unbarred. – Juvenile is more *rufous-brown* (not sandy-buff) and *unstreaked* (only finely marked on breast of some). The bill is slightly heavier on average.

VOICE Calls very similar to those of Imperial Eagle, if not identical.

Golden Eagle

Imperial Eagle

Spanish Imperial Eagle

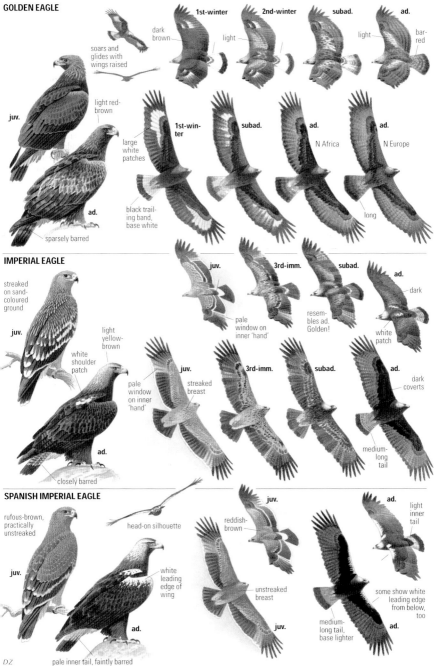

GOLDEN EAGLE

soars and glides with wings raised

dark brown

1st-winter

light

2nd-winter

subad.

light

ad.

bar-red

barred

juv.

light red-brown

large white patches

1st-win-ter

subad.

ad.
N Africa

ad.
N Europe

black trailing band, base white

long

ad.

sparsely barred

IMPERIAL EAGLE

streaked on sand-coloured ground

juv.

light yellow-brown

white shoulder patch

juv.

pale window on inner 'hand'

3rd-imm.

subad.

resembles ad. Golden!

ad.

dark

white patch

pale window on inner 'hand'

juv.

streaked breast

3rd-imm.

subad.

ad.

dark coverts

medium-long tail

ad.

closely barred

SPANISH IMPERIAL EAGLE

rufous-brown, practically unstreaked

head-on silhouette

juv.

reddish-brown

ad.

light inner tail

juv.

white leading edge of wing

unstreaked breast

juv.

medium-long tail, base lighter

some show white leading edge from below, too

ad.

ad.

pale inner tail, faintly barred

DZ

Lesser Spotted Eagle *Aquila pomarina* —

55–65 cm, WS 143–168 cm. Summer visitor Apr–Sep (Oct), winters in Africa; locally rather numerous migrant through Turkey and Middle East. Breeds in forests on open or wooded plains. Food small mammals, amphibians, some birds and insects. Nests in tree.

IDENTIFICATION Medium-sized, dark and compact eagle. Wings evenly broad, tips well 'fingered', although not quite so prominently as on the other, larger *Aquila* eagles; 'hand' less ample, 7th primary 'finger' minute (juv.) or short (ad.). Tail rounded, tail length ⅔ to ¾ of width of wing. In head-on profile, *wings are slightly angled at carpal joints and primaries lowered*, especially when gliding, somewhat also when soaring (lowered primaries when gliding occur among other species too, notably Spotted and Steppe Eagles). Wingbeats rather quick. Head and neck buzzard-like, *bill small* for an eagle. Nostrils round (characteristic of spotted eagles). Best identified by plumage: *dark brown with contrastingly paler head/neck and upperwing-coverts*; a *small whitish primary patch above* is characteristic; a little white on uppertail-coverts on most; underwing usually has *wing-coverts paler than flight-feathers* (milk-chocolate brown against dark grey; when seen well in good light, very few ambiguous). Flight-feathers generally densely barred dark (at distance usually invisible), dark bars at least as wide as paler bars in between; barring prominent right out to tip; some birds are completely unbarred. – Adult: Lesser and median upperwing-coverts *pale yellowish-brown*, forming well-defined area on forewing; upper head pale; back dark (most often) or somewhat paler, depending on moult and wear. White primary patch small and well defined. No obvious white tips to greater coverts, secondaries or tail-feathers. – Juvenile: Wing-coverts (lesser and median, both sides) darker than on adult, medium brown, still usually slightly paler than greater coverts and flight-feathers (though some have confusingly dark under primary coverts). Head brown, with *rufous-golden* (white when bleached) *patch on nape*. White primary patch is rather extensive, often 'spreading' across inner primaries. Greater coverts (both sides), trailing edge of wings and tail narrowly tipped white; outer upper median coverts also tipped white, but not always visible in the field. Tendency to have slightly bulging secondaries (unlike ad.). – Immature: Adult plumage acquired over a period of *c.* 5 years, but ageing in the field is difficult except for adults and juveniles; however, moult of flight-feathers can give a clue—only inner primaries renewed in 1st summer, both some inner and some outer in following summers.

VOICE Vocal in breeding area. High-pitched bark, 'k-yeep', sometimes likened to yapping of small dog. ♂ has drawn-out whistle, 'wiiiik', during aerial display.

(Greater) Spotted Eagle *Aquila clanga* V***

L 59–69 cm, WS 153–177 cm. Breeds in forests, often interspersed with rivers and marshes. Short-range migrant, wintering in southern part of range and in Middle East. Rare. Food mammals, carrion. Nests in tree.

IDENTIFICATION Large, dark, compact eagle. Flight silhouette very similar to Lesser Spotted Eagle (which see); differs very slightly only in having more ample 'hand' with longer 'fingers'. Bill medium-large. Nostrils round. Best identified by plumage: dark brown, with usually *darker coverts than flight-feathers below* (the opposite of Lesser Spotted) and *lacking well-defined pale upperwing-coverts*. White *primary patch above less distinct*, formed mainly by basally white shafts of primaries, and more 'spread out', *reaching almost to leading edge of wing*. Flight-feathers below generally densely barred dark, dark bars narrow and becoming fainter towards tip; some birds are unbarred. – Adult, typical: *Dark brown* with slightly and diffusely paler brown head, back and upperwing-coverts, dark plumage relieved only by diffuse, whitish primary patches and, on many birds, some white on uppertail-coverts. Under forewing often darker than greater coverts and flight-feathers, but many look uniformly dark below. A *prominent single white crescent or patch below at the base of the outer primaries* is a good mark, but some have two narrow crescents, one at the primary base and a fainter second at the base of the primary coverts, just as on Lesser Spotted. – Adult, pale: Some are pale brown on head and wing-coverts, recalling Lesser Spotted Eagle, but lack dark back and sharp division between pale covert area above and dark rest of wing, are only *diffusely* paler brown on forewing and mantle. – Juvenile, typical: Purplish *brown-black* with buff/white spots and feather tips of varying number and prominence. Birds with large spots very typical, *spots forming prominent rows along all wing-coverts*; those with smaller spots approach most prominently spotted juvenile Lesser Spotted Eagle. Exceptionally, pale spots on head merge to form patch on nape as on Lesser Spotted. *Head very dark with contrasting yellow gape-flange.* Under forewing brown-black, clearly darker than medium grey greater coverts and flight-feathers. Secondaries long and 'bulging' in flight silhouette, plumage evenly fresh/worn. – Juvenile, pale: Variable; less dark ground colour, partly or extensively rufous-brown, often heavily spotted or striped yellowish, can be confused with Lesser Spotted at long range, but generally distinguished by dark brown feathers or pattern on head, neck and lesser upperwing- and underwing-coverts, thus less homogeneously brown; washed-out primary patch above also good clue. – Palest form (var. *fulvescens*; very rare) has all body-feathers pale golden (wear to whitish in 1st summer) and pale tips so extensive that it looks more like pale-morph N African Tawny Eagle or bleached juv. Imperial Eagle; distinguished—with difficulty—by size, proportions, size of bill and sometimes head-on silhouette and plumage details. Palest form probably occurs among immatures, too. – Immature: The spotted plumage of juvenile repeated in at least one more plumage (spots only slightly smaller and less distinct), thus adult plumage is not developed until after 5–6 years.

VOICE Calls similar to Lesser Spotted Eagle's but lower-pitched. Main call barking 'kyak', singly or repeated.

Lesser Spotted Eagle   Spotted Eagle

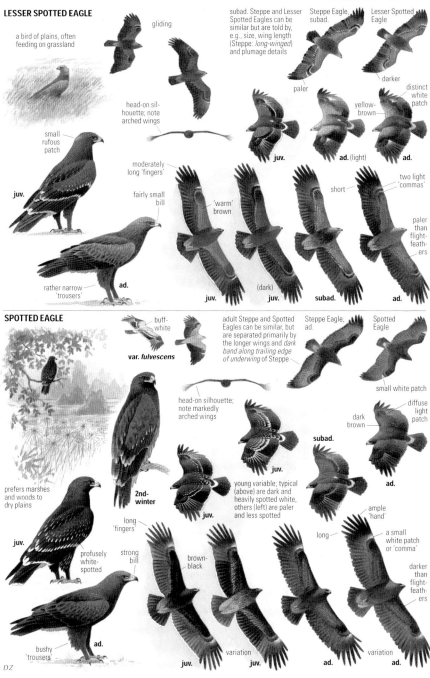

LESSER SPOTTED EAGLE

a bird of plains, often feeding on grassland

gliding

subad. Steppe and Lesser Spotted Eagles can be similar but are told by, e.g., size, wing length (Steppe: *long-winged*) and plumage details

Steppe Eagle, subad.

Lesser Spotted Eagle

paler

darker

distinct white patch

yellow-brown

juv.

ad. (light)

ad.

head-on silhouette; note arched wings

small rufous patch

juv.

moderately long 'fingers'

fairly small bill

'warm' brown

short

two light 'commas'

paler than flight-feathers

rather narrow 'trousers'

ad.

juv.

juv. (dark)

subad.

ad.

SPOTTED EAGLE

buff-white

var. *fulvescens*

adult Steppe and Spotted Eagles can be similar, but are separated primarily by the longer wings and *dark band along trailing edge of underwing* of Steppe

Steppe Eagle, ad.

Spotted Eagle

small white patch

head-on silhouette; note markedly arched wings

diffuse light patch

dark brown

subad.

juv.

ad.

prefers marshes and woods to dry plains

juv.

2nd-winter

long 'fingers'

strong bill

profusely white-spotted

brown-black

young variable; typical (above) are dark and heavily spotted white, others (left) are paler and less spotted

juv.

ample 'hand'

long

a small white patch or 'comma'

darker than flight-feathers

bushy 'trousers'

ad.

juv.

juv.

variation

ad.

variation

ad.

DZ

Steppe Eagle *Aquila nipalensis* —

L 62–74 cm, WS 165–190 cm (ssp. *orientalis*). Closely related to Tawny Eagle, and by some regarded as conspecific. Summer visitor (Mar–Oct/Nov) breeding on open, dry plains and foothills, wintering in Africa; locally numerous migrant in Middle East. Food rodents and other mammals, bird nestlings, insects (in winter especially termites), carrion, etc. Nests in tree or on ground.

IDENTIFICATION (Ssp. *orientalis*.) *Large* to very large. Wings long and broad, tips prominently 'fingered'. *Head and neck* somewhat more *prominent* than on the spotted eagles, and *'arm' proportionately longer*. Other clues are *heavy bill* and *long, conspicuous, yellow gape-flange* (reaching to rear edge of eye). With experience, the more ample 'hand', with more prominent, longer 'fingers' with long 7th primary, separates from Lesser Spotted Eagle. Size helpful only for largest birds and in direct comparison. Nostrils oval (round on spotted eagles). *Flight- and tail-feathers coarsely barred dark, bars well spaced and always prominent* at close range, covering central 'hand' ('palm') too (spotted eagles unbarred there); barring not so obvious at a distance, but often shows on distal parts of inner primaries; *terminal band wider on adult, forming dark trailing edge of wing*, visible on most birds at moderate range. Chin and throat pale in all plumages. Only tips of primaries ('fingers') black below, *'palm' paler grey*. On perched birds, 'trousers' are wider and more prominent than on especially Lesser Spotted Eagle (which has tight 'stockings' only). Many have a small white patch on the centre of the back, but this can be seen on both spotted eagles as well. – Adult: Dark or mid brown with coarsely barred flight- and tail-feathers, dark trailing edge of wings unbroken; nape often diffusely paler brown. Dark birds recall Spotted Eagle, but have *dark trailing edge to wings and tail*, and have slightly longer wings. Pale birds recall Lesser Spotted Eagle, but, apart from structural differences (cf. above), often (many exceptions!) have back and upperwing-coverts uniformly light brown (back always darker than wing-coverts on Lesser Spotted); underbody darker than underwing; rather prominent darkish carpal area below. – Juvenile: Characteristic, mid brown with *broad white band along centre of underwing* (exceptionally vestigial) and *broad white trailing edge to wings and tail*. On some, white midwing-band expands to large cream-white patch at carpals. Upper greater coverts broadly tipped white, merging with usually prominent whitish primary patch. Uppertail-coverts with much white. Plumage uniformly fresh/worn. – Immature: Variable, but has complete or partial white midwing- band, and traces of white trailing edge to wings and tail, especially on inner primaries. Plumage unevenly worn or in moult. – Subadult: Similar to adult,

but a few flight-feathers remaining without a prominent dark tip, and traces of the white midwing-band generally visible (remaining for longest on inner primary coverts).

VOICE Rather silent. Calls basically similar to those of two spotted eagles, but somewhat lower-pitched.

Tawny Eagle *Aquila rapax* —

L 62–72 cm, WS 165–185 cm. Closely related to Steppe Eagle. N African race (ssp. *belisarius*) resident in mountains and forests, rare. Food as for Steppe Eagle; piracy often recorded. Nests in tree.

IDENTIFICATION Compared with Steppe Eagle a smaller, somewhat more chunky bird, only marginally larger than Spotted Eagle. Plumages differ from Steppe Eagle in being more variable and *often quite pale. Flight- and tail-feathers densely but insignificantly barred*, or unbarred, some adults with a faint dark trailing edge. *Lower back to uppertail-coverts almost invariably very pale* (typical of young Imperial Eagle, too, but rare for Steppe). Pale birds usually have *markedly pale inner three primaries* (and sometimes base to rest of primaries below), recalling pattern of young Imperial Eagle. Yellow gape-flange prominent but reaching only to centre of eye (rear edge on Steppe; tiny difference, still useful when seen well). *Throat not markedly paler than rest of underbody* (Steppe Eagle has pale throat). *Young birds lack striking white band on underwing* of young Steppe Eagle. – Adult: Dark, medium, light or rufous-brown with darker flight- and tail-feathers. Upperwing-coverts and many body-feathers dark-centred, giving streaked overall impression, and through gradual moult a ragged, less uniform appearance shown by many (except for the darkest, but these are very rare within region). Pale patch at base of inner primaries insignificant. Iris light (dark in Steppe). – Juvenile: Usually pale rufous-brown, bleaching to creamy-white; a few are darker mid brown. Underwing-coverts are pale, the greaters dark-centred. Plumage uniformly fresh/ worn.

Verreaux's Eagle *Aquila verreauxii* —

L 78–88 cm, WS 190–210 cm. Extremely rare breeder in SE corner of region (Sinai). Found in mountains in desert. Favourite food hyrax. Nests on cliff-ledge.

IDENTIFICATION Almost size of Golden Eagle (may look larger owing to dark plumage). Adult striking, with *black plumage, large whitish 'windows' on primaries* above and below, and *white stripes to mantle and white rump/uppertail-coverts*, together forming a large U (in flight) or V (at rest) on upperbody. An approaching bird at long range can be taken for a dark-morph Long-legged Buzzard before silhouette and upperparts are revealed. Flight silhouette very characteristic, with *bulging secondaries, narrow wing-base and narrow inner 'hand'*. At distance, wing-tips often appear rather pointed. *Soars with wings raised in distinct V.* – Juvenile: Vaguely reminiscent of adult Golden Eagle, being rather dark with pale rufous-golden nape-shawl, differing in having *distinctly light-based primaries, different wing shape, whitish uppertail-coverts*, slightly shorter tail, proportionately smaller head and longer, slimmer black neck, longer legs and larger feet. Sides of head and throat black. Upperwing-coverts dark, tipped pale buff, appearing 'scaly'.

Steppe Eagle

Tawny Eagle

STEPPE EAGLE

juv.

long gape-flange

juv.

head-on silhouette; note markedly arched wings

often buff-brown nape

white trailing edge

ad.

juv.

white trailing edge

gliding

subad.

broad white band

broad white band

juv.

coarse well-spaced bars

subad.

ad.

ample 'hand'

ad.

variation

similar to Lesser Spotted

similar to Spotted

'palm' paler grey

dark carpal

broad black trailing edge

dark belly

ad.

ad.

TAWNY EAGLE

often steals prey from other predators

juv.

compared with Steppe, larger head, heavier bill-base and paler iris

juv.

light back/rump

similar to Imperial

juv.

variation

juv.

subad.

indistinct barring

subad.

ad.

similar to Lesser Spotted

variation

ad.

ad.

no dark trailing edge

black wing-tips and pale 'windows' on inner wing

ad.

VERREAUX'S EAGLE

ad.

perched young at long range can recall both Imperial and Steppe Eagles

juv.

juv.

juv.

ad.

ad.

pure white rump area

light 'window'

typical wing shape: narrow base, broad centre and narrow 'hand'

DZ

Short-toed Eagle *Circaetus gallicus* —

L 62–69 cm, WS 162–178 cm. Summer visitor (late Mar–Oct), winters in Africa. Scarce, *c.* 4000 pairs within region, mostly in southwest. Breeds in mainly open, arid country with mountains and scattered woods, in north also in river valleys, forests. Food reptiles. Nests in tree.

IDENTIFICATION Large, pale eagle with both *long and broad wings*. Tail length about ⁴/₅ of or equal to width of wing, *tail narrow at base and square-cut* when folded, corners sharp. *Neck short and head broad*, almost owl-like on perched birds (but not always apparent on flying). Flight silhouette when gliding characteristic, *carpals held well forward* and *wings bowed* or arched when seen head-on. Outer secondaries and inner primaries long, giving rather *straight rear edge of wing even when carpals are pressed forward*. Soars on flattish wings. *Hovers*, or hangs motionless in the wind by making small wing adjustments. *Very pale underparts* separate it from most other species; silvery-white with *sharply set-off dark grey head/breast* is typical, rows of dark spots across belly and wing-coverts and loosely barred flight- and tail-feathers. *Tail has three evenly spaced dark bars*, with a hint of a fourth on some, bars visible above as well. Distinguished from Osprey and pale-morph buzzards by *lack of dark carpal patches*, and by tail pattern. Some are darker-patterned, others so pale that only a hint of the tail-bands and some faint barring are visible. Tips of outer primaries shaded grey, darkest along edges, unlike buzzards (which have solidly blackish tips). – Adult/Juvenile: Ageing difficult. Juvenile has more bulging secondaries and narrower 'hand', and all flight-feathers are evenly fresh/worn, finely tipped white.

VOICE Rather vocal in breeding season. One call likened to 'kyo' call of Golden Oriole, given singly or repeated. Also a plaintive 'mee-ok'.

Booted Eagle *Hieraaetus pennatus* —

L 42–51 cm, WS 110–135 cm. Summer visitor (late Mar–Oct), winters in Africa (a few in SW Spain). Breeds in forests with mixture of open ground and hills or mountains. Food mammals, reptiles, birds, mostly caught on or near ground after spectacular stoop with wings folded. Nests in tree or (rarely) on cliff.

IDENTIFICATION Small eagle, of similar size and shape to a buzzard, though 'hand' is more ample with one more 'finger' (6 instead of 5), making the wing more evenly broad than on buzzards. Flight is also more eagle-like, with straighter course, often faster speed and longer glides. *Tail* ⁴/₅ of or about equal to width of wing, *square-cut, sides straight* (or even slightly concave near tip). Two morphs: pale has *white underbody* (with some brown or dusky shades on breast and around eyes) and *white underwing-coverts* (with scattered

dark spots) *strongly contrasting against black flight-feathers* (*inner three primaries typically paler* and barred); dark morph has dark brown underbody (rufous tinge, streaked) and underwing-coverts (often somewhat paler towards leading edge), and flight-feathers similar to pale morph although on average not so black, more brown and barred; most striking feature is *paler three inner primaries*. Undertail on both morphs grey with *darker tip and centre*. (There is some variation in both morphs: pale morph with rufous tinge on underbody; and—more common—dark morph being mid-brown with paler rufous leading edge of underwing, sometimes called 'rufous morph'.) About 75% of all show very characteristic *pure white small patch on base of leading edge of wing*, visible when seen head-on ('landing lights'); exceptionally, something similar can be seen on Honey Buzzard (though not such pure white and well-marked patches). Upperparts on both morphs have *pale ochrous-buff panel across inner upperwing, whitish uppertail-coverts* and some pale feathers on scapulars.

VOICE Highly vocal in breeding season. Main call shrill 'kli kli kli'. Also buzzard-like 'hiyaah' and long series of 'gü'.

Bonelli's Eagle *Hieraaetus fasciatus* —

L 55–65 cm, WS 145–165 cm. Breeds in forests or mountains. Rare, *c.* 600 pairs within region, mainly in SW. Food usually medium-sized mammals or birds. Nests in cave or on ledge on steep, inaccessible cliff, sometimes in tall tree.

IDENTIFICATION Medium-large, powerful eagle with broad wings and *straight, rather broad, square-cut* tail of about the same length as width of wing, or slightly less. *Wing-tips only moderately 'fingered'* for such a large raptor. *Carpals pressed forward when gliding*, and combination of this and *fairly small head* and length of tail recalls Honey Buzzard. Soars and glides on flattish wings, primaries at times slightly lowered. – Adult: At distance in flight, combination of *whitish body and dark wings and tail* unique. When seen closer from below, *leading edge of wings is white* (extent variable, involving lesser and sometimes some median coverts), outer primaries are basally diffusely pale, and greater coverts are darkest, being blackish; *tail is pale grey with broad dark terminal band*. White areas narrowly streaked dark. Upperparts dark grey with characteristic *whitish patch on back* (of varying size; can be missing). – Juvenile: Underbody and underwing-coverts *pale rufous-buff* (finely streaked dark), *wing-tips blackish*, flight- and tail-feathers pale grey and narrowly barred dark, no broad terminal band on tail. Greater coverts can be rufous-buff without any dark, or have some dark bases forming a faint band on outer and on primary coverts. – Immature: At first, underbody is pale brown, *prominently streaked dark*. Gradually, greater coverts become darker and body whiter. Dark terminal tail-band developed from 3rd winter, adult plumage from 5th.

VOICE Apparently rather silent. Various barks and shrill notes have been recorded at breeding sites.

Short-toed Eagle

Booted Eagle

Bonelli's Eagle

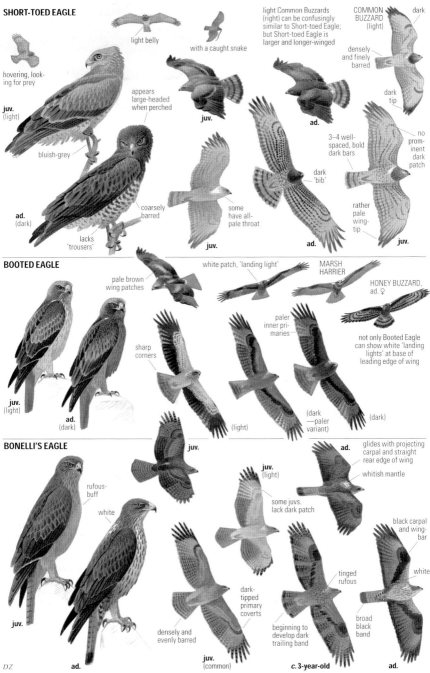

SHORT-TOED EAGLE

light belly

with a caught snake

hovering, looking for prey

juv. (light)

appears large-headed when perched

bluish-grey

ad. (dark)

coarsely barred

lacks 'trousers'

juv.

some have all-pale throat

dark 'bib'

juv.

ad.

light Common Buzzards (right) can be confusingly similar to Short-toed Eagle; but Short-toed Eagle is larger and longer-winged

COMMON BUZZARD (light)

dark

densely and finely barred

dark tip

3–4 well-spaced, bold dark bars

no prominent dark patch

rather pale wing-tip

juv.

BOOTED EAGLE

pale brown wing patches

white patch, 'landing light'

MARSH HARRIER

HONEY BUZZARD, ad. ♀

paler inner primaries

not only Booted Eagle can show white 'landing lights' at base of leading edge of wing

juv. (light)

sharp corners

ad. (dark)

(light)

(dark —paler variant)

(dark)

BONELLI'S EAGLE

juv.

ad. glides with projecting carpal and straight rear edge of wing

whitish mantle

rufous-buff

white

juv. (light)

some juvs. lack dark patch

black carpal and wing-bar

white

tinged rufous

dark-tipped primary coverts

broad black band

juv.

ad.

densely and evenly barred

juv. (common)

beginning to develop dark trailing band

c. **3-year-old**

ad.

DZ

Red Kite *Milvus milvus* r**B**4

L 61–72 cm, WS 140–165 cm. Breeds in forests near lakes, interspersed with open fields. Mainly migratory in northern part of range. In Britain, smaller population (130–150 pairs) resident in Wales; reintroduced at several sites in England and Scotland. Food fish, offal, refuse, insects. Often steals food from other birds. Nests in tall tree.

IDENTIFICATION Medium-large, long-winged, with characteristic *long, deeply forked tail. Wings rather narrow and evenly broad, held somewhat arched and flexed at the carpals, long 'hand' lowered*. In profile, *looks stooped, with tail and head hanging down*. Flight buoyant and leisurely, almost crow-like, with *constant twisting of tail. White 'windows' below on inner 'hand'* typical. *Tail rufous above, paler below. Pale yellowish-brown panel diagonally across dark inner wing*, paler and more prominent than on Black Kite, and visible in head-on profile as pale wing-bend. Head pale. – Adult: No light tips to greater upperwing-coverts. Breast and belly deep rufous, narrowly streaked black. Undertail-coverts darkish. – Juvenile: Narrow white tips to upper greater coverts. Breast and belly rufous with yellowish-buff central streaks, giving a paler appearance than dark under-wing. Undertail-coverts pale.

VOICE Rather silent. Thin, piping, Common Buzzard-like mewing followed by drawn-out notes rising and falling, 'weee-ooh, ee oo ee oo ee oo'. Also 'wee-oh' repeated.

Black Kite *Milvus migrans* V**

L 48–58 cm, WS 130–155 cm. Summer visitor, winters in Africa. Breeds in forests near lakes, rivers or wetlands, also close to human settlements. Annual vagrant to Britain & Ireland. Food fish, offal, refuse, sometimes picked up in harbours or by motorways. Social habits, and where numerous fairly large flocks can be seen. Nests in tree.

IDENTIFICATION Medium-sized, with slightly forked tail. Distinguished from Red Kite by dark plumage, slightly smaller size, proportionately shorter wings and tail, *broader wing-tip* and *less forked tail*, which is *grey-brown above*, never rufous. Dark brown with paler bases to primaries below (European adults only slightly paler; juveniles, and many eastern migrants in Middle East, much whiter, approaching Red Kite). Upperparts dark brown with *pale mid brown panel across inner wing* (same pattern as on Red Kite but darker and duller). If tail-fork not seen (or fork missing through moult, wear, or fanning of tail), possible to confuse with dark-morph Booted Eagle, but latter has light upper-tail-coverts, usually white patch at base of forewing and somewhat larger head. Marsh Harrier in dark plumage separated by much less 'fingered' wing-tips, lack of pale primary bases below, and by head-on silhouette with raised

'arm' and flatter 'hand', not arched wings with lowered primaries. – Adult/Juvenile: Ageing much as for Red Kite.

VOICE Main call recalls Red Kite but is faster, a whinnying 'pee-e-e-e-e'. Also a Common Buzzard-like mewing call.

Marsh Harrier *Circus aeruginosus* m**B**4 / **P**5

L 43–55 cm, WS 115–140 cm. Breeds on shallow freshwater lakes or rivers. Except in south and west migratory, wintering in Africa. Small population in E Britain. Food small mammals, birds, insects. Nests in tall reedbed.

IDENTIFICATION Largest harrier, somewhat bigger than Common Buzzard but with slimmer body, narrower wings and longer tail. *Soars with wings raised in shallow V, glides with 'arm' raised and 'hand' more level*. At distance possible to confuse with Black Kite and dark-morph Booted Eagle, but has *less 'fingered' wing-tips, rounded tail* and different head-on profile. – Adult ♂: *Distinctly set-off black wing-tips, uniformly pale blue-grey tail*, head and breast pale yellowish-white, upperwing three- or four-coloured. Some are very pale, at distance recalling ♂ Hen Harrier, but have *chestnut belly* and chestnut on upperwing-coverts. – Adult ♀: Dark brown with creamy-white crown, throat and forewing (variable amount). Often *pale patch on breast*. ♂-like pale birds distinguished by *lack of well-marked black wing-tips* and by *brown tail*. – Juvenile: Blackish-brown with golden crown and throat, sometimes also forewing; a rare morph is all dark. Differs from adult ♀ in narrow golden line along greater upperwing-coverts, very dark underwing-coverts, darker tail, narrower 'hand' and more bulging 'arm'.

VOICE ♀ has thin, piping whistle, 'psee-ee', repeated a few times, when receiving food from ♂. Alarm a rapid 'quek-ek-ek-ek-ek'. In breeding season during aerial display, has whining, nasal 'way-**e**', repeated twice with 2-sec. pause, in tone recalling Lapwing alarm.

Black-winged Kite *Elanus caeruleus* —

L 31–36 cm, WS 71–85 cm. Breeds in semi-deserts, open plains, forest fringes by rivers. Very rare. Food small mammals, birds, insects. Nests in tree.

IDENTIFICATION Unmistakable: the *size of a Hobby*, but has bulkier body, *pointed* but *broad wings* and *short, square-cut tail*. Pale blue-grey above with black forewing, white below with blackish primaries; head white with *black 'face-mask'*. *Hovers* like a Kestrel, *soars and glides with raised wings* like a harrier, when hunting recalls Short-eared Owl and in active flight large Black Tern. – Juvenile: Back and shoulders dark grey, feathers tipped white; greater upperwing-coverts tipped white. Crown brownish. Breast tinged rufous.

VOICE Mainly silent. Sharp 'kree-ak' heard from both sexes. High-pitched whistle used as alarm.

Red Kite   Black Kite   Marsh Harrier   Black-winged Kite

RED KITE

juv.

white-tipped greater coverts

juv.

juv.

pale rufous

often flies with flexed wings

ad.

paler buff-brown

deeply forked

deep rufous

long

ad.

very distinct light 'window'

short legs and drawn-out rear parts typical of kites

ad.

BLACK KITE

dark eye-surround

juv.

paler buff-brown

juv.

grey-brown

ad.

ad.

note that tail-fork disappears when tail is spread

slightly forked

dark brown

white-tipped greater coverts

juv.

distinct light 'window'

diffuse light 'window'

easterly variant (Central Asia)

ad.

ad.

MARSH HARRIER

♂ Marsh Harrier (unusually pale)

♂ Hen Harrier

ad. ♀

ad. ♂

brown

note difference in shape: Marsh Harrier has longer wings, but somewhat shorter tail

red-brown

grey

black tip

2nd cal-year ♂, autumn

pale brown coverts

ad. ♀

ad. ♂

juv.

♂ features most obvious on underwing

ad. ♀

brown-bellied

ad. ♂

BLACK-WINGED KITE

white tips

rusty-tinged

pointed wings

finely scaled

hovering, often seen over dry fields

juv.

ad.

juv.

short

ad.

DZ

juv.

ad.

ad.

Hen Harrier *Circus cyaneus* r(m)**B4**

L 45–55 cm, WS 97–118 cm. Breeds on bogs in open taiga, marshes or shallow lakes with much vegetation, also on moors and heathland in flat country or hills. Open country in winter. Food small mammals, birds. Nests on ground.

IDENTIFICATION Recognized as a harrier by *long wings and tail*, and *low flight with wings raised in shallow V when gliding*. Separated from Marsh Harrier by plumage, lighter build and flight, from the two narrow-winged species by *shorter and more ample 'hand' with 5th primary long*, and *broader 'arm'*. – Adult ♂: Wing-tips black, *underparts white with blue-grey head and breast sharply set off*, darkish trailing edge to underwing; upperparts blue-grey with *white uppertail-coverts*. – Adult ♀: Upperparts brown with white uppertail-coverts, inner wing with variable yellowish panel; underparts buffish-white, streaked brown. – Juvenile: Distinguished from adult ♀ by more *rufous-yellow underparts* with fewer streaks, especially on belly, and *more prominent and more rufous panel above on inner wing*, not so yellowish and indistinct; *pale tips to greater upperwing-coverts*.

VOICE ♀ has thin whistling 'piih-eh' when receiving food from ♂. Alarm of ♀ a twittering 'chit-it-it-it-et-it-et-it-et...' with varying pitch towards end; ♂ has a more display-like, straighter 'chek-ek-ek-ek'. In breeding season during aerial display, ♂ gives rapid, bouncing series of notes, 'chuk-uk-uk-uk-uk', somewhat recalling alarm of Little Gull.

Montagu's Harrier *Circus pygargus* m**B5**

L 39–50 cm, WS 96–116 cm. Summer visitor (Apr–Sep), winters in Africa. Breeds on open plains, bogs, wasteland among arable fields, heathland with low bushes. In Britain, sporadic breeder only, fewer than 10 pairs. Food small birds or mammals, lizards, insects. Nests on ground.

IDENTIFICATION Very long and narrow wings (5th primary short, unlike on broader-winged Hen Harrier), *slim body* and narrow, long tail. *Flight buoyant and tern-like*, especially ♂. ♀ very similar to ♀ Pallid Harrier. Melanistic birds occur rarely in W Europe. – Adult ♂: Resembles ♂ Hen Harrier, but differs in shape, flight and in having *black bands across secondaries* (two below, one above), more extensive black on wing-tips, *darker grey back / inner wing* (*upperparts appearing tricoloured*, with paler grey-white outer wing inside black tip). Chestnut streaks on belly detectable at close range. (Very old ♂♂ have extensive blue-grey breast/upper belly and lose much, occasionally all, of the chestnut streaking on belly.) – Adult ♀: Best separated from Hen Harrier by shape. From Pallid by slightly narrower wing-base; *obvious dark band across brown secondaries above*, just outside coverts; widely spaced prominent dark bands across pale buff secondaries below, *pale colour not darkening towards body* as

on Pallid; *dark trailing edge on 'hand' below*; and larger underwing-coverts and *axillaries distinctly cross-barred*. – Juvenile: Darker and more rufous than adult ♀, *underparts uniformly chestnut or golden-rufous*, except for some dark streaks on sides of breast on many (very rare on Pallid). *Secondaries* dark, unbarred above and *almost unbarred dark grey below*. Narrow pale band along greater coverts. Best distinguished from similar juvenile Pallid by *lack of prominent unstreaked buff-white neck-collar* or uniform dark brown sides of neck—there is *no dark 'boa'*. ♂♂ have more irregular barring below on primaries. – 1st-summer ♂: Variable amount of dark grey feathers on head, neck and upper breast, often creating (potentially misleading) effect of pale collar. Central tail-feathers often moulted to greyish from Apr. Flight-feathers still juvenile (brown, barred).

VOICE ♀ and fledged young have thin whistle, 'pee-ee' (not falling in pitch), when receiving food. Alarm similar for both sexes, a rapid bouncing 'chit-er chit-er chit-it-it-it-it', slightly recalling Turnstone. In summer during aerial display, ♂ has a rather nasal, Jackdaw-like 'kyeh kyeh kyeh'.

Pallid Harrier *Circus macrourus* **V*******

L 40–50 cm, WS 97–118 cm. Summer visitor (Mar–Sep), winters in Africa. Vagrant to Britain, about one every three years. Habitat, food and nest much as for Montagu's Harrier.

IDENTIFICATION Shape similar to Montagu's Harrier, but differs on average in having *slightly broader wing-base* and, especially on adult ♂, shorter and more ample 'hand', thus is *a trifle more compact* and buzzard-like. This comes through in mode of flight as well, which is, again especially in ♀, somewhat less light and tern-like. Reliable identification, however, can be made only by using plumage characters, too. – Adult ♂: Very pale; *pearl-grey above* (*without prominent white uppertail-coverts* of ♂ Hen Harrier), white below with *only faintly darker head and upper breast, wing-tips with narrow black wedges*. – Adult ♀: Very similar to ♀ Montagu's but told by: almost *uniformly dark brown secondaries above*, lacking a dark band (but can have a hint); overall *darker secondaries below with denser dark bands*, and *pale bands darkening towards body*; trailing edge of 'hand' paler than on Montagu's, and barring of primaries less strong distally; larger underwing-coverts and *axillaries dark*, only finely spotted pale, or diffusely streaked rufous. Told from very similar ♀ Hen by different wing shape. – Juvenile: Very similar to juvenile Montagu's but separated by *prominent, unspotted pale buff-white neck-collar*, enhanced by *uniform dark brown sides of neck* ('boa'). Primary bases below often unbarred, leaving *pale 'boomerang' outside dark tips of coverts*. – 1st-summer: Usually like juvenile (but paler and worn), though a few ♂♂ moult early and show pale belly, a few thin rufous streaks on breast, and greyish central tail-feathers even in Mar.

VOICE ♀ has thin, whining, monosyllabic whistle, 'piih', when receiving food from ♂. Alarm similar to Montagu's but on average shorter. Display-call of ♂ high-pitched whinnying trill, 'dir-r-r-r-r'.

Hen Harrier Montagu's Harrier Pallid Harrier

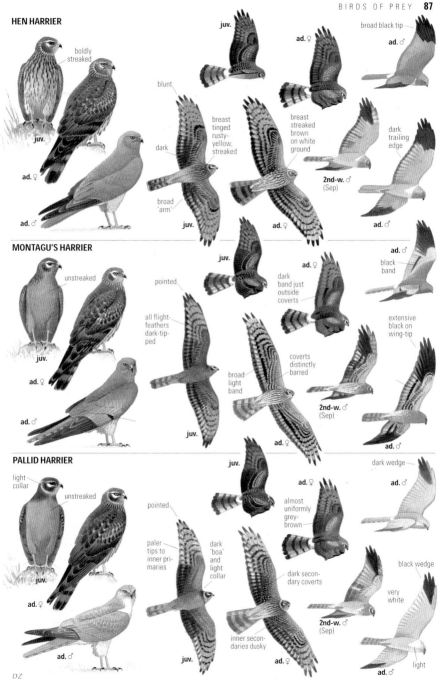

HEN HARRIER

juv.

ad. ♀

ad. ♂

broad black tip

boldly streaked

juv.

blunt

breast tinged rusty-yellow, streaked

breast streaked brown on white ground

dark trailing edge

dark

ad. ♀

broad 'arm'

2nd-w. ♂ (Sep)

juv.

ad. ♀

ad. ♂

ad. ♂

MONTAGU'S HARRIER

unstreaked

juv.

ad. ♀

ad. ♂

black band

pointed

all flight-feathers dark-tipped

dark band just outside coverts

extensive black on wing-tip

broad light band

coverts distinctly barred

2nd-w. ♂ (Sep)

juv.

ad. ♀

ad. ♂

PALLID HARRIER

light collar

unstreaked

juv.

ad. ♀

ad. ♂

dark wedge

ad. ♂

pointed

paler tips to inner primaries

dark 'boa' and light collar

almost uniformly grey-brown

dark secondary coverts

black wedge

very white

inner secondaries dusky

juv.

ad. ♀

2nd-w. ♂ (Sep)

light

ad. ♂

DZ

BUZZARDS *Buteo* and *Pernis*

Medium-sized, broad-winged raptors. They frequently soar high up using rising warm air. Hover or sit motionless watching for prey, which is taken on ground. The two genera are not closely related but appear similar at a distance.

Rough-legged Buzzard *Buteo lagopus*   **P / W5**

L 49–59 cm, WS 123–140 cm. Breeds on fells, in mountain valleys or upland tundra, sometimes in lowland forests with minor hills or crags. In Britain & Ireland, rare passage and winter visitor. Food mainly small mammals. Nests on cliff-ledge or steep slope, at times quite accessible, or in tree.

IDENTIFICATION Typical buzzard, with broad wings and medium-length tail, but compared with Common Buzzard larger and *longer-winged*. Glides on *wings clearly bent at carpal joints* (bend slightly more marked than on Common), inner wing raised and primaries flat. *Active flight with slower wingbeats* than Common Buzzard. *Hovers frequently*, much more commonly than Common Buzzard. Best recognized by *white inner tail above and below* (pale-morph Common can have whitish inner tail, too, but not so clearly contrasting against dark upperwing/rump and distal tail, more diffusely set off, and coinciding with white upperwing-coverts and rump not found on Rough-legged Buzzard). Underside whitish with bold pattern, always incl. *blackish carpal patches* and *dark belly*. Plumage variation largely referable to differences between sexes and ages. (Very rarely a *dark morph* has been recorded within region, blackish on whole body and wing-coverts, with white tail- and flight-feathers heavily barred black; very difficult to distinguish from dark Long-legged Buzzard, and except for size from dark 'Steppe Buzzard' *B. buteo vulpinus*.) – Adult ♂: Ample 'hand', evenly broad wings and rather short tail; trailing edge often somewhat uneven through wear and moult. *2–4 black cross-bars inside broad black end-band above on outer tail*, 1–3 of these visible from below; flight-feathers narrowly but distinctly cross-barred; typically has *head/breast darker than belly*, latter profusely broken up by light barring; 'trousers' cross-barred; *underwing-coverts dark*, often giving Common Buzzard-like impression, not seen on adult ♀; *upperparts usually all dark with small, diffuse paler patch at base of outermost primaries*, and leading edge of 'arm' a little paler. – Adult ♀: Differs from adult ♂ in having *only one narrow black bar* (very rarely two bars) *inside broad black end-band on tail*, visible above and below; *dark belly patch usually prominent and almost invariably darker than head/breast*; underwing-coverts variable but not so dark as on darkest adult ♂. – Juvenile: *Narrower 'hand' and slightly bulging secondaries*; all flight-feathers uniformly fresh/worn. Ground colour yellowish-white, *breast and underwing-coverts typically are* loosely streaked; belly solidly black without light barring; tail has diffusely defined dark grey broad end-band, often rather pale from below, on ♂ frequently with hint of several cross-bars through it; flight-feathers only diffusely barred, end-band diffuse; *upperwing typically with large pale primary patches*. – Subadult ♂: Often intermediate between adult ♂ and adult ♀, making sexing in the field more difficult except for typical extremes. Underwing-coverts and head/breast not so dark as on typical adult ♂, and tail with fewer bands.

VOICE Vocal in breeding season. Main call a wailing miaow, recalling Common Buzzard, but drop in pitch perhaps more pronounced, and tone often sounds more whining and piercing. Also used as alarm, at times vibrant (esp. when taking off from perch).

Long-legged Buzzard *Buteo rufinus*   —

L 50–61 cm, WS 130–150 (ssp. *rufinus*; SE Europe, Asia); L 43–50, WS 105–125 (ssp. *cirtensis*; N Africa). Breeds in arid steppe or semi-desert, also in mountains (Africa). Food small mammals, reptiles, insects. Nests often on cliff-ledge.

IDENTIFICATION Ssp. *rufinus*: Large and long-winged buzzard, similar in shape to Rough-legged Buzzard. *Silhouette and flight as for Rough-legged Buzzard* (incl. hovering), but at times glides and soars on slightly more raised wings. Often best distinguished by plumage, but, with some very similarly plumaged 'Steppe Buzzards' *B. buteo vulpinus* (cf. under Common Buzzard and below), size and flight must be considered, too. At least three different colour morphs: pale (commonest), rufous and dark, but difference between first two far from clear-cut. Common to all are *dark carpal patches* (slightly on upperwing as well, which is very rare for 'Steppe Buzzard'), *dark trailing edge of wings, very white primary bases* below, and for adults *unbarred pale rufous tail* (there may be a hint of a dark end-band); in strong light at a distance, the adult tail can look whitish, especially when bleached. All pale and many rufous morphs have *pale head and breast and progressively darker belly*. Upperwing has pale greyish-white primary bases and often *pale rufous or yellowish-brown forewing, paler than dark grey flight-feathers*. Easily confused with rufous morph of 'Steppe Buzzard', and best recognized by larger size, proportionately longer wings and slower wingbeats, by dark belly and paler head in pale morph and by usually paler upperwing-coverts. Note that tail of juvenile is greyish-buff and finely barred, very similar to some 'Steppe Buzzards'. *Dark morph* (easternmost parts of range) has body and wing-coverts blackish, tail- and flight-feathers white with distinct barring; very similar to dark-morph Rough-legged Buzzard (but hardly occurring in same area) and dark-morph 'Steppe Buzzard', but is larger and longer-winged than latter. – Adult: Tail unbarred pale rufous above, slightly paler and greyer below; broad black band along trailing edge of wing. – Juvenile: Tail greyish-buff, finely barred grey; indistinct dark band along trailing edge of wing. – Ssp. *cirtensis*: Smaller and a little more compact, similar to Common Buzzard in size and shape. Head often pale and belly dark; dark carpal patches below can be missing. Cere and feet of juveniles often pale brownish blue-grey rather than yellow. No dark morph.

VOICE Rather silent. Calls resemble those of Rough-legged Buzzard, but are shorter and more mellow in tone.

Rough-legged Buzzard   Long-legged Buzzard

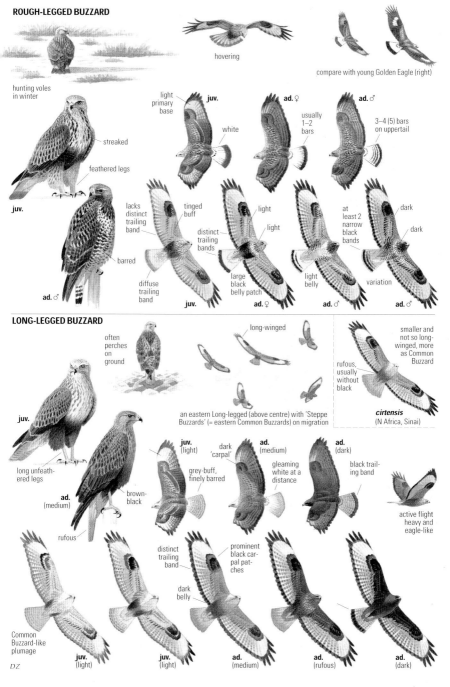

ROUGH-LEGGED BUZZARD

hovering

compare with young Golden Eagle (right)

hunting voles
in winter

light
primary
base

juv.

ad. ♀

ad. ♂

white

usually
1–2
bars

3–4 (5) bars
on uppertail

streaked

feathered legs

juv.

lacks
distinct
trailing
band

tinged
buff

light

at least 2
narrow
black
bands

dark

distinct
trailing
bands

light

dark

barred

diffuse
trailing
band

large
black
belly patch

light
belly

variation

ad. ♂

juv.

ad. ♀

ad. ♂

ad. ♂

LONG-LEGGED BUZZARD

often
perches
on
ground

long-winged

smaller and
not so long-
winged, more
as Common
Buzzard

rufous,
usually
without
black

cirtensis
(N Africa, Sinai)

juv.

an eastern Long-legged (above centre) with 'Steppe
Buzzards' (= eastern Common Buzzards) on migration

long unfeath-
ered legs

ad.
(medium)

brown-
black

rufous

juv.
(light)

dark
'carpal'

grey-buff,
finely barred

ad. (medium)

gleaming
white at a
distance

ad.
(dark)

black trail-
ing band

active flight
heavy and
eagle-like

distinct
trailing
band

prominent
black car-
pal pat-
ches

dark
belly

Common
Buzzard-like
plumage

juv.
(light)

juv.
(light)

ad.
(medium)

ad.
(rufous)

ad.
(dark)

DZ

Common Buzzard *Buteo buteo*   rB3

L 46–58 cm, WS 110-132 cm. Fairly common. Breeds in forests or small woods with access to open land, farmland, meadows or marshes. Food mainly voles, also birds, rabbits, reptiles, amphibians, insects, earthworms. Nests in tree.

IDENTIFICATION Medium-sized, *broad-winged*, rather compact raptor with *broad, short neck* and medium-length tail. Often seen perched on fence posts or telegraph poles watching for prey. Also soars (moderate height), showing *fan-shaped, spread tail*, and wings held pressed forward and *lifted in shallow V*. Glides on flatter wings, generally with slightly raised inner wing and slightly lowered outer wing, *showing more angled carpal bend than Honey Buzzard*. In fast glide carpals are pushed forward and primaries flexed back. As with all *Buteo* buzzards, *tail is slightly or obviously shorter than width of wing, has straight sides and sharp corners* (Honey Buzzard usually has slightly longer tail, equalling width of wing, slightly convex sides and round corners). 'Steppe Buzzard' ssp. *vulpinus* (E Europe, winters in Africa) on average slightly smaller, more narrow-winged and appearing longer-tailed than ssp. *buteo* (W Europe, short-range migrant or resident); for plumage differences, see below. *Active flight with rather quick, stiff wingbeats*, with experience appreciably faster pace than Honey and Rough-legged Buzzards. Plumage variable, from very dark to very pale; still, several characters useful. Off-white *tail densely barred grey*; regardless of colour morph *a pale band across lower breast*, separating dark upper breast from (sides of) belly (exception: some uniformly dark *vulpinus*); from below, trailing edge of wing and wing-tips blackish, involving whole 'fingers'; rest of flight-feathers whitish, barred dark (5–7 bars; outer primaries have only faint bars). *Pale morph* vaguely similar to pale-morph Booted Eagle, but base of primaries extensively white on underside, and *dark carpal patch* diagnostic; upperparts frequently with some degree of *pure white on forewing* (lesser and median coverts) and rump. – Adult: *Terminal tail-band blackish, distinct and much broader than inner bars*. Light feathers of breast, lower belly/'trousers' and greater underwing-coverts *finely cross-barred*, not blotched or streaked. Wings rather evenly broad with more ample 'hand', and tail slightly shorter, (esp. on ♂) than juvenile. – Juvenile: *No distinctly broader terminal tail-band*. Underparts coarsely *streaked*, especially on breast; some feathers blotched or with indication of cross-bars, but streaking predominates. 'Hand' narrow, tail often slightly longer than on adult. Eye paler than adult's. – 'Steppe Buzzard', ssp. *vulpinus*: Main plumage differences from ssp. *buteo* are (1) paler tail, inclining to rufous, the most red-tailed sometimes strongly recalling adult Long-legged Buzzard (which see); (2) on upperwing,

pale bases to outer primaries form small light patch; (3) from below, primaries whiter, and (4) trailing edge to wing on adults black and more prominent; (5) rufous morph and dark morph both frequently have underbody uniform, or almost so, lacking obvious pale breast-band.

VOICE Highly vocal for a bird of prey, especially in spring. Main call a loud, mewing 'piiiyay', falling in pitch (and skilfully mimicked by Jay!); given mainly in flight. Begging call of fledged young similar but drawn out and with tremolo, and more whining in tone.

(European) **Honey Buzzard** *Pernis apivorus*   mB5

L 52–59 cm, WS 113–135 cm. Summer visitor (late Apr/May–late Aug/Sep), wintering in tropical Africa. Breeds in forests with clearings, glades, small wetlands, fields. In Britain, rare away from few breeding sites (only *c.* 15 in all). Food mainly larvae and nests of wasps, which are dug out from the ground, also reptiles, amphibians, nestlings of small birds, worms, etc. Nest in tall tree, lined with fresh leaves during breeding.

IDENTIFICATION Slightly larger and more *long-winged* than Common Buzzard, but at distance easily confused with it. At closer range, several finer points of distinction: *neck slim* and *head held forward* in flight in Cuckoo fashion; *tail rather long, about as long as width of wing, sides slightly convex and corners rounded*; head-on silhouette in glide with *smoothly downcurved wings*, unlike Common Buzzard in lacking obvious bend at carpal joints; soars on flattish wings; *active flight with slower, more elastic wingbeats*. Plumage variable, incl. dark, medium, pale and rufous morphs both as adults and as juveniles. Adults usually distinctive, but juveniles much more similar to Common Buzzard. – Adult ♂: Ample 'hand' and rather long tail. *Only tips of longest primaries black, sharply set off*; prominent black trailing edge to wing; *long step to next dark bar across pale grey flight-feathers*; tail similar, *prominent dark end-band and long step to inner one or two narrower dark bars at base*; head largely blue-grey; *upperparts brown-grey, with black bars of underside visible above as well*; cere grey, eye yellow. – Adult ♀: Differs from adult ♂ in having slightly *more extensive dark on 'fingers', diffusely set off; shorter step between dark bars at end and base of tail- and flight-feathers, showing more bars*; secondaries often dusky; no or rather little blue-grey on head; *upperparts dark brown, hardly showing any bars*. – Juvenile: Slightly shorter inner primaries and sometimes shorter tail, giving *more Common Buzzard-like silhouette*; wing-tips more extensively dark, as on Common Buzzard; *flight-feathers more densely barred than on adult* (4–5 bars instead of 2–3), recalling juvenile Common Buzzard (but latter has *c.* 6); *secondaries and tail often darkish, with 4 or 5 evenly spaced bars*; cere yellow, eye dark. Dark morph (fairly common) uniformly dark brown on underbody, *lacking pale breast-band* of most Common Buzzards (ssp. *buteo*); lightest part on inner underwing is greater coverts (bases of secondaries on Common Buzzard). Pale and medium morphs often coarsely *streaked on breast/belly*, not cross-barred as most adults.

VOICE Silent except in breeding season. Main call a plaintive whistling '**pee**e-lu' or 'glü-**i**-yü', at times recalling Grey Plover in general structure. Near nest an odd, mechanical, rapidly ticking call as from a distant mowing-machine.

Common Buzzard

Honey Buzzard

COMMON BUZZARD

quietly watching for voles from fence post

Honey   Marsh Harrier   Common Buzzard

compare silhouettes – Common Buzzard is more compact

young are streaked below

juv.

extremely light variant

paler breast, finely barred

juv.   **ad.**

ad. (dark)

juv. (light)

black 'comma'

lacks broad terminal band

juv. (light)   **juv.** (medium)

vulpinus ('Steppe Buzzard') (E Europe, Asia)

pale rufous

(dark)

(medium)   (rufous)

head-on silhouette

gliding

short-winged and compact in flight, fairly quick wingbeats

broad black terminal band

pale band
pale breast

ad. (medium)   **ad.** (dark)

HONEY BUZZARD

dark eye   yellow cere

juv. (dark)

yellow eye   dark

ad. ♂

♀ gliding

♂

dark 'mask'

convex side

juv. (light)

rounded corners

juv. (rufous)

dark wing-tip

sparsely but evenly barred

lacks pale breast-band

juv. (dark)

juv.   **ad. ♀**   **ad. ♂**

more bars than on ad. ♂

dusky 'fingers' on ♀

ad. ♀ (dark)   **ad. ♀** (common)

smoothly downcurved wings in head-on silhouette

appearing long-winged when gliding

only 'fingertips' black on ♂

translucent primary base

ad. ♂ (dark)

typically well-spaced barring

dark carpal patch

ad. ♂ (common)   **ad. ♂** (light)

DZ

(Eurasian) **Sparrowhawk** *Accipiter nisus* r**B**3

L ♂ 29–34 cm, ♀ 35–41 cm, WS ♂ 58–65 cm, ♀ 67–80 cm. Breeds in forests, also near human settlements; sometimes in dense parts of large parks. Food small birds. Nest in tree, often 6–12 m up, newly built each year.

IDENTIFICATION Small raptor with rather short, broad, blunt-tipped wings and long tail. *Tail* always *longer than width of wing* and *has 4–5 bars, also on central tail-feathers* (though often indistinct on ad. ♂). Flight characteristic, a few quick wingbeats relieved by a short glide, *pigeon-quick wingbeats* making the bird ascend, and brief glides descend, thus *flightpath slightly undulating*, not so steady as that of Goshawk. ♀ could be confused with ♂ Goshawk (as size difference not always obvious) but, apart from quicker wingbeats and lighter, more undulating flight, the flight silhouette is slightly different, with *narrower tail-base, sharper corners to squarer tail, proportionately shorter inner wing and larger head, shorter neck and slimmer body*. Often flies low over ground making surprise attacks; can even pursue small birds on foot under bushes; does not shun urban areas and gardens (as Goshawk normally does). Perched birds (upright stance) identified by *comparatively small bill, thin legs and slim lower body*. – Adult ♂: Small; slate-grey upperparts, often tinged bluish; rufous cheeks; barring on breast and belly is rufous (rarely brown-grey like ♀). – Adult ♀: Larger than ♂, with steadier flight; slate-grey upperparts; barring below is brown-grey (rarely faintly tinged rufous, and then similar to the least rufous ♂♂). – Juvenile: Dark brown upperparts, *feathers of forewing edged rufous*, visible at close range. Barring of underparts often coarse, broken up and irregular on breast.

VOICE Mainly silent outside breeding season. Main call rapid chattering or cackling 'kewkewkewkewkew...', with minor variations used for contact, display, and alarm. Food-call of ♀ a thin wailing '**pii-ih**'.

Levant Sparrowhawk *Accipiter brevipes* —

L 30–37 cm, WS 63–76 cm. Summer visitor (Apr–Sep), winters in Africa. Breeds in forests, also undisturbed copses, orchards. Food lizards, large insects, small birds. Nest in tree, often 5–10 m up, lined with green leaves.

IDENTIFICATION Resembles Sparrowhawk, but sexes more similar in size, *wings narrower and more pointed, tail slightly shorter*, giving almost falcon-like silhouette when gliding, but action hawk-like. *Dark wing-tips above and below* characteristic (esp. on ♂, less so on juv.), as are *unbarred central tail-feathers*. *Thin dark central line on throat* of adult ♀ and juvenile characteristic (when seen). At close range, *dark eye* of adults and *grey cheeks of ♂* are useful points. Underwing appears whitish on adults (but is finely barred rufous). Habit

of migrating in dense, at times large flocks separates it from Sparrowhawk. – Adult ♂: Blue-grey above, with marked blackish wing-tips. – Adult ♀: Slate-grey above, with slightly darker wing-tips; somewhat larger than ♂; often a faint throat-line. – Juvenile: Dark brown above with somewhat darker wing-tips. Underside streaked or blotched dark. Throat-line well marked.

VOICE Characteristic, shrill, clear 'kee-wick', often repeated a few times.

(Northern) **Goshawk** *Accipiter gentilis* r**B**4

L ♂ 49–56 cm, ♀ 58–64 cm, WS ♂ 93–105 cm, ♀ 108–127 cm. Breeds in forests. In Britain rare (about 250–300 pairs). Food birds and mammals, up to size of Pheasant and hare. Nest in tree, bulky, about 10–16 m up, often re-used.

IDENTIFICATION Medium-large, strong raptor, broad-winged and long-tailed. Marked sexual size difference, wingspan of ♂ similar to Carrion Crow, of ♀ to Common Buzzard. Usually seen flying at treetop level, a few *relaxed wingbeats* (slower pace than Jackdaw) relieved by short *straight glide* (unlike Sparrowhawk, does not lose height when gliding). Often soars or sits watching, body erect, showing *strong lower body* ('hip-heavy') *and tarsi/toes*. Adult ♂ confusable with ♀ Sparrowhawk despite larger size; note somewhat slower wingbeats, *proportionately longer and more pointed wings, rounded tail-corners, broader tail-base*, and *slightly longer neck*. – Adult: Bluish- (♂) or slate-grey (♀) above; whitish below, barred grey. Supercilium white. – Juvenile: Brown above; *buff-white below, coarsely streaked brown* ('armpits' blotched, can look 'chequered' below in flight).

VOICE Mainly silent outside breeding season. Calls, heard mostly at dawn, much as Sparrowhawk's but distinctly louder, lower-pitched and more fierce, and cackling slower, 'kya-kya-kya-kya-...'. Begging-call of ♀ and young a wild, melancholy 'piii-lih'.

Dark Chanting Goshawk *Melierax metabates* —

L 39–47 cm, WS 85–105 cm. Local in Morocco (main distribution south of Sahara), breeding in open parkland, semi-deserts and scrub. Nests in dense tree.

IDENTIFICATION Like a mixture of ♂ Goshawk and ♂ Hen Harrier, broad-winged with fairly long tail, *blue-grey* (belly and underwing finely barred white), with *dark iris, red feet and cere; wing-tips and central uppertail black*. Juvenile brown, breast streaked, belly coarsely barred dark; on flying bird, note *pale rump*. Iris, feet and cere yellow. Rather long-legged. *Accipiter*-like habits.

VOICE Vocal during breeding season. Series of loud, clear whistling notes, 'pee-pee-pee-...'. Alarm a rapid cackling 'klew-klew-klew-...'.

Sparrowhawk   Levant Sparrowhawk   Goshawk   Dark Chanting Goshawk

SPARROWHAWK

Kestrel
Sparrow-hawk

Goshawk
Sparrow-hawk

long 'arm'

'fat-bellied'
long neck

long, narrow 'hand'

juv.

blunt

banded

ad. ♂

plain grey wing-tip

coarsely barred

light eye

rufous cheek

ad. ♀

ad. ♂

juv.

ad. ♂

sparse bands

ad. ♀

sharp corners

Sparrowhawk

ad. ♀

'knitting-needle thin' tarsi

LEVANT SPARROWHAWK

pointed

diffusely barred

ad. ♂

black tip

juv.

black tip

ad. ♀

boldly streaked

very pale

throat-line

ad. ♂

dark eye

grey cheek

juv.

rather dense bars

ad. ♀

ad. ♂

GOSHAWK

round corners

Goshawk

long-necked

juv.

streaked

juv.

ad. ♀

orange eye

'hip-heavy'

ad. ♂

juv. ♀

very strong tarsi

ad.

ad. ♂

DARK CHANTING GOSHAWK

watches from exposed perch (unlike *Accipiter* hawks)

broad wing-tip

ad.

yellow eye

dark eye

ad.

red

juv.

red

long-legged!

ad.

FALCONS *Falconidae*
Small to medium-sized raptors, wings rather pointed, flight agile and quick, most take their prey in air. Bill has blunt 'tooth' on cutting edges of upper mandible.

(Common) Kestrel *Falco tinnunculus* r(m)**B**3

L 31–37 cm, WS 68–78 cm. Found in open country, on plains, by airfields, motorways, arable fields, heaths and marshes interspersed with woods or copses, also lower fells up to birch and willow zones. Food voles, insects. Nests in tree, often in old nest of corvid; or building, in hole or niche.

IDENTIFICATION Medium-sized falcon with *long wings and tail*, wings rather narrow at base and slightly blunt at tips when spread. *Hovers frequently* with hanging tail spread like a fan. Active flight with *rather looser* (relaxed, mechanical) *wingbeats* than other falcons. General shape at times recalls Sparrowhawk, but confusion prevented by *continuous flight with much less gliding*, by narrower wings which are held more straight out (Sparrowhawk has somewhat flexed wings at carpals, with projecting wing-bend), and plumage: *back and upperwing-coverts reddish-brown, contrasting with darker flight-feathers*. – Adult ♂: Rump and uppertail *unbarred blue-grey*, tail with wide dark terminal band; head greyish, finely streaked; back and upperwing-coverts *deep chestnut with small black spots*. – 1st-summer ♂: Some are distinguished by obvious dark barring of rump and uppertail. – Adult ♀: Rump and uppertail *brown, finely barred dark*, terminal tail-band somewhat broader; head brownish, distinctly streaked; upperparts warm brown, *less reddish than* ♂, barred dark rather than spotted. (Rarely, head, rump and inner tail are greyish, but *tail* virtually *always barred*.) – Juvenile: Similar to adult ♀ but more yellowish red-brown above, and breast more boldly and diffusely streaked; a *hint of a pale band along upper primary coverts* often visible. A few ♂♂ have (barred) blue-grey rump and uppertail.

VOICE Main call a fast series of short, sharp notes, 'kee-kee-kee-kee-...', rather shorter than Hobby and Merlin calls. Young and ♀ beg with whining, vibrant trills, 'keerrrl...', repeated a few times.

Lesser Kestrel *Falco naumanni* V***

L 27–33 cm, WS 63–72 cm. Mainly summer visitor (Mar–Sep). Breeds *colonially* in towns, steep cliffs, ruins, etc., usually at low level. Social also on migration. Rare vagrant to Britain & Ireland. Food insects, caught on ground (frequently walks briefly on ground between dives, like Red-footed Falcon) or in the air. Nests in niche or hole in building, on cliff-ledge; scrape, no material.

IDENTIFICATION Small, elegant falcon, very similar to Kestrel but separated by *diagnostic call* (see below) and *slightly*

shorter wings and tail, which when fully spread are broader. On a windy day, still looks elegant, with pointed wings, narrow tail and *quick wingbeats*. Slightly elongated central tail-feathers on some (only exceptionally so on Kestrel). *Claws pale* (Kestrel: dark). – Adult ♂: Similar to Kestrel but *lacks black spots on upperparts*, and has a narrow *bluish wing-panel above* between chestnut forewing and dark flight-feathers. Head blue, with *no dark moustachial stripe* as on Kestrel (but shadow can create this effect). *Underwing* more *whitish* with *darker wing-tip* than on Kestrel (but some are more similar to Kestrel). Spots on underparts smaller and rounder than on Kestrel, and *breast* often *darker rufous-buff* (tinged vinous). – 1st-summer ♂: Very Kestrel-like, as *blue-grey on upperwing is missing*, and *dark spots are present on chestnut upperparts* (on coverts and tertials). Often only central tail-feathers of adult type, rest barred. No real dark moustaches. – Adult ♀/Juvenile: Similar to Kestrel, and often inseparable by plumage alone. On average paler under-wing and underbody, and finer moustachial stripe and streaks on underparts. Often slightly paler cheek patch than on Kestrel, too, reaching up behind eye, giving 'kinder' expression. (Blue-grey rump/uppertail is not a clue.)

VOICE Diagnostic contact-call trisyllabic, hoarse, rather high-pitched, rasping 'chay-chay-chay' (tone recalls Grey Partridge), often in chorus in colonies. Also Kestrel-like series of short notes, though faster and more chattering. Begging-call is very like Kestrel's, a vibrant 'keerrrl...'.

Red-footed Falcon *Falco vespertinus* V*

L 28–34 cm, WS 65–76 cm. Summer visitor (Apr–Sep), winters in Africa. Vagrant to Britain & Ireland, usually about 5–10 annually. Breeds colonially, rarely singly, in open country with stands of trees, on steppe, by meadows and in open river valleys. Food mainly insects. Nests in old nest of corvid, often in rookery; may breed among Rooks.

IDENTIFICATION Medium-small falcon, *silhouette recalling both Kestrel and Hobby* depending on how long tail length is perceived. *Active flight* often Kestrel-like *with rather loose wingbeats*, but habit of *catching insects in flight* strongly recalls Hobby. *Often hovers, alights on ground, walks, hovers again*, etc. – Adult ♂: Unique combination of *dark blue-grey body and coverts, dull red 'trousers' and undertail*, and *pale silvery-grey flight-feathers*. Cere and feet are deep orange. – 1st-summer ♂: Variable amount of blue-grey in plumage, but invariably *underwing is barred* as on juvenile, and *under-body at least partly rufous*. – Adult ♀: *Virtually unstreaked* pale rufous-buff *underparts*; *back slate-grey, barred dark*; head yellowish-white; feet and cere orange. – Juvenile: Underparts rich buff, *streaked dark*; short, dark moustachial stripe and mark through eye; *underwing has prominent dark trailing edge*; cere and feet yellow.

VOICE Vocal in breeding season and at roosts. Chattering calls, 'kekekeke...', ♂ generally faster and higher-pitched than ♀. Flight-call of ♂ resembles similar call of Hobby, a whining 'kew kew kew kew...'.

Kestrel

Lesser Kestrel

Red-footed Falcon

KESTREL

dark moustachial stripe

bold, dense spotting

black claws

ad. ♀

ad. ♀

ad. ♀

ad. ♂

black spots

watching for voles while hovering, or from perch

at times confusingly rounded wing-tips

ad. ♂

LESSER KESTREL

plain grey cheek

small, sparse, rounded spots

pale claws

ad. ♀

ad. ♂

ad. ♀

1st-s. ♂

ad. ♂

unmarked red-brown

blue-grey panel

pale

deep rufous-buff

ad. ♀

ad. ♂

RED-FOOTED FALCON

brown with a tinge of grey

streaked

blue-grey, barred

rufous-buff

ad. ♀

juv.

ad. ♂

red

often briefly alights on ground while chasing insects

rufous-buff

ad. ♀

silvery-grey primaries above

ad. ♂

dark trailing edge

juv.

juv.

1st-summer ♂

1st-summer ♂

2nd-winter ♂ (Sep)

mixture of old and new flight-feathers

amount of blue-grey varies individually

ad. ♀

dark outer wing from below

ad. ♂

DZ

(Eurasian) **Hobby** *Falco subbuteo* m**B**4

L 29–35 cm, WS 70–84 cm. Summer visitor (Apr/May–Sep), winters in Africa. Breeds in variety of habitats: arable land with lakes and woods; bogs and rivers in taiga; mountain forests. In Britain < 500 pairs. Food insects and birds, caught in the air by supreme velocity in chase or stoop. Nests in tree, using abandoned nest of other bird, often crow.

IDENTIFICATION Medium-sized, elegant falcon with *long, pointed wings* and *medium-length, square-cut tail*. *Dashing flight*, and ability to catch birds in the air (incl. Swallows and even Swifts) generally causes alarm when Hobby appears; often seen in low, fast flight over reedbeds or marshes, *wingbeats powerful, somewhat spaced, clipping*. When catching dragonflies at the height of summer flight is more relaxed, with short accelerations and turns; prey then eaten in the air during brief glide. Silhouette often typical, with quite pointed wings when *long primaries* are flexed back, but at times wing-tips appear more blunt, recalling Red-footed Falcon (which has only a trifle longer tail and shorter wings, and thus might be mistaken for a Hobby at a distance). At normal range, adult looks *dark grey above* and *darkish below with white throat*; at closer range *rusty-red 'trousers' and vent* show, as does bold streaking of breast and belly, and black moustachial stripe. In the Mediterranean area, Eleonora's Falcon is a potential confusion risk, too, but is slightly larger and has proportionately somewhat longer tail. Also, Hobby has more uniform wings and tail below. – Juvenile: Differs from adult in lack of red 'trousers' and vent (still lacking in 1st summer), having pale tips to upper primary and greater coverts, paler forehead, browner cast on upperparts, and yellowish-buff (instead of whitish) underparts.

VOICE Main call a scolding 'kew-kew-kew-kew-...', not unlike song of Wryneck but with less whining, pleading ring; considerable variations in tempo. Also, repeated, agitated, sharp 'kit-chic' from both sexes in air; single sharp 'kit'. Begging-call drawn-out, urging 'peee-eh', recalling Merlin (but different from vibrant trill of Kestrel).

Eleonora's Falcon *Falco eleonorae* **V*****

L 36–42 cm, WS 87–104 cm. Summer visitor (late Apr/May–Oct), winters in Africa. In Britain, vagrant twice. Breeds colonially on mainly Mediterranean islands and coastal cliffs. Breeding postponed until late summer–autumn to coincide with autumn migration of small passerines, which are caught over sea. Food small birds. Nests on cliff-ledge or in rock crevice.

IDENTIFICATION Medium-large, with *long, comparatively narrow wings, long tail and rather slim body*. Like a large Hobby or slim ♂ Peregrine, but separated from both by longer tail and from the latter by proportionately longer and narrower wings. However, the difference does not always appear significant, e.g. at long range or from tricky angles, and it is unwise invariably to expect immediate recognition by silhouette alone; a prolonged and more all-embracing observation, or closer range, will be conclusive, though. *Flight relaxed, with soft but forceful wingbeats* (recalling a skua *Stercorarius*!), but very quick in pursuit-flight. Spends much time gliding on flattish wings, looking out for prey over the sea. – Adult, light morph: In plumage resembles juvenile Hobby, but separated by *contrast between very dark underwing-coverts and paler grey bases to flight-feathers*; also, *underbody is deeper rufous-buff or rusty-brown* (not buff-white). – Adult, dark morph: Entirely dark brownish-black but, just as light morph, shows contrast between blackish underwing-coverts and somewhat paler bases to flight-feathers. – Juvenile: Rather similar to juvenile Hobby, but distinguished by silhouette, size, and *paler bases to barred flight-feathers below, contrasting with dark wing-tip and wing-coverts*. Rich buff below, finely streaked dark. Throat buffish, not so white as on Hobby.

VOICE Main call a nasal, somewhat grating 'kyeh kyeh kyeh kyah'. Various sharp notes as alarm in vicinity of nest, e.g. 'kak kak' and 'kekekeke...'.

Sooty Falcon *Falco concolor* —

L 32–37 cm, WS 78–90 cm. Summer visitor to extreme SE corner of range (Israel, Egypt, Red Sea) in (Apr) May–Nov; winters in E Africa. Breeds in lower mountains or on cliffs in deserts and on coral islands and coastal cliffs. Habits much as those of Eleonora's Falcon. Food small birds, in winter insects, too. Nests on cliff-ledge or in rock crevice.

IDENTIFICATION Medium-sized, *slightly larger than Hobby*, which it otherwise resembles in silhouette, and is somewhat smaller than Eleonora's Falcon. *Head proportionately larger than Eleonora's, and tail shorter*. Yellow cere generally more prominent than on adult Eleonora's. *Uniform bluish-grey plumage of adult* is unique—dark-morph Eleonora's has blackish underwing-coverts contrasting with paler bases to flight-feathers (Sooty uniform); and adult ♂ Red-footed Falcon has silvery-grey primaries, paler than blue-grey body, and has dull dark red 'trousers' and vent (lacking on Sooty). Darkness of adults varies from rather pale blue-grey (paler than any Eleonora's) to dark, blackish lead-grey, extremes bridged by intermediates. ♂♂ apparently more frequently pale, but plumage-wear and age might also play a part. – Juvenile: Resembles both juvenile Hobby and juvenile Eleonora's (also, juv. Red-footed Falcon; p. 94). Distinguished, apart from by size and silhouette, by *broad dark trailing edge to undertail and underwing* (unlike Hobby) and lack of contrastingly dark underwing-coverts (unlike Eleonora's); *dark and unbarred central tail-feathers* (visible from below as well) which are somewhat longer than rest, giving *slightly wedge-shaped tail*; and tendency towards *dark breast-band*.

VOICE Little known. Some calls resemble Kestrel's but are slower and coarser.

Hobby   Eleonora's Falcon   Sooty Falcon

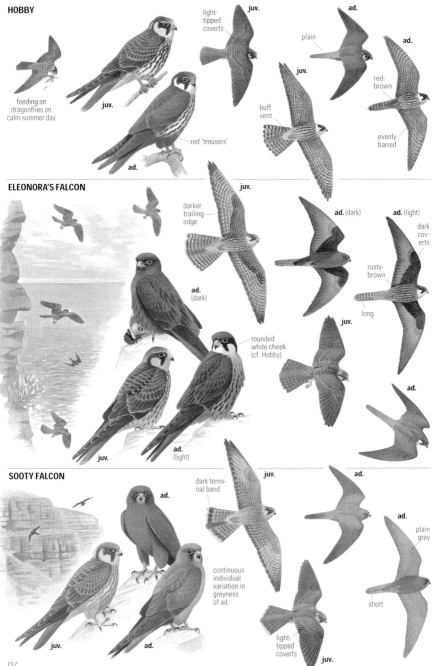

HOBBY

feeding on dragonflies on calm summer day

juv.

light-tipped coverts

ad.

plain

red-brown

juv.

buff vent

evenly barred

juv.

red 'trousers'

ad.

ELEONORA'S FALCON

juv.

darker trailing edge

ad. (dark)

ad. (dark)

ad. (light)

dark coverts

rusty-brown

long

ad.

rounded white cheek (cf. Hobby)

juv.

juv.

ad. (light)

SOOTY FALCON

ad.

dark terminal band

juv.

ad.

ad.

plain grey

continuous individual variation in greyness of ad.

short

light-tipped coverts

juv.

juv.

ad.

DZ

Peregrine Falcon *Falco peregrinus* rB4

L ♂ 38–45 cm, ♀ 46–51 cm, WS ♂ 89–100 cm, ♀ 104–113 cm. Circumpolar. Drastic decline owing to biocides and persecution in 1950s and 1960s, since when some recovery. Breeds on steep coastal cliffs or in mountains, also on cliffs in lowlands and on ground on open bogs in taiga. Migrant in north and east. Food small or medium-sized birds, caught in the air after quick horizontal pursuit or spectacular stoop from height with closed wings. Nests on cliff-ledge, rarely in old nest in tree or (esp. in northeastern taiga) on ground.

IDENTIFICATION Medium-sized to large; pronounced sexual size difference, ♀ larger. Strongest of falcons in relation to size, *bulky body, 'chest-heavy'. Wings pointed, 'arm' rather broad, tail medium-length*. In flight, wings are usually slightly flexed, *carpal bends showing well*. Active flight with fairly quick, rather shallow wingbeats, speed moderate. When prey spotted, wing action more determined, and speed suddenly increases. – Adult: *Slate-grey above, lower back/rump/uppertail-coverts paler blue-grey*. Underparts white, lower breast/belly finely barred, leaving cheeks/throat/upper breast plain white (most extensive white on ♂) and contrasting strongly with *black hood and broad, distinct moustachial stripe*. – Variation: Mediterranean ssp. *brookei* is slightly smaller, darker above, tinged rufous below, and has some rufous on nape (cf. Barbary Falcon). – Juvenile: Best recognized by prominently *streaked* (not cross-barred) *breast and belly*; further, *upperparts are brownish*, with thin pale fringes along tips of primary and greater coverts; cere and feet dull yellowish-green or bluish-green. Confusion is possible with dark juvenile Gyr Falcon (p. 100), but, apart from silhouette and, for ♂♂, size, the *moustachial stripe is more distinctly broad and black, and does not merge with streaked cheek; underwing uniformly greyish* (Gyr has contrastingly dark coverts); undertail-coverts barred or marked with wedge-shaped blotches (not streaked as on Gyr); colour of cere and feet differ on average, Gyr Falcon often having purer blue in 1st winter.

VOICE Mostly silent away from breeding site. Main call harsh cackling at medium pace, scolding and persistent, sometimes repeated at length, 'rehk rehk rehk rehk...', used as alarm and contact-call. Both sexes have a disyllabic, sharp 'ee-chip' during display, often in air. Begging-call a vibrant 'kyi-i-i-ih'.

Barbary Falcon *Falco (peregrinus) pelegrinoides* —

L ♂ 33–37 cm, ♀ 36–39 cm, WS ♂ 76–86 cm, ♀ 89–98 cm. Closely related to Peregrine Falcon (by many regarded as conspecific). Breeds in semi-desert with cliffs and smaller mountains, further E also in foothills and mountains. Food as that of Peregrine Falcon. Nests on cliff-ledge.

IDENTIFICATION Very much a smaller version of Peregrine, and at times difficult to identify reliably. In size, ♂ only marginally larger than Hobby (but bulkier and 'chest-heavy', like Peregrine). In flight silhouette, 'arm' is fractionally narrower than on Peregrine. Owing to size, wingbeats on average slightly quicker in comparable situations. Identification based primarily on plumage. – Adult: Compared with Peregrine, *upperparts are paler blue-grey; flight-feathers from below paler* with *darker wing-tips and rear edge of outer wing; underbody and underwing-coverts tinged rufous* (fresh) *or creamy* (bleached), but note that Peregrine of ssp. *brookei* has faint rufous tinge, too. Other criteria for Barbary are: *barring of underparts less extensive* (least barring on ♂); tendency to show *dark terminal band on undertail; hint of dark 'comma' below on tips of primary coverts; moustachial stripe narrower; nape rusty-red* (requires close range, and note that Peregrine ssp. *brookei* has rufous tinge on nape, too). – Juvenile: Resembles juvenile Peregrine, but *head is not so dark*, forehead, nape and supercilium being rufous-buff; *moustachial stripe narrower*; tendency to show *dark end-band on undertail*; and *streaking on underbody narrow* and concentrated into central area, *throat/upper breast and 'trousers'/lower belly almost unmarked buff-white*.

VOICE Like Peregrine's, but slightly more high-pitched.

Merlin *Falco columbarius* r+mB4 / W4

L 26–33 cm, WS 55–69 cm. Breeds mainly in birch and willow zones in fells, also on bogs in taiga and in open coastal areas and heathland. Migrant in north. Food mainly small birds, caught in the air after dashing horizontal chases or prolonged aerial pursuits. Nests in tree (in abandoned nest of crow or raptor), in scrub or on ground.

IDENTIFICATION Smallest falcon. Flight silhouette not unlike Peregrine, rather *'chest-heavy' with pointed 'hand', fairly broad 'arm' and medium-length tail*, and confusion for a brief moment actually possible when size not apparent. However, active flight with *much quicker wingbeats*. Hunts in low flight, at times with *thrush-like camouflage-flight* (gently bouncing, tendency for series of wingbeats relieved by fleeting close-winged glides), or in quick aerial pursuit. Very agile on wing. – Adult ♂: *Upperparts blue-grey with broad black terminal band*, primaries dark. *Breast rusty-yellow, finely streaked* dark, throat white. Rather indistinct narrow moustachial stripe. – Adult ♀: *Upperparts brown-grey, tail heavily barred dark* (c. 5 dense, broad bars, terminal only slightly wider). *Breast buff-white, boldly streaked dark*. Moustachial stripe rather narrow, not so distinct. – Juvenile: Very similar to adult ♀, and generally not separable in the field. On average richer brown above, without the greyish cast on back and tail apparent on many adult ♀♀. Primary coverts barred pale rufous (on ad. ♀ more uniform).

VOICE Silent except in nest area. Alarm quick accelerating series of sharp notes, 'kikikiki...', slightly higher-pitched and more rapid in ♂ than in ♀. Begging-call resembles Hobby's (even Curlew's), a plaintive 'pee-eh'.

Peregrine Falcon

Barbary Falcon

Merlin

PEREGRINE FALCON

juv.

Peregrine

Gyr

ad.

note darker wing-coverts and
broader wings of Gyr Falcon

paler
tail-base

juv.

ad.

variation

juv.

streaked

broad
mous-
tache

juv.

barred

pointed

ad.

dark
'hand'

BARBARY FALCON

evenly barred

darker
towards tip

LANNER
erlangeri

← compare →

ad.

ad.

rufous

small
mous-
tache

finely bar-
red

juv.

lightly
streaked

ad.

juv.

ad.

MERLIN

SPARROWHAWK (to compare)

dark marking on
cheek appears
as 'double
moustache'

wing-
and tail-
feathers
boldly
barred

chasing passerines

dark outer
wing

black termi-
nal band

juv.

♀

blue-
grey

orangey
hue

ad. ♂

♀

ad. ♂

ad. ♂

DZ

Gyr Falcon *Falco rusticolus* **V**∗∗
L 53–63 cm, WS 109–134 cm. Resident in mountains and tundra, preferring canyons in birch zone, or tundra with crags and patches of trees and scrub. Vagrant to Britain & Ireland, about 3–4 records annually. Food taken on ground or in air, birds (mainly Ptarmigan), lemmings and other small mammals. Nest on cliff-ledge, often revealed by abundance of yellowish-green lichens growing beneath on rock.

IDENTIFICATION Largest falcon, *wingspan as Common Buzzard. Wings broad, wing-tips rather rounded* for a falcon. *Tail slightly longer than on Peregrine Falcon*, the other large falcon within same range. Body weighty, as Peregrine's, but longer, and *base of tail broad* (undertail-coverts bulky, as on Goshawk). Flight similar to Peregrine, but owing to larger size and *slightly longer 'arm'* more stable, with *somewhat slower and more shallow, elastic wingbeats.* Aerial hunts mainly by horizontal pursuit, often low over ground; ♂ and ♀ can co-operate to exhaust prey; only rarely stoops from height like Peregrine; prey often taken on ground. Plumage variation basically geographical, but overlap and variation substantial: attractive white morph (predominating Greenland, also occurring Siberia) is *white with dark wing-tips* and some dark spotting; light grey morph (Iceland) is pale grey with whitish barring; dark grey morph (Fenno-Scandia, Russia) is medium grey with pale grey barring. Last two have *narrow and indistinct moustachial stripe, pale supercilium,* and *finely streaked or dusky cheeks.* – Adult, grey morphs: Cere and feet are yellow; upperparts greyish (or greyish-brown), barred or spotted pale ash-grey; underparts rather finely spotted and streaked dark, some cross-barring on flanks and 'trousers' on most. – *Juvenile: Cere and feet bluish* (at least through 1st winter); upperparts are dark brown-grey, with very little or no pale barring or spotting except on tail; *underparts boldly streaked dark*, no barring.

VOICE Has a loud, hoarse rasping or harsh cackling, 'wray (-eh) wray(-eh) wray(-eh)…', pace slower, voice gruffer and individual notes more clearly disyllabic than Peregrine's.

Saker Falcon *Falco cherrug* **[V**∗∗∗**]**
L 47–55 cm, WS 105–129 cm. Breeds in wooded steppe, by grassland close to foothills or forests, in gallery forests along rivers in open country. Partial migrant. Food rodents (susliks, voles), also birds. Nests on cliff-ledge or in old stick nest in tree, often in heronry. Rare (only *c.* 600 pairs in Europe).

IDENTIFICATION *Large*, almost as Gyr Falcon, and resembles that in flight silhouette, with *rather broad wings with blunt tips.* Separated with practice by slightly narrower wings and slimmer base of tail and 'hips', but as a rule necessary to consider plumage characters as well. – Adult, normal: Most birds distinguished from similar Lanner by *tawny-brown back and inner wing, contrasting with darker grey flight-feathers* almost as on ♀ Kestrel (Lanner usually slate-grey with darker flight-feathers, like ♀ Red-footed). *Head usually rather pale brown*, with *whitish supercilium* (absent on Lanner, or rufous-buff and indistinct), *crown finely streaked* (lacking dark forecrown and rufous nape of Lanner), *moustachial stripe narrow*, indistinct on many, more prominent on some; *some look almost white-headed at distance. Uppertail often looks uniform brown* when folded, but variable amount of buff bars present on outer or all tail-feathers (Lanner on average more prominently and more completely barred, but much overlap makes this character unreliable). (Caution: Young Lanners in N Africa and Middle East are cinnamon-brown above, often have very pale head, and unbarred uppertail!) Underparts usually prominently *streaked from lower throat and down, often boldly on flanks*, and often *'trousers' are all dark* (Lanner is more finely spotted on breast, and has cross-bars on flanks and 'trousers'). Underwing similar to Lanner, with more or less contrasting dark underwing-coverts forming a *dark forewing* (unlike Peregrine and Barbary). – Adult, grey morph ('saceroides'; very rare in Europe): Upperparts greyish and barred, much resembling Lanner, possibly told by size, shape, and head pattern. – Juvenile: Very similar to adult; *upperparts tawny earth-brown, underparts boldly streaked*; head on average darker than on adult but with more distinct white supercilium. Difficult to distinguish by plumage from juvenile Lanner, but *'trousers' often all dark* (almost like Rough-legged Buzzard), and *upperparts slightly paler with a tawny tinge* compared with European juvenile Lanners. Cere and feet dull grey-green, or grey tinged bluish-green.

VOICE Rather similar to Peregrine Falcon's, though somewhat slower and more whining, less hoarse.

Lanner Falcon *Falco biarmicus* —
L 43–50 cm, WS 95–105 cm. Resident in desert, arid steppe, lower mountains. Food mainly small and medium-sized birds, caught in the air by fast stoop or chase; ♂ and ♀ often co-operate when hunting. Nests on cliff-ledge, rarely in tree, using old stick nest. Rare (only *c.* 300 pairs in Europe).

IDENTIFICATION Slightly smaller than Saker, with *somewhat narrower wings and tail* (like a short-tailed Kestrel in silhouette). – Adult: *Upperparts slate-grey or brownish-grey, barred dark* (European ssp. *feldeggii*), or ground colour paler bluish-grey (N African ssp. *erlangeri*), not cinnamon-brown as most Sakers. *Underparts less streaked* than Saker, more finely *spotted*, and *are cross-barred on flanks/'trousers'. Tendency towards dark forecrown-band. Nape and supercilium* (if present) *pale chestnut.* Blackish moustachial stripe prominent but narrow. (For further distinctions, cf. Saker.) – Juvenile: Very similar to both adult and juvenile Saker, but the *'trousers' are streaked, never all dark. Upperparts* either *very dark* on mantle (Europe), or paler, warmer brown (N Africa, Middle East) like many Sakers.

VOICE Resembles that of Gyr Falcon, but is less loud.

Gyr Falcon

Saker Falcon

Lanner Falcon

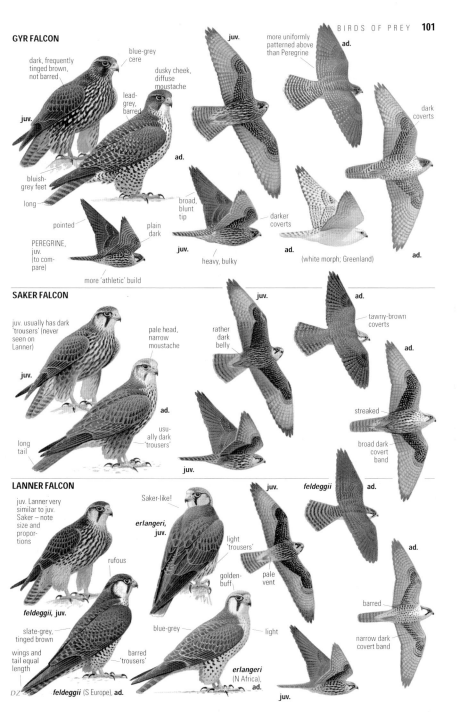

GYR FALCON

dark, frequently tinged brown, not barred

blue-grey cere

dusky cheek, diffuse moustache

lead-grey, barred

juv.

bluish-grey feet

long

pointed

juv.

PEREGRINE, juv. (to compare)

more 'athletic' build

plain dark

juv.

more uniformly patterned above than Peregrine

ad.

dark coverts

broad, blunt tip

darker coverts

heavy, bulky

ad.

(white morph; Greenland)

ad.

SAKER FALCON

juv. usually has dark 'trousers' (never seen on Lanner)

pale head, narrow moustache

juv.

rather dark belly

juv.

ad.

tawny-brown coverts

ad.

usually dark 'trousers'

long tail

juv.

ad.

streaked

broad dark covert band

LANNER FALCON

juv. Lanner very similar to juv. Saker – note size and proportions

Saker-like!

erlangeri, juv.

rufous

juv.

feldeggii

ad.

ad.

light 'trousers'

pale vent

golden-buff

***feldeggii*, juv.**

slate-grey, tinged brown

wings and tail equal length

DZ

feldeggii (S Europe), **ad.**

barred 'trousers'

blue-grey

light

erlangeri (N Africa), **ad.**

barred

narrow dark covert band

juv.

GROUSE *Tetraonidae*
Medium-sized to large, sturdy and thickset, non-migratory birds of mountain slopes and boreal forests. Spend much time on ground. Feathered nostrils, strong completely or partly feathered feet and lack of spurs are common features, as are rounded wings with stiff, downcurved primaries and, in flight, noisy, rapid bursts of wingbeats interrupted by glides. Mainly vegetarians, but take insects in summer. Nest on ground. Young precocial, already capable of short flights after 1–2 weeks; tended solely or primarily by ♀.

Willow Grouse *Lagopus l. lagopus* —
L 35–43 cm. Sedentary in boreal forests, preferably birch (but also found in coniferous and willow), and on tundra with willows, dwarf birch, heather, etc. In winter often at lower altitudes and in more sheltered habitats, coniferous and denser birch forests.
  IDENTIFICATION The two *Lagopus* species are very similar, best separated by calls, fine details in plumage, size of bill, and choice of habitat. With the exception of Red Grouse (the Willow Grouse race of the British Isles; see below), they are told from other grouse by largely *white wings* all through the year. Rounded body, smallish head, feathered toes and short tail are other characteristics. In winter, almost completely white, in summer mainly rufous-, tawny- or greyish-brown. Basically, ♂ has three plumages, ♀ two. – Adult ♂ spring (*c.*Mar–early Jun): *Head, neck and upper breast deep rufous* or chestnut-red, *almost uniform* without much barring; *belly* and parts of flanks and back *white*, white gradually reduced, partly replaced by brown; upperparts black with brown barring. – Adult ♂ summer (Jun–Sep): Gradually acquires *barring on head, neck and upper breast*, and more *ochrous and tawny colours*, less rufous. – Adult ♀ breeding (–Sep): Similar to summer ♂, but plumage on average tawnier, less rufous, and more obviously barred buff and black. – Winter (Nov–Mar): From Sep, slowly attaining nearly *all-white plumage* (except for black tail); told from Ptarmigan by invariably *white lores*, not black, and slightly larger size (esp. ♂♂); habitat also good (though not infallible) clue, Willow Grouse preferring cover in birch and coniferous forests, rarely entering willow and alpine zones in winter. When seen close, note that the *bill is heavier* than Ptarmigan's (and claws on average paler).
  VOICE Main call (with function of song) from perched cock during spring nights is an accelerating series of loud, nasal, bouncing barks, ending in a trill, 'kau, kau kau-ka-ka-kakarrrrrrr'. Alternative call, uttered partly in flight, is 'ke-u, ke-kerrrrr-ke-kerr ehe ehe ehe', slowing down at end and often followed (or preceded) by a few 'kowah' ('go back!'). ♀ call 'njau' (clever mimic will attract ♂♂).

Red Grouse *Lagopus lagopus scoticus* r**B**2
L 33–38 cm. A local race of Willow Grouse. Sedentary on heather moors and in highlands of N and W Britain and in Ireland, largely avoiding forests.
  IDENTIFICATION Shape and habits as Willow Grouse, differing in summer in *dark, not white, wings* and, especially ♂♂, in darker plumage overall; striking difference in winter, when *no white plumage* is adopted. In *all plumages basically dark brown with reddish tinge*, ♂ always more uniform and darker and deeper rufous, ♀ paler and with ochrous edges or bars. Sexing possible when breeding pair seen together; often more difficult when single birds are encountered.
  VOICE Identical to that of Willow Grouse.

(Rock) Ptarmigan *Lagopus mutus* r**B**3
L 31–35 cm. Breeds on mountainsides and tundra, barren and rocky terrain with only little vegetation. Sedentary, but in winter sometimes in more sheltered habitats, e.g. in willow scrub and open birch forests at upper tree-limit.
  IDENTIFICATION Slightly *smaller* than Willow Grouse but very similar in shape, with rounded body and smallish head; toes feathered. In winter, nearly all white with short, black tail. In summer, brown colours are more grey-tinged than rufous, making it reasonably distinctive if seen well. – Adult ♂ spring (May–Jun [Jul]): *Head, neck and upper breast* and parts of flanks and back *dark grey-brown and black, finely vermiculated* black and edged or barred buff and white, giving a mainly *dark grey general impression* in the field (Willow Grouse deep red-brown and hardly barred at all); *lores blackish; belly, wings and parts of flanks white*. – Adult ♂ summer (Jul–Sep [Nov]): As in spring, but colour *paler grey*, less dark brown-grey; *sparse black patches on back* typical; lores brown, speckled white. Paler than Willow Grouse at same time of year, lacking rufous tinge. – Adult ♀ spring–summer: Differs from ♂ in having more *coarsely barred plumage* with *more yellowish tinge*, dark brown and black, barred and spotted yellowish-buff and off-white. Lores rather pale. Compared with Willow Grouse, *throat and sides of head are a little darker and more greyish* (not tinged buff and ochrous, respectively). – Winter: Plumage *all white*, except for black tail and *black loral stripe on all* ♂♂ and, thinly, on some ♀♀; most ♀♀ have white lores (and may therefore be difficult to distinguish from Willow Grouse). When seen close, note that the *bill is smaller* than on Willow Grouse (and claws are on average darker). Generally forms large flocks in winter, keeping on open mountainsides or in scrub and heather rather than in forests (cf. Willow Grouse).
  VOICE Rather less vocal than Willow Grouse, but far from mute (in spite of scientific name)! All calls rather similar, mostly low belching or dry, snoring sounds. Actually only one call typical, an almost Garganey-like creaking with characteristic rhythm, 'arr orr ka-**karr**' ('here comes the bride'; sometimes only two or three syllables); appears to have song function (but at times given by ♀, too), mostly delivered from ground in spring, sometimes when flushed. A related shorter 'urr-errr' has been described as 'perch-song'. In song-flight in early spring, ♂ gives a belching sound while descending on stiff wings, ending in a cackle, 'ahrrrr-ka-ka-ka-ka-ka-ka'. Alarm or aggression shown by a 'kwa' and variations. Call of ♀ a soft 'kee-a'.

Willow Grouse / Red Grouse

Ptarmigan

WILLOW GROUSE

juv.

dark, short central primary

ad. ♂ summer

displaying ♂ in Apr

heavy bill

♀

winter

ad. ♀ late summer

ad. ♂ late summer (Aug/Sep)

tawny-brown, barred

ad. ♀ spring

big red eyebrow

deep rufous

ad. ♂ spring (May/Jun)

RED GROUSE

on a Scottish moor

retains brown plumage all the year around

ad. ♀

ad. ♂

ad. ♂

PTARMIGAN

among lichen-covered rocks on bare mountain slope

ad. ♀ late summer

ad. ♂ late summer (Aug/Sep)

ad. ♂ summer

♀

delicate bill

black lores

buff with grey admixed

greyish, spangled white

winter

♂

ad. ♀ spring

ad. ♂ spring (May/Jun)

DZ

Capercaillie *Tetrao urogallus* r**B4**

L ♂ 74–90 cm (tail *c*.25), ♀ 54–63 cm. Sedentary in mature coniferous forests, preferring areas with old pines on rocky ground with abundance of berry-bearing shrubs and moss and with element of aspen and spruces, avoiding open ground. Spectacular communal display in *late* spring.

IDENTIFICATION *Very large*, ♂ being about a third larger than♀. Takes off with *very loud wing noise*; longer flights fast and direct, with bursts of rapid wingbeats interspersed between glides. – ♂: Not likely to be confused with any other grouse through mere size; that aside, has *very long tail* (cocked and spread as a fan during display), *long neck* (erect in display, with raised feathers) and *dark colours*. Heavy, strongly curved *bill straw-yellow*. A conspicuous *rounded, white patch at base of forewing*. In flight characteristic, with *long, folded, straight tail* and *long, thick, outstretched neck* making wings look comparatively small. – ♀: Considerably smaller than ♂, still distinctly larger than♀ Black Grouse. In spite of size difference can be confused with Black Grouse, which it resembles, the two being brown, barred dark, and found in similar habitat, but told by: *throat and parts of upper breast unmarked orange-brown*; *more obvious strings of white patches on scapulars* ('braces'); often slightly paler and more rufous plumage; slightly longer and more rounded tail, which is somewhat more rufous (though rufous tinge to some degree often found on ♀ Black Grouse, too).

VOICE At evening gathering of ♂♂, belching, bellowing 'ko-**krerk**-korohr' and variants. Call of ♀, mainly from perch in tree, a slowly repeated cackling 'grak', often at peak lek season (early May in N). Song, at dawn, first from tree perch, then from ground in group, consists of clicking double notes, accelerating into 'cork-pop' note, immediately followed by fine, grinding hissing, ground-displaying ♂♂ at times replacing last element with noisy wing-flutter. Whole song lasts 5–7 sec., audible at only 200–300 m.

Black Grouse *Tetrao tetrix* r**B3**

L ♂ 49–58 cm (tail *c*.15), ♀ 40–45 cm. Sedentary in variety of habitats, ranging from moors, bogs, and clear-fellings in forested areas to heaths and barren islands. Communal display in *early* spring, *many* ♂♂ on ground in *open* area (incl. ice-covered lakes). Also, single ♂♂ may sing from treetops, even in summer. In winter often seen in birches, eating buds.

IDENTIFICATION Medium-large, small-headed grouse with small bill. Wing noise on take-off moderately loud. Flight as Capercaillie, but Black Grouse appears more compact. – ♂: *Black* (with purplish gloss) except for *white undertail-feathers* (prominently exposed during display), white underwing, and a *white wing-bar*; comb-shaped *red eyebrows*. Most striking feature is *lyre-shaped tail*, cocked and spread during

display, but in flight folded and simply appearing *long*. – ♀: Black-barred greyish-brown all over, incl. throat and breast (cf. ♀ Capercaillie). Tail grey-brown, often showing slight tinge of rufous (less than on Capercaillie), square or slightly forked. In flight, shows *narrow whitish wing-bar*.

VOICE ♀ has a rapid, cackling call, often ending with a nasal, drawn-out note, 'kakakakaka**keh**-ah'. Song of ♂ a far-carrying, bubbling, prolonged rookooing, 'rro-perre-**oo**-ohr rro-per**roo**…'. Another distinctive call, partly with song function, is a strong, harsh hissing 'choo-**iiish**'.

Caucasian Grouse *Tetrao mlokosiewiczi* —

L ♂ 50–55 cm (tail *c*.18), ♀ 37–42 cm. Sedentary in Caucasus and NE Turkey on mountainsides (at 1500–3000 m) at tree-limit and on open slopes with low *Rhododendron* scrub and herb meadows; somewhat lower in winter.

IDENTIFICATION ♂ resembles Black Grouse, differing in following points: *longer, straighter tail, deeply forked* but with less obvious lyre-shape; *black undertail-coverts*; *no white wing-bar*. – ♀ is similar to Black Grouse, but (at close range) separated by: *greyer*, less rufous tinge; *longer tail*; barring of underparts finer and less regular; somewhat less extensive white visible on undertail-coverts; and paler supercilium and darker cheek patch.

VOICE ♂ almost mute. During display, flutter-jumps produce thin, whistling wing sound, audible at *c*.150 m. ♀ has cackling call reminiscent of Black Grouse.

Hazel Grouse *Bonasa bonasia* —

L 34–39 cm. Sedentary in mixed coniferous (rarely broad-leaved), closed forests, preferring damp and densely undergrown areas with old spruces. Spends much time on the ground in shaded places, but may walk along the limbs of trees, and take a perch high up in trees. Difficult to see, cleverly keeps in cover; does not squat, flies early.

IDENTIFICATION Rather *small*, roughly Jackdaw-sized, has plump body, small head and bill. Intricate plumage pattern with greyish upperparts, brownish wings and whitish underparts, latter marked dark brown and rufous. – ♂: *Short crest*, which can be erected; *throat bib blackish, bordered white*; *tail greyish with prominent black terminal band*. – ♀: Like ♂, but smaller crest, and *throat brown, speckled white*, not black; colours duller, upperparts less clean grey.

VOICE Anxiety-call of ♀ a liquid 'piih-tettettettett'. Alarm repeated 'plit'. Song of ♂ a characteristic rhythmic phrase of *very fine notes* (comparable only to Yellow-browed Warbler, Goldcrest and Penduline Tit), 'tsiii-u-**iih** ti, ti-ti-ti-ti', the last series of notes, after a hint of a pause, rapid and falling slightly in pitch. Wing noise from flushed birds (often not seen in dense forest!) typical, 'burr, burr, burr,…'.

Capercaillie

Black Grouse

Caucasian Grouse

Hazel Grouse

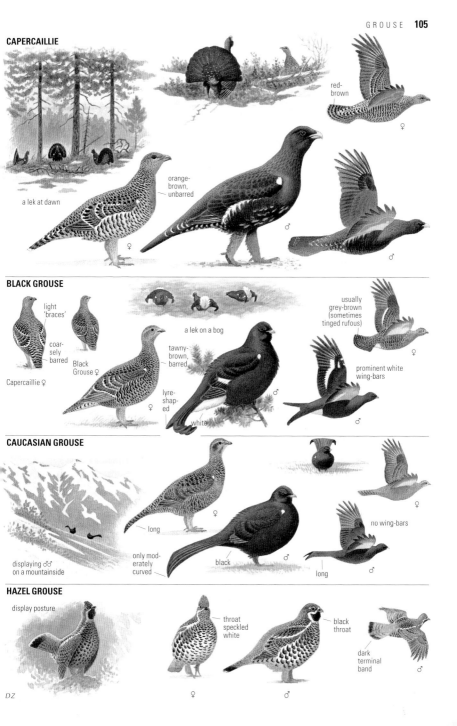

CAPERCAILLIE

a lek at dawn

red-brown ♀

orange-brown, unbarred

♀

♂

♂

BLACK GROUSE

light 'braces'

coarsely barred

Black Grouse ♀

Capercaillie ♀

a lek on a bog

tawny-brown, barred

lyre-shaped

white

♀

♂

usually grey-brown (sometimes tinged rufous)

♀

prominent white wing-bars

♂

CAUCASIAN GROUSE

displaying ♂♂ on a mountainside

long

only moderately curved

black

♀

♂

no wing-bars

♀

long

♂

HAZEL GROUSE

display posture

throat speckled white

black throat

♀

♂

dark terminal band

♂

DZ

PARTRIDGES and PHEASANTS *Phasianidae*

A very heterogeneous group, but all preferring open terrain rather than woodland. Found both on open plains and on mountain slopes above treeline. Even more ground-dwelling than the grouse; run quickly and athletically, flying only when need dictates. Nostrils unfeathered. Most have bare tarsi, and ♂♂ of several species are equipped with spurs. Food plant material and insects. Nest on ground.

Caucasian Snowcock *Tetraogallus caucasicus*

L 50–60 cm. Very closely related to other snowcocks, including Caspian (see below). Endemic to Caucasus. Breeds on bare, rocky, boulder-strewn mountains at 2000–4000 m (rarely lower, mostly in winter), with only patchy low vegetation. Gregarious when not breeding, but flocks small. Shy and difficult to approach; soon takes wing and drops like a stone out of sight behind precipice edge or runs off even when several hundred metres away. Food plant matter.

IDENTIFICATION *Big and robust* with very large head, thick neck and long tail. Plumage intricately marked in grey, brown, white and black, but looks *mostly grey at distance*. *White patch on neck-side* and *rusty-red nape*. Flanks tinged reddish-brown, feathers heavily patterned black. *Breast and mantle finely vermiculated dark*. Large *white wing-panels* (as on bustard or young Golden Eagle; common to all snowcocks). Sexes similar, but ♀ slightly duller and with nape not so obviously rusty-brown. (For differences from Caspian Snowcock, see latter.) Agile and persistent mountain-climber, bounds and runs nimbly up slopes, often with tail raised enough to reveal white, *fluffed-up undertail-coverts*. Flies down at breathtakingly steep angle with long glides and short bursts of wingbeats. – Juvenile: Like ♀ but duller; upperparts lack red-brown elements and flanks lack contrasting markings.

VOICE Essentially as for other snowcocks. See Caspian Snowcock for a description. Song differs from latter's in that final notes drop in pitch.

Caspian Snowcock *Tetraogallus caspius* —

L 56–63 cm. Close relative of Caucasian Snowcock. Breeds at scattered sites in mountain regions, including in E Turkey (and so is the species most easily seen by W Europeans) and Armenia. Habits and habitat much as Caucasian but less of a high-alpine bird, mostly found lower down (1800– 3000 m).

IDENTIFICATION *Big and hefty* like Caucasian Snowcock, or even marginally bigger. Plumage pattern similar, but overall appearance is *slightly paler*. If seen through telescope at moderate range, some minor differences are revealed: *nape is grey*, lacking rusty-red; *breast patch light grey* with only obscure small spots, not vermiculated; *mantle and breast-*

sides uniform grey, not vermiculated; *a small orange-brown spot behind eye; flanks more grey-brown* than red-brown. Sexes similar, but slightly smaller ♀ is duller.

VOICE Flight-call a series of loud cackles, 'chok-ok-ok-ok-...'. Rather muffled, chuckling conversational notes 'buk-buk-buk...', which now and then (when agitated) turn into drawn-out, bubbling trills (recalling ♀ Cuckoo) terminating in a whining 'loop', 'buk-buk-bu-bubububrrrrr-rrrrreyah'. Song, given with head thrown back and, near end, bill wide-open, a desolate, very far-carrying and echoing whistle ascending the scale in clear stages, 'sooo-luuu-dlee-**iiih**'; at distance somewhat like Curlew's call. Song heard almost solely at daybreak and in early morning.

Black Francolin *Francolinus francolinus* —

L 33–36 cm. Breeds on dry plains with access to water, especially cultivated fields but also tall-grass fields, untilled areas, e.g. riversides, with tamarisks and other shrubbery. Sedentary. Terrestrial. Shy and unobtrusive.

IDENTIFICATION Barely the size of a Grey Partridge but often with fairly *upright posture*, thus looks rather large. Somewhat slimmer build than Grey Partridge. – Adult ♂: Distinctive, with *black head and breast* separated by *broad reddish-brown neck-band*. White chin patch, white spots on mantle and breast-sides. Belly black with white U-shaped spots. – ♀: More anonymous-looking: yellowish-brown with heavy dark barring and spotting. Told by *red-brown nape* and *black lateral tail-feathers*.

VOICE Song highly characteristic and normally the first sign of the bird's presence, a constantly repeated, seven-syllable call with distinctive rhythm and cracked, mechanical voice, 'kyok, **kiiik** ki-**kii**-ko ki-**kiik**'; heard mostly at dawn.

Double-spurred Francolin *Francolinus bicalcaratus* —

L 30–33 cm. Local and rare breeder in Morocco (main range S of Sahara) in open woodland, wooded pasture, palm groves, cultivated fields, along river shores with thickets and also in vegetated wadis. Sedentary. Habits as Black Francolin. Shy, difficult to see, slips away smartly.

IDENTIFICATION Size of Barbary Partridge (which occurs in same area) but has *red-brown crown and nape, all-brown tail* without red-brown outer feathers, *heavily black-streaked underparts* (not barred flanks), black forehead and narrow white supercilium. Bill and legs yellowish-grey or greenish. Sexes alike, but ♂ has small spurs.

VOICE Utters an irregularly repeated, disyllabic 'i-**teck**'. Best located by its song, delivered mostly at dawn from an elevated perch (tree, rock, mound, post), a repeated, low-pitched 'kuarr kuarr'. Also gives loud hacking and jarring calls, 'krrrrr krrrrr...'.

Caucasian Snowcock

Caspian Snowcock

Black Francolin

Double-spurred Francolin

CAUCASIAN SNOWCOCK

display posture

rusty-red

dark, finely patterned

♀ similar, only with slightly duller colours

♂

CASPIAN SNOWCOCK

dark grey

grey

♀ similar, only with slightly duller colours

♂

BLACK FRANCOLIN

♂

♀

red-brown

white cheek patch

black

♀

♂

DOUBLE-SPURRED FRANCOLIN

sometimes perches in trees

light supercilium

red-brown

grey rump

BARBARY PARTRIDGE (to compare)

DZ

Red-legged Partridge *Alectoris rufa* rB2

L 32–35 cm. Breeds mainly in lowlands, selecting varied habitats, including cultivated farmland with pasture, heathland, unworked sandy or stony terrain with low vegetation, coastal meadows; sometimes found also in mountain areas above treeline. Introduced in Britain. Resident. Gregarious, often in flocks. Wary. Runs away quickly when disturbed. Flies only if pressed, flight then low with rapid beats and stiff-winged glides. Most often located by its calls.

IDENTIFICATION Virtually no range overlap exists between the four similar *Alectoris* species. Nevertheless, best to check: *small white bib* framed by coarse, *broad black border* which at lower edge breaks up into *heavy black streaking on breast*; *brown hindneck* (greyer on other species). Like Grey Partridge has *reddish-brown tail-corners*, but is *grey on lower back, rump and central tail*, this well visible when flushed.

VOICE Rhythmic series of hoarse notes. Territorial call, often heard morning and evening (but midday, too), begins with a few clucks only to turn into a three-syllable phrase at cantering pace, the last two notes raucous, 'chu chu chu chu ka-**cheh-cheh**, ka-**cheh-cheh**, ka-**cheh-cheh**,...'; the final phrases are sometimes five-syllabled, 'ku-**kak** kaka-**cheh**,...'.

Rock Partridge *Alectoris graeca* —

L 33–36 cm. Breeds on rocky alpine slopes generally above treeline (but also in clearings and among scattered trees), mostly at 1000–2000 m, often with grass, scrub and low bushes; avoids N-facing slopes. Has declined. Resident. Gregarious. Behaviour as for Red-legged Partridge.

IDENTIFICATION Like Chukar; differs in: *pure white bib*; *sharply demarcated black border to bib* (varying in width in breast-centre: broad in Alps, narrow or even broken in Sicily); *narrow* white supercilium which often *also crosses forehead*; a little *black bordering base of upper mandible*.

VOICE Territorial call usually irregular series of short, throaty, very hard notes, now and then interrupted by a rapid choking series, 'chi chek pe-ti-**chek** chik chi-chek chi-**cheay-cheay-cheay**, pe-**te**-ti-ti**chek** chik te...' and so on, thus often without the repetitive pattern of its relatives.

Barbary Partridge *Alectoris barbara* —

L 32–35 cm. Breeds in a wide variety of habitats and at different altitudes, from bare, rocky mountain slopes (up to 3000 m) among boulders and shrubs, through open woodland and clearings at lower levels, down to dry, open terrain in lowlands. Occurs in Canary Islands (incl. Lanzarote, Fuerteventura); introduced in Madeira. Sedentary. Gregarious. Behaviour as for Red-legged Partridge.

IDENTIFICATION Has *broad, dark reddish-brown neck-collar bestrewn with white spots*; dark *red-brown central crown-band*;

no white bib, is instead *light grey on throat and head-sides* with diffuse light brown band backwards from cheek; *shoulders attractively patterned in pale blue-grey and rusty-brown*.

VOICE Territorial call often typical: series of short, impure notes (sometimes hint of double syllable) with an occasional hoarse, drawn-out interjection, 'tre tre tre tre tre tre **cheeh**che tre tre tre tre tre...' (trotting rhythm with a stumble). But at times very like Red-legged Partridge, with series of trisyllabic 'tra-**che-che**'. Also an unslurred 'tshuuih'.

Chukar *Alectoris chukar* [V***]

L 32–35 cm. Breeds in similar habitats to closely related Rock Partridge, but also descends lower and is found around cultivations, pasture on barren terrain etc.; also in mountain deserts. Has declined in Europe. Said to be shyer and more difficult to see than Rock Partridge.

IDENTIFICATION Like Rock Partridge; differs in: *yellow-tinged* white bib; sometimes some *black spots at bottom of bib* in breast-centre; *broad, diffuse pale supercilium* not reaching forehead; *no black bordering base of upper mandible*; *brown streak behind eye*; browner upperparts.

VOICE Territorial call variable, often rhythmic series at fast galloping pace and with hoarse voice, introduced by several short, monosyllabic, shrill notes, 'ga ga ga ga cha-**chak**era-**chak**era-**chak**era-...'; structure at times simpler, e.g. 'chak chak chak che-chak **truc**-ku **truc**-ku **truc**-ku **truc**-ku...'.

Sand Partridge *Ammoperdix heyi* —

L 22–25 cm. Breeds in mountain deserts, on rocky slopes, in wadis and similar but with access to water. Often not shy, and easy to approach. Behaviour otherwise as *Alectoris*.

IDENTIFICATION Like a *small pale* Grey Partridge, and has similar *red-brown tail-corners*. – ♂: Sandy-brown with *blue-grey head* and *white loral / cheek patch*. Bill orange-yellow. Flanks with *wavy striping* of white / black / brown. – ♀: Much plainer than ♂; lacks white on head. Bill dull yellow.

VOICE Song a usually rapidly repeated short call (1½–2 per sec.), slightly downslurred and ending sharply, 'kiwa kiwa kiwa...', or (at distance) slightly softer 'ua ua ua...'.

See-see Partridge *Ammoperdix griseogularis* —

L 22–25 cm. Breeds locally in SE Turkey, N Syria and eastwards; found in similar terrain to Sand Partridge, but sometimes also at somewhat higher altitude (to 2000 m).

IDENTIFICATION Like Sand Partridge, but ♂ has *tapering black band from forehead to nape*, bordering white cheek patch; grey *neck-sides are speckled white*. ♀ duller.

VOICE Song a repeated upslurred whistle (a good 1 per sec.), at distance recalling Spotted Crake (of all species out in middle of the desert!), 'hoit, hoit, hoit,...'.

Red-legged P.   Chukar   Rock Partridge   Barbary Partridge   Sand Partridge

RED-LEGGED PARTRIDGE
brown back
reddish-brown
broad, black-streaked 'neck-shawl'

ROCK PARTRIDGE
black rim along entire base of upper mandible; narrow light supercilium
white

BARBARY PARTRIDGE
dark median crown-stripe
light grey
reddish-brown

CHUKAR
black rim along base of upper mandible only on forehead; broad, diffuse light supercilium
cream

SAND PARTRIDGE
white patches on cheek and lore
like a washed-out version of ♂
plain
♀
♂

SEE-SEE PARTRIDGE
♂
black supercilium and forehead
speckled white
very similar to ♀ Sand Partridge
♀
♂

DZ

Grey Partridge *Perdix perdix* r**B**2

L 28–32 cm. Breeds in open farmland with some hedges and other shelter, preferably in or beside cultivated fields; also meadowland. Has declined greatly in Britain. Resident. Terrestrial. Gregarious, flocks keep tightly together. Nervous and wary. Freezes or runs away in good time. Food seeds and leaves. Nests on ground; clutch large, 10–20 eggs.

IDENTIFICATION Compact, *rounded body* and small, rounded head. Usually encountered as an entire flock is flushed, all at once, and with excited calls and noisy, rapid series of wingbeats and short stiff-winged glides flies a short way low over the ground; the image caught is of grey-brown birds with *rusty-red on the tail*. Seen closer, this is a handsome bird, with *orange-brown 'face' and throat*, chestnut-brown flank-bars, delicately vermiculated *ash-grey breast* and a large *horseshoe-shaped blackish-brown belly patch*. Sexes similar (♂ 'cleaner', with better-marked pattern). ♀'s belly patch smaller, less clear. – Juvenile: Yellow-brown and grey-brown; lacks orange throat, grey breast and dark belly patch. (More like a chick Pheasant or adult Quail than a Grey Partridge.) After 2–3½ months assumes adult-like plumage.

VOICE On rising, gives sharp, excited, short 'prri prri prri...' or 'rick-rick-rick...'. Song (by both sexes) a hoarse and abruptly clipped 'kierr-ik', repeated a few times at moderate intervals, often heard at night.

(Common) Quail *Coturnix coturnix* m**B**4

L 16–18 cm. Breeds on open farmland, drawn to vast plains with clover pasture and young corn fields. Warmth-loving; winters in Africa. Heavily hunted on passage in Mediterranean region. In warm springs quite a number of night-flying migrants 'overshoot' their destination and end up farther N, when far more than usual heard calling in May/Jun. Nests on ground, often in crops; clutch 8–13.

IDENTIFICATION Often heard but rarely seen; keeps well hidden, reluctant to fly by day. *Very small*, like a rather small Pheasant chick, which it somewhat resembles in plumage: *buff-brown* with dark brown markings above and on breast and head, and with narrow whitish streaks above and on flanks. ♂ is black on centre of throat (extent variable, often just a narrow band, thus best judged in front view), ♀ is dirty white. If you do flush a Quail, or see a raptor do so, it looks unexpectedly *long-winged*, different from other gallinaceous birds; *wingbeats fast, flightpath low and direct*; quickly drops back into cover.

VOICE When flushed, a wader-like soft, rolling 'wrree'. Song, mainly at dusk and daybreak (but also at other times of day), a rhythmic, trisyllabic phrase rapidly (1 per sec.) repeated 3–8 times: a sharp whistle, far-carrying, with stress on first and last syllables and with the final two sylla-bles close together, '**büt** bül-**üt**' ('wet-my-lips'); close to, a throaty mechanical secondary note (roughly as that of Spotted Crake) is audible; sometimes also a few muffled, nasal, creaky 'mau-wau' introductory notes. (Only confusion risk is distant Curlew, whose '**vi**-vi-**vü**' alarm-call may be heard at night in same habitat in early summer.)

Small Button-quail *Turnix sylvatica* —

(Old evocative name: Andalusian Hemipode.) L 15–17 cm. One of Europe's least-known species. Actually belongs to same order as the cranes. Most like Quail, but lives mostly on dry heaths with low dwarf palm, asphodel etc. Resident. Roles of sexes reversed (as in phalaropes). Nests on ground; clutch 3–5. Protracted breeding season, Apr–Sep.

IDENTIFICATION Rarely seen, presence noted mostly by its voice. Hard to flush more than once. *Very small*. Short-tailed. Brown above and whitish below, with *orange patch on breast* and *coarse dark spotting on breast-sides*. ♀ more brightly coloured and somewhat bigger than ♂. Rises with loud *wing noise*. Is quite *short- and round-winged*, unlike Quail. On landing, stands momentarily in characteristic upright manner with wings held out. *Upperwing-coverts yellowish-brown, contrastingly paler than dark primaries*.

VOICE ♀'s territorial call a low-pitched, straight, second-long hoot, repeated a few times at 2–3-sec. intervals, 'hoooo... hoooo... hoooo...', reminiscent of a distant fog-horn. Heard most at dusk and dawn.

Corncrake *Crex crex* m**B**4–5

L 22–25 cm. Belongs to the rails and crakes (pp. 114–117), but is not so tied to wet marshland as its relatives. Breeds on damp meadows by marshy lowland lakes, but also on lush meadowland and hay fields (where usually wiped out by silage-cutting, haymaking etc.) with access to wetter spot with taller vegetation. Has declined. Now very rare and local in Britain & Ireland. Summer visitor, winters E Africa.

IDENTIFICATION Half the size of a Grey Partridge and much *slimmer*, like a Water Rail in shape (quite long neck, rounded body) but with *short, stubby bill*. Plumage *greyish yellow-brown* with *blue-grey band over eye* and grey on breast-sides (grey colour less obvious on ♀); *heavily dark-spotted above*. In flight, which appears 'flappy' and unsure, shows *red-brown wing patch* and *prominent, dangling legs*. Hard to flush, sneaks away cleverly. Most often seen at dusk and dawn, when courting ♂'s head sticks above the vegetation.

VOICE Display-call is heard from dusk to morning (at times briefly in daytime, too), a persistently repeated hoarse and mechanical, sharp rasping 'ehrp-ehrp' (or, if you like, 'crex-crex'), once per second and for hours on end with only brief rests. Otherwise rather silent.

Grey Partridge   Quail   Small Button-quail   Corncrake

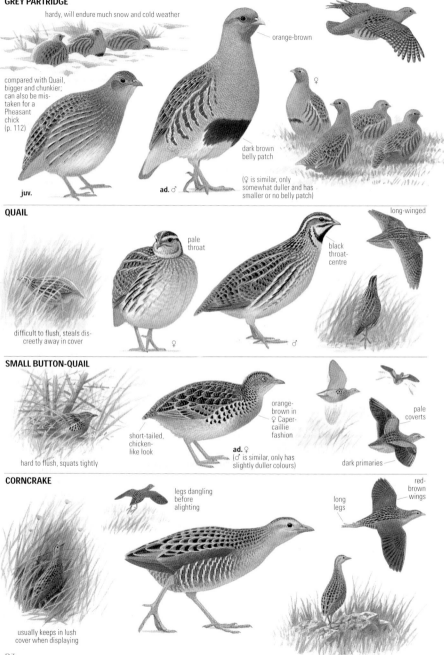

GREY PARTRIDGE

hardy, will endure much snow and cold weather

orange-brown

compared with Quail, bigger and chunkier; can also be mistaken for a Pheasant chick (p. 112)

dark brown belly patch

♀

(♀ is similar, only somewhat duller and has smaller or no belly patch)

juv.

ad. ♂

QUAIL

long-winged

pale throat

black throat-centre

difficult to flush, steals discreetly away in cover

♀

♂

SMALL BUTTON-QUAIL

orange-brown in ♀ Capercaillie fashion

short-tailed, chicken-like look

ad. ♀
(♂ is similar, only has slightly duller colours)

pale coverts

hard to flush, squats tightly

dark primaries

CORNCRAKE

legs dangling before alighting

long legs

red-brown wings

usually keeps in lush cover when displaying

DZ

(Common) **Pheasant** *Phasianus colchicus*   rB2

L ♂ 70–90 cm (of which tail *c.* 35–45), ♀ 55–70 cm (tail *c.* 20–25). Introduced in Europe (in Britain probably from 11th/12th century); wild populations occur E Black Sea and in Caucasus, eastwards to China. Breeds in farmland areas with cover such as copses with dense undergrowth, scrubby thickets, conifer plantations, also in large gardens and parks. Resident. Roosts in trees, sometimes in reeds. Food plant material, insects etc. Nests on ground.

IDENTIFICATION Adult ♂: Unmistakable with *long, barred brown tail*, the dark *head glossed greenish-black and violet* and with bare, warty, *red head-sides*. Many in Britain have narrow *white neck-collar* and grey rump (ssp. *torquatus* from China), but ♂♂ lacking white collar and with brown rump (typical of nominate *colchicus* from SW Asia, incl. Caucasus) not uncommon; most, however, a mixture of these (and other, also introduced) races. – ♀: Buff-brown with dark angular spots and feather centres. Rather nondescript, but long tail identifies it as a pheasant. See also under the other pheasant species.

VOICE Alarm, often when flushed, a hacking series of disyllabic, slightly hoarse calls with stress on first syllable, '**ku**-tuk **ku**-tuk **ku**-tuk...', often decreasing in strength. ♂'s song far-carrying, abrupt, an allied hacking call of two syllables, not unlike clearing one's throat, usually immediately followed by a short, noisy wing-flutter, '**koohrk**-kuk (burrrr)'; the cock repeats this at long intervals (1–15 min.) from a well visible perch on the ground, log pile, fence post or similar site. A range of other soft calls.

Golden Pheasant   *Chrysolophus pictus*   [rB4?]

L ♂ 90–105 cm (of which tail *c.* 60–70), ♀ 60–80 cm (tail *c.* 30–35). Indigenous in mountains of C China. Introduced in Britain since late 1800s; several self-sustaining populations (main ones SW Scotland, S & E England, Anglesey), inhabiting younger dense, dark, rather bare-floored pine and larch forest, rarely also mixed forest with richer understorey. Closely related to Lady Amherst's Pheasant (see below).

IDENTIFICATION Adult ♂: Unmistakable. Despite its *bright red colours on underbody and tail-sides*, and the yellow areas on its crown and back, the cock often avoids detection by slipping stealthily through the vegetation. *Orange-yellow nuchal cape* can be raised like a *fan* when displaying. – ♀: Resembles ♀ Common Pheasant, though proportionately longer tail and legs impart more elegant impression. Both this and ♀ Lady Amherst's differ from ♀ Pheasant in overall slightly darker, more *densely barred* plumage and subtly discrete 'cloak' of feathers over nape. ♀ Golden has somewhat *paler* yellow-brown *forehead*/forecrown, comparatively *unobvious yellowish-pink orbital skin, yellow-tinged*

legs, barred belly and a little *less boldly barred tail* than ♀ Lady Amherst's.

VOICE ♂'s song a one- or two-syllable, gruff, piercing 'ehk' or 'eh-aik' (with second syllable one note higher), usually heard in spring; higher in pitch than Common Pheasant's territorial call. Otherwise rather silent.

Lady Amherst's Pheasant *Chrysolophus amherstiae* [rB5]

L ♂ 105–120 cm (of which tail *c.* 75–90), ♀ 60–80 cm (tail *c.* 25–30). Breeds in mountain forests of SW East Asia. Introduced in Britain in 1900s; a few small feral populations survive very locally in S England (esp. Bedfordshire), where they live in woods and thickets with rich, dense understorey (e.g. bramble, rhododendron). Close relative of Golden Pheasant, and the two occasionally hybridize in England.

IDENTIFICATION Adult ♂ unmistakable, pyrotechnical display of feathered splendour! The broad white feathers with black (blue-glossed at certain angles) tips which adorn the nape and normally droop like a *silver-white cape* can be raised to form a *fan* when courting the ♀. The herringbone-patterned *grey-white tail is extremely long*. – ♀: Basically like Common Pheasant, but is more *finely and evenly barred above and on neck*, not so coarsely spotted as latter. Very like ♀ Golden Pheasant; differs in *darker red-brown forehead, crown and throat*, more conspicuous *pale greyish orbital skin, greyish legs*, unbarred belly and *more boldly barred tail*.

VOICE Song often heard at nightfall, an 'aahk aik-aik', thus as Golden Pheasant's but with *double-note* ending.

Helmeted Guineafowl   *Numida meleagris*   —

L 58–68 cm. Only a remnant survives in Morocco of the once healthy NW African population. Introduced and domesticated in e.g. S France. Breeds in drier, savanna-type country with bushes and scattered trees, also in farmed areas with some clumps of trees and bushy cover; shuns deserts and marshes. Gregarious, seen mostly in small or rather large (often of *c.* 25 birds) flocks. Roosts in trees, like pheasants; also takes 'siesta' in shade. Resident. Food mostly plant material, some insects. Nests on ground among bushes.

IDENTIFICATION Fully as *big as a chicken*, with heavy, *compact body*, narrow neck, small head, broad, rounded wings, rather long tail and fairly long legs (thus somewhat turkey-like). Plumage violet-tinged *grey, sprinkled with white spots*. Head striking: a brownish *knob* on crown, and *bare blue-white and red skin on sides and on forehead*. Greyish-black upper neck and sparse, 'unkempt' hair on nape and hindneck. Sexes alike. When disturbed, the flock runs quickly into cover, all birds with neck extended. – Juvenile: grey-brown with pale spots. Head markings much as those of a ♀ pheasant.

VOICE All calls raucous, unmusical, with several loud. Wide variation, and many calls merge into each other depending on mood etc. ♀'s include a disyllabic 'ka-bak'. Other calls are hard staccato 'tek-tek-tek-tek-...', at times mixed with hard rolling calls, 'tk trrrrrrrrrrr tk tk tk...', also a plaintive 'cher-chih, cher-chih,...' and so on.

Pheasant

Golden Pheasant

Lady Amherst's Pheasant

PHEASANT

white neck-collar

'*torquatus* group'

♂

♂

complex geographical variation further muddled in Europe, where introduced stock often are crosses of several races

'*colchicus* group'

mainly Chinese species introduced in Europe as game-bird at least since the Middle Ages, and possibly as early as in Roman times

♀

spotted

GOLDEN PHEASANT

quickly runs for cover

unmistakable!

♂

♀

yellow-brown

barred

yellowish-brown

LADY AMHERST'S PHEASANT

unmistakable!

♂

can exceed 1 m in length

♀

rufous-brown

unbarred

grey

HELMETED GUINEAFOWL

sociable, usually keeps together in family groups or larger flocks

in S Europe often introduced C African race:

sabyi
(Morocco)

meleagris
(Ethiopia, Kenya)

DZ

RAILS and CRAKES *Rallidae*

Small to medium-sized, aquatic birds living in marsh vegetation, usually concealed. Podgy body, in some species laterally flattened, and rounded wings. Several species have loud calls, heard mostly at night. Migrate at night. Food plant material, small animals. Nest in dense vegetation, generally in marshes. (One species, Corncrake, is treated on p. 110.)

Water Rail *Rallus aquaticus* rB4 / W3

L 23–26 cm (bill 3–4½). Breeds at thick-reeded shallow lakes and sedge marshes. Northern breeders winter in W and SW Europe. Usually hidden away on reedbed floor or among dense sedge, but sometimes seen scurrying across a muddy gap in reeds; in winter, may come out on to open ice.

IDENTIFICATION Rather small with rounded rear body, flat breast and quite long neck, and *long, narrow, slightly decurved bill*. At distance looks *rather dark*; just *undertail-coverts gleaming light* (white with buff admixed). Moves cautiously one moment, nimbly the next; flies into cover with rapid wingbeats and dangling legs. – Adult: Black-spotted olive-brown above, 'face' and breast dark blue-grey, flanks and belly barred black and white. *Bill red* with darker culmen and tip, legs dirty red. – Juvenile: *Throat and centre of breast white*, sides of head and breast brownish and diffusely barred; often suggestion of *darker mask* and *narrow pale line over lores*. Reduced red on bill.

VOICE Rich repertoire: a discontented piglet-like squeal, soon dying away (cf. Red-necked Grebe), 'grüiit grroit grui gru'; a weary, 'all-in', choking moan, 'ooouuuh'; short 'kip' notes when disturbed. ♂'s song, often at night, a persistent pounding 'küpp küpp küpp küpp...' in long, slightly accelerating series; ♀♀ (unmated?) at times utter a high, characteristic 'püp püp pü-errrrr' (structure as call of ♀ Little Crake, but higher-pitched and with distinct Water Rail voice); the terminal trill, 'pü-errrrr', is heard in spring from flying rails (probably also ♀♀) at night.

Spotted Crake *Porzana porzana* mB5 / P5

L 19–22½ cm. Breeds mostly in soggy sedge bogs and damp tussocky meadows (avoids reedbeds). Hard to flush, slips away unseen even in low sedge. Rare and local in Britain.

IDENTIFICATION A bit smaller than Water Rail, which it resembles in general shape and habits. Told by *short, straight bill*, usually buff undertail-coverts, *greenish legs* and, in fluttering flight, *white leading edge to wing*. Close to, shows *fine white spotting on neck, breast and upperparts*, *yellow-grey bill* with spot of red at base. – Juvenile: Lacks lead-grey colour on supercilium, throat and breast; throat often whitish.

VOICE Song highly distinctive, a high, gently upslurred, sharp 'wolf-whistle' (first part only), rhythmically repeated

(fully 1 per sec.) at night, 'huitt, huitt, huitt,...'; audible at 1–2 km on still nights, at distance can recall dripping water; close to, a cracked, grunting secondary note heard.

Sora *Porzana carolina* V✱✱✱

L 18–21 cm. Very rare vagrant from N America. Like Spotted Crake in appearance and habitat choice. In all plumages differs in *unstreaked dark median crown-stripe* (Spotted is streaked), *lack of white spots on head, neck and breast*, and dark *tertials with pale edges* (not wavy bars as on Spotted). Calls include a Little Grebe-like trill which rapidly drops in pitch and slows down; song a slowly repeated, low-pitched, drawling whistle rising at end, 'ku-vü' (like prelude to Bar-tailed Godwit's display-call).

Little Crake *Porzana parva* V✱✱✱

L 17–19 cm. Breeds in reeds in somewhat deeper water. Most at home in natural reedbeds with some bulrush, open areas and channels. Mostly E European species, rare vagrant in Britain & Ireland. Located almost solely by loud calls.

IDENTIFICATION *Small*. Like Baillon's Crake; differs in *long primary projection*, rather *long tail*, in adult *a touch of red at base of bill*, *no white markings above* or, on younger birds, some white *streaks or spots* (not loops and squiggles), along with *restricted barring on rear body*. Sexes differ: ♂ blue-grey below, ♀ buffy grey-white with a hint of blue-grey on head. Immature like ♀ but has strikingly *whiter face and underparts*, with more *extensive barring on body-sides*; told from young Baillon's by longer primary projection.

VOICE ♂'s song is heard at night, a far-carrying (often audible at 1–2 km), nasal yapping 'kua', repeated slowly at first, then faster and faster, finally dropping in pitch and becoming a stammer; many renditions left unfinished. ♀ has a short phrase with the same nasal, high-pitched tone, 'kua-kua-kvarrrr' (cf. Water Rail).

Baillon's Crake *Porzana pusilla* V✱✱✱

L 16–18 cm. Breeds in sodden sedge bogs where water no more than knee-deep, sometimes with a few reeds. Rare in S Europe, more numerous in E; a rare vagrant in Britain.

IDENTIFICATION *Small*. Like Little Crake; told by *short primary projection* (primary tips reaching only a little bit outside tertials), rather *short tail*, *no red on bill-base*, some *white loops and squiggles on reddish-brown upperparts*, and also, below, *more distinct and more extensive dark and white barring on rear body*. Sexes similar (♂ cleaner and darker blue-grey); immature dirty brown below, with no blue-grey.

VOICE Song a soft, dry rattle varying in volume, very reminiscent of edible frog (and to lesser extent of Garganey), 2–3 sec. long, not audible beyond 250 m (often only 75 m!).

Water Rail

Spotted Crake

Little Crake

Baillon's Crake

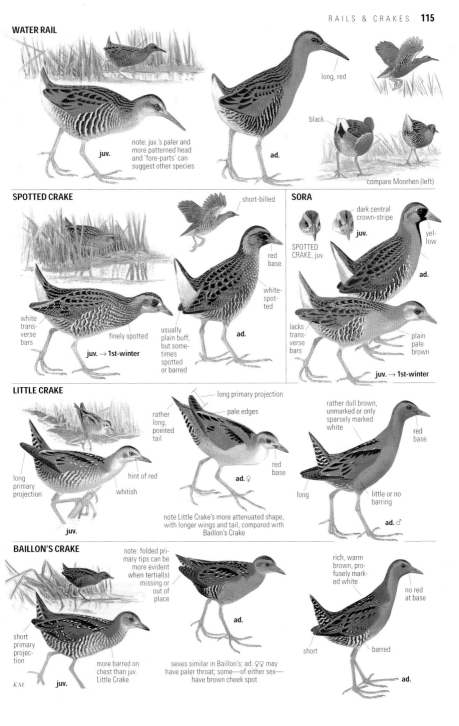

WATER RAIL

long, red

black

note: juv.'s paler and more patterned head and 'fore-parts' can suggest other species

juv.

ad.

compare Moorhen (left)

SPOTTED CRAKE

short-billed

red base

white-spotted

white transverse bars

finely spotted

usually plain buff, but sometimes spotted or barred

juv. → 1st-winter

ad.

SORA

dark central crown-stripe

juv.

SPOTTED CRAKE, juv.

yellow

ad.

lacks transverse bars

plain pale brown

juv. → 1st-winter

LITTLE CRAKE

long primary projection

pale edges

rather long, pointed tail

red base

ad. ♀

note Little Crake's more attenuated shape, with longer wings and tail, compared with Baillon's Crake

long primary projection

hint of red

whitish

juv.

rather dull brown, unmarked or only sparsely marked white

red base

long

little or no barring

ad. ♂

BAILLON'S CRAKE

note: folded primary tips can be more evident when tertial(s) missing or out of place

short primary projection

more barred on chest than juv. Little Crake

juv.

ad.

sexes similar in Baillon's; ad. ♀♀ may have paler throat; some—of either sex— have brown cheek spot

rich, warm brown, profusely marked white

no red at base

short

barred

ad.

KM

(Common) **Moorhen** *Gallinula chloropus*   r**B**2 / **W**2
L 27–31 cm. Common breeder on smaller lakes, ponds, pools and rivers with dense vegetation cover. Usually secretive but in some places quite bold, and may be seen strolling in open on grass and waterside meadows. Northern breeders migrate to W and S Europe, returning in Mar–Apr. Nest a roofed basket well hidden in dense vegetation.
IDENTIFICATION A pigeon-sized, *dark* bird with rather long tail and *long green legs with long toes*. *Bill red with yellow tip.* Slate-grey plumage (upperparts brown-tinged) with a *white line along side of body* and *white sides to undertail-coverts* (form inverted white V in rear view). Carries tail high and *jerks it* when walking, also jerks head when swimming. – Juvenile: Grey-brown with dirty white chin and throat; identified by shape and actions, also by pale line along side and white undertail-coverts. Downy young is like that of Coot, black with red bill, but *lacks yellow-brown collar.*
VOICE Wide repertoire, and heard more often than seen. Most typical is a short, explosive, bubbling or gargling call, 'kyorrrl!', which reveals its presence within reeds. Other calls are a sharp 'ki-keck' (annoyance) and a trisyllabic, fast, cracked 'kreck-kreck-kreck', which may be repeated for long periods and is also given at night in flight.

(Eurasian) **Coot** *Fulica atra*   r**B**3 / **W**2
L 36–42 cm. Breeds on lakes and slow rivers with ample vegetation but also open-water areas. Many overwinter in northern harbours, others migrate to W Europe; large winter flocks on some British & Irish reservoirs. Nest a pile of dead reeds at reedbed edge, often fairly visible. Defends territory fiercely, swims menacingly at intruders and charges them.
IDENTIFICATION *Plump*, broad body, short tail and small, rounded head. *Sooty-grey body* and *black head* with *white bill and white frontal plate*. In flight shows narrow *white trailing edge to secondaries*. Legs strong, toes long and lobed (like grebes; not webbed as on ducks). Swims with gently *nodding head*. Dives with a small leap, then resurfacing (floats like a cork). When taking off from water, runs along surface with splashing feet. For differences from similar Red-knobbed Coot, see latter. – Juvenile: Greyish-white on head-sides, foreneck and breast, otherwise grey-brown. Note that undertail is dark (pale on young Moorhen). Downy young is black with *red and blue on head* and with *yellow-brown collar.*
VOICE Repertoire rich and varied; livens up lowland lakes at night. Loudest call is a cracked, monosyllabic 'kowk' or 'kruke', often repeated. Frequently utters an explosive, sharp 'pitts!' (like striking a stone with a metal bar). On spring nights, a nasal trumpeting 'pe pe-**eu**', somewhat jolting in rhythm, is often heard from Coots flying around territory. Young beg with pitiful, whimpering, lisping '**üh**-lif' notes.

Red-knobbed Coot *Fulica cristata*   —
L 39–44 cm. Breeds in N Morocco, and locally (rare) in SW Spain. Habitat the same as for Coot, and the two can co-exist. Perhaps a trifle shyer than Coot, and seems to be more reclusive than that species. Resident.
IDENTIFICATION Very like Coot, and safely identified only at reasonable range and with some experience of variation in latter. During breeding season *small dark red nodules on forehead* diagnostic, but these rapidly shrink after breeding and are often surprisingly hard to see in the field at a distance (look simply dark). Best characters: *feathering on side of upper mandible is gently rounded* (not forming pointed wedge as on Coot); bill white with *tinge of blue-grey* (not creamy-white or pinky-white as on ad. Coot); frontal shield extends a bit more towards crown and is *squared off at top*; *neck is narrower*; in flight *wing all dark* (lacks Coot's white trailing edge to secondaries). Often swims with weight at front and 'stern' raised, and head looks conical (but beware that shape and posture at times very like Coot). Bends neck at centre when picking food from water's surface ('neck gives way in middle'; Coot bends entire neck).
VOICE Very different from Coot's. Often gives a disyllabic, very fast 'ker**re**', nasal and shrill (can recall Little Crake), also a hollow, nasal, slightly hoarse 'ka-hah'. Occasionally utters long series of rolling 'krre' notes.

Purple Swamp-hen *Porphyrio porphyrio*   —
L 45–50 cm. Breeds at marshes and smaller lakes with lush but rather low growth of reeds, bulrushes and sedges, often with plenty of broken and fallen stems for clambering about; at times climbs high up in reed clumps, unlike its relatives.
IDENTIFICATION Almost *size of Black Grouse*, with smart *shimmering dark blue and purple plumage*, *big red bill* (with *large* frontal plate) and powerful, prawnshell-red legs with long toes. *Undertail-coverts white.* Bill a little duller in winter, but frontal plate usually remains deep red. Immatures have somewhat duller plumage with greyer head, a few greyish-white feathers on central underparts, and initially more greyish-pink on bill and legs. Flies with fast-cranking wing-beats and long, dangling legs. Swims if need be. – Variation: Egyptian population (ssp. *madagascariensis*) has green colour on back, scapulars and tertials; Caspian and Turkish breeders (*caspius*) have paler, greyish head.
VOICE Very loud and startling (almost as if someone is pulling your leg!). Rich repertoire. Often emits (esp. at night) drawn-out tooting calls with nasal, bleating tone and alternating in pitch, repeated in long series. Also hard, straight, mechanical trills with cracked voice, 'prrrih prrrih prrrih...', varying in intensity, at times very shrill and 'indignant'. Contact-call a clicking 'chuck'.

Moorhen   Coot   Red-knobbed Coot   Purple Swamp-hen

MOORHEN

white undertail with black central stripe

white patchy line along flanks

pair with chicks

juv.

ad.

COOT

territorial fight

juv.

pointed black wedge in front of eye

1st-winter

white trailing edge

pink hue

ad.

RED-KNOBBED COOT

two Red-knobbed Coots (upper two in left row) and three Coots

raised 'stern'   flat-backed

rounded black feathering in front of eye

1st-winter

lacks white edge

blue-grey hue

ad. breeding

PURPLE SWAMP-HEN

blue

white

caspius (Turkey, SW Syria) **ad.**

pale blue-grey

green

madagascariensis (Egypt) **ad.**

K M

juv.   **ad.**

CRANES *Gruidae*
Very large wading birds with long legs and long neck. Bill straight, medium-long, dagger-shaped. Toes unwebbed. Tertials elongated and bulky, seem to form the tail (true tail short, hidden underneath). Experts in soaring flight, flying with neck extended like storks; form V or oblique line on migration, flock formation thus as for geese but instantly told by outstretched legs, slower pace, much gliding, incidence of soaring on thermals and higher flight altitude. Gait stately and measured. Wary. Food plants, insects, amphibians, small mammals. Nests on ground.

(Common) **Crane** *Grus grus*   **P4–5/V**∗
L 96–119 cm, WS 180–222 cm. Breeds sparsely on bogs in boreal forests, in reedbeds in lakes or along rivers in forested areas, mainly in deserted regions. Long-distance migrant (arriving late Mar–1st half Apr, leaving 2nd half Sep). Spectacular dancing display mainly in spring by pair, or involving hundreds of birds (mostly imm.) at favoured sites: walking with erect, stiff neck, sometimes with raised wings, leaping into air with beating wings, bowing, picking up items from ground and tossing them up; freezes in erect posture before shaking plumage. Food plant material, grain, old potatoes, insects. Nest mound of vegetation.

IDENTIFICATION *Huge*, with *very long legs* and *long, narrow neck*. Plumage mainly *pale bluish-grey*, but most breeding birds acquire *rusty-brown back* from staining with (ferruginous and muddy) bog water during incubation. *Head and upper neck black and white*; bare skin of *hindcrown red* (size of red varying). *Elongated tertials extremely bulky* and disorderly, giving impression of almost Ostrich-like, bushy 'tail'. Flight-feathers grey-black, contrastingly darker than coverts and body. Sexes similar, but ♂ on average slightly larger when pair seen together. When duetting (neck erect, bill pointing up, tertials and breast-feathers fluffed up), wings of ♂ half-open, of ♀ not. *Wings long and rectangular*, tips deeply 'fingered'. Majestic flight with slow wingbeats and rather flat wings, *neck and legs outstretched* as on a stork (though White Stork has proportionately slightly shorter legs and neck, at least the shorter legs often discernible in flight; Grey Heron differs in having neck withdrawn, wings deeply arched on downstroke, wing-tips not deeply 'fingered'). Expert in soaring flight but will also use active flight on migration, then forming V-shaped flocks or oblique line, flight altitude often supremely high, speed moderate. Gait measured and stately, but can be quite quick when chasing a fox away from young (performed confidently!). – Juvenile: Immediately distinguished by rather *pale rufous-brown head and upper neck*, lacking the black, white and red pattern of adult, and by less bulky tertials.

VOICE Vocal, calls loud and far-carrying. Contact-call (mainly in flight) deep, resounding, trilling or jarring 'krro' and 'karr'. Young in autumn have peculiar piping 'cheerp', mixing with deep adult calls. Pair sounds the reveille (duet-call) at breeding site in early dawn (or during light summer nights in N), ♂ uttering loud trumpeting 'krrroo' and ♀ (immediately after) lower-pitched 'kraw' and sometimes also hard, knocking 'ka-ka-ka'. Other duets may run 'krruu-**ih** kraw, **krru**-kraw, ...'.

Siberian White Crane *Grus leucogeranus*   —
L 105–135 cm, WS 205–245 cm. Extremely rare breeder in Siberia, and migrant through region, which is seen annually in small numbers in the Volga delta, on their way to and from winter grounds in N Iran. *Huge, pure white* with *black wing-tips* and *red 'face'*. Legs reddish. (Not illustrated.)

Demoiselle Crane *Anthropoides virgo*   —
L 85–100 cm, WS 155–180 cm. Breeds on, or in vicinity of, dry natural steppe with access to fresh water, sometimes at high altitudes. Avoids forests. Long-distance migrant, western population wintering in Africa, arriving in spring at breeding sites at same time as Crane (late Mar/early Apr), but leaving one month earlier (mainly late Aug); passage through Middle East largely unnoticed (seen regularly only in Jiddah, so may take easterly route; however, also often in Cyprus in Aug). Gregarious; often forms larger flocks than Crane on migration, at times several hundreds of birds. Apparently decreasing.

IDENTIFICATION *Very large*, with similar proportions to Crane, but has slightly larger, more rounded head, and somewhat shorter bill and shorter and thinner neck. The fact that it is almost 20% smaller than Crane is not always evident when seen in the field, and plumage difference not obvious at long range, especially in flight. As with Crane, *body and wing-coverts are pale ash-grey* with contrastingly *darker flight-feathers*; unlike Crane, breeding birds do not acquire rusty-brown back in summer (no bog water available; breed in drier habitats), but stay pale grey. On ground, at long range, differently shaped *tertials* best clue, being *long, pointed, straight* and *hanging down in orderly fashion*, lacking 'bushy' look of Crane. At closer range, different pattern of head and neck evident: *black on neck reaches further down*, to breast, and consists of *elongated, loose black feathers*. No red on crown as on Crane. Sexes similar, though ♂ slightly larger on average. In flight, Demoiselle Crane is very similar to Crane but in good light distinguished by *black breast*, and by having *greyer primary coverts* creating *less distinct contrast with black primaries*. The proportionately *slightly larger, more rounded head* is sometimes noticeable. Any moult-gap in the wing (Jun–Oct) indicates Demoiselle Crane (Common Crane moults all primaries simultaneously, like wildfowl). – Juvenile: Generally duller than adult, having *very pale head* (appearing whitish at distance) with vestigial tufts; foreneck and breast slate-grey (not black) in centre, feathers only slightly elongated.

VOICE In general recalling Crane, but slightly more high-pitched and drier, not so resounding. Contact-call from migrating birds 'grro', at distance similar to Crane. Courtship-calls said to be more guttural and hoarse than in Crane.

Crane   Demoiselle Crane

CRANE

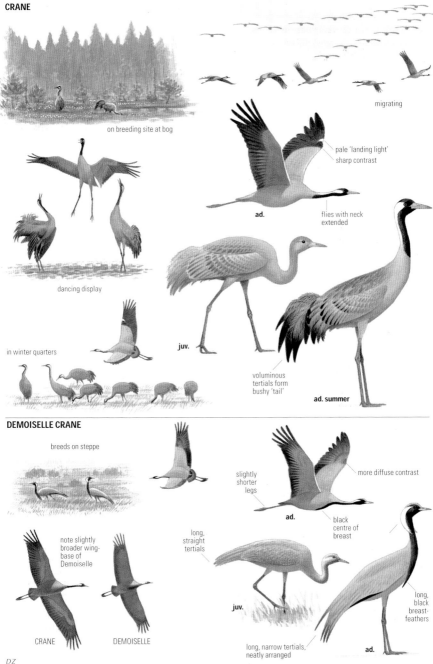

on breeding site at bog

migrating

pale 'landing light'
sharp contrast

ad.

flies with neck extended

dancing display

juv.

in winter quarters

voluminous tertials form bushy 'tail'

ad. summer

DEMOISELLE CRANE

breeds on steppe

slightly shorter legs

ad.

more diffuse contrast

black centre of breast

note slightly broader wing-base of Demoiselle

long, straight tertials

CRANE   DEMOISELLE

juv.

long, narrow tertials, neatly arranged

long, black breast-feathers

ad.

DZ

BUSTARDS *Otididae*
Medium-sized to very large, heavily built terrestrial birds with rather long, strong feet. Wings long and broad with 'fingered' tips and striking white patterns visible in flight. Birds of large plains, semi-cultivated or natural steppe or desert with scrub, but also on grassy fields and open slopes. Gait slow and deliberate if undisturbed. Feeding action recalls cranes: 'near-sighted', petty scrutiny, flashing pick-up of food. Wary, will often withdraw by running in vegetation to avoid close encounter. Often gregarious, especially outside breeding season. All species are declining in numbers, and some are endangered. Omnivorous. Nest on ground.

Great Bustard *Otis tarda* V***
L ♂ 90–105 cm, ♀ 75–85 cm, WS ♂ 210–240 cm, ♀ 170–190 cm; weight ♂ 8–16 kg, ♀ 3½–5 kg. Breeds on dry, flat and large, open plains, preferably natural steppe but accepting presence of arable fields if sufficiently undisturbed. Marked decline in numbers. Gregarious all year, having spectacular communal displays in spring and summer, when ♂♂ turn much of plumage 'inside-out', showing, and shaking, loose white feathers all over ('foam bath'), with head and neck completely withdrawn on to back.

IDENTIFICATION *Huge*, and largest ♂♂ heaviest birds in region, about 30% larger than ♀♀, and more than twice as heavy. Strongly built, with *heavy chest*, obvious especially in flight. Wings long and deeply 'fingered', flight action not unlike White-tailed Eagle, uninterrupted, measured wing-beats, majestic. On ground, recognized by *rufous tinge on breast* and *plain greyish head. Wing has much white above*, broad panel on wing-coverts contrasts with blackish secondaries and ochrous-brown or tawny forewing, white invading *washed-out outer wing* (primaries and primary coverts are diffusely tipped brown, not black). – Adult ♂: *Huge; breast and sides of lower neck rufous* (less in non-breeding); *head and upper neck blue-grey; neck very thick*, even when relaxed; *long bristle-like white feathers at sides of chin* (erected in display, lost in non-breeding); often some white visible on wing, even when folded. Displaying ♂ immediately recognized by *much white exposed*. – ♀: Smaller than ♂ (though largest close to some immature ♂♂, and sexing not always possible by size alone). Plumage differs from breeding ♂ in *less blue tinge to head*, being pale ash-grey with yellow tinge; *often lacking rufous on lower neck* (being pale blue-grey) *and breast* (being more pale ochrous-brown); and having less white on upperwing, *white only rarely showing on folded wing*; still, some ♀♀ are very similar to subadult ♂♂, especially in winter.

VOICE Mostly silent. Alarm-call is a short, nasal bark, 'ongh'. Young have a fine, plaintive whistle, 'cheeoo'.

Houbara Bustard *Chlamydotis undulata* V***
L 55–65 cm, WS 125–151 cm. Breeds in deserts and semi-deserts with sandy soil and scrub and bushes, also on steppe and in open wadis with low bushes. Display includes raising of feathers of crown and lower throat, retracting head on to back (eventually invisible among white feathers) and trotting gait. Sensitive to disturbance. Has declined.

IDENTIFICATION *Very large*, with long, narrow neck and rather *elongated body and long tail*. Wings long and rather narrow, well 'fingered'. Flight recalling giant Short-eared Owl (impressive like eagle, though wingbeats deeper, and hint of jerky upstroke as with *Asio* owls). Main feature *black band along side of neck*. Upperparts pale pink-brown with dark vermiculation. In flight, *white primary-base patch on* upperwing striking, *contrasting with black secondaries and rest of primaries*; black alula forms isolated spot. Sexes similar, but ♀ smaller, and has greyer tinge above, less pale forehead, and less clean-cut black neck band. – Variation: A local and rare race on Fuerteventura and Lanzarote, Canary Is (*fuertaventurae*), is darker above and smaller. Birds in Sinai and eastwards (*macqueenii*) are larger and paler, and this form has recently been suggested to be a separate species.

VOICE Practically mute. Young have thin piping notes.

Little Bustard *Tetrax tetrax* V***
L 40–45 cm, WS 83–91 cm. Breeds in open, flat or undulating terrain with grass or cultivation, requiring vegetation tall enough to give cover. Display, apart from call, includes foot-stamping and sometimes wing-flash with short leap in the air. Monogamous, or one ♂ can have 2–3 ♀♀. Food mainly plant material and invertebrates.

IDENTIFICATION Smallest bustard within the region, still roughly of ♀ Pheasant size. Mainly because of size, *flight* differs from that of larger relatives and is more *grouse-like*, with noisy take-off, and quick, shallow wingbeats, interrupted by short glides on medium-long wings with rounded tips and somewhat arched primaries. *Much white on wing, including secondaries*, contrasting with *black tips to outer primaries and primary coverts*. – Adult ♂ breeding: Striking pattern of head and neck, *neck being black with two white collars*; also, neck-feathers erected in display, making neck look inflated (even in flight!); *head and throat lead-grey*. Body dark-marked sandy-brown above, whitish below. Outermost 4th primary short and peculiarly emarginated to produce high-pitched whistling wing sound. – ♀ and non-breeding ♂: Like breeding ♂ but lacking black, white and grey pattern of head and neck, being sandy-brown with fine dark marks. Upperparts more heavily marked dark on ♀ than on non-breeding ♂, latter looking paler at distance.

VOICE Rather silent. Most frequently heard call is song of ♂, a slowly repeated (about every 10 sec.) dry snort, 'prrt', rather soft but still audible at 500 m. Also, ♂ has whistling wingbeat sound. When flushed, ♀ may utter a low staccato chuckle. Young have a fine, plaintive call, 'cheeoo', very similar to that of Great Bustard.

Great Bustard

Houbara Bustard

Little Bustard

GREAT BUSTARD

grazing ♂♂

lacks white 'moustache'

imm. ♂

in flight heavy, like an eagle

much white in wing

♀

ad. ♂

thick-necked

very heavy chest

early stages of the display

full display ('foam bath')

HOUBARA BUSTARD

lacks black

heavily barred

white primary patch

lacks black on neck

undulata (N Africa)

hiding from passing Bedouin party

macqueenii (Middle East)

juv.

ad.

display

LITTLE BUSTARD

much white in wing

black neck

throat-feathers can be inflated even in flight

two ♂♂ displaying with neck-feathers erected

♀

♂

♂

DZ

WADERS *Charadriiformes*

Waders comprise a large group of long-legged birds, usually living near water along shores or on bogs and marshes; a few have adapted to drier habitats. On migration and in winter often seen in dense flocks on tidal mudflats and on seaweed along the shoreline. They include several families, two of which are large: plovers and lapwings *Charadriidae*, and sandpipers and allies *Scolopacidae*; see below. Waders are closely related to skuas, gulls, terns and auks, all being members of the same large order, *Charadriiformes*.

Waders feed on insects, worms, molluscs and crustaceans; sometimes also on plant material, small fish, etc.

The nest is usually a simple scrape on the ground, and the incubating parent relies either on camouflaging plumage or on cryptic egg pattern. Young are down-covered on hatching and immediately leave nest, those of most species being self-feeding. They are tended by both parents (commonest), by the female alone (Ruff, Jack Snipe, Great Snipe, Woodcock) or by the male alone (e.g. Painted Snipe, Dotterel, Purple Sandpiper, Spotted Redshank, Wood Sandpiper, phalaropes). Among those species where both parents tend the young it is common for the female to leave the young, before they are fledged, whereas the male stays longer.

Waders are among the most interesting of all birds. Their often long-distance migrations, their association with wild places, their adaptations of structure and bill shape for different feeding techniques, and their beautiful plumages are all part of their appeal. For experienced birdwatchers, the challenge of identification adds to the attraction.

The plovers (pp.128–135) form a distinctive group of 14 species. They are all short-billed, and when relaxed have a compact, rather rounded, horizontal and short-necked shape. When approached, they head-bob nervously, and when feeding have an especially characteristic 'run-stop-peck' action. *Charadrius* plovers have particularly striking head patterns and breast-bands. The region's five lapwings (pp.136–137) are closely related to the plovers, but are usually larger and have broader, more blunt-tipped wings.

The family *Scolopacidae* (pp.138–163) includes 51 of the region's waders. It contains such well-known groups as the *Calidris* sandpipers, the curlews and godwits, the snipes, the *Tringa* sandpipers ('shanks'), and the phalaropes. Most breed in northern Europe and Siberia, nesting in open, sparsely vegetated upland or arctic habitats. In the rest of Europe they are seen mainly during winter or on migration, forming flocks on marshes and coasts. Sandpipers feed by restless picking from the surface or by probing in the mud or seaweed with their usually long and slender bill.

IDENTIFICATION OF WADERS

Beginners usually find waders difficult. This is because waders have different winter, summer and immature plumages, as well as transitional stages as they moult from one plumage to the next. Also, there is a confusing array of vagrants, most of which are very similar to their regular European counterparts. Then there is the practical problem that they are often seen at a distance, making it difficult to make out sufficient detail.

The first steps

The following suggestions should remove most of the initial confusion and uncertainty about wader identification.

Most of the main plumages displayed during the course of a year are described and illustrated. Bear in mind that they are not all seen at the same time of year, so the situation is not so complex as a first look at the plates might suggest. *Only those plumages relevant to the season need to be considered.*

If you find a 'different' wader in a flock, the overwhelming likelihood is that it will be another common species (or one in a different plumage from others of the same species around it) rather than a rarity. With this in mind, we have *grouped the regular European sandpipers together* on pp.138–153, with similar species compared on the same or an adjacent page. All of these species are fairly distinctive, and, given reasonable views (admittedly not always easy), it should be possible to identify the species fairly quickly. Until the common species can be identified with confidence, it is best to ignore the remote chance that you will find one of the vagrant species, which are treated on pp.152–163 (plus two on pp.142–143). This approach, and the arrangement of the plates, should simplify things. (For plovers and lapwings the number of possible vagrants is smaller, and regular species and vagrants are therefore treated together.)

Although you will quickly be able to identify distinctive waders such as Curlew, Redshank or an adult summer Dunlin even at a distance, most species require close views. The ideal situation is a close flock, such as from a hide at a bird reserve. A *telescope* greatly increases the potential for identification, and is essential for any serious wader-watching.

Waders are identified by a combination of features, especially size (though beware of pitfalls; see p.11), *bill shape and length, leg length, plumage patterns, colour, voice, and behaviour.* Note that shape can vary: for example, resting birds hunch their neck into the shoulders, whereas it is extended when feeding; in cold weather waders fluff up their body plumage, looking fatter and shorter-legged.

With experience, waders can be identified at increasing distances, mainly on the basis of silhouette, behaviour, and especially their distinctive flight-calls.

Advanced techniques

Wader identification can be taken much further. It may be possible to tell the sex, or what subspecies it belongs to; the various plumages can be recognized, including first-winter and first-summer, which are rarely illustrated in the plates. These abilities make identification easier. To identify difficult vagrants, it is essential to make comparisons with similar species in the same plumage. All this requires detailed observation, and knowledge of topography and moult.

A typical plover, the Ringed Plover. It has a short bill suitable for picking up.

A typical sandpiper, the Dunlin. Long bill suitable for probing.

Autumn is the best time for studying waders, because juveniles are present and it is the main moult period. Try spending an hour or two on a flock of close waders and practise ageing techniques, locating the various feather tracts, or studying their moult. Practice of this kind, repeated whenever the opportunity arises, provides the only real way of mastering wader identification and ageing.

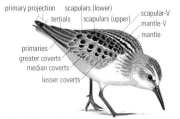

A Little Stint moulting from juvenile into 1st-winter plumage.

Topography. Practise locating the features labelled on the chart above when you look at the plates, or when studying magazine and book photographs, and birds in the field.

Moult. *Adults* have two moults each year, the 'spring' moult (mainly Jan–Apr) which produces summer plumage, and the 'autumn' moult (mainly Aug–Nov) which produces winter plumage. The spring moult is partial (head, body and variable amount of inner wing-coverts), and the autumn moult is complete (including wings and tail). Waders thus change their body plumage twice each year, but the wing-and tail-feathers only once.

J J A S O N D	J F M A M J J A S O N D

post-juvenile   spring moult   autumn moult
moult   (partial)   (complete)

Typical moult cycle of wader.

Unlike the adult, juveniles have only a partial moult in autumn, the 'post-juvenile moult' (mainly Sep–Nov), which produces first-winter plumage. Subsequent moults are as for adult. All moults take place in or near the wintering areas. The post-juvenile moult starts soon after arrival, and the spring moult is completed before the northward migration.

Ageing. Typical juvenile, adult winter and adult summer plumages, as well as any sexual difference in summer plumage, are described and illustrated in the plates. Note the following points about these plumages, including the period in which each occurs:

Juvenile: Jul–Oct (Nov). Juveniles do not usually move far from the breeding areas until mid Aug; later they usually outnumber adults in migrant flocks. Juvenile plumage is all fresh and neatly patterned, unlike the worn, variegated appearance of adults in autumn. The difference is sometimes difficult to see, and is best looked for on the tertials and greater coverts (unworn and neatly patterned on juveniles, much worn and plainer on adults).

Adult summer: (Mar) Apr–Sep (Oct). In spring, the fresh summer plumage of most *Calidris* and some other species has whitish fringes giving a distinctive 'frosted' appearance. These not very resistant broad fringes disappear quickly to reveal full summer colour, usually by the time the birds arrive in the breeding areas. By late summer, the plumage is generally highly worn and darker above. In autumn, any wing moult indicates adult; this is useful for ageing adults in flight, on which the tatty, moulting wings are obvious.

Adult winter: Sep–Mar. In most species, winter plumage is plainer, less colourful, and quite unlike juvenile and adult summer plumages.

The following plumages are usually not described:

First-winter: (Sep) Oct–Mar. Because the wings are not included in the post-juvenile moult, first-winters can be told from adult winter by the pattern of the retained juvenile wing-feathers. The difference shows best on the tertials or greater coverts. As shown in the plates, the pattern on these feathers is, on most species, quite different from the usually plainer adult winter ones. Wear reduces the difference, however, and it is usually difficult to discern after midwinter.

First-summer: May–Jul. First-summers often stay in the wintering areas all summer, and do not return north with the adults. In most species, the first spring moult produces only partial summer plumage, or a plumage little different from winter. In some species, adult summer females are less bright than males, so only extreme winter-like birds can safely be aged as first-summer. First-summers often start their moult early, so any individuals in full winter plumage in Jul–Aug are probably second-winter. Before May and after Jul, it is not safe to distinguish between first-summers and late- or early-moulting adults.

Transitional plumages: Moulting birds show mixed characters of adjacent plumages, and are referred to as e.g. 'adult winter moulting to summer' or 'juvenile moulting to first-winter'. Transitional plumages are especially noticeable in autumn, with the usually plainer and less colourful winter feathers producing a patchy appearance against the summer or juvenile plumage.

Juvenile Dunlin moulting to 1st-winter plumage.

1st-winter Dunlin: note diagnostic retained juvenile wing-feathers. Cf. adult winter.

Adult winter Dunlin: note plain wing-feathers. Cf. 1st-winter.

Adult summer Dunlin moulting to winter plumage.

(Eurasian) **Oystercatcher**
Haematopus ostralegus r+m**B**3

L 39–44 cm (incl. bill 6½–9), WS 72–83 cm. Breeds on open, flat coasts. Commonly feeds on tidal flats or fields and other open ground (generally no more than *c.* 20 km from sea, but locally much further inland); roosts communally in winter. Food mainly cockles, mussels, worms; also crustaceans, insects. Vertically flattened, blade-like blunt-tipped bill specially adapted for hammering and opening cockles, mussels, etc. Nest is bare scrape on ground, preferring pebbly patches, sand or rocky ground to grassy meadows.

IDENTIFICATION Large, compact and deep-chested. Striking combination of *long and straight orange-red bill* and *black and white plumage*. Broad *white wing-bar* conspicuous in flight. Flight direct with quick wingbeats, somewhat recalling a duck. – Adult summer: Orbital ring orange-red, eye deep red. ♂ has on average shorter, thicker bill than ♀; sometimes ♂ also has brighter red base of bill, but sexing of single birds usually not possible. Legs pink. – Adult winter: Like adult summer, but has obvious white 'chinstrap'. – Juvenile: Dull brownish-black above, not black; extensive black tip to pale orange bill; legs greyish. – 1st-year: Distinguished from adult by narrower black tail-band; extensively dark-tipped bill; brownish upperparts; dull flesh legs; white chinstrap usually retained in 1st summer; wings (retained from juv.) much faded, brownish by 1st summer; orbital ring dull yellow-orange and eye brownish-red. Some older birds may retain dark bill-tip, so 1st-year safely ageable only by notation of full range of features.

VOICE Noisy. Common flight-call (also when perched) is distinctive far-carrying, shrill 'peep' or 'k-peep!'. So-called piping call (usually from ground, open bill pointing down, often maintained by pair or dense little group) is of similar shrill quality; typical phrases, often run together, are accelerating 'kip kip kip-kip-kip-...' running into a fast 'kli-klikli...', and a distinctive bubbling trill, 'prrrrrrrrr...'. Flight-song (by ♂, or ♂+♀, in wide-circling display-flight, typically with slow-motion, deep wingbeats) contains slower 'plee-ah plee-ah plee-ah...' in time with wingbeats.

(Pied) **Avocet** *Recurvirostra avosetta* r+m**B**4

L 42–46 cm (incl. bill *c.* 8; excl. leg projection *c.* 10), WS 67–77 cm. Breeds on flat, open seashores or shallow lagoons with brackish or salt water, with bare margins and sandy shoals; in winter, also frequents estuaries, mudflats. Migratory in N and E, wintering in Mediterranean and Africa. In Britain & Ireland, uncommon away from well-known breeding colonies and wintering sites in E and S England. Food mainly insects and small crustaceans, typically obtained by distinctive feeding action in which slightly opened bill-tip is swept from side to side through water or soft mud, detecting prey by touch. Also feeds by pecking at surface of mud; occasionally swims, upending to feed like a duck. Nest is sparsely or fully lined scrape on bare ground near water, occasionally more substantial collection of vegetation forming raised mound in shallow water. Wary, giving full alarm in flight when disturbed during breeding.

IDENTIFICATION In quick or distant view, can be overlooked as a gull because of general white appearance. Otherwise *unmistakable pattern of black and white*, slender *upcurved black bill* and *long pale blue legs*. In flight, pied pattern distinctive, though at long range can be taken for ♂ Goosander or Shelduck. – Adult: ♂ told by longer bill which appears less sharply curved, and head markings always black and neat; ♀ has shorter, sharply curved bill, and head markings are sometimes less clear-cut and tinged brownish. – Juvenile: Markings dull brownish, not black; white areas sullied brownish or barred; legs dull grey. – 1st-year: Distinguishable from adult so long as juvenile features retained; primaries much faded and brownish by 1st summer.

VOICE Common call is loud, piping 'klüp klüp klüp...' with characteristic ring; used also for alarm.

Black-winged Stilt *Himantopus himantopus* V**

L 33–36 cm (incl. bill *c.* 6½; excl. leg projection 14–17). Frequents areas of shallow fresh, brackish or salt water, e.g. lagoons, saltpans, estuaries. Migratory, generally wintering in Africa. Vagrant to Britain & Ireland. Food mainly insects; long legs enable feeding in deeper water than used by other waders. Nest is lined scrape on islet or near water, occasionally a raised mound of vegetation in shallow water.

IDENTIFICATION Extraordinarily elegant wader; unmistakable, with *needle-fine, straight bill*, amazingly *long reddish-pink legs*, and *black and white plumage*. In flight, head and legs extended, giving bizarrely elongated outline; *all-black underwing* and flicking wing action with quite *pointed wings* add to distinctive appearance. – Adult: ♂ readily told by whole upperparts green-glossed black; ♀ has glossy brown mantle and scapulars forming brown saddle that contrasts with black wings. ♂ averages more black on head than ♀, but much overlap and head and neck pattern not safe difference between sexes. – Juvenile: Dull brown with scaly pattern of pale feather fringes, and pale-tipped secondaries and white-tipped inner primaries; legs dull flesh. – 1st-year: Told from adult so long as dull legs and juvenile flight-feathers retained; many indistinguishable by 1st summer.

VOICE Very noisy during breeding season, otherwise rather silent. Common call is shrill, squeaky, quickly repeated 'kyik kyik kyik...', recalling Avocet (similar fluty, ringing tone, but higher-pitched and harder, less liquid). Potential predators near colony chased with loud and grating 'kreet kreet kreet...', rather like Spur-winged Lapwing. A rolling 'krre' can sound rather like Black-headed Gull. Juvenile has different call, 'gip!', recalling Wood Sandpiper, which can be heard still in 2nd cal.-year spring.

Oystercatcher Avocet Black-winged Stilt

OYSTERCATCHER

display

ad. summer

not pure black

dark tip

lacks dark tip

brownish-black

greyish-pink

1st-summer

pink

greyish

juv.

ad. winter

ad. summer

AVOCET

can be surprisingly difficult to spot among gulls

ad.

thin, black upturned bill unique

juv.

ad. ♀

ad. ♂

BLACK-WINGED STILT

1st-winter

white trailing edge

white wedge

all-dark wings

brown-tinged back

ad.

amazingly long legs

jet-black back

♂ has on average more black on head than ♀, but note that *head pattern varies in both sexes*

juv.

ad. ♀

ad. ♂

KM

Stone-curlew *Burhinus oedicnemus* m**B**4

L 38–45 cm, WS 76–88 cm. Breeds on bare or sparsely vegetated open ground (heathland, dry, stony pastures, dried mud, steppe margins, etc.). Summer visitor (Mar–Oct), winters in SW Europe and Africa. In Britain & Ireland, rare away from few breeding areas in S and E England. Most active dusk to dawn, but daytime activity and calling not unusual. Food mainly insects. Nest is bare scrape.

IDENTIFICATION General shape and actions like oversized plover. Walks stealthily or runs with long body held horizontal and head often hunched into shoulders. Well camouflaged when stationary; *large yellow eye* and *black-tipped bill* are often most eye-catching features. Distinctive in flight, with *strong black and white wing pattern*, hunchbacked profile, and *shallow beats of long, stiffly bowed wings*. Will sometimes squat on ground to avoid detection. – Adult: Standing ♂ has horizontal white covert bar more strongly bordered with black than ♀, difference obvious when pair seen together. – Juvenile: Lacks prominent whitish supercilium; coverts plain, sandy (lacking adult's obvious blackish and whitish bars); greater coverts broadly fringed white.

VOICE Noisy during breeding season. Some calls rather reminiscent of Curlew, like rising, whistling 'küü-**lii**e' or 'kur-li-**lii**'and alarm, a rapid 'kü-vü-**vü**', repeated in long series. Also heard is a thin piping 'kiiiie'. Display-call often heard at night, a series of loud, wailing, mournful notes with first syllable coarsely trilled and second clear, 'klii-ürr-**lee**, klürrr-**lee**, klürrr-**leee**, klürrr-**leee**, klürrr-**leee**,...'.

Senegal Thick-knee *Burhinus senegalensis* —

L 35–39 cm. Resident Egypt, mainly Nile delta and Cairo region. Inhabits open ground like Stone-curlew, but showing marked preference for wet habitats and water margins.

IDENTIFICATION Like Stone-curlew, but *bill longer, stouter*, with relatively *small area of yellow at base*, and broad, *uniform pale grey midwing-panel*, lacking adult Stone-curlew's dark double wing-bars with a narrow white bar between. Legs on average duller greyish-yellow, not so bright yellow.

VOICE Long series of mournful, ringing whistles, first rising and accelerating, then falling and fading, 'pü pi pi-pi-pi-**pii**-**pii**-**pii**-pii-pi pi...', vaguely recalling Oystercatcher.

Cream-coloured Courser *Cursorius cursor* **V*****

L 24–27 cm. Requires bare, flat terrain to accommodate ground-running behaviour, especially sandy semi-desert. Uncommon, but sometimes in small groups. Vagrant to Europe, including Britain & Ireland. Food mainly insects.

IDENTIFICATION Unmistakable through its *all sandy-buff plumage* and *pale legs*. Smaller than Golden Plover. Rather plover-like in feeding action and structure, but *much longer-legged*, and *bill curved*. Flight action flicking, rather dove-like, interspersed with short glides. Distant flight pattern very distinctive: *black outer wing* and 'flashing' *black underwing* contrast sharply with pale sandy-buff remainder. Juvenile has plainer head and faint scaly pattern above.

VOICE Usual flight-call is subdued, ventriloquial 'quett'.

Collared Pratincole *Glareola pratincola* **V***

L 24–28 cm, WS 60–70 cm. Breeds in loose colonies in extensive flat, dry terrain with low vegetation, canals and areas of bare ground (e.g. drained deltas); also wet meadows, reedbeds, by saltpans, etc. Summer visitor (Apr–Oct), winters in Africa. Vagrant to N Europe; annual in Britain & Ireland. Catches insects in flight, interspersing graceful Black Tern-like action with erratic swooping or dashing manoeuvres over wide area. Nest is scrape on bare ground.

IDENTIFICATION Long wings and forked tail giving *tern-like shape* but with longer legs and stubby bill. At distance look for distinctive combination of *agile feeding flight* (see above) and *square white rump and white belly contrasting with all-dark remainder*. Collared difficult to tell from Black-winged: at close range, *dull red underwing-coverts* and *white trailing edge of inner wing* are diagnostic of Collared, but even then both may be surprisingly difficult to discern. Also generally paler above than Black-winged, and adult has more red at base of bill. (Cf. also rare vagrant Oriental Pratincole, p. 380.) At very close range, adult summer ♂ has black lores (brownish on ♀) and slightly sharper head pattern than ♀. Neat black throat-surround lost in winter – Juvenile: Dense dark spotting forming broad breast-band. Head plain; scaly above; all-black bill.

VOICE Calls nasal but piercing. Common flight-call is a high-pitched, sharp 'kit' or 'kittik' recalling Little Tern, from flocks in spring (song) excited, rhythmic five-syllable calls, '**kür**re-kek kit**tik**'.

Black-winged Pratincole *Glareola nordmanni* **V****

L 24–28 cm. Breeding habitat as for Collared Pratincole but more often found at wet meadows, reedy marshes and in vegetated areas. Summer visitor (Apr–Oct), winters mainly in S Africa. Vagrant to W Europe.

IDENTIFICATION Very similar to Collared Pratincole, but *darker and more uniform upperwing* (invariably lacking light trailing edge to inner wing), *black underwing* (Collared, too, can look black in poor light!), at rest *slightly longer legs* and on average *shorter tail*. Adult has *less red at base of bill* than Collared and often slightly *darker lores and forehead*.

VOICE Similar to Collared Pratincole's but slightly lower-pitched and harder and drier ('knocking'), often 'kettek' 'ke-ti-tik' or 'kett'. Alarm is dry, hard, rolling 'tr-r-rt'.

Stone-curlew

Cream-coloured Courser

Collared Pratincole

Black-winged Pratincole

STONE-CURLEW

relies on camouflage to avoid detection

large yellow eye

wing-bars less prominent than on ad.

juv.

ad.

SENEGAL THICK-KNEE

larger white patch than on Stone-curlew

heavier bill with less yellow than Stone-curlew

lacks black-bordered whitish band

usually plainer outer tail than on Stone-curlew

CREAM-COLOURED COURSER

blue-grey

diffusely spotted

all-black underwing

runs with head held high

juv.

ad.

COLLARED PRATINCOLE

winter

white trailing edge

ad. summer

red-brown

often appears black in shadow

obvious contrast between coverts and flight-feathers

scaly pattern

juv.

medium brown

obvious red

ad. winter

tail often longer than wing-tip

ad. summer

BLACK-WINGED PRATINCOLE

1st-winter

no white edge

ad. summer

black

short-tailed

rather uniform upperwing

at rest, juv. Black-winged (not shown) and Collared Pratincoles (see left) are practically identical

black on lores and forehead tends to be extensive

less red

dark

ad. winter

tail invariably clearly shorter than wing-tip

rather long

ad. summer

KM

Little Ringed Plover *Charadrius dubius* m**B**4

L 15½–18 cm, WS 32–35 cm. Breeds on bare, usually sandy or gravelly terrain near fresh water, e.g. river or lake edges or islands, often at man-made sites such as gravel-pits, reservoirs or saltpans. Summer visitor to Europe (mostly Apr–Sep/Oct), winters in Africa. Rather scarce in most areas, but sometimes seen in small groups on migration. Generally prefers freshwater margins and estuaries to coastal mudflats. Food mainly insects. Nest is shallow scrape on bare ground.

IDENTIFICATION Slightly smaller than Ringed Plover, with slimmer, longer bill and more slender rear end. Often appears slightly *longer-legged* owing to less 'full' chest and belly. *No light wing-bar or only a very faint one; dark ear-covert patch often rather pointed at lower rear corner*, not rounded. Long tertials cover most of primaries (thus shorter primary projection than on Ringed Plover). – Adult: Distinctive combination of *obvious yellow orbital ring*, all-black bill, and pale brownish- or greyish-pink (not orange) legs. ♀ has much brown in black head markings and breast-band. In winter, black on head and breast becomes brown, forehead and supercilium buffish; yellow orbital ring usually still visible. – Juvenile: Distinguished from Ringed by *smaller and more diffuse pale area on forehead, not extending back behind eye* in obvious supercilium (is tinged buff above lores and eye), and *pale yellow orbital ring* visible at close range.

VOICE Commonest call, often heard from lone bird in flight, a slightly downslurred, short, piping '**piu**' (or 'pew'). Alarm-call a similar but straighter and more strident and hard 'pree'. On territory, sometimes an almost Sand Martin-like rasping 'rererere...'. Song, either in daytime in slow-winged, bat-like display circuit or heard at night, consists of quick, hard 'pri-pri-pri-...' and rather slow, rhythmic, coarse, buzzy '**cree**-a, **cree**-a, **cree**-a, ...'.

(Common) Ringed Plover

Charadrius hiaticula r(m)**B**3 / **P+W**

L 17–19½ cm, WS 35–41 cm. Breeds on open shores by sea or lakes, preferring gravelly or sandy patches among short grass; also above treeline on fells and tundra. Outside breeding season fairly common on inland water margins, estuaries and tidal flats; may form sizable groups on migration and in winter. Food is wide variety of freshwater and marine invertebrates. Nest is scrape on sand, shingle or other bare ground near inland water or on the coast.

IDENTIFICATION Compared with Little Ringed Plover, more compact and full-chested with slightly shorter tertials and longer primary projection. Flight rapid with rather loosely 'clipped' wingbeats; compared with e.g. Dunlin, is longer-winged with less protruding head. Adult's *orange legs and bill-base*, and *prominent white wing-bar* striking; ♀

has often much brown in black head markings and breast-band, giving less clear-cut and smart appearance than ♂. In winter, legs are sometimes a little duller orange, and bill sometimes is all dark. – Juvenile: *Dark brown* instead of black *on head and breast*; *breast-band reduced* or broken in centre; upperparts finely pale-fringed; bill all dark or with a little yellowish at the base, *legs* dull orange to *yellowish*. Black on head and breast acquired by Dec/Jan, after which 1st-winter rarely distinguishable from adult. – Variation: Very slight; northerly birds of Fenno-Scandian mountains and arctic coasts (ssp. *tundrae*) on average slightly smaller and slimmer than in rest of Europe (*hiaticula*) and a tinge darker above; they also moult flight-feathers in winter quarters, instead of near breeding grounds as *hiaticula*.

VOICE Call very characteristic: a soft, distinctly disyllabic, rising '**poo**-eep'. Alarm is a monosyllabic, piping 'peep'. Song usually alternates between a quick, rhythmic, mellow 'tee-**too**-e tee-**too**-e tee-**too**-e tee-**too**-e...' and a hurried, more simple 't'**wee**a-t'**wee**a-t'**wee**a-t'**wee**a-...', usually in slow-winged, bat-like display circuit low over the ground.

Semipalmated Plover *Charadrius semipalmatus* **V**∗∗∗

L 16–17½ cm. Vagrant from N America; only two British records, and one Spanish, but probably overlooked.

IDENTIFICATION Very similar to Ringed Plover, except in slightly smaller, and all *front toes are obviously webbed* (Ringed has tiny web only between middle and outer toes), *bill averages shorter and thicker-based* (but some have same bill size), and slightly smaller and more slim-bodied shape recalling Little Ringed Plover (but beware smaller northern Ringed Plover ssp. *tundrae*). In all plumages has *thin pale orbital ring* (lacking on Ringed except some ad. ♂♂, and note that juv. Ringed often shows a suggestion of a pale eye-ring or crescent in front of or below the eye). – Adult: Dark breast-band averages narrower, and on most lacks obvious breast-side bulges, *often strikingly thin and of even width*; ♂ usually lacks white supercilium behind eye (almost always present on Ringed). – Juvenile: At close range, look for more or less large wedge of white extending from side of throat above corner of gape (juv. Ringed practically always dark from lores down to gape). Also, upperwing-coverts often more contrastingly pale-fringed, and breast-band seldom if ever broken in centre.

VOICE Differs markedly from Ringed's: either a quick, hoarse, rising whistle, 'che**wee**', not so distinctly disyllabic as Ringed's, and with stress on second syllable, recalling a distant Spotted Redshank; or a more drawn-out 'che-**wee**'.

Killdeer *Charadrius vociferus* **V**∗∗

L 23½–26 cm. Vagrant from N America, annual in Britain & Ireland. Mostly recorded in winter. Prefers meadows and short-grass fields, but can also be seen on sandy seashores.

IDENTIFICATION Obviously larger than Ringed Plover and with longer neck, long all-dark bill, and much *longer tail producing strikingly elongated rear end. Double dark breast-band* and *orange-brown rump* diagnostic in all plumages. 1st-year distinguishable only by faint pale fringes on retained juvenile upperpart feathers.

VOICE Thin, far-carrying, high-pitched, rising 'klüee', sometimes breaking into fast, whinnying 'klüee-i-i-i-...'.

Little Ringed Plover   Ringed Plover

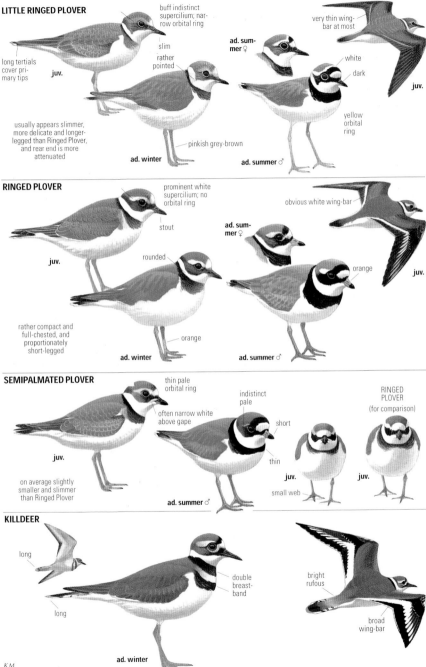

LITTLE RINGED PLOVER

buff indistinct supercilium; narrow orbital ring

very thin wing-bar at most

ad. summer ♀

long tertials cover primary tips

juv.

slim

rather pointed

white

dark

juv.

usually appears slimmer, more delicate and longer-legged than Ringed Plover, and rear end is more attenuated

pinkish grey-brown

yellow orbital ring

ad. winter

ad. summer ♂

RINGED PLOVER

prominent white supercilium; no orbital ring

obvious white wing-bar

stout

ad. summer ♀

juv.

rounded

orange

juv.

rather compact and full-chested, and proportionately short-legged

orange

orange

ad. winter

ad. summer ♂

SEMIPALMATED PLOVER

thin pale orbital ring

indistinct pale

RINGED PLOVER (for comparison)

often narrow white above gape

short

juv.

thin

on average slightly smaller and slimmer than Ringed Plover

juv.

juv.

small web

ad. summer ♂

KILLDEER

long

double breast-band

bright rufous

long

broad wing-bar

ad. winter

KM

Kentish Plover *Charadrius alexandrinus* P5

L 15–17 cm. Breeds on mudflats or sparsely vegetated ground near coasts. Summer visitor to N Europe (mostly Mar–Oct). Locally common, but has declined in many areas. Food insects, crustaceans, worms. Nest on bare ground.

IDENTIFICATION Slightly smaller, longer-legged and *thinner-billed* than Ringed Plover, with *short 'stern'* and *flat-crowned, broad, large head. Paler than Ringed*. In all plumages has *small dark breast-side patches* rather than complete or centrally broken breast-band; bill black; *legs blackish* (or sometimes paler grey-brown); in flight, shows prominent wing-bar and *all-white tail-sides*. – Adult: ♂ has neat black markings on head and breast-sides, and *crown and nape with* variable amount of *rusty colour*; pattern and colour less well marked in winter. ♀ has grey-brown (not black) markings on head and breast (rarely, may have complete brown breast-band), and no or very little rusty on crown. – Juvenile: Like adult ♀, but head and breast-side markings paler and has fine pale fringes on upperparts. – 1st-summer ♂: Lacks fully developed black markings and rusty crown.

VOICE Calls on ground, often in anxiety, are a quiet, rolling 'dr'r'rp' and an ascending, soft whistle, 'bew-it' (almost like Spotted Crake). Flight-call is a short 'bip' or 'bipip'. The song is rarely heard, a mixture of rhythmical '**che**-ke **che**-ke **che**-ke...' and somewhat Dunlin-like hard rolling, guttural 'drruu**rree-rre-rre**', usually in butterfly-like display-flight.

Kittlitz's Plover *Charadrius pecuarius* —

L 14–16 cm. Found on mudflats, shores, near ponds, etc. Locally common in Egypt. Mainly sedentary; vagrant to Israel. Nest is scrape on bare ground, often near water.

IDENTIFICATION Adult summer *head pattern and orange-washed underparts unmistakable*. Winter adult and juvenile more difficult: resemble Kentish Plover but slightly smaller (appear to have a shorter body), *longer-billed*, and *longer-legged*. In all plumages (esp. breeding), has rather *patterned, 'faded-looking' upperparts* caused by diffuse pale feather fringes, not uniform upperparts as on Kentish Plover; dark lesser coverts sometimes show as dark 'shoulder'; and *obvious buff or pinkish tone to supercilium, hindneck-collar, breast-side patches and across breast*, not whitish as on Kentish Plover. Legs are grey, sometimes faintly tinged green or brown. Toes project well beyond tail in flight.

VOICE Rather silent. Short 'chik' in flight, and a dry 'drrr'.

Lesser Sand Plover *Charadrius mongolus* V***

L 17–19 cm. Vagrant to Europe from Central or E Asia; scarce migrant in Middle East. Often seen on shorelines, mudflats and fields. Winters E Africa and S Asia.

IDENTIFICATION Only slightly larger than Ringed Plover but proportionately somewhat longer-legged and longer-billed. All plumages very similar to Greater Sand Plover, esp. non-breeding, so size and structure important: is slightly *smaller*; structure recalls Kentish owing to proportionately *rather large head*, similar leg length *without noticeably long tibiae*, and *small bill*, length of which is equal to or less than distance from bill-base to rear of eye, and *bill-tip is blunter* (Greater often has *noticeably long tibiae*, and usually *heavier bill*, length of which is usually greater than bill-base to rear of eye, and *bill-tip is more pointed*); *legs dark* grey-green (often paler grey-green or yellowish-grey on Greater); and *even-width, full-length wing-bar* (on Greater, inner wing-bar faint, outer wing-bar broad). Tends to take fewer steps (1–4) between shorter pauses when feeding (Greater often takes 3–10 steps and pauses longer, but much overlap). – Adult: Summer ♂ has on average broader rufous breast-band and more black on head than often somewhat duller ♀, but sometimes sexes are more similar. – 1st-summer: Only partly acquires adult plumage. Winter adult and immature plumages recall Kentish, from which told by larger size, absence of white hindneck-collar and lack of all-white tail-sides. – Variation: In Central Asia (ssp. *pamirensis* of *atrifrons* group), legs and bill slightly longer, wings shorter, forehead on summer ♂ black with only tiny white loral spots, and rufous breast-band lacks black upper border; in E Asia (*mongolus* group), legs and bill shorter, wings longer, forehead on summer ♂ with large white patch, and rufous breast-band has thin black upper border.

VOICE Hard, short 'trik' or 'tirrik'; also has soft, more rolling 'trrrp', very similar to call of Greater Sand Plover.

Greater Sand Plover *Charadrius leschenaultii* V**

L 19–22 cm. Scarce breeder in C Turkey and Middle East on dry, sparsely vegetated steppe. Uncommon migrant Middle East; vagrant to Europe. On migration and in winter frequents beaches or water margins near coast. Food insects, small crustaceans and marine worms.

IDENTIFICATION Proportions recall Grey Plover rather than Kentish, but smaller, slimmer, much longer-legged (esp. tibiae), and bill longer. In all plumages resembles Lesser Sand Plover, which see for detailed comparison. Note particularly *slightly larger size, longer legs and bill*, latter with somewhat stronger base and *more pointed, attenuated* tip, also often noticeably *longer body* and *slightly longer and thinner neck*. Legs on average *paler* greenish- or yellowish-grey than on Lesser. Sexes appear to differ clearly, ♀ being much duller and greyer. – Variation: Breeders in Turkey and W Middle East (ssp. *columbinus*) have slightly shorter bill, and summer ♂ much rufous on breast and often on flanks and back, too. Birds E of Caspian Sea (*crassirostris*) similar but with longer, stronger bill. In E Asia (*leschenaultii*), rufous breast-band is narrow.

VOICE Call a trilling 'trrr', often quickly doubled or trebled; quality recalls Curlew Sandpiper or Turnstone. Difficult to tell from some Lesser Sand Plover calls without much practice.

Kentish Plover

Kittlitz's Plover

Greater Sand Plover

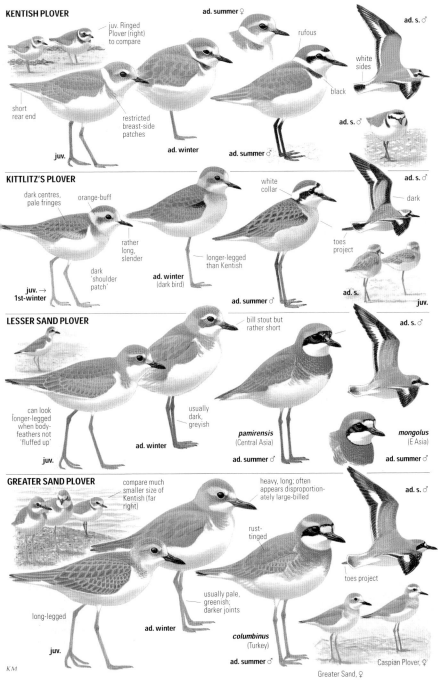

KENTISH PLOVER

juv. Ringed Plover (right) to compare

ad. summer ♀

rufous

black

ad. s. ♂

white sides

ad. s. ♂

short rear end

restricted breast-side patches

juv.

ad. winter

ad. summer ♂

KITTLITZ'S PLOVER

ad. s. ♂

dark centres, pale fringes

orange-buff

white collar

dark

toes project

rather long, slender

longer-legged than Kentish

dark 'shoulder patch'

juv. →
1st-winter

ad. winter
(dark bird)

ad. summer ♂

ad. s.

juv.

LESSER SAND PLOVER

bill stout but rather short

ad. s. ♂

can look longer-legged when body-feathers not 'fluffed up'

usually dark, greyish

pamirensis
(Central Asia)

mongolus
(E Asia)

juv.

ad. winter

ad. summer ♂

ad. summer ♂

GREATER SAND PLOVER

compare much smaller size of Kentish (far right)

heavy, long; often appears disproportion-ately large-billed

ad. s. ♂

rust-tinged

toes project

long-legged

usually pale, greenish; darker joints

columbinus
(Turkey)

juv.

ad. winter

Caspian Plover, ♀

KM

ad. summer ♂

Greater Sand, ♀

Grey Plover *Pluvialis squatarola*   **P / W**3

L 26–29 cm, WS 56–63 cm. Breeds in high Arctic on tundra, where adults spend Jun–Jul, then migrates to W Europe, where some stop to moult, and even stay through winter (mostly ♂♂), whereas a majority pass through to winter W Africa (mostly ♀♀ in tropical Africa); juveniles migrate *c.* 1½ months later (late Aug–Sep) than adults in autumn. On autumn migration seen on coastline, often singles or a few birds only, loosely spread out along shore or on shingle bank, behaviour poised (even sluggish). In winter frequents tidal flats and adjacent freshwater pools, can be seen in large gatherings at high tide. In spring crosses N Europe in one or two long legs in May, usually passing unnoticed at great height in fair weather, but in cold, adverse conditions large, dense flocks can sometimes be seen resting. Food mainly marine worms, molluscs and crustaceans.

IDENTIFICATION Distinctively big plover with *bulky body*, *large head* and *heavy bill*; posture more hunched and feeding action more ponderous than with smaller plovers. In flight, *black axillaries* diagnostic, *bold white wing-bar* and *whitish rump* characteristic. – Adult summer: ♂ has solid black below, ♀ has white intermixed. – Adult winter: Underparts whitish, and grey upperpart feathers and wing-coverts diffusely fringed or barred whitish. – Juvenile: Greyish-black upperparts and wing-coverts neatly spotted and notched *yellowish-buff*; underparts pale yellowish-buff with fine grey streaking; *black 'armpits'* distinctive in flight; general coloration often yellowish-brown, recalling juvenile Golden Plover, and since it has a well-marked pale supercilium and often a hint of a dark ear patch it may even resemble an American Golden Plover (p. 134). – 1st-summer: Like adult winter or with very little black below. Many stay through summer in W Europe and W Africa.

VOICE Vocal. Call is a distinctive, mournful, trisyllabic whistle with middle syllable lower-pitched and sometimes stressed, 'peee-**uu**-ee'; at times, often with juveniles, voice is shrill and hoarse. Display-song, often in butterfly-like slow-motion flight, is a different trisyllabic whistle with first and last syllables lower and stressed, '**plu**-ee-**uu**'; other calls heard on breeding grounds, usually in anxiety, are a straight 'plüüh' and a Curlew-like 'pluu-ee'.

(Eurasian) Dotterel *Charadrius morinellus*   m**B**4

L 20½–24 cm. Breeds high in mountain areas with low cover and scree, often preferring partly flat areas; also on open tundra. Occurs on northerly breeding sites mostly mid Jun–mid Aug. Rare on migration, often singles or in small groups on arable or short-grass fields. Food insects. Nest is bare scrape. ♂ does most of incubation and care of young. Some ♂♂ are extremely tame just before eggs hatch.

IDENTIFICATION Somewhat smaller than Golden Plover, and is slightly more compact, with shorter neck and wings and proportionately larger head with smaller bill. In all plumages, has *long white or ochrous-buff supercilium* and *plain upperwing* with narrow pale leading edge (white shaft to outermost primary). – Adult summer: Combination of *orange-rusty breast*, *black belly*, narrow *black and white breast-band* and well-marked *white supercilium* contrasting with *dark hindcrown* makes it unmistakable; as with Phalaropes, ♀ is brighter-coloured, smarter than ♂. – Adult winter: Greyish breast and flanks tinged buff, with *faint whitish breast-band*, and upperpart feathers and wing-coverts dark (slaty-) grey with thin rufous-buff fringes. – Juvenile: Like adult winter, but upperparts and larger wing-coverts blackish-brown with neat *creamy-buff fringes broken at tip by black central streak*; underparts have on average more obvious dark mottling on breast and upper flanks. – 1st-winter: Told by retained juvenile wing-coverts.

VOICE Flight-call on migration (often on take-off) is a soft, rolling, somewhat descending 'pjürr'. Contact-call also a simple 'kwip-kwip'. Song by ♀ is a simple, repeated whistling, 'pwit pwit pwit...', *c.* 2 calls per sec., delivered in flight over territory with shallow, shivering wingbeats.

Caspian Plover *Charadrius asiaticus*   **V**★★★

L 19–21 cm. Breeds in Central Asia, mainly N and E of Caspian Sea, on dry plains, often lowland and saline habitats near water; often forms loose breeding colony, nests *c.* 50 m apart. Summer visitor (mostly late Apr–early Aug), winters Africa. Rare in Middle East on migration, vagrant Europe (recent British records on Scilly Is and in Scotland). Nest is sparsely lined scrape on bare or thinly vegetated ground.

IDENTIFICATION Resembles the sand plovers, but *shape and carriage much more elegant, with slimmer, more elongated rear end*, has longer, slimmer bill than Lesser and *long legs* like Greater. Slightly larger than Ringed Plover, about size of Lesser Sand Plover, but slender, elegant shape makes it appear larger than it actually is. In all plumages, has *much bolder pale rear supercilium* than sand plovers, lacks obvious white on tail-sides (white confined to terminal fringe), and has only a *faint wing-bar*. – Summer ♂: Pure white forehead, lores and cheeks, dark ear-coverts, and *broad chestnut breast-band* distinctly *bordered black at lower edge*; 1st-summer can be less well marked. – Summer ♀: Supercilium and cheeks *off-white*, not pure white; ear-coverts very *pale brown*; breast-band grey-brown with just a little chestnut, and *no black lower border*; border between off-white throat and grey-brown breast-band diffuse. – Winter: Adult plumage resembles sand plover (cf. p. 130), but has *an extensive grey-brown unbroken breast-band*, not defined breast-side patches, and *more grey underwing*. Juvenile similar to adult winter, but has more obvious pale fringes on upperparts.

VOICE Call on ground a short 'chüp', often quickly repeated twice, but usually given singly in flight. Song is a repeated ringing trisyllabic call.

Grey Plover

Dotterel

Caspian Plover

GREY PLOVER

two ad. summers and one 1st-summer

juv.

bold white wing-bar

white

black axillaries

ad. summer ♂

neatly spotted and notched yellow-buff

heavy

juv.

ad. winter

ad. summer ♀

ad. summer ♂

DOTTEREL

juv.

white shaft

plain above

ad. s. ♀

lacks wing-bar

dark with creamy-buff fringes; some scapulars renewed

broad supercilium, buff at rear

more evenly grey than ♂

bright rufous

pale breast-band

juv. → 1st-winter

ad. winter

ad. summer ♀

ad. s. ♂

CASPIAN PLOVER

juv.

ad. s. ♂

short white wing-bar

toes project

♂ and ♀

rather prominent pale fringes

broad white

much white

long, thin

long tibia

grey-green

black rim

juv.

ad. winter

ad. summer ♀

ad. summer ♂

KM

(European) **Golden Plover** *Pluvialis apricaria* †**B**3 / **W**2

L 25–28 cm, WS 53–59 cm. Breeds on moors, bogs, upland pastures, mountainsides above treeline, tundra; on British breeding sites mostly late Mar–mid Jul, but on northern tundras Jun–Aug. In winter on lowland fields or pastures, often with Lapwings and locally in large flocks. Migrating flocks dense, flight rapid; roosting movements at dawn and dusk involve much manoeuvring (flock flicking from yellow-brown to white as birds turn). Rarely seen wading, prefers drier ground. Rather shy and wary. Food insects, worms, berries and seeds. Nest is scrape in heather or grass.

IDENTIFICATION Slightly smaller and daintier than Grey Plover, and has somewhat *narrower and more pointed wings* and faster wingbeats. At distance looks brown above, but seen close has dark grey upperparts with feather edges densely notched greenish- or ochrous-yellow and white. In flight, shows *diffuse, rather narrow whitish wing-bar*, dark rump and flashing *white axillaries and inner underwing*. For separation from very similar Pacific and American Golden Plovers, see under those. – Adult: Summer ♂ shows more black below than ♀, but because of individual variation only very dark adult summer ♂♂ in N Europe, or breeding pair seen together, safely sexable. In winter, underparts lack black. – Juvenile: Very similar to adult winter but more uniformly fresh and neatly patterned, and *much of belly and flanks finely barred grey-brown* (ad. not so neatly patterned, and has *whiter belly*). – 1st-summer: Often like adult winter or with very little black below. – Variation: Birds from S of breeding range ('*apricaria*' type) on average acquire less striking summer plumage than N birds ('*altifrons*'), which average more black below, but much variation in all parts of breeding range, so subspecific status not fully justified.

VOICE Plaintive flat whistle, 'püü' or 'tüü(u)' (only slightly downslurred), in flight or persistently repeated on ground when alarmed. Plaintive, rhythmic song given in butterfly-like display-flight, 'pü-**peee**-oo, pü-**peee**-oo, pü-**peee**-oo...', often followed by a quicker, subdued 'per**purr**lya-per-**purr**lya-per**purr**lya-...' when alighting, or on ground; latter call can be heard outside breeding season, too.

Pacific Golden Plover *Pluvialis fulva* **V**∗∗

L 21–25 cm. Closely related to American Golden Plover and formerly treated as conspecific with it. Breeds in N Siberia and W Alaska. Vagrant to W Europe, mostly in late summer (ads.) and autumn (juvs.). Often seen on coastal lagoons and mudflats, but sometimes on fields and pastures.

IDENTIFICATION Very similar to Golden Plover, size and structure differing in following ways: slightly *smaller* and *slimmer-bodied*, with proportionately slightly *larger head* and longer neck, *longer legs*, and in flight *slimmer wings* and *toes projecting somewhat beyond tail-tip*. On average, the bill is slightly *longer* and more evenly thick (Golden has bill a little shorter with finer tip and deeper base, but subtle difference and overlap). In all plumages, *axillaries and inner underwing are grey-brown* (same as on

Golden Plover

American, but diagnostic compared with Golden, which is pure white). Even more difficult to separate from American Golden Plover, but note this: a trifle *smaller* size; *wings shorter* but *tertials longer*, resulting in moderate primary projection with *3 primary tips showing beyond tertials* (note that longest two primaries are close together), instead of 4 (or even 5) as on American; some juvenile Pacific have shorter tertials and a 4th primary tip barely showing; beware also of moult or wear altering this feature. Further, Pacific has *slightly longer legs* than American. – Adult summer: Like Golden Plover but: has *more white on forehead* and *along sides of neck and upper breast* (forming hint of white 'bulge') but less along flanks; *narrow white rim along flanks* often *boldly marked black* or even vestigial; undertail-coverts variably pied or predominantly black (rarely appearing all black in the field); *upperparts more coarsely patterned*. – Juvenile: Very similar to juvenile Golden, best told by size, structure, underwing colour, and voice. On average *slightly more yellow-buff tinge on head, neck and breast*, with finer and more distinct spots, but some are practically alike in field. Cf. American for distinctions from that.

VOICE Flight-call is whistled, disyllabic 'chu-it!', remarkably similar to Spotted Redshank (higher-pitched?) or with more drawn-out end, 'chu-**ee**'. Straight 'peee', as from Golden, or downslurred 'pluu-e', have been noted on migration.

American Golden Plover *Pluvialis dominica* **V**∗∗

L 24–27 cm. Closely related to Pacific Golden Plover and formerly treated as conspecific with it. Breeds in N America. Vagrant to Europe. Seen in same habitats as Pacific.

IDENTIFICATION Very similar to Pacific Golden Plover, sharing with it *grey-brown axillaries and inner underwing* (white on Golden), but on average *slightly larger* and *slimmer-bodied*, *longer-winged* and *shorter-legged* (*toes usually do not project beyond tail-tip* in flight). Crucial to establish long primary projection on resting bird: *4* (sometimes even 5) *primary tips visible beyond tertials*, and *wing-tips usually project clearly beyond tail-tip* (same length as tail, or only slightly beyond, on most Pacific). Told from Golden by colour of underwing, slightly *smaller size* and *slimmer build*, with *wings appearing longer and thinner* in flight. Several plumage characters are important, too (see below). – Adult summer ♂: *All-black underparts* including under-tail-coverts; *clear-cut white shawl* along sides of neck and upper breast ending in *prominent white 'bulge'*; *no white along flanks*. – Adult summer ♀/1st-summer: Plumage can be very similar to Pacific, best told by structure and proportions. – Juvenile: Compared with Golden, and especially Pacific, a *more greyish* bird, lacking yellowish-buff tinge on head, neck and breast; *supercilium* on average *more whitish* and *ear-spot and 'loral smudge' darker*; dark cap and *dark mantle* but paler greyish nape; *golden spangling on upperparts* often *confined to fore-mantle, upper scapulars and tertials*, remainder of upperparts and wing-coverts spangled whitish or buff (Pacific and Golden have whole upperparts and wing-coverts more uniformly gold-spangled).

VOICE Common call is a '**clu**-ee', unlike Pacific (and Spotted Redshank) with more stress on first syllable, and second syllable sometimes barely audible, 'cluu(e)'. Also a trisyllabic '**dlu**-ee-uh', second note higher and trembling.

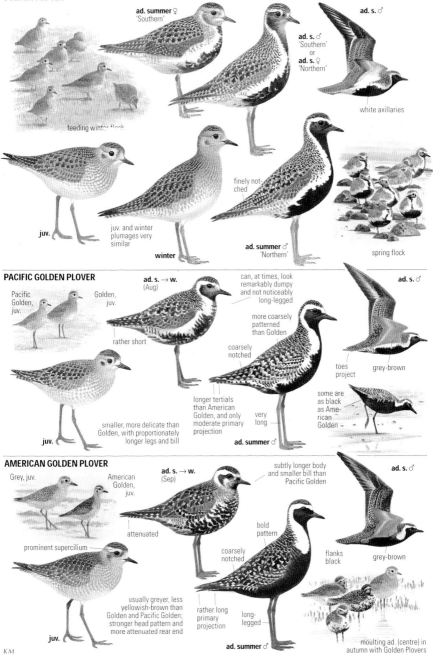

GOLDEN PLOVER

ad. summer ♀
'Southern'

ad. s. ♂

ad. s. ♂
'Southern'
or
ad. s. ♀
'Northern'

white axillaries

feeding winter flock

finely notched

juv.

juv. and winter
plumages very
similar

winter

ad. summer ♂
'Northern'

spring flock

PACIFIC GOLDEN PLOVER

Pacific
Golden,
juv.

Golden,
juv.

ad. s. → w.
(Aug)

can, at times, look
remarkably dumpy
and not noticeably
long-legged

ad. s. ♂

rather short

more coarsely
patterned
than Golden

coarsely
notched

toes
project

grey-brown

longer tertials
than American
Golden, and only
moderate primary
projection

very
long

some are
as black
as American
Golden

smaller, more delicate than
Golden, with proportionately
longer legs and bill

juv.

ad. summer ♂

AMERICAN GOLDEN PLOVER

Grey, juv.

American
Golden,
juv.

ad. s. → w.
(Sep)

subtly longer body
and smaller bill than
Pacific Golden

ad. s. ♂

attenuated

prominent supercilium

bold
pattern

coarsely
notched

flanks
black

grey-brown

usually greyer, less
yellowish-brown than
Golden and Pacific Golden;
stronger head pattern and
more attenuated rear end

juv.

rather long
primary
projection

long-
legged

ad. summer ♂

moulting ad. (centre) in
autumn with Golden Plovers

KM

(Northern) Lapwing *Vanellus vanellus* r(m)**B**2 / **W**1

L 28–31 cm, WS 67–72 cm. A common breeding bird of a variety of inland and coastal open country, usually on arable fields, pastureland or sea- or lakeside meadows; in winter forms sometimes large flocks on farmland, marshes. Food worms and insects. Nest is lined scrape on ground.

IDENTIFICATION Unmistakable *black and white*, pigeon-sized, stocky plover. Has unique *long, thin, wispy crest*, and at close range beautiful *green and purple iridescence on dark upperparts*. In flight, has extraordinary *strongly rounded wing-tip* ('frying-pan wings') and deliberate, flappy beats, wings alternately showing white below and dark above, so that the typically rather closely packed flocks give a distinctive 'flickering' effect even at great distance. – Adult summer: ♂ told by longer crest and solid black on foreneck and face; also, in flight, broader, rounder 'hand'. ♀ has shorter crest, and black on foreneck is less extensive and speckled white, giving less smart head pattern; also narrower, more pointed 'hand'. – Adult winter: Chin and foreneck become white, and upperparts and coverts fringed with buff at tips, giving scaly pattern. – Juvenile: Crest stumpy; resembles adult winter, but pale fringes on upperparts, coverts and tertials complete (not confined to tips) and finely scalloped or spotted. – 1st-winter: Told from adult winter by pattern of retained juvenile coverts and tertials, but difference lost quickly through wear of feather fringes.

VOICE Highly vocal, and often heard at night. Flight-call when fully alarmed is a heartbreakingly shrill, breathy 'pwaay-**eech**' or 'wa**ay**-ach'. Highly aerobatic rolling and tumbling display-flight of ♂ low over field in early spring accompanied by bubbling, wheezy 'song' and (at close range) vibrant throbbing produced by beating wings; song goes 'chae-widdle**wip**, i-**wip** i-wip... cheee-o-**wip**'.

Spur-winged Lapwing *Vanellus spinosus* —

L 25–28 cm. Scarce breeder in SE Europe; locally numerous in Middle East. Vagrant to W Europe. Frequents bare or sparsely vegetated open ground, usually near water. Food mainly insects. Nest is lined scrape on bare ground.

IDENTIFICATION Slightly smaller than Lapwing, and a little slimmer and *longer-legged*. At all ages, distinctive *large white cheek patch* on otherwise black head and has *black breast, flanks* and *tail*, black bill and dark grey legs. In flight at distance, best told from Sociable Lapwing by *black secondaries*. – Adult: Upperparts uniform pale brown. – Juvenile: Like adult, but has some pale scaly feather fringes above (e.g. on forehead) and black parts are tinged brownish-grey.

VOICE Vocal and noisy. Squeaky single or quickly repeated 'p(v)ik', somewhat recalling Black-winged Stilt. Song a series of rapidly repeated high-pitched '**ti**ti-**ter**it'.

Red-wattled Lapwing *Vanellus indicus* —

L 32–35 cm. Breeds across southern Asia; within treated region, found regularly only on Tigris river around Cizre in SE Turkey. Accidental outside breeding area in Middle East.

IDENTIFICATION Structure, actions and general coloration as Spur-winged Lapwing, but somewhat *larger*. Has diagnostic combination of *long yellowish legs, black throat and central breast* but *white flanks*, (in flight) *white tail crossed by even-width, fairly narrow black band*, and (at close range) *red bill-base, lores and orbital ring*. Juvenile separable by white forehead and chin, and white-mottled black throat patch.

VOICE Strident, grating 'cree', 'crik' and other variations, repeated or extended into tern-like chattering, e.g. 'cree-crik cree-ki-koo-it cree-ki-koo-it...'.

Sociable Lapwing *Vanellus gregarius* **V**∗∗

L 27–30 cm. Breeds on wide, dry steppes of Central Asia and SW Siberia, often rather far from water; winters in NE Africa, Iraq and India, sometimes also in S Israel (Negev). Scarce passage migrant in SE Europe and Middle East; vagrant elsewhere, usually appearing with Lapwings, which have similar habitat and food requirements.

IDENTIFICATION Behaviour and structure as Lapwing, but slightly smaller and *longer-legged*. At all ages, unmistakable combination of *bold white supercilium, blackish legs*, and *three-coloured upperwing pattern* (recalling Sabine's Gull). Recalls White-tailed Lapwing, but not so slender or long-legged and has prominent supercilium, black legs and *black-banded tail*. – Adult summer: Crown and eye-stripe black, breast pinkish grey-buff, *belly black* with deep chestnut rear part. – Adult winter: Breast paler, *belly white*. – Juvenile: Diffusely streaked breast and prominent scaly pattern above. – 1st-winter: Told by retained juvenile coverts and tertials.

VOICE Utters single harsh 'kretch' or repeated, chattering 'kretch-etch-etch...' in flight.

White-tailed Lapwing *Vanellus leucurus* **V**∗∗∗

L 26–29 cm. Breeds Central Asia W to Iraq, winters E Africa and India. Scarce migrant SE Europe and Middle East; very rare vagrant to W Europe. Often seen at well-vegetated ponds, lush river edges, along canals and ditches with good cover, rather than on open mudflats. Behaviour often rather skulking, taking cover and being flushed rather close.

IDENTIFICATION Slightly smaller than Spur-winged Lapwing and with much more elegant shape and *very long legs*. At all ages, rather uniformly *pale grey-brown head and body* without prominent supercilium, and *very long yellow legs* diagnostic, even before sight of striking flight pattern with *all-white tail*. Juvenile has obvious scaly pattern above.

VOICE Migrants usually silent.

Lapwing Spur-winged Lapwing Red-wattled Lapwing Sociable Lapwing

LAPWING

short

pale-scalloped

juv.

pale fringes

ad. winter

forms large flocks in winter

ad. s. ♀

even-width wing

ad. summer ♂

ad. s. ♀

ad. s. ♂

very broad 'hand'

SPUR-WINGED LAPWING

ad.

(small spur)

black belly

patchy, pale fringes

juv.

ad.

wide black band

ad.

RED-WATTLED LAPWING

ad.

ad.

broad white band outside black

red

yellow

ad.

ad.

SOCIABLE LAPWING

white secondaries

Dotterel-like head markings

juv.

black band

broad supercilium

dark

ad. winter

ad. summer

dark

WHITE-TAILED LAPWING

ad.

ad.

all white

rather plain

long

heavily spotted

juv.

yellow

very long

ad.

M

(Red) **Knot** *Calidris canutus*   **P** / **W**1–2

L 23–26 cm, WS 47–53 cm. Breeds in high Arctic. Winters on wide tidal flats, locally in huge flocks; smaller numbers occasionally on freshwater pools near coast. Concentrated spring migration late May–early Jun largely unnoticed.

IDENTIFICATION Rather *short-legged, plump wader*, larger and stockier than Dunlin. Bill usually *straight and rather thick and short* (about same length as head), but some have surprisingly long and slightly decurved bill. In flight, has long-winged, short-bodied outline with thin white wing-bar and *pale grey* (actually finely barred) *rump patch*. In winter and juvenile plumages, best told by *shape, general greyness*, prominent light *supercilium* and rather short *grey-ish-green legs*. (Also, cf. similar but very rare vagrant Great Knot, p. 380.) – Adult summer: ♂ averages more uniform and richer *rufous-orange below* than ♀. – Adult winter: Plain grey above with thin white fringes to scapulars, white supercilium, grey-streaked breast, and grey bars and chevrons on flanks and undertail-coverts. – Juvenile: Like adult winter at distance, but usually with *orange-buff wash on underparts* (occasionally so strong as to suggest adult summer) and breast and flanks more finely spotted and barred with grey; at close range, upperparts and especially wing-coverts *neatly pale-fringed, with dark subterminal crescents*.

VOICE Flight-call a short, nasal, rather soft 'whet-whet'.

Sanderling *Calidris alba*   **P** / **W**3

L 18–21 cm. Breeds in high Arctic; seen on passage and in winter in sometimes large flocks on sandy beaches, mudflats or pools near coast; rare inland. Feeds with *distinctive dashing running action ahead of breaking waves*, but also more methodically on calmer, shallow shorelines or grassy areas.

IDENTIFICATION Dunlin-sized, but more compact. Could be confused with stints owing to lively action, especially lone bird away from typical shore habitat, but note *larger size, stouter bill, much broader black-bordered white wing-bar*, and diagnostic lack of hind toe. In winter, appears *strikingly pale* among other shore waders and shows *distinctive blackish wing-bend* (when this is not covered by breast-side feathers). – Adult summer: In spring, head and *clear-cut dark-spotted breast-band* grey/rufous, and upperparts blackish and rufous with broad pale fringes; in summer, head, breast and upperparts become strongly rufous. – Adult winter: Generally plain, very pale grey above with blackish lesser coverts; wing-coverts and tertials diffusely white-fringed. – Juvenile: General pattern like juvenile stint, but whole plumage more contrastingly black and white, *mantle and scapulars more spangled or spotted with white* (not neat scaly pattern) and lacks white mantle- and scapular-Vs.

VOICE Flight-call is an emphatic, slightly liquid 'plit'.

Purple Sandpiper *Calidris maritima*   **P** / **W**1–2

L 19–22 cm, WS 37–42 cm. Breeds on coasts, rocky tundra and in marshes on barren mountainsides up to snowline; in winter and on passage found on coastal rocks (look for it or extensive areas of wave-washed, seaweed-covered rocks), usually in flocks, often with Turnstones, occasionally also at pools near coast; rare inland. Nest is scrape on bare ground.

IDENTIFICATION A little larger than Dunlin and with similar bill shape, but *fatter body* and *shorter legs* give distinctive *dumpy, rather shuffling look*, and *tail longish*, projecting beyond wing-tips. In winter, told by habitat and distinctive combination of shape, *uniform brown-grey head* (no supercilium), *upperparts and breast*, and *mustard-yellow* (or sometimes pale reddish-brown) *legs and bill-base*. Dark general coloration contrasting with whitish belly, 'armpits' and rump-sides, and *narrow, poorly marked wing-bar* distinctive in flight. Lone bird feeding in manner of other waders, in untypical habitat (e.g. muddy pool edge), can be temporarily very confusing, especially juvenile in neat scaly plumage. – Adult summer: Breast and flanks are mottled blackish; *mantle/scapulars edged whitish and rufous*. – Juvenile: Neat whitish fringes on scapulars and wings form *strong scaly pattern*; rusty on crown and mantle; actually rather like a juvenile Dunlin, but *legs and bill-base paler* and *tail longer*.

VOICE Usual flight-calls sharp 'quit' or 'quit-it'. Alarm is a loud, rapid laughing 'pehehehehe...'. In display-flights, utters Dunlin-like buzzing 'prruee-prruee-prruee-...' and hard twittering 'kewick-kewick-wick-wick-wick-...'.

(Ruddy) **Turnstone** *Arenaria interpres*   **P** / **W**2–3

L 21–24 cm, WS 43–49 cm. Breeds on mainly stony or rocky coasts and in treeless archipelagos; wary, keeping watch from top of shore or boulder. Winters in a variety of coastal habitats. Food highly varied; uses bill to turn over stones or seaweed to obtain prey beneath. Nests on ground.

IDENTIFICATION Medium-sized, *stocky* wader with distinctive *wedge-shaped, pointed bill, orange legs* and *pied wing pattern*. – Adult summer: ♂ has extensive bright orange-brown on scapulars and wing-coverts, and clear black-and-white head pattern; ♀ (and 1st-summer ♂) has less clear orange (often lacking on wing-coverts) and less smart head pattern. – Adult winter: Distinctive pale-centred breast-side patches; rather dark grey-brown above, often with some dull orange on scapulars; wing-coverts and tertials *plain* grey-brown or *diffusely* edged paler; legs bright orange. – Juvenile: Like adult winter, but with neat ginger-brown or whitish fringes giving *distinct scaly pattern* above.

VOICE Flight-calls chuckling 'tuk-a-tuk-tuk' and short, yelping 'k(l)ew'. Both alarm and display-song an emphatic, accelerating rattle, 'chuvee-chuvee-vitvitvitvitvit'.

Knot   Sanderling   Purple Sandpiper   Turnstone

KNOT

juv. (fresh)

obviously scaly

buff tinge

ad. winter

grey-green

rather short

compare smaller Dunlin (right)

juv.

pale grey

ad. summer

cf. Curlew Sandpiper (p. 141)

SANDERLING

dark feather centres with three 'spears'

juv.

ad. winter

black

lacks hind toe

rather stout

pale

ad. spring (Apr–May)

Sanderling

Dunlin

ad. summer (Jul–Aug)

ad. w.

wide wing-bar, edged black

runs quickly along edge of surf

PURPLE SANDPIPER

juv.

streaked

tail projects

ad. winter

bright orange

yellowish base

short, yel- lowish-grey

ad. summer

ad. winter

in flight, appears dark

Dunlin

Purple Sandpiper

TURNSTONE

pale fringes

juv.

very dark upperparts

ad. winter

orange

wedge- shaped

bold dark breast pattern

ad. summer ♂

ad. w.

in flight, boldly patterned

KM

Dunlin *Calidris alpina*　　　　r(m)**B**4 / **P**1 / **W**1

L 17–21 cm, WS 32–36 cm. Breeds on low or high ground, in wet short-grass or tundra habitats; on migration (in autumn ads. in late Jul–Aug, juvs. in late Aug–Oct) and in winter the region's commonest small wader, found in a variety of marshy or coastal habitats, but most numerous on tidal flats or on banks of seaweed on shallow shores.

IDENTIFICATION The standard small wader of the region. Familiarity with all Dunlin plumages and their variations will provide yardstick against other species. It will also help in initially picking out other species as 'something different'. – Starling-sized wader with variable bill length (see Variation), the shortest and straightest almost stint-like, the longest and most decurved approaching Curlew Sandpiper. – Adult summer: *Black belly patch* diagnostic; variable *rufous on mantle/scapulars*, becoming more obvious through wear; ♂ brighter than ♀, with contrasting pale grey nape (brownish on ♀). – Adult winter: Drab and rather featureless plumage is in itself rather distinctive, combining plain brownish-grey upperparts (fine whitish fringes, esp. on wing-coverts); rather clear-cut pale grey breast-band contrasting with white belly and finely streaked or clear white flanks; *rather plain head* with indistinct short supercilium; and usually fairly long decurved black bill (but beware long and short extremes). – Juvenile: Dark brown above, neatly fringed pale rufous or rich rufous, usually with white scapular- and mantle-Vs; *pattern of underparts* distinctive, with neat breast-band of diffuse streaks and *band of rather bold blackish spots on belly-sides* leaving broad, *usually unmarked white flank-band*; whole *head, nape and upper breast washed ginger*, without obvious supercilium: even at long range, therefore, shows distinctive combination of rather plain gingery head, spotted belly-sides and white flank-band. Note variability of belly-side spotting, from often very dense (easily confused with moulting adult summer) to very rarely totally lacking. – Variation: Three subspecies occur within treated region, differing in average bill length and brightness of rufous on upperparts: *arctica* (Greenland) winters mainly W Africa) shortest-billed, least rufous; *schinzii* (Iceland, W Europe; winters mainly W Africa) intermediate bill length and rufousness; and *alpina* (Arctic; winters W Europe, Mediterranean) longest-billed, richest rufous. Only extreme individuals safely identifiable; ♀♀ average longer-billed than ♂♂, so shortest-billed individuals probably ♂ *arctica/schinzii*, and longest-billed probably ♀ *alpina*.

VOICE Flight-call a buzzing or harshly rolling 'chrrreet'. Conversational calls from flocks short, rippling 'plip-ip-ip'. In display-flight, utters ascending, strained '**rrüee-rrüee-rrüee-**...', which turn into a hard, descending, slightly slowing trill, '**rürrüü**rürürürürü-rü-ru-ru ru ru'.

Curlew Sandpiper *Calidris ferruginea*　　　　**P**4–5

L 19–21½ cm. Breeds in arctic Siberia; winters mainly in Africa, scarcely in Mediterranean region, and rarely W Europe. On passage, usually rather scarce, but much commoner in some autumns; frequents marshes and coast, often in mixed flocks with Dunlin. Food mainly invertebrates.

IDENTIFICATION Slightly larger than Dunlin, but with *longer, finer-tipped and more evenly decurved bill*; longer neck and legs (esp. tibiae) give *more elegant outline*; *white rump* obvious in flight. – Adult summer: ♂ averages more uniform (less white-flecked) and brighter *brick-red below* than ♀. – Adult winter (rarely seen in Europe): Resembles Dunlin (esp. long-billed *alpina*) except for more elegant shape, paler-grey upperparts, *prominent white fore-supercilium*, and white rump. – Juvenile: Greyer than Dunlin, with *uniform scaly pattern* (lacking Vs), more *prominent and whiter supercilium, streaking on underparts confined to breast-sides*, and usually obvious *orange-buff wash across breast*.

VOICE Flight-call a short trilling or jingling 'chürrip' or 'kürürip', a little like call of Temminck's Stint but lower-pitched and coarser, quite different from buzzing call of Dunlin (but note that giggly conversational calls from flocks of feeding Dunlins can sound rather similar).

Broad-billed Sandpiper *Limicola falcinellus*　　　　**V**∗∗

L 15–18 cm. Breeds in wettest parts of upland or taiga bogs; summer visitor (mostly late May–Aug), winters E Africa, S Asia on or near coasts. Scarce passage migrant anywhere in Europe but more common in E than W; in Britain & Ireland, 2–3 records annually. During migration seen resting both on inland marshes and on coasts. Nest is lined cup in tussock.

IDENTIFICATION Easily overlooked as a young Dunlin, but is *slightly smaller*, enhanced by somewhat *shorter legs*, and usually slower feeding action giving more stocky and furtive impression; bill Dunlin-like but rather long and straighter in profile, with subtle *downward kink only near tip*; even at long range juveniles often picked out by size, slow movements, *dark upperparts* and *white belly*; while in Europe, has *boldly striped head pattern* (obvious dark eye-stripe, strong pale supercilium, and *thin pale lateral stripes on dark crown*). – Adult summer: Distinctive combination of *heavily streaked flanks* (often with arrowheads) and *complete breast-band* with *dark upperparts* with thin white mantle- and scapular-Vs; in fresh plumage whitish fringes give frosted look, but when worn *upperparts and breast become very dark* and Vs reduced or lacking. – Adult winter: Dunlin-like, but a hint of distinctive head pattern retained. – Juvenile: Upperparts like strongly marked Dunlin, but underpart pattern is very different, with well-marked, brown-washed breast-band streaked at sides, contrasting with *all-white belly and flanks*.

VOICE Flight-call is a dry, high-pitched, buzzing trill, a little upward-inflected, 'brrre-eet'; also short 'chep'. In display-flight has rhythmic, buzzing 'brre, brre, brre **ber**re **ber**re brebrebrebre...', recognized by the call-note voice (Sand Martin-like).

Dunlin　　　　Curlew Sandpiper

Broad-billed Sandpiper

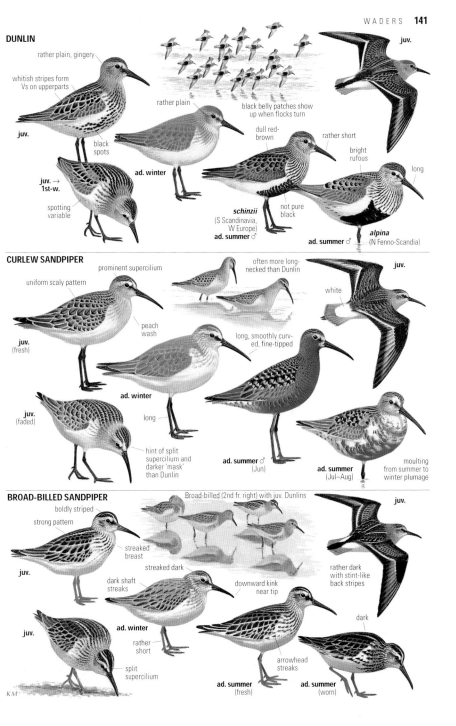

DUNLIN

rather plain, gingery

whitish stripes form Vs on upperparts

juv.

black spots

**juv. →
1st-w.**

spotting variable

rather plain

ad. winter

black belly patches show up when flocks turn

dull red-brown

rather short

bright rufous

long

not pure black

schinzii
(S Scandinavia, W Europe)
ad. summer ♂

alpina
(N Fenno-Scandia)
ad. summer ♂

juv.

CURLEW SANDPIPER

prominent supercilium

uniform scaly pattern

peach wash

juv.
(fresh)

juv.
(faded)

long

ad. winter

often more long-necked than Dunlin

white

long, smoothly curved, fine-tipped

hint of split supercilium and darker 'mask' than Dunlin

juv.

ad. summer ♂
(Jun)

ad. summer
(Jul–Aug)

moulting from summer to winter plumage

BROAD-BILLED SANDPIPER

boldly striped

strong pattern

streaked breast

dark shaft streaks

juv.

juv.

Broad-billed (2nd fr. right) with juv. Dunlins

streaked dark

ad. winter

rather short

split supercilium

downward kink near tip

arrowhead streaks

ad. summer
(fresh)

juv.

rather dark with stint-like back stripes

dark

ad. summer
(worn)

KM

Temminck's Stint *Calidris temminckii*   mB5 / P5

L 13½–15 cm. Breeds on bogs, marshes or river deltas in upland taiga or on tundra and fells; also in coastal habitats. Winters mainly Africa. On passage (mostly May and Aug) frequents pools and marshes, lakesides or rivers; in Britain & Ireland, much less common than Little Stint, but just as likely to occur in spring as in autumn. Nest is lined scrape in open or in low vegetation, often willow scrub, in damp area.

IDENTIFICATION Same size as Little Stint, but slightly *longer-bodied* (tail projects slightly beyond wing-tips) and *shorter-legged*, with finer, *slightly decurved bill*. Unobtrusive, unlike Little Stint typically choosing thinly vegetated rather than open sections of mudflats; also, usually *feeds with distinctive creeping action* on flexed legs and with slower pecking rate. Unlike Little Stint, *flies off high on erratic course*, continuously giving *distinctive trilling call*. Outer tail-feathers all white (grey on Little). *Legs pale* (yellowish, greenish or brownish). In winter and juvenile plumages *recalls a miniature Common Sandpiper* because of shape, rather plain brownish upperparts, and well-marked breast. Beware that winter Little Stint frequently misidentified as Temminck's, especially one with sleek plumage, thus looking slimmer and longer-bodied than usual, with mud-coated (thus pale-looking) legs, and in bright sun (when outer tail-feathers can look white in flight); Temminck's, however, has *brownish* upperparts (pale grey with dark feather centres on Little), rather *plain brownish head* (strong supercilium and whitish face on Little), *clear-cut brownish breast* (pale grey on Little) and *shorter legs*. – Adult summer: Variable number of black-centred, rufous-edged feathers on upperparts, mainly among scapulars and on mantle, at distance giving distinctive spotted effect. – Adult winter: Plain, dull grey-brown upperparts and breast contrasting with pure white underparts. – Juvenile: At close range, *pale fringes and dark subterminal line on scapulars and wing-coverts*; upper scapulars contrastingly dark-centred.

VOICE Flight-call when flushed distinctive, a loud, dry trilling, usually repeated 'tirrr-tirr-tirr...'. In display-flight, ♂ hovers giving continuous cricket-like reel, 'tititititititi...'.

Little Stint *Calidris minuta*   P4 / W5

L 14–15½ cm, WS 27–30 cm. Breeds on tundra, usually near coast. On passage in W Europe, less common in spring than in autumn (due to more easterly route in spring), and in autumn numbers highly variable depending on breeding success. Frequents muddy edges of pools, coastal flats etc., often in sizable flocks, and often mixing with Dunlins.

IDENTIFICATION A small wader, about ⅔ length of Dunlin. The standard stint of region; familiarity with all its plumages essential for picking out Temminck's or vagrant stints

(p. 154, and below). *Small size*; 'runs around feet' of other small waders, e.g. Dunlin, but even when alone small size indicated by usually *quicker actions and pecking rate*. Fine-tipped, *straight, short bill* (shorter than shortest-billed Dunlin) gives distinctive *spiky-billed look* at distance; *more extensive white on head and breast* gives whiter front end than other small waders except Sanderling. *Legs black*, but look brownish against dark background, or pale when mud-coated. – Adult summer: Rusty-orange tones on head, breast and upperparts variable (strongest on ♂), becoming more obvious during summer as whitish fringes of fresh plumage disappear. *Split supercilium* and *yellowish mantle-V* usually obvious. – Adult winter: Grey above, with dark feather centres giving mottled effect; grey breast-sides (or breast-band: then easily confused with Temminck's). – Juvenile: *Blackish-centred upperpart feathers* and wing-coverts with neat *pale or rich rufous fringes* and usually prominent mantle- and scapular-Vs; underparts white except for cluster of fine streaks over rusty wash at breast-sides; *strong white split supercilium*, and *dark 'ridge' down centre of crown*.

VOICE Flight-call is single or repeated sharp, high-pitched 'stit'. Song (in flight or from ground) a weak 'swee-swee-swee-swee-...', now and then relieved by silvery 'svirrr-r-r'.

Long-toed Stint *Calidris subminuta*   V***

L 14–15½ cm. Breeds in Siberia. Rare vagrant to Europe.

IDENTIFICATION Like Least Sandpiper (*pale legs, no primary projection*), but *slightly larger*, with bill usually obvious *pale base to lower mandible*, and *longer neck and legs* (esp. tibiae) giving *general outline often recalling miniature Wood Sandpiper* rather than stint; *toes noticeably long*, with middle toe slightly longer than tarsus (a little shorter on Least); toes project somewhat beyond tail in flight; *forehead* often dark down to bill (supercilia usually join across forehead on Least); *supercilia whiter and broader*, often *with split over eye*; *lores rather pale* (usually darker on Least); and often rufous-tinged 'cap'. – Adult summer: *Broad rufous fringes on upperparts and tertials*. – Adult winter: Clear-cut dark centres to grey-brown scapulars. – Juvenile: At least *median and lesser coverts fringed whitish*, contrasting with rufous-fringed scapulars / tertials (juv. Least has wing-coverts also fringed rufous, thus no contrast).

VOICE Call a trilled 'chrip', like weak Pectoral Sandpiper.

Least Sandpiper *Calidris minutilla*   V**

L 13–14½ cm. N American species. Vagrant to W Europe, mostly Jun–Oct. Averages one annually Britain & Ireland.

IDENTIFICATION Similar to Long-toed Stint, which see for differences. Told from other stints by *pale* (usually yellowish or greenish) *legs* (except otherwise dissimilar Temminck's), and *short or non-existent primary projection*; more *extensive breast streaking* (often complete breast-band), *duller head pattern*, and *browner coloration* jointly give *less white, more drab general appearance*. – Adult summer: *Thin* rufous fringes on upperparts and tertials, often lacking when worn. – Adult winter: Mousy grey-brown above, with *diffuse* dark feather centres giving scaly impression at distance. – Juvenile: Often bright rufous fringes on upperparts and wings, and has thin white mantle- and scapular-Vs.

VOICE Call a soft, high-pitched, vibrant, rising 'trre-eep'.

Temminck's Stint   Little Stint

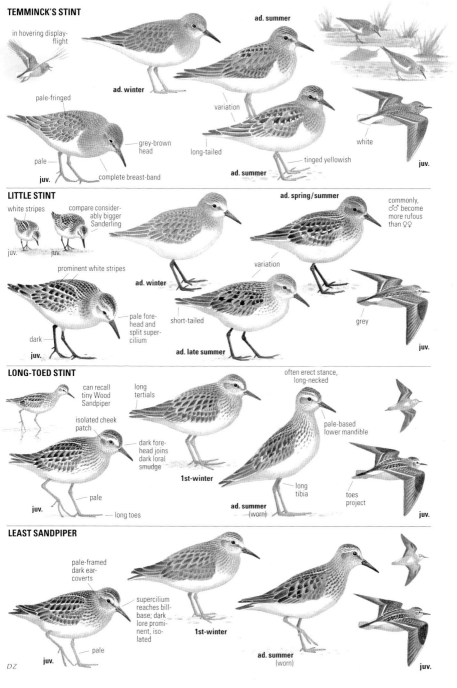

TEMMINCK'S STINT

in hovering display-flight

ad. summer

ad. winter

pale-fringed

variation

grey-brown head

long-tailed

pale

white

juv.

complete breast-band

tinged yellowish

ad. summer

juv.

LITTLE STINT

white stripes

compare considerably bigger Sanderling

ad. spring/summer

commonly, ♂♂ become more rufous than ♀♀

juv.   juv.

prominent white stripes

ad. winter

variation

pale forehead and split supercilium

short-tailed

dark

grey

juv.

ad. late summer

juv.

LONG-TOED STINT

often erect stance, long-necked

can recall tiny Wood Sandpiper

long tertials

isolated cheek patch

pale-based lower mandible

dark forehead joins dark loral smudge

1st-winter

long tibia

pale

juv.

long toes

ad. summer (worn)

toes project

juv.

LEAST SANDPIPER

pale-framed dark ear-coverts

supercilium reaches bill-base; dark lore prominent, isolated

1st-winter

juv.   pale

ad. summer (worn)

juv.

DZ

Wood Sandpiper *Tringa glareola*   m**B**5 / **P**4

L 18½–21 cm, WS 35–39 cm. Breeds on bogs and marshes in taiga. On passage, frequents inland or coastal marshes, shallow pools, often in large flocks (except in NW); winters mainly Africa. Nest is usually in dense vegetation on ground.

IDENTIFICATION General shape similar to Redshank, but ⅓ smaller in size and bill length. Similar to Green Sandpiper, differing in *paler brown* colour; *larger pale markings on upperparts*; *longer legs*; *fine barring of outer tail*; breast and flanks loosely streaked and barred, *markings not forming a clear-cut breast-band*; light *supercilium extends behind eye*; and *yellowish-green legs*. Bobs rear body like Common Sandpiper when agitated. In flight, unlike Green Sandpiper, shows *pale underwing, whole of toes projecting beyond tail*, and no strong black/white contrast. – Adult summer: Upperparts coarsely and irregularly mottled whitish and buff. – Adult winter: Plumage greyer and breast rather plain. – Juvenile: Upperparts *densely*, neatly and *strongly spotted buff-white. Breast finely streaked*, not nearly uniform.

VOICE Flight-call distinctive, a quick, high-pitched whistling 'chiff-if-if', all syllables on same note. Alarm is persistent sharp 'gip gip gip...'. Song (in display-flight) a rapid burst of fluty, yodelling 'tü-**lülltilülltilülltilüll**ti...'.

Green Sandpiper *Tringa ochropus*   **P** / **W**4

L 20–24 cm, WS 39–44 cm. Breeds in waterlogged wooded areas, on bogs and marshes. Summer visitor (mostly Mar/Apr–Aug); winters in S Europe and Africa. On passage, shows preference for ditches, pond edges, lakesides, etc., seldom open mudflats. Occurs singly or in small groups. Nest is in tree in old nest of other bird, usually thrush.

IDENTIFICATION Size and structure as Wood Sandpiper but *more robust*, with *slightly shorter legs*. Typically sighted when flushed unexpectedly from some unlikely ditch or puddle, flying off with distinctive calls, showing *blackish wings* (even below) and *white rump*, pattern like oversized House Martin; *toes barely project beyond tail*. Outer tail has just *a few very broad, dense black bars*, looking *all dark*. On ground, differs from Wood Sandpiper in *much finer speckling* and darker colour which make *upperparts look uniform blackish*; *dark breast clear-cut against white underparts*; eyering white; *white supercilium does not extend beyond eye*; and *greenish-grey legs*. – Adult winter: Breast and upperparts almost uniform dark. – Juvenile: Upperparts *neatly and finely spotted* with buff-white (thus more like Wood).

VOICE Flight-call a clear, ringing whistle, '**tlu**eet-wit-wit', first note with rising inflection, the next two higher-pitched. Alarm-call a clipping 'tlip-tlip-tlip-...'. Song (in display-flight) more complex than Wood Sandpiper's, a rapid, rhythmical phrase, '**tluui-tüi tluui-tüi tluui-tüi tluui-tüi**...'.

Common Sandpiper *Actitis hypoleucos*   m**B**3 / **P**2 / **W**5

L 18–20½ cm, WS 32–35 cm. Breeds near water in forested areas, preferring stony or gravelly shores, most common at lakes and rivers in taiga, also at coasts, in archipelagos. Summer visitor (mostly Apr/May–Aug), winters in Africa, rarely in S Europe. Migrates singly or in small parties, frequently by night, when revealed by its calls. Nest is placed in vegetation, usually in forest, close to water.

IDENTIFICATION Told by behaviour and shape long before plumage is seen: a medium-small wader with horizontal, semi-crouched carriage, short-necked, *long-tailed*, rather short-legged, which habitually *bobs rear body*, especially after every quick movement or on landing (the other sandpipers on this page share this habit, but in less exaggerated form). Flight action highly distinctive, with *flightpath close over water* and quick bursts of *shallow, pulsating beats interrupted by fleeting glides on stiffly down-bowed wings. Brown above, with *distinctive white divide between carpal area and clear-cut breast-side patch*; legs greenish, brownish or dull yellowish-grey. – Adult: Plainer than juvenile, especially in winter. – Juvenile: More obvious barring above, wing-coverts and tertials finely tipped and edged pale buff.

VOICE Vocal. Flight-call a rapid series of clear, high-pitched whistling notes falling in pitch slightly, 'swee-swee-swee-swee-swüü', often heard on dark August nights. Alarm-call is a drawn-out whistling note, 'heeeep'. Song, in pulsating song-flight, is rhythmic repetition of finely twittering phrase, 'swidi**dii**-dide-swidi**dii**-dide-swidi**dii**-dide-...'.

Terek Sandpiper *Xenus cinereus*   **V**∗∗

L 22–25 cm. Breeds in lowland boreal taiga zone by rivers and oligotrophic lakes; also in harbours or at sawmill factories with floating logs. Winters in Africa, Asia and Arabia. On passage, seen mainly on coastal mudflats and pools, rare in W Europe. Nest is lined scrape in short vegetation.

IDENTIFICATION Shape rather like large Common Sandpiper, but *very long upcurved bill*. Occasionally wags rear body, and habitually picks insects from surface with *quick, dashing actions*. In flight, *broad white trailing edge* to wing recalling Redshank's, but narrower and less contrasting; *rump and tail grey*. Upperparts and breast *pale grey*, with *dark carpal area* and (on adult summer only) prominent *irregular dark stripes on upper scapulars*. Bill black (adult summer) or with dull yellow or orange base; short legs dull or bright yellow, or (on adult) often orange.

VOICE Flight-call a rapid series of 2–5 short, whistling notes, a high-pitched ringing 'vüvüvü', at times recalling Whimbrel, though softer. Song a repetition of a usually trisyllabic unit, e.g. 'ka klee-**rreee**, ka klee-**rreee**, ka klee-**rreee**, ...', somewhat recalling song of Stone-curlew.

Wood Sandpiper   Green Sandpiper   Common Sandpiper   Terek Sandpiper

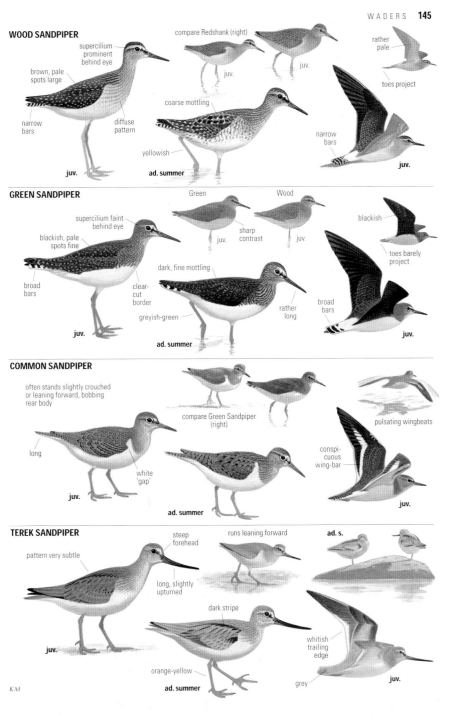

WOOD SANDPIPER

supercilium prominent behind eye

brown, pale spots large

narrow bars

diffuse pattern

juv.

compare Redshank (right)

juv.

juv.

coarse mottling

yellowish

ad. summer

rather pale

toes project

narrow bars

juv.

GREEN SANDPIPER

supercilium faint behind eye

blackish, pale spots fine

broad bars

clear-cut border

juv.

Green

juv.

sharp contrast

Wood

juv.

dark, fine mottling

greyish-green

rather long

ad. summer

blackish

toes barely project

broad bars

juv.

COMMON SANDPIPER

often stands slightly crouched or leaning forward, bobbing rear body

long

white 'gap'

juv.

compare Green Sandpiper (right)

ad. summer

pulsating wingbeats

conspi-cuous wing-bar

juv.

TEREK SANDPIPER

pattern very subtle

juv.

steep forehead

long, slightly upturned

runs leaning forward

dark stripe

orange-yellow

ad. summer

ad. s.

whitish trailing edge

grey

juv.

KM

(Common) **Redshank** *Tringa totanus* r(m)**B**3 / **P**+**W**2

L 24–27 cm, WS 47–53 cm. Breeds on inland and coastal marshes, wet meadows and moorland. On passage and in winter, singly or in flocks mainly on or near coast; less commonly far inland. Wary and noisy. Nests on ground.

IDENTIFICATION Commonest medium-sized wader in most of region. *Red legs and bill-base* shared only by Spotted Redshank, but beware that some Ruffs can be similar, having orange-red legs and bill-base). In all plumages, brownish above, with streaked breast and flanks, and whitish eye-ring and fore-supercilium. In flight, pointed white rump and diagnostic *broad white trailing edge to wing* obvious. – Adult summer: Upperparts and underparts with irregular, coarse dark markings; often, whitish eye-ring only prominent feature on head. – Adult winter: Rather *plain grey-brown above and on breast*; flanks and undertail-coverts *only sparsely barred or streaked*. – Juvenile: Feather fringes on *upperparts neatly notched with buff*; neck and breast distinctly streaked; flanks and belly finely but *evenly patterned*; *legs yellow-orange* (less red than adult).

VOICE Call a distinctive, musical 'teu' or melancholy, down-slurred '**teu**-hu' or '**teu**-huhu'. Alarm-call a persistent 'kyip-kyip-kyip...'. Song (often in flight) a loud, musical 'tül-tül-tül-tül-tu**liu**-tu**liu**-tu**liu**-...' and '**lee**o-**lee**o-**lee**o-...'.

Spotted Redshank *Tringa erythropus* **P**4 / **W**4

L 29–33 cm. Breeds in open, arctic taiga near bogs and marshes, and on tundra. On passage, singly or (mainly in spring) in small groups, on inland and coastal marshes, lagoons, less commonly on coasts; ♀♀ move S as early as Jun.

IDENTIFICATION Like Redshank, but *outline slimmer* and more elegant, with slightly *longer legs* and *longer, finer bill* which has *distinctive but very subtle downward droop near tip*; also, *red on bill restricted to base of lower mandible* (not whole bill-base as Redshank); winter and juvenile plumages show much more *clear-cut white fore-supercilium*. When feeding, typically wades more deeply than Redshank, often swims and upends. Flight dashingly fast and direct; wings plain, with *white rump extending in thin 'slit' far up back*. – Adult summer: ♂ *all black* (with fine white speckling above); legs blackish. ♀ similar, but with extensive white flecking on flanks, belly, undertail-coverts. – Adult winter: Pale grey above, with *clear white underparts* and whitish head/neck (Redshank obviously browner above and on breast); legs red. – Juvenile: *Underparts rather uniformly barred* (lacks Redshank's breast-band); feather edges on greater coverts and tertials more finely barred than adult winter. Legs red.

VOICE Call is very distinctive, quick, emphatic, disyllabic whistle, 'chu-it!'. Song (in flight) is a rhythmic, 'grinding' or rolling whistle, 'crrru**eee**-a crrru**eee**-a crrru**eee**-a ...'.

(Common) **Greenshank** *Tringa nebularia* r+m**B**4 / **P**3

L 30–34 cm, WS 55–62 cm. Breeds mainly on dry ground in northern mature pine forests near bogs and water. On migration to Africa, usually travels alone or in small, loose parties only. Food insects and worms, but a very agile bird and also habitually dashes after small fish in shallow water.

IDENTIFICATION Slightly larger and more heavily built than Redshank, with slightly *longer and broader-based bill with slight or distinct upcurve*; bill-base and *legs grey* or *greenish-grey*. At distance, adult winter and juvenile look grey above with *whitish head/neck*. In fast and powerful flight, wings dark, with *white rump extending in point up back*, and very *pale tail*. – Adult summer: Variable number of scapulars dark-centred, contrasting with otherwise brownish-grey upperparts; head, breast and flanks coarsely streaked and barred. – Adult winter: Rather *pale grey above* with fine scaly pattern; *foreneck and centre of breast white*. – Juvenile: Fairly *dark grey-brown above*, with neat pale fringes giving rather *striped* pattern; *breast neatly and uniformly streaked*.

VOICE Vocal. Call is distinctive, powerful, trisyllabic whistling 'tyew-tyew-tyew', all on one note (juv. often with shrill voice). Alarm a persistent 'kyu!'. Song (in flight, high up) is sustained grinding 'clu-**wee** clu-**wee** clu-**wee** clu-**wee** ...'.

Marsh Sandpiper *Tringa stagnatilis* **V**∗∗

L 22–25 cm. Breeds in grassy lowland marshes, including on steppe, or on open taiga bogs. Migrates through E Europe to winter in Africa and S Middle East (also in India), usually resting at inland marshes, ponds and mudflats.

IDENTIFICATION Size between Wood Sandpiper and Redshank, but *long, straight* (very subtly upturned on some), *needle-fine bill*, slim body and neck, and *very long, rather spindly legs* (esp. long tibiae) give extreme slenderness and elegance unlike any other *Tringa*, at times even reminiscent of Black-winged Stilt. In flight, dark wings, *long white 'slit' up back* (extending almost to nape!), and *long leg projection beyond tail-tip*. Diffusely white supercilium and feathering around base of bill prominent in all plumages. Legs dull yellowish (rarely orange on ad. summer) or greenish-grey. – Adult summer: Brown-grey above, *prominently spotted and barred black*. – Adult winter: Grey above, white below, with whitish head/neck, giving impression of small, 'delicate' Greenshank. – Juvenile: Upperparts dark with neat pale feather fringes and finely notched greater coverts and tertials, rather like juv. Greenshank but whiter centre of breast.

VOICE Flight-call 'kyew', with diphthong, or 'kyu-kyu-kyu', like Greenshank but quicker and higher-pitched. Song a melodious, rhythmic 'tu-**lee**-a tu-**lee**-a tu-**lee**-a...', recalling Redshank but more drawling and woeful in tone, and rapid twittering series, 'chip! chip! chip-ipepepepepepepep'.

Redshank

Spotted Redshank

Greenshank

Marsh Sandpiper

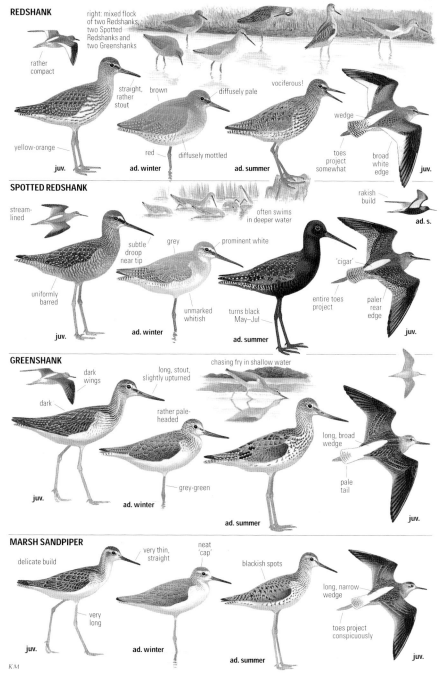

REDSHANK

right: mixed flock of two Redshanks, two Spotted Redshanks and two Greenshanks

rather compact

straight, rather stout

brown

diffusely pale

vociferous!

wedge

yellow-orange

red

diffusely mottled

toes project somewhat

broad white edge

juv.

ad. winter

ad. summer

juv.

SPOTTED REDSHANK

rakish build

ad. s.

streamlined

often swims in deeper water

subtle droop near tip

grey

prominent white

'cigar'

uniformly barred

unmarked whitish

turns black May–Jul

entire toes project

paler rear edge

juv.

ad. winter

ad. summer

juv.

GREENSHANK

chasing fry in shallow water

dark wings

long, stout, slightly upturned

dark

rather pale-headed

long, broad wedge

grey-green

pale tail

juv.

ad. winter

ad. summer

juv.

MARSH SANDPIPER

very thin, straight

neat 'cap'

delicate build

blackish spots

long, narrow wedge

very long

toes project conspicuously

juv.

ad. winter

ad. summer

juv.

KM

Black-tailed Godwit *Limosa limosa* r(m)**B**5 / **P**3 / **W**4

L 37–42 cm (incl. bill 8–11), WS 63–74 cm. Breeds on extensive wet meadows, grassy marshes, boggy moorland. On passage and in winter, frequents mainly estuaries, saltings, coastal mudflats and lagoons; also inland marshes.

IDENTIFICATION About the size of Whimbrel, but outline slimmer. When plumage differences not discernible, told from Bar-tailed Godwit on ground by *longer tibiae*, slightly *longer and straighter bill* (straight or very slightly upcurved, more obviously curved on Bar-tailed). Unmistakable in flight: *broad white wing-bar, black tail-band, square white rump*, and equally long projection of bill/head and tail/legs at each end of body giving *distinctive elongated look*. Bill in summer yellowish or orange-flesh with dark tip, pink-based in winter. – Adult summer: ♂ acquires much more extensive and brighter orange-rufous summer plumage than ♀; *belly and undertail-coverts whitish*, and *flanks barred* (ad. summer ♂ Bar-tailed entirely dark rufous below). – Adult winter: *Plain* brown-grey breast and upperparts (Bar-tailed streaked). – Juvenile: *Head and breast tinged cinnamon-buff* (of variable strength); *wing-coverts pale-fringed with black subterminal spots* (Bar-tailed more streaked pattern). – Variation: Icelandic birds (ssp. *islandica*) have shorter bill and legs, and deeper rufous summer plumage below extending further down on the breast, than in rest of Europe (*limosa*).

VOICE Flight-call a quick, reedy, slightly nasal 'vi-vi-ve!' and a Lapwing-like 'vääh-it'. Noisy when breeding: song (partly in complex display-flight) opens with nasal, drawling 'kehi-e-**itt** kehi-e-**itt** kehi-e-**itt** ...', turning into rapid, rhythmic 'weddy-**whit**-o weddy-**whit**-o weddy-**whit**-o ...'.

Bar-tailed Godwit *Limosa lapponica* **P** / **W**3

L 33–41 cm (incl. bill 7–11), WS 62–72 cm. Breeds on open tundra and taiga bogs. Migrates (late May and late Jul–Aug) mainly along coasts and over sea to and from winter grounds in W Europe and W Africa. Large flocks on some tidal flats.

IDENTIFICATION About equal in size to Black-tailed Godwit, from which told by *shorter legs* (esp. tibiae) and slightly shorter, usually *clearly upcurved bill* (beware that bill is longer on ♀ than on ♂ and hence more like Black-tailed). The two godwits best told by plumage: *barred tail*; white rump extending in *point up back* (as on Curlew); plain wings *lacking wing-bar*. Leg projection shorter than on Black-tailed. Bill dark with pink base. – Adult summer: ♂ has *whole underparts dark rufous* (darker than Black-tailed), whereas much paler underparts of ♀ (off-white, washed pale apricot) usually *entirely lack rufous*, and breast is streaked. Bill black with a little pale at base. – Adult winter: Upperparts pale brownish-grey, with dark feather centres giving *streaked effect* (Black-tailed plain); off-white below without

buff; faintly streaked on breast-sides only. Bill pink-based. – Juvenile: Like adult winter but darker above, with *neatly buff-spotted edges to scapulars and* (most obvious) *tertials*; breast all streaked; buff wash on foreneck/breast (cf. ad. ♀).

VOICE Call is nasal 'cew**ee**-cew**ee**' (sharper than Knot). Song (in display-flight) is persistent, nasal 'ku**we**-ku**we**-ku**we**-...', often preceded by series of rapid 'witwitwet'.

(Eurasian) Curlew *Numenius arquata* r(m)**B**3 / **P**+**W**2

L 48–57 cm (incl. bill 9–15), WS 89–106 cm. Breeds in taiga on open bogs or arable fields along rivers, on wide coastal (usually wet) meadows, wide pastures, arable plains with patches of wet meadows, moorland, etc. On passage (mostly Apr and Jun–Sep) and in winter, usually in flocks on coasts or pasture. Often wary during breeding.

IDENTIFICATION *Largest wader*, with *unmistakable very long, evenly decurved bill* (longest on ♀, shorter on ♂ and juv.). Easily confused only with usually less common Whimbrel. Uniformly streaked and barred grey-brown, with no outstanding plumage features. Flight rather slow, gull-like. Note *pointed white rump* and darker outer primaries.

VOICE Call a far-carrying, rising, fluty, melancholy whistle, 'cour-**lii**'; on migration often a 'cue-cue-**cew**'. Alarm a fierce 'vi-vi-vü!'. Song (in flight with shivering wings, then descending glide) starts with drawling notes, merging into distinctive rhythmic, rippling trill, 'oo-**ot**, oo-**ot** oo-**eet** trru-**ee** trrru-**eel** trrrru-**eel** trrrru-**eel** trrru-**uhl**'.

Whimbrel *Numenius phaeopus* m**B**4 / **P**4

L 37–45 cm (incl. bill 6–9), WS 78–88 cm. Breeds on taiga bogs, on mountainsides above tree-limit (e.g. cranberry scrub), tundra. On passage (mostly late Apr–May and Jul–Aug) seen singly or in small parties; frequents mainly pasture and coasts; winters on African coasts, rarely in Europe.

IDENTIFICATION Like Curlew but slightly *smaller*, and has proportionately somewhat *shorter bill* (beware juv. Curlew, especially ♂, also with rather short bill), *dark crown-sides* and *rather dark eye-stripe* giving *strong supercilium* and (when viewed head-on) neat *light median crown-stripe* (beware faint crown-stripe often shown by Curlew, too). Wing-beats faster, and underwing looks on average slightly darker than Curlew's (wing-coverts are more patterned). – Variation: American birds (ssp. *hudsonicus*), rarely recorded in W Europe, lack white rump.

VOICE Call a loud, fast, rippling whistle, 'püpüpüpüpü-püpü', all on same note, vaguely recalling ♀ Cuckoo or Little Grebe. Alarm at breeding site similar to call but longer and not so even-pitched. Song begins like Curlew's but breaks into bubbling, long-drawn-out, straight trill, *lacking Curlew's pulsating rhythm*, and has more woeful ring.

Black-tailed Godwit   Bar-tailed Godwit   Curlew   Whimbrel

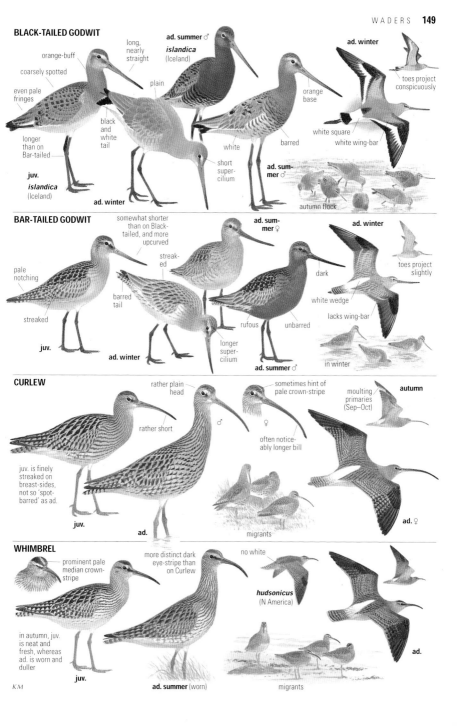

BLACK-TAILED GODWIT

orange-buff

coarsely spotted

even pale fringes

long, nearly straight

ad. summer ♂
islandica (Iceland)

plain

black and white tail

longer than on Bar-tailed

juv.
islandica (Iceland)

ad. winter

toes project conspicuously

orange base

barred

white

short supercilium

white square

white wing-bar

ad. winter

ad. summer ♂

autumn flock

BAR-TAILED GODWIT

somewhat shorter than on Black-tailed, and more upcurved

pale notching

streaked

streaked

barred tail

juv.

ad. winter

ad. summer ♀

ad. winter

dark

rufous

unbarred

longer super-cilium

ad. summer ♂

toes project slightly

white wedge

lacks wing-bar

in winter

CURLEW

rather plain head

rather short

♂

♀

sometimes hint of pale crown-stripe

often noticeably longer bill

moulting primaries (Sep–Oct)

autumn

juv. is finely streaked on breast-sides, not so 'spot-barred' as ad.

juv.

ad.

migrants

ad. ♀

WHIMBREL

prominent pale median crown-stripe

more distinct dark eye-stripe than on Curlew

no white

hudsonicus (N America)

in autumn, juv. is neat and fresh, whereas ad. is worn and duller

juv.

ad. summer (worn)

migrants

ad.

KM

(Eurasian) **Woodcock** *Scolopax rusticola* r(m)**B**3 / **P**3
L 33–38 cm (incl. bill 6–8), WS 55–65 cm. Breeds in moist woodland (deciduous or mixed), interspersed with glades, rides or fields, with wet soil, shade and at least some undergrowth. On passage and in winter, also sometimes drier scrub or bushy terrain; usually solitary. Crepuscular habits; rarely active in daytime unless accidentally flushed. Best chance of seeing Woodcock is *dusk* visit to panoramic viewpoint in known breeding area, especially Apr-Jun when 'roding' ♂ patrols large area in level, direct flight over treetops. Nest is lined cup in sparse cover in shaded wood.

IDENTIFICATION Pigeon-sized, *thick-bodied* 'snipe of the woods'. If flushed from day roost, flies off with whirring, rather loud *wing noise*, twisting through trees, showing much *rusty-brown on rump and tail*. In roding flight, note unmistakable *fat-bodied, long-billed silhouette* with *stiff, flickering action* (actually rapidly doubled wingbeats) of *broad, blunt-ended wings*, slightly tail-heavy carriage and with bill pointing obliquely down. All plumages similar.

VOICE Roding ♂ repeatedly gives 3–4 grunted or growling notes followed by high-pitched, short explosive sound, 'wart wart wart-wart **pissp**!'; moderately far-carrying (300 m). When encountering rival (or mate?) in air, close pursuit accompanied by frenetic 'plip-plip pissp psi-plip...', etc.

Great Snipe *Gallinago media* V**
L 26–30 cm (incl. bill 6–7), WS 43–50 cm. Breeds on open wet meadows in lowland or (in N Europe) on mountainside, where ♂♂ meet on traditional leks. On passage frequents wet meadows, lush pastures and drier fields. Scarce; only a vagrant to British Isles (often Sep–Oct). Winters in Africa.

IDENTIFICATION Slightly *larger, stockier* and shorter-billed than Snipe, with flight steadier and not so high or lengthy, but beware slow-flying (tired or injured) and thus large-looking Snipe. Flushes (at *c.* 5 m) with *audible wing sound*; on upperwing, best clues are *white-bordered, dark midwing-panel* on greater coverts and *white-tipped primary coverts* (not white trailing edge as on Snipe); *underparts and underwing coarsely barred* (not extensive white belly and striped underwing as on Snipe); and *much white on outer tail-feathers* (not visible in normal flight: best looked for when tail spread on landing or take-off). On ground, *white tips form obvious lines on wing-coverts*, and *underparts wholly barred* (only slightly less complete on centre of belly). All plumages similar; juvenile has less white on tail than adult.

VOICE Quiet; gruff croak occasionally given when flushed. Song from ♂♂ gathered at display 'arena' lasts 4–6 sec., in three merging parts: rapid rising then falling twittering ('bibbling'); accelerating clicking (like bouncing table-tennis ball); then whining 'whizzing' (audible *c.* 300 m).

(Common) **Snipe** *Gallinago gallinago* r(m)**B**3 / **P**+**W**2
L 23–28 cm (incl. bill *c.* 7), WS 39–45 cm. Breeds in marshes, bogs and damp meadows with short, dense vegetation; on passage and in winter, also small muddy patches, pool margins, ditches, seashores, pastures, etc., often in small groups. Nest usually well concealed in vegetation.

IDENTIFICATION Medium-sized wader; prefers cover, but when seen in open shows distinctive combination of *disproportionately long, straight bill*, rather *dumpy shape*, *short-legged, crouching posture*, and *striped head and body*. When flushed (usually within 10–15 m), *zigzags fast*, giving *distinctive call* and showing *thin white trailing edge to wing*, then *towers quickly* on *twisting course*. Plumage basically brown, with boldly striped head and upperparts. Flanks barred dark, *belly white* (which from some angles is difficult to see, falsely 'signalling' Great Snipe). All plumages similar.

VOICE Flight-call on take-off is abrupt, scraping 'catch!' (like a rubber boot being pulled out of soft mud); tends to be disyllabic, 'ca-**atch**!' (like a muffled sneeze). Vocal song (from post or other perch) often long-sustained '**chip**-per **chip**-per **chip**-per...'; but as main display has distinctive 'drumming' sound, a throbbing, bleating 'hühühühühühü-hühühü...', produced by air vibrating through spread outer tail-feathers in intermittent short, steep dives during wide-circling display-flight, mostly at dusk.

Jack Snipe *Lymnocryptes minimus* **P** / **W**3
L 18–20 cm (incl. bill 4), WS 33–36 cm. Breeds in extensive waterlogged bogs in N Europe. On passage (mostly Apr–early May and Sep–Oct) and in winter, muddy pool margins etc. Uncommon or local, but probably overlooked owing to skulking habits in often inaccessible patches.

IDENTIFICATION About ⅔ size of Snipe, with *much shorter bill* (about 1½ times length of head; Snipe's bill at least twice head length), but which is proportionately deeper-based. Skulking: *flushes only when almost trodden on*, flies up *silently*, showing more *rounded wing-tips, pointed tail* and less erratic flight than Snipe, *usually landing not far away*. When seen on ground, head shows strong pattern, with *split supercilium, dark crescent below eye*, always strong dark loral patch, and *lacks median crown-stripe*; *breast and flanks strongly streaked* (not barred); *bold yellowish back-stripes*; green sheen on mantle and scapulars; and unique, often prolonged *bouncing action* when feeding, as if whole body on springs ('sewing machine'). All plumages similar.

VOICE Rarely, gives quiet, harsh 'gatch' when flushed. In long, fast, shallow descent during display-flight, hollow 'ogog**ok**-ogog**ok**-ogog**ok**-...', like distant cantering horse, lasting *c.* 8 sec., followed by a few muffled, high-pitched, fizzing notes; sound distinctive, but hard to locate.

Woodcock   Great Snipe   Snipe   Jack Snipe

WOODCOCK

head held high

usually rapidly doubled
wingbeats when 'roding'

broad-winged, tip rounded

broad trans-
verse bands

pot-bellied

'roding' ♂ at dusk

ad.

GREAT SNIPE

various stages of display

much
white

dark

medium-
length

prominent
white
wing-bar

displaying
♂ on
favourite
tussock

barred

only narrow, indis-
tinct pale edge

ad.

SNIPE

diving
in dis-
play

pale
crown-
stripe

pale-banded

white belly

long

feeding

singing from perch

white, unbarred

prominent
white edge

ad.

JACK SNIPE

dark

short

short

squatting

ad.

quickly 'bouncing' forebody when feeding

DZ

Red Phalarope (Grey Phalarope)

Phalaropus fulicarius **P**4–5

L 20–22 cm, WS 36–41 cm. Breeds in Arctic on mainly coastal wet tundra, sometimes in drier area, but always near fresh or brackish water. Winters in Atlantic off S and W Africa, via migration routes well out in N Atlantic. In W Europe, very rare in late spring; more regular Sep–Oct (esp. W coast Britain & Ireland), when gales bring singles or small groups (at times large numbers) close inshore, or odd birds to coastal pools. Nest in tussock near shallow water. Common sex roles reversed; more attractively plumaged ♀♀ gather in flocks to compete for ♂♂, which tend eggs/young.

IDENTIFICATION Dunlin-sized, usually very tame wader. Outside breeding areas, in black, pale grey and white plumage, often seen swimming (when shape and colour recall miniature Little Gull) or in flight over sea, when could be overlooked as Sanderling (but *white wing-bar pronounced only on the 'arm'*, thinner on primaries, dark 'mask' often discernible at long range, and looks *distinctly strong-chested*) until it *plops down and swims*; also, flying parties over sea usually looser, not so cohesive as Sanderling (and other *Calidris*). When swimming, pecks quickly all around for food on surface. In all plumages, told from Red-necked by *slightly thicker and* (when viewed head-on) *flattened bill*; identification difficult at distance if bill shape not discernible, especially if in moult (e.g. juvenile to 1st-winter), when plumage differences obscured. – Adult summer: Rarely seen away from breeding areas; unmistakable. ♂ has underparts often white-flecked and slightly less bright, and head pattern less clear-cut than ♀. Bill yellow with dark tip. In flight, distinctive *contrast between dark body and white underwing-coverts*. – Adult winter: *Almost plain pale blue-grey upperparts* and wings (Red-necked has whitish mantle-V and scapular fringes); *dark-bordered white crown* (ad. Red-necked white crown, juv. solidly black); bill dark, usually with hint of *yellow-brown base*. – Juvenile: Resembles juvenile Red-necked Phalarope, but *ochre-yellow mantle-V thinner and scapular-V usually lacking*, and rather quickly acquires its first pale grey 1st-winter scapulars (juv. Red-necked moults somewhat later). Has *light apricot-buff wash on neck/breast* (more pinkish-tinged grey at first on Red-necked).

VOICE Flight-call sharp, high-pitched, metallic 'pit' (can recall Coot). Song (by ♀ in slow-winged, circling display-flight) buzzing, far-carrying 'brrreep', vaguely recalling Broad-billed Sandpiper. Excited 'bip bip bip...' on water.

Red-necked Phalarope *Phalaropus lobatus* m**B**5 / **P**4

L 17–19 cm, WS 30–34 cm. Breeds on wet marshes and pools and osier delta lands on mountainsides above tree limit or on tundra; extends farther inland and to higher altitude

than Red Phalarope. Migrates in late Jul-Aug/early Sep (earlier than Red), mainly non-stop towards SE across Europe to winter in Arabian Sea, where it leads pelagic life far from land. Scarce on autumn passage, feeding at coasts, inland marshes and pools. In W Europe rare in spring, too, but in N Baltic and further east may occur in very large flocks in late May. Nest in vegetation near water. Sex roles reversed as with Red Phalarope.

IDENTIFICATION General size, shape and behaviour much as described for Red, but a little *smaller and daintier*, with slightly *shorter body* (less gull-like when swimming), and *bill very thin* (not laterally flattened) and always all black. – Adult summer: Crown, cheeks, back of neck, breast-sides and mantle lead-grey, *throat and small spot above eye white*. Variable amount of *red or rufous-ochre on sides of neck*, neater and more intense on ♀, less colourful and with less clear-cut pattern on ♂. – Adult winter: (Rarely seen in Europe.) Medium grey above, with distinct whitish mantle-V and scapular fringes (Red Phalarope paler and almost plain). – Juvenile: Unlike Red Phalarope, has prominent *ochrous-buff* (or whitish when faded) *Vs above* on both mantle and scapulars, a *solid dark cap*, and a *faint pinkish-grey hue on neck/breast-sides* (which, however, quickly fades to white).

VOICE Common call is a short, nasal and slightly throaty 'chep' or longer (almost disyllabic) 'cherre'. The throaty call, and sharper variants, 'chik', are used in chorus in display.

VAGRANT WADERS

Most of the waders on the following pages are vagrants to Europe from N America and Asia (as are a few species on pp. 128–129, 134–135 and 142–143). Accordingly, they are unlikely to be seen, and will therefore require careful observation and full description before they can be reported, confirmed, and details published. Some vagrants are unmistakable, but most are similar to regular European species, and identification requires much caution and thorough familiarity with commoner counterparts. Read the general advice on wader identification on pp. 122–123, too.

Wilson's Phalarope *Phalaropus tricolor* **V**∗∗

L 22–24 cm. Breeds in N America. Vagrant to Europe. A few records annually in Britain & Ireland, mostly 1st-winter birds in Aug–Oct, seen at coastal pools, marshes.

IDENTIFICATION Slightly larger than the other phalaropes, and oddly proportioned, with *longer neck, longer, needle-fine bill*, and *longer legs*. Swims, but also *commonly walks in* shallow water or on muddy edges, snapping at insects in *stealthy, crouched posture, rear end pointing up, breast almost touching ground*, or pecks with distinctive rocking-horse action as if whole body on pivot. *Legs* black on adult summer, otherwise *yellow*. In flight, *plain wings* and *square white rump*; toes project beyond tail. – Adult summer: Unmistakable; ♀ brighter than ♂. – Adult winter: Uniform *very pale grey upperparts and wing-coverts*, white below: *looks strikingly white at distance*; long white supercilium; diffuse greyish stripe on side of neck; *lacks dark head markings*. – Juvenile/1st-winter: Commonest plumage seen in Europe: as adult winter, but brown, pale-fringed juvenile wing-coverts/tertials and often some scapulars retained.

VOICE Flight-call a short, nasal 'vit'.

Red Phalarope   Red-necked Phalarope

RED PHALAROPE

thin stripes

broad wing-bar

chunky build

juv. → 1st-w.

ad. s. → ad. w.

juv.

1st-winter

ad. summer ♀

thick

juv. → 1st-winter

forecrown white with black sides, hindcrown black

plain

ad. winter

yellow

ad. summer ♂

ad. summer ♀

RED-NECKED PHALAROPE

prominent stripes

narrow wing-bar

'dainty' build

juv.

juv.

ad. summer ♀

♂

♀

light pinkish-grey hue on neck and breast quickly fades to white

thin

a little black on hindcrown

juv. → 1st-winter

white stripes

ad. winter

ad. summer ♀

all dark

ad. summer ♂

WILSON'S PHALAROPE

unusually proportioned wader owing to long neck and rather short legs

lacks distinct 'mask'

long-necked

white

plain

juv. → 1st-w.

1st-winter

ad. summer ♀

yellow

long, needle-fine

juv. → 1st-winter

ad. summer ♀

ad. summer ♂

KM

ad. winter

Baird's Sandpiper *Calidris bairdii* V*

L 14–17 cm. Breeds in N America, NE Siberia. Vagrant to Europe. Often on dry or short-grass terrain but also beaches, especially with banks of storm-deposited seaweed.

IDENTIFICATION Slightly smaller than Dunlin, with delicate build like a stint. Unusual 'flattened oval' shape to body when viewed from in front or behind. *Wing-tips project beyond tail*, and *long-bodied, short-legged outline* often even more striking than on White-rumped Sandpiper, from which it differs in all plumages in *lack of white rump*, less prominent supercilium, *finer-based bill with straighter culmen*, and all-black bill. – Adult summer: Grey-buff upperparts with variable amount of dark feather centres; *buffy wash across breast, streaked brown at sides*. Beware of Sanderling in confusing, somewhat similar transitional plumages (Sanderling has chunky build, longer legs, stouter bill). – Adult winter: As adult summer, but upperparts plainer grey-brown with pale feather fringes. – Juvenile: General coloration on head and breast *usually strikingly buff*; upperparts a shade greyer, with broad whitish tips forming a *uniform scaly pattern* (similar to juv. Curlew Sandpiper), lacking obvious white Vs or rufous fringes; throat and indistinct supercilium pale buff; *usually complete gorget of brown breast streaking* on otherwise white underparts.

VOICE Flight-call short purring trill, 'prrreet'.

White-rumped Sandpiper *Calidris fuscicollis* V*

L 16–18 cm. Breeds in N America. Vagrant to Europe.

IDENTIFICATION A little smaller than Dunlin. With Baird's Sandpiper shares distinctive *long-bodied, rather short-legged outline*, unlike other small waders; *wing-tips project beyond tail*. In all plumages, white uppertail-coverts forming *U-shaped white patch*, prominent *whitish supercilium*, a medium-length, rather thick-based *bill slightly decurved at tip*; at close range, *brownish base to lower mandible*. – Adult summer: When fresh, greyish above with neat black feather centres; breast and *flanks streaked black*. Narrow white *mantle, stripes* and, when worn, *conspicuously pale bases to second lowest row of scapulars*. – Adult winter: Closely resembles winter Dunlin, best told by: small size; slim, attenuated shape; shorter bill. – Juvenile: Attenuated shape, *whiteness of underparts* and *prominence of supercilium* usually most striking differences from Dunlin. Pattern of upperpart feathers rather like juvenile Baird's, but usually *obvious rufous edges to mantle, upper rows of scapulars and tertials*. Also, has distinct, stint-like *white mantle- and scapular-Vs*, crown tinged rufous, and flanks finely streaked grey.

VOICE High, squeaky, mouse- or bat-like 'tzeet'.

Semipalmated Sandpiper *Calidris pusilla* V**

L 13–15 cm. Breeds in N America. Vagrant to Europe.

IDENTIFICATION Compare Little Stint (p. 142) and Western Sandpiper. Typically stockier than Little Stint, with *short, straight, thick-tipped bill* (on average thicker and straighter than Little's), but beware some longer-billed birds with slight decurve occur. *Toes half-webbed* (eliminates all stints except Western). – Adult summer: *No obvious rufous colour or light Vs on upperparts*, thus rather *drab grey-brown with black scapular centres*; rather *well-marked breast-band* with a few streaks extending to upper flanks. – Adult winter: Best

told by palmations and call; from Western by *more diffuse breast-side streaks* and very *slightly longer primary projection*. – Juvenile: Usually noticeably less bright and overall *more uniformly patterned* than Little Stint. May show faint, diffuse pale mantle-V (often more obvious at long range) and slightly darker upper-scapular tract, but generally *lacks contrasting rufous zones or distinct light Vs. Ear-coverts and lores usually a shade darker*, and *crown more evenly streaked*, contrasting with rather clear-cut supercilium. Breast-sides more diffusely streaked and *primary projection shorter* than on Little Stint. A few are rather bright above, being very difficult to distinguish from juvenile Western, but still are more uniformly coloured, with upper rows of scapulars same shade as crown (tend to be brighter rufous on Western).

VOICE Most distinctive flight-call a short, harsh 'tchrp', but also a more Little Stint-like 'tüpp'.

Western Sandpiper *Calidris maura* V***

L 14–17 cm. Breeds in N America. The rarest of the American stints in Europe.

IDENTIFICATION Compare Little Stint (p. 142) and Semipalmated Sandpiper. *Bill usually fine-tipped, slightly decurved and rather long*: this, and flat-backed, longish-legged shape, *typically recall miniature Dunlin rather than stint*. Crown-sides and ear-coverts typically rather pale; white supercilium prominent in front of eye. *Toes half-webbed* (eliminates all stints except Semipalmated). – Adult summer: *Extensive rufous on black-centred scapulars*, contrasts with *rather plain grey wing-coverts*; usually *rufous on crown-sides and ear-coverts*; breast streaking breaks into *obvious arrowhead markings on upper flanks*. – Adult winter: Very difficult to distinguish from winter Semipalmated. Sharp, fine streaks *often extend across breast*. – Juvenile: *Prominent rich rufous on upper scapulars* contrasts with basically *grey lower scapulars and wing-coverts*; lower scapulars typically have *pointed* blackish centres and tips (broader, more anchor-shaped black markings on Semipalmated); faint mantle- and scapular-Vs; neat breast-side streaks.

VOICE Flight-call a high, vibrant 'jeet'.

Red-necked Stint *Calidris ruficollis* V***

L 13–16 cm. Breeds in NE Siberia. Rare vagrant to Europe.

IDENTIFICATION Compare Little Stint (p. 142), and juvenile and adult winter Semipalmated Sandpiper. Usually subtly but *distinctly shorter-legged/longer-bodied shape* and shorter-billed than Little Stint. – Adult summer: Throat/upper breast *plain, bright orange, bordered below with black streaks or arrowhead marks*; orange tones extend to supercilium and nape; scapulars black-centred with rufous fringes, contrasting with plain or dark-centred *grey wing-coverts and tertials*; sometimes prominent *whitish mantle-V*. Orange on breast/head and rufous above often largely obscured by whitish fringes in fresh plumage. – Adult winter: Told from Semipalmated by shape and *unwebbed toes*; probably not safely told from Little Stint, but possibly by shape (of classic individual) and call. – Juvenile: Like Little Stint, but lower scapulars and wing-coverts greyer, thus *contrast* with black-centred, rufous-fringed upper scapulars and mantle; mantle- and split supercilium less prominent or lacking.

VOICE Flight-call a high-pitched, slightly hoarse 'chriit'.

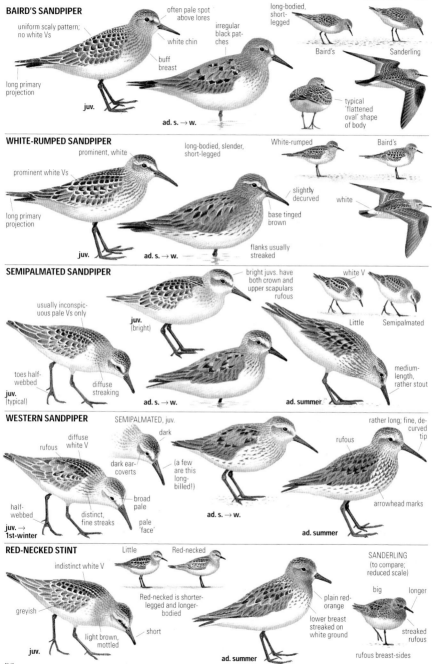

BAIRD'S SANDPIPER

uniform scaly pattern; no white Vs

often pale spot above lores

white chin

irregular black pat- ches

buff breast

long primary projection

juv.

ad. s. → w.

long-bodied, short-legged

Baird's

Sanderling

typical 'flattened oval' shape of body

WHITE-RUMPED SANDPIPER

prominent, white

long-bodied, slender, short-legged

prominent white Vs

long primary projection

slightly decurved

base tinged brown

flanks usually streaked

juv.

ad. s. → w.

White-rumped

Baird's

white

SEMIPALMATED SANDPIPER

usually inconspic- uous pale Vs only

bright juvs. have both crown and upper scapulars rufous

juv. (bright)

white V

Little

Semipalmated

toes half- webbed

juv. (typical)

diffuse streaking

ad. s. → w.

ad. summer

medium- length, rather stout

WESTERN SANDPIPER

SEMIPALMATED, juv.

dark

diffuse white V

rufous

dark ear- coverts

(a few are this long- billed!)

half- webbed

juv. → 1st-winter

distinct, fine streaks

broad pale

pale 'face'

ad. s. → w.

rather long; fine, de- curved tip

rufous

arrowhead marks

ad. summer

RED-NECKED STINT

indistinct white V

Little

Red-necked

greyish

Red-necked is shorter- legged and longer- bodied

light brown, mottled

short

juv.

plain red- orange

lower breast streaked on white ground

SANDERLING (to compare; reduced scale)

big

longer

streaked rufous

rufous breast-sides

ad. summer

DZ

Ruff *Philomachus pugnax* mB5/P+W4

♂ L 29–32, WS 54–60 cm, ♀ L 22–26 cm, WS 46–49 cm.
Not a rare vagrant but a common European breeder, treated here to facilitate comparison with some similar-looking species. Breeds on taiga bogs, in marshes and pools on mountainsides and tundra, and in wet grass meadows at lakesides or seashores. Summer visitor, winters mainly in Africa; on passage and in winter frequents marshes, shallow pools, estuaries, ploughed and stubble fields. Usually seen as a few or in smaller parties, but in spring at favoured sites can occur in very large flocks. ♂♂ display in communal lek on traditional arenas, which ♀♀ visit for mating. Arena, commonly used by *c.* 5–20 ♂♂, open grassy patch, often with bare soil on favourite spots, *c.* 1 m apart. Display silent, involves wing-flutter, short jumps, crouching with ruff erected, brief fluttering attacks on rivals with bill, legs or wings, sudden erect stance, or forward-bent stance with ruff raised and drooped wings and tail.

IDENTIFICATION Marked sexual size difference: ♂♂ (Ruffs) considerably larger than ♀♀ (Reeves). Largest ♂♂ slightly bigger and bulkier-bodied than Redshank; smallest ♀♀ only slightly larger-bodied than Dunlin (but with longer neck and legs). Small-headed/large-bodied look, *rather long neck* (when not hunched), and *medium-length bill* which, unlike some confusion species, is *slightly curved,* give rather distinctive shape which is especially useful for identifying some immatures or ♀ plumages that are otherwise confusingly variable in pattern, bare-part colours and size. Frequent habit (shared only with Black-tailed Godwit) of slightly raising mantle-feathers when feeding, appearing as *loose, pointed 'crest' at top of back.* Wingbeats subtly deeper and slower than other small or medium-sized waders, giving rather distinctive *lazier flight action*; often long glides before alighting. Thin, indistinct light wing-bar but *bold white oval patch on each side of uppertail.* Bill and leg colour variable: some non-breeding ♂♂ with bright orange bill-base and legs easily confused with Redshank (cf. p. 146), but shape different, and *upperparts largely scaly* (with some coarse bars at rear), not largely plain (with some fine barring and spotting). – Adult summer: Display-plumage of ♂ has *erectable crest and ruff* in variable combinations of plain or coarsely barred *black, deep rufous, orange or white*; worn only in May–Jun and rarely seen away from breeding areas; bill, warty skin on face, and legs usually orange. ♀ brown, variably mottled or boldly spotted with black; typically, bill all dark but legs orange or dull red (rarely brown or greyish-green). – Adult winter: Sexes similar except for size. Bare parts usually duller and darker. ♂ has no crest, ruff or bare skin on face (but *pale feathering at bill-base*). Rather *plain pale grey-brown*, but some are more whitish on head and neck; tertials and large scapulars diffusely pale-fringed or *coarsely barred dark*. – Juvenile: Like adult winter, but often *stronger buff tinge below*, and *upperparts have neat scaly pattern* with *solidly dark feather centres.*

VOICE Nearly mute, has only low grunting sounds.

Ruff

Buff-breasted Sandpiper *Tryngites subruficollis* V*

L 18–20 cm. Breeds in N America. Occurs annually in Britain & Ireland, often appearing in small groups. Often seen on short-grass fields (pasture, airfields, golf courses) but also on pools and mudflats on seashores.

IDENTIFICATION Dunlin-sized wader *preferring dry or short-grass terrain.* Like small juvenile ♀ Ruff, but *bill shorter, finer, straighter and black* (Ruff's usually pale-based); head and underparts more uniform sandy-buff, with *neat dark-streaked cap* and *black eye prominent on plain face*; *breast-sides neatly spotted*; and *legs mustard-yellowish.* In flight resembles miniature Golden Plover, *shows no white above* and has *white underwing with dark crescent* on primary coverts. Adult has broadly pale-edged scapulars and plainer wing-coverts, whereas juvenile has neat and uniform scaly upperparts with intricately patterned wing-coverts.

VOICE Usually silent; low, muffled, monosyllabic 'gerf'.

Pectoral Sandpiper *Calidris melanotos* V*

L 19–23 cm, WS 38–44 cm. Breeds in N America, NE Siberia. Commonest American vagrant to Britain & Ireland, most records Sep–Oct; in rest of Europe often in May.

IDENTIFICATION Slightly larger than Dunlin, with rather short, slightly decurved *pale-based bill*; general shape and flight pattern recall small Ruff, particularly when alert and adopts *erect stance with neck stretched.* In all plumages, has *sharply demarcated gorget of streaks* coming to point in centre of breast (belly thus unmarked), and *pale legs tinged yellowish* (at times more grey-green). – Adult summer: Like juvenile, but rusty fringes and white Vs less prominent or lacking, less neat scaly pattern especially on worn wing-coverts, and supercilium less prominent. ♂ has coarsely mottled, not neatly streaked, breast-band. – Adult winter (extremely rare in Europe): Grey-brown above, with dark feather centres more diffuse than on juvenile. – Juvenile: Upperpart feathers blackish-centred with rufous fringes, forming neat scaly pattern; white mantle- and scapular-Vs usually prominent; creamy, finely streaked supercilium.

VOICE Flight-call a short, trilling, slightly throaty 'krrrt', a little like that of Curlew Sandpiper (or Baird's) but deeper.

Sharp-tailed Sandpiper *Calidris acuminata* V**

L 17–21 cm. Breeds in E Siberia. Rare vagrant to Britain & Ireland. European records in May and Jul–Sep.

IDENTIFICATION Resembles Pectoral Sandpiper, but in all plumages *lacks its distinctive breast pattern*, has *whiter supercilium* (esp. behind eye) against *clear-cut rustier cap* and more *prominent white eye-ring.* – Adult summer: Streaked upper breast, with variable but usually *extensive dark chevrons* (or arrowheads) *on breast-sides, flanks and undertail-coverts.* – Adult winter: Streaked breast, *extending as streaks or chevrons* (arrowheads) *onto flanks and undertail-coverts* (where streaks, if any, are very few and fine on Pectoral). – Juvenile: Usually strong orange-buff wash on breast, with streaking confined to thin necklace across upper breast; cap brighter, more fiery-rufous than on Pectoral, with clear white supercilium very prominent, especially behind eye.

VOICE Flight-call a very distinctive mellow, plaintive, rather subdued 'wheep' or 'pleep', often doubled or repeated several times; can recall Swallow.

RUFF

juv. ♂

juv. ♀

juv. ♂

juv. ♀

ad. ♂

autumn flock show-
ing variation in
size and
plumage

white
sides

project far

often
raised,
appear
'loosely
attached'

plain

long
tertials

juv. ♀

pale bill-
surround

communal lek in spring

flock in spring

♂

♂

♀

ad. ♀
spring

ad. ♂
breeding

ad. ♂ winter

BUFF-BREASTED SANDPIPER

pale eye-ring

neatly
scalloped

spotted
sides

patchy

lacks
obvious
wing-bar

recalls small
plover

conspic-
uous dark
crescent

mustard-
coloured

ad. s.
→ w.

no
white

juv.

long
primary
projection

juv.

PECTORAL SANDPIPER

Dunlin,
juv.

short

point

'full'
chest

Pectoral, juv.

inconspicuous
wing-bar

conspicuous white
stripes

breast streaks
end abruptly

sharp 'cut-off'

longer
primary
projection
than Ruff
or Dunlin

juv.

white,
unmarked

ad. s. → w.

SHARP-TAILED SANDPIPER

juv.

stronger head
pattern than
Pectoral

streaked necklace

plain orange-buff, streaking restricted to sides

ad. summer

juv.

streaked

rufous

hint of 'spot-
bars'

ad. s. → w.

KM

Lesser Yellowlegs *Tringa flavipes* V*

L 23–25 cm. Breeds in N America. Fairly regular vagrant to Europe, mainly in late summer and autumn, and about 5–10 records annually in Britain & Ireland. Frequents short-grass marshes, muddy coastal pools, or inland marshy lakesides.

IDENTIFICATION Resembles Redshank but smaller (about same size as Marsh Sandpiper), with noticeably rakish build, *long, slender neck*, *long wings* and *long legs*. Unusual shape and proportions as likely to attract attention as any plumage feature or colour of legs. Bill virtually *straight, fine* and *practically all dark; long legs* always *bright yellow*. Distinguished from Marsh Sandpiper and Greenshank in flight by having *square white rump patch* (without pointed extension up back). Can be confused with Wood Sandpiper (which has similar white rump patch and rarely has dull yellowish rather than greenish legs) but, apart from differences in structure (note esp. Lesser Yellowlegs' *longer primary projection* and *extension of the wing-tips beyond tail*), Lesser Yellowlegs has *shorter supercilium* (not continuing behind eye) and lacks the distinct dark cap and two-tone bill of Wood Sandpiper. In flight, has much less compact look than Wood Sandpiper owing to longer neck, longer legs and longer wings. When size is not apparent can easily be confused with Greater Yellowlegs, but note: *slender build*; *narrow* and slightly *shorter bill* (only slightly longer than head; clearly longer on Greater); *straighter bill* (straight or only faintly upturned; obviously upturned on Greater); and darker bill (all dark or with only faint hint of yellow-brown base; always paler-based on non-breeding Greater). Also, secondaries and primaries are uniformly dark (secondaries and inner primaries at least partly finely spotted light on Greater). – Adult summer: Unlike Greater Yellowlegs, has *flanks sparsely barred or unmarked*, and belly usually completely unmarked white. – Adult winter: Plumage much as Greater Yellowlegs. – Juvenile: Differs from adult winter in having darker mantle, wing-coverts and tertials with more contrasting light spots. Plumage similar to juvenile Greater Yellowlegs, but *breast more diffusely and finely streaked*.

VOICE Call rather high-pitched, clear 'tew', often uttered singly, sometimes 2–4 notes in quick succession at same pitch; voice a mixture of Redshank and Marsh Sandpiper.

Greater Yellowlegs *Tringa melanoleuca* V**

L 29–33 cm. Breeds in N America. Rare vagrant to Europe. Almost annual in Britain & Ireland.

IDENTIFICATION Greenshank-like, but in all plumages has *bright yellow legs* (sometimes slightly orange-yellow), *generally browner* (less grey) coloration, upperpart feathers more prominently notched with white, and *white rump not extending in V up back*. Can be confused with Lesser Yellowlegs, which see for detailed comparison, but *size and shape like Greenshank*, especially *stouter*, slightly *longer bill* (considerably more than head length), which is *obviously upturned* and *grey-based*. Caution: some Greenshanks have dull greyish-yellow legs, and some juvenile Redshanks have pale orange legs. – Adult summer: Much *more and coarser barring on flanks* than Lesser Yellowlegs, sometimes *also on belly*. – Adult winter: Largely grey above and white below. Like juvenile, but paler, greyer and less strongly patterned above. – Juvenile: Dark brownish above with neat pattern of not-

ches and spots on feather fringes; *breast is more strongly streaked* than on Lesser Yellowlegs.

VOICE Flight-call three-syllable whistle, very like Greenshank, but sometimes seems 'livelier', and slightly higher-pitched and almost invariably with lower-pitched third syllable, 'peu-peu-pew'. Typically somewhat louder and clearer than call of Lesser Yellowlegs (though some calls close), three-syllabic pattern often good clue.

Solitary Sandpiper *Tringa solitaria* V***

L 18–21 cm. Breeds in N America. Vagrant to Europe, usually in summer–autumn.

IDENTIFICATION Very similar to Green Sandpiper except *lacks white rump* (rump is dark, with barred tail-sides), and strength of white spotting above intermediate between Green and Wood Sandpipers. In flight, *rather dark underwings* recall Green Sandpiper, but Solitary is noticeably slighter in build, with longer-looking, narrower wings. When seen well on the ground, *bill and legs average slightly longer*, and *bill usually slightly decurved* (unlike Green and Wood Sandpipers); *white eye-ring usually bolder than on Green Sandpiper*. – Adult summer: Head, neck and breast more coarsely streaked with white than Green Sandpiper; usually prominent white spotting on mantle and scapulars, with contrastingly darker-looking wing-coverts. – Juvenile: Compared with juvenile Green Sandpiper, a shade lighter brown above, with longer primary projection and extension of wing-tips beyond tail. Both have short supercilium and white eye-ring, but eye-ring often more conspicuous on Solitary Sandpiper.

VOICE Call like Green Sandpiper's in quality, but softer, 'tewit-weet'.

Spotted Sandpiper *Actitis macularia* V*

L 18–20 cm. Breeds in N America. Fairly regular vagrant to Europe, with annual records in Britain & Ireland, including one breeding attempt in Scotland; usually in late summer and autumn, but a few spring and overwintering records.

IDENTIFICATION Very similar to Common Sandpiper; in all plumages generally *greyer above* (less brown), *tail projection short*, and *short wing-bar* not reaching to body. – Adult summer: *Black spots below* diagnostic, but sometimes sparse and difficult to see. – Adult winter: Plain brown-grey above, no spots below. Very similar to Common Sandpiper; at very close range tertial edges unmarked (faintly barred on Common), but identification best confirmed by tail length, extent of wing-bar, and call. – Juvenile: *Tertials and greater coverts plain, with barring restricted to tips*, leaving *strongly barred area confined to median and lesser coverts* (tertial fringes and coverts fully barred on Common); *legs pale, yellowish* (usually dull brownish or greenish on Common). Juvenile also differs from Common Sandpiper in more uniform ('smoother') and greyer breast-side patches; bill often rather pale pinkish-horn with darker tip. In flight, shows less white on outer tail than Common Sandpiper (and seems less inclined than Common to spread tail).

VOICE Variable. Single vagrants often frustratingly silent! Can at times sound very like Common Sandpiper, but more often utters a short, whistled 'peet!', or doubled 'peet-weet' with tone reminiscent of Green Sandpiper.

LESSER YELLOWLEGS

winter

REDSHANK

note smaller size, more delicate build and more attenuated rear end than Redshank (above, right)

juv.

fine, all dark

diffusely streaked

more rakish than Wood Sandpiper in flight

WOOD SANDPIPER

long

rather short

WOOD (to compare)

GREATER YELLOWLEGS

winter

Greater Yellowlegs resembles Greenshank in size and shape, but legs are brighter yellow and upperparts more strongly marked white

juv. → 1st-winter

square white rump

white wedge on back

GREENSHANK (to compare)

longer, stouter and more upturned than on Lesser; paler base

strongly streaked

barred

LESSER, ad. s.   GREATER, ad. s.   GREENSHANK, ad. s.

SOLITARY SANDPIPER

dark

white

GREEN (to compare)

more attenuated rear end than Green Sandpiper

hint of barring

juv.

GREEN, juv. (to compare)

white eyering often bolder than on Green

more delicate build

Solitary   Green

Solitary looks more slender and narrower-winged than Green

ad. s.

GREEN, ad. s.

SPOTTED SANDPIPER

ad. summer

COMMON, juv. (to compare)

tertial fringes finely notched

shorter tail projection than Common

tertial fringes plain

juv.

breast-sides tend to be greyer and more uniform on juv. Spotted

Common

Spotted

wing-bar reduced towards inner wing

wing-bar extends to inner wing

winter

in winter, shape and leg colour are helpful clues

COMMON, winter (to compare)

KM

160 WADERS

Slender-billed Curlew *Numenius tenuirostris* **V**∗∗∗

L 36–41 cm (incl. bill *c.* 8), WS 77–88 cm. Now extremely rare: very few recent sightings, and along with Bald Ibis possibly the most endangered species within the treated region. Breeds locally in W Siberia; winters Morocco (only 1–2 birds known recently), SE Italy (flock of *c.* 20 in 1995), Tunisia (?), Middle East (?); migration via SE Europe or Middle East. In winter, frequents meadows or saline steppe near marshes.

IDENTIFICATION Whimbrel-sized (cf. p. 148), but slightly more delicate build, and *bill thinner* and *tapering to finer tip* (making it appear longer than it is). Ground colour on *sides of head, throat and breast whiter*, and black streaks more sharply contrasting than on both Whimbrel and Curlew; breast streaking gradually breaks up into diagnostic *distinct rounded or drop-shaped spots on lower breast and flanks*, contrasting sharply against white ground. Head pattern intermediate between Curlew and Whimbrel, has *rather dark loral stripe and crown-side* creating impression of *light supercilium* (though nothing like on Whimbrel, and lacks distinct pale median crown-stripe of that species). *Underwing-coverts all white*; rump white and *uppertail very pale* (looking whitish, paler than on Curlew and Whimbrel); secondaries and inner primaries distinctly barred light, giving obvious contrast with darker outer wing (but hardly a diagnostic difference unless directly compared with the other two species). – Juvenile: Flanks streaked, not spotted (some spots acquired in 1st winter). Caution: Curlew can have proportionately as short a bill, white underwing, and contrasting flank markings, so important to be sure of small size, different bill shape, and (on adults) shape of flank spots.

VOICE Call is a Curlew-like 'cour-lee' but *sweeter, higher-pitched*, and when repeated *faster*. Alarm in flight a sharper and shorter 'cu-ee'.

Little Curlew *Numenius minutus* **V**∗∗∗

L 29–32 cm (incl. bill *c.* 4½), WS 57–63 cm. Breeds in NC and NE Siberia, winters mainly in N Australia. Extremely rare vagrant to Europe in late summer–early autumn.

IDENTIFICATION Obvious curlew, but *tiny* (slightly smaller than Golden Plover, which it resembles in actions and flight) and has *small head*, rather *short neck* and a proportionately *much shorter and less decurved bill* than its congeners. In all plumages, *Whimbrel-like head pattern* (dark crown-sides, narrow light median crown-stripe), wholly *grey-brown underwing-coverts*, rather finely mottled *buffish underparts*, and *lacks white rump* (caution: Whimbrel of the N American ssp. *hudsonicus*, p. 148, lacks white rump, too; see also Upland Sandpiper). Forehead and lores often pale, and this together with prominent light buff supercilium gives *pale-faced impression*. Primaries and secondaries are rather uniformly dark, contrasting with *pale upperwing-coverts* on inner wing. Base of lower mandible pinkish. – Very similar also to exceedingly rare (possibly now extinct) N American relative Eskimo Curlew *Numenius borealis*

Slender-billed Curlew

(p. 387), but this has shorter legs, slightly longer, more downcurved bill, longer wings (wing-tips projecting beyond tail when folded), and darker-patterned underparts.

VOICE Flight-call is a rapid laughing 'kui-kui-kui-kui-...', distinctly higher-pitched and softer than Whimbrel. In anxiety, may utter a slightly sharper 'quit-quit'.

Upland Sandpiper *Bartramia longicauda* **V**∗∗

L 28–32 cm, WS 50–55 cm. Breeds in N America. Vagrant to Europe, annual in Britain & Ireland. Prefers grass fields (pastures, airfields, golf courses) but will feed on stubble fields and low-growing crops, too.

IDENTIFICATION Redshank-sized wader with small head and shape like miniature Curlew or Whimbrel, thus not unlike Little Curlew, but with *short, straight bill* (with pale yellow-brown lower mandible), *very long tail extending well past wing-tips*, and long, *very thin neck* when alert; *no obvious white above in flight*. In all plumages has *dark cap* with *thin light median crown-stripe, prominent dark eye on plain face*, and dark arrowhead marks on breast and flanks. Legs are dull yellowish. Wing-feathers strongly barred. – Adult: Dark-barred scapulars, tertials and wing-coverts. – Juvenile: Pale-fringed feathers and pale-notched tertials, giving neater, stronger scaly pattern than adult.

VOICE Clear, whistled, bubbly 'quip-ip-ip-ip' in flight, strongly recalling ♀ Cuckoo or Little Grebe.

Stilt Sandpiper *Micropalama himantopus* **V**∗∗∗

L 18–23 cm, WS 37–42 cm. Breeds in N America. Vagrant to Britain & Ireland, mostly adults in late summer. Generally found with flocks of *Calidris* species on coastal lagoons or mudflats, but also inclined to mingle with *Tringa* species (e.g. Redshank) and Ruff, which may be wading in water too deep for *Calidris* species.

IDENTIFICATION Slightly larger than Dunlin, but longer-winged, *longer-necked* and *much longer-legged*. Curved bill, general shape and *white rump* recall Curlew Sandpiper, but *legs noticeably longer*, giving stilt-like impression (and longer foot projection in flight), *legs yellowish to dull green* (not black), and *bill more even in thickness, less fine-tipped*, giving rather tubular impression. Distinctive body shape, remarkably *angular* in profile and peculiarly *laterally compressed* when viewed from in front or behind (not so rounded as e.g. Redshank). Wings rather uniformly dark above, *lacking obvious wing-bars*, but trailing edge rather pale. Often wades in deep water, and extraordinary length of legs may then not be obvious. – Adult summer: Partially or completely *barred underparts; rusty ear-coverts* contrasting with white supercilium. Indistinct short pale median crown-stripe towards rear of 'cap'. At long range looks plain and rather dark, prompting thoughts of dowitcher or even juvenile Spotted Redshank. – Adult winter: Plain grey-brown above; breast more extensively streaked than Curlew Sandpiper, extending to flanks and undertail-coverts. – Juvenile: Blackish feather centres and whitish fringes give less grey, more contrasting scaly pattern on upperparts than Curlew Sandpiper; prominent supercilium contrasts with dark cap and dark mask across ear-coverts.

VOICE Flight-call is a soft trilled 'trrrp' recalling that of Curlew Sandpiper.

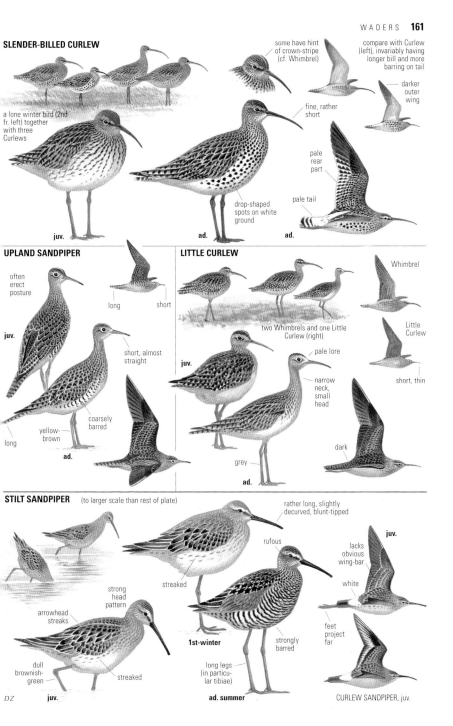

SLENDER-BILLED CURLEW

some have hint of crown-stripe (cf. Whimbrel)

compare with Curlew (left), invariably having longer bill and more barring on tail

darker outer wing

a lone winter bird (2nd fr. left) together with three Curlews

fine, rather short

pale rear part

pale tail

drop-shaped spots on white ground

juv.

ad.

ad.

UPLAND SANDPIPER

often erect posture

long   short

juv.

short, almost straight

coarsely barred

yellow-brown

long

ad.

LITTLE CURLEW

Whimbrel

two Whimbrels and one Little Curlew (right)

Little Curlew

short, thin

juv.

pale lore

narrow neck, small head

grey

dark

ad.

STILT SANDPIPER (to larger scale than rest of plate)

rather long, slightly decurved, blunt-tipped

rufous

streaked

strong head pattern

arrowhead streaks

dull brownish-green

streaked

juv.

1st-winter

strongly barred

long legs (in particular tibiae)

ad. summer

juv.

lacks obvious wing-bar

white

feet project far

CURLEW SANDPIPER, juv.

DZ

Long-billed Dowitcher *Limnodromus scolopaceus* **V***
L 27–30 cm (incl. bill 5½–7½), WS 42–49 cm. Breeds in N America and E Siberia. Vagrant to Europe; several records annually in Britain & Ireland.

IDENTIFICATION Dowitchers are Snipe-sized, with shape, actions and plumage suggesting cross between Snipe and Bar-tailed Godwit; very *long bill*, prominent supercilium, *greenish* moderate-length *legs* and (in flight) *thin white 'slit' up back* and *prominent whitish trailing edge to wing*. Typical of dowitchers is that *blunt-tipped bill is a fraction decurved distally*. Given good views, identification of juveniles straightforward, but adult summer and adult winter difficult, often requiring diagnostic voice to confirm. Bill lengths overlap extensively, and useful only for extremes: *twice head length or more indicates Long-billed*, about 1½ times head length indicates Short-billed; on Long-billed *black bars on tail-feathers broader than light bars*, on Short-billed black bars narrower than light bars (those with equal-width bars are indeterminate). – Adult summer: Underparts (often except undertail-coverts) rusty-orange, *including belly*, with *dense spotting on foreneck and upper breast*, and *strong barring on breast-sides, flanks and undertail-coverts*. – Adult winter: Flank barring and *whole breast* grey, with *rather abrupt border against white belly*. – Juvenile: Tertials, greater coverts and scapulars *solidly dark-centred*, with neat (sometimes finely scalloped) whitish or rufous fringes (or sometimes small internal markings near tips).

VOICE Single shrill, short, sharp 'yip' or 'kyip', quality recalling Wood Sandpiper or distant Oystercatcher; often calls singly every 2–3 sec. in flight, or quickly doubled or trebled ('kyip-ip' or 'kyipipip'), especially when alarmed.

Short-billed Dowitcher *Limnodromus griseus* **V*****
L 25–29 cm (incl. bill 5–6½). Breeds in N America. Very rare vagrant to Europe (actually only two accepted records, both in Oct, in Ireland and Germany, following the rejection of many previous reports). Obviously highly unlikely to occur on this side of the Atlantic, so any presumed sighting should be thoroughly documented.

IDENTIFICATION See Long-billed for general characters of dowitchers, and for bill-length and tail-pattern differences. – Adult summer: Base colour of underparts usually washed-out orange (paler than Long-billed), either with *faintly spotted breast* (looking plain orange at distance), *sparsely barred flanks* and *spotted* undertail-coverts (ssp. *hendersoni*) or with *white belly* and at times stronger markings on breast, flanks and undertail-coverts as Long-billed (ssp. *griseus*). – Adult winter: Near-identical to Long-billed. Flank barring and *upper breast* grey, breaking up into *very fine mottling and speckling on lower breast* before white belly. – Ju-

venile: Breast and upperparts usually tinged stronger rufous than on Long-billed; tertials, greater coverts and scapular have obvious *internal rufous cross-bars, spots or stripes*.

VOICE Flight-call is a fast, clear double or triple note, 'tüdü or 'tüdlü', with rattling quality like Turnstone's flight-call.

Pin-tailed Snipe *Gallinago stenura* —
L 25–27 cm (incl. bill c. 6). Breeds in N Ural range and E through N Siberia, in open tundra and flat river valleys winters in S Asia; rare vagrant to E Europe and Middle East

IDENTIFICATION Similar to Snipe (p. 150), but note: *very thin and diffuse pale trailing edge to wing* (not prominent white as on Snipe); median and lesser coverts form *pale panel on upperwing*; *bill slightly shorter* and rather stout especially at base; rather *short-tailed*, and *toes often project beyond tail-tip* in flight; *wings rather blunt-tipped*, and primaries more brownish (darker on Snipe); *primary coverts narrowly tipped pale* (on average more so than on Snipe) *underwing darker and uniformly barred* (lacking white bands of Snipe); *creamy stripes on upperparts not so prominent* as on Snipe; and *different voice*. When seen on ground, main colour of *back is brown with much barring and spotting* (not so unmarked brown-black as on Snipe), median and lesser coverts are rather *barred* brown (not predominantly spotted and streaked as on Snipe), and lower scapulars are fringed whitish *around tips* (not broadly fringed white only on outer webs and ochrous-brown on inner webs as on Snipe). *Thin pin-like outer tail-feathers* unique.

VOICE Call when flushed is short, sharp, harsh and throaty monosyllabic 'chree!', slightly lower-pitched and coarser than Snipe's. The 'song', delivered in dives during display-flight, mostly in evenings, is a peculiar scratchy, sharpening sound culminating in vibrating and whizzing notes.

Painted Snipe *Rostratula benghalensis* —
L 23–26 cm. Breeds in Egypt in overgrown swamps, pools, ditches; vagrant in Israel. Rather secretive, and rarely seen unless flushed. As with phalaropes, sex roles reversed; ♀ may lay several clutches, incubated by different ♂♂.

IDENTIFICATION Roughly Snipe-sized, but looks distinctly heavier, more lethargic when it takes off on *broad round-tipped wings*, with long legs obvious, *entire toes projecting beyond tail-tip*. Shortish, rather *drooping bill which is fairly thick and pale* (dull pinkish); *thick light eye-ring continuing in stripe behind eye*; and *yellow-buff breast / shoulder-stripe joining mantle-V* striking (especially on ♀). Narrow buff median crown-stripe. Underwing white, broadly bordered dark. – Adult ♂: *Dull grey-brown on throat* (upper throat mottled white), *neck and upper breast*; *narrow grey-black breast-band*. Indistinct buff-white eye-stripe. Upperwing and scapulars brownish-green, *wing-coverts broadly barred buff*. – Adult ♀: Brighter than ♂; *rufous on throat, neck and upper breast*, bordered with a *wide black band across breast*. Distinct white eye-stripe bordered blackish. *Upperwing and scapulars rather uniform greenish*, finely vermiculated dark. – Juvenile: Resembles adult ♂ but breast more diffusely mottled, lacking distinct border towards belly, and upperparts have more buff barring.

VOICE ♀ gives low hooting 'koot' in Woodcock-like roding display-flight at dusk; otherwise mainly silent.

Pin-tailed Snipe   Painted Snipe

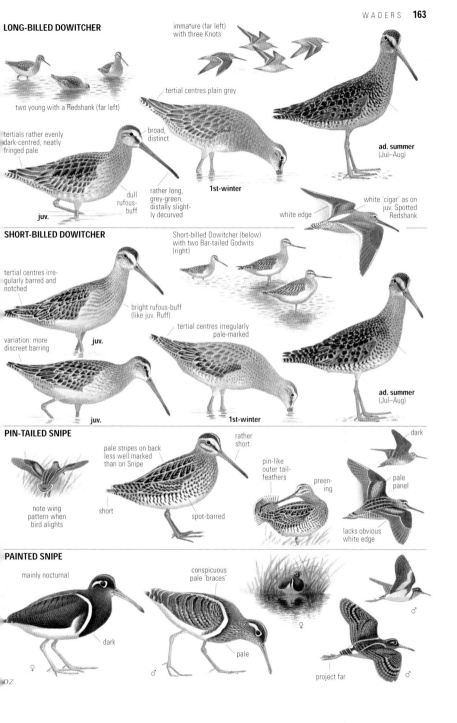

LONG-BILLED DOWITCHER

immature (far left) with three Knots

two young with a Redshank (far left)

tertial centres plain grey

tertials rather evenly dark-centred, neatly fringed pale

broad, distinct

dull rufous-buff

rather long, grey-green, distally slightly decurved

1st-winter

juv.

ad. summer (Jul–Aug)

white 'cigar' as on juv. Spotted Redshank

white edge

SHORT-BILLED DOWITCHER

tertial centres irregularly barred and notched

Short-billed Dowitcher (below) with two Bar-tailed Godwits (right)

juv.

bright rufous-buff (like juv. Ruff)

tertial centres irregularly pale-marked

variation: more discreet barring

juv.

1st-winter

ad. summer (Jul–Aug)

PIN-TAILED SNIPE

rather short

dark

pale stripes on back less well marked than on Snipe

note wing pattern when bird alights

short

spot-barred

pin-like outer tail-feathers

preen-ing

pale panel

lacks obvious white edge

PAINTED SNIPE

mainly nocturnal

dark

♀

conspicuous pale 'braces'

pale

♂

♀

♂

project far

♂

DZ

SKUAS *Stercorariidae*

Medium-large, darkish, gull-like birds, mostly maritime. Breed in N Europe on tundra, coastal moors, remote islands, etc. Migrate along coasts and at sea, and to a lesser extent overland, to winter in N Indian Ocean and off W Africa, S America and southern N America, where they lead a pelagic life. Food during breeding lemmings, eggs and young of other birds, fish, insects and berries, during rest of year mainly fish; also other small animals, carrion and offal. Fish generally obtained through piracy from other birds.

Predatory habits reflected by hooked tip of bill and sharp, curved claws. Piratical chases of other birds performed with impressively rapid and acrobatic flight; victim, usually gull or tern, pursued incessantly and very closely, the skua demonstrating fabulously quick reactions, until victim disgorges the contents of its crop, which are caught in the air by the pursuing skua. Auks and other fish-eating birds are also attacked. Gulls and terns generally fly up when a skua approaches, as for a bird of prey.

Skuas are mainly grey-brown and off-white with a light pattern at the primary bases. Dark, light and intermediate morphs occur in some species. Sexes alike. Adults of the smaller species have long, projecting tail-feathers of characteristic shape. Often rest on sea, but alight 'reluctantly' after long glide and short hovering.

FIELD IDENTIFICATION OF SKUAS

The successful identification of skuas in the field requires a lot of practice. Below, some advice is offered, addressed especially to the beginner.

Most skuas look dark in the field, and this generally holds true for young and light-morph birds as well. They normally *appear even darker than most juvenile gulls*, a common alternative at long range (>1 km) or at tricky angles. As a rule, the lighter head and back of young gulls are visible even at a distance, as are the more conspicuous light rump and, on most, paler inner primaries. Apart from plumage distinctions, skuas are recognized by *more pointed 'hand'* (not so valid for the broad-winged Great Skua, of course), faster flight, more elegant movements, in relaxed flight *more shallow, even and powerful wingbeats*; in short, more 'purposeful' flight in comparison with the rather deliberate, almost lazy (in strong winds somewhat hesitant) wingbeats of gulls, which also are deeper in corresponding relaxed flight.

A skua is chasing a tern to force it to disgorge the fish in its crop.

The remote risk of confusion with a shearwater remains to be eliminated, especially in strong winds and at long range. In gales, the skuas, too, practise the shearwater mode of banking flight: a fast low glide before the wind along the waves and a steep climb obliquely into the wind, banking to one side, again followed by low glide before the wind, etc. As soon as the bird beats its wings (usually immediately before the climb) the experienced eye can tell them apart: the flight of skuas is falcon-like, buoyant and 'athletic' with rather slower and shallow wingbeats; the *shearwaters give quick bursts of beats* (though somewhat slower for the larger species) with their narrower and *more straight wings*.

The most difficult part of skua identification is to separate non-adults of Arctic, Pomarine and Long-tailed Skuas. The crucial points to note are given in the species accounts. Some general advice: *Size* is, as always, difficult to be certain of when watching a bird through a telescope far out over the sea, but an attempt should be made to establish whether the bird is decidedly large or small. Note that the dark plumage of skuas gives a misleading impression when comparing with the whiteness of gulls: dark birds seen against a bright sky appear larger than white ones; and, conversely, dark birds against a dark sea often appear smaller than white ones, which appear big, especially so if seen in strong light.

Then pay attention to *structure and proportions* (such as width of the 'arm') and to *mode of flight*. Check whether the bird has a central tail projection of any kind, and whether there are any prominent light areas in the plumage. For birds approaching closer, it is useful to note prominence of primary patches, size and coloration of bill, and shape of short tail projections (if any). And do not expect to be able to identify all skuas in flight at the beginning. It takes a great deal of experience before the more difficult individuals can be sorted out. Even experts (at least sensible experts!) leave some birds unidentified.

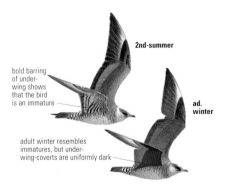

2nd-summer

bold barring of under-wing shows that the bird is an immature

ad. winter

adult winter resembles immatures, but under-wing-coverts are uniformly dark

Ageing of skuas (Arctic Skua shown above) in autumn and winter is made easier if you pay attention to the underwing.

Great Skua

Pomarine Skua

GREAT SKUA

juv.
ad.
juv.

juv.
(dull)

on average
smaller
wing
'flashes'
than ad.

imm. / **ad.** (dark)

short
tail

ad.
(pale)

wing 'flashes'
conspicuous
at long range

juv.
(bright)

head
darker
than body

barrel-shaped

plain

ad. in threat/
display posture

very
heavy

variable pale
markings

conspicuous white
wing 'flash'

Great Skua attacking Gannet

juv.

ad.

plain (unbarred)
underbody and
undertail-coverts

dark

K M

Great Skua *Stercorarius skua*   m**B**4 / **P**3

L 50–58 cm, WS 125–140 cm. Breeds on rocky islands and damp, elevated coastal moors, usually in loose colony; winters in N and S Atlantic. In Britain & Ireland, breeds in Scotland and seen irregularly along coasts, especially during or after autumn storms. Food mainly fish, taken from surface of sea or from other birds, or behind trawlers. Nest a shallow depression, defended with fierce dives.

IDENTIFICATION Large and heavy, roughly of Herring Gull size. In flight, *all dark with large white primary patches above and below*. Bill heavy. *Head and neck powerful*. Central tailfeathers broad, tips rounded, not or only slightly projecting. Soars more frequently than congeners, can give Buzzard-like impression. Floats high on sea. – Adult summer: Coarsely streaked yellow-brown on nape, neck and upperparts, ♀ on average more so. – 1st-year: More uniformly brown than adult and *tinged reddish-brown*, especially below; the white 'flashes' on upper 'hand' often less extensive and prominent than on adult. – Main risks of confusion with young large gull (esp. an oiled one) and with juvenile Pomarine Skua or, at distance, adult dark-morph Pomarine. Told from young gull by *flight being more steady and purposeful, wings beating more flexibly* (wingbeat pace otherwise similar); proportionately *heavier body* ('flying barrel'); *broader wing-bases* but often more pointed 'hand'; and—most reliably—*white wing patches* (see above). From juvenile Pomarine by *heavier body and flight*; *lack of light cross-barring* (thus never has contrasting pale rump, vent or underwing-coverts); often *slightly darker head than rest of body* (Pomarine usually uniformly dark, or head a shade paler than chest); broader and proportionately somewhat shorter wings; and generally clearly larger and purer white wing patches reaching right in to arm. (However, some juv. Great Skuas have confusingly restricted patches on upper-

wing.) From adult dark-morph Pomarine by silhouette and flight, and certainly by lack of broad, long tail projections (though can be absent through moult on Pomarine).

VOICE Silent away from breeding grounds. There, single or series of short, slightly nasal 'gok' can be heard; in display utters squeezed, rolling 'chirr'.

Pomarine Skua *Stercorarius pomarinus*   **P**4

L 42–50 cm (excl. ad. summer tail projections 5½–11), WS 115–125 cm. Breeds on arctic tundra; passes N and W Europe on migration, mostly in May and Oct–Nov, to and from winter areas e.g. off W Africa. Rare but regular on passage in Britain (esp. E and S coasts) & Ireland. Usually seen singly or in small groups, sometimes very large parties (50+). Juveniles can be quite fearless.

IDENTIFICATION In flight, appears definitely larger than Common Gull and *slightly smaller than Herring Gull*. On the ground surprisingly small, smallest birds appear hardly as big as Kittiwakes but always look heavy-chested. Longwinged; *'arm' rather broad*, appears somewhat wider in distance from rear edge of wing to tip of tail (projections disregarded); 'hand' pointed, much as on Arctic Skua. *Flight relaxed and steady*, wingbeats measured and path more direct, not light and jerky with energetic wingbeats as sometimes with Arctic. In all plumages, *light primary patch above and below* roughly as on Arctic and considerably less than on normal Great. – Adult summer: *Long and broad tail projections*, look blunt-ended in profile (central tail-feathers twisted 90°; 'carries a spoon'); moulted twice annually, Nov–Dec and Mar–Apr (and at other times very rarely broken off). Two morphs: light (commoner) has dark cap (reaches below gape), dark and *coarse* breast-band (on ♂ fairly often broken on centre of breast, and can be missing), insignificant or prominent barring of flanks, and

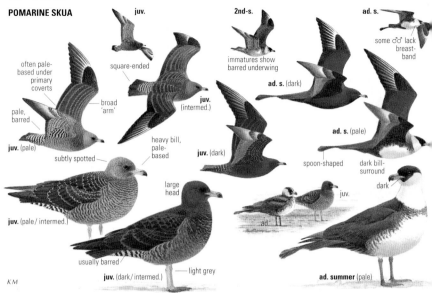

POMARINE SKUA

often pale-based under primary coverts

square-ended

juv.

broad 'arm'

2nd-s.

immatures show barred underwing

ad. s. (dark)

ad. s.

some ♂♂ lack breast-band

juv. (intermed.)

pale, barred

juv. (pale)

heavy bill, pale-based

subtly spotted

juv. (dark)

large head

ad. s. (pale)

spoon-shaped

dark bill-surround

juv.

dark

juv. (pale / intermed.)

usually barred

light grey

juv. (dark / intermed.)

ad.

ad. summer (pale)

K M

extensive dark vent distinctly demarcated (element of light barring on many); dark morph is all dark (except for wing patches). – Juvenile: Varying from mid brown with yellowish-buff bars, especially on rump and vent, to uniform dark blackish-brown, but *almost always looks dark in the field.* Told from similar juvenile Arctic Skua by *calmer, more steady flight; broader 'arm'; fuller belly; heavier bill* being more noticeably *pale blue-grey* (readily visible at 300 m), *tipped dark*; light morph has pale 'double patch' on underwing, i.e. *both primaries and primary coverts basally light* on most (hard to judge beyond 300 m); and *blunt-ended, broad central tail-feathers which project only insignificantly, if at all.* Juvenile practically never has strongly contrasting pale head or belly (cf. Arctic and Long-tailed). Darkest dark morphs unbarred like dark adult. – 2nd cal.-year, light morph: Neck and belly paler, central tail-feathers shortish or half-length and not twisted. – 3rd cal.-year, light morph: Neck and belly pale, dark cap beginning to show, but underwing-coverts still barred, not all dark as on adult. – Adult winter, light morph: Similar to 3rd cal.-year, tail projections being half-length, but told by all-dark, unbarred underwing-coverts.

Arctic Skua *Stercorarius parasiticus*   **mB**4 / **P**3
L 37–44 cm (excl. ad. summer tail projections 5–8½), WS 108–118 cm. Breeds on tundra, coastal moors and barren islands, locally in loose colony; winters mainly S of the Equator. In Britain fairly common locally in N Scotland. Nest a shallow depression. Often keeps watch from top of island or a moorland ridge.

IDENTIFICATION Like a *dark* gull with pointed wings and *fast, flexible, almost falcon-like flight.* At closer range, *light primary patches* and on adult *half-length, pointed tail projections.* In flight, appears to be of *Kittiwake size.* Wings long and fairly narrow, 'hand' pointed; width of 'arm' ap-

pears equal to or slightly less than distance from rear edge of wing to tip of tail (projections disregarded). Flight lighter than Pomarine's, but beware, may at times show some weightiness; in strong winds Arctic recalls a Kittiwake in lightness, quick wingbeats and sudden lunges, whereas Pomarine is decidedly heavier and more steady, like a large gull. *Bill a little finer* than on Pomarine. Plumages much as for Pomarine—thus large variation—but note the following distinctions: dark cap of adult less black, does not solidly surround gape, and always excludes a *small light patch above base of bill*; if breast-band present, usually a dark illdefined shade, not coarsely patterned; palest juveniles lighter than Pomarine, have *contrasting light head and neck* (finely streaked; discernible at close range) and *often belly, too.* Darkest juveniles extremely similar to darkest Pomarine, most reliably identified by bill size, tail shape and overall proportions; note also pointed central tail-feathers projecting 1–3 cm, forming tiny *'double point'* at rear of tail, primary coverts below lacking pale base (exceptions: 1 out of 20) and *bill generally looking dark*, not strikingly palebased (tendency to paler base hardly visible beyond 150 m).

VOICE Most often heard is a nasal, mewing 'eh-glow', repeated a few times in display. Alarm a short 'pjew!'.

Long-tailed Skua *Stercorarius longicaudus*   **P**4
L 35–41 cm (excl. ad. summer tail-streamers 12–24), WS 105–112 cm. Breeds on heathy fells above tree-limit and on drier tundra; winters mainly in S Atlantic. Feeds largely on lemmings in summer, and accordingly fluctuates in numbers. Scarce passage migrant in W Europe in May and Aug–Sep (Oct, rarely later). Occasionally, juveniles rest on inland fields, appearing fearless.

IDENTIFICATION *Small and slim*, body like Black-headed Gull, but *long, slender wings* give a larger impression in

ARCTIC SKUA

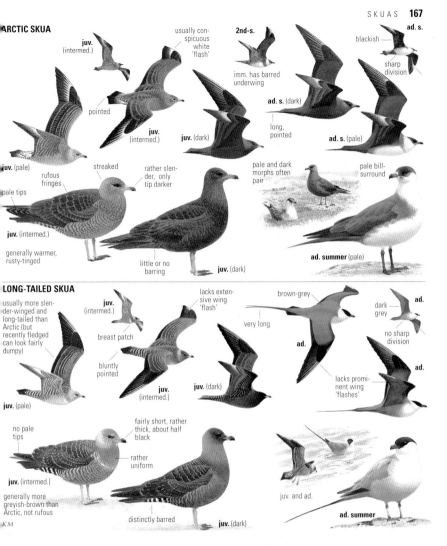

juv. (intermed.)

usually conspicuous white 'flash'

2nd-s.

imm. has barred underwing

blackish

ad. s.

sharp division

pointed

juv. (intermed.)

juv. (dark)

ad. s. (dark)

long, pointed

ad. s. (pale)

juv. (pale)

rufous fringes

streaked

rather slender, only tip darker

pale tips

pale and dark morphs often pair

pale billsurround

juv. (intermed.)

generally warmer, rusty-tinged

little or no barring

juv. (dark)

ad. summer (pale)

LONG-TAILED SKUA

usually more slender-winged and long-tailed than Arctic (but recently fledged can look fairly dumpy)

juv. (intermed.)

lacks extensive wing 'flash'

brown-grey

ad.

dark grey

no sharp division

very long

breast patch

bluntly pointed

juv. (intermed.)

juv. (dark)

ad.

lacks prominent wing 'flashes'

ad.

juv. (pale)

no pale tips

juv. (intermed.)

generally more greyish-brown than Arctic, not rufous

fairly short, rather thick, about half black

rather uniform

distinctly barred

juv. (dark)

juv. and ad.

ad. summer

K M

flight. *Flight light*, almost tern-like. Inclined to stall and settle on the sea, even on migration. Often hovers on breeding grounds. – Adult summer: Distinct black cap, *contrast above between dark remiges and paler brown-grey wing-coverts* and back, *no light primary patch below*, and *very long and pointed tail-streamers*. – Juvenile: Variation as pronounced as in Arctic Skua; told from that by silhouette (slim body, narrow wings, longer-looking rear end) and flight, and in light and median morphs *greyer, less brown general coloration* (but dark morph very like Arctic), by similarly (1–3 cm) protruding central tail-feathers being rather rounded, and by *bill being short with pale base*. A few have longer stubby 'points' at rear of tail than any juvenile Arctic.

VOICE Higher-pitched than that of congeners, repeated 'kew' and 'kri**ep**' and quarrelling 'kre-krep'. In display wailing '**glee**-ah', reminiscent of Common Gull.

Arctic Skua

Long-tailed Skua

GULLS *Laridae*

Some of the region's 16 breeding species are very common, and frequently occur near man, with the result that gulls are a familiar group of birds. For breeding, they require habitats near coasts, marshes or inland waters, often forming large colonies. Nest is a collection of twigs and plant material sited on bare ground or among low vegetation.

Especially outside the breeding season, some species are common inland, and they also then form large nocturnal roosts of mixed species in sheltered coastal waters, or on lakes or reservoirs. The distance between roosting and feeding areas can be as much as 40 km: morning and evening flights are often high, with flocks frequently in lines or V-formations. The smaller species are generally rather dainty feeders, picking from the surface (sometimes plunging more deeply for fish, etc.), and in summer large numbers often gather to hawk flying ants high in the sky. The larger species are scavengers or take fish, and are often predatory on eggs and young of seabirds. Gulls are attracted to fishing ports, trawlers, rubbish tips and sewage outfalls, and some species form large flocks, mainly in search of worms, on arable fields and pasture, especially when ploughing is in progress.

IDENTIFICATION OF GULLS

Adult gulls are usually fairly easy to identify, because each species has a diagnostic combination of size, upperpart colour, wing-tip pattern, and bill and leg colour. The immatures are generally more difficult, having comparatively nondescript brown or barred plumage, and bill and leg colours which have yet to acquire adult coloration. The great variety of immature plumages can at first seem very complex and daunting, but the picture will be greatly clarified if the two following areas of basic information about gull plumages and moult are fully understood:

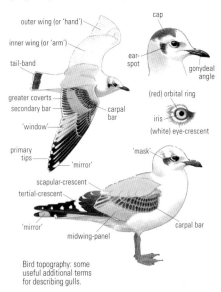

Bird topography: some useful additional terms for describing gulls.

(1) Length of immaturity

Each species belongs to one or other of three categories:

Two age-groups. This category contains most of the small species. Black-headed Gull is a common example of a species with two age-groups. Adult plumage is acquired when the bird is just over one year old. Thus, for most of the year, only two different age-groups are recognizable, i.e. 1st-year (juv., 1st-winter, or 1st-summer) and adult (ad. winter or ad. summer). Note that during Jul–early Sep, however, three age-groups can be recognized: juvenile (recently fledged); 1st-summer (just over one year old); and adult summer (just over two or more years old).

Three age-groups. This category contains the medium-sized species and Little Gull. Common Gull is a familiar example of this category. Adult plumage is acquired at just over two years of age. Thus, for most of the year, three age-groups are recognizable, i.e. 1st-year (juv., 1st-winter, or 1st-summer); 2nd-year (2nd-winter or 2nd-summer); and adult (ad. winter or ad. summer). During Jul–early Sep, however, four age-groups can be recognized: juvenile (recently fledged); 1st-summer (one year old); 2nd-summer (two years old); and adult summer (three or more years old).

Four age-groups. This category contains all the large species. Herring Gull is a common example of a gull with four age-groups. Adult plumage is acquired at just over three years of age. Thus, for most of the year, four age-groups are recognizable, i.e. 1st-year (juv., 1st-winter, or 1st-summer); 2nd-year (2nd-winter or 2nd-summer); 3rd-year (3rd-winter or 3rd-summer); and adult (ad. winter or ad. summer). During Jul–early Sep, however, five age-groups can be recognized: juvenile (recently fledged); 1st-summer (one year old); 2nd-summer (two years old); 3rd-summer (three years old); and adult summer (four or more years old).

(2) Moult

The change from juvenile to adult plumage is achieved by regular moults, in which old feathers are replaced by new ones. The first moult of all gulls is the *post-juvenile moult*, which for most species takes place shortly after the bird first flies: it is a partial moult, replacing only the juvenile head- and body-feathers, and results in 1st-winter plumage. In every year following the one in which it hatched, every gull has a *spring moult* (a partial moult, in which only the head- and body-feathers are renewed) and an *autumn moult* (in which the whole plumage is renewed).

In all moults, the feathers are replaced a few at a time. The partial moults take 1 or 2 months, and complete autumn moult takes 3 or 4 months. In the case of an immature gull, each moult brings its appearance gradually closer to that of the adult. In adults, summer plumage is acquired by the spring moult, and winter plumage by the autumn moult. The diagram (opposite) shows the complete sequence of moults (and the resulting appearance from juvenile to adult) of a gull with two, three, and four age-groups. Note that the wing- and tail-feathers are retained for a whole year, and by the summer can appear as a very worn and faded version of their original pattern, especially on first-summer birds.

Like the plumage, the colour of the bill and legs of immatures changes gradually until the adult colour is acquired, and thus provides further clues to the age of a young gull.

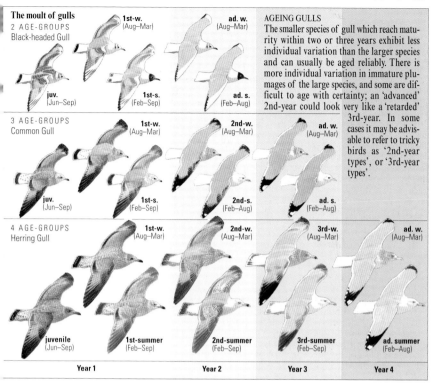

The moult of gulls

2 AGE-GROUPS
Black-headed Gull

1st-w. (Aug–Mar)

ad. w. (Aug–Mar)

juv. (Jun–Sep)

1st-s. (Feb–Sep)

ad. s. (Feb–Aug)

3 AGE-GROUPS
Common Gull

1st-w. (Aug–Mar)

2nd-w. (Aug–Mar)

ad. w. (Aug–Mar)

juv. (Jun–Sep)

1st-s. (Feb–Sep)

2nd-s. (Feb–Aug)

ad. s. (Feb–Aug)

4 AGE-GROUPS
Herring Gull

1st-w. (Aug–Mar)

2nd-w. (Aug–Mar)

3rd-w. (Aug–Mar)

ad. w. (Aug–Mar)

juvenile (Jun–Sep)

1st-summer (Feb–Sep)

2nd-summer (Feb–Sep)

3rd-summer (Feb–Sep)

ad. summer (Feb–Aug)

Year 1 | **Year 2** | **Year 3** | **Year 4**

AGEING GULLS

The smaller species of gull which reach maturity within two or three years exhibit less individual variation than the larger species and can usually be aged reliably. There is more individual variation in immature plumages of the larger species, and some are difficult to age with certainty; an 'advanced' 2nd-year could look very like a 'retarded' 3rd-year. In some cases it may be advisable to refer to tricky birds as '2nd-year types', or '3rd-year types'.

WATCHING GULLS

Perhaps the best time to study gull plumages is in winter, when their patterns are relatively fresh after the complete autumn moult. Find a close flock to start with, and begin to identify the two age-groups of Black-headed Gull (1st-winter and ad. winter), the three age-groups of Common Gull (1st-winter, 2nd-winter and ad. winter), and the four age-groups of Herring Gull (1st-winter, 2nd-winter, 3rd-winter and ad. winter). In spring, note the progress of the spring moult of adults (Black-headed acquiring its hood, or Herring Gull losing its head streaks and acquiring an all-white head). In summer and autumn, notice how the wing pattern of immatures becomes sometimes much worn and faded,

and also how gulls look very ragged in flight as their wing- and tail-feathers are renewed during the autumn moult.

Such studies will increase your skill at identifying and ageing common species, and thus also increase the chance of noticing some rare gull among them. Note that a few gulls, especially immatures of species with four age-groups, can be very tricky to identify or age, even for the expert.

Because they are common, large and approachable, gulls provide valuable exercises in studying moult and the progress of immature plumages. This knowledge can also be applied to many birds other than gulls, so time spent studying gulls is worthwhile not only for its own interest.

Two adult summer Lesser Black-backed Gulls *Larus fuscus graellsii*. Note that tone of grey changes to some extent with angle of view (or light), important to bear in mind when looking at gulls.

juv.

1st-summer

Note that retained juvenile wing- and tail-feathers can become much worn and faded by 1st-summer plumage, when they are one year old, as shown on these Kittiwakes.

Black-headed Gull *Larus ridibundus* r(m)**B**2 / **W**1

L 35–39 cm, WS 86–99 cm. Common colonial breeder at lakes in vast reedbeds or marshy areas, also on ponds near coasts. Migratory in far north, retreating in winter from ice. Abundant feeder on ploughed fields and in towns. Not shy.

IDENTIFICATION Two age-groups (see p. 168). In flight, told instantly from other common gulls by *white leading edge to outer wing*; this is its best field mark, often being visible at extremely long range. Similar wing pattern shared only by Slender-billed Gull and vagrant Bonaparte's Gull; see also Grey-headed Gull (p. 381). Also note: *obvious blackish area bordering white leading edge of underwing*; *pointed* (rather tern-like) *wings*; and proportionately *smaller head, longer neck* and *shorter tail*: these all add to distinctive appearance compared with other common gulls. When standing, also told by combination of small size, *head pattern* (hood or dark ear-spot) and (on adult) *reddish bill and legs*. – Adult summer: *Dark brown hood* (often looks black) and *dark, dull red bill and legs*. – Adult winter: *Bold dark ear-spot* and *red or brown-red legs and bill*, latter with dark tip. – Juvenile (Jun–Sep): Looks strikingly 'different', having extensive ginger-brown upperparts and head markings, brown wing markings, black tail-band, and yellowish-flesh legs and bill, latter with a dark tip. –1st-winter: Juvenile wings, tail, and bill and leg colour retained, but head and body like adult winter. –1st-summer: Like 1st-winter, but many acquire partial hood (at times full hood like ad. summer); brown on wings often faded and much reduced in extent (look for brown-centred tertials); and bill-base and legs more orange-red.

VOICE Noisy at colonies and when feeding in flock; the noise from large colonies in spring can be earsplitting, also at night. Common calls are a strident, downslurred, single or repeated 'krreearr', with many variations, and short, sharp 'kek' or 'kekekek'.

Slender-billed Gull *Larus genei* **V*****

L 37–42, WS 90–102 cm. Habitat and habits much as Black-headed Gull, but more coastal outside breeding season. Rather scarce even in Mediterranean breeding areas, where much rarer than Black-headed. Vagrant to S Britain.

IDENTIFICATION Mainly two age-groups (see p.168). A little larger than Black-headed Gull, which it closely resembles in wing pattern and general appearance, but *head white* (lacks hood) in summer; has only *faint ear-spot, if any*, in winter; and has usually obvious *yellowish or whitish iris* (however, can look dark-eyed depending on light; Black-headed Gull always dark-eyed). Also very important for identification is its *peculiar head-and-bill shape*, produced jointly by *longer* (but actually not more slender) *bill*, more *elongated forehead*, and very long neck when fully extended; beware

BLACK-HEADED GULL

prominent ear-spot

large dark tip

ad. w.

faint ear-spot

ad. w.

small dark tip

SLENDER-BILLED GULL

Slender-billed Gull has longer bill, forehead and, when alert, longer neck than Black-headed Gull.

that Black-headed can give a rather similar impression (but never quite so exaggeratedly), so important to check other differences carefully to avoid misidentification. Legs comparatively long. Adult summer differs further in: usually *strong pink wash on underparts*; and darker red bill (often looking blackish). Adult winter has no pink, has a pale grey ear-spot (if any), and less dark red bill and legs. In addition to the structural differences from Black-headed, 1st-year has usually paler brown wing markings; paler ear-spot (if any); *paler yellowish-brown or orange-flesh bill and legs*, and bill with dark tip much smaller or lacking. – Some 2nd-year birds told by dark-centred tertials.

VOICE Vaguely recalling Black-headed's, but the rolling call is a lower, drier and harder 'krerrr' with a somewhat strained voice. At breeding site some low, gruff, nasal calls.

Bonaparte's Gull *Larus philadelphia* **V****

L 31–34, WS 79–84 cm. Vagrant from N America; a few records annually in Britain & Ireland.

IDENTIFICATION Two age-groups (see p.168). Small version of Black-headed, which it closely resembles in upperwing pattern and general appearance. Small size and quicker wingbeats may suggest Little Gull. Lacks Black-headed's dark grey on outer underwing, thus *from below primaries are translucent white* or pale grey *with distinct black trailing edge*. Beware of 1st-summer Black-headed with faded and translucent primaries, and which are often slightly smaller than adults! Other all-plumage differences from Black-headed are its *proportionately smaller bill*, which is *black* or mainly black; proportionately *shorter legs*; and slightly darker grey upperparts which accentuate the white leading edge on the outer upperwing. Adult summer differs further in *blackish hood* (not brown), usually pink-flushed underparts (unusual on summer Black-headed), and more orange-red or pinkish legs. Adult winter usually has larger ear-spot, grey extending more strongly onto hindneck; and *pale flesh-pink legs* (not red). 1st-year differs from Black-headed in blacker (less brown) upperwing markings; *different pattern on primary coverts*, inner being whitish, outer marked dark (1st-year Black-headed rather dark inner, white central, and one or two dark-marked outer); larger ear-spot; and grey often extending strongly onto hindneck and breast-sides (head/neck pattern thus can recall ad. winter Kittiwake).

VOICE Common feeding call a high, nasal, tern-like 'chirp', quite unlike Black-headed Gull's.

Black-headed Gull   Slender-billed Gull

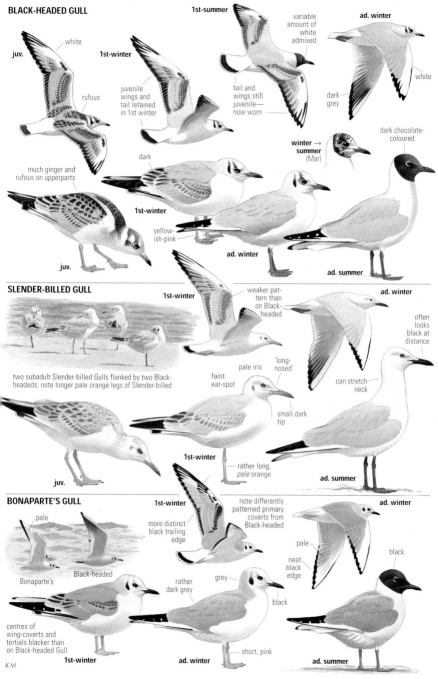

BLACK-HEADED GULL

white

juv.

rufous

1st-winter

juvenile wings and tail retained in 1st winter

much ginger and rufous on upperparts

dark

1st-summer

variable amount of white admixed

tail and wings still juvenile—now worn

ad. winter

white

dark grey

winter → summer (Mar)

dark chocolate-coloured

1st-winter

yellow-ish-pink

ad. winter

ad. summer

juv.

SLENDER-BILLED GULL

1st-winter

weaker pattern than on Black-headed

ad. winter

often looks black at distance

can stretch neck

two subadult Slender-billed Gulls flanked by two Black-headeds; note longer pale orange legs of Slender-billed

pale iris

faint ear-spot

'long-nosed'

small dark tip

juv.

1st-winter

rather long, *pale* orange

ad. summer

BONAPARTE'S GULL

pale

Black-headed

Bonaparte's

1st-winter

more distinct black trailing edge

note differently patterned primary coverts from Black-headed

ad. winter

pale

neat black edge

black

rather dark grey

grey

black

centres of wing-coverts and tertials blacker than on Black-headed Gull

1st-winter

short, pink

ad. winter

ad. summer

K·M

Common Gull (Mew Gull) *Larus canus* r**B**3 / **W**2

L 40–46 cm, WS 99–108 cm. Breeds colonially or singly along coasts, on islands, in marshes, along rivers or at inland lakes. Lined nest usually near water on ground, preferably somewhat elevated, on boulders, poles in harbours, occasionally low trees, roofs of buildings, etc.

IDENTIFICATION Three age-groups (see p. 168). Somewhat larger than Black-headed Gull. *Much larger* Herring Gull (p. 174) is the only similar common species; when size difficult to judge, look for *smaller, narrower bill*, more *rounded head*, much daintier general shape and quicker actions, less heavy, more active flight with often *deeper and more energetic wingbeats*, and *narrower wings*; adult also often shows *more obvious tertial-crescent* and *larger 'mirrors'*; 1st-year has *plain* (not barred) *midwing-panel* giving neater upperwing pattern, and broad black, *clear-cut band on white tail*; also *more neatly patterned underwing* than immature Herring. Standing adult summer also resembles Kittiwake, but *legs long and pale* (not short and black), *forehead less steeply rounded*, and *primaries are white-tipped* and more extensively black. –Adult: Head white (streaked grey in winter), bill and legs greenish-yellow (bill duller in winter, with thin dark band). –Juvenile: Grey-brown head and breast, scaly brown upperparts. –1st-winter: Head and body similar to adult winter, but retains juvenile wings and tail; bill greyish with clear-cut black tip. –1st-summer: Like 1st-winter, but wings and tail often much faded, and bill-base yellowish or pinkish. –2nd-year: Like adult, but more black on outer wing, lacks prominent white primary tips, has smaller 'mirrors', and legs and black-banded or black-tipped bill often bluish green-grey.

VOICE All calls much higher-pitched than Herring Gull's, including 'laughing' call, 'ke ke ke **kleeeh**-a... **kleeeh**-a... kay-a kay-a kay-a kay-a ke ke'. Call a distinctive, thinly yelping 'keea', often repeated. Persistent 'klee-**u** klee-**u**...' when alarmed (often good hint of bird of prey in vicinity!).

Ring-billed Gull *Larus delawarensis* **V**∗

L 41–49 cm, WS 112–124 cm. Vagrant from N America. Numerous records annually in Britain & Ireland.

IDENTIFICATION Three age-groups (see p. 168). Resembles Common Gull, but slightly larger, heavier-bodied, and has *thicker bill*. – Adult: *Clear-cut, broad black bill-band* (beware sometimes obvious band on ad. winter or 2nd-year Common); *yellow iris* (brown on Common); *paler grey upperparts* (similar to Black-headed); *faint tertial-crescent* (prominent on Common); and *smaller mirror*. – 1st-year: Told from Common Gull by *paler grey upperparts and midwing-panel*, often *a few obvious dark crescents among scapulars* (unmarked or with only faint shaft streaks on Common), *narrower pale tips to tertials*, and *more variegated tail*

Note how posture can change hood shape of gulls.

MEDITERRANEAN GULL, ad. summer

pattern (broad band on white tail on Common). – 2nd-year: Like adult, but has more black on outer wing; white primary tips and 'mirror' (if any) smaller, and often greenish-yellow or greyish bill-base and legs; commonly has *variable tail-band* (usually lacking on Common). Beware that immature Herring Gull can provide easy pitfall if actually much heavier and longer bill and much larger size are not apparent (e.g. on lone bird); 2nd-year Herring resembles 1st-year Ring-billed, but tertials and coverts more mottled or barred (rather solidly dark-centred on Ring-billed), underwing rather uniformly dusky (neatly dark-flecked, and secondary bar showing through, on Ring-billed), and tail more extensively dark; 3rd-year Herring resembles 2nd-year Ring-billed, but wing and tail patterns less neat, and legs pink. – Has habit of walking about a lot. Also, adults and 2nd-winter birds appear to have remarkably loose plumage.

VOICE Like Herring Gull's but higher-pitched and nasal.

Mediterranean Gull *Larus melanocephalus* m**B**5 / **W**4

L 37–40 cm, WS 94–102 cm. Nests colonially. Breeding populations of W and S Europe small, usually among Black-headed colonies, including (rare) S and SE England. Scarce annual visitor to Britain & Ireland, mainly in S and E (mostly migrants from Black Sea).

IDENTIFICATION Three age-groups (see p. 168). A trifle larger than Black-headed Gull, with *shorter, thicker, more obtuse bill*; less pointed, *broader, slightly shorter wings*; and longer legs. Flight with *quicker and stiffer wingbeats* than Common Gull. – Adult: Unmistakable; *all-white flight-feathers*, very *pale grey upperparts* (silvery-white at distance), *scarlet bill and legs* (less bright in winter), and *large black hood* (dark 'mask' in winter). – 1st-year: Resembles Common Gull, but differs in *all-white underwing-coverts*, *paler grey midwing-panel*, slightly thinner tail-band, *reddish-based dark or wholly black bill*, *reddish or black legs*, and (from Sep) *paler grey upperparts*, *dark 'mask'* (or partial hood in 1st summer) and *white underparts*. – 2nd-year: Like adult, but with variable, small black markings on wing-tip.

VOICE Call is distinctive, rising-then-falling note, enthusiastic, nasal 'yeah!', but with slightly whining tone.

HERRING GULL   RING-BILLED GULL

Common Gull

Mediterranean Gull

2nd-winter

tertials and coverts variably finely vermiculated or barred

rather plain

1st-winter

Beware of similarity between immature Herring and Ring-billed Gulls (see text).

COMMON GULL

1st-winter

dusky brown-grey

dark grey

broad, clear-cut band

more black than on ad.

small 'mirror'

2nd-winter

large white 'mirror'

ad. winter

coarsely marked

ad. w.

thick band

dark grey

neat

juv.

pale

1st-winter

white primary tips small

2nd-winter

broad white

ad. summer

yellow-green

RING-BILLED GULL

1st-winter

pale grey

pale grey

variegated band

more black than on ad.

little or no 'mirror'

2nd-winter

often partial band or dark spots

small 'mirror'

ad. winter

coarsely marked

pale grey, some dark crescents

thin pale fringes

stout

pale grey

ad. w.

pale iris on ad.

broad band

pale

1st-winter

white primary tips small

2nd-winter

faint white crescent

ad. summer

yellowish

MEDITERRANEAN GULL

when fully spread, small white spots are revealed

black

1st-winter

variable black markings

white

2nd-winter

ad. winter

pale grey

narrow band

unmarked white

white

rather plain

strongly scalloped

dark 'mask'

short, stout

very pale

ad. w.

black

blood-red

whiter below than juv. Common

juv.

long, dark

1st-winter

variable black markings

2nd-winter

white

ad. summer

red

KM

Herring Gull *Larus argentatus* ⌐**B**2 / **W**2

L 54–60, WS 123–148 cm. Very common near coasts; frequent inland, too, feeding on fields, rubbish dumps, etc. Roosts on harbour piers or secluded islands; flights to these at height, often in formation. Frequently soars high up. Nests, often colonially, on coastal islands, cliffs or at lakes.

IDENTIFICATION Four age-groups (see p. 168). Told from all other common gulls by *large size* and *pale grey upperparts* (cf. much smaller Common Gull, p. 172), but see very similar Yellow-legged Gull. Grey on upperparts develops only from 2nd-winter onwards, so 'all-brown' 1st-years more difficult to tell from Lesser and Great Black-backed Gulls (p. 176). *Head of adult white in summer, streaked in autumn.* Bill colour develops gradually, from dark with variable pale base on juvenile/1st-winter to yellow with orange-red spot on adult; iris from brown of juvenile to yellow (with yellow or orange orbital ring) of adult. *Legs pink* at all ages. See Great Black-backed Gull (p.176) for general comments on ageing large gulls. – Variation: Birds of W Europe and Iceland (ssp. *argenteus*) are relatively small and round-headed and have back pale grey. Breeders in Scandinavia and around the Baltic (*argentatus*), wintering partly in W Europe, average larger, slightly darker grey on back, extremes having little black and much white on wing-tip; birds of E Baltic and N Fenno-Scandia like *argentatus*, but locally some or most have legs yellowish or yellow (var. '*omissus*').

VOICE Calls include strident 'kyow', repeated and loud when used as alarm. In anxiety a distinctive 'gag-ag-ag'. Familiar exalted 'laughing' display-call is a loud, deep and clanging 'aau...kyy**aa**-kya-ky**a**-kya-ky**a**-kya kya...ky**au**'.

Yellow-legged Gull *Larus cachinnans* **V**∗ / **P**+**W** 4

L 52–58 cm, WS 120–140 cm. Habits similar to Herring Gull, to which it is closely related (sometimes treated as conspecific, but may be even closer to Lesser Black-backed Gull). Sedentary. Increasing in many areas, and now frequently straggles in Jul–Oct to NW, NC Europe and Baltic.

IDENTIFICATION Four age-groups (see p. 168). Very similar to Herring Gull in adult and subadult plumage. Immatures more like Lesser Black-backed. Consistently adults have *whiter head in autumn* (no or very little streaking) and *bright yellow legs* all year, and often show all or many of following characteristics (referring to ssp. *michahellis* of W France, SW Iberia, Mediterranean and SW Black Sea) compared with Herring Gull: in flight *slightly longer wings*; on adults, *outer primaries have more black* and *smaller white spots*; *larger red spot on bill*; *red or orange orbital ring*; on average *slightly darker grey back* with *less bluish cast*; more *nasal calls*; immatures have *neater tail-band* and *paler rump*, somewhat *darker inner primaries* (recalling Lesser Black-backed),

lighter head and underparts and on average a *darker bill*. – Variation: Birds of of Atlantic Islands (*atlantis*) are rather dark grey on back. Adults of N Black Sea and Caspian Sea (*cachinnans*; possibly full species) very like *michahellis* but slightly paler grey above, with on average less black on wing-tip but larger white spots, and have more dark marks on head/nape in winter (thus closer to Herring Gull), are slimmer and longer-winged and longer-legged, and bill is long and lacking strong gonydeal angle; immatures told by shape and often by on average paler underwing and by plainer dark bases to upper greater coverts (wing-bar effect), but differences subtle and a cautious approach advisable. Breeders in E Turkey and Armenia (*armenicus*; possibly full species) are small and slim and usually have darkish eye, dark-banded bill-tip, and a comparatively *short bill*.

VOICE All calls more similar to Lesser Black-backed Gull's than Herring's owing to the nasal, rather deep voice.

Audouin's Gull *Larus audouinii* —

L 44–52, WS 117–128 cm. Still one of world's rarest gulls, but significant increase in W Mediterranean in recent years. Nests colonially or singly on rocky, small islands. Strictly coastal or pelagic, frequenting wave-washed rocky coasts and bays or sandy beaches. Rarely scavenges like other large gulls, but feeds almost exclusively on fish, snatched in flight from near surface or in deeper plunge-dives.

IDENTIFICATION Four age-groups (see p. 168). Slightly smaller than Herring Gull, with more elegant general appearance; *shorter, stubbier bill*; *more elongated forehead* with feathering expanding towards nostrils; *longer neck* when alert; *longer, narrower wings*; flies more gracefully, with more gliding; bill often pointing slightly down when perched. In breeding areas, Yellow-legged Gull is only similar adult gull, from which told by *dark red bill* (looks black at distance), *dark iris*, *dark grey or greenish legs* (often visible in flight, too), *much paler grey* and slightly two-toned *upperwing lacking broad, clear-cut white trailing edge*, and has *only tiny white 'mirror'* at wing-tip; *small white primary tips*, like *'string of beads'*. – 1st-year: Juvenile similar to Yellow-legged and Lesser Black-backed Gulls, but underwing more strongly patterned with *dark-barred coverts and dark flight-feathers separated by light midwing-panel*; *rump darkish*, but *white uppertail-coverts forming prominent U*; largely *black tail-feathers broadly tipped white*; lower flanks usually dark; *legs dark grey*; *bill deepest at tip, two-toned*, tip black and inner two-thirds grey. Develops adult-like upperbody early, gaining many pale grey feathers on scapulars and mantle Feb–May. – 2nd-year: Told by *pale grey upperparts*; 'smart' wing pattern with *dark and neat secondary bar*; *narrow black tail-band*; *dark legs*; and usually *red-based bill*. – 3rd-year: Like adult, but a little black on primary coverts; 'mirror' lacking; and sometimes hint of tail-band.

VOICE Calls when breeding include a nasal 'gleh-i-eh', low 'ug-ug-uk' (alarm) and harsh, raucous 'argh' in endless series, recalling the noise in a rookery.

Herring Gull

Yellow-legged Gull

Audouin's Gull

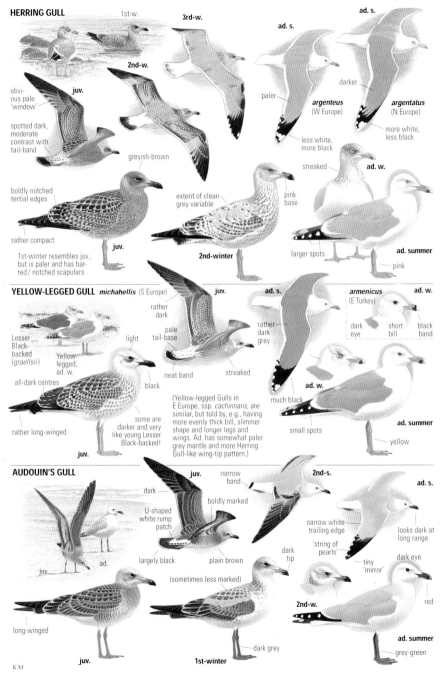

HERRING GULL

1st-w.

3rd-w.

ad. s.

ad. s.

2nd-w.

juv.

obvious pale 'window'

spotted dark, moderate contrast with tail-band

paler

argenteus
(W Europe)

darker

argentatus
(N Europe)

less white, more black

more white, less black

greyish-brown

boldly notched tertial edges

extent of clean grey variable

streaked

ad. w.

rather compact

pink base

juv.

1st-winter resembles juv., but is paler and has barred / notched scapulars

2nd-winter

larger spots

ad. summer

pink

YELLOW-LEGGED GULL *michahellis* (S Europe)

juv.

ad. s.

rather dark

pale tail-base

rather dark grey

armenicus
(E Turkey)

ad. w.

dark eye

short bill

black band

Lesser Black-backed (*graellsii*)

light

Yellow-legged, ad. w.

neat band

streaked

all-dark centres

black

some are darker and very like young Lesser Black-backed!

much black

ad. w.

rather long-winged

(Yellow-legged Gulls in E Europe, ssp. *cachinnans*, are similar, but told by, e.g., having more evenly thick bill, slimmer shape and longer legs and wings. Ad. has somewhat paler grey mantle and more Herring Gull-like wing-tip pattern.)

small spots

ad. summer

yellow

ad. summer

juv.

AUDOUIN'S GULL

juv.

narrow band

2nd-s.

ad. s.

dark

boldly marked

narrow white trailing edge

looks dark at long range

U-shaped white rump patch

'string of pearls'

tiny 'mirror'

dark eye

juv.

ad.

largely black

plain brown

dark tip

red

2nd-w.

(sometimes less marked)

long-winged

juv.

1st-winter

dark grey

ad. summer

grey-green

KM

Lesser Black-backed Gull *Larus fuscus* m+r**B**2/**P**+**W**2

L 48–56 cm, WS 117-134 cm. Breeds colonially along coasts and at lakes. In N and E Europe long-distance migrant, crossing Europe along rivers to reach Africa, in W Europe shorter-distance migrant, and many winter British Isles.

IDENTIFICATION Four age-groups (see p. 168). *Blackish upperparts* develop from 2nd winter onwards, instantly narrowing choice to this species or Great Black-backed, from which told by *smaller size* (same as or slightly smaller than Herring), *slimmer body* and *longer, more pointed wings, and thinner*, less massive *bill*. In addition, adults have *yellow legs* (not pink); *smaller white 'mirror'* at wing-tip and smaller white spots on primary tips, so *lack continuous white rear edge to 'hand'*; in W Europe *obvious grey smudging on head Sep–Feb* (head white or faintly streaked on Great Black-backed). 1st-year more difficult to tell from Great Black-backed and, especially, Yellow-legged and Herring Gulls (p. 174). Bare parts develop gradually: bill from all black on juvenile to yellow with red spot on adult; iris from brown to yellow (with red orbital ring); and legs from pink to yellow. See Great Black-backed for general comment on ageing large gulls. – 1st-summer birds mainly stay longer in wintering areas, thus uncommon in breeding areas, at least in early summer. – **Variation**: Birds of W Europe and Iceland (ssp. *graellsii*), wintering south to W Africa, have upperparts slate-grey, contrasting with blacker wing-tips; breeders in SW Scandinavia (*intermedius*), which winter commonly in W Europe and south to W Africa, have upperparts dark blackish-grey; birds of Baltic (*fuscus*), wintering in Middle East and E Africa, have upperparts all (brownish-)black, with little or no contrast with wing-tips, and head much less streaked in winter; birds of N Russia (*heuglini*; taxonomic position not quite clear) are slate-grey above like *graellsii*, but are on average slightly larger and bulkier.

VOICE All calls similar to Herring Gull's, but noticeably *deeper and more nasal*, thereby recalling Yellow-legged Gull.

Great Black-backed Gull *Larus marinus* r(m)**B**3

L 61–74 cm, WS 144–166 cm. Breeds along coasts, singly or in small colonies, locally at larger lakes. Sedentary. Food fish, offal, birds (incl. fledged); kleptoparasitic, robbing sea ducks, cormorants, etc. Nest often high on rocky islands.

IDENTIFICATION Four age-groups (see p. 168). *Largest gull*, with bulky body, thick neck, and *very heavy bill*. *Blackish upperparts* (which generally develop in spring during 3rd calendar-year) and *large size* instantly indicate this species (or Lesser Black-backed Gull, which see for differences). 1st-year and most 2nd-winter lack black on upperparts, thus also difficult to tell from Herring Gull (p.174). Bare parts develop gradually: bill from all black on juvenile/1st-winter

to yellow with orange spot on adult; iris from brown to yellowish-grey (with red orbital ring). *Legs pale fleshy* at all ages. Given reasonable views, most immature large gulls can be aged by wing and tail patterns: – Juvenile: Whole plumage neat; scapulars and tertials mainly solidly dark-centred; head mottled. – 1st-winter: Resembles juvenile, but scapulars are more barred and head becomes slightly paler. – 2nd-winter: Resembles 1st-winter, but wing-coverts not so strongly chequered, greater coverts rather plain or finely patterned, and usually acquires pale base of bill. Extensively blackish scapulars and some mantle-feathers usually acquired in spring moult of 3rd calendar-year (2nd summer). – 3rd-winter: Most wing-coverts blackish; a few barred. – 4th-winter: Many as adult, but a few retain some slight signs of immaturity on wing-coverts, tail, and bill-tip.

VOICE Like that of Lesser Black-backed and Herring Gulls, but *much deeper* and typically always *hoarse and gruff*; 'laughing' display-call is also slower and shorter.

Pallas's Gull (Great Black-headed Gull)
Larus ichthyaetus **V*****

L 58–67 cm, WS 146–162 cm. Nests colonially on marshes, lake islands etc. in SE Russia. Scarce but regular in Middle East in winter; vagrant to Europe, with only one record in Britain (in 1859); none in Ireland. Food fish, crustaceans, insects (also swarming in flight), small mammals etc.

IDENTIFICATION Four age-groups (see p. 168), but plumage development initially quick as in a three-year gull. As large as or larger than Herring Gull, but slightly slimmer-bodied and *longer-winged*, with *elongated forehead* which accentuates *length and heaviness of bill*. In flight, slightly slimmer-winged than other large gulls, with deep chest, long head, and large bill giving front-heavy look. *Very large size* and *black hood* make adult summer unmistakable, but standing birds in other plumages could easily be overlooked as Yellow-legged Gulls, except for usually *obvious dark 'mask'* and *white eye-crescents*. Also, important always to bear in mind pitfall of some other large gull with oil-stained head, so essential to check other diagnostic features described below, especially the distinctive wing and tail patterns. – Adult: *Outer wing mainly white, with black crescent across tip*; black-banded yellowish bill (with red towards tip in summer); and yellowish legs. – Juvenile: Scaly brown above; brown breast-sides or breast-band contrasting with *white underparts*; striking *pale grey midwing-panel*; *underwing-coverts white*; *broad, clear-cut, black tail-band*; pale, dark-tipped bill; and greyish or brownish-flesh legs. – 1st-winter/1st-summer: As juvenile, except adult-like *pale grey upperparts, dark hindneck*; bill and legs often show some yellowish in 1st summer. – 2nd-year: Like adult, but much black on outer wing, and thin tail-band. – 3rd-year: Like adult, but more black on wing-tip, and sometimes trace of tail-band.

VOICE Noisy at colonies. Flight-call is a deep, rather nasal 'aagh', rather similar to the call of Lesser Black-backed Gull. Mostly silent when not breeding.

Lesser Black-backed Gull   Great Black-backed Gull   Pallas's Gull

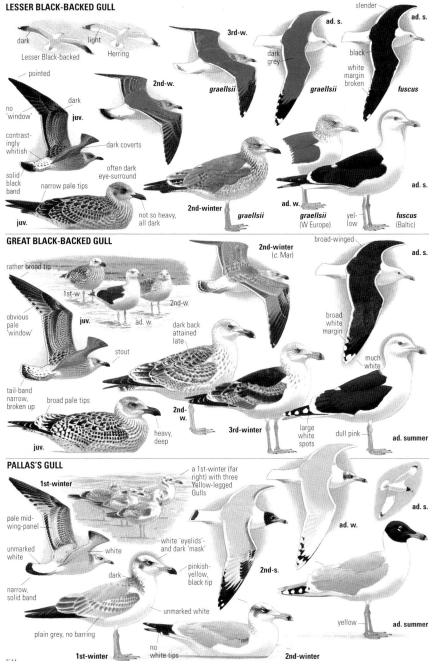

LESSER BLACK-BACKED GULL

dark   light
Lesser Black-backed   Herring

pointed

no 'window'   dark   **juv.**

3rd-w.

dark grey   **graellsii**

2nd-w.   **graellsii**

ad. s.

graellsii

slender   ad. s.

black
white margin broken   **fuscus**

contrastingly whitish   dark coverts

solid black band   narrow pale tips   often dark eye-surround

juv.   not so heavy, all dark

2nd-winter   **graellsii**

ad. w.   **graellsii** (W Europe)

yellow   **fuscus** (Baltic)

ad. s.

ad. s.

GREAT BLACK-BACKED GULL

rather broad tip

1st-w.   **2nd-w.**

2nd-winter (c. Mar)   broad-winged   ad. s.

juv.   ad. w.

obvious pale 'window'

stout

tail-band narrow, broken up   broad pale tips

juv.   heavy, deep

dark back attained late

2nd-w.   **3rd-winter**

broad white margin

much white

large white spots   dull pink   ad. summer

PALLAS'S GULL

1st-winter

a 1st-winter (far right) with three Yellow-legged Gulls

pale mid-wing-panel

unmarked white   white

dark

narrow, solid band

plain grey, no barring

1st-winter

white 'eyelids'-and dark 'mask'

pinkish-yellow, black tip

unmarked white

no white tips

2nd-winter

ad. w.

2nd-s.

ad. s.

yellow   ad. summer

KM

Ross's Gull *Rhodostethia rosea*   V**

L 29–32 cm, WS 73–80 cm. Breeds in High Arctic of NE Siberia and N America. Vagrant to N Europe, recently with a few records annually in Britain & Ireland.

IDENTIFICATION Two age-groups (see p. 168). Resembles Little Gull in habits and size, but slightly larger, with *longer, more pointed wings* and *long tail* with *pointed tip*. At distance, likely to be overlooked as Little Gull. – Adult summer: Neat *black neck-ring*, pink-flushed underparts, white trailing edge to wing *broader than on Little Gull* and *not extending around wing-tip*. – Adult winter: Like adult summer, but neck-ring replaced by small dark ear-spot, dark area in front of eye, and pale grey on crown, neck and breast-sides; underparts often white. – 1st-year: Dark 'W-pattern' like Little Gull, but less black on primaries and lacks secondary bar, giving *broader white trailing edge*, accentuated below by *ashy-grey greater underwing-coverts*; lacks Little Gull's full tail-band and blackish cap. 1st-summer may have partial or full neck-ring.

VOICE Vagrants usually silent.

Little Gull *Larus minutus*   P4 / W4–5

L 24–28 cm, WS 62–69 cm. Breeds in usually small colonies on freshwater marshes. Winters in W Europe and Mediterranean area, migrants (mainly Apr–May, Aug–Oct) seen along coasts, sometimes even at sea, or at inland waters. Picks small food items from water surface; hawks flying insects. Nest usually among vegetation in shallow water.

IDENTIFICATION Three age-groups (see p. 168). *Very small* (²⁄₃ size of Black-headed) and dainty, with quick wingbeats and more erratic, indirect flightpath giving tern-like impression. Adult and 2nd-year flash alternately *blackish underwing* and pale grey upperwing, giving distinctive appearance even at long range; *distinct white border to entire wing* gives impression of *rounded wing-tip*. – Adult summer: *Black* hood, reddish-brown bill (looks black), scarlet legs, and pink-flushed underparts. – Adult winter: Black ear-spot and blackish cap; underparts white; bill black; legs dull red. – Juvenile: Extensive blackish-brown on head and upperparts, *dark 'W pattern' across wings*, faint secondary bar, black tail-band, all-white underwing (except for small dark patch where rear edge of wing meets body), black bill, and pink legs. – 1st-winter: Head and body like adult winter, remainder as juvenile. – 1st-summer: Like 1st-winter, or with partial or full hood; by midsummer wings often worn, and 'W' faded pale brown; tail-band often broken in centre. – 2nd-year: As adult, but variable *black markings on upperwing-tip*, and *underwing-coverts paler or whitish*.

VOICE Short, hard, nasal 'keck', at times quickly repeated. Noisy display-call a rhythmic '**kay**-ke-**kay**-ke-**kay**-ke-…'.

(Black-legged) Kittiwake *Rissa tridactyla*   m(r)**B**2 / **P**3

L 37–42 cm, WS 93–105 cm. Rarely seen far from sea. Breeds colonially (at times several tens of thousands of pairs) on steep sea-cliffs, sometimes on buildings. Common near colonies and fishing ports, or boats at sea. Food invertebrates and fish, including waste from commercial fishing.

IDENTIFICATION Three age-groups (see p. 168). A trifle larger than Black-headed, with slight notch in tail and short legs. Stiff, quick wingbeats and narrow outer wing give less 'lazy', more tern-like flight than other gulls. – Adult: *Small black triangle on wing-tip*; dark grey upperparts *shade to whitish before black wing-tip*, adding to distinctiveness of almost three-coloured wing pattern; bill yellowish; legs dark brown or blackish (rarely red, orange or flesh); head white in summer, with grey hindneck and crescentic blackish ear-spot in winter. – 1st-year: *Dark 'W-pattern' across wings* and black tail-band; juvenile and some 1st-winters have white head with black ear-spot and *black half-collar*; otherwise head as adult winter; W often much faded by 1st summer, and bill becomes dull yellowish with dark marking at tip. Juvenile/1st-winter similar to 1st-year Little Gull but, with practice, recognized by different structure (Kittiwake is bigger-headed) and flight action. Kittiwake is darker grey above, has *cleaner white rear portion of wing*, and lacks Little Gull's dark cap and small black patch where under secondaries meet body. – 2nd-year: Like adult, but told at close range by e.g. black fringes on outermost primaries, some black on bill, or winter head pattern in summer.

VOICE Noisy at or near colonies; commonest call is repeated, quick, nasal 'kitt-i-**waa**ke'. In flight, a short, nasal 'kya!'. Alarm short, knocking 'kt kt kt…'.

Sabine's Gull *Larus sabini*   V* / **P**5

L 30–36 cm, WS 80–87 cm. Breeds in High Arctic of N Siberia and N America. Numerous records annually off mainly W coasts of Britain & Ireland, mostly Aug–Oct, especially when mid-Atlantic southward migration route of N American population (which winters off SW Africa) is diverted by northwesterly gales.

IDENTIFICATION Two age-groups (see p. 168). Size between Little Gull and Black-headed Gull. Neat body but large wings. Notched tail. *Sharply contrasting upperwing pattern* distinctive at all ages, but beware that wing pattern of 1st-year Kittiwake can look very Sabine's-like even at fairly close range. Important, therefore, to note other confirmatory features before making firm identification: adult summer has *blackish-grey hood*, which is retained much later into autumn than that of other hooded gulls; adult winter and 2nd-year birds have variable, usually extensive blackish nape and hindneck; juvenile (Jul–Dec) has *pale-scaled mousegrey upperparts*, much grey on head and breast-sides (*head looks mainly dark at distance*, not white like Kittiwake); also, *flight* is somewhat *lighter*. – 1st-summer: Like adult, but head as in winter, or only partial hood.

VOICE Juveniles have a piping 'prree' like a young tern.

Little Gull · Kittiwake · Sabine's Gull

ROSS'S GULL

1st-w.   1st-w.

ad. w.

ad. s.

white

1st-winter

Little Gull

Ross's

pale

pointed

'black eye'

white wedge reaches tip

long

ad. winter

grey

lacks secondary bar

grey

broad edge

ad. w.

long, pointed

pointed

1st-winter

ad. summer

LITTLE GULL

juv.

variably marked black

rounded, white tip

ad. w.

ad. s.

1st-winter

narrow white

blackish

grey secondary bar

faint band

paler than ad.

2nd-winter

dark patch

dark

juv.

1st-winter

ad. winter

ad. summer

KITTIWAKE

juv.

solid black

ad. winter

breeding site

1st-winter

pure white (cf. juv. Little Gull)

two-toned grey

worn 1st-s. moulting to 2nd-w.

black W-pattern

plain grey

at long range and at certain angles confusingly similar to Sabine's (see below)

ad. w.

juv.

rather short-legged, feet dark

ad. summer

SABINE'S GULL

juv.

juv.

ad. w.

ad. s.

juv.

large wings on neat body

looks dark at long range

pale tip

ad. w.

compare with juv. Kittiwake (above left)

mouse-grey, pale-scaled

small head, slender bill

forked

long, pointed 'stern'

juv.

ad. summer

KM

Glaucous Gull *Larus hyperboreus* P / W4

L 63-68 cm, WS 138–158 cm. Nests singly or in loose colonies on cliffs, islands, or other open ground near sea. South of breeding range, uncommon or rare (mostly Oct–Apr), mainly near coast among flocks of other large gulls. Food in summer mainly fish, eggs and young of other birds; in winter, mainly waste from fishing ports, rubbish tips, etc.

IDENTIFICATION Four age-groups (see p. 168). Glaucous and Iceland Gulls are the only *large* gulls with *whitish primaries*. Adults have paler grey upperparts than Herring Gulls; 1st- and 2nd-years in fresh plumage are rather *uniformly pale ochrous-brown* or café-au-lait-coloured, with fainter and finer barring on upperparts and wing-coverts than other large gulls; *unmarked* pale or white flight-feathers diagnostic at all ages, obvious in flight, especially from below, when they appear strikingly translucent (but beware of moulting Herring Gulls in Aug–Nov). Because they are similar in plumage at all ages, telling Glaucous from Iceland rests entirely on differences in size, structure, bill pattern (on 1st-years), and bill colour (on some adults and 3rd-years). Given good views, identification of most is easy: Glaucous is *obviously or slightly larger and longer-legged than Herring Gull* and more heavily built, with large bill, small eye, and sloping forehead and often angled hindcrown giving a mean, aggressive look; as a rule, *the bill is as long as or longer than the length of the* (short) *projection of primaries beyond the tail-tip*. Glaucous Gull is also correspondingly broader-winged, longer-necked and larger-headed, and more lumbering in flight than Iceland, but the structural and size differences are often more difficult to appreciate in flight than on the ground. Identification of 1st-years is made easier because of diagnostic difference in bill pattern: Glaucous invariably has *bill two-thirds pale* (pinkish) *with sharply demarcated black tip* (Iceland has more extensive black tip, shading into often only slightly paler base). Adult's orbital ring is yellow (reddish on Iceland). Occasional small or small-looking Glaucous or large or large-looking Iceland can be more difficult: in such cases, bill pattern (on 1st-years) and bill-length/primary-projection difference are the most useful features. – Caution is necessary over all-white albinistic individuals of other species, paler-than-normal (so-called leucistic) immature Herring Gulls, and Glaucous × Herring Gull hybrids. All-white albinistic gulls are rare, however, and in any case no Glaucous or Iceland is ever entirely pure white (although some much-faded 1st- and 2nd-years may appear so at long range). Leucism and hybridity show on immature gulls through the outer primaries, secondary bar or tail-band being at least slightly darker than the general colour of the rest of the plumage, and adult hybrids will show dark markings on the wing-tip; pure

Glaucous and nominate Iceland never show such features.
VOICE Resembles Herring Gull's, but some notes coarser.

Iceland Gull *Larus glaucoides* P / W4–5

L 52–60 cm, WS 123–139 cm. Breeds in Greenland and in N Canada (but not in Iceland!); rare winter visitor to NW Europe, usually much rarer than Glaucous. Habitat and food much as for Glaucous Gull.

IDENTIFICATION Four age-groups (see p. 168). Very similar to Glaucous Gull, having *whitish primaries*, adults with pale grey back and yellow bill with red spot, immatures with finely brown-barred plumage. However, Iceland Gull is smaller, even *slightly* or obviously *smaller and shorter-legged than Herring Gull* and usually more lightly built, with 'normal-sized' bill, proportionately larger eye and rather rounded head giving a comparatively gentle appearance; in flight, it often gives a short-necked and small-headed impression. As a rule, the *bill is obviously shorter than the length of the* (long) *projection of primaries beyond the tail-tip*. 1st-years are usually told by bill pattern: *extensive dark tip* covering about half of bill, *shading into only slightly paler* (dull flesh or grey) *base*. Some Iceland retain diagnostic bill pattern well into 2nd year, but others subsequently acquire Glaucous-like pattern. Some adult and 3rd-year Iceland have *slightly greenish-yellow bill colour* (always yellowish on Glaucous, without greenish tone). Adult's orbital ring reddish. – Variation: Breeders in arctic NE Canada (*L.g. kumlieni*; vagrant to NW Europe, about 1–2 records annually) like nominate *glaucoides* except often slightly larger and heavier-billed, and adults have diagnostic wing-tip pattern (see illustration), frosty-grey when fresh (though darkness variable) or grey-brown when faded, and often dark iris; 3rd- and 2nd-years have dark areas on outer webs of outer 3–4 primaries (reflecting eventual adult pattern) and often a darker tail-band; 1st-year indistinguishable from *glaucoides*. Breeders in arctic NW Canada (*thayeri*; apparently at least two records in Europe) overall darker, with darker and more extensive markings on wing-tips, approaching very pale Herring Gulls; on present knowledge difficult to identify reliably.

VOICE Like Herring Gull's, but slightly higher-pitched.

Ivory Gull *Pagophila eburnea* V**

L 41–47 cm, WS 100-113 cm. Rare vagrant south of High Arctic (just about annually recorded in Britain & Ireland), usually near fishing ports or at carrion on beach; often attracted to seal or cetacean corpses.

IDENTIFICATION Two age-groups (see p. 168). Size of Common Gull, but has *broader wings, shorter neck,* plumper body, longer tail and *shorter legs*. Flight light, wingbeats rather quick. – Adult: *All white*, but essential to note peculiar shape, *dark-based, yellow-tipped bill* and black legs to rule out chance of an all-white albinistic other gull. – 1st-year: Distinctive *finely black-spotted white plumage*; 'swarthy' face.

VOICE Tern-like 'krreeo'.

Glaucous Gull Iceland Gull Ivory Gull

GLAUCOUS GULL

buff-white tip

Glaucous

translu-cent

dark   Herring, 1st-w.

juv. / 1st-w.

pink, outer third black; long

little or no tail-band

less evenly patterned than 1st-w.

2nd-winter

3rd-winter

ad. w.

long 'weigh-tier' neck, 'front-heavy'

broad wing, blunt tip

pale iris   pale tip

ad. s.

juv. / 1st-winter

1st-winter (faded, spring)

2nd-winter

'blotchier' than 1st-w.

short wing-tip   **ad. winter**

ICELAND GULL

Herring

Glaucous

Iceland

at all ages, shape (compared with Herring Gull) is safest way to identi-fication; all three above are 1st-w.

juv. / 1st-w.

usually all-dark bill

attenuated 'stern'

2nd-winter

3rd-winter

ad. w.

'short-necked'

often acquires pale base in 1st winter

often surprisingly 'chunky' in flight; best to concentrate on head and bill

rather pointed   *kumlieni*

tinged green-ish-yellow

ad. s.

juv. / 1st-winter

1st-winter (faded, spring)

2nd-winter

long wing-tip   **ad. w.**   grey   **ad. w.**

kumlieni (arctic Canada)

IVORY GULL

bill colours diagnostic

unmarked white

black spots

dusky 'face'

feeding on seal carcase

ad.

juv. / 1st-w.

juv. / 1st-winter

short, black   **ad.**

ad.

KM

Sooty Gull *Larus hemprichii* —

L 42–45 cm, WS 105–113 cm. Breeds Jul–Sep in S Red Sea to Persian Gulf; in winter, occasionally wanders as far north as Suez and Eilat. Strictly coastal. Omnivorous; commonly scavenges along shores.

IDENTIFICATION Three age-groups (see p. 168). The size of Common Gull, but *dark colour* and *long wings* can give larger impression at distance; dark colour, especially dark underwing, can also give skua-like impression. Darkness and long-winged flying and perched silhouette, and *exceptionally long bill*, are characters also shared by slightly smaller White-eyed Gull, from which best told at all ages by *thick bill* (equally long but *thinner* on White-eyed), two-coloured and *sharply dark-tipped bill* (all dark-looking bill on White-eyed), and heavier build. – Adult summer: *Hood dark brown* (black on White-eyed); *white crescent* usually *above eye only* (thicker white crescents above and below eye on White-eyed); *breast and upperparts sooty-brown* (purer greyish and slightly paler on White-eyed); and *bill greenish with dark end and red tip* (dark red with black tip on White-eyed). – Adult winter: Hood less clear, and white half-collar obscured (on both species). – Juvenile: *Plain, pale greyish-brown head and neck* (darker brown on White-eyed); inconspicuous *thin pale crescent above eye* (prominent white crescents both above and below eye on White-eyed); and *sharply two-toned bill* (all dark on White-eyed). – 2nd-year: Like adult winter but head pattern less developed, and has variable black tail-band.

VOICE Resembles that of Kittiwake, especially falsetto laughing display-call 'veee**aa**h ve ve **vah**, veee**aa**h...'. Some calls are both shriller and harsher than White-eyed Gull's.

White-eyed Gull *Larus leucophthalmus* —

L 39–43 cm, WS 100–109 cm. Breeds in Red Sea and Gulf of Aden; small numbers straggle regularly north to Eilat. Mainly coastal. Food mainly fish.

IDENTIFICATION Three age-groups (see p. 168). Sooty Gull is only likely confusion species, sharing with White-eyed *dark colour, dark underwing*, slim shape and *long bill*; at all ages told from Sooty by following characters: slightly *smaller* size and lighter build; *thinner bill*, appearing *all dark* at distance. – Adult: *Black hood, thick white crescents above and below eye*, and *slightly paler and purer grey breast and upperparts*; bill at close range seen to be *dark red with black tip* (lacking greenish tinge of Sooty). – Juvenile: *Darker overall* than Sooty owing to duller pale tips to wing-coverts, and *darker and browner head and neck*; *prominent white crescents above and below eye*; and *all-dark bill*. – 2nd-year: Like adult winter, but has blackish 'mask' rather than hood, variable black tail-band, and all-dark bill.

VOICE Like Sooty Gull's, but usually slightly lower-pitched and less harsh.

Laughing Gull *Larus atricilla* V*

L 36–41 cm, WS 98–110 cm. Breeds in N America. Vagrant to Europe, a few records annually in Britain & Ireland.

IDENTIFICATION Three age-groups (see p. 168). Size between Black-headed and Common Gulls. Franklin's Gull is only likely confusion species, but also beware 2nd- or 3rd-winter Lesser Black-backed Gull, which could look similar if its actually much larger size not apparent (e.g. distant or brief views of lone bird). Laughing and Franklin's are much *darker grey above* than other small European gulls (nearly as dark as W European Lesser Black-backed *L. f. graellsii*). Laughing is slightly larger than Franklin's, with *longer bill*, legs and wings, latter giving *elongated rear end* when perched (Franklin's is more compact, Little Gull-like in shape). Adult and 2nd-year Laughing differ further from 1st-summer or older Franklin's in *all-black wing-tip* with *white primary tips tiny or lacking* (bold black and white pattern on Franklin's); tail all white (pale grey centre on Franklin's, although this not always obvious); *thinner white crescents* above and below eye (thick on Franklin's, and joined at rear); *less extensive dark on head* in winter (Franklin's has distinctive 'half-hooded' pattern in 1st-summer and adult winter plumages); and *dull red* bill and legs in adult summer (when Franklin's bright red). – 1st-winter: Note *grey on breast, flanks and underwing-coverts* (these areas white on Franklin's); less grey on head ('half-hood' on Franklin's); all primaries evenly dark (paler 'window' on Franklin's); and *greyish tail with full, broad black band* (white with smaller band on Franklin's). – 1st-summer: As 1st-winter but upperwing-coverts often faded, pale brown (upperwing of Franklin's adult-like in 1st summer). – 2nd-year: As adult, but possible to age by black of wing-tip extending more or less strongly onto primary coverts, and (on most) variable black band on tail.

VOICE Flight-call Common Gull-like, yelping 'kee-agh'.

Franklin's Gull *Larus pipixcan* V***

L 32–36 cm, WS 81–93 cm. Breeds in N America. Rare vagrant to Europe, often in summer but in other seasons, too.

IDENTIFICATION Two age-groups (see p. 168). Size of Black-headed Gull or slightly smaller. Only likely confusion species is Laughing Gull, which see for detailed comparison (but beware adult winter Kittiwake could look similar in brief or distant view). Main differences from Laughing: *slightly smaller size* and *more compact shape*; *shorter bill*; in adult plumage *bold black and white pattern at wing-tip*; *thicker white crescents above and below eye*, joining at rear; and *bright red bill and legs*. – 1st-summer: After complete moult in 1st spring, resembles adult winter, but with *white division* between grey of upperwing and black of wing-tip *narrow or lacking*; white primary tips smaller (but still obvious); and never acquires full hood (thus useful difference from adult summer); quite different appearance from 1st-summer Laughing Gull, which retains juvenile wings and tail. – 2nd-winter: Like adult, but sometimes possible to age by less extensive white on wing-tip.

VOICE Soft 'krruk' or shrill, repeated 'guk' when feeding.

Sooty Gull   White-eyed Gull

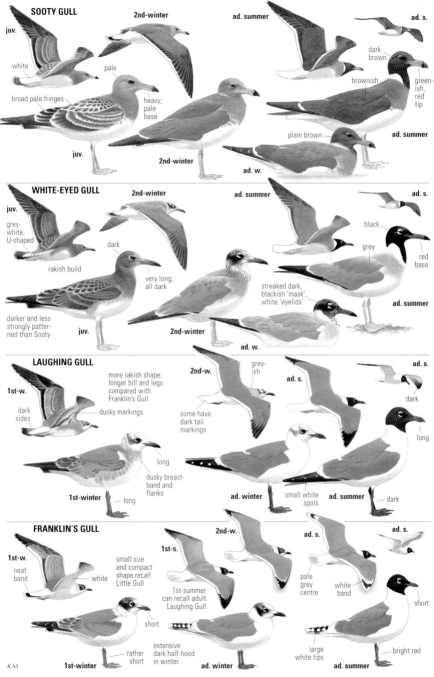

SOOTY GULL

juv.

white

broad pale fringes

pale

heavy; pale base

juv.

2nd-winter

2nd-winter

ad. summer

ad. s.

dark brown

brownish

greenish, red tip

plain brown

ad. summer

ad. w.

WHITE-EYED GULL

juv.

grey-white, U-shaped

rakish build

dark

very long; all dark

darker and less strongly patterned than Sooty

juv.

2nd-winter

2nd-winter

ad. summer

ad. s.

black

grey

red base

streaked dark, blackish 'mask', white 'eyelids'

ad. summer

ad. w.

LAUGHING GULL

1st-w.

dark sides

dusky markings

more rakish shape, longer bill and legs compared with Franklin's Gull

2nd-w.

some have dark tail markings

long

dusky breast-band and flanks

1st-winter

long

grey-ish

ad. s.

ad. s.

dark

long

ad. winter

small white spots

ad. summer

dark

FRANKLIN'S GULL

1st-w.

neat band

white

2nd-w.

1st-s.

small size and compact shape recall Little Gull

1st-summer can recall adult Laughing Gull

short

rather short

1st-winter

extensive dark half-hood in winter

ad. winter

ad. s.

pale grey centre

white band

large white tips

ad. summer

ad. s.

white band

short

bright red

KM

TERNS *Sterninae*

Relatively small to medium-sized, slender seabirds with long, narrow and pointed wings, usually long and deeply forked tail, and long and pointed bill. Masterly fliers, some migrating longer distance than any other birds. Flight light and elegant, at times buoyant, with elastic wingbeats, wings often kept bent at the carpal joint. Frequently hover before plunging into water for fish, but do not glide in the air, and only rarely swim like gulls. Nest on ground, often colonially.

Little Tern *Sterna albifrons*　　　　　　mB4

L 21–25 cm, WS 41–47 cm. Breeds in loose colonies along sandy, shallow coasts or islands with shingle and shells and low grass; also at lakes and wide rivers. Summer visitor (mid Apr–Oct), winters in Africa. Food mainly small fish.

IDENTIFICATION *Tiny* tern, appearing only about half the size of Common Tern, with *noticeably narrow wings* and *very fast wingbeats; hovers low over surface*, often prolonged, then plunges to catch fish; typically *repeats dives more quickly* than other terns. – Adult summer: *White forehead* and *black lores*; bill *yellow with small black tip*; legs orange-yellow; 2–3 outer primaries blackish. – Adult winter: Like adult summer, but from Aug lores white and forecrown paler. – Juvenile: Bill dark (with dirty yellow base), mantle/scapulars with dark scaly pattern, and upper forewing dusky; best identified by *flight action* and *small size*.

VOICE Distinctive sharp, rasping, often repeated 'kriet'; rapid chattering in display and alarm, '**ker**re-kiet **ker**re-kiet **ker**re-kiet...'. Young beg for food with a light, ringing 'plee' or 'plee-we'.

Sandwich Tern *Sterna sandvicensis*　　mB3 / P3–4

L 37–43 cm (incl. tail-streamers 6–9 on ad.), WS 85–97 cm. Breeds colonially on sandy beaches or low islands in salt or brackish water. Summer visitor to N Europe (mainly late Mar–late Sep), winters in S Europe and Africa. Scarce inland, unlike Caspian Tern strictly following Atlantic coasts on migration. Food mainly fish. Nest a scrape on ground.

IDENTIFICATION *Large size* (about same size as Black-headed Gull, but certainly slimmer) and *long, 'pencil' bill* distinctive. Rapid fishing flight with *measured, forceful wingbeats, wings slightly flexed, long and evenly narrow; also, appears short-tailed* (front-heavy) in flight. When feeding, often patrols at greater height than Common or Arctic Tern, with bill pointing down, making sudden and bold dive to catch fish. In stronger winds, typically feeds where waves break, sometimes in large and noisy gatherings. – Adult summer: Pale grey upperparts, white underparts (actually lightly washed creamy-pink) and broad white trailing edge give *very whitish impression* compared with Common or Arctic Tern; outer

4–5 primaries darken during summer to form blackish wedge or tip; *legs and bill black*, latter with *small yellow tip*. – Adult winter: *Forehead and crown white* (from Jun onwards), leaving thin dark 'mask', and (Nov–Mar) upperwing uniform frosty-grey. – Juvenile: *Bold scaly pattern above*, especially on scapulars; *complete dusky cap*; bill usually dark, shorter than adult's. – 1st-year: Head and body like adult winter, but retains juvenile dark markings on coverts, secondaries and tail; outer primaries and tail-feathers worn, blackish by spring. Yellow bill-tip tiny or lacking.

VOICE Noisy at colonies, and when feeding during summer–early autumn. Flight-call distinctive, a loud, grating 'ker**rick**' (like pressing amalgam into tooth). Begging-call of juvenile/1st-winter thin, high-pitched, ringing 'sree-sri'.

Gull-billed Tern *Sterna nilotica*　　　　V**

L 35–42 cm, WS 76–86 cm. Breeds colonially in open, flat country at lakes, marshes (fresh, brackish or saline), sheltered coastal waters, fields on irrigated plains, and mountain lakes (to *c.* 2000 m) with grassy meadows and sandy shores. Summer visitor (Apr–Sep), winters in Africa; in Britain & Ireland a very few records annually. Food mainly insects, also frogs, small mammals, etc.

IDENTIFICATION Distinguished from Sandwich Tern at all ages by *short, thick, all-black* bill only half length of cap (about same length as cap on Sandwich, but beware of not fully grown, all-black bill of immature Sandwich); slightly *broader wing-bases* (though wings still both long and pointed); shorter neck (the tail is shorter, too, but appears equal in practice); and *longer legs* when perched. Feeding behaviour and *inland habitats* also distinctive: *does not normally plunge-dive* like Sandwich, but with leisurely flight *hawks insects in air*, often over dry meadows, at times even in open forests, or swoops to pluck prey from water surface or vegetation. – Adult summer: *Uniform frosty-grey* upperparts, including *rump and* (white-sided) *tail*; primaries often uniform (though, on most, outer 4–5 wear to darker grey during summer, at times creating dark wedge on 'hand' much as on Sandwich); from *below, dark trailing edge on outer primaries longer and more clear-cut* than on Sandwich, often also showing from above. – Adult winter: *Isolated patch or streak behind eye*, not continuing across nape. – Juvenile: Bill slimmer than adult's; most have much *less patterned upperparts and wings* than juvenile Sandwich, and all have *less black on head*. – 1st-summer: Head and body as adult winter; retained juvenile wings and tail have less obvious dark markings than Sandwich. Slightly more Common Gull-like wing shape (on adult 'arm' is slightly broader, making outer wing look shorter and more pointed).

VOICE Noisy at colonies. Flight-call is a deep, nasal, rising 'gur-**wick**' (slightly reminiscent of Bar-tailed Godwit display); alarm is a quick, laughing 'gwic-gwic-gwic'. Also, from breeders a bubbly or rattling 'br-r-r-r-...'. Juveniles beg with a piping, high-pitched 'pe-eep' (lacking the ringing tone of juv. Sandwich).

Little Tern　　　　Sandwich Tern　　　　Gull-billed Tern

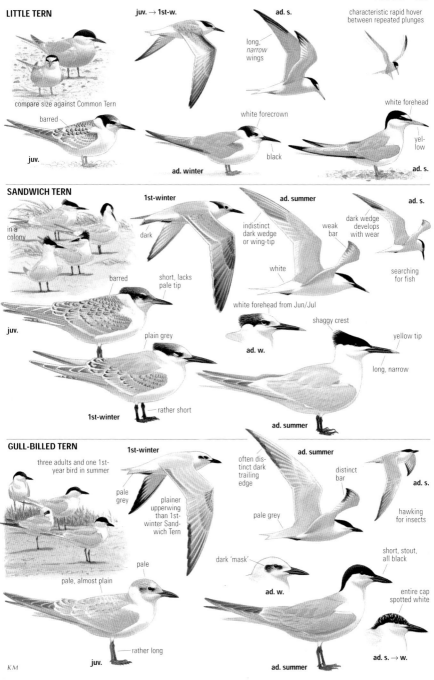

LITTLE TERN

juv. → 1st-w.

ad. s.

characteristic rapid hover between repeated plunges

compare size against Common Tern

long, *narrow* wings

white forehead

barred

juv.

white forecrown

black

ad. winter

white forehead

yel-low

ad. s.

SANDWICH TERN

1st-winter

ad. summer

ad. s.

in a colony

dark

indistinct dark wedge or wing-tip

weak bar

dark wedge develops with wear

barred

short, lacks pale tip

white

searching for fish

juv.

plain grey

white forehead from Jun/Jul

shaggy crest

yellow tip

ad. w.

1st-winter

rather short

long, narrow

ad. summer

GULL-BILLED TERN

1st-winter

ad. summer

three adults and one 1st-year bird in summer

pale grey

often distinct dark trailing edge

distinct bar

ad. s.

plainer upperwing than 1st-winter Sandwich Tern

pale grey

hawking for insects

pale

dark 'mask'

short, stout, all black

pale, almost plain

ad. w.

entire cap spotted white

rather long

juv.

ad. summer

ad. s. → w.

KM

Common Tern *Sterna hirundo* mB3 / P2

L 34–37 cm (incl. tail-streamers 5–8 on ad.), WS 70–80 cm. Breeds colonially or singly both at coasts and at inland waters (lakes, rivers, etc.). Summer visitor (Apr–Oct), winters in W and S Africa. Food fish. Nest is scrape on ground.

IDENTIFICATION Very similar to Arctic Tern, but, with practice, separation nearly always possible. Apart from being slightly larger, different structure when perched useful: *longer bill* (often looking slightly decurved) and head, and *longer legs* (belly well clear of ground). Different structure also in flight: *longer neck/head* and *slightly broader wings*, which appear to be more or less central on body. Hovers, and dives directly for fish. – Adult summer: *Bill orange-red with black tip*, but note that black tip can be very small, especially by midsummer; underparts pale grey, usually without obvious contrast with white cheek; *short tail-streamers not extending beyond wing-tip*; outer 4–6 primaries darker than rest, forming *dark wedge on upperwing*, but note that wedge often is very faint in spring (only a dark 'notch' at trailing edge), becoming obvious by midsummer through wear; from below, *primaries white with broad, rather diffuse dark trailing edge*; translucency strongest on inner primaries. – Adult winter (some start moult in Jul; Arctic not until reaching winter range): White forehead and underparts, dark carpal bar, and all-black bill. – Juvenile: Upperwing has *pale square-shaped midwing-panel* between *narrow grey secondary* bar and *obvious dark carpal bar*; other differences from Arctic include: a little *orange at base of bill* (bill all black on Arctic from late summer); *forehead and upperparts obviously ginger-brown in tone* when recently fledged; extensive *carpal bar usually visible when perched* (smaller on Arctic, usually concealed). – 1st-summer (usually stays in winter range; rare in Europe): White forehead and underparts; blackish bill; wholly or partly retained juvenile wings and tail much worn, giving striking variegated pattern. – 2nd-summer (many stay in winter range, scarce in Europe): Like adult summer, but has immature features such as white on forehead, patchy grey underparts, and blackish bill.

VOICE Noisy at colonies, including short, sharp 'kit', rapid series of quarrelling 'kt-kt-kt-kt-...' and typical '**kier**ri-**kier**ri-**kier**ri-...' with variations. Alarm is a disyllabic, drawn-out, downslurred 'kreee-arrr' or a sharp 'chip!'.

Arctic Tern *Sterna paradisaea* mB3 / P2

L 33–39 cm (incl. tail-streamers 7–11½ on ad.), WS 66–77 cm. Breeds in colonies (in N often very large and dense) or singly along coasts, on islands in sea-bays, locally at ponds in taiga or barren mountains, and on tundra near water. Summer visitor (end Apr–Oct), winters off S Africa and Antarctica. Probably has the longest migration of all birds.

IDENTIFICATION Very similar to Common Tern (which see); Arctic told by: slightly smaller size; *shorter bill, head and neck* and *longer tail*, making wings look ahead of centre of body; *very short legs*; slightly *narrower wings*. Flight often more elastic and gracefully bouncing than Common Tern's, but display-flight of latter is just as elegant. Often dives with 'stepped hover', dropping short distance and hovering again before final plunge; at times snatches prey from surface in Black Tern fashion. – Adult summer: *Bill dark red* (blood-red) *without black tip*; *lower throat, breast and belly washed grey*, creating subtle contrast with white upper throat and cheeks, stronger than on most Common Terns; *long tail-streamers* extending beyond wing-tip when perched. *Upperwing uniformly pale grey* (lacking dark wedge or 'notch' of Common), and *all flight-feathers near-white and translucent from below*, outer primaries with neat black trailing edge (narrower than on Common). – Juvenile: Carpal bar often fainter than on normal Common Tern, and *secondaries are whitish*, not shaded grey as on Common Tern; often a *white triangular area on hindwing*. Dark bill first red-based, from Aug/Sep all black. Forehead white (more clearly demarcated than on Common). – 1st-summer (scarce in Europe): White forehead, dark bill, a faint dark carpal bar (thus resembles adult winter).

VOICE Recalls Common Tern; includes piping, clear 'pi-pi-pi-pi-...', 'pyu pyu pyu', and ringing '**pree**-eh', and quarrelling, hard rattling 'kt-kt-kt-krrr-kt-...'; alarm disyllabic 'krri-errrrr' (variable, like Common's or harder, drier).

Roseate Tern *Sterna dougallii* mB4

L 33–36 cm (incl. tail-streamers 8–11 on ad.), WS 67–76 cm. Breeds colonially at maritime coasts, on beach or offshore island. Summer visitor (mainly mid May–Aug), winters in W Africa. Scarce and local. Nest often in hollow.

IDENTIFICATION Compared with Common or Arctic, Roseate Tern has shorter wings and faster, shallower wingbeats, giving faster-looking more direct flight; hovers less and uses distinctive *angled power-dive, as if 'flying into water'* to catch fish. – Adult summer: Extreme paleness of grey upperparts and white-looking underparts give *outstanding whitish look* among greyer Common and Arctic; *bill all black or with red at base* (red becomes more extensive during summer); legs rather long, bright red; *underparts flushed very pale pink* (lacking any grey); *very long, flexible tail-streamers*; only outer 2–4 primaries darker than rest, forming *thin dark leading edge*; at rest, *whitish inner primaries* leave 'small dark wing-tip' (all primary tips rather dark on Common/Arctic). – Adult winter: White forehead and underparts, dark carpal bar, black bill; tail-streamers moulted Jul–Aug. – Juvenile: *Like miniature juvenile Sandwich Tern*, because of *bold scaly pattern on upperparts*, complete blackish cap (but forehead gradually turns white from Sep), all-black bill, and *blackish legs*.

VOICE Calls distinctive, a quick, disyllabic '**chiv**vick', slightly recalling Spotted Redshank, and a straight, deep, raucous 'krraahk'.

Common Tern

Arctic Tern

Roseate Tern

COMMON TERN

juv.

diffusely darker rear edge

dark carpal bar

dark secondary bar

pale grey

1st-summers in flight:

worn outer (juv.) primaries dark

all primaries fresh

dark wedge, faint in spring, more distinct in summer

only inner primaries translucent

ad. s.

Common

Arctic

broad diffuse bar

ad. s.

longer head/bill

bill-base orange

rather long

gingery

juv. (faded)

short tail-streamers

juv. (fresh)

ad. winter

oranged-red, usually black tip

pale grey

ad. summer

ARCTIC TERN

juv.

distinct dark bar

white secondaries

white

rather narrow and diffuse dark carpal bar

white

juveniles in flight:

Common

Arctic

upper 'hand' plain light grey

narrow distinct bar

all primaries translucent

ad. s.

ad. s.

short neck/ head/bill

rapidly darkens

black, rather short

usually little ginger-brown

juv. (faded)

on average more black on head than on juv. Common

juv. (fresh)

long tail-streamers

1st-summer

very short

dark red, usually no black on tip

grey

ad. summer

ROSEATE TERN

juv.

upperwing similar to juv. Common Tern, but usually more contrast with 'saddle'

variably strong bar

narrow dark wedge

ad. s.

lacks obvious dark rear edge

very white plumage

ad. s.

juv. and ad. Roseate (2nd and 3rd from left) with a juv. Sandwich and two Common

looks short-winged and long-tailed in flight

broad white inner edge

bold pattern

whitish

all dark, shorter than adult

dark

juv. (pale)

ad. spring

all dark

red base when breeding

very pale

light rosy flush

dark

juv. (typical)

ad. winter

inner primaries pale with broad white inner edge

ad. summer

KM

Caspian Tern *Sterna caspia* **V**∗

L 48–55 cm, WS 96–111 cm. Breeds colonially or singly, mostly on more remote offshore, low islands. Summer visitor (Apr–Oct; in Britain & Ireland about 5 records annually), winters in W Africa, occasionally Mediterranean Sea. Migration partly over land, following rivers over European continent, and crossing W Sahara in Mar and Nov. Food mainly fish, which during breeding can be caught far from colony (30–60 km, or more), often in fresh water. Nest is bare scrape on ground (sand or rocks).

IDENTIFICATION Largest tern; *wingspan larger than Common Gull*. Slow wingbeats and flight more ponderous than other terns, is more gull-like; also, looks decidedly *front-heavy* in flight. *Very large red bill* and *extensive dark* (blackish) *under primaries* at all ages. – Adult: *Bill bright red*, with small dark subterminal mark on most; legs black. In winter, *black on head extensive*, not thin-masked pattern of most other terns. – Juvenile: Full dark cap, extending further down on lores and cheeks than on adult; dusky-tipped orange bill; *pale legs*; rather faint dark markings on upperparts and tail; and inner wings rather uniformly pale, lacking obvious dark carpal bars of other large terns. – 1st-winter: Orange-red bill (only slightly paler than ad.winter) and dark legs develop quickly during first autumn. Forehead usually becomes slightly paler, too (still streaked dark), much as on adult winter. – 1st-summer: As adult winter, except wings and tail much worn or with obvious variegated pattern through moult.

VOICE Flight-call deep and fierce 'krre-ahk!' with hoarse, heron-like quality; the noise in colonies can be earsplitting. Begging-call of juvenile/1st-winter a repeated squeaky, whistled 'wee-**vi**'.

Royal Tern *Sterna maxima* **V**∗∗∗

L 42-49 cm, WS 86–92 cm. Primarily an American species. In E Atlantic, breeds only in Mauritania, wandering north to NW African coast (exceptionally Spain). Rare vagrant to rest of W Europe, including Britain & Ireland, probably from N American population.

IDENTIFICATION Size between Sandwich and Caspian Terns. Distinguished from Caspian Tern at all ages by *smaller size*, *less stout bill*, slimmer wings, *more attenuated rear end*, *more forked tail*, and *dark below primaries confined to narrow trailing edge*, thus invariably lacking extensive blackish area of Caspian. Also similar to Lesser Crested Tern, which see for comparison (below). Told from Crested Tern (p. 381; a very rare vagrant to treated area) of Middle East race *velox* by distinctly paler grey back and upperwing (Crested is almost lead-grey) and orange bill (Crested yellow or duller greenish-yellow) which is straight and dagger-shaped (Crested

slightly slimmer and more downcurved). Also, in breeding plumage note white rump and tail-centre (Crested greyish), and black forehead (Crested narrowly white). Could also be confused with Elegant Tern (p. 381), extremely rare vagrant from C America, but is somewhat larger, has stouter, straighter and slightly more reddish-orange bill (Elegant slimmer, longer, slightly decurved bill which is orange with yellowish tip), and often more extensive white forehead and eye-surround in non-breeding plumage (Elegant invariably solidly black eye-surround). – Adult: Told from Caspian by *unmarked orange* or *orange-yellow bill* (red only exceptionally), which is slightly slimmer and more pointed; *shaggier crest*; and fact that cap fall only briefly in spring, then quickly reduced to *thin dark 'mask' in winter plumage*, developing progressively from as early as May–Jun. – 1st-year: Told from Caspian Tern by *yellowish or pale orange bill* (not orange-red); prominent dark carpal bar, greater-covert and secondary bars; and pale head pattern (like ad. winter). – Variation: Breeders in W Africa (ssp. *albididorsalis*), frequently (mainly in Jun–Oct) seen along Moroccan Atlantic coast, differ from American (*maxima*) in having on average longer, narrower and more yellowish-orange (less reddish-orange) bill, and in being slightly smaller and slimmer, but still much larger than Sandwich Tern. – NB: The identification of a vagrant orange-billed tern often depends on the assessment of a number of subjective criteria. Observe critically and carefully judge size, bill shape and length, mantle shade, colour of rump, etc.

VOICE Flight-call throaty 'kerriup' or 'krree-it', recalling Sandwich Tern but coarser and lower-pitched.

Lesser Crested Tern *Sterna bengalensis* **V**∗∗∗ / (m**B**5)

L 33–40 cm (incl. tail-streamers *c.* 7 on ad.), WS 76–82 cm. Libyan breeding population winters along NW African coast; scarce in Gulfs of Suez and Aqaba (from Red Sea population). Very rare vagrant to Europe. Has bred a few times (Italy, Spain), in England some years in mixed pair with Sandwich Tern (apparently involving same bird which has been present each year since 1984). Habitat, food and breeding much as for Sandwich Tern.

IDENTIFICATION Size and plumage as Sandwich Tern, except that *bill is pale orange* (1st-year) *to bright orange* (adult), often shading to yellowish tip, and averaging slightly thicker-based and shorter than on Sandwich; compared with Sandwich Tern, *upperparts more uniform and slightly darker grey, including rump and tail-centre*; on juvenile, legs at first are dull brown-grey but quickly become blackish like adult. Distinguished from Royal Tern at all ages by: distinctly *smaller size*; *slimmer and more slender-tipped bill*; proportionately longer wings forming more upcurved rear end when perched; lighter flight action; more deeply forked tail; *upperparts darker grey* and (on adults) more uniform grey of about similar tone to Common Tern (Royal same tone as or paler grey than Sandwich Tern); and *rump and tail-centre grey* (white on Royal, but rump-centre grey on 1st-year Royal). – Juvenile/1st-winter: Like Sandwich Tern, but note yellowish-orange bill. (Very rarely, however, juvenile Sandwich Tern has a mostly pale orange or yellowish bill with just a dark culmen and tip.)

VOICE Flight-call a grating 'kerrick', like Sandwich Tern's.

Caspian Tern   Lesser Crested Tern

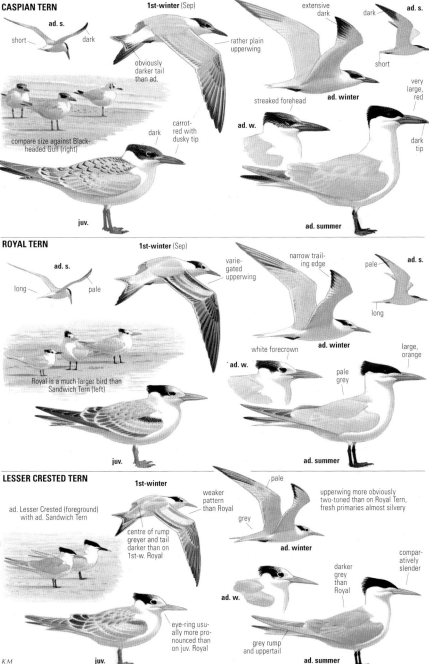

CASPIAN TERN

ad. s.
short
dark

1st-winter (Sep)

obviously darker tail than ad.

rather plain upperwing

extensive dark

dark

ad. s.

short

compare size against Black-headed Gull (right)

dark

carrot-red with dusky tip

juv.

streaked forehead

ad. winter

ad. w.

very large, red

dark tip

ad. summer

ROYAL TERN

ad. s.
long
pale

1st-winter (Sep)

variegated upperwing

narrow trailing edge

pale

ad. s.

long

Royal is a much larger bird than Sandwich Tern (left)

juv.

white forecrown

ad. w.

ad. winter

pale grey

large, orange

ad. summer

LESSER CRESTED TERN

1st-winter

pale

ad. Lesser Crested (foreground) with ad. Sandwich Tern

weaker pattern than Royal

centre of rump greyer and tail darker than on 1st-w. Royal

grey

ad. winter

upperwing more obviously two-toned than on Royal Tern, fresh primaries almost silvery

ad. w.

darker grey than Royal

comparatively slender

eye-ring usually more pronounced than on juv. Royal

juv.

grey rump and uppertail

ad. summer

KM

Sooty Tern *Sterna fuscata* V∗∗∗

L 42–45 cm (incl. tail-streamers 7–10 on ad.), WS 72–80 cm. Breeds on islands in southern oceans and tropical waters, e.g. S Red Sea, Persian Gulf, and West Indies. Outside breeding, leads a partly pelagic life, rather like a skua. Rare vagrant to treated region, most often to W Europe and in summer.

IDENTIFICATION *Black-and-white* plumage, *dark rump, long, narrow and pointed wings* and *long, deeply forked tail* narrow choice down to this species and Bridled Tern (which see for comparison). Sooty Tern is *larger* (almost of Sandwich Tern size), with a proportionately *somewhat heavier head* and *longer bill*. Wings are slightly broader, and flight more powerful and steady (Bridled more narrow-winged with lighter flight). Primaries dark below (paler with dark tips on Bridled). – Adult: *Upperparts black* or very nearly black (clearly darker than Bridled, which is brown-grey, though beware of light effects making Sooty appear paler grey or Bridled look dark, too); *white forehead patch broad*, and *black loral stripe narrow at gape*. – Juvenile: Plumage largely sooty-grey, only lower belly whitish, and upperparts and upperwing-coverts having *white tips forming bars*. In flight recalls oversized, long-winged Black Tern, but note whitish lower belly (dark grey on Black) and dusky 'armpits' (light on Black). – Variation: Breeders of West Indies and S Atlantic (ssp. *fuscata*) have pure white underparts and underwing-coverts; breeders in Indian and Pacific Oceans (*nubilosa*) have a light grey wash below in fresh plumage.

VOICE Vagrants mainly silent, but occasionally utters very characteristic 'ker-**wack**i-wack'.

Bridled Tern *Sterna anaethetus* V∗∗∗

L 37–42 cm (incl. tail-streamers 8–10 on ad.), WS 65–72 cm. Breeding areas include Caribbean, Mauritania, Red Sea and Persian Gulf. Habits similar to Sooty Tern's. Scarce vagrant to treated region, most often in summer.

IDENTIFICATION *Dark upperparts*—including rump and *deeply forked tail*—distinctive, shared only by similar Sooty Tern, but at long range White-cheeked Tern can be similar. Compared with Sooty, size and structure more like Common Tern, with narrow wings, long tail and rather small head, and *flight* often appears more *elegant and light*. – Adult: *White forehead patch narrow*, extending behind eye in a *sharp point*, and *bold black loral stripe*; pale collar on some (but can be absent; invariably lacking on Sooty); *upperparts paler, brown-grey*, with contrasting darker flight-feathers (at long range recalling adult Long-tailed Skua) and white outer tail-feathers (on Sooty, upperparts and upperwing uniform blackish, but beware effects of light making Sooty appear paler greyish, or Bridled look very dark). – Juvenile: Basic

pattern similar to adult, including whitish throat and breast, and whitish underwing with thin dark trailing edge, but head pattern less clear-cut, tail lacks obvious white outer feathers, and upperparts are either fringed buff, giving obvious scaly pattern, or darker and almost plain (1st-year Sooty quite different: sooty-grey on throat and breast, and sooty-black above, distinctly barred or spotted white).

VOICE Vagrants mainly silent.

White-cheeked Tern *Sterna repressa* —

L 32–34 cm, WS 58–63 cm. Breeds in Red Sea, S Sinai and in N Indian Ocean. Summer visitor (mainly Apr–Oct). Occasional in Gulf of Aqaba (Eilat).

IDENTIFICATION Rather similar to Common Tern, except slightly *longer bill*, narrower wings, and often more elegant, bouncing flight. – Adult summer: Like Common Tern, having black-tipped red bill, but: *darker grey above*; *grey rump and tail* concolorous with back; *darker grey underbody* with a clear contrast with *white cheeks* (recalling Whiskered Tern); whole *underwing has broad, diffuse, grey trailing edge*, contrasting with greyish-white underwing-coverts (often lightest along midwing-panel). – 1st-year: Like Common Tern, but juvenile usually more strongly marked dark above, and *rump/uppertail grey as back*; *plainer, more uniform grey upperwing* than on Common, with less obvious secondary bar (above) and, from most angles, a rather pale silvery-grey sheen on the primaries; bill soon becomes all black. Told from rather similar young Whiskered Tern by *longer, strongly forked tail*, and *longer bill* and longer, narrower wings.

VOICE Similar to that of Common Tern.

Forster's Tern *Sterna forsteri* V∗∗

L 33–36 cm (incl. tail-streamers *c.* 7½ on ad.), WS 64–70 cm. North American species. Vagrant to W Europe; in Britain & Ireland about one record annually.

IDENTIFICATION Size and shape much as Common Tern, except *slightly larger head, more wedge-shaped, conical bill*, *longer legs*, and *longer tail-streamers* extending well beyond wing-tips on perched adults. – Adult summer: Much as Common Tern, with orange-red black-tipped bill, but note: *tail centred pale grey*, leaving only rump pure white; *all primaries frosty-white above* (lacking dark outer wedge of Common); and *white underbody*. – Adult winter: *White crown*, leaving only a *prominent black 'mask'* around eye and on ear-coverts, and black bill, recalling Gull-billed Tern. Upperwing-coverts all grey, lacking dark carpal bar of winter Common Tern. (European records mainly in winter, so worth careful check of any tern in this season. Beware pitfall of distant adult winter Sandwich Tern, which has frosty-grey primaries Nov–Mar.) – 1st-year: Compared with young Common Tern, less contrasting dark wing and tail markings (lacks obvious carpal bar), and outer primaries only slightly darker than on adult, especially at tip; when perched, *dark-centred tertials* often obvious. As with adult, *heavy-based, long and pointed bill* useful clue. Overall whiteness and front-heavy, short-tailed look in flight recall Sandwich Tern, but Forster's has more distinct dark tips to outer primaries, bolder, more discrete 'mask', and reddish legs.

VOICE Call a rolling, slightly harsh 'kreerr', somewhat recalling Black-headed Gull.

Bridled Tern   White-cheeked Tern

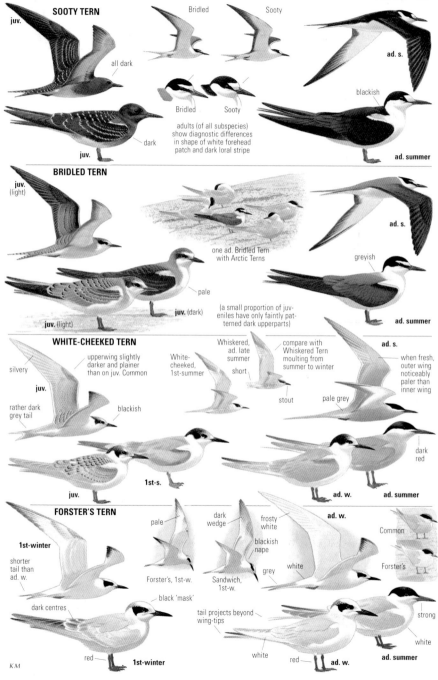

SOOTY TERN

juv.

all dark

dark

juv.

Bridled   Sooty

Bridled   Sooty

adults (of all subspecies) show diagnostic differences in shape of white forehead patch and dark loral stripe

ad. s.

blackish

ad. summer

BRIDLED TERN

juv. (light)

one ad. Bridled Tern with Arctic Terns

pale

juv. (dark)

juv. (light)

(a small proportion of juveniles have only faintly patterned dark upperparts)

ad. s.

greyish

ad. summer

WHITE-CHEEKED TERN

silvery

upperwing slightly darker and plainer than on juv. Common

juv.

rather dark grey tail

blackish

juv.

1st-s.

Whiskered, ad. late summer

White-cheeked, 1st-summer

short

stout

compare with Whiskered Tern moulting from summer to winter

pale grey

ad. s.

when fresh, outer wing noticeably paler than inner wing

dark red

ad. w.   ad. summer

FORSTER'S TERN

1st-winter

shorter tail than ad. w.

dark centres

red   **1st-winter**

pale

Forster's, 1st-w.

dark wedge

blackish nape

Sandwich, 1st-w.

black 'mask'

tail projects beyond wing-tips

white   red   ad. w.

frosty white

grey

white

ad. w.

Common

Forster's

strong

white

ad. summer

KM

MARSH TERNS *Chlidonias*

The three 'marsh terns' *Chlidonias* differ from 'sea terns' *Sterna* in their lazier flight with more banking from side to side (sea terns have generally firmer wingbeats and steadier, more direct flight). Marsh terns also differ in having slightly shorter and broader wings and less forked tail than the sea terns. The marsh terns feed by dipping down to the water surface to take insects (only occasionally plunging more deeply after fish, etc.), or by catching insects in the air with agile, hawking flight. They do not hover-and-dive after fish like sea terns, but note that sea terns—especially immatures—will also dip-feed or hawk insects in the manner of marsh terns. Marsh terns breed in loose colonies in shallow freshwater or marshy habitats. On migration they also frequent coasts or large, open inland waters.

Black Tern *Chlidonias niger*   P4

L 22–26 cm, WS 56–62 cm. Commonest marsh tern, breeding in freshwater marshes with patches of low, floating vegetation, often among Black-headed Gulls for protection. Summer visitor (mainly late Apr–Sep), winters in Africa. In Britain & Ireland, occasional large migrant gatherings or coastal passage, but seldom numerous.

IDENTIFICATION Adult summer: All-black head and body, rather *uniform dark grey upperparts*, white undertail, and dark legs and bill; head and underparts mottled or patched with white on moulting adults in spring (before May) and summer/autumn (white feathers on head already appearing in Jun). – Adult winter (head and body plumage fully acquired Sep onwards): Much as juvenile, but *upperparts plain grey*, lacking scaliness, and *outer 5–7 primaries darker than rest*. – Juvenile: *Extensive black cap* and *obvious dark breast-side patches*; scaly pattern on darkish saddle and wing-coverts; darker carpal and secondary bars; and outer primaries not contrastingly darker than inner. Could be mistaken for juvenile Common/Arctic Tern, but note smaller size, *shorter, less forked tail*, slightly *shorter wings*, and dark breast-side patches; mode of flight (cf. above under 'Marsh terns') also good clue. – 1st-summer (usually stays in winter range): Variable; like adult winter but usually differing in having darker, more worn outer primaries and darker secondaries, and on some a few scattered dark feathers on underbody and head (these safely told only in May–Jun from moulting ad.).

VOICE Flight-call a harsh, almost multisyllabic 'k'shlet' (slightly recalling Little Tern), and short, nasal 'klit' and 'klee-a'. Alarm-call energetic 'ki-ki-ki...', or a shrill 'kyeh'.

White-winged Tern *Chlidonias leucopterus*   V*

L 20–24 cm, WS 50–56 cm. A rarer and more easterly relative of Black Tern, breeding in similar habitat. Summer visitor (May–Sep), winters in Africa. Vagrant to Britain & Ireland, 10–40 records annually.

IDENTIFICATION Structure subtly different from Black Tern: bill shorter, legs longer, wings broader, and tail only faintly notched. – Adult summer: *White forewing* (diffusely demarcated); *white rump*; contrasting *black saddle and underwing-coverts*; and *bright red legs*; moulting adults have white-mottled head and underparts as Black Tern, but are easily told by their retained *black underwing-coverts*. – Adult winter (head and body plumage fully acquired Sep onwards): Told from Black Tern by *whiter crown* and *lack of breast-side patches*; *whitish-grey rump and tail-sides*; and (at least while still in Europe) *narrower dark leading edge to outer wing* (only 1–4 outer primaries darker than rest), and often *some black retained on underwing-coverts*. – Juvenile/1st-winter: Told from Black Tern by *lack of dark breast-side patches*, and from late summer by *more white on forecrown*; *brownish-black saddle contrasting strongly* with *pale grey inner wing* and *white rump* (though beware of some Black Terns with pale saddle and very pale grey rump); tertials and rear scapulars rather plain (tipped pale on Black); *tail pale grey with white sides*. At first glance can look surprisingly like young Little Gull before different shape and upperpart plumage become apparent. – 1st-summer: As for Black Tern.

VOICE Lower-pitched and often harsher than Black Tern's: conversational, soft 'kek'; and typical rasping 'chr-re', recalling Grey Partridge (and Little Tern) in tone.

Whiskered Tern *Chlidonias hybridus*   V**

L 24–28 cm, WS 57–63 cm. Breeds at lakes, rivers and marshes. Summer visitor (late Apr–Sep), winters in Africa, locally Mediterranean Sea. Vagrant to Britain & Ireland.

IDENTIFICATION Larger, longer-legged and often *stronger-billed* than other marsh terns, and flight action less 'nimble'; plumage can recall Common/Arctic Tern, so *shallow tail-fork* and *greyish rump and tail* important to note. – Adult summer: *Breast and belly dark grey*, contrasting strongly with *white cheek and underwing-coverts*; bill dark red; legs red. Can look quite pale at long range. – Adult winter: Rear crown finely streaked black, and a *solid black patch behind eye*; told from Black Tern by *dark smudge at breast-sides being faint or lacking*, from White-winged Tern by *plainer upperwing* lacking any contrastingly darker outer primaries. – Juvenile: Could be overlooked as White-winged Tern, but note: *broader wings*; often *stronger bill*; *pale grey rump and tail* (latter usually with thin dark end-band); *faint or no carpal bar*; *more coarse, black-spotted and scaly pattern on saddle*. From juvenile Common/Arctic Tern by: *grey rump and tail*; *paler wings*; and *contrasting saddle*. From juvenile Arctic also by *darkish secondaries*. – 1st-winter (head and body plumage moulted early Jul–mid Sep): Much as adult winter except juvenile wings (with dark secondaries) and tail retained. – 1st-summer: As for Black Tern.

VOICE Flight-call is a dry, harsh, rasping 'cherk' (or 'krche'), almost recalling Corncrake in tone.

Black Tern

White-winged Tern

Whiskered Tern

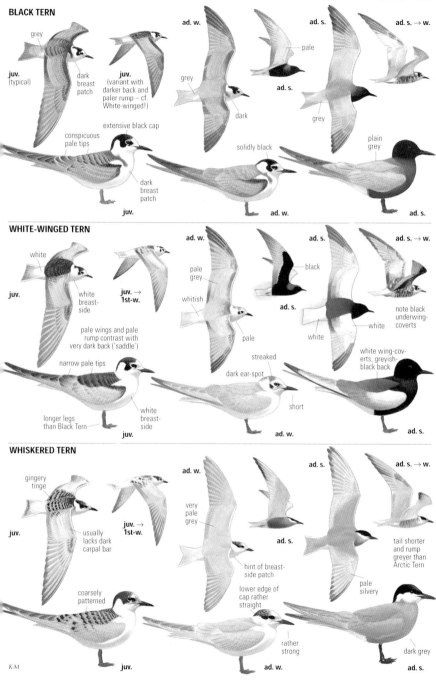

BLACK TERN

grey

juv. (typical)

dark breast patch

juv. (variant with darker back and paler rump – cf. White-winged!)

extensive black cap

conspicuous pale tips

dark breast patch

ad. w.

grey

dark

ad. s.

pale

ad. s.

ad. s. → w.

grey

plain grey

solidly black

juv.

ad. w.

ad. s.

WHITE-WINGED TERN

white

white breast-side

juv.

juv. → 1st-w.

pale wings and pale rump contrast with very dark back ('saddle')

narrow pale tips

longer legs than Black Tern

white breast-side

juv.

ad. w.

pale grey

whitish

pale

ad. s.

black

ad. s.

white

ad. s. → w.

note black underwing-coverts

white

streaked

dark ear-spot

short

white wing-coverts, greyish-black back

ad. w.

ad. s.

WHISKERED TERN

gingery tinge

juv.

usually lacks dark carpal bar

juv. → 1st-w.

coarsely patterned

juv.

ad. w.

very pale grey

ad. s.

hint of breast-side patch

lower edge of cap rather straight

rather strong

ad. w.

ad. s.

ad. s. → w.

tail shorter and rump greyer than Arctic Tern

pale silvery

dark grey

ad. s.

KM

AUKS *Alcidae*

Black and white, medium-large or rather small marine birds, which come to land only to breed. Body elongated, with webbed feet placed far back; wings rather small and narrow. The 'penguins of the Northern Hemisphere', they dive skilfully to catch fish and crustaceans. Dive from surface with a flick of wings and 'fly' under water, using feet for steering. They practically always fly close to the water, with rapid, whirring wing-beats, in small 'trains' of several birds in closely spaced line. Winter at sea, more commonly seen at coasts during and after gales. Nest on cliff-ledge or in crevice.

An auk opens its wings and dives with typical flick.

'Train' of auks flying close to the water with rapid wingbeats. Here a Razorbill (last in line) and three Guillemots.

Little Auk (Dovekie) *Alle alle* W4

L 19–21 cm, WS 34–38 cm. Arctic species, breeding in huge colonies on coastal mountainsides, in places far from sea; winters south to North Sea. In N Britain, regular winter visitor, rare on other coasts, usually after gales. Often migrates and dives closer to land than its relatives. Food primarily planktonic. Nests in a crevice or under boulders in scree.

IDENTIFICATION *Very small*, appears only half size of Puffin, almost like small wader. *Bill very short* and stubby. Scapulars edged white. Flight light, more prone to veer than its relatives. Usually floats very low between dives, wings dragging; otherwise swims higher, with wings tucked in; may stretch neck. Takes off freely and without splash. Most obvious risk of confusion is with 1st-year Puffin because of latter's rather small, dark bill and fairly small size and similar *dark underwing*: best distinguished by *c*.50% smaller size; *moth-quick, whirring wingbeats* where individual beats difficult to discern; somewhat narrower and *more backswept wings*, which appear central on body; white trailing edge to secondaries; smaller head; and lack of complete dark breast-band. Confusion with the larger auks possible, too, if observation is only fleeting and angle of view

poor; usually the whirring, quick wingbeats are obvious, but note also the grey (all-blackish looking) underwing.

VOICE Noisy at colonies, mostly silent elsewhere. Twittering, chattering notes turning into a laughter, 'krrii-ek ak ak ak ak', merge into a buzzing chorus. Alarm given on wing, a whinnying 'huhuhuhuhu...'.

(Atlantic) Puffin *Fratercula arctica* m(r)B2

L 28–34 cm, WS 50–60 cm. Nests colonially in burrows on grassy, steep slopes by coastal cliffs. Common near colonies; winters farther out to sea than other auks.

IDENTIFICATION Adult summer: *Parrot-like, huge, colourful bill*. At close range, unmistakable combination of bill, *large, pale, rounded 'cheek patch'* and dark unbroken breast-band. Floats high. Appears 60% the size of Guillemot. At distance in flight, told from that by *shorter, thicker body*; *larger, rounder head, pale in summer*; rather *dark underwing* (some greyish-white visible at close range); lack of white trailing edge to arm; rump lacks white sides; 'stern' short, giving impression of *wings placed far back on body*; and orange feet often surprisingly obvious. – Adult winter: Bill smaller, eye-surround dark greyish. – Juvenile / 1st-winter: Resembles adult winter, but bill much smaller and darker; can be confused with Little Auk (which see).

VOICE Deep, grunting 'arrr-uh' etc., mostly uttered from burrow.

Black Guillemot *Cepphus grylle* r(m)B3

L 32–38 cm, WS 49–58 cm. Nests among boulders and in rock crevices, singly or in small, loose colonies. In Ireland and NW Britain fairly common; mainly sedentary.

IDENTIFICATION Clearly smaller than Guillemot, slightly larger than Puffin. Bill pointed, black. Head rather small, body plump and pot-bellied, appears pear-shaped. Flight close above water with *quick, whirring wingbeats*; *stern-heavy*. – Adult summer: *All black with large oval upperwing patches*; underwing largely pure white. Feet red. Heavy 'stern' together with rapid wingbeats immediately rules out drake Velvet Scoter (p. 64), even when long range makes different assessment of white wing patches difficult to see. – Adult winter: Very different, with *white underparts* and variable *white barring above*. In flight, superficially resembles a winter grebe, but told by shape, mode of flight, still obvious oval white upperwing patches, and extensively white underwing and rump area. – Juvenile / 1st-winter: Light wing patch profusely barred dark; head, breast and rump usually duskier than on adult. – 1st-summer: Black body like adult, but barring on wing patch retained, some birds more extensively and making wing look dark. (A rare all-black adult variety, *'motzfeldi'*, occurs in far N.)

VOICE Displaying ♂♂ call with a series of very fine pipit-like notes, 'sipp-sipp-sipp-...'. Sometimes a similar but scraping version is heard, 'sipp-sü-sipp-sü-sipp-sü...'. Also to be heard are very fine, drawn-out piping 'seeeeeeuu' calls.

Little Auk   Puffin   Black Guillemot

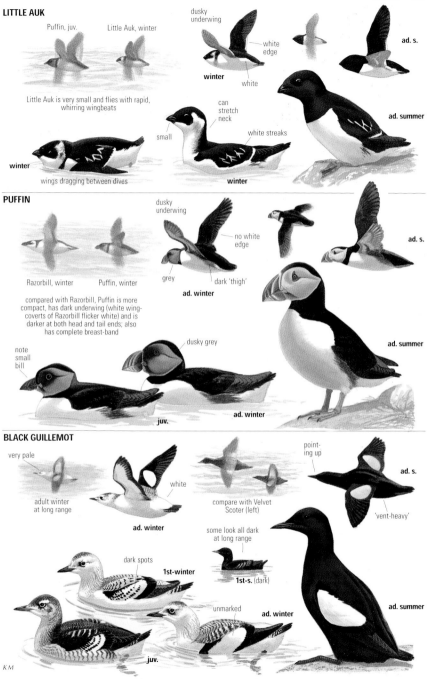

LITTLE AUK

Puffin, juv.

Little Auk, winter

Little Auk is very small and flies with rapid, whirring wingbeats

dusky underwing

white edge

winter

white

ad. s.

ad. summer

can stretch neck

small

white streaks

winter

wings dragging between dives

winter

PUFFIN

Razorbill, winter

Puffin, winter

compared with Razorbill, Puffin is more compact, has dark underwing (white wing-coverts of Razorbill flicker white) and is darker at both head and tail ends; also has complete breast-band

dusky underwing

no white edge

grey

dark 'thigh'

ad. winter

ad. s.

ad. summer

note small bill

dusky grey

juv.

ad. winter

BLACK GUILLEMOT

very pale

adult winter at long range

ad. winter

white

compare with Velvet Scoter (left)

some look all dark at long range

1st-s. (dark)

point-ing up

ad. s.

'vent-heavy'

dark spots

1st-winter

unmarked

ad. winter

juv.

ad. summer

K M

(Common) Guillemot *Uria aalge* r+m**B**1

L 38–46 cm (excl. exposed feet *c.* 4), WS 61–73 cm. Commonest auk in British Isles. Nests on bare, narrow cliff-ledge on steep coastal cliffs, in often large colonies. Single egg laid directly on ledge, pear-shaped to prevent rolling off, incubated by bird standing up. Parents recognize egg by pattern and young by voice. Young jumps from cliff when three weeks old, still not fledged, tended at sea by ♂ alone.

IDENTIFICATION Head and upperparts brownish, underparts white. Percentage of distinctive 'bridled' variety (see plate) increases towards north. At close range *slender, pointed bill* obvious. Greatest risk of confusion with Brünnich's Guillemot (which see), but much more common problem is to distinguish Guillemot from Razorbill at long range, when bill shape becomes surprisingly difficult to see. Guillemot has *paler greyish-brown upperparts* (Razorbill appearing almost black); difference obvious in W Europe (esp. small race *albionis* of S Britain is pale), less obvious but still present in N Norway. Also, Guillemot is *slightly larger* than Razorbill— in mixed 'trains' Guillemots are usually longer-bodied (but beware of variation, and in winter larger birds from the north may in some areas mix with smaller in the south). Variable amount of *dark streaking on flanks*, in 'wingpits' and on underwing-coverts, but some populations (e.g. S Britain and Baltic) average less streaked and some unstreaked (Razorbill always pure white). Further, flying Guillemot usually told by *wide, dark brown rump area, generally with uneven border to narrow white rump-sides* (Razorbill has narrower, black central rump band, broadly and evenly bordered pure white in Long-tailed Duck fashion); feet projecting beyond tip of short tail, giving *'untidy' end to stern* (feet tucked neatly beneath tail on Razorbill); slightly *hunchbacked outline* (Razorbill appears straighter-backed); and wings set a trifle ahead of centre (wings appear central on Razorbill). – Adult winter: Amount of white on side of head varies, just as on Razorbill, but Guillemot generally appears *more white-headed*. Acquires summer plumage early, (Nov) Dec–Feb, and can then be distinguished from 1st-winters, which moult later. – 1st-summer: Like adult, except variable amount of white on throat, and retained juvenile flight-feathers much faded, brownish.

VOICE Vocal in colony, e.g. 'stomach-rumbling' 'mmm...'; hard and nasal notes repeated in staccato, 'ha ha ha ha...', turning into prolonged bellowing '...ha-aahr', etc. Young give high-pitched, disyllabic 'plee-ü' after leaving nest.

Brünnich's Guillemot *Uria lomvia* V**

L 40–44 cm (excl. exposed feet *c.* 4), WS 64–75 cm. Arctic species. Nest site and breeding much as Guillemot (though selects narrower ledges on average), often in mixed colonies. Winters south to C Norway; rare vagrant to British Isles.

IDENTIFICATION Told from Guillemot by *shorter, stouter bill* with pronounced gonydeal angle (but beware some variation in Guillemot); usually obvious *whitish line along upper edge of gape* (but note that exceptional Guillemots have hint of pale gape streak); *lack of obvious dark streaking on flanks* (a few have faint streaks low down); in summer, *white comes to sharp point on foreneck* (not rounded as on Guillemot). At longer range, flying birds can generally be separated from Guillemots by *slightly shorter body and more tucked-in neck* (valid only at breeding sites; in winter, comparison with smaller W European Guillemot *albionis* may be necessary, giving reversed size difference); *darker, almost blackish upperparts* with *broader white sides to black rump*, more *round-backed and pot-bellied outline*, and largely white 'wingpits'. At distance in flight, Razorbill-like impression because of blackish upperparts and similar rump pattern, but Brünnich's told by slightly larger size, *shorter tail* and projecting feet, *round-backed outline, and pointed bill held inclined downwards*. – Adult winter: Wholly dark ear-coverts with no white behind eye. Greatest identification pitfall juvenile/1st-winter Razorbill, dark birds of which can have head pattern close to that of Brünnich's and a considerably weaker and more pointed bill than adult Razorbill; they are smaller, however, and usually have at least some white visible around ear-coverts and behind eye. – 1st-summer: Same differences as for Guillemot.

VOICE Calls are similar to Guillemot's, but tone is harder, 'meaner' and more crow-like.

Razorbill *Alca torda* m(r)**B**2

L 38–43 cm, WS 60–69 cm. Breeds on steep coastal cliffs, preferring broader, sheltered ledges; also among boulders or in burrows. Will accept lower rocks and islets if sufficiently remote.

IDENTIFICATION Distinctive combination of *deep, blunt bill*, flattened laterally, *black with white lines*; blackish upperparts (always blacker than Guillemot, but difference subtle in far N); powerful neck; long, pointed tail; and consistently *smaller size* than Guillemot at breeding sites (difference slightest in England and France). Bill shape surprisingly difficult to use when watching flying birds at some range. Concentrate on blacker upperparts, *straighter back, whiter underwing* and 'wingpit', and *more neatly defined white rump-sides*. Long tail covers feet, whereas these generally visible at rear end on guillemots. See also Guillemot and Brünnich's Guillemot for detailed comparisons. – Adult summer: White line across tip of bill; white loral line. – Adult winter: Generally retains white bill line but lacks loral. – 1st-winter: Lacks white bill line (but often has hint of loral) and has *considerably weaker and more pointed bill*. At least has a small white smudge behind eye on ear-coverts. – 1st-summer: Same differences as for Guillemot.

VOICE Rather silent. Very deep, creaking 'urrr' heard from breeding birds.

Guillemot Brünnich's Guillemot Razorbill

GUILLEMOT

ad. winter

dusky 'armpit'

brown

restricted white on sides

long, pointed

rounded

('bridled' variety)

ad. s.

ad. s.

long, pointed

projecting feet

ad. ♂ escorting unfledged young

variably streaked flanks

1st-winter

long

white

ad. winter

albionis (W Europe)

aalge (N Europe)

BRÜNNICH'S GUILLEMOT

ad. winter

white 'armpit'

blackish

much white on sides

white gape stripe

point

ad. s.

short, strong, down-curved culmen

compact and 'neckless', slightly hunchbacked ('flying barrel'), bill somewhat pointing down

projecting feet

ad. s.

un-streaked flanks

ad. summer

1st-winter

short, small

dark

ad. winter

RAZORBILL

ad. winter

white 'armpit'

black

much white on sides

blunt

feet tucked beneath long tail

ad. s.

short, deep, blunt

ad. ♂ escorting unfledged young

long tail, often raised

ad. summer

1st-winter

small

white

ad. winter

KM

SANDGROUSE *Pteroclididae*
Medium-sized birds with small head, short neck and sturdy, compact body. Closely related to pigeons and waders, but also have partridge-like traits. Fast, strong flyers with long, pointed wings. Some species have pointed tail projections. Inhabit mostly deserts or arid plains. Flocks seen visiting freshwater sources in morning or evening, flying long distances to reach these. Partly nomadic in dry season, but details poorly known. Lay 2–3 eggs directly on ground.

Black-bellied Sandgrouse *Pterocles orientalis* —
L 30–35 cm. Breeds on poorly vegetated level plains; ascends to higher levels, is not so dependent on warm conditions as most congeners. Visits waterholes mostly in morning, sometimes flying tens of miles. Wary and often shy.

  IDENTIFICATION Big and *sturdy*, with *rather broad wings* and *distended silhouette*. Immediately told by *large black belly patch* on both sexes (but at long range can therefore recall Golden Plover, also suggested by golden-brown upperwing and rapid, straight flight on long, pointed wings). Strong contrast below between black remiges and white coverts. – ♂: *Unmarked greyish breast patch*. Rusty-yellow throat with black centre. Upperparts densely covered with large rusty-yellow spots. – ♀: *Yellow-brown breast patch finely spotted black*. Upperparts finely vermiculated.

  VOICE Flight-call a rolling or bubbling '**chürrr`r**'re-ka', slowing down at end (final syllable lower), at close range with a musical overtone, at distance roughly like a snorting horse (and then blurred into 'cheurrr`r'). On rising sometimes a high 'chiiu', almost like Little Owl's call.

Pin-tailed Sandgrouse *Pterocles alchata* —
L 28–32 cm (plus tail projection 2–10), WS 55–63 cm. Breeds on open, dry lowland plains, sandy uncultivable tracts or dried-out lake beds and river mouths. Visits waterholes in morning. May be seen in flocks of thousands.

  IDENTIFICATION Smaller and slimmer than Black-bellied Sandgrouse. *Long, narrow tail projection* (longest on adult ♂). *Belly and underwing-coverts white*, contrasting strongly with black remiges. Both sexes have *black loral stripe* and black-framed breast patch. – ♂: *Wing-coverts golden-green* with narrow black cross-bars, shoulders and back have rounded yellow-green spots. *Narrow black bib*. Crown, nape and neck band plain olive-green. *Breast patch reddish-brown*. – ♀: Like ♂ but has *less greenish and more black-vermiculated wing-coverts*, densely black-vermiculated crown and nape, *whitish chin, two black bands between throat and breast* (♂ only one), and paler brown breast patch.

  VOICE In flight a hard grating, descending 'rrreh-a' (nasal; at distance vaguely recalls Mediterranean Gull).

Spotted Sandgrouse *Pterocles senegallus* —
L 29–33 cm (plus tail projection 3–6). Like Crowned Sandgrouse, breeds in flat, desert-like, stony terrain at lower levels. Visits waterholes in morning, in often large flocks.

  IDENTIFICATION Medium-sized, pale yellow-buff sandgrouse with protracted, attenuated rear body and *narrow tail projection*. In flight, *secondaries are contrastingly black below* (primaries, however, diffusely paler). A narrow black patch down belly-centre. – ♂: Crown, nape and breast light blue-grey, *throat, cheeks and neck-sides bright orange*. – ♀: Rather like ♂ Crowned, but has *tail projection*, more *buff ground colour* and *sparser spotting above*. Finely *dark-streaked across breast*, also on crown and hindneck.

  VOICE Flight-call in chorus from flocks visiting waterholes a disyllabic, sharp 'ku**itt**-o' (akin to Lichtenstein's), sometimes preceded by a monosyllabic 'kvi'.

Crowned Sandgrouse *Pterocles coronatus* —
L 25–29 cm. Breeds at lower levels in deserts and semi-deserts and on dry, stony plains with sparse vegetation. Visits waterholes normally only in morning. Not over-shy.

  IDENTIFICATION Between Lichtenstein's and Spotted Sandgrouse in size and plumage. In flight, *blackish remiges* contrast with paler coverts both above and below. – ♂: *Plain pinky-grey below*. Head- and neck-sides pale orange. A white-edged *black vertical mark on chin and forehead*, with white around eye. Crown-sides blue-grey and crown-centre reddish-brown. Upperwings have *dull yellow drop-shaped spots*. – ♀: Densely *spot-barred with black* (thus like Lichtenstein's), but has almost *unmarked buff-white throat*.

  VOICE Flight-call a (four- or) five-syllable, rather hard, somewhat nasal 'chu-ku chu-ku-kurr' with jolting rhythm.

Lichtenstein's Sandgrouse *Pterocles lichtensteinii* —
L 22–25 cm. Within the region breeds in S Morocco, Sinai and S Israel in wadis and flatter mountain tracts in barren or desert-like, stony terrain. Visits waterholes at late dusk, flocks usually small (<50). Vigilant but not really shy.

  IDENTIFICATION Compact, with *dark, densely vermiculated plumage*. Rather tall, and with rear end not so protracted and pointed as on congeners, and walks with tail somewhat more raised. Yellow bare skin around eye. – ♂: *Broad black and white bars on forecrown. Rusty-buff and black bands across lower breast* and greater wing-coverts. Bill orange. – ♀: *Finely vermiculated all over*, without ♂'s head and breast markings. Bill grey.

  VOICE Evening gatherings at waterholes give evocative, full 'ku**itt**(a)l' in chorus; the call has a metallic secondary note. Alarm-call a croaky, noisy, dry and excited 'krre-krre-krre-krre-...', also uttered on rising.

Black-bellied Sandgrouse   Pin-tailed Sandgrouse

Spotted Sandgrouse   Crowned Sandgrouse

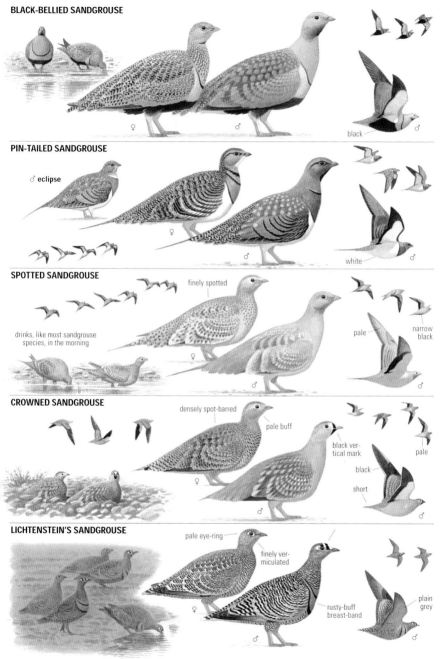

BLACK-BELLIED SANDGROUSE

♀ ♂

black ♂

PIN-TAILED SANDGROUSE

♂ eclipse

♀ ♂

white ♂

SPOTTED SANDGROUSE

finely spotted

drinks, like most sandgrouse
species, in the morning

♀ ♂

pale narrow
black ♂

CROWNED SANDGROUSE

densely spot-barred

pale buff

black ver-
tical mark

pale

black

short

♀ ♂ ♂

LICHTENSTEIN'S SANDGROUSE

pale eye-ring

finely ver-
miculated

rusty-buff
breast-band

plain
grey

♀ ♂ ♂

DZ   drinks late at dusk

PIGEONS and DOVES *Columbidae*
Medium-sized, compact birds with full, rounded breast and small head. Fly rapidly with clipped wingbeats. Can drink with bill lowered in water (can suck up water, unlike other birds). The young are fed on 'pigeon-milk' from the crop.

Rock Dove *Columba livia*   r**B**4
L 30–35 cm, WS 62–68 cm. Breeds in caves and on steep cliffs, mostly on sea coasts but also in mountains. Resident.
   IDENTIFICATION Rather like Stock Dove in plumage and shape, but is *paler grey on back and upperwings* and has *white underwings*. Flight fast and strong. Has *snow-white rump* (light grey in Asia) and *two complete black wing-bars*. Eye reddish, bill dark. In display, glides with wings held in V.
   VOICE Coos like Feral Pigeon, a moaning 'drru**oo**-u', repeated several times, often with faint increase in volume.

Feral Pigeon *Columba livia* (domest.)   r**B**2
L 29–35 cm, WS 60–68 cm. City pigeons (gone wild from pigeon-houses) originate from the wild Rock Dove. Widespread and abundant in towns and cities, breeding on ledges of buildings and bridges, in attics, etc. Resident.
   IDENTIFICATION Identical to Rock Dove in shape, and some of the numerous plumage variants are also exactly the same as latter (see above); other variants are e.g. variegated white and grey, all dark grey, reddish-grey, dark piebald, or as Rock but without white rump. Voice as Rock Dove's.

Stock Dove *Columba oenas*   r**B**2
L 28–32 cm, WS 60–66 cm. Breeds in wooded areas, forest edge and larger, undisturbed parks with mature oaks and other deciduous trees which provide nest holes, locally also on rocky coasts or buildings. Rather shy. Nests in cavities.
   IDENTIFICATION Rather like a Feral Pigeon in size and shape, thus smaller and *shorter-tailed than Wood Pigeon*, this obvious in mixed flocks in flight. Somewhat more vigorous flight with *faster flicking beats* than Wood Pigeon (though difference not great). Plumage blue-grey with shimmering green and vinous neck patch. In flight, shows *grey underwings* (Rock Dove and Feral Pigeon largely white) and *paler blue-grey back and wing-covert panel above*. Small black wing patches near body (cf. Rock Dove). Sexes and ages similar. Flight display with slow, deep beats followed by glide on slightly raised wings.
   VOICE Song a rather monotonous series of disyllabic, hollow moaning '**ooo**-ue' notes, weaker at start of series.

(Common) **Wood Pigeon** *Columba palumbus* r**B**1/**W**+**P**1
L 38–43 cm, WS 68–77 cm. Breeds in woods (esp. in arable farmland areas), parks and gardens, even in city centres.

Forages on grass lawns and fields. Has increased greatly, and also become less shy, in Britain and N Europe. Resident in Britain & Ireland, where large numbers also visit in winter from N and E Europe, with flocks 1000-strong seen in October. Nest a simple platform of sticks in tree.
   IDENTIFICATION The largest pigeon, *clearly bigger than Feral Pigeon* and with proportionately somewhat longer tail and smaller head, and is also fuller-breasted but nonetheless *more elongated*. Best identified by *large white patch on neck-side* and in flight a *white transverse band on upperwing*. In flight, differs from Stock Dove also in somewhat *slower wingbeats*, larger size and marginally *longer tail*. Sexes alike. Typical flight display with short steep climb, a few loud wing-claps and downward-sloping glide on stiff wings and with spread tail. – Juvenile: Lacks white neck patches (usually acquired Aug–Dec).
   VOICE Clattering wing noise on take-off serves as alarm-call. During breeding season often a hollow, hoarse, stifled, growling 'hooh-hrooo...'. Song a five-syllable, hollow cooing with characteristic rhythm (first syllable emphasized, slightly longer pause before short fifth), '**dooh**-doo, daaw-daaw...doo'; the phrase is repeated 3–5 times without pause (which results in the short final syllable appearing to begin the next series).

Trocaz Pigeon *Columba trocaz*   —
L 42–45 cm. Breeds in Madeira (<2500 pairs) in caves and on rocky mountain slopes in the tree-heath and laurel zone. Resident. Shy. Feeds at lower levels.
   IDENTIFICATION Looks like a big, short-winged Wood Pigeon without white markings but with *silver-grey neck patch*. *Rump dark*, as back. *Underwing dark grey* (cf. Rock Dove). Pale eye. Song as Wood Pigeon's but weaker.

Bolle's Pigeon *Columba bollii*   —
L 37–40 cm. Rare breeder in Canary Islands (Palma, Gomera, Tenerife) in laurel forests on mountain slopes; nest often in tree. Resident. Shy, hard to observe when perched.
   IDENTIFICATION Looks like a *very dark* Wood Pigeon without white markings. Rather short, rounded wings. Rapid flight. *Grey plumage* with *contrastingly dark flight-feathers*. Tail long, *banded dark and light*, often held closed (looks square-ended). Song a soft four-syllable, hoarse cooing.

Laurel Pigeon *Columba junoniae*   —
L 40–43 cm. Breeds in Canaries (Palma, Gomera, Tenerife) in or immediately below the tree-heath and laurel zone on rocky mountain slopes. Resident. Often seen flying singly or in pairs. Wary, but not really shy.
   IDENTIFICATION *Uniform dark brown* (with metallic gloss) *without contrast between coverts and remiges*, but with head/neck pale grey and with *paler grey rump/upper-tail* and diffuse *buff-white terminal tail-band*. Long-necked and *short-winged* in flight, which is *rather unsteady*, with *slow wingbeats*. Song a hoarse 'hiccuping' cooing.

Rock Dove   Stock Dove   Wood Pigeon

ROCK DOVE

narrow black border — white — light grey

fast, powerful flight

wing-bar

rather narrow

white rump patch

ad.

FERAL PIGEON

vast plumage variation; some look just like wild-origin Rock Dove

STOCK DOVE

contrast

ad.

uniform with grey of head

rather small; stocky build

short wing-bars

blue-grey

broad tail-band

broad dark rear edge

juv.

ad.

WOOD PIGEON

rather plain

large, heavy, rather long-tailed

ad.

broad white transverse bands

grey-white subterminal bar

white

broad black tail-band

juv. lacks white neck patch, but has white wing-bands

juv.

long

ad.

TROCAZ PIGEON

silvery patch

BOLLE'S PIGEON

somewhat smaller and darker than Trocaz Pigeon

LAUREL PIGEON

broad buff-white tail-band

long neck

very dark

pale

KM

(Eurasian) Collared Dove *Streptopelia decaocto* ⌐B2

L 31–34 cm, WS 48–56 cm. Breeds around farmyards and in towns, in parks and gardens wherever there are dense trees for nesting; tends to avoid open, unbroken country; absent from uplands. Invaded Europe from SE in recent decades. Now declining somewhat in N and W. Resident. Food mostly vegetable matter; often spilled grain, frequents grain silos and cultivated fields, in winter often in flocks. Confiding.

IDENTIFICATION A medium-sized, *elongated*, rather 'elegant' dove with *long tail* and pale plumage. Best identified by narrow (white-edged) *black bar across neck-side*. Rather *uniformly pale buff-grey* with somewhat browner tone on back and blue-grey tinge to greater wing-coverts (some variation: some look browner, others more blue-grey). Dark eye contrasts with the uniformly pale head. *Outer tail-feathers broadly tipped white* (obvious in flight, when tail is spread). Closed *tail looks almost all white from below*, contrasting with *ash-grey undertail-coverts*. – Juvenile: No black neck mark, has somewhat duller, browner colours.

VOICE In conflicts and on landing a noisy 'krreair', not unlike Black-headed Gull. Song a trisyllabic coo, repeated a few times, 2nd syllable drawn out and stressed and 3rd lower, 'doo-**doooo**-do', somewhat Cuckoo-like at distance.

(European) Turtle Dove *Streptopelia turtur* mB3

L 25–27 cm, WS 49–55 cm. Breeds in open lowland deciduous woods and copses with rich undergrowth, mainly in agricultural areas, also in more open country with dense shrubbery and isolated trees. Summer visitor (mostly May–Aug), winters S of Sahara. Rather shy and hard to observe closely, keeps well hidden in tree canopy but may be seen at distance on telephone wires and foraging on ground. Heavily hunted on passage through Mediterranean.

IDENTIFICATION Rather small and slim dove with fast, somewhat fitful or slightly pitching flight, e.g. when landing. In practice most like Laughing Dove, but differs in: *bright orange-brown feather edges* and *clearly demarcated black feather centres above* on scapulars and lesser wing-coverts (Laughing darker reddish-brown and almost uniform); *more restricted grey-blue panel in centre of wing*; *longer and more pointed wings* and *somewhat shorter tail*; *narrower white tail-sides* with *complete black inner border*; at close range shows *neck patch of black and white stripes* (the white at times blue-tinged), noticeable *black tail-base below*, and orange eye surrounded by rather distinct, reddish bare skin. (Cf. also Oriental Turtle Dove.) – Juvenile: More uniformly dirty brown and buffy greyish-white, and lacks neck patch. Can be confused with juvenile Collared Dove, but note tail markings.

VOICE Wing-clatter on take-off. Song a deep, hard purring, 'turrrrrr turrrrrr turrrrrr', repeated several times.

Oriental Turtle Dove *Streptopelia orientalis* V***

L 30–35 cm, WS 54–62 cm. Breeds in C Siberian taiga (ssp. *orientalis*), also in SW Siberian forest-steppe and Central Asia (*meena*). Rare vagrant in N and W Europe.

IDENTIFICATION Like Turtle Dove in plumage, but almost always clearly *bigger* and *heavier-built*; in flight can recall a small Wood Pigeon more than a Turtle Dove, with more *loosely flicking beats* and *steadier course*. Adult differs from Turtle Dove in: upperwing feathers have *bigger and more diffusely defined dark grey* (not jet-black) *centres* and narrower and more buffy-brown (not orange-brown) fringes; tends to show two *narrow pale wing-bars* along tips of greater and median coverts; *blue-grey panel on wing darker* and more restricted; *breast darker brownish-pink*; rump more blue-grey; less conspicuous bare facial skin. Tail-tip pale blue-grey and belly greyish-pink (*orientalis*). – Juvenile: Very like juvenile Turtle Dove, but has darker mantle and breast and cruder proportions. – Variation: Ssp. *meena* is a little smaller and has white tail-tip and whiter belly.

VOICE Song hollow and rather throaty: two hoarse notes followed by two somewhat clearer ones, then two hoarse and so on, 'hru-hru oo-oo hru-hru oo-oo...'.

Laughing Dove *Streptopelia senegalensis* [V***]

L 23–26 cm, WS 40–45 cm. Breeds in small woods, plantations (e.g. of date palms) and gardens, often close to houses, also in urban areas so long as vegetation (e.g. lines of trees) exists; typical bird of desert oases (where partly introduced). Resident. Bold. Nests in thick bushes and trees.

IDENTIFICATION A *small and slim*, rather long-tailed and short-winged dove. In the field appears mainly *reddish-brown* at moderate range; close to, shows *blue-grey panel on wings* between dark grey remiges and blotchy red-brown upperparts (blue more extensive than on Turtle Dove), and *all-white undertail* (and belly). *Black and ochre pattern on crop* is diagnostic. In flight rather like Turtle Dove (e.g. similarly patterned uppertail and dark underwing), but told by *more uniformly brown back* (without black feather centres) and usually visibly *slightly longer tail and shorter wings*.

VOICE Song a hollow coo of five short syllables at fast, slightly jolting pace, 3rd and 4th a little higher-pitched and more stressed, 'do-do-**du**-du-do'; several calling in unison in distance can sound almost like Black Grouse cooing.

Namaqua Dove *Oena capensis* —

L 22–26 cm, WS 28–33 cm. Within the region a rare breeder in S Israel; African species. Found by cultivations in semi-desert with acacias and bushes. Often seen on ground.

IDENTIFICATION *Very small and slim. Long black, wedge-shaped tail*. Often flies low with fast, clipped beats. Rusty-brown primary patch (seen in flight). – Adult ♂: *Black forehead, throat and breast.* Belly white. *Bill yellow and red.* – Adult ♀: Lacks black on head and breast. Bill grey with reddish base. – Juvenile: Upperwing-coverts and shoulders coarsely marked in white, buff and dark grey.

Collared Dove

Turtle Dove

Laughing Dove

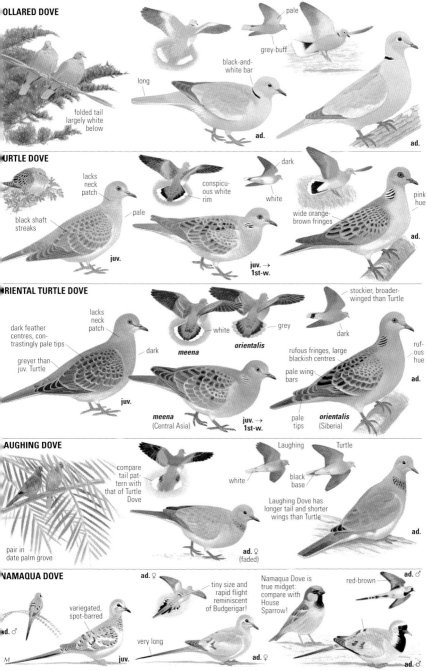

OLLARED DOVE

folded tail largely white below

long

pale

grey-buff

black-and-white bar

ad.

ad.

URTLE DOVE

lacks neck patch

black shaft streaks

pale

juv.

conspicuous white rim

dark

white

juv. → 1st-w.

wide orange-brown fringes

pink hue

ad.

RIENTAL TURTLE DOVE

dark feather centres, contrastingly pale tips

greyer than juv. Turtle

lacks neck patch

dark

juv.

white

meena

orientalis

grey

meena (Central Asia)

juv. → 1st-w.

stockier, broader-winged than Turtle

dark

rufous fringes, large blackish centres

pale wing-bars

pale tips

orientalis (Siberia)

rufous hue

ad.

AUGHING DOVE

pair in date palm grove

compare tail pattern with that of Turtle Dove

white

Laughing

Turtle

black base

Laughing Dove has longer tail and shorter wings than Turtle

ad. ♀ (faded)

ad.

NAMAQUA DOVE

ad. ♂

M

variegated, spot-barred

juv.

ad. ♀

tiny size and rapid flight reminiscent of Budgerigar!

very long

Namaqua Dove is true midget: compare with House Sparrow!

ad. ♀

red-brown

ad. ♂

ad. ♂

CUCKOOS *Cuculidae*
Four breeding species, plus two vagrants from N America. Medium-sized, long-bodied birds with long tail. Short legs. Three of the breeding species are nest parasites.

(Common) Cuckoo *Cuculus canorus* m**B**3
L 32–36 cm, WS 54–60 cm. Seen in all kinds of woodland, farmland, alpine terrain, coastal heath—versatile in habitat choice. Summer visitor (Apr–Sep), winters in tropical Africa. Easy to observe in breeding season, perches in open, call very familiar. Parasitizes various hosts, each ♀ Cuckoo specializing on a certain species, laying mimicking eggs.

IDENTIFICATION Medium-sized, *slim*, with *long, rounded tail* and *pointed wings*. Flies with regular wingbeats (glides uncommon and short), wings mostly *beaten below horizontal plane* (unlike Kestrel and Sparrowhawk); moderate speed; 'straight-backed' posture with *forward-pointing bill*. Often settles right in open on telephone wire or fence post, landing a little clumsily. Perched bird often droops its wings and cocks tail a little. – Adult ♂: Plain blue-grey above and on head and breast; sharp border below against finely dark-barred white belly. Iris, orbital ring, bill-base and feet yellow. – Adult ♀: Two morphs: grey like ♂, but at close range told by rusty-buff tinge and some dark barring on breast; brown morph rusty-brown above and on breast and often has wholly dark-barred plumage. – Juvenile: Slate-grey with ± obvious element of rusty-brown. Best told by *white patch on nape* and *narrow white feather fringes above*.

VOICE Song the familiar disyllabic call with emphasis on first syllable, '**goo**-ko', when excited sometimes trisyllabic. In pursuit-flight often a guttural hoarse 'goch-che-che-che'. ♀ has a loud, rapid bubbling trill, somewhat recalling Little Grebe, 'pühühühühühü...'. Young has a squeaky, uninflected, slightly throaty call, 'psrih', stubbornly repeated; may also be heard from migrating juveniles.

Oriental Cuckoo *Cuculus saturatus* V***
L 30–34 cm. Breeds in taiga and scrubby forest. Arrives at its European breeding grounds mid May–Jun; winters in SE Asia. Insectivorous. Nest parasite.

IDENTIFICATION Very like Cuckoo, and usually hard to separate by appearance alone; close, lengthy observation always essential. Fractionally *smaller* size with *proportionately slightly heavier bill*. Grey morph of both sexes is a shade darker on back and upperwings than Cuckoo (hard to judge in field). Dark barring on white belly basically the same as on Cuckoo, but some have slightly thicker and sparser bars. *Vent often rusty-buff and almost unmarked* (some Cuckoos similar). Under primary coverts often unmarked or with reduced barring (also shown by some

Cuckoos, and is difficult to use in field!). Brown morph (only ♀; common) always entirely and heavily barred, usually with *broader black bars above than red-brown ones* (normally the reverse on ♀ Cuckoo), especially on tail.

VOICE ♂'s song differs clearly from Cuckoo's, is safest way to separate the species: a *fast* series of *equally stressed* paired notes with *Hoopoe-like tone*, usually introduced (e.g. on landing) by stuttering series of 4–8 hoots, '(pupupupupu) pu-pu pu-pu pu-pu pu-pu...'. ♀ has a trill like ♀ Cuckoo's.

Great Spotted Cuckoo *Clamator glandarius* V***
L 35–39 cm. Breeds in savanna-like heathland, often with cork oak or stone pine, also in olive groves and the like. Nest parasite on crows (mostly Magpie). Flies around a lot, frequently hops on ground with raised tail. Food insects.

IDENTIFICATION Size of Cuckoo, but *wings broader and blunter*, and *tail somewhat longer and narrower. Dark above, bestrewn with small white spots*, pale below. – Adult: Primaries dark grey. *Crown and ear-coverts silvery-grey*, hind-crown with hint of crest. Tertials and secondaries broadly tipped white. Throat and breast-sides yellowish-white. – 1st-summer: Variable, usually with *rusty-brown shade on primaries*, also slightly darker head and back than adult. – Juvenile: *Primaries bright rusty-brown, tipped white. Cap dull blackish*. Upperparts blackish with slightly smaller white spots than on adult. Tertials and secondaries with only narrow white tips. Throat and breast ochre-buff.

VOICE Noisy and loud. Usually gives a rattling, cackling call, 'cherr-cherr-che-che-che-che' or 'ki-ki-ki krie-krie-krie...', sometimes recalling Turnstone or alarm of ♀ harrier. When agitated, a nasal, gruff 'cheh'.

Yellow-billed Cuckoo *Coccyzus americanus* V**
L 29–32 cm. Vagrant from N America. Differs from similar Black-billed Cuckoo in *yellowish bill-base*, paler upperparts, brighter rusty colour on primaries and *more obvious white terminal spots on tail-feathers*. Orbital ring yellowish.

Black-billed Cuckoo *Coccyzus erythropthalmus* V***
L 28–31 cm. Very rare vagrant from N America. Told from similar Yellow-billed Cuckoo by grey-based *blackish bill*, darker upperparts, less obvious rusty tone on primaries and *narrower, more obscure pale tips to tail-feathers*. Adult has red orbital ring (juv. yellowish).

Senegal Coucal *Centropus senegalensis* —
L 35–41 cm. Breeds in Egypt in open terrain with bushes and tall grass; occasionally seen in gardens. Resident. Shy, mostly stays hidden in vegetation or runs on ground.

IDENTIFICATION *Big*. Long tail. *Strong, black bill. Wings rusty-brown, rounded*, flight flappy and slow with brief glides. *Head and tail black*, back dark brown, underparts buff-white. – Juvenile: Dark-barred above.

VOICE A series of bubbling, hollow notes, like pouring a bottle of water, 'boo-boo bu-bu-bu-bu...'.

Cuckoo

Oriental Cuckoo

Great Spotted Cuckoo

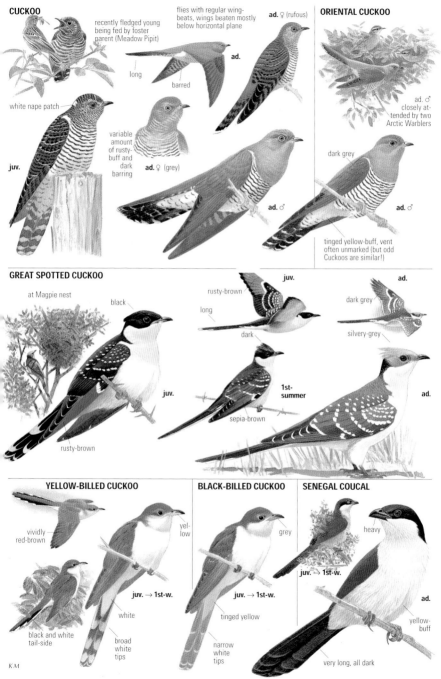

CUCKOO

recently fledged young being fed by foster parent (Meadow Pipit)

flies with regular wing-beats, wings beaten mostly below horizontal plane

ad. ♀ (rufous)

ad.

long

barred

white nape patch

variable amount of rusty-buff and dark barring

ad. ♀ (grey)

juv.

ad. ♂

ORIENTAL CUCKOO

ad. ♂ closely attended by two Arctic Warblers

dark grey

ad. ♂

tinged yellow-buff, vent often unmarked (but odd Cuckoos are similar!)

GREAT SPOTTED CUCKOO

at Magpie nest

black

rusty-brown

juv.

rusty-brown

long

dark

juv.

1st-summer

sepia-brown

juv.

ad.

dark grey

silvery-grey

ad.

YELLOW-BILLED CUCKOO

vividly red-brown

yellow

juv. → 1st-w.

white

black and white tail-side

broad white tips

BLACK-BILLED CUCKOO

grey

juv. → 1st-w.

tinged yellow

narrow white tips

SENEGAL COUCAL

heavy

juv. → 1st-w.

ad.

yellow-buff

very long, all dark

KM

OWLS *Strigiformes*
Birds of prey, many with nocturnal habits; 17 species. Catch prey primarily with surprise attack. Plumage dense and soft-surfaced, allowing noiseless flight. Very good hearing and vision. Head large, with often characteristic facial pattern. Eyes directed forwards. Some have ear-tufts. Sexes similar, ♀ usually slightly larger than ♂. Nest in cavity, in old twig nest, or on ground; eggs white and rounded.

Tawny Owl *Strix aluco* **rB**3
L 37–43 cm, WS 81–96 cm. Breeds in forests, parkland, wooded farmland, preferring old broadleaf trees (ancient oaks etc. providing large holes); frequently found near man in gardens and towns. Fairly numerous. Sedentary. Nocturnal. Food, mainly voles and insects, taken on ground after watch from perch. Nests in hole. Aggressive when young leave nest, can attack intruder.

IDENTIFICATION Medium-sized, compact; *wings broad and rounded, head large and rounded*. Flight direct with fairly quick wingbeats; often makes long, straight glides. Ground colour variable from rufous-brown (predominant in Britain, absent in NW Africa) to greyish-brown, whole plumage mottled, finely streaked and vermiculated dark. Facial discs rather plain. *Thin whitish 'extra eyebrows' on forecrown* add to 'kind' expression. *Eyes black*. (Note that yellow-eyed species, e.g. Long-eared Owl, can look dark-eyed at night in headlights owing to large pupils.) Scapulars lined with white spots. No prominent pale patch on inner primaries above (cf. Long-eared and Short-eared Owls). Tail finely and indistinctly barred.

VOICE Rather vocal. Most common call the well-known 'kew**ick**', shrill and repeated; fierce variations used as alarm. Song a 'mourning' hooting, tone ocarina-like, can be mimicked by blowing in hands, first a drawn-out note falling in pitch at end, followed by *c.* 4-sec. pause, then an abrupt note quickly followed by a rapid series of shivering notes ending with a drawn-out note falling in pitch like the initial one, '**hoooo**uh.......ho, ho'ho'ho'**hoooo**uh'. A hoarse and more wailing variation of the song is used by the ♀ (and allegedly rarely by ♂, too). During courtship either sex utters a low-pitched, shivering tremolo (the so-called 'xylophone trill'), 'o'o'o'o'o'o'o'o'o'o'o'o...', audible only to *c.* 50 m. Begging-call of young a squeaking '**psee**-ep'.

(Eurasian) **Eagle Owl** *Bubo bubo* **V*****
L 59–73 cm, WS 138–170 cm. Resident in mountains and forests, preferring areas with rocks, steep cliffs and mature trees (preferably conifers); often in rocky archipelagos. Scattered distribution, generally rare and local. Sedentary. Only a handful of genuine records in Britain, all in last century.

Nocturnal and partly crepuscular. Day roost in dense mature spruces or firs, or in cave or crevice. Food mammals (voles, rats, hedgehogs, hares) and birds (corvids, gulls, wildfowl, etc.). Nests on inaccessible cliff-ledge or, less often, on the ground by rock or tree, exceptionally in abandoned raptor's nest or in barn.

IDENTIFICATION *Largest* owl, strong build enhanced by dense, 'fluffy' plumage; large-headed. When relaxed can appear *barrel-shaped*, when alert may display surprisingly long (but thick) neck. *Ear-tufts long*, visible except in flight, held flattish when relaxed or anxious, more erect when calling or disturbed. Flight powerful and steady, wingbeats rather shallow, glides straight, recalling large buzzard (but head of course huge, and wings more arched when gliding). *Eyes orange-red, large*. Main colour below *yellowish-brown with dark streaks*, broad on breast. Upperparts darker brown, boldly streaked and vermiculated blackish. Throat white, exposed when calling. In flight, primary bases only slightly paler (yellowish-brown) than rest (cf. Great Grey Owl), boldly and evenly cross-barred. – Juvenile: Downy young recognized by proportionately huge bill and talons, and by nest site. Fledged young have fully feathered body at a few weeks of age, but told first few months by partly downy, rounded head with only small ear-tufts. – Variation: A smaller and in some areas paler (though variable) race (*ascalaphus*) in N Africa and parts of Middle East.

VOICE Call of ♀ a harsh barking '**rhä**ev'. Alarm a fierce, startlingly loud, nasal barking '**kwa**!', often 3–5 notes quickly repeated, '**kwa**-**kwá**-**kwa**!'. Anxiety-call nasal, muffled, gull-like 'gaw'. Song deep sonorous booming '**oo**-hu', second syllable falling in pitch, voice surprisingly faint at close range, still audible at 1½–4 km, usually repeated at intervals of 8–12 sec., at long range only first note heard (confusable with Long-eared Owl, but pace much slower). ♀ has higher-pitched, hoarse version. Begging-call of young a loud, husky, scraping 'chu**eesh**' (as when planing wood), heard through calm summer and early-autumn nights.

Brown Fish Owl *Ketupa zeylonensis* —
L 50–58 cm, WS 125–140 cm. Extremely rare and local (if not extinct?) in N Israel (and adjacent areas?), breeding in wadis with scrub and trees. Nocturnal and crepuscular. Stalks fish from perch at bankside or by wading in shallow water, or will fly low over water with legs dangling. Day roost in crevice or dense tree.

IDENTIFICATION *Large*, with *horizontal, broad ear-tufts*. Looks flat- and broad-headed. *Pale mid brown* above, finely streaked darker brown; paler buffish- or pinkish-cream below, *rather sparsely and finely streaked brown*. On upperparts pale lower scapulars form a light band. *Eyes yellow*. Feet unfeathered and greyish. Flight-feathers are brown, barred dark. Tail boldly barred brown. Facial discs poorly developed. Faint wing sound heard from flying bird.

VOICE Imperfectly known. Song a very deep, muffled (not audible very far!), trisyllabic 'huu, **whoo** huu' (second 'inhaling' note higher), slowly repeated. According to one description, has series of deep, muttered hoots, rising at end and with distinct pause after first note, 'ku, ku-ku ku-ku ku-ku...'. Also said to have strange screaming sound reminiscent of Stone-curlew. Alarm is hissing sound.

Tawny Owl   Eagle Owl

TAWNY OWL

pale crown-stripes

large, rounded head

iris black

looks compact in flight, wings rounded and fairly short, comparatively plain dark

(grey)

(rufous)

two young (left), *c.* 4 weeks old

a certain colour variation, with continuous gradation from greyish to more rufous

EAGLE OWL

long ear-tufts

fledged young, *c.* 2½ months old

iris orange-red

dark brown (colour of pine-tree bark)

buff-brown

young on cliff-ledge nest, *c.* 6 weeks old

ascalaphus (N Africa, Middle East)

plumage variable, some are dark as in Europe

short

iris yellow

'face' lined dark

small

mobbed by screaming Hooded Crows

upperwing rather uniformly rusty-brown

'boxing gloves'

tufts invisible

BROWN FISH-OWL

on lookout for fish

bushy ear-tufts

white 'braces'

iris yellow

plain 'face'

boldly barred flight-feathers

'skinny' legs

DZ

Great Grey Owl *Strix nebulosa* —

L 59–68 cm, WS 128–148 cm. Mainly resident in lowland boreal forests, often near bogs or infields; rare and local. Partly nomadic. Mainly crepuscular (incl. on light northern summer nights). Food almost exclusively voles (in spite of size—bulk made up of feathers, not muscles and bones!), caught on ground after watch from perch. Nests in abandoned raptor's nest or on top of broken tree trunk, rarely on ground. Some are aggressive when their young are about to leave nest, others fairly tame and will permit rather close observation.

IDENTIFICATION *Large*, with thick neck and proportionately *very large and rounded head*, looking like a *sawn-off log in profile*. Wings very long, broad and rounded, tail fairly long, well rounded. Impressive-looking in flight, with *measured, slow wingbeats* (heron-like), capable of long glides. Basically *dusky grey* with darker grey pattern, underside paler, breast and belly coarsely streaked and finely vermiculated. Facial pattern surrounding *small yellow eyes* and bill striking. Upperwing shows conspicuous *large pale buff patch at base of primaries* and dark grey carpal area and forewing; shoulders pale grey ('braces'). *Uppertail has broad dark terminal bar* (lacking on Ural and Eagle Owls). When pair seen, ♀ larger and often with proportionately slightly smaller head.

VOICE The call of ♀ is a hoarse, high-pitched 'chi**ep**-chi**ep**-chi**ep**'. Alarm or aggression-call is a deep, subdued growling 'grrook-grrook-grrook', and ♀ has a related remarkable drawn-out growling 'grrrrrrrrrrrk'; snaps bill loudly when angry. Song is a very deep, pumping series (9–12) of booming hoots, well spaced (c. 1½ per sec.), falling slightly in pitch and loudness at end, 'bvoo, bvoo, bvoo,...'; normally audible no farther than 400 m. Begging of young reminiscent of call of ♀, 'psiep-psiep', deeper when older.

Ural Owl *Strix uralensis* —

L 50–59 cm, WS 103–124 cm. Resident in old boreal forests interspersed with bogs, often also open water, clearfellings and small fields. In S Europe also mountain forests, beech woods. Food voles, frogs and insects (taken after watch from low perch), but is strongly built and takes also a variety of birds (incl. other owls!). Nests in tree trunk ('chimney'), nestbox or abandoned raptor's nest. *Caution:* Very aggressive when young about to leave nest and can attack intruder fiercely; keep your eyes fixed on the parents if you stumble on an inhabited nest, and leave area quickly!

IDENTIFICATION Medium-large, head rounded, *tail long* and rather wedge-shaped (noticeable in flight); wings rounded. Flight direct, purposeful, recalling Common Buzzard. Plumage *pale buffish grey-brown* (paler than Tawny),

streaked darker brown; in brief encounters, *paleness* is usually best clue. *Eyes black*, stand out well on *plain buffish-grey facial discs*. Bill yellowish. Upperwing evenly barred dark, *lacking conspicuous pale patch* on inner primaries of Great Grey Owl and Short-eared Owl. *Uppertail evenly and boldly barred dark* (cf. Great Grey).

VOICE Call of ♀ a raw, very harsh (recalling both Grey Heron and Eagle Owl) disyllabic '**kre**-ef!'. Alarm a loud, nasal barking 'wak'. Song of ♂ a deep cooing-like hooting, 7 notes in constant pattern, first two notes, then pause of c. 4 sec., then two notes immediately followed by three more, 'wo-ho...... woho uh**wo**-ho', audible at 2 km in calm weather; ♀ has higher-pitched, hoarse version. Alternative song of ♂ (courtship, nest-showing, anxiety) a rapid series of 6–8 short, deep hoots, slightly increasing in pitch, pace and stress but decreasing at end, 'po po po po po po'; ♀ has harsher version. Begging-call of young much as for Tawny Owl (though deeper), a high-pitched, throaty 'peechep'.

Snowy Owl *Nyctea scandiaca* V***

L 53–65 cm, WS 125–150 cm. Breeds on tundra or high plateaux above tree-limit, preferring areas with scattered rocks and good view. Apparently nomadic, fluctuating with food supply. One pair bred in 1960s–70s in Shetland; otherwise irregular and extremely rare winter vagrant in Britain. Food mainly lemmings and other voles, also birds and rabbits. Nest scrape on ground, in lemming-years with large clutches and lined with store of dead prey.

IDENTIFICATION *Large, strikingly white* in most plumages. *Eyes yellow.* Flight powerful, and wings have proportionately shorter 'arm' and more pointed 'hand' than other large owls. – Adult ♂: Pure white (except for a few scattered tiny dark spots). – Adult ♀: White, with dark spots on crown, dark cross-barring below (except white centre of breast), and dark 'scalloping' on back and shoulders; flight-feathers and wing-coverts coarsely barred dark on white ground. – 1st-winter ♂: Very similar to adult ♀ but slightly smaller; plumage rather off-white when fresh; upperparts more distinctly cross-barred, on average slightly finer barring below; *tips of tertials, inner greater coverts, and flight-feathers diffusely vermiculated grey*. Bleached to predominantly white in 1st summer. – 1st-year ♀: Like adult ♀, but dark spots and bars heavier and denser, at distance creating strong contrast of white face and neck, and almost uniform dark body and crown; also, more dark barring on crown and breast.

VOICE Alarm a loud, grating bark, 'krek-krek-krek-krek-krek-...' (Mallard-like!), ♂ lower-pitched than ♀; ♀ also has a mewing call, 'pyeey, pyeey, pyeey,...', like a falsetto bark, and a thin whistling 'seeuuee'. Song a far-carrying, deep 'gawh', repeated at c. 5-sec. intervals, audible at 1–3 km; apparently somewhat variable in tone (soft, clean voice like Eagle Owl or more hoarse; even said to recall Great Black-backed Gull) and pattern (single or combination of notes). Begging-call of young a high-pitched whistling squeal.

Great Grey Owl

Ural Owl

Snowy Owl

GREAT GREY OWL

in profile like a steamship flue funnel

swarthy 'face'

stately look

large head, small yellow eyes

grey

hunting voles in 'taiga barn country'

young, *c.* 5 weeks old

broad band

pale buff-brown primary base

broad-winged

broad dark tail-band

thick neck

URAL OWL

typical nest site in hollow tree trunk ('chimney')

deceptively gentle look

pale, plain 'face', straw-yellow bill

buff-grey

iris black

rounded profile

lacks paler patch

evenly barred

young, 4–5 weeks old

long (cf. Tawny Owl)

SNOWY OWL

densely barred

dusky tertial tips marked grey

1st-w. ♀

ad. ♂

young, *c.* 7 weeks old

ad. ♀

white tertials distinctly barred

narrowly barred

ad. ♀

ad. ♀

DZ

(Northern) Hawk Owl *Surnia ulula*   **V**∗∗∗
L 35–43 cm, WS 69–82 cm. Mainly resident in boreal forests, often in upper tree zone on mountain slopes (mixed conifers and birch), preferring vicinity of bog, meadow or clearfell. Fluctuating in numbers, some years locally fairly common. In some autumns considerable numbers move south. About five records in Britain this century. Partly diurnal. Food voles (main prey, taken on ground after watch from treetop) and birds (e.g. thrushes; capable of catching prey as large as Willow Grouse). Nests in tree-hole ('chimney' or vertical) or abandoned raptor's nest. *Caution:* Can fiercely attack intruders when young leave nest; do not go near, and keep your eyes fixed on the parents while in sight of young just out of a nest!

IDENTIFICATION Medium-sized with distinctive proportions: *very long tail* and *rather narrow, bluntly pointed wings*, thus recalling a hawk more than other owls, this enhanced by *direct, agile flight* with short series of wingbeats relieved by brief glides. Perches in treetops, also fearlessly exposed on bare dead spruces. Head rather large and often *flat-crowned* (alert, alarmed). Upperparts dark brown with *pale hind-neck and scapulars*, latter forming prominent V on perched bird in rear view ('braces'). Underparts whitish and finely cross-barred except on *upper breast*, which is *pure white*. Face *whitish, strongly outlined black*, expression 'stern'. Eyes yellow. Nape has a pale and dark pattern ('false face', defence purpose), and side of head has a black patch. – Juvenile: Similar to adult but a little greyer and duller, with dusky eye-surround and diffusely patterned throat and upper breast.

VOICE Alarm shrill, like ♀ Merlin, 'ki-ki-kikikikikiki'. Food-begging call of ♀ a hoarse, squeezed, drawn-out 'ksheee-lip', ending abruptly. Song (early spring, dark night) a very long and rapid bubbling, almost ventriloquial trill, 'lülülülülülülülü...', 8–9 sec., pauses 8–25 sec., audible to at least 1 km. When agitated (anxiety, courtship) utters a gargling, short cooing, almost like Black Grouse. Begging of young resembles that of ♀ but is more hissing, 'pssss-lip'.

Tengmalm's Owl *Aegolius funereus*   **V**∗∗∗
L 22–27 cm, WS 50–62 cm. Breeds in dense forests with small bogs and glades. Fairly common in N Europe; about 50 records in Britain. Mainly sedentary, but in some autumns many move south, possibly predominantly ♀♀ and young. Strictly nocturnal, difficult to see other than in vicinity of nest. Food mainly voles. Nests in tree-hole (old nest of Black Woodpecker) or box.

IDENTIFICATION Medium-small (about as Little Owl), *large-headed* (flattish crown). Medium-sized eyes yellow, *facial expression 'astonished'*. Upperparts brown, with whitish spots and diffuse blotches on shoulders; underparts whit-

ish, diffusely blotched brownish. Wings rounded, *flight rather direct* with series of quick wingbeats and brief straight glides. Greatest risk of confusion Pygmy Owl (small, same range and habitat), but this is only the size of a Starling, has proportionately smaller head, has different, 'stern' facial expression, shows tendency to bounding flight, and has proportionately shorter wings; also, Pygmy often perches in treetops, whereas *Tengmalm's prefers canopy*. – Juvenile: Mainly *chocolate-brown*, with variable amount of white on face.

VOICE Rather vocal. Commonest call squirrel-like 'chi**a**k'. Song a rapid series of deep whistling notes (5–8; when excited, drawn out to much longer series), initially slightly rising in pitch and pace, surprisingly loud (audible to well over 3 km on calm nights), 'pu-po-**po-po-po-po**'; pitch and speed vary somewhat; possible to mimic (lowest possible whistling). Begging-call of young a thin, abrupt 'ksi!'.

(Eurasian) Pygmy Owl *Glaucidium passerinum*   —
L 15–19 cm, WS 32–39 cm. Breeds in coniferous or mixed forests in boreal zone or in C European mountains, with a preference for mature spruce or fir forests. Mainly sedentary. Crepuscular habits (night vision poor in complete darkness). Rather fearless, and can sometimes be attracted by imitation of song. Food birds, voles; very bold for its size, and capable of killing thrushes (which are larger). Stores food supply in holes. Nests in hole in a tree (often old nest of Great Spotted Woodpecker).

IDENTIFICATION *Very small* (Starling size), round-headed (vestigial ear-tufts rarely indicated). *Head is proportionately smaller* than on Little and Tengmalm's Owls. Flight dashing, over longer distances *obviously bounding* (in woodpecker fashion). Perches in spruce tops. At times waves tail or raises it slowly in flycatcher fashion. Facial discs poorly developed, but *short, narrow white supercilia prominent*, and yellow *eyes small* and closely set, giving *'stern' expression*. Lower hindneck has diffuse light pattern creating faint suggestion of 'false face' (defence purpose). Grey-brown above, speckled with *tiny white dots*; whitish below, with brown breast (more extensive on sides) and thinly streaked belly. – Juvenile: Very similar to adult, but lacks white spotting on crown, back and wing-coverts.

VOICE Call of ♀ a very thin, drawn-out 'tseeeh' (recalling Blackbird or Robin, but more 'determined'). In autumn (but also at other times) commonest call is so-called scale-song, a series of 5–10 sharp, squeezed whistles, rising in pitch, 'chuuk-chüük-cheek-chiihk-...' (like bicycle pump with finger over hole). Song is repeated mellow, piping whistle, 6–7 per 10 sec., recalling Bullfinch and Scops Owl, but is a fraction more drawn out, slightly higher-pitched and has hint of accentuated end, 'pjük'; audible at 500 m–1 km. In excitement, a fine, subdued stammering is interfoliated between regularly spaced whistles, 'pjük... (popopo)... pjük... (popo-po)... pjük...', etc. Begging-call of young is a fine 'tseeh', recalling ♀'s call but shorter.

Hawk Owl   Tengmalm's Owl   Pygmy Owl

HAWK OWL

grim look

on the lookout from top of a dead tree

pale nape pattern creates 'false face'

large pale shoulder patches

finely barred, like a hawk

long

young just out of nest, *c.* 4 weeks old

hawk-like silhouette in flight, but head is proportionately bigger

TENGMALM'S OWL

♀ looking out of nest hole in old aspen tree

three young just out of nest, *c.* 4 weeks old

'astonished' look

plain dark brown

PYGMY OWL

austere look

no white spots

short white eyebrows

barred

grey-brown

more distinct pattern than juv.

with a captured Willow Tit

juv.

ad.

flight woodpecker-like, smoothly bounding

DZ

Long-eared Owl *Asio otus* rB(3–)4 / **W**4

L 31–37 cm, WS 86–98 cm. Breeds in forests in vicinity of open country, in copses among arable fields, in larger parks with conifers, etc. Migratory in northern part of range, sedentary in S. Not scarce in Britain in optimum habitats, but declining. Nocturnal and crepuscular. Food mainly voles. Nests in old nest of other bird in tree (usually crow).

IDENTIFICATION Clearly *smaller than Tawny Owl*, slightly smaller than Short-eared Owl. *Wings long and rather narrow. Long ear-tufts* often visible (in courtship; when alarmed; in erect camouflage posture), but can be practically invisible (in flight; when relaxed). *Flight rather slow and wavering*, a few rowing wingbeats (markedly slower than Tawny, very similar to Short-eared) interspersed with glides. Similarity to Short-eared enhanced by similar upperwing pattern— *large yellowish-buff patch on base of outer primaries* accentuated by dark carpal patch and dark wing-tip: separated by *lack of whitish trailing edge to 'arm'; wing-tip being evenly barred dark; underbody rather evenly streaked*; tail densely and indistinctly barred; lack of contrasting dark tertials below; eyes orange; wings proportionately slightly shorter and broader. – Sexes similar, ♂ being on average paler, less heavily streaked below, face paler and less buff.

VOICE Adult rather silent. Call of ♀ a weak, nasal, somewhat cracked '**peh**-ev', repeated. Alarm a rather impetuous, hoarse, nasal 'wrack, wrack-wrack'. Song a series of deep hooting 'oh', repeated every 2½ sec., at first more feeble and deep, audible 500 m–1 km but already faint at 200 m. At times, ♂ and ♀ perform duets (call of ♀ muffled). Begging-call of young *loud* and 'heartbreaking', a disyllabic, drawn-out, *plaintive*, high-pitched '**pee**-eh', audible over 1 km.

Short-eared Owl *Asio flammeus* rB4 / **W**3

L 33–40 cm, WS 95–105 cm. Breeds on heathland, in scrub among meadows, on bogs, esp. in upper tree zone in open boreal forests. In Britain local in N, sporadic in S. Mainly migratory in N Europe, sedentary in rest. Partly diurnal. Food mainly voles. Nest a scrape on ground.

IDENTIFICATION Medium-sized, wings very long, narrow and rather pointed, *head comparatively small, rounded.* Ear-tufts minute and rarely seen. Plumage *pale yellow-brown* and buff-white, heavily streaked. In certain lights, e.g. dusk or overcast weather, can look surprisingly whitish. Palish face with *distinct black patches around yellow eyes*, expression 'mean'. Flight buoyant and wavering, *wingbeats rowing in slow-motion fashion, wings rigid-looking*, glides freely. Often perches on ground. In flight, distinguished from similar Long-eared Owl (which see) by *white trailing edge to 'arm'*; wing-tip almost solidly black with only one bold bar inside tip; *contrast between streaked breast and largely unstreaked*

belly; tail coarsely barred; tertials contrastingly darker below; wings proportionately somewhat longer and narrower. – Sexes similar, ♂ on average paler below and on face, and less heavily streaked.

VOICE Call of ♀ a hoarse, baleful '**cheh**-ef '(drawn out when begging, '**cheeeh**-op'). Alarm a harsh 'chef-chef-chef'. Song given in flight (often high up), a quick series of subdued, deep hoots, 'uh-uh-uh-uh-uh-uh-...', 6–20 notes at a time, audible to *c.* 1 km. Short, quick wing-claps also given during song-flight. Begging-call of young like call of ♀ but more hissing.

Marsh Owl *Asio capensis* —

L 30½–37 cm, WS 80–95 cm. Breeds in marshland or wet meadows with long grass, within region only locally and rarely in NW Morocco; declining. Sedentary. Partly diurnal. Nest on ground, a hollow in tuft of grass.

IDENTIFICATION Like a small Short-eared Owl (and habitat much the same, too) with the following distinctions: size a trifle *smaller* even than Long-eared Owl; *wings shorter, broader and blunter-tipped*; flight more like that of Long-eared than Short-eared Owl, *glides on slightly arched wings*; upperbody, chest and upperwing-coverts almost uniform dark brown, making *cream-white face contrast strongly*; *eyes black*; *secondaries dark above*, coarsely barred below; belly pale, finely barred. – Juvenile: Has a diffuse, pale panel on upperwing-coverts. At closer range, breast and upperparts can be seen to be coarsely barred.

VOICE Call a harsh, croaking bark, 'qurark', frog-like. Song apparently a repetition of the bark, several notes in a series. Begging-call of young a disyllabic rather musical 'too-ee' with rising inflection.

Barn Owl *Tyto alba* rB4

L 33–39 cm, WS 80–95 cm. Breeds in farmland with scattered copses, gardens, rarely in villages close to fields. In Britain not scarce, but local. Sedentary. Nocturnal and crepuscular. Food voles, frogs, insects. Nests in hole in tree, building or ruin, often using nestboxes inside farmhouses.

IDENTIFICATION Medium size, *slim body*, long wings, *long legs. Face* pale and *heart-shaped. Eyes dark.* Flight recalls Long-eared Owl, slow, wavering, elegant. Appears *long-necked and short-tailed in flight, feet often dangling* when hovering. *Plumage typically very light* (♂ normally palest), notably so in flight. – Variation: Underparts practically pure white in W and S Europe, and on W Canaries (mainly ssp. *alba*) and in N Africa and Middle East (*erlangeri*), whereas they are yellow-orange in N, C and E Europe (*guttata*) and on E Canaries (*gracilirostris*) and Madeira (*schmitzi*). Upperparts grey and ochre in entire range.

VOICE Call of ♀ (rarely ♂) a purring shriek (Nightjar voice), repeated. Alarm, often in flight, a shrill, hoarse squeal. Song a drawn-out (*c.* 2 sec. long) rattling or gargling shriek, 'shrrreeee', often repeated. Begging-call of young is a drawn-out, wheezy snoring.

Long-eared Owl

Short-eared Owl

Barn Owl

LONG-EARED OWL

alert bird with tufts erect

orange iris

when relaxed tufts are folded and become barely visible

rusty-buff tinge, strongest on ♀

in camou-flage posture

finely barred

lacks white rear edge

finely barred wing-tip

streaking continues onto belly

4–5 narrow bands

finely barred

nestling, c. 4 weeks old

SHORT-EARED OWL

alert bird with vestigial tufts erect

yellow iris

pink-buff tinge, strongest on ♀

alarmed

boldly barred

white rear edge

black tip

nestling, 3–4 weeks old

streaking concentrated on breast

2–3 black bands

boldly barred

MARSH OWL

plain dark brown

iris black

alert bird with vestigial tufts erect

plain dark breast

alarmed

dark brown

white edge

primary pattern recalls that of Short-eared Owl

BARN OWL

heart-shaped 'face', black eyes

alba, erlangeri et al. (W and S Europe, W Canaries, N Africa, Middle East)

nestling, c. 4 weeks old

white

very pale in flight (and lacks dark carpal patches)

white

yellow-orange

long-legged

guttata et al. (C and E Europe, E Canaries)

alba

often dangling legs

K M

Little Owl *Athene noctua* ᵣ**B**3

L 23–27½ cm. Breeds in open country with mixture of fields, copses, cliffs, gardens, parks, hedgerow trees; also semi-deserts. Sedentary. Introduced in Britain 19th century. Partly diurnal; this and habit of *perching fully exposed* mean that it is often seen. Food insects, birds, small amphibians and snakes. Nests in hole in tree or building.

IDENTIFICATION *Small*, with *large, broadly rounded head, long legs* and short tail. Often squat posture when alarmed, bobbing in excitement. *Flight* fast, over longer stretches *bounding* like woodpecker. Brown above, speckled white; whitish below, densely streaked brown. *Whitish oblique eyebrows* give 'stern' expression. Eyes yellow. – Juvenile: Plumage pattern duller, lacking white spots on crown. – Variation: In S Middle East a pale grey-brown race (*lilith*). Intermediate populations in SE Europe and Asia Minor (*indigena*) and in Central Asia (*bactriana*).

VOICE Commonest call a sharp, complaining '**kee**-ew', in falsetto, falling in pitch, often eagerly repeated. Alarm short, explosive, high-pitched 'chi, chi, chi-chi,...'. Song a full and mellow, *slightly drawn-out rather low-pitched hoot with ending upward-inflected*, repeated about every 5–10 sec., 'goooek' ('querying' tone), each song note longer than song of Scops Owl; ♀ has higher-pitched, more nasal, less mellow version. Begging-call of young a hissing 'shree'.

(Eurasian) Scops Owl *Otus scops* **V**∗∗∗

L 19–21 cm, WS 47–54 cm. Breeds in broadleaved and mixed open woodland, copses in farmland, churchyards, town parks, larger gardens; also found in wooded lower mountains. Migratory, wintering in southernmost Europe and Africa S of Sahara. In Britain only a few records per decade. Nocturnal. Food mainly insects. Nests in hole.

IDENTIFICATION Small, somewhat *smaller than Little Owl*. Sits upright, showing little of ear-tufts when relaxed (merely as *sharp corners of crown*), more when alert (can adopt erect camouflage posture like Long-eared Owl). In flight, shows proportionately long and narrow wings, path hardly bounding (cf. Little). Except at close range, appears *rather uniform brown* (rufous or more greyish; variable) with *pale* (grey-white) *shoulder line*, slightly paler face and underbody; seen well, shows intricate pattern of black streaks and vermiculations, diffuse whitish spots and rufous patches. Eyes yellow. For separation from at times extremely similar Pale Scops Owl, see that species.

VOICE Song most commonly heard call, a constantly repeated short, deep, whistling 'tyuh' every 2–3 (4) sec., easy to mimic, audible to *c.* 1 km; ♀ has slightly higher-pitched version, often duetting with ♂. Distinguished from midwife toad by slightly longer note and fuller, more musical clang-

ing quality (not completely straight and mechanically whistling like the toad).

Pale Scops Owl *Otus brucei* —

L 20–22 cm. Distribution and habits not well known. Habitat apparently as Scops Owl. Partly migratory, some wintering in S Israel. Often roosts in dense acacia. Nocturnal. Food mainly insects, also small mammals, birds. Nests in hole.

IDENTIFICATION *Small*, a trifle larger than Scops Owl (although difference normally impossible to perceive in the field), but in shape and habits identical to that species: *broad, thick ear-tufts*, hardly discernible on relaxed bird; erect posture; long wings; short tail. Main distinctions apart from song (see below) are *paler, more dull sand-grey plumage*, especially face; distinct, thin streaking below (though a few streaks on breast bolder), enhanced by pale ground colour, but lacks *bold white cross-bars and obvious dark barring* (is only *evenly and finely* vermiculated); pale *shoulder line always buff* (not whitish as on some Scops); *no rufous* in plumage, and pale spotting above reduced (though some Scops Owls in S Europe and Middle East rather similar). Rudimentary feathering on bases of toes (Scops unfeathered) difficult to make out in the field. – Juvenile: Finely cross-barred below but *without distinct streaks*, which separates it also from juvenile Scops.

VOICE On breeding ground, best distinction from similar-looking Scops Owl. *Calls are softer and much less loud*, usually audible only at very close range. Song a *long series of slowly repeated* (once per 1 or 2 sec., ♂ allegedly faster) *low cooing notes*, 'whoh whoh whoh whoh...'; tone subdued and ventriloquial, not softly but loudly whistling as that of Scops. A four-note variant has been described as 'oo-oo oo-oo ...', singly or repeated. A high-pitched, squeaky 'tzir tir tir ir' is uttered in excitement.

Hume's Owl *Strix butleri* —

L 29–33 cm. Resident in arid lower mountains, in deserts with deep, rocky wadis or cliffs. Breeds very rarely in Sinai, S Israel, and Jordan. Nocturnal habits. Food voles, mice, insects. Nests on cliff in crevice or hole.

IDENTIFICATION Medium-sized, large-headed, like a small Tawny Owl, but *eyes yellow* (juv. more orange-yellow), and *plumage pale and rather plain*, underparts not streaked, only finely and diffusely barred pale ochrous-buff.

VOICE A pumping 'do-do-do-do-do-do', rising slightly in pitch at end, appears to serve as defensive call. ♀ begs with a fine, fluty, upward-inflected hooting 'dooa'. Song a rhythmical, sonorous hooting of five syllables with a voice more reminiscent of Collared Dove than Tawny Owl (voice 'kind', soft and recalling toy ocarina), first a single note falling slightly in pitch, then *c.* 1½-sec. pause followed by four short notes almost in Ural Owl rhythm, '**hoo**u... **ho**-hu ho-**ho**', audible to *c.* 200 m and repeated 1–4 times/min. ♀ has deeper-voiced slightly muffled version. Young said to have fine 'sneezing' begging-calls.

Little Owl

Scops Owl

Pale Scops Owl

LITTLE OWL

often perched in daylight on telephone poles

plain

lilith, saharae
(desert forms in
N Africa and
S Middle East)

pale grey-brown

white spots,
head broad and rounded

bounding flight

juv.

noctua

noctua, vidalii
(Europe
except
in SE)

SCOPS OWL

tufts some-times invisible

streaked dark,
spotted white

white spots

whitish 'braces'

(rufous)

streaked

juv.

streaked
and with
bold
cross-barring

(grey-brown)

PALE SCOPS OWL

merely
streaked
(no white
spots)

sand-brown

bar-red

yel-lowish-buff 'braces'

juv.

frequently
shorter wing
than Scops Owl

predom-inantly
streaked,
barring
faint

HUME'S OWL

rounded
head

iris
deep
yellow

at day roost

pale ochre,
discreetly
barred

typical breeding site in
wadi in desert area

boldly barred flight-
and tail-feathers

pale, unmarked

DZ

NIGHTJARS *Caprimulgidae*
Medium-sized birds specialized for catching largish flying insects in flight at dusk and at night: have large gape, strong bristles at bill-corners (to enlarge diameter of 'trapping funnel'), long, narrow wings and tail, large head, short neck and legs, small bill. Plumage soft and brown-mottled, often with white spots ('signal flashes') on wings and tail. By day rest motionless on branch or ground. Noticed mostly at night, by calls. Nest on ground.

(European) Nightjar *Caprimulgus europaeus* mB4
L 24–28 cm, WS 52–59 cm. Breeds in open pine forest on sandy soils, often with some drier, sparsely vegetated bogs and clearings with pine saplings; also in more open sandy mixed and deciduous woods with glades and felled areas. Summer visitor (mostly May–Sep), wintering in Africa.

IDENTIFICATION *Mottled brown, buff-white, grey and black*, and with screwed-up eyes, the Nightjar resting lengthwise on a branch is hard to detect. Adult ♂ has *snow-white spots on wings and tail-corners*, which ♀ and 1st-autumn ♂ lack. ♂ also has a small narrow white patch across lower throat-side (lacking or indistinct on ♀). When hunting insects, flight noiseless, light and pitching with slight climbs, brief hovers, sudden fast glides disappearing from view etc.

VOICE Normally heard only during breeding season and at night. Call a frog-like but sonorous 'krru**it**'. Song a far-carrying (often audible at 1 km) hard reel, at close range amazingly rattling and intense, which, with only brief pauses, carries on 'in two gears' for hours on end, 'errrrrrrurrrrrrr-urrrrrerrrrrrrr...', from late dusk to dawn. When ♀ is in the vicinity, reeling sometimes changes into a hacking 'fi**orr**, fi**orr**'and ends with a halting rattle (sounds like engine break-down!); wing-claps also form part of courtship.

Red-necked Nightjar *Caprimulgus ruficollis* —
L 30–34 cm, WS 60–65 cm. Breeds on sandy heath with tree clumps and bushy vegetation or in closed spine-pine forest. Summer visitor (end Apr–mid Oct), winters W Africa.

IDENTIFICATION The region's largest nightjar, *bigger and longer-tailed* than Nightjar. Plumage is similar in pattern, but has *rusty-ochre neck band, throat and upper breast*. All wing-coverts broadly pale-tipped. Both sexes have pale wing and tail spots (most obvious and whitest on ♂) and rather *large white throat patch* (ditto). – Variation: In N Africa (ssp. *desertorum*) much paler and more rusty.

VOICE A hoarse 'tsche-tsche-tsche...' (like steam engine) is given by ♀. Song a far-carrying disyllabic knocking sound with hollow, slightly nasal quality, repeated in long series, 'kyo**tok**-kyo**tok**-kyo**tok**-...'; volume waxes and wanes a little during course of song. Also wing-claps in courtship.

Egyptian Nightjar *Caprimulgus aegyptius* V***
L 24–27 cm, WS 53–58 cm. Breeds in deserts and semi-deserts with limited vegetation, e.g. sand dunes with low shrubs and scattered trees, often near spring or stream.

IDENTIFICATION Size of Nightjar, with *long, narrow wings* as latter and rather long tail, but is *paler and more sandy-coloured*. Finely patterned above, *without Nightjar's heavy black streaking*. *Lacks obvious white wing patches* (has much white on inner web of outer primaries, so *under primaries conspicuously white*, but on upper side white glimpsed only when wing fully spread). In flight, upperwing pattern can recall a ♀ Kestrel, with *'hand' darker than yellow-brown 'arm'*. *Tail pale*, on ♂ with *distinct white corners*. Flies with *rather slow, almost Long-eared Owl-like jerky wingbeats*. (During winter months in Middle East beware small, pale race *unwini* of Nightjar on passage from Iran; this, however, has fully barred primaries below and heavy black streaking on back, like European birds.)

VOICE Song long series of rapidly repeated hollow and mechanical-sounding short churrs, 'krroo-krroo-krroo...', at distance like an engine (e.g. old-fashioned 2-stroke engine on fishing sloop); tempo drops somewhat towards end of each series.

Nubian Nightjar *Caprimulgus nubicus* —
L 20–22 cm, WS 46–50 cm. Breeds in barren, arid, open terrain, in semi-desert with bushes (acacia, tamarisk, beside low-growth palm groves). Keeps late hours; not active until it is pitch-dark. Often sits on roads and bare fields.

IDENTIFICATION The region's *smallest* nightjar. Proportionately *shorter tail* than Nightjar, and *somewhat broader and blunter wings*. Colours much as Red-necked Nightjar, predominantly *grey with rusty-ochre neck band* and reddish-brown bars on inner remiges. ♂'s *white wing and tail spots* very conspicuous (the former contrast with otherwise *almost black wing-tips*), ♀'s almost as big.

VOICE Song a hollow, clanging sound repeated in couplets barely once per second, 'kyau kyau'(or 'trül trül'); audible to only *c.* 200 m. Also wing-claps.

(Common) Nighthawk *Chordeiles minor* V***
L 23–25½ cm, WS 54–60 cm. N American species; very rare vagrant Sep–Oct, mainly in Britain. Size of Nightjar, but has *more pointed wings* and *medium-length, shallowly forked tail*. Seen head-on, glides with *wings in V and bent at carpal*. The unbarred *blackish* primaries have a *distinct broad, white cross-band* (halfway between carpal and tip) on ♂; less distinct on ♀. ♂ has *broad white subterminal band on tail*, also a clear *white throat patch* (smaller and buff-tinged on ♀). Immatures have white trailing wing-edge.

Nightjar Red-necked Nightjar Egyptian Nightjar Nubian Nightjar

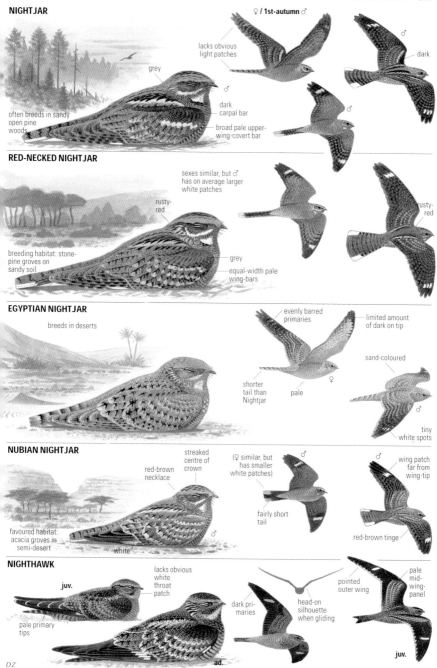

NIGHTJAR

♀ / 1st-autumn ♂

lacks obvious light patches

grey

dark

often breeds in sandy open pine woods

♂

dark carpal bar

broad pale upper-wing-covert bar

♂

RED-NECKED NIGHTJAR

sexes similar, but ♂ has on average larger white patches

rusty-red

rusty-red

breeding habitat: stone-pine groves on sandy soil

grey

equal-width pale wing-bars

EGYPTIAN NIGHTJAR

breeds in deserts

evenly barred primaries

limited amount of dark on tip

sand-coloured

shorter tail than Nightjar

pale

♀

♂

tiny white spots

NUBIAN NIGHTJAR

streaked centre of crown

red-brown necklace

(♀ similar, but has smaller white patches)

♂

wing patch far from wing-tip

♂

fairly short tail

favoured habitat: acacia groves in semi-desert

white

red-brown tinge

NIGHTHAWK

lacks obvious white throat patch

pointed outer wing

pale mid-wing-panel

juv.

dark primaries

head-on silhouette when gliding

pale primary tips

juv.

DZ

ad.

SWIFTS *Apodidae*

Streamlined birds with long, pointed wings, accomplished and indefatigable flyers. Have 'clinging feet' which (unlike those of swallows) are unsuited for perching, therefore seen almost solely in flight. Can copulate in flight (!), and even sleep on the wing. Food insects, which are gathered at altitudes of up to 1 km or more. Nest in cavities in buildings.

(Common) Swift *Apus apus*   m**B**3 / **P**2

L 17–18½ cm, WS 40–44 cm. Breeds in towns and villages and, rarely, in deserted wooded areas or cliffs. Summer visitor (mostly May–Aug), winters in S Africa. Nests in ventilation shafts, cracks etc. in walls, under convex roof tiles or in church towers, sites used regularly year after year. Pairs stay together throughout their life.

IDENTIFICATION Seen incessantly hunting insects in the air, often with swallows (and confused with these by the layman); told by *dark underparts* (only throat pale), somewhat larger size, different wing shape and flight. *Wings sickle-shaped* with long 'hand' and very short 'arm' (carpal joints indiscernible, right next to body). Flight one minute with *frenziedly fast wingbeats* (action so rapid that wings appear to 'beat alternately'), the next with long glides or sailing, motionless against the wind (swallows flutter, or have more backward-clipping action). – Juvenile: Blacker ground colour; pale forehead and lores (white feather fringes); whiter throat patch; finely white-edged wing-coverts.

VOICE Various shrill, monotone, ringing screams, 'srriiirr', sometimes faintly downslurred (or upslurred). Especially striking are the choruses of screams from tight flocks flying around low over the rooftops on summer evenings.

Pallid Swift *Apus pallidus*   **V*****

L 16–18 cm, WS 39–44 cm. Breeds in cavities in buildings or rock faces. Migrant, winters S of Sahara.

IDENTIFICATION Very like Swift; marginally *broader wings* (seen best on outer wing), *broader head/neck* and *plumper body*. Flies with (subtly) *slower wingbeats* and longer glides. *Forehead and throat* are on average *paler*, and a *dark eye patch* normally shows up against paler brown head-side. Upperwings show *slightly paler brown secondaries, inner primaries and primary coverts* contrasting with almost blackish outer primaries and mantle. *Back / rump subtly paler brown than mantle* (hint of 'saddle effect'; Swift is more evenly dark above). Underparts are somewhat *paler and more scaly* than on Swift.

VOICE Like Swift's (and at times hard to separate), but commonest call almost always has *lower pitch*, is *more clearly downslurred* (is thus *disyllabic*), and voice is somewhat drier, *more mechanical and hard*, 'vrrii-e'.

Alpine Swift *Apus melba*   **V****

L 20–23 cm, WS 51–58 cm. Breeds colonially, usually in tall buildings, also in rock faces. Summer visitor (mostly Apr–Sep), winters in S Africa. Pairs for life.

IDENTIFICATION Immediately identified by its *large size*, and for a swift its *rather slow wing action with deep beats* (can momentarily be taken for a Hobby), also by the *white belly*. Also has *throat white*, but this (surprisingly) not always so easy to see (can be in shadow or have restricted white). Colours above and on breast-band *drab grey-brown*.

VOICE Easily recognized, drawn-out twittering series which accelerate or (normally) slow down and drop a little in pitch at end, e.g. 'ti ti tititititititititiit-ti-ti-ti-ti ti tü tü'.

Plain Swift *Apus unicolor*   —

L 14–15½ cm, WS 36–39 cm. Breeds in Madeira and the Canary Islands. Summer visitor (Mar–Aug), but also overwinters; winter area of migrants unknown (Morocco?).

IDENTIFICATION Very like Swift, but is *slightly smaller* and a little *slimmer* and *narrower-winged*. *Tail* proportionately *somewhat longer with narrower base. Pale throat patch smaller, not so bright*, and lower edge less clearly demarcated. A shade paler grey-brown than Swift (not sooty-black), but this difference perceptible only under optimal conditions.

VOICE To all intents inseparable from Swift's.

White-rumped Swift *Apus caffer*   —

L 14–15½ cm, WS 33–37 cm. Breeds locally in S Spain and NW Africa in old Red-rumped Swallow nests. Summer visitor (May–Oct), winters S of Sahara.

IDENTIFICATION Very *dark* with *white rump patch*, white and *well-defined small throat patch* and *diffusely pale-tipped secondaries*. Slim rear end and *long, deeply forked tail*.

VOICE A jolting, hard, staccato series which may change into a trill, 'chüt-chüt-chüt-chüt-ürrrrrrrr'.

Little Swift *Apus affinis*   **V*****

L 12–13½ cm, WS 32–34 cm. Breeds in towns and villages but also on cliff faces. Partially resident.

IDENTIFICATION *Dark*, with quite *broad white rump patch* which *extends onto flanks* (and so can be seen from below). In flight, characteristic silhouette with *broad tail-base* and *short but quite broad, square-cut* (rounded when spread) *tail* and rather broad inner primaries but short secondaries, so *wing looks ample in centre* but *trailing edge looks pinched in near body* (effect amplified in spring by inner primaries having been shed in species' early start of moult). Flight often fluttering almost like House Martin, not that fast.

VOICE A high, bouncing twitter pulsating a little in volume (and vaguely recalling Great Snipe display at distance).

Swift   Pallid Swift   Alpine Swift   Little Swift

SWIFT

screaming flock on summer evening

narrow, long, sickle-shaped

forked

rather plain dark

pointed

PALLID SWIFT

upperpart colour easiest to see against dark background

somewhat broader head than Swift's

pale

dark

broad 'hips'

pale fringes visible in good light

dark 'mask' contrasting

large white throat patch

stronger contrast between dark outer primaries and paler inner than on Swift

a trifle broader wings than Swift

subtly blunt

ALPINE SWIFT

white throat (at times difficult to see at long range)

plain brown above

short

clean white belly patch

very large and long-winged, wingbeats clearly slower than those of the smaller species

PLAIN SWIFT

subtly smaller and more slender than Swift

uniformly sooty brown-grey

deeply forked

diffuse, small pale throat patch

WHITE-RUMPED SWIFT

partly albinistic Swift for comparison

narrow white patch

pointed

pale tips to secondaries

deeply forked

LITTLE SWIFT

broad white patch

rather broad outer wing

much white visible also from below

square end

DZ

(Eurasian) **Hoopoe** *Upupa epops*　　　　**P**5
L 25–29 cm (of which bill 4–5), WS 44–48 cm. Breeds in farming districts and open, grazed country with copses, hedges and bushes; often seen in vineyards and orchards. Summer visitor (mostly end Apr–Sep), winters in Africa. Spends much time on ground, and needs some short-grass or bare areas for feeding (food mostly worms, insects). Wary (but not exactly shy), keeps a certain distance from man. Nests in hole in tree, stone wall, nestbox, house foundations.

IDENTIFICATION One of the most striking and distinctive birds of the whole region: *buffy-pink with black- and white-striped, broadly rounded wings*, and crown with an erectile *crest like Indian chief's* (though normally raised only momentarily on landing, otherwise rarely). Bill long, narrow, slightly decurved. Tail black with broad white band. Flight flappy and rather unsteady with short undulations, hint of gliding, and uneven rhythm, often low over ground. Moves energetically and jerkily on ground, like a starling.

VOICE When agitated and excited a high, noisy 'scheer' with traits of Collared Dove and distant Black-headed Gull. Also a dry rolling 'cherrr' in mate/brood-feeding and other situations. Song a trisyllabic hollow, muffled 'oop-oop-oop', repeated several times; weak at close range yet carries.

KINGFISHERS *Alcedinidae*

Small and medium-sized, compact birds with proportionately large head and bill, short neck and small legs. Most live by water and are accomplished in plunge-diving for fish.

(Common) **Kingfisher** *Alcedo atthis*　　　　r**B**4
L 17–19½ cm (of which bill *c*.4). Breeds at small and moderate-sized fish-rich slow-flowing rivers with some trees and suitable nesting banks; occasionally lakes; also estuaries and coasts in winter. Perches motionless on lookout for small fish, caught following vertical dive. Also hovers occasionally when scanning. Rather shy and restless. Excavates nest in sandy bank, a good metre-long tunnel leading to nest chamber, where young reared on bed of piled fish bones.

IDENTIFICATION A small, *plump, short-tailed* and short-legged bird with *big head* and disproportionately *long bill*. Perches upright. Beautifully bright colours: *crown and wings greenish-blue* (look more greenish from some angles depending on how light falls), *back and tail bright blue* (shifting from azure to cobalt!), *underparts and cheek patch warm orangey brownish-red*, throat and a patch on neck-side snow-white. Despite this display of colour can be difficult to pick out if perched motionless in shadow on a waterside branch. More often noted as it flies straight and fast low over water, calling. Sexes similar, but in breeding pairs ♂ has all-black bill and ♀ reddish base to lower mandible.

Legs light red. – Juvenile: Like adult, but plumage somewhat duller and greener. Legs greyish.

VOICE Normal call, often given in flight, is a short, sharp whistled 'zii', sometimes with afternote, '**zii**-ti', and in excitement repeated in brief series. Song, seldom heard, a simple series of call-like notes in jerky, irregular rhythm.

White-throated **Kingfisher** *Halcyon smyrnensis*　—
L 26–30 cm (of which bill *c*. 6). Breeds in various habitats, and unlike its relatives not strictly tied to water but can be seen among trees in drier farmland, in palm groves and in town parks, sometimes even in pure forest with smallish glades. Usually, however, lives near water. Takes fish, amphibians, lizards, insects. Nests in hole in bank.

IDENTIFICATION *Biggest* kingfisher in the region, size of a large thrush. Vivid colours make it unmistakable, with head, belly, flanks and lesser coverts chestnut-brown, *throat and upper breast pure white, back, uppertail and most of upperwings blue-green*. Bill coral-red. In flight, gleaming sky-blue primary patches above and *large white wing-panels below*. – Juvenile: Somewhat duller, and white breast often with fine dark vermiculation. Bill yellow-brown or orange with darker tip.

VOICE Very noisy and loud, its voice can dominate a locality. The alarm is a croaky, metallic series, 'krix krix krix-ix...'. Song a very loud and aggravatingly repeated, rapid trilling whistle, dropping in pitch and sounding indignant and bleating, '**ti-ti-tü-tü-tu-tu-**...', often delivered from top of a tall eucalyptus tree.

Belted **Kingfisher** *Ceryle alcyon*　　　　**V**∗∗∗
Very rare vagrant from N America. See text p. 382.

Pied **Kingfisher** *Ceryle rudis*　—
L 25–27 cm (of which bill *c*. 5). Breeds at rivers, lakes, river mouths, canals and fishponds; also on coasts, where it may be seen hovering a fair way out above the surf. Resident. Takes fish, mostly after hovering and then diving in stages from at times high up (often 5–20 m). Sociable.

IDENTIFICATION A rather large and lively kingfisher. Hovers and perches in open, easy to see. As its name implies, plumage is entirely *black and white*. Underparts white, ♂ with *two black bands across breast* and ♀ with one. White supercilium between black crown and black eye-stripe. Tail fairly long, white with black centre and terminal band. Outer wing black with white primary-base patches. Bill black.

VOICE Loud, sharp and chirpy whistled notes, often delivered at furious tempo and without any clear pattern (can recall Great Snipe display) but now and then crystallizing into a rhythmic 'titi-**tütt**-titte**ritt**'.

Hoopoe　　　　　　Kingfisher

White-throated Kingfisher　　Pied Kingfisher

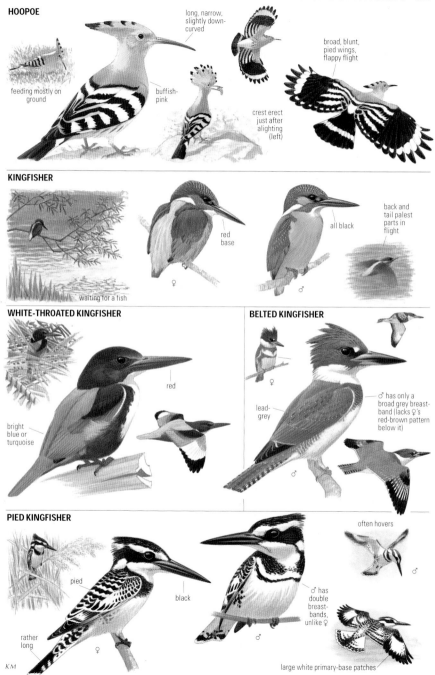

HOOPOE

long, narrow, slightly down-curved

feeding mostly on ground

buffish-pink

crest erect just after alighting (left)

broad, blunt, pied wings, flappy flight

KINGFISHER

waiting for a fish

red base

♀

all black

♂

back and tail palest parts in flight

WHITE-THROATED KINGFISHER

red

bright blue or turquoise

BELTED KINGFISHER

♀

lead-grey

♂ has only a broad grey breast-band (lacks ♀'s red-brown pattern below it)

♂

PIED KINGFISHER

often hovers

♂

pied

black

rather long

♀

♂ has double breast-bands, unlike ♀

♂

large white primary-base patches

KM

BEE-EATERS *Meropidae*

Rather small or thrush-sized, slim birds with slender, pointed, downcurved bill, long, pointed wings and long tail, usually with tail projection. Three species in the region, many more in rest of Africa and in S Asia; warmth-loving. Specialists in catching flying insects, not least *Hymenoptera*. Sociable habits, often seen in flocks, breed in colonies. Nest in ground holes, often in river bank or sand-pit.

(European) **Bee-eater** *Merops apiaster*   **V**∗

L 25–29 cm (incl. tail projection 0–3), WS 36–40 cm. Breeds in open country in warm regions, in cultivated areas or in broken, open terrain with pastureland, bushes, odd trees or copses, often by rivers with steep banks. Summer visitor (mostly May–Aug), winters in S Africa. Wary.

IDENTIFICATION Medium-sized bee-eater with exotically rich and gaudy plumage colours. Adult should be unmistakable with *bright yellow throat, yellowish-white shoulder patches* and *red-brown crown / back and inner wing-panel* above. Juvenile on other hand can at distance be confused with Blue-cheeked Bee-eater (which see), owing to duller and more greenish colours above. Flies in long, shallow undulations. Hunts often high up with straight-winged glides and brief periods of fast wingbeats (much as House Martin).

VOICE Call a frequently repeated, soft rolling 'prrüt' with lilting tone, given in chorus from flocks in flight, carries far. When agitated at nest a purer, short, whistled 'wüt'.

Blue-cheeked Bee-eater *Merops persicus*   **V**∗∗∗

L 28–32 cm (incl. tail projection 4–8), WS 35–39 cm. Breeds in dry, open terrain, but often near watercourses. Summer visitor (mostly Apr–Sep), winters in Africa.

IDENTIFICATION An *almost entirely green* bee-eater, same size as Bee-eater but adult has *longer and narrower tail projection*. Like Bee-eater has *rusty-red underwings*, so resembles latter from below in flight (unless shape of tail projection discernible). Note *uniform green back* (lacks any hint of pale shoulder patches), *red-brown throat patch* with only *little yellow on chin* and *narrower dark trailing edge to arm below*. – Juvenile: Duller green. Only rudimentary tail projection. Has almost no yellow on chin and lacks blue-green on head.

VOICE Call like Bee-eater's but is drier and a bit harder, also somewhat higher-pitched, 'prri prri prri...'.

Little Green Bee-eater *Merops orientalis*   —

L 21–25 cm (incl. tail projection 5–8). Breeds in arid, open terrain with scattered trees, also in palm groves and gardens etc. Often seen perched on wires and bushtops. Not shy.

IDENTIFICATION Smallest bee-eater in region, no bigger than a wheatear, with almost *entirely green* plumage and *black eye-stripe* and a *black cross-band between throat and breast*. Sexes alike. – Variation: In Israel and Jordan (ssp. *cyanophrys*) entire *throat and a narrow supercilium bright blue*, black band below throat usually broad and diffuse, also *tail projection short*. In Nile Valley (*cleopatra*) has *throat green*, throat band always narrow, and *tail projection long*.

VOICE Call or alarm short, hard 'kitt' notes. Song seems to consist of various hard, rolling, shrill whistles in rapid series, e.g. 'krrih krrih kru-kru krieh kr-krü'.

(European) **Roller** *Coracias garrulus*   **V**∗∗

L 29–32 cm, WS 52–57½ cm. Breeds in dry, warm, open country with scattered trees, copses and open woods (mainly oak, locally also pine) and plenty of largish ground-dwelling insects (beetles, grasshoppers etc.). Summer visitor (mostly May–Aug), winters in S Africa. Nests usually in tree-hole.

IDENTIFICATION A Jackdaw-sized, heavily built, green-tinged *pale blue* bird with *brown back*. Large head and *strong black bill*. In flight, shows contrast between blue wing-coverts and blackish remiges. Leading wing-edge and rump ultramarine-blue. Over longer stretches flies with rather slow but powerful, slightly clipped beats and on straight course, but at times makes minor turns and swerves. – Juvenile: Duller and more green-grey plumage; breast and median upperwing-coverts tinged brown.

VOICE Call and alarm a hard 'rack-ack' (sometimes mono- or trisyllabic). When nervous etc. raucous series, 'reehr-eehr-eehr-...' (voice like scolding Jackdaw or Rook). Call during almost Lapwing-like display-flight starts with a few hard notes followed by 1–4 fast, hoarse drawn-out 'kraah' notes. Structure of call varies somewhat.

Rose-ringed Parakeet *Psittacula krameri*   [r**B**4]

L ad. ♂ 39–43 cm (of which tail *c.* 22–26), younger ♂ and ♀ 27–36 cm; WS 42–48 cm. Breeds in open woods, parks and gardens in Egypt, Israel, Greece, Spain, England, Holland, Belgium and W Germany; introduced from its natural range in S Asia and C Africa. (Cf. Monk Parakeet, p. 390.)

IDENTIFICATION Medium-sized and slim like a bee-eater, and with its *wholly pale green* plumage possibly confusable at distance in flight with Blue-cheeked Bee-eater; but note bill, and that *underwing is pale green with dark grey remiges* (not uniform rusty-red). Unmistakable at close range: *parrot bill with rosehip-red upper half*, also extremely wedge-shaped, long tail. Yellowish-white eye with orange-red bare surrounding skin. – ♂: Small black bib. Narrow black and orangey-pink neck-ring. Very narrow black loral streak. Older birds have very long tail. – ♀: Head all green.

VOICE Very loud, squawking 'kyik kyik kyiek' and the like; somewhat reminiscent of begging Fieldfare fledglings.

Bee-eater   Blue-cheeked Bee-eater   Little Green Bee-eater   Roller

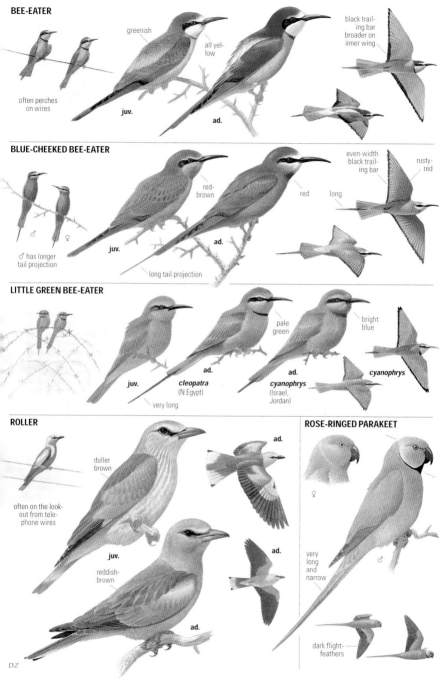

BEE-EATER

greenish

all yellow

black trailing bar broader on inner wing

often perches on wires

juv.

ad.

BLUE-CHEEKED BEE-EATER

♂

♀

♂ has longer tail projection

red-brown

red

even-width black trailing bar

rusty-red

long

juv.

ad.

long tail projection

LITTLE GREEN BEE-EATER

pale green

bright blue

juv.

cleopatra
(N Egypt)

ad.

ad.

cyanophrys
(Israel, Jordan)

cyanophrys

very long

ROLLER

ROSE-RINGED PARAKEET

duller brown

ad.

often on the lookout from telephone wires

♀

juv.

reddish-brown

ad.

ad.

very long and narrow

♂

ad.

dark flight-feathers

DZ

WOODPECKERS *Picidae*

Eleven species, all but the aberrant Wryneck specialists in climbing and excavating nest holes in vertical tree trunks. Anatomical adaptations include strong feet with mobile toes (species with four toes have two directed backwards) and sharp claws, stiff tail-feathers which serve as support on vertical surfaces, also powerful awl- or chisel-shaped bill and 'shock-absorbent' braincase. Food includes wood-boring insects; have greatly elongated tongue base for scouring and emptying deep insect burrows. Most species use drumming as a 'song' (both sexes drum). Only the Wryneck is a long-distance migrant, others largely residents.

Black Woodpecker *Dryocopus martius* —

L 40–46 cm, WS 67–73 cm. Nests in mature forest, often pine and mixed forest, but also beech. Expanding in NW Europe. Wary but also inquisitive, can be called up by imitating its voice. Nest entrance oval, *c.* 9×12 cm.

IDENTIFICATION Crow-sized and *entirely black* with *whitish eye* and *all-red crown* (♂) or just a red patch on hindcrown (♀). Compared with e.g. Green Woodpecker, *narrower neck* and longer head with *angular nape*. *Flight flappy* and rather clumsy with *head held up*, with mostly downward jerks of *broad, rounded wings, on straight course* (not dipping as other woodpeckers), recalling Nutcracker if anything.

VOICE Rich repertoire of loud calls. Often heard year round is the flight-/alarm-call, 'krrück krrück krrück...'. On landing it may utter a shrill **'kliii-**eh'. Song a shrill whistled series, quite distinct from Green Woodpecker's laugh in its more tentative intro, even pitch throughout and 'wilder' voice, 'kuih kvi kvi-kvi-kvi-kvi-kvi-kvi-kvi'. In spring drums very loudly in open bursts (like machine-gun salvos; audible at 2–4 km), 1.75–3 sec. long (♂ longer than ♀).

(European) Green Woodpecker *Picus viridis*   r**B**3

L 30–36 cm, WS 45–51 cm. Breeds in open deciduous and mixed woods, mature farmland with pasture and trees, parkland and commons, also in large gardens. Common. As all woodpeckers, absent Ireland. Food mainly ants; spends much time on ground. Shy, wary. Nest entrance *c.* 6×7 m.

IDENTIFICATION Often seen passing in *strongly undulating flight*, and so long as you see *green upperparts with yellow rump* confusion is possible only with Grey-headed Woodpecker (which see for differences); ♀ Golden Oriole, also greenish above and with dipping flight, is much smaller and slimmer, with narrower wings, longer tail. Once the bird perches, on the alert, and can be watched through binoculars, note the *red crown* and *black-enclosed white eye*. Sexes differ in ♂ having *red centre to black moustache*, ♀ not. – Juvenile: Much as adult but whole plumage is spotty and

vermiculated. – Variation: Iberian birds (ssp. *sharpei*) have almost no black on head, are dusky grey around eye, and ♂ has red moustache with black border below only.

VOICE Usually noticed by calls. Often utters a shrill, explosive 'kyü-kyü-**kyück**' in flight, sometimes drawn out in long series with stress on e.g. every second or fourth syllable. Song a loud, laughing series of 10–18 'klü' notes falling somewhat in pitch and accelerating slightly at end, 'klüh-klüh-klü-klü-klü-klü-klü-klü-...'. Drums only rarely, a fast but soft roll *c.* 1½ sec. long. Young beg with hoarse, rasping series of notes.

Grey-headed Woodpecker *Picus canus*   —

L 27–30 cm. Breeds in several quite different habitats, e.g. in swamp-forests along rivers and lakeshores with plenty of insect-rich decayed deciduous trees; in open or park-like mature deciduous forest; in open woodland in uplands (often to 600 m, at times higher) and with good coniferous element. Food insects, often ants. Nest-entrance diameter *c.* 5½ cm.

IDENTIFICATION Between Green and White-backed Woodpeckers in size, but confusable of course only with former. Compared with Green, the *head is slightly smaller and more rounded*, this reinforced by the slightly *shorter and more slender bill* ('kinder' appearance), the different, more *uniform grey head pattern* with less black around eye (only lores black) which is *amber-coloured*, the *narrower dark stripe on chin-side*, also *red crown patch restricted to forecrown* (♂) or *no red at all on crown* (♀). Back is moss-green (lacks Green Woodpecker's yellow-green tone), underparts unvermiculated *light grey* (with hint of green), not yellow-tinged. – Juvenile: Very like adult, only somewhat more subdued colours.

VOICE When agitated, series of choking 'chk'. Song a series of 6–9 mechanical-sounding whistles which gradually drop in pitch, 'kii kii küü küü, küü, kuu', and often slow down markedly after fast opening; easy to imitate by whistling; lacks Green Woodpecker's laughing, almost bubbling tone, sounds more desolate. Drums more often than Green, rolls loud and rather fast, *c.* 1½ sec. long.

Levaillant's Green Woodpecker *Picus vaillantii*   —

L 30–33 cm. Breeds in mountain forests of oak, poplar, cedars and pine, mainly close to treeline at around 2000 m.

IDENTIFICATION Very like Iberian ♀ of Green Woodpecker (see latter), but has *pale border above the all-black moustache* (*both sexes*) right up to the bill, also is *less dusky grey behind and above eye*. ♂ has fully red crown, ♀ is red only on hindcrown (black-spotted on rest of crown).

VOICE Like Green Woodpecker's, but song often slightly faster in tempo, with more even pitch and not so laughing in tone. Drums more often than Green, rolls 1–1½ sec.

Black Woodpecker   Green Woodpecker   Grey-headed Woodpecker   Levaillant's Green Woodpecker

BLACK WOODPECKER

flight flappy and slightly clumsy, course straight

all-red crown

angular hindcrown

thin neck

♂

red only on hindcrown

♀

♂

sexes already differ as nestlings

♀

GREEN WOODPECKER

undulating flight, folds wings completely between wingbeat bursts

juv. ♀

black

red

juv. ♂

spotted black

yellow-green

♂

black eye-surround

red centre

black

♀

no black around eye

♀

♂

sharpei
(Iberia)

GREY-HEADED WOODPECKER

small red patch on forehead

narrow

grey

♂

lacks red

♀

plain

looks neckless, snub-nosed and rather short-billed in flight

lacks black and white bars on tail-sides

often visits old aspen trees

LEVAILLANT'S GREEN WOODPECKER

♂

obvious pale border above all-black moustache

♂

lacks red

♀

prefers ancient oak and cedar woods at high altitudes in Atlas mountains

DZ

Great Spotted Woodpecker *Dendrocopos major* ⌐B3

L 23–26 cm, WS 38–44 cm. Breeds in all kinds of woodland, especially with stands of spruce and pine (conifer seeds important winter food), also larger parks and gardens; in Britain mostly in deciduous / mixed woods, often with good element of aspen and waterlogged regrowth. Alert and cautious, but in winter may visit birdtables, suet bags etc., can cling upside-down like a tit. Food insects, conifer seeds, at times also bird eggs and nestlings. To extract seeds wedges cones firmly in special bark crevices ('anvils'); piles of empty cones lie beneath. In some autumns, when cone crop fails in northern taiga, makes invasion-like migrations to S and SW (some reach Britain). Nest entrance *c.* 5×6 cm.

IDENTIFICATION The commonest of the 'pied' woodpeckers, i.e. those with basically *black and white plumage*. Usually easily identified by *saturated red vent* sharply demarcated from whitish belly, by *unstreaked flanks*, and by its two *large, white, oval shoulder patches*. The black wings are barred white. *Flies in deep undulations*, in straight direction. – Adult ♂: Sugar-lump-sized *red patch on hindcrown*. – Adult ♀: Black *crown with no red*. – Juvenile: Combination of mostly red crown (red patch larger and brighter in ♂), more poorly developed black stripe between moustache and nape, paler red vent and sometimes faint streaks on flanks makes it confusable with Middle Spotted and White-backed Woodpeckers; note *white ovals on shoulders* as on adult (eliminating White-backed), *black moustachial stripe reaching bill, black sides to red crown patch* and *black hindcrown* (eliminating Middle Spotted). – Variation: Birds in W and S Europe usually more dusky (grey-tinged) brownish-white below and on forehead, also have slightly more slender bill. In Algeria and Tunisia (ssp. *numidus*) breast has a mottled black and red band, and red of vent extends well (but to variable degree) up onto belly.

VOICE Call a short, sharp 'kick!', sometimes slowly repeated (*c.* 1 per sec.) in longer series. When agitated gives a very fast series of thick-voiced chattering notes, 'chrett-chrett-chrett-chrett-...'. Drums in spring, rolls being characteristically short (0.4–0.8 sec.), very fast (difficult to hear individual strikes) and ending abruptly. Young beg with incessant series of thin, high twitters, 'vivivivivi...'.

Syrian Woodpecker *Dendrocopos syriacus* —

L 23–25 cm. Breeds in open, cultivated country, in orchards, gardens, parks, lines of trees, vineyards etc. Has expanded NW during 1900s. Food insects, also fruit and berries. Nest entrance *c.* 5 cm in diameter.

IDENTIFICATION Very like Great Spotted Woodpecker: a black and white 'pied' woodpecker of same size and with *only small red patch on hindcrown* on ♂ and all-black crown

on ♀, also with *large white shoulder patches* and *red vent*. Close observation needed for safe distinction; note: *no black line joining black central nape band with black angled stripe on neck-side* (safest feature on adults); *somewhat longer bill*; *pale nostril feathering* (Great Spotted black); *less white on outer tail-feathers* (only a few white spots at tip of black outer rectrices; Great Spotted has narrowly barred white tail-corners); on average cleaner white head-side and paler forehead (Great Spotted usually has dirty white cheek and brownish-white forehead, but occasionally identical); sometimes a few faint grey streaks on lower flanks and belly (never shown by post-juv. Great Spotted); on average less intensely red vent (but odd birds are similar); often slightly bigger red hindcrown patch on ♂ than corresponding one on Great Spotted (but a few are the same). – Juvenile: Streaked flanks. Often *reddish on breast*.

VOICE Common kick-call is softer than Great Spotted's and often surprisingly like Redshank's alarm-call, 'gipp'; when highly agitated this can be repeated in rapid series, 'gip-gip-gip-...', and also intermixed with a 'chirrr'. Also has thick chattering 'chre-chre-chre-...' (like Great Spotted's). Drumroll resembles Great Spotted's, but can usually be separated by being longer, 0.8–1.2 sec., and by decreasing somewhat in volume towards end (Great Spotted's short roll is more abruptly cut off); faster strike frequency and shorter duration than White-backed Woodpecker's. Young quieter than Great Spotted Woodpecker young.

Middle Spotted Woodpecker *Dendrocopos medius* —

L 19½–22 cm. Breeds in lofty deciduous woods with some old oak, hornbeam and elm and mixture of clearings, pasture and denser parts. Warmth-loving. Food insects and sap. Spends much time high up in tree crowns, and often hops along horizontal, thick branches in search of insects. Nest often excavated in decayed, rotten trunk or thick branch, sometimes strongly sloping or almost horizontal; entrance-hole diameter *c.* 4 cm.

IDENTIFICATION Only negligibly smaller than Great Spotted Woodpecker, but still looks clearly smaller owing to the *short, slender bill* and the *rounded, pale head*. Sexes similar, with: *red crown* (reaches further back on ♂, and colour is brighter red); *lack of black moustachial stripe*; white forehead and head-side, on which eye stands out as a dark spot; *white oval shoulder patches* (cf. White-backed Woodpecker); *pinkish vent* which fades into yellowish-brown belly; and fine *dark streaks on flanks*. Often perches across branches in slightly hunched posture and with drooped tail.

VOICE Kick-call rather weak; little used; very like Lesser Spotted Woodpecker's. More often gives a series of such calls *at fast trotting pace* with slightly different first syllable higher-pitched, 'kick kück-kück-kück-kück-kück-...'. Territorial assertion by song, 4–8 (or more) whining, nasal notes at slow pace (*c.* 2 per sec.), 'gvayk gvayk gvayk gvayk gvayk'. *Does not drum* for territorial purposes (only *very rarely* as auxiliary action).

Great Spotted Woodpecker

Syrian Woodpecker

Middle Spotted Woodpecker

GREAT SPOTTED WOODPECKER

two white oval shoulder patches

tail-sides barred black and white

black

♀

all-red crown

black rim

often hint of a gap

shoulder patches faintly barred

red black band

long

♂

black-spotted red breast

black

♂

red

deep red

large white spots

versatile in habitat choice: spruce-cone specialist in taiga zone, but thrives also in mixed forests and in parks and gardens

a variable amount of red on belly

juv. ♂

numidus (N Algeria, N Tunisia)

pale red, diffuse border

(juv. ♀ is similar, but has less red on crown)

SYRIAN WOODPECKER

black

black rim

red

rather large red nape patch

♀

pale

long

usually pale-cheeked

♂

gap

often red-tinged breast

streaked

sparsely streaked

pale red

few white spots

breeds in mature deciduous woods in cultivated open country; also in villages and towns

juv. ♂

(juv. ♀ is similar, but has less red on crown)

MIDDLE SPOTTED WOODPECKER

weak

thrives in mature oak forests

rounded head

gap

♂

moustachial stripe does not reach bill

tinged yellowish, streaked

♀

sexes similar, but red on crown on ♀ is somewhat duller, and the red does not reach so far back on nape

pale red, diffuse border

DZ

White-backed Woodpecker *Dendrocopos leucotos* —
L 25–28 cm. Breeds in wet mixed forest, often by lakes and rivers, with plenty of dead and dying deciduous trees (aspen, sallow, alder, birch); thus requires areas undisturbed by forestry operations, so now greatly threatened. Food insects, including larvae of longhorn beetles. Spends much time near ground pecking at willow and alder bases etc., often leaving traces in form of large, deep craters (almost as Black Woodpecker). Mobile and unpredictable, but not particularly shy. Large territory (esp. winter). Nest hole *c.* 5½×6½ cm.

IDENTIFICATION Slightly *bigger* than Great Spotted Woodpecker, longer-necked, with more angular head profile and *longer bill*. Vent light red, poorly demarcated, *belly faintly tinged buffy-pink*. Flanks streaked. Black band on head-side does not reach crown, leaves white 'throughway'. Despite its name, white back can be hard to see, but at least in flight *lower back is conspicuously white*. Perched bird in side view told by *white median coverts forming broad horizontal patch*, broader than white remex bars. ♂ has *all-red crown*, ♀ black. – Variation: Birds in SE Europe and Turkey (ssp. *lilfordi*) have *vermiculated* white back and can also have vermiculated flanks.

VOICE Kick-call is lower-pitched, 'thicker' and not so sharp as Great Spotted's, 'byück', when excited repeated in irregular series, 'byück, byü-byück...'. Drumming usually identifiable by powerful, 'loose' opening and weaker and accelerating ending ('ping-pong ball bouncing to halt'), also by being normally clearly longer (often 1.6–2.1 sec.) than Three-toed Woodpecker's, the most likely confusion risk. (Beware: ♀ White-backed often gives slightly shorter drum, sometimes approaching Three-toed.)

Three-toed Woodpecker *Picoides tridactylus* —
L 21½–24 cm. Breeds in coniferous and mixed forest with some older spruce stands and (often dying) deciduous trees. Food mostly insects; specializes on larvae of spruce bark-beetle, often strips dead spruces; also drills rings of holes in spruces to get at the sap. Usually shy. Nest entrance 4½×5 cm.

IDENTIFICATION Almost as big as Great Spotted Woodpecker. Rather dark-looking because *wings are very dark* and *flanks are diffusely vermiculated grey*. Head-side, too, looks dark with its *broad black bands*. Note *white panel from nape and right down entire back*. ♂ has pale *lemon-yellow crown*, crown of ♀ is black-streaked. – Variation: In C Europe (ssp. *alpinus*) white back-panel is vermiculated.

VOICE Kick-call softer than Great Spotted's, 'bick'. Drumming powerful, well articulated, of medium length (often 1.1–1.4 sec.), often with hint of rise in volume at start (and faint acceleration towards end), most like half a Black Woodpecker roll (and can be confused with that!). Begging-call of young sounds like an insect or distant engine.

Lesser Spotted Woodpecker *Dendrocopos minor* rB4
L 14–16½ cm, WS 24–29 cm. Breeds in deciduous woods, old orchards, parkland and, particularly in Britain, river valleys with alders. Nest entrance 3×3½ cm.

IDENTIFICATION *Smallest* woodpecker, a real dwarf with *short, plump body, round head* and *short, pointed bill*. Black above with *white bars across wings and back*. Black bar on head-side does not reach crown, leaving narrow white 'throughway' (as on White-backed Woodpecker). Flanks usually weakly streaked. ♂ has *red crown patch* with black sides; ♀ lacks all red in plumage, has small black-edged dirty brownish-white crown patch. Superficially like White-backed Woodpecker if size not apparent, but differences include *lack of red on vent*. Flies in deep undulations.

VOICE Kick-call short and sharp, generally more feeble than Great Spotted's, though still at times confusingly similar. Territory proclaimed with both drumming and song. Song a series (8–15) of piping, straight notes sometimes rising at end, 'piit piit piit piit piit piit, piit'; lacks Wryneck's whining tone. Drumming rather weak but typically open, more rattling than whirring; tempo constant throughout, and length often 1.2–1.8 sec.; often two drumrolls are given in succession with just a microsecond pause in between.

(Eurasian) Wryneck *Jynx torquilla* P4–5
L 16–18 cm. Breeds in open country with orchards, scrub-by pasture, open woodland with fields, copses etc. Summer visitor (mostly May–Sep), winters in Africa. In Britain now ± extinct, rare on passage. Ants are favourite food. Nests in existing tree-hole or nestbox (does not excavate own hole).

IDENTIFICATION Size about that of a small shrike or a Barred Warbler. *Mottled brown and grey above* (merges well with bark of trees), *vermiculated dark below on pale ground* like a small hawk (dirty white on belly, buffish-ochre on breast). *A dark line runs through eye and down neck-side*, with another *dark line along centre of crown and back*. The long *tail is sparsely barred*. Bill rather short and pointed, with strong base. Unlike other woodpeckers, does not climb using tail as support, but behaves more like a passerine; often perches crosswise on horizontal branches, chisels rather than digging with its bill. Flight, too, is more passerine-like, fast with only moderately undulating course. Frequently hops on ground (with slightly raised tail) in search of ants; otherwise rather discreet, quiet habits, and easily escapes detection but for its voice. Sexes alike.

VOICE Alarm a series of hard 'teck' notes. Hisses (and twists head snake-like) if discovered in nest hole or otherwise startled. Young beg with a fast, shuttling 'zizizizizi...'. Song a series of 12–18 loud, whining notes, 4 per sec., 'tie-tie-tie-tie...'; rather long intervals between phrases.

White-backed Woodpecker

Three-toed Woodpecker

Lesser Spotted Woodpecker

Wryneck

WHITE-BACKED WOODPECKER

favours damp deciduous forests with plenty of dying trees

white back / rump ♂

black

♀ red long

♂ gap

barred back

barred flanks

unmarked white back

pale buffish-pink, streaked

pale red

lilfordi
(Pyrenees, SE Europe, Turkey, Caucasus)

leucotos
(N and E Europe)

THREE-TOED WOODPECKER

often 'ring-barks' spruces to get at the sap

lacks red

long white panel along back ♂

lacks yellow

black-cheeked

yellow ♂

♀

streaked

barred back

densely barred

unmarked white back

alpinus
(Alps, E and SE Europe)

tridactylus
(N Europe)

LESSER SPOTTED WOODPECKER

climbs quietly on underside of thick branches like a large tree-creeper

♂

red weak ♂

gap

barred

black

♀

lacks red

lacks red

WRYNECK

throat ochrous-buff

can be confused with a ♀ Red-backed Shrike in flight

frequently searches for ants on ground

short, pointed

dark band

sexes alike

barred

long, sparsely barred

DZ

LARKS *Alaudidae*
Ground-living passerines, mostly brown and off-white. 20 species. Hindclaw long and straight. Many have sustained, hovering or fluttering song-flight and are excellent singers, capable of mimicry, too. Nest on the ground in tuft of grass. Young often leave nest before fledged. Juveniles recognized by pale-fringed feathers on back and wings.

(Common) Skylark *Alauda arvensis* rB1
L 16–18 cm. Breeds commonly in open, cultivated land, also on meadows and heaths. Mainly resident, but influx in winter from N. Large flocks may congregate on stubble fields and grass steppe in winter.
    IDENTIFICATION *Greyish-brown, streaked* above and on breast; breast buff, belly white. Streaking of breast ends rather abruptly above unmarked belly. ♂ can erect *blunt crest* on crown (Crested Lark has longer and more pointed crest). Often seen on fields and along roadsides; when approached, it first squats, then 'catapults' up, retreating a short distance low over ground with *fluttering wings* and half-spread, lowered tail, the brown bird showing *thin, diffuse* (brownish-white) *trailing edge to wing* and *white sides of tail*. Sings sometimes (often at dawn) from perch but usually in *typical song-flight*, climbing higher and higher on fluttering wings, and eventually stays at one spot at 50–100 (150) m, difficult to detect. At end of song-flight descends while singing, but falls silently to ground the last stage with folded wings.
    VOICE A variety of calls, all rather dry rolling sounds, e.g. 'prreet', 'prrlyh', 'prrüt-üt' and 'preeh-e'. Sometimes, often when anxious, a more piping 'p(r)eeh'. Sings from late winter until midsummer, from first light to evening. Song is an incessant outpour of rolling, chirruping and whistling notes at fast pace and for periods lasting 3–15 min., some notes being repeated and varied, and with a few imitations (of e.g. Green Sandpiper, Barn Swallow) woven in.

Oriental Skylark *Alauda gulgula* —
L 14–16 cm. Breeds on cultivated fields and natural steppe in S Asia and Central Asia (W to Iran); northern populations short-range migrants. Rare winter visitor in Israel.
    IDENTIFICATION Very similar to Skylark; slightly smaller, though more reliably separated by: *shorter primary projection*; more *uniformly pale buff underparts*; on many, *primaries edged red-brown*; outer tail-feathers usually light buffish-grey (but at times almost white, and difficult to judge against the sky); trailing edge of wing not obviously pale; and on average slightly longer bill and shorter tail than Skylark. Can erect small crest like Skylark.
    VOICE One flight-call very different from any of Skylark, a short, strident, buzzing or 'mechanical' 'bzrü'. Other calls

include somewhat Barn Swallow-like 'plip' and several more Skylark-like notes, 'prit-üt', 'drreeü' etc. Song very like Skylark's (only more feeble), delivered in similar song-flight.

Crested Lark *Galerida cristata* V***
L 17–19 cm. Breeds in fields, on open industrial sites, among railway tracks in harbours, etc. (with easily accessible weed seeds); in S parts of range also in more arid areas. Resident. In Britain & Ireland extremely rare vagrant.
    IDENTIFICATION A fraction larger than Skylark, greyish-brown with *long, pointed crest*, visible at rear crown even when folded (short crest of Skylark invisible when folded). Compared with Skylark, usually a slightly more greyish and dark bird (though races of N Africa paler and browner) with more *diffuse streaking on breast* (though some are more distinctly streaked). Lacks pale trailing edge of wing (cf. Skylark), and has *buff-brown outer tail-feathers*, not white. Underwing, and often uppertail-coverts, tinged red-brown. *Bill is long and pointed with straight lower edge* (a certain variation in bill length: longest in N Africa, shorter in N Europe and Middle East; cf. very similar Thekla Lark).
    VOICE Vocal. Commonest call consists of variable combination of 2–4 whistling, straight notes, one or several drawn out, with desolate ring, e.g. 'treelee**püü**' or 'vü tee **vüü**'. This call used as 'eager' contact-call, but also as alternative song, uttered repeatedly in the territory. Other calls are e.g. cheerful mewing, soft but usually slightly cracked, upward-inflected 'dvuuee', often in flight and repeated, and a more strident, whimpering 'brshü'. The real song is long and often given in flight, richly varied, containing quite a lot of the melancholy, straight whistling notes (cf. above); often difficult to separate from song of Thekla Lark!

Thekla Lark *Galerida theklae* —
L 15–17 cm. Breeds in more natural and arid habitats than Crested Lark, often at higher altitudes on barren mountain slopes or dry steppes; sometimes also in orchards, in cork oak savanna or shrubbery on sandy soil.
    IDENTIFICATION Very similar to Crested Lark, and reliable identification generally requires close view. Marginally smaller. *Bill is shorter* and usually *not so pointed—lower edge slightly convex* on most (exception: Balearics), which creates 'more cute' appearance; bill is often slightly darker, too. *Streaking of breast* generally *more distinct* and finer on paler ground (though some are very similar). Plumage is *greyer*, *mantle and back* on average somewhat *more distinctly streaked*, *tertials more contrasting*, and *uppertail-coverts more reddish-brown* than on Crested. Now and then perches in bushes or trees (as Crested Lark only exceptionally does).
    VOICE Similar to Crested Lark's, but softer and more melodious (not such melancholy piping with straight notes), and often more syllables, e.g. 'tu-telli-**tew**-tilli-**tee**'; certain calls, however, are more like Crested's. Flight-song is similar to Crested's, but is slightly softer, *more varied* and pleasing, not so sharply piping. Both use mimicry.

Skylark   Crested Lark   Thekla Lark

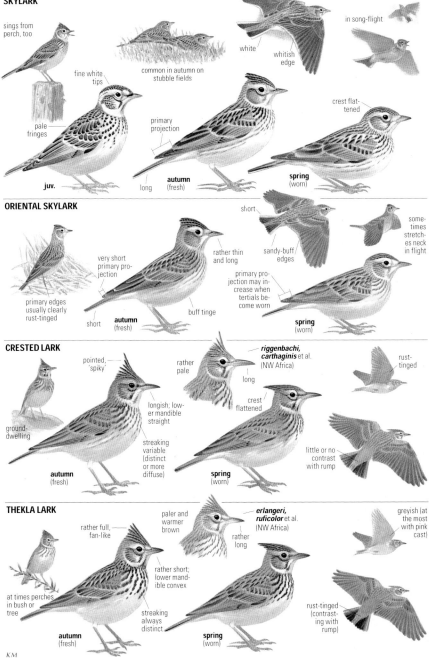

SKYLARK

sings from perch, too

fine white tips

common in autumn on stubble fields

white

whitish edge

in song-flight

crest flat-tened

pale fringes

primary projection

long

juv.

autumn (fresh)

spring (worn)

ORIENTAL SKYLARK

short

rather thin and long

sandy-buff edges

some-times stretch-es neck in flight

very short primary projection

primary edges usually clearly rust-tinged

short

autumn (fresh)

buff tinge

primary projection may increase when tertials become worn

spring (worn)

CRESTED LARK

pointed, 'spiky'

rather pale

riggenbachi, carthaginis et al. (NW Africa)

long

rust-tinged

ground-dwelling

longish; lower mandible straight

crest flattened

streaking variable (distinct or more diffuse)

little or no contrast with rump

autumn (fresh)

spring (worn)

THEKLA LARK

paler and warmer brown

erlangeri, ruficolor et al. (NW Africa)

greyish (at the most with pink cast)

rather full, fan-like

rather long

at times perches in bush or tree

rather short; lower mandible convex

streaking always distinct

rust-tinged (contrasting with rump)

autumn (fresh)

spring (worn)

KM

Woodlark *Lullula arborea* r(m)**B4**

L 13½–15 cm. Breeds in open forests, preferring pine on sandy soil, but also in mixed or broadleaved forests with clearings and on heathland with scattered copses. Resident in Britain; increasing. N European birds migrate to S Europe. Rather shy and difficult to approach.

IDENTIFICATION Rather small, brown and *short-tailed.* Often perches exposed in trees, bushes or on wires, unlike other larks (though spends most of the time on ground). *Can recall small woodpecker in undulating flight with short, broad wings* and stubby tail! *Tail tipped white* (adding to the short impression when seen against a bright sky). Sides of tail not white (as on Skylark) but pale brown, and trailing edge of wing on adult not light. When perched, note characteristic *light-dark-light pattern near bend of wing* (primary coverts dark with buff-white tips, and white patch at their base); also *broad buffish-white supercilia reaching far back* (almost joining on hindneck). Song mostly delivered in drifting song-flight high up (100–150 m), often at very first light, or even beneath stars on pitch-dark night.

VOICE Call a soft whistling yodel, '**tlew**ee-**tlew**ee' or more feebly '**dü**dlu**ee**', often revealing overflying small parties in autumn or spring. Song is one of the most attractive, consisting of pleasant and 'sweet but melancholy' notes in series, opening hesitantly, accelerating, often falling in pitch and gaining in loudness, e.g. 'lee, lee-lee-leelee**leelü**lu... **ee**-lü **ee**-lü **ee**-lü-**eelu-eelu**eelu... tluee, tluee tluee vi vi vi **tellellellell**...', etc.

(Greater) **Short-toed Lark**
Calandrella brachydactyla V**

L 14–16 cm. Breeds in open, dry areas, on cultivated fields or more arid plains. Annual vagrant to Britain late spring or autumn, favouring sandy wasteland, arable fields or open seashores.

IDENTIFICATION Rather small and pale, greyish-brown and off-white. Underparts of adult practically *unmarked*, with only *a dark patch on side of breast* ('dwarf Calandra Lark'; some have faint patch, others have several streaks rather than one patch, but never streaked on *whole* breast; cf. Lesser Short-toed Lark). Important distinction from Lesser Short-toed is *long tertials*, reaching to or very near tip of wing. Median coverts dark with broad pale tips (in pipit fashion). Broad off-white supercilium and largely unstreaked grey-brown cheek, outlined in pale, give distinct facial expression. Bill pointed and rather pale. Some birds (both sexes; more commonly in Spain and Africa) have faint red-brown tinge on crown (often with reduced streaking), others are more evenly grey-brown and obviously streaked (normal plumage in E Europe, Turkey). Song-flight usually slowly drifting around at some height, *undulating*, tail folded, *song phrases generally delivered in phase with bursts of quick, fluttering wingbeats* (end of descent, whole ascent). More prolonged song phrases (from agitated bird) or strong winds (forcing singer to beat wings in longer and quicker bursts) at times alter typical pattern. – Juvenile: Apart from pale fringes on upperparts, has sparse and diffuse blotching across whole breast; separated from juvenile Lesser Short-toed by primary projection, bill shape and calls.

VOICE Call a dry chirruping 'drit', drier, shorter and more 'bouncing' than Skylark's, like House Martin call; or more full 'trilp', a bit reminiscent of Tawny Pipit. At times tantalizingly similar to Lesser Short-toed's, 'drrr-t-t'. Song of two types, the simpler being characteristic: brief phrases (1–2 sec.), dry chirruping voice, faltering opening, acceleration and clattering or shuttling end, pauses between phrases 1–3 sec. A more ecstatic song prolongs phrases to 5–30 sec., includes imitations and displays a greater variation, making it easily confusable with Lesser Short-toed (and other larks!) unless the call and faltering sections are woven in.

Lesser Short-toed Lark *Calandrella rufescens* V***

L 13–14½ cm. Breeds on dry plains (clay), by salines and on desert-like steppe. Mainly resident, but eastern populations migrate to Middle East.

IDENTIFICATION Small, usually fractionally smaller than Short-toed Lark (but some eastern races equal in size), *greyer* and *more evenly streaked.* Best separated by: *streaked breast* (incl. centre of breast, recalling dwarf Skylark); *shorter tertials* (ending 10–15 mm short of wing-tip); *shorter, more bulbous bill*; and voice. Often 'cute-looking' from *rounded head shape,* small bill and wide pale eye-ring. Supercilium is usually less obvious. Cheek finely streaked. Song-flight often drifting around with fluttering wingbeats and partly spread tail, in suitable winds now and then shifting to clearly *slower wingbeats* (never seen from Short-toed). – Marked geographical variation: Birds of Spain (ssp. *apetzii*) small and rather grey-brown, breast heavily streaked, flanks streaked, too. Birds in S Middle East and N Africa (*minor*) and in the Canaries small but brown, less greyish, streaking of breast fine, flanks unstreaked. Birds of E Europe (*heinei*) and Turkey (*aharonii*) large and greyish, breast finely and diffusely streaked, flanks faintly streaked.

VOICE Most common call a dry, trilling or buzzing 'drrrrd', often slightly falling in pitch or slowing at the end; usually repeated a few times; voice reminiscent of Sand Martin. NB: Short-toed Larks can at times have very similar calls! Song consistently richer, more varied, and pace quicker than Short-toed's; excellent imitations (incl. of other larks, making identification so much more problematic—can mimic Crested or Short-toed for several seconds!); will mix imitations with own drier trills and softer, piping notes in Thekla fashion. Some phrases shorter, more like Short-toed Lark; mixed-in dry trilling calls and 'frizzling' fast pace are then best clues.

Woodlark

Short-toed Lark

Lesser Short-toed Lark

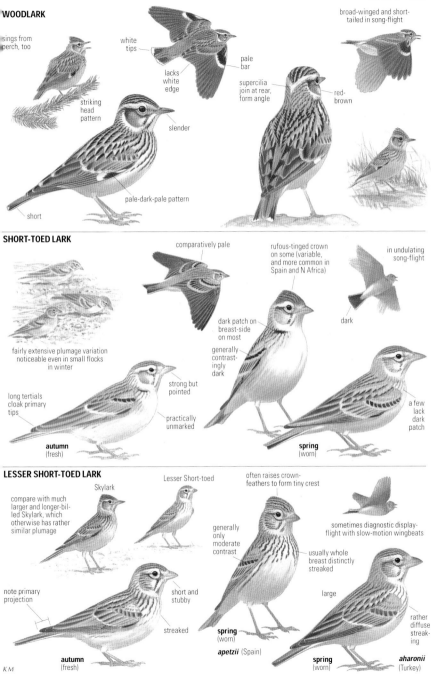

WOODLARK

sings from perch, too

white tips

lacks white edge

striking head pattern

slender

short

pale-dark-pale pattern

broad-winged and short-tailed in song-flight

pale bar

supercilia join at rear, form angle

red-brown

SHORT-TOED LARK

comparatively pale

rufous-tinged crown on some (variable, and more common in Spain and N Africa)

in undulating song-flight

dark patch on breast-side on most

dark

generally contrastingly dark

fairly extensive plumage variation noticeable even in small flocks in winter

long tertials cloak primary tips

strong but pointed

practically unmarked

a few lack dark patch

autumn (fresh)

spring (worn)

LESSER SHORT-TOED LARK

Skylark

Lesser Short-toed

often raises crown-feathers to form tiny crest

compare with much larger and longer-bil-led Skylark, which otherwise has rather similar plumage

generally only moderate contrast

sometimes diagnostic display-flight with slow-motion wingbeats

usually whole breast distinctly streaked

note primary projection

short and stubby

large

streaked

rather diffuse streaking

autumn (fresh)

spring (worn)

apetzii (Spain)

spring (worn)

aharonii (Turkey)

KM

Desert Lark *Ammomanes deserti* —

L 15–16½ cm. Breeds in arid (desert-like), open, often sloping or rocky terrain, in wadis or on mountainsides with boulders and smaller stones. Generally avoids flat and sandy desert. Resident. Usually seen singly, in pairs or a few together. Discreet habits; often confiding, and allows quite close approach; unpredictable, often flies off silently.

IDENTIFICATION Chaffinch-sized, robust lark, front-heavy with tapered rear. *Bill fairly heavy and long*, culmen curved (bill size varies geographically to some extent, e.g. larger in S Morocco, smaller in Sinai and Israel), *base pale brownish-yellow* with slightly darker culmen and tip. Plumage evenly grey-brown above, pinkish grey-buff below, usually with *obvious diffuse streaking on breast*. Short supercilium and ill-defined eye-ring pale; loral streak faintly darker. Tertials brown-grey, tinged red-brown, when fresh obviously pale-edged. *Tail rather dark*, tail-feathers edged rufous-buff. Outer webs of primaries edged red-brown. Sexes alike. (For geographical variation, see plate.) Resembles Bar-tailed Lark, but most reliably distinguished by size and colour of bill, and lack of *distinct black band on outer tail*. Further helpful differences: Desert Lark's usually more streaked breast and neck-sides, slightly longer primary projection, and different voice and choice of habitat.

VOICE Rather silent, still has several calls, some perhaps only variations of same: a common call is a rolling 'churrr' (almost like distant Alpine Chough!); also, a more subdued whistling, slowly repeated 'cheealp', 'chu-ül', 'chü(u)' or 'chup' (obviously varying!). Song rather deep-voiced, loud and resonant with desolate ring, a quickly repeated phrase of 3–6 syllables, often uttered in undulating song-flight, e.g. 'chu-we-chacha, **wooee**' or 'chu-**weeü** chuwe-trutru'.

Bar-tailed Lark *Ammomanes cincturus* —

L 13–14 cm. Breeds in flat, sandy deserts, but also in semi-desert with pebbles and scattered low vegetation. *Not found in mountains* or in rocky, broken terrain. Resident, locally nomadic. Often seen in larger flocks outside breeding; restless, an industrious runner, making brief stops only.

IDENTIFICATION Recalls Desert Lark, but distinguished by the following (apart from habitat and voice): *smaller size* and more chubby, with *rounded head* and *shorter bill*—has a 'cuter' look, though shape rather variable, being fluffed up and rounded on chilly mornings but remarkably slender and noticeably 'leggy' in midday heat; in autumn, upperparts (mantle/scapulars) *often* contrastingly *greyer* than head/nape and wing; tail pale red-brown with *distinct black terminal band*, obvious when alighting (when the tail is briefly spread); *bill off-white* in strong sunlight, faintly *pinkish* in overcast weather; tertials *pale rufous* (best judged from be-

hind); and *outer primaries tipped blackish*, sometimes noticeable in flight, and *contrasting with tertials* on folded wing.

VOICE Some calls resemble Desert Lark's. Often a dry, somewhat strained and hard trilling 'cherr'; also a short, nasal 'chüp'. A possibly more diagnostic call is a harsh 'bshee' (recalling autumn call of Reed Bunting). Song characteristic, a thin squeaky note repeated rhythmically a few times, preceded by one or two low notes (audible only at close range), rather like the sound of a distant, old, rusty pump, '(tleo) weeeh, (tleo) weeeh, (tleo) weeeh, ...'; often delivered in song-flight, undulating in phase with the song.

Dunn's Lark *Eremalauda dunni* —

L 14–15 cm. Local and scarce breeder in flat and sandy desert and semi-desert in Middle East (e.g. Jordan); range poorly known. Resident or nomadic; some scattered winter and breeding records in S Israel, more regularly in recent years. Runs readily, but will also make longer stops than Bar-tailed Lark to 'rough up' some plant with its strong bill.

IDENTIFICATION Between Desert and Bar-tailed Larks in size. Note: *heavy bill pinkish* (sometimes with orange cast at tip) but *lacking markedly dark culmen and tip*; bill thick even *near tip*, culmen strongly curved; red-brown tinge in sand-brown plumage; red-brown *streaking on crown, mantle and sides of breast*; *long tertials* practically reach tip of wing (virtually *no primary projection*); grey, *narrow moustachial and malar stripes; tail-sides black, central tail-feathers buff*; rather obvious light buff-white eye-ring and short supercilium; wings (incl. coverts) fairly uniform and pale.

VOICE Call a throaty upward-inflected 'dshrooee'; also a more sparrow-like 'chilp'. More subdued 'prt' and trilling 'drrree-ü' also heard from foraging flocks. Song a rapid stanza of sparrow-like chirpings and drier lark-type notes.

Black-crowned Sparrow-lark

Eremopterix nigriceps —

L 11½–12½ cm. Not a regular breeder within treated region, occurs further S (Cape Verde, S Morocco, Sahel region, SE Egypt, S Iraq, etc.); occasional breeder in Israel. Recorded in Algeria. Typically seen in flocks, usually in flat semi-desert and on arid plains with scattered bushes or trees.

IDENTIFICATION *Very small*, Serin-sized, but with proportionately rather large head. Bill large and *conical*, finch-like, comparatively pale grey-white. *Underwing dark* (blackish on ♂). Outer tail-feathers are black, central pale, like back.—Adult ♂: *Black underparts* (from chin to undertail), sand-coloured above, and *boldly pied head pattern*.—Adult ♀: Entire upperparts pale rufous-buff (rufous tinge decreases with abrasion), crown, scapulars and sides of breast finely streaked. Rest of underparts pale buffish-white. Median coverts a little darker brown, often forming darker band. Colour and tail pattern recall Dunn's Lark, but note smaller size, dark underwing, heavy conical bill (lacking pinkish tinge), and shorter, blunter wings in flight. Alights again surprisingly quickly after having been flushed.

VOICE Call e.g. a sparrow-like 'chep'. Song, heard mostly at dawn and dusk, a rhythmically repeated (every 4–5 sec.) phrase of 2–4 notes with melancholy ring, e.g. 'wit ti-weee', last note slightly lower-pitched and drawn out. Usually delivered in drifting, low song-flight with fluttering wings.

Desert Lark   Bar-tailed Lark

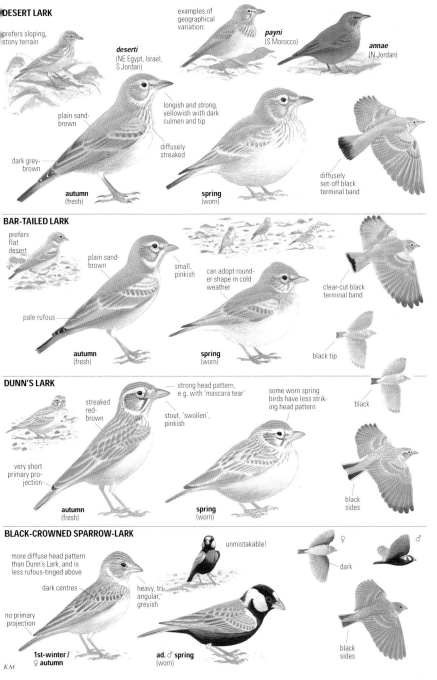

DESERT LARK

prefers sloping, stony terrain

examples of geographical variation:

deserti (NE Egypt, Israel, S Jordan)

payni (S Morocco)

annae (N Jordan)

plain sand-brown

longish and strong, yellowish with dark culmen and tip

diffusely streaked

dark grey-brown

diffusely set-off black terminal band

autumn (fresh)

spring (worn)

BAR-TAILED LARK

prefers flat desert

plain sand-brown

small, pinkish

can adopt rounder shape in cold weather

clear-cut black terminal band

pale rufous

black tip

autumn (fresh)

spring (worn)

DUNN'S LARK

streaked red-brown

strong head pattern, e.g. with 'mascara tear'

stout, 'swollen', pinkish

some worn spring birds have less striking head pattern

black

very short primary projection

black sides

autumn (fresh)

spring (worn)

BLACK-CROWNED SPARROW-LARK

more diffuse head pattern than Dunn's Lark, and is less rufous-tinged above

unmistakable!

♀

♂

dark centres

dark

heavy, triangular, greyish

no primary projection

black sides

1st-winter / ♀ autumn

ad. ♂ spring (worn)

KM

Calandra Lark *Melanocorypha calandra* V★★★

L 17½–20 cm. Breeds in open cultivated country and on natural steppe. Migrant in E, mainly resident in W. In winter often in larger flocks.

IDENTIFICATION Strongly built and large lark, with *heavy yellowish-brown bill* and characteristic *large black patch on side of breast* (varying in shape and size: sometimes very large, sometimes running across breast, sometimes narrow). Pale supercilium and pale eye-surround. Typically has *blackish underwing* with a *wide, distinct white trailing edge* (obvious in flight, and glimpse of white trailing edge at times detectable even on folded wing). Upperparts roughly as Skylark, greyish-brown, streaked dark. White sides to tail. Legs brownish-pink. Song-flight often characteristic, the lark 'hanging' (at times drifting around) at some height (25–100 m) with, provided there is some wind, *slow-motion wingbeats* with stiff, straight wings and folded tail; slow wingbeats may give impression of larger than actual size.

VOICE Call either very characteristic dry rolling, almost frizzling 'schrrrreep', or more Skylark-like 'trreeh', 'trip-trip', etc. Song like Skylark's, protracted, full of chirping notes at fast pace, mixed up with a few imitations; recognized by slightly slower pace, hinted pauses, and abundance of dry rolling call-like notes woven in. (Cf. Bimaculated Lark.)

Bimaculated Lark *Melanocorypha bimaculata* V★★★

L 16–18 cm. Breeds on arid, stony plains (semi-desert) and mountainsides; also on arable fields like Calandra Lark, but then usually at higher elevation, near upper limit of cultivation. More migratory habits than Calandra Lark.

IDENTIFICATION Resembles Calandra Lark (heavy bill and dark breast patch the same), but differs in following: slightly smaller (and with a little shorter tail); *underwing brownish-grey; trailing edge of wing just a little paler brown* (not white); *tip of tail white* (sides not); on average more *contrasting and well-marked head pattern* with more obvious supercilium, and dark lines through and below eye; upperparts on average with lighter feather edges in fresh plumage. In song-flight, wingbeats are usually *continuously fast and fluttering*, but in brisk wind slower (bat-like), and in very strong wind can keep wings motionless for long spells. Stiff wingbeats with straight wings in slow motion apparently not executed. *Tail* also often *kept well fanned*, unlike Calandra's.

VOICE Calls resemble Short-toed Lark's, e.g. short, dry twittering 'tripp, tripp', but voice is coarser and calls more varied, including rasping 'tcher' and the like. Song confusingly similar to Calandra's, consisting largely of fast, dry, rolling twitter, but pitch slightly deeper and voice harder, almost 'bouncing' (not so 'lightly frizzling'), and is more monotonous with fewer imitations and soft notes.

Thick-billed Lark *Ramphocoris clotbey* —

L 17–18 cm. Breeds in arid, open terrain in NW Africa (e.g. S Morocco) and locally in Middle East (Jordan?). Resident.

IDENTIFICATION Large, with *huge bill. Wide white trailing band on wing* and *dark underwing*. – Adult ♂: Sides of head black with distinct white spots; bill pale bluish-grey; underparts heavily blotched black. – Adult ♀: More limited area of dark grey on head, pale spots less well marked; bill pale horn with at most only faint shade of blue; underparts less heavily blotched. – Winter: Pale fringes cover most of dark areas in plumage. – Juvenile: Head almost uniform, without dark pattern, and bill somewhat less heavy.

VOICE Call whistling 'tsu-ee?' ('querying') or open, rolling 'zrrroüh' (rising). Song a rapid stanza of twittering notes.

White-winged Lark *Melanocorypha leucoptera* V★★★

L 17–19 cm. Breeds on natural steppe, dry heaths and to some degree on cultivations. Partly migratory.

IDENTIFICATION Characteristic *wing pattern of white, black and brown* (sexes largely alike). Wide white trailing edge of wing makes wings look peculiarly narrow against a light sky. Most similar to Mongolian Lark (*M. mongolica*), but that is larger, has heavier bill, and has a Calandra-like black patch on the breast side. – Adult ♂: Crown unstreaked red-brown. Breast usually sparsely streaked only. – Adult ♀: Crown streaked, grey-brown with only tinge of rufous. Breast generally prominently streaked.

VOICE Call a dry, hard twitter, 'drrit-drrit', recalling Bimaculated Lark. Song most of all recalls Skylark, but recognized by sections of faltering notes (as from Short-toed or Horned Larks) and by somewhat harder, drier voice.

Black Lark *Melanocorypha yeltoniensis* —

L 18–20½ cm. Breeds on natural steppe, often near marshes and salines. Locally common. Partly migratory.

IDENTIFICATION Adult ♂: Large, all black, with bill heavy and straw-coloured; in autumn, pale fringes cover much of black. Song-flight often with *wingbeats in slow motion*. Display-flight at low level with very high, stiff wingbeats or dove-like glides; tumbles down to court ♀ with raised tail and lowered wings and neck. – Adult ♀: Brown-grey, blotched dark; plumage rather variable, some resemble Calandra Lark, having a larger dark patch on side of breast. Note, however, dark legs, no wide white trailing edge of wing, and usually obvious blotching below. Underwing-coverts almost black, clearly darker than wing-feathers.

VOICE Song like Skylark's but slightly higher-pitched and even more frizzling and frantically twittering (like 'quarrelling young Starlings'); loudness frequently varied. Soft, miaowing, 'pleading' notes are frequently mixed in.

Calandra Lark   Bimaculated Lark   White-winged Lark   Black Lark

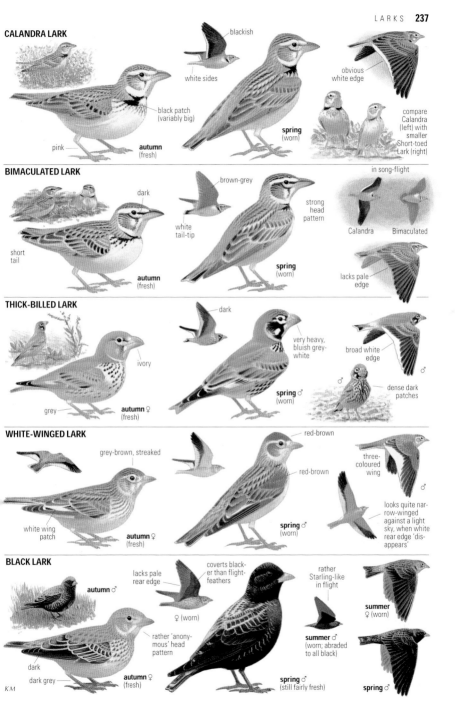

CALANDRA LARK

blackish

white sides

black patch (variably big)

pink

autumn (fresh)

spring (worn)

obvious white edge

compare Calandra (left) with smaller Short-toed Lark (right)

BIMACULATED LARK

dark

brown-grey

white tail-tip

strong head pattern

short tail

autumn (fresh)

spring (worn)

in song-flight

Calandra   Bimaculated

lacks pale edge

THICK-BILLED LARK

dark

ivory

grey

autumn ♀ (fresh)

very heavy, bluish grey-white

spring ♂ (worn)

broad white edge

dense dark patches

♂

WHITE-WINGED LARK

grey-brown, streaked

red-brown

red-brown

white wing patch

autumn ♀ (fresh)

spring ♂ (worn)

three-coloured wing

♂

looks quite narrow-winged against a light sky, when white rear edge 'disappears'

BLACK LARK

autumn ♂

lacks pale rear edge

coverts blacker than flight-feathers

♀ (worn)

rather 'anonymous' head pattern

dark

dark grey

autumn ♀ (fresh)

rather Starling-like in flight

summer ♂ (worn; abraded to all black)

spring ♂ (still fairly fresh)

summer ♀ (worn)

spring ♂

KM

Horned Lark (Shore Lark)
Eremophila alpestris   **P**+**W**4

L 16–19 cm. Breeds in mountains above tree-limit, on alpine moors and dry stony ground, often on crown of lowest fells, in extreme north on tundra at sea-level. Migrant in north. Scarce and local in Europe, has decreased.

IDENTIFICATION Slightly smaller than Skylark. In all plumages, recognized by characteristic *head pattern of black and yellow* (Europe, N Turkey, Caucasus, N Africa) *or white* (rest of Asia). Along sides of crown elongated black feathers forming tiny, narrow 'horns' (not always visible in the field). Sexes and ages similar, but when pair-members seen together on breeding ground adult ♂ is: larger; more well marked on head; has longer 'horns'; practically unstreaked pinkish-brown crown and nape; less streaking on mantle; and unstreaked pinkish-brown lesser coverts. In winter flocks, immature ♀ can sometimes be picked out: small size; head pattern more ill-defined (lores grey, not black, and dark cheek patch small); 'horns' missing; crown, nape and mantle rather distinctly streaked dark. Still, many autumn birds are difficult to sex or age. – Juvenile: Upperparts and breast with pale and dark dots, and hint of dark cheek patch. – Variation (apart from yellow or white ground colour on head; see above): Birds in N Europe (ssp. *flava*) have black on head separated from black breast patch; birds in SE Europe (*balcanica*), N Turkey and Caucasus (*penicillata*) have black on head merging with black breast patch. In Middle East (*bicornis*), upperparts are warmer rufous-tinged.

VOICE Call fine, short squeaky notes, single 'eeh', or with 'echo', '**eeh**-dü' or '**eeh**-deedü', rather metallic, 'rippling' ring, and calls fairly anonymous. Sometimes more harsh 'prsh' or 'tsrr'. Song, delivered from rock or in flight, usually promptly repeated brief phrases (1–2½ sec.) with characteristic acceleration after faltering, 'fumbling' opening (same song pattern as Short-toed Lark) and desolate chirruping, jangling voice (rather like Lapland Longspur).

Temminck's Lark *Eremophila bilopha*   —

L 14–15 cm. Breeds in semi-desert, on drier steppe, lower mountainsides (< 1000 m), etc., at lower altitude than Horned Lark. Mainly resident. Discreet habits; not shy.

IDENTIFICATION Like a small Horned Lark of Middle East (ssp. *bicornis*), but separated by following: upperparts, incl. wing-coverts and whole tertials, vividly rufous (lacking dark centres); primary projection short; primary tips blackish (fringed pale in fresh plumage), contrasting strongly with rufous tertials. Note that black breast patch never merge with black of cheek (as in some races of Horned Lark), and that ground colour of head is white (never yellow).

VOICE Voice similar to Horned Lark, but song consistently

sounds slightly finer and contains some cracked, thin notes; phrases frequently short, without much variation. Pace also more even (accelerations not so obvious as with Horned).

Dupont's Lark *Chersophilus duponti*   —

L 17–18 cm. Breeds on dry, sandy soil with tufts of grass, on natural steppe or in semi-desert and flatter mountainsides, high plateaux as well as low plains near sea. Will also feed on arable fields. Mainly resident. Extremely shy and elusive, quickly running for cover. Nervous and jerky movements.

IDENTIFICATION Size as Skylark but slimmer; slimness enhanced by *narrower, longer neck*, *longer legs* and *long, slightly downcurved bill*. Sometimes adopts upright stance. The plumage is rather like Skylark's (brown above, breast streaked, white sides of tail), but is slightly darker with (in fresh plumage) fine pale feather tips, and has *thin pale central crown-stripe* (best visible head-on), lacks pale trailing edge of wing, and has thin dark malar stripes (much as in Crested Lark). – Variation: The description refers to birds in Spain and NW Africa north of Atlas (ssp. *duponti*). In S Algeria and in Libya (*margeritae*), the plumage is distinctly more red-brown, and the bill is longer.

VOICE Sings mostly at dawn and dusk, a slowly repeated, brief, melancholy phrase, opening with a few short whistles followed by a nasal, miaowing, drawn-out note, 'wu-**tlee**-tre-weeüüih'. Song-flight at great height, also at night.

(Greater) Hoopoe Lark *Alaemon alaudipes*   —

L 19–22½ cm. Breeds in flat desert, semi-desert, in open wadis, etc. Resident. Usually seen singly or in pairs; larger flocks rare. Fairly tame. Prefers to run away rather than fly.

IDENTIFICATION *Large, slim, pale sand-coloured* (colour variation: some are more grey) lark with rather *broad wings with black and white pattern* (vaguely recalling Hoopoe in flight). *Legs and bill long* (bill-tip slightly downcurved). Head pattern well marked, with black moustachial stripe and eye-streak. Breast usually finely but distinctly blotched. Starts singing from top of bush or ground (or in Hoopoe-like, flappy, low flight), continuing in *spectacular song-flight* with steep climb for 1–5 m with spread tail, followed by vertical collapse, wings folded, landing on ground or ending with a short, low flight.

VOICE Commonest call a strong, rolling, upward-inflected 'zrrruee'. Song consists of characteristic thin piping and melancholy-sounding notes, starting tentatively, accelerating and then slowing down again, e.g. 'voy voy... **vüüü**(cha) **vüüü**(cha) swe-swe-swe-swe-swe sisisi... svee, sveeh', where '**vüüü**' is piercingly thin and most far-carrying. In Middle East, an almost Black Woodpecker-like 'kri-kri-kri-kri-kri' is inserted in the phrase.

Horned Lark   Temminck's Lark

Dupont's Lark   Hoopoe Lark

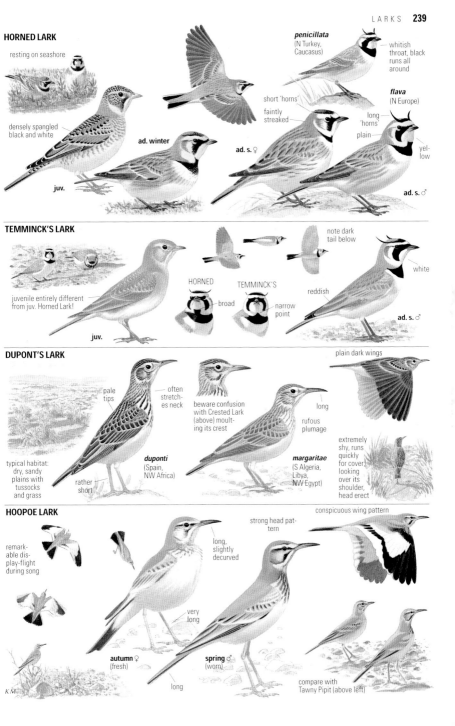

HORNED LARK

resting on seashore

penicillata
(N Turkey, Caucasus)

whitish throat, black runs all around

densely spangled black and white

ad. winter

short 'horns'

faintly streaked

ad. s. ♀

flava
(N Europe)

long 'horns'

plain

yellow

juv.

ad. s. ♂

TEMMINCK'S LARK

note dark tail below

juvenile entirely different from juv. Horned Lark!

HORNED

TEMMINCK'S

broad

narrow point

reddish

white

juv.

ad. s. ♂

DUPONT'S LARK

plain dark wings

pale tips

often stretches neck

beware confusion with Crested Lark (above) moulting its crest

long

rufous plumage

typical habitat: dry, sandy plains with tussocks and grass

rather short

duponti
(Spain, NW Africa)

margaritae
(S Algeria, Libya, NW Egypt)

extremely shy, runs quickly for cover, looking over its shoulder, head erect

HOOPOE LARK

conspicuous wing pattern

strong head pattern

remarkable display-flight during song

long, slightly decurved

very long

autumn ♀
(fresh)

spring ♂
(worn)

long

compare with Tawny Pipit (above left)

K M

SWALLOWS and MARTINS *Hirundinidae*

Relatively small passerines with long, pointed wings, adapted for a life largely in the air, where they catch insects by means of fast, agile flight and their large mouth. Bill small, legs short. Most are long-distance migrants which winter in the tropics. Sexes alike. Nest either in excavated holes in sandy banks or in cup skilfully built of mud, plants and saliva.

Sand Martin *Riparia riparia*   m**B**2

L 12–13 cm. Breeds colonially in vertical sandy or earth banks, e.g. in gravel-pits and river banks, where nest is excavated (often a good metre horizontally into the earth). Rather tied to water, often seen in numbers hunting insects in low flight over lakes and rivers. Summer visitor to Britain & Ireland (Mar–Oct), winters in tropical W Africa. Prior to and during migration roosts communally in large reedbeds.

IDENTIFICATION One of the smallest swallows. Dull *grey-brown above* (primaries slightly darker) *and white below*, with *grey-brown breast-band* separating white throat from white belly. *Underwings dark* (grey-brown, wing-coverts somewhat darker). Tail shallowly but clearly forked and without white 'windows' (cf. Crag Martin). Differs from closely related Plain Martin in somewhat larger size, dark breast-band, white throat and *contrastingly darker underwing-coverts*. Flight rapid and light. When accelerating, wings beaten backwards and in towards body, so then look narrow; does not glide that often. – Juvenile: Pale, rusty-buff or whitish fringes, especially on tertials and upper-wing-coverts, are visible at close range; at distance these areas look a little paler than on adult.

VOICE Call a dry, voiceless rasp as from coarse sandpaper, 'trrrsh'; when excited, e.g. in throng around colony entrance holes, this harsh call is uttered in long series at rapid and often quickening rate, 'trrrsh, trre-trre-trre-rrerrerre...'. These series, or very similar combinations of calls, seem to constitute the song. Alarm-call a higher, excited 'chiir'.

Plain Martin *Riparia paludicola*   —

L 10½–11½ cm. Breeds in winter in small colonies and groups in sandbanks, much as Sand Martin, but, within the region treated here, only in Morocco (more numerous in S Africa). Habits as for Sand Martin, but is a resident.

IDENTIFICATION The *smallest* hirundine in the region. Has proportionately slightly *shorter wings* than Sand Martin, and these therefore look somewhat broader and blunter. The different shape combined with *lack of dark breast-band*, and diffusely dark-spotted or *dusky throat*, can recall Crag Martin unless the small size is apparent. The underwing is rather plain (wing-coverts only moderately darker than flight-feathers). Flight lighter and more fluttering than Sand Mar-

tin's, with more frequent changes in direction and speed. – Juvenile: Same differences as for Sand Martin.

VOICE As Sand Martin's, but higher, softer and less rasping and hard,'chirr', 'prri' and the like.

(Eurasian) **Crag Martin** *Ptyonoprogne rupestris*   **V**∗∗∗

L 14–15 cm. Breeds in caves and cavities on cliff faces, rarely also in holes in buildings and walls. Found at all levels, even high up (>2000 m) in remote mountain areas. Migrant in N, resident or short-distance migrant in S.

IDENTIFICATION Rather large and compact swallow with *heavy body, broad neck and broad but pointed wings*. Drab *grey-brown above* with flight-feathers a shade darker, and dirty brown-tinged greyish-white below on breast and *gradually darkening rearwards* towards undertail-coverts. At moderate range and in good light, *throat* is seen to be *faintly streaked or dusky*. Underwing pattern characteristic, with *rather pale brown-grey remiges and clearly contrasting sooty-black coverts*. An important character is visible only when the shallowly forked tail is spread: *small white 'windows' on most tail-feathers*. Flight powerful and agile, often glides on flat wings held straight out, twists and turns, sweeps rapidly along, gives a few quick beats, and so on. Often seen high up in air like a swift, or patrolling back and forth along vertical cliff high in mountains. – Juvenile: Same plumage differences as for Sand Martin.

VOICE Rather discreet repertoire. Calls often heard include a short, high, clicking 'pli', a cheerful Linnet-like 'piieh', also short, chirpy, somewhat House Martin-like 'tshir' and 'trit'. Song consists of a quiet, fast, twittering series.

Rock Martin *Ptyonoprogne fuligula*   —

L 12–13 cm. Breeds in desert or desert-like terrain on cliff faces, in ravines, locally also on ruins and other buildings. Resident. Widely distributed in Africa and Middle East.

IDENTIFICATION Like Crag Martin, with same shape and basic pattern, including *white 'windows' on most tail-feathers* (visible only if tail spread), but is slightly but *clearly smaller* and a shade *paler grey-brown above*, especially on lower back / rump (discernible in direct comparison or with sufficient experience) and *paler pure white below*. Throat is *pale*, not washed grey-brown as on Crag Martin, and *undertail-coverts are fairly pale*, not dark as on Crag. An important distinction in flight is that *only the carpal area on underwing is darker than rest of wing* (on Crag Martin all coverts are dark, so a greater area dark), and that the *contrast is less strong* than on Crag Martin.

VOICE Unobtrusive. Soft, rather dry 'trrt' like House or Sand Martin, also more Barn Swallow-like, slightly nasal 'vick'. Song a muffled, somewhat raucous twitter.

Sand Martin   Plain Martin   Crag Martin   Rock Martin

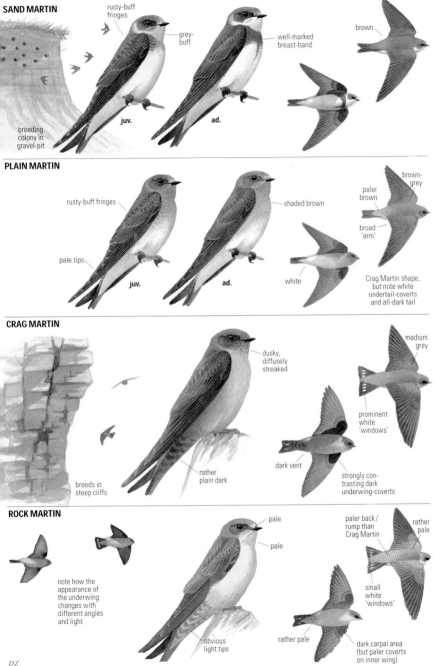

SAND MARTIN

rusty-buff fringes

grey-buff

well-marked breast-band

brown

breeding colony in gravel-pit

juv.

ad.

PLAIN MARTIN

rusty-buff fringes

shaded brown

pale tips

juv.

ad.

white

brown-grey

paler brown

broad 'arm'

Crag Martin shape, but note white undertail-coverts and all-dark tail

CRAG MARTIN

dusky, diffusely streaked

medium grey

prominent white 'windows'

breeds in steep cliffs

rather plain dark

dark vent

strongly contrasting dark underwing-coverts

ROCK MARTIN

pale

pale

paler back / rump than Crag Martin

rather pale

note how the appearance of the underwing changes with different angles and light

small white 'windows'

obvious light tips

rather pale

dark carpal area (but paler coverts on inner wing)

DZ

Barn Swallow *Hirundo rustica*   mB2 / P1

L ad. 17–21 cm (of which tail projection 3–6½), juv. 14–15 cm. Breeds commonly in cultivated areas with farmyards, small villages etc. Summer visitor (in Britain & Ireland mainly Apr–Oct), winters in Africa. Often roosts communally in reedbeds outside breeding season. Nest an open mud cup reinforced with plant material, placed on roof beam or projection inside barn, boathouse, under bridge, in culvert etc. Commonly hunts insects low over ground, often around legs of grazing cattle, but also at treetop height.

IDENTIFICATION The symbolic swallow, well known to one and all through its breeding habits and through its characteristic appearance with *long, pointed wings* and *deeply forked tail with wire-thin elongated streamers*. Blue-glossed black above, white or buffish-white below (in most of Europe; see Variation below) with *blue-black breast-band and blood-red throat and forehead*. The red colour is surprisingly difficult to see on flying bird and at a little distance, when the swallow then looks mostly all dark on head and breast. When tail is spread while braking and turning, *small white 'windows' are visible on outer tail-feathers. Flight fast and powerful with clipped beats*, passing back and forth and often low above ground or water surface (may then drink in flight); less inclined than House Martin to make long, slow, curving glides. Sexes alike (but ♂ has on average narrower and longer tail-streamers). – Juvenile: Short, blunt tail-streamers. Forehead and throat rusty buffish-white or brownish-pink (not blood-red). Upperparts with minimal blue gloss. – Variation: Birds along E Mediterranean coast (ssp. *transitiva*) are reddish-buff below, and those in Egypt (*savignii*) deep rusty-red.

VOICE Noisy, its loud calls enlivening farmsteads and small villages. In 'itinerant flight' gives cheerful sharp 'vit!', often repeated two or more times. Mates preen each other and entertain the barn livestock with cosy chatter almost like Budgerigars. Cats are announced with sharp 'siflitt' notes and birds of prey with similar 'flitt-flitt!'. The rather loud song consists of a rapid twitter now and then interrupted by a croaking sound which turns into a dry rattle.

Red-rumped Swallow *Hirundo daurica*   V**

L 14–19 cm (ad. with tail extension 3–5). Breeds on cliffs in mountain areas and along steep coasts, sometimes also in cavities on ruins, under bridges etc. Migrant, winters in tropical Africa. Builds a closed nest of mud with entrance tunnel, fixed to roof of cave, recess or similar site. Rare but regular vagrant to Britain & Ireland, mostly Mar–May and Aug–Nov. Often hunts insects high up in remote mountain districts.

IDENTIFICATION Resembles Barn Swallow, having similar size and shape with *long, pointed tail-streamers*, but immediately told by *pale rump*, which at distance can look white

(cf. House Martin) but at close range is *light rusty-red* at top and somewhat paler (sometimes whitish) to rear. Close views also reveal that *nape has a narrow rusty-brown band* and that *head-sides are pale*, not blue-black. Wings and tail dark brownish-black (tail without Barn Swallow's white 'windows'), mantle, scapulars and crown shiny blue-black. Red-rumped Swallows in flight are also identifiable from below at distance by their *pale throat and breast* and *squared-off black undertail-coverts* (white on Barn Swallow). At close range, underparts are seen to be pale rusty-buff or buff-white with very discreet, thin streaks. Flight intermediate between Barn Swallow and House Martin, clipped wingbeats but also a lot of slow gliding on straight wings. – Juvenile: Shorter tail-streamers, less blue gloss above, buff-white tips to tertials and many wing-coverts.

VOICE Noisy, but not so loud as Barn Swallow. Call, often given by flocks hunting insects, a rather soft but spirited, nasal 'tveyk' (recalling Tree Sparrow in tone). Alarm a sharp 'kiir!'. Song allied to Barn Swallow's in structure, contains croaking sounds and rattles, but the introductory twitter is much lower in pitch and harsher, slower and shorter (with rhythm and ring almost like song of Black-headed Bunting).

(Common) House Martin *Delichon urbica*   mB2 / P2

L 13½–15 cm. Breeds commonly and colonially in villages, farms, towns, also all kinds of open country; attracted to houses, but also cliff faces in undeveloped areas. Summer visitor (Apr–Oct), winters in Africa. Outside breeding period roosts communally in trees (not reeds). Confiding towards man, building its closed, convex mud nest beneath eaves on house walls, on bridge girders etc., sometimes even on ferryboats in regular service, oblivious to the boat's movements or to rather intrusive human activities; those breeding in the species' original sites attach their nests to rock walls on fault faces or mountain precipices. When young have fledged, birds often perch in numbers on telephone wires ('music score'). Hunts insects at all levels, but often high in air.

IDENTIFICATION Easily recognized by *pure white rump* contrasting sharply with otherwise *black upperparts*, with crown, mantle and scapulars *glossed blue. Underparts white*. Black tail short and moderately forked (lacks streamers). On ground, e.g. at pool of water to collect mud for nest, the white-feathered feet (as on a grouse) are noticeable. Flight not so swift as Barn Swallow's, more *fluttery* with frequent and at times *long glides on straight wings*, often in gentle curves at slow speed. – Juvenile: Like adult but with hardly any blue gloss above, and has throat and upper breast sullied brownish-grey. Slight touch of yellow at base of lower mandible (adult has all-black bill).

VOICE Noisy, especially at colonies. Gives incessant dry but pleasing twitter, 'prrit', with variations according to mood and requirements. When agitated, utters a higher, emphatic and drawn-out 'chierr'. Song little more than a chatty burst of chirps with no clear structure, but the whole sounds rather sweet and 'eager'.

Barn Swallow

Red-rumped Swallow

House Martin

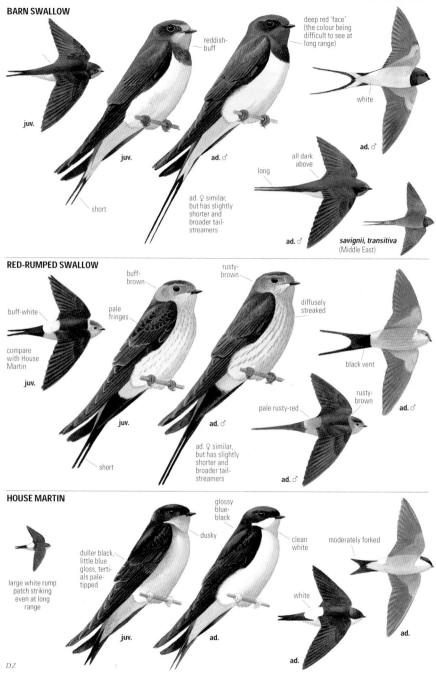

BARN SWALLOW

juv.

juv.

reddish-buff

ad. ♂

ad. ♀ similar, but has slightly shorter and broader tail-streamers

short

deep red 'face' (the colour being difficult to see at long range)

white

ad. ♂

all dark above

long

ad. ♂

savignii, transitiva (Middle East)

RED-RUMPED SWALLOW

buff-white

compare with House Martin

juv.

buff-brown

pale fringes

juv.

short

rusty-brown

diffusely streaked

black vent

rusty-brown

pale rusty-red

ad. ♂

ad. ♂

ad. ♂

ad. ♀ similar, but has slightly shorter and broader tail-streamers

HOUSE MARTIN

large white rump patch striking even at long range

duller black, little blue gloss, tertials pale-tipped

glossy blue-black

dusky

juv.

clean white

white

ad.

ad.

moderately forked

ad.

DZ

PIPITS and WAGTAILS *Motacillidae*

Rather small, slim, long-tailed passerines with pointed bill which spend much time on the ground. Migratory in N and E. Insectivores. Pipits (ten breeding species, three vagrants) are brown and white with varying degree of streaking on breast and upperparts; have characteristic songs, usually delivered in typical song-flight. Nest on ground among grass tufts. Wagtails (four species) have more contrasts in plumage and simpler songs, also very long tail which they wag up and down. Nest in holes, recesses or cover of vegetation.

Tawny Pipit *Anthus campestris* **V**∗

L 15½–18 cm. Sparse breeder on sand dunes, sandy open ground, at gravel-pits and in clearings, in S Europe also on barren mountain slopes. In Britain & Ireland rare but regular on passage (esp. Aug–Oct). Winters in Africa.

IDENTIFICATION A large, slim pipit with relatively uniform *sandy-coloured* plumage. *Dark loral stripe* in all plumages (occasionally less obvious owing to angle of light or wear). *Hindclaw relatively short* (cf. Richard's Pipit). Legs pinkish or light brown. – Adult: *Crown to back almost unstreaked* (only hint of diffuse spotting), *underparts unstreaked buff-white*, sometimes with a few narrow streaks on upper breast-side. Distinct *pale supercilium*; usually dark moustachial stripe and very thin malar stripe. *Median coverts contrastingly dark, in fresh plumage broadly tipped buff-white*. – Juvenile: Crown to back heavily dark-patterned, feathers finely fringed white. *Upper breast dark-spotted* (varying in extent; at times some streaks on flanks, too). Resembles Richard's Pipit (see latter).

VOICE Call a full 'tshilp' (soft ending; slightly House Sparrow-like, but can also recall Short-toed Lark) or shorter 'chüp'. Song simple, usually delivered in undulating song-flight, two or three syllables with ringing tone, often stressed and drawn out at end, slowly repeated in time with peaks in flight, e.g. 'tsirliih...tsirliih...tsirliih...'. (In the Balkans it may sound like 'sr'r'rüih', trembling and dropping in pitch.)

Long-billed Pipit *Anthus similis* —

L 16–17½ cm. Breeds in N Israel, W Syria and Lebanon (also W Jordan?) on bare, open slopes with plenty of (often flat) rock outcrops and grass, herbs and other low vegetation (± garrigue). Resident or short-distance migrant.

IDENTIFICATION Like Tawny Pipit and roughly the same size (marginally larger), but slightly *longer-tailed* and *longer-billed*. Plumage somewhat *greyer* and *less contrasty* than Tawny Pipit's, uppertail darker. *Supercilium* often rather narrow and *reaches far back towards nape*, longer than on Tawny. Breast lacks clear dark streaking, is merely obscurely spotted. Belly and flanks often tinged warm buff.

Tawny Pipit   Long-billed Pipit

Median coverts proximally dark. Bill-base light pink.

VOICE Call resembles Desert Lark's, a short 'chupp'. Alarm 'siih'. Song delivered from rock or in fluttering, slow song-flight, simple, vaguely like Tawny Pipit's but a bit more varied, three or four chords randomly strung together in slow drawl, e.g. 'siu...chürr...siu...chivü...srrüi...siu...' and so on.

Richard's Pipit *Anthus richardi* **V**∗

L 17–20 cm. Rare but regular Siberian vagrant in (mostly) W Europe, primarily in autumn (mid Sep–Nov), extremely rare at other seasons; thus does not breed within region.

IDENTIFICATION A touch bigger than Tawny Pipit, this reinforced by *longer legs and tail* and by habit of *standing more upright and stretching neck*. When perched on wire against pale background (sky), a useful pointer is *very long hindclaw* (longer than hind toe). Bill averages somewhat longer and stouter than Tawny Pipit's (like small thrush, but difference not always striking). *Flight powerful with long dips*. Often *hovers* briefly before landing in grass (only exceptionally a sign of this in Tawny). Plumage similar to juvenile Tawny Pipit (dark-streaked on back and breast), but has *pale lores* (at certain angles, however, e.g. in oblique front view, can appear dusky). – Adult: *Breast and flanks usually warm buff* (even rusty-tinged), contrasting with whiter belly-centre, *upper breast distinctly streaked*; often streaks coalesce to form dark wedge on lower throat-side. Greater and median coverts and tertials rather *broadly tipped rusty-brown* when fresh. – Juvenile (often even into Oct): Like adult, but upperpart streaking darker, and the blackish median coverts and tertials *narrowly and sharply edged white*.

VOICE Call typical, esp. when flushed or on migration, a frothy, grating or hoarse, drawn-out and uninflected (or faintly downslurred) 'pshee!' (or 'shreep'; some House Sparrows can sound similar, but on other hand is very different from Skylark's calls). Straight, less typical, weaker 'cheep' calls heard at breeding site, and sometimes given by vagrants). Song simple, delivered in deeply undulating song-flight, a grinding '**tschi**vü-**tschi**vü-**tschi**vü-**tschi**vü-**tschi**vü'.

Blyth's Pipit *Anthus godlewskii* **V**∗∗∗

L 15½–17 cm. Extremely rare autumn vagrant in NW Europe from Mongolia and adjacent regions.

IDENTIFICATION Very like Richard's Pipit in plumage, but is *slightly smaller* and has *shorter legs, shorter and somewhat more pointed bill, shorter tail* and tendency to more distinct wing-bar. In hand, differs in certain measurements (e.g. shorter hindclaw) and in amount of white on second outermost tail-feather (short, broad white wedge on Blyth's, long and narrow on almost all Richard's), but safe identification in the field requires detailed study at close range and preferably close check of call. *Underparts somewhat more uniformly buff* (belly not so white). Most reliably identified are birds with adult-type median coverts (often odd ones present even in 1st autumn): these have *broad and sharply defined light ochre-buff tip, against which the dark centre has blunt, broad edge* (not darker rusty-brown, somewhat more diffuse and narrower tip, with dark centre projecting in broad wedge).

VOICE Call like Richard's Pipit's but slightly higher in pitch, a little purer in tone, somewhat reminiscent of Yellow Wagtail, 'pshiu', often interspersed with low 'chip-chüp'.

TAWNY PIPIT

plain upperparts

ad.

at long range juv. Yellow Wagtail (left) may be confused with Tawny Pipit, but note black legs and breast pattern

invariably dark lores

rather plain

well-defined dark centres

dark loral stripe

streaked

a few fine streaks

spotted

clean whitish

juv. is very like Richard's Pipit, but note different head pattern and length of hind-claw

juv.

ad.

rather short hindclaw

LONG-BILLED PIPIT

favours stony hillsides with rock outcrops

rather long and strong

long

side of head slightly less contrasting than Tawny Pipit's

diffuse dark centres

malar stripe usually indistinct

diffuse streaks

often washed buffish

ad.

RICHARD'S PIPIT

often attracts attention by calling overhead

Richard's Pipit

long

from some angles may appear to have darker loral stripe—best to evaluate in profile!

compare with Skylark (right): note, e.g., shorter bill and legs (and different gait)

head and particularly bill almost thrush-like

stout

pale loral stripe

streaked

streaked

ad.

close-up of three me-dian coverts:

moulted adult type (centre) has *pointed* dark central point

long

long

1st-winter

BLYTH'S PIPIT

rather short

often washed buffish

more compact, not so 'gangly' as Richard's

shortish, pointed

often appears more neatly streaked than Richard's

close-up of three median coverts:

shorter than Richard's

moulted adult type (centre) has *blunt* dark central point

shorter and more curved than Richard's

1st-winter

KM

Water Pipit *Anthus spinoletta* **W**4

L 15½–17 cm. Breeds in mountain regions on bare alpine slopes and upland plains. Short-distance migrant, winters in lowland areas at freshwater marshes, ponds, watercress-beds, flooded fields etc., also at coasts on waterlogged meadows with fresh water. Very closely related to Rock and Buff-bellied Pipits (the three until recently regarded as conspecific).

IDENTIFICATION In winter plumage very like Rock Pipit (incl. usually *dark legs*) but *a shade paler and browner above* (not olive-grey), and *ground colour of underparts is purer white with more distinct streaks*. Supercilium and wing-bars *generally paler* and better marked. *Pure white on outer tail-feathers* (but note that Rock Pipit's light dusky tail-sides can appear white in strong light). – Summer: Moults into characteristic plumage in Mar, with *almost unmarked pale pinkish underparts* (streaked only on flanks) and dark *ash-grey head and nape* which usually contrast with *brown mantle, distinct white supercilium* and *whitish wing-bars*. – Variation: Birds in the Caucasus (ssp. *coutellii*), whose winter range includes Middle East, are *more distinctly streaked above* and more buff below (on whole of underparts; *spinoletta* has pink hue strongest on breast).

VOICE Call like Rock Pipit's or often faintly upslurred, 'vüisst'. Song extremely similar to Rock Pipit's, but to the practised ear sometimes recognizable by certain more rhythmic motifs and thin, fine, drawn-out notes (vaguely recalling Red-throated Pipit), e.g. 'zrü zrü zrü-zrü-zrü-zrü-zü-zü-züzü-zü-zü-züzü-zü-züzüzüzüzü svirir**irr**-svirir**irr**-svirir**irr** suuü-suuü psiii**eh**-psiii**eh**-psiii**eh**' (though note that certain geographical variations occur!).

Rock Pipit *Anthus petrosus* r**B**3 / **W**3(2?)

L 15½–17 cm. Breeds on rocky coasts and islands. Most N European breeders migrate to W European coasts in winter.

IDENTIFICATION A relatively sturdy pipit with predominantly *dark plumage* and *smudgy markings*. Best characters are usually *dark legs* (sometimes not-so-dark reddish-brown but never pink as e.g. Meadow Pipit) and *relatively long, dark bill*. Outer tail-feathers pale greyish, not pure white (except sometimes at tip). *Supercilium usually indistinct and short*. Narrow white eye-ring. Underparts dirty white, often tinged buff; breast and flanks *heavily but diffusely streaked dark*. Upperparts brown-grey with *faint olive tinge*, mantle indistinctly dark-streaked. – Variation: Nordic and Russian birds (ssp. *littoralis*) virtually identical to W European (*petrosus*) in winter, but some acquire distinctive summer plumage in which underparts tinged pink and dark streaking somewhat reduced. Extreme examples may closely resemble Water Pipit but have greyer mantle and rump area and bold dark malar stripe.

VOICE Call a sharp, explosive, drawn-out 'viisst', usually given singly or repeated less quickly than in Meadow Pipit. Song confusingly similar to Water Pipit's (and not that unlike Meadow Pipit's!), series of repeated, sharp, fine notes with three or four theme changes during the song, the full version always delivered in typical climbing and then descending song-flight on rigid wings, 'zrü-zrü-zrü-zrü-zrü-zre-zre-zre-zre-zre-zre-zre-sui-sui-sui-sui-zri-zri-zri…' or similar. Told from Meadow Pipit's by slightly sharper, almost 'electric' voice and harder and less pure introductory 'zrü' series on lower pitch.

Buff-bellied Pipit *Anthus rubescens* **V**∗∗∗

L 15–16 cm. Very rare vagrant from America or Asia. Ssp. *rubescens* breeds in N America and W Greenland and has been recorded in autumn in W Europe; ssp. *japonicus* (very different in appearance; see below) breeds in E Asia (so far as known not W of Lake Baikal) and is regular in winter in e.g. Israel. Very closely related to Rock and Water Pipits (all three until recently regarded as conspecific).

IDENTIFICATION A touch smaller than Water Pipit, with somewhat *more slender bill* and *paler lores* which may suggest Meadow Pipit, but Buff-bellied always *much less distinctly streaked on upperparts* than Meadow. – Winter: Ssp. *rubescens* is clearly *buff below* with rather narrow but distinct dark streaks and, usually, *dark legs*. Ssp. *japonicus* is *whiter below* with *distinct blackish streaks* (incl. large dark malar patch, roughly as on young Red-throated Pipit), *darker and greyer above*, often has neat eye-ring and distinct supercilium, sometimes with dark border above (can recall Olive-backed Pipit!); legs reddish-brown, often paler than on *rubescens*.

VOICE Call like Meadow Pipit's 'psipp' but slightly more squeaky and emphatic; usually uttered singly.

Berthelot's Pipit *Anthus berthelotii* —

L 13–14½ cm. Breeds commonly in Canary Islands and Madeira on dry plains, stony and sandy terrain with low vegetation and also mountain slopes. Resident.

IDENTIFICATION *Small* as a Meadow Pipit, but with somewhat different proportions: *short rear end* (legs thus appear placed far back), *rather big head* but slender bill. Adult is predominantly *grey and dirty white*, whereas juvenile often is tinged rufous above. Dirty white *distinct supercilium* characteristic. Pale eye-ring and diffuse pale area beneath eye and in centre of ear-coverts, together with *dark eye-stripe* (incl. lores), *dark moustachial stripe* and *narrow dark malar stripe*, give head a bold and almost striped appearance. *Breast clearly streaked on dirty white ground colour* (no buff tones). Upperparts unstreaked (nape) or with very meagre fine streaks. Pale tips to median coverts form obvious wing-bar. Actions more like a Desert Lark than a pipit, makes rapid mouse-like dashes interrupted by fleeting stops; hard to flush, prefers to run away.

VOICE Call not unlike Yellow Wagtail's, 'tsri(e)', also a shorter soft 'chup'. Song, given in undulating song-flight, a rather energetically delivered, somewhat Tawny Pipit-like call slowly repeated 4–7 times, 'tschilp…tschilp…tschilp…', at times a bit faster and with almost prinia-like rattling and rolling quality, 'tsivirr, tsivirr, tsivirr, tsivirr'.

Water Pipit Rock Pipit

WATER PIPIT

ad. s.

prominent wing-bars

white

greyish-white

winter
coutellii
(Middle East)

yellow-buff tinge

brown

yellow

summer
spinoletta

off-white, unmarked

grey or paler red-brown

winter
spinoletta
(Europe)

white tail-sides

ROCK PIPIT

Rock Pipit

compare Rock Pipit (left) with much brighter and more contrastingly marked Meadow Pipit; note leg colour, too

MEADOW PIPIT

extreme (and rare) Water Pipit-like bird

grey

dark malar patch

spring
littoralis
(variation)

(many have shorter and less well-marked supercilium than this bird)

summer
littoralis
(Fenno-Scandia)

underparts usually sullied-looking

winter
petrosus
(W Europe)

greyish buff-white tail-sides

BUFF-BELLIED PIPIT

autumn
(fresh)

streaked

autumn
(fresh)

spring
(worn)

MEADOW PIPIT
(to compare)

pink

japonicus

rubescens

boldly streaked

diffusely streaked

red-brown

autumn
(fresh)
japonicus
(E Asia)

buff-white

autumn
(fresh)
rubescens
(N America)

BERTHELOT'S PIPIT

ad. s.
(worn)

broad and long, off-white

large-headed

pink

ad. winter
(fresh)

legs appear placed far back—gives peculiar look

juv. is browner above than ad. and is more boldly marked

contrastingly white

pale

juv.

KM

Meadow Pipit *Anthus pratensis* r**B**1 / **P**1 / **W**1

L 14–15½ cm. Breeds in open country, on heaths and moors (very common), coastal meadows, pastures and bogs. Resident in Britain & Ireland, where also large passage (Mar–May, and esp. Sep–Oct) and many winter visitors from NE.

IDENTIFICATION Typical pipit, with olive-tinged grey-brown and buff-white or dirty white, ± streaked plumage. Like Tree Pipit, but usually distinguished from latter without difficulty by calls and habitat. Both species can, however, occur in same places (wooded pasture, edges of raised bogs, on passage on meadowland), and close study of appearance then needed unless calls heard. Note *somewhat slimmer bill* (which often looks all dark at distance, lacking Tree Pipit's pink base to lower mandible), slightly *more diffuse*, less contrasty head pattern with *less marked supercilium* and slightly narrower and not so pale submoustachial stripe. A *narrow dirty white eye-ring* is often palest part of face. *Upperparts more heavily streaked* than on Tree Pipit (but some in fresh plumage are rather similar). Hindclaw is long and not so curved (cf. Tree Pipit), but close views and good observation conditions needed to confirm this. Legs pinkish. Ground-dwelling, prefers to land *on ground* after flight excursions but often also on fence wires and posts, at times also on bushtops, low isolated trees and telephone wires. Song-flight characteristic, first climbing with rapid wingbeats, then dropping on stiff wings.

VOICE Call, from bird rising with jerky springing flight, a few heated, thin 'ist ist ist' notes; birds flying over give similar or shorter 'ist', 'ist üst' or the like. Alarm a tremulous double note, 'sitt-itt' (or 'tirri'). Song like Rock Pipit's: series of rapidly repeated thin, piercing notes with motif changing three or four times during verse, which is fairly constant in structure, 'zi zi zi zi zi zi zi zi zi zi zi zü-zü-zü-zü-zü-zü-svisvisvisvisvi **tüü tüü tüü tüü tüü** tii-svia' (note that initial notes are higher and less 'jangling' than Rock Pipit's, and that verse often ends with a slight flourish). Complete verse only in song-flight; perched bird reels off intro after intro, 'zi zi zi zi zi...'.

Tree Pipit *Anthus trivialis* m**B**2 / **P**2

L 14–16 cm. Breeds locally in open woodland, in Britain often young conifer plantations, sparsely timbered heaths and commons, downland with scrub, woodland glades, but in N and W Britain mainly older oak and birch woods in uplands. Summer visitor (mainly Apr–Sep), winters in Africa.

IDENTIFICATION Like Meadow Pipit, but has *somewhat heavier bill*, rather more bold head markings with slightly stronger supercilium and broader and paler submoustachial stripe, as well as suggestion of dark eye-stripe (though differences often minor and hard to see). Underparts show *more contrast between warm buff breast and white belly* and between *heavy*

streaking on breast and thin streaks on flanks (Meadow Pipit more evenly yellowish- or off-white below, with equally coarse streaks both on breast and on flanks). Mantle / back normally less distinctly dark-marked than Meadow Pipit (but difference not always evident). At close range, short and curved hindclaw can sometimes be seen. Legs and bill-base pink. Slightly heavier in build than Meadow Pipit, and flight is a little more direct, not quite so light and skipping. Rather shy and difficult to approach. Often forages on ground, but when startled is more likely to fly up and *perch in tree*; in open country it tends to fly off farther than Meadow Pipit. Song-flight characteristic, starts from tree, climbs up, *then parachutes down on rigid wings, legs dangling near end of descent*, to perch in different tree. Often pumps tail downwards when perched.

VOICE Call is a drawn-out, uninflected, hoarse 'spihz'. Alarm a discreet but penetrating, clear 'sütt'. Song repeated frequently, even in middle of day when many species take a siesta, a jaunty, loud verse made up of trills and series of repeated notes with varied tempo, e.g. 'zit-zit-zit-zit cha-cha-cha-cha sürrrrrrrrrrrr **siiiii**-a tvet-tvet-tvet-tvet **si**va **si**va **si**iiva **si**iihva cha-cha-cha'; the sequence of the various components varies.

Olive-backed Pipit *Anthus hodgsoni* **V**∗∗

L 14–15½ cm. Breeds in open woodland in Siberia and in far NE of Europe, winters in S Asia. Rare but annual autumn vagrant in W Europe (a few spring and even winter records).

IDENTIFICATION Very like Tree Pipit (with similarly short, curved hindclaw; all other pipits have slightly longer and less curved hindclaw), but has somewhat different head pattern, more *green-tinged* brown-grey and *less clearly marked mantle and crown*, also on average *heavier black spotting on breast* (extremes, however, the same with regard to breast markings). *Supercilium bold, whitish and unstreaked* (Tree Pipit has finely streaked pale yellow-brown supercilium of variable prominence), *distinctly tinged rusty-buff in front of eye* (at best faintly buff on Tree Pipit). Above supercilium a *dark border to crown-side* (never obvious on Tree Pipit). Behind ear-coverts, diagonally below rear end of supercilium, almost invariably has an *isolated pale spot, and below this a dark spot* (sometimes a faint hint of such spots on Tree Pipit). In autumn always shows *fresh tertials with broad olive-brown edges* (imm. Tree Pipits have narrow grey-white edges to often slightly worn tertials).

VOICE Call very like Tree Pipit's, a straight, slightly hoarse, high-pitched 'spiz' (doubtfully distinguishable from Tree Pipit, but Olive-backed Pipit's call on average a little less hoarse, somewhat finer and less drawn out). Alarm a fine, sharp 'sitt'. Song as Tree Pipit's, but the verses are often a bit shorter, the voice softer and higher, the tempo fast throughout (does not slow down intermittently like Tree Pipit's) and the trills are drier (which together with some very thin, high notes can bring to mind song of Red-throated Pipit); the voice at times recalls Dunnock (which Tree Pipit's song never does).

Meadow Pipit

Tree Pipit

Olive-backed Pipit

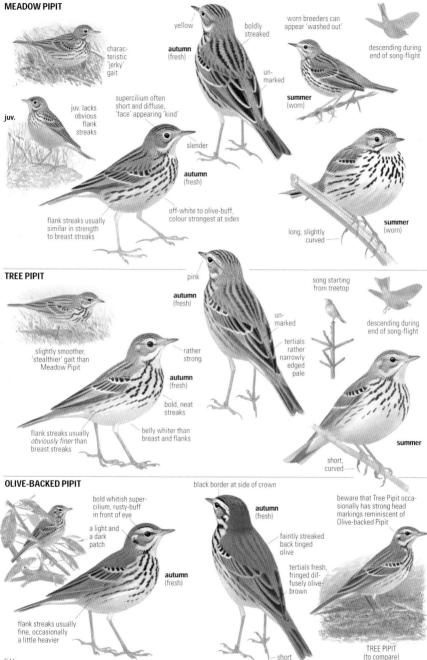

MEADOW PIPIT

characteristic 'jerky' gait

juv.

juv. lacks obvious flank streaks

yellow

boldly streaked

autumn (fresh)

worn breeders can appear 'washed out'

descending during end of song-flight

un-marked

summer (worn)

supercilium often short and diffuse, 'face' appearing 'kind'

slender

autumn (fresh)

off-white to olive-buff, colour strongest at sides

flank streaks usually similar in strength to breast streaks

summer (worn)

long, slightly curved

TREE PIPIT

pink

autumn (fresh)

un-marked

tertials rather narrowly edged pale

song starting from treetop

descending during end of song-flight

slightly smoother, 'stealthier' gait than Meadow Pipit

rather strong

autumn (fresh)

bold, neat streaks

belly whiter than breast and flanks

flank streaks usually *obviously finer* than breast streaks

summer

short, curved

OLIVE-BACKED PIPIT

bold whitish supercilium, rusty-buff in front of eye

a light and a dark patch

autumn (fresh)

black border at side of crown

autumn (fresh)

faintly streaked back tinged olive

tertials fresh, fringed diffusely olive-brown

beware that Tree Pipit occasionally has strong head markings reminiscent of Olive-backed Pipit

flank streaks usually fine, occasionally a little heavier

short

TREE PIPIT (to compare)

KM

Red-throated Pipit *Anthus cervinus* **V**∗∗

L 14–15 cm. Breeds sparsely on bare mountains and tundra in northernmost Europe, on swampland in willow zone and open, low upland birch forest with grassy patches. Summer visitor, winters in Africa and locally in Middle East. Vagrant Britain & Ireland (mostly Apr–Jun, Aug–Nov).

IDENTIFICATION Resembles Meadow Pipit in size and shape, and occurs on passage (at times also breeds) in same habitats as that species. Normally, however, only autumn immatures present identification challenge. In all plumages *heavily black-streaked above, including back and rump* (Meadow Pipit only poorly marked on rump), with *brown ground colour* and some rufous and whitish fringes (lacks olive tinge shown by most autumn Meadow Pipits). – Adult: Easily identified by *rusty-red throat*. Some (prob. mostly ♂♂) also have rusty-red on supercilium, forehead and upper breast, as well as having these areas completely unpatterned (thus lack dark malar stripe); others (prob. mostly ♀♀) have more restricted rusty-red and are heavily streaked. The rusty colour is retained in autumn (winter plumage), but is initially more yellow-brown in tone. – 1st-autumn: Lacks rusty-red on throat, which is buff-white. Note *heavily dark-streaked upperparts* with brown rather than olive-grey ground colour, *distinct pale tertial edges, pale lores, complete narrow whitish eye-ring*, thin bill with usually yellowish base to lower mandible, *whitish stripes along mantle*, and often strong black wedge shape on lower throat-side.

VOICE Call a fine, drawn-out, squeaky 'pssiih', with hint of hoarseness at close range (but much higher, purer and longer than Tree Pipit's call). Alarm a 'chüpp' like Ortolan Bunting's. Song very characteristic in its rhythmic theme with ringing tone, its needle-fine, drawn-out notes (with call-note quality) and its redpoll-like dry buzzing sound, e.g. 'svü-svü-svü-**svü**, svü-svü-svü-**svü**, svü-svü-svü-**svü**, psiu psiiiü psiiiüüh sürrrrrrrrr wi-wi-wi-wi tsvü-tsvü-tsvü'.

Pechora Pipit *Anthus gustavi* **V**∗∗∗

L 14–15 cm. Breeds in boggy areas with open conifer forest and willows, on damp tundra with scattered trees and bushes, by swampy river banks with rushes, willows and isolated trees. Summer visitor (Jun–Sep), winters in SE Asia. Rare vagrant in W Europe, mostly Sep–Oct; odd spring records. Terrestrial. Hard to flush, scampers mouse-like in vegetation.

IDENTIFICATION Owing to boldly streaked upperparts, with *whitish stripes along mantle-sides* (often a hint of a secondary stripe) and frequently dark malar patch on throat-side, most resembles young Red-throated Pipit, but differs as follows: somewhat *heavier bill* with usually pinkish or light brown base; *shorter tertials*, which do not cover primaries right to the tips; more prominent pale, almost *whitish wing-bars*; contrast between *white belly and buff breast* (Red-

throated Pipit more uniform yellowish-white below); *crown / nape and ear-coverts rather light rufous-brown, finely but distinctly streaked dark*; tendency to have dark lores but indistinct moustachial and malar stripes; supercilium short and diffuse, finely streaked; tail-sides not pure white.

VOICE Can call frequently on passage, *but much less inclined to call when* (reluctantly) *flushed* than other pipits, a short, sharp, clicking 'dzepp' with almost electrical overtone, repeated a few times. Song soft with strained, 'mechanical' voice, hard, dry trills broken by double note,'turrrrrr-tirrrrrrr-**chu**chi-turrrrrrrr-**chu**chi-tirrr-turrrrrr...'.

White / Pied Wagtail *Motacilla alba* r(m)**B**2 / **P**1

L 16½–19 cm. Common breeder in various habitats, often in open cultivated country close to habitation and water, e.g. farmyards and lakesides, as well as villages, towns and cities, in N also far from habitation in open forest or on bogs. Partial resident in W and S Europe, summer visitor in N (Apr–Oct), wintering in Middle East and NE Africa. Nests in stone walls, beneath roof tiles, in ventilation shafts, banks, among ivy, under stones etc. Attracted to bare areas such as grass lawns, golf courses, flat rocks, roofs and asphalt roads, where this fast-running bird can easily see and catch insects.

IDENTIFICATION Slender, with *long, narrow black and white tail* which *is constantly wagged up and down*. Walks with jerking head movements, rushes after prey only to pull up suddenly with tail pumping excitedly. – Adult ♂ summer (WHITE WAGTAIL ssp. *alba*): Black crown and nape with *sharp border against ash-grey mantle*. White forehead / forecrown. Jet-black bib (bill to breast). White wing-bars and white tertial fringes. – Adult ♀ summer (*alba*): Like ♂, but less black on nape and *diffuse border against grey back*, or only a little black on crown, or even *all-grey crown and nape*. – Winter: White chin and throat, on some tinged yellow; black breast-band. Forehead white, white with greenish-yellow tinge, or light grey with greenish tinge (adult ♂ whitest; immatures can have no white at all). – Juvenile: Dark crown-sides. Wing-bars greyish. *Breast patch grey*, not black. – Variation: In Britain & Ireland, and sporadically on adjacent Atlantic coasts, PIED WAGTAIL ssp. *yarrellii* breeds, summer-plumaged adult ♂ of which has *jet-black upperparts* and ♀ (and imm. ♂) *dark sooty-grey with black rump*; flanks dark olive-grey. Winter and immature plumages somewhat less dark above. Breeding in rest of Europe (passage migrant in Britain & Ireland) is ssp. *alba*, with light grey upperparts. In Morocco *subpersonata*, with distinctive head pattern.

VOICE Call is easily recognizable, a two- or three-syllable, cheerful 'tsli-**vitt**' or 'zi-ze-**litt**'. Normal song very plain and simple, a few twittering notes, a pause, then a few more notes followed by further pause etc.; the whole gives impression of being casual and reflective and does not always sound like 'proper' song. The opposite is so with the ecstatic song variant, used in excitement, in territorial conflicts and when mobbing Cuckoo or Sparrowhawk, a long, very fast series of indignant chirping notes.

Red-throated Pipit

Pechora Pipit

White / Pied Wagtail

RED-THROATED PIPIT

♂ type
♀ type

most adults have orange-brown throat in winter, too, ♀♀ usually less prominently than ♂♂

ad. winter

whitish mantle stripes

streaked (cf. Meadow Pipit)

1st-winter

ad. summer (♂ type)

fine bill with (greenish-tinged) yellow base

underparts pale cream-white, lacking contrast between breast and belly

1st-winter

PECHORA PIPIT

broad whitish mantle stripes

prominent white wing-bars

hard to flush, steals away shrewdly in the grass

tertials shorter than wing-tip

finely but distinctly streaked crown and nape

malar stripe usually narrow

stout, pinkish

contrast between whitish belly and buff breast

WHITE / PIED WAGTAIL

looking for insects on bare surfaces

♂

♀

deeply undulating flight

1st-winter

ad. winter *alba*

alba never has such dark grey flanks as *yarrellii*

dark grey, often blotchy

blackish

ad. summer ♀ *yarrellii*

ad. winter ♂ *yarrellii*

glossy black

ad. s. ♂ *yarrellii* (Britain & Ireland)

PIED WAGTAIL

diffuse transition black to grey

plain grey

ad. summer ♀ *alba*

sharp border

WHITE WAGTAIL

ad. w. ♂

subpersonata (Morocco)

ad. s. ♂

ad. s. ♂ *alba* (Continental Europe)

KM

Yellow Wagtail *Motacilla flava* mB3 / P3

L 15–16 cm. Breeds in lowland areas on marshy pastures, waterlogged meadows, beside lakes and at sewage-farms, in N Europe also on forest bogs and mires and in wet clearings. Summer visitor (mainly Apr–Sep/early Oct), winters in Africa. Migrants on pastures and golf courses on autumn passage (roost in reedbeds). Nests in tussocks on ground. Complex geographical variation in appearance, especially of ♂♂, and this cannot be treated in detail here; at least eight different races just within the region covered.

IDENTIFICATION The least extreme of the wagtails in proportions, with tail slightly shorter than White Wagtail's and clearly shorter than that of Grey. ♂ is *saturated yellow below*, ♀ a little duller, especially on breast. Autumn immatures are pale below, *buff-white with only faint yellow tinge on vent* (the yellow at times difficult to see in the field, or can even be lacking altogether; cf. Citrine Wagtail). *Mantle and back greyish-green or grey-brown*, with *olive tinge barely discernible* in the field. *Black legs.* Wing brownish-grey, with rather distinct but narrow wing-bars pale yellow or dirty white. – Variation in ♂♂: In greater part of Continental Europe (ssp. *flava*), the head is blue-grey with prominent white supercilium and white submoustachial stripe between dark grey cheek and yellow throat; small white patch below eye. In Britain (*flavissima*), crown, nape and ear-coverts are yellow-green, and rest of head bright yellow like underparts. Typical ♂♂ of other races illustrated on opposite plate. Note that intermediate forms from border areas between two races occur.

VOICE In much of Europe call a fine 'psit' or slightly fuller 'tslie' (also 'tsrlie'), but in Balkans and in parts of E Europe (*feldegg*) usually a more grating, frothy 'zrri(e)' (with more obvious 'r'; cf. Citrine Wagtail). Song is one of the most modest of all bird songs, usually consisting of two (occasionally one or three) scraping notes, with the last generally slightly stressed, 'srrii-**srriiht**'; often delivered from top of a post, low bush or fence-wire perch.

Citrine Wagtail *Motacilla citreola* V**

L 15½–17 cm. Breeds on waterlogged meadows, open bogs in forest with low vegetation and sparse willow bushes, and soggy river banks. Migrant, winters in SE Asia (a few in Middle East). Rare but increasingly numerous vagrant to W Europe. Expanding westwards (now breeds e.g. Poland).

IDENTIFICATION Like Yellow Wagtail in size and proportions, but tail on average somewhat longer. *Double broad white* (or whitish) *wing-bars* important character in all plumages (exception: heavily worn breeding birds). – Adult ♂ summer: Unmistakable, with entirely *lemon-yellow head, black nuchal band, ash-grey mantle/back*, yellow belly (but usually *whitish undertail-coverts*; always yellow on Yellow

and Grey Wagtails). Flanks dusky grey (as on White Wagtail, unlike the other wagtails). – Adult ♀ summer / adult ♂♀ winter: Crown and cheeks have grey tone, nape lacks black, yellow of underparts is usually paler. Note *yellow supercilium* and *yellow-framed dirty grey ear-coverts*, as well as *white wing-bars*. In winter plumage especially, some dark spots on breast. – 1st-winter: Lacks pure yellow in plumage (but breast and forehead often have tinge of yellow-buff) and can be confused with pale immature Yellow Wagtails. Note following: *broad white wing-bars*; *grey or brownish-grey upperparts* (never olive-toned); *pale lores* and often forehead (Yellow Wagtail dark); *light-framed ear-coverts*; *all-dark bill* (Yellow Wagtail has slightly paler base to lower mandible); *never any yellow on undertail-coverts*; *flight-call.*

VOICE Contact-call often very like Yellow Wagtail's, 'tslie'. Alarm and flight-call (often heard from vagrants in W Europe) a characteristic loud, ripping, straight (voice as in Yellow Wagtail song) 'tsriip', repeated several times. (Black-headed Yellow Wagtails, *feldegg*, also have r-sound in call, but call not so loudly ripping and straight, more soft, frothy and with faint terminal upslur.) Song most like White Wagtail's, a few uncomplicated syllables at a time, delivered from top of a willow bush (slightly longer phrases in song-flight); individual notes also not unlike Yellow Wagtail call (*flava*).

Grey Wagtail *Motacilla cinerea* rB3 / P3

L 17–20 cm. Breeds in scattered pairs on small, fast-flowing watercourses with plenty of exposed rocks in and alongside the water and with woodland or at least rows of trees along the banks; at times also on lakeshores and slower rivers. Mostly resident in Britain & Ireland; also migrants and winterers from N Europe (passage Aug–Oct). Nests in rock crevice, cavity in stone bridge, mill foundations etc. beside water.

IDENTIFICATION Compared with the other wagtails, Grey Wagtail has *longest tail* and *shortest legs.* Constantly pumps its long tail, and so strongly that *whole rear end rocks* with it. In all plumages *bright yellow vent* and also *yellow-green rump.* *Legs brownish-pink* (other wagtails black). *Grey upperparts* contrast with *black wings.* Tertials edged (yellow-)white. Distinct pale supercilium. In *deeply undulating flight*, when long tail is very striking, shows a *broad white wing-bar*, most evident from below. – Adult ♂ summer: *Black bib.* Pure *white supercilium and submoustachial stripe.* Rest of underparts yellow (but flanks sometimes a little paler). – Adult ♀ summer: Throat white with some greyish-black; sometimes more ♂-like with much black on throat, but always shows some white, and has buff-white supercilium and indistinct submoustachial stripe. – Winter: Pale throat with no dark feathering. Older birds are yellower on breast and whiter on throat, younger ones paler yellow on breast and buff-tinged on throat.

VOICE Call basically like White Wagtail's but sharper and higher-pitched, 'zi-zi'. Alarm a repeated 'süiht', often interspersed with call. Song a short, mechanical series of sharp notes, 'ziss-ziss-ziss-ziss', often mixed with alternative phrase of higher notes, 'si si si si süi'.

Yellow Wagtail

Citrine Wagtail

Grey Wagtail

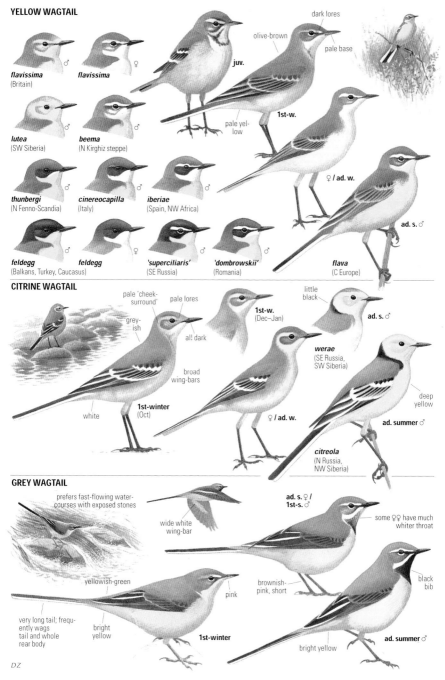

YELLOW WAGTAIL

flavissima
(Britain) ♂

flavissima
♀

lutea
(SW Siberia) ♂

beema
(N Kirghiz steppe) ♂

thunbergi
(N Fenno-Scandia) ♂

cinereocapilla
(Italy) ♂

iberiae
(Spain, NW Africa) ♂

feldegg
(Balkans, Turkey, Caucasus) ♂

feldegg
♀

'superciliaris'
(SE Russia) ♂

'dombrowskii'
(Romania) ♂

juv.

dark lores

olive-brown

pale base

pale yel-low

1st-w.

♀ / ad. w.

ad. s. ♂

flava
(C Europe)

CITRINE WAGTAIL

pale 'cheek-surround'

pale lores

grey-ish

al! dark

broad wing-bars

white

1st-winter
(Oct)

1st-w.
(Dec–Jan)

♀ / ad. w.

little black

ad. s. ♂

werae
(SE Russia, SW Siberia)

deep yellow

ad. summer ♂

citreola
(N Russia, NW Siberia)

GREY WAGTAIL

prefers fast-flowing water-courses with exposed stones

wide white wing-bar

yellowish-green

very long tail; frequently wags tail and whole rear body

bright yellow

1st-winter

pink

ad. s. ♀ /
1st-s. ♂

some ♀♀ have much whiter throat

black bib

brownish-pink, short

bright yellow

ad. summer ♂

DZ

(Winter) **Wren** *Troglodytes troglodytes* r**B**1 / **W**
L 9–10½ cm. Breeds in woodland with dense undergrowth, in overgrown clearings and scrub, often in rank streamside growth and gardens, also on barren islands with hedges, shrubbery, walls etc. Resident; migratory in N Europe.

IDENTIFICATION *Very small*, and this reinforced by ludicrously *small tail that is often raised vertically*, also by short neck; thus looks like a little ball. *Reddish-brown above and brownish-white below with fine dark vermiculations*. Bill quite long, pointed and slightly decurved. Sexes and ages alike.

VOICE When nervous, a rattling, hard 'zerrrr' as well as single hard clicking 'zeck!' notes, the two sometimes combined in long series. Song amazingly loud for so small a bird, series of metallic ringing notes and trills roughly like a Canary or Tree Pipit, e.g. 'zitrivi-si **svi-svi-svi-svi-svi** zivüsu **zü-zü-zü-zü** si-**zirrrrrrr svi-svi-svi** siyu-**zerrrrr** sivi!'. Sings mostly from cover.

(White-throated) **Dipper** *Cinclus cinclus* r**B**3 / (**W**)
L 17–20 cm. Breeds along shallow watercourses in upland tracts, often forested, preferably beside fast-flowing torrents with exposed boulders as convenient perches, less on lowland rivers with weirs. Dives for aquatic invertebrates, *swims underwater* using wings and can walk on bottom; is also a 'winter bather', hopping in from edge of ice. Also swims on surface, body very low. Nest of straws and moss, domed and with side entrance, placed out of reach on wall of rock or mill over water, or even behind waterfall. Mostly resident.

IDENTIFICATION *Compact build* with strong legs and *short tail, which is often held somewhat cocked*. Plumage *dark with big white bib*, usually sooty-black (birds in north and large parts of France) or brownish on head and rusty-brown beneath bib (Britain & Ireland; less obviously in C Europe). Nictitating membrane white. *Flight straight*, with *fast whirring beats of the rounded wings*. Often curtseys when perched. – Juvenile: Dull grey with pale wavy bars above and dark ones below. May show hint of pale bib.

VOICE Call a short, hoarse 'stretts!' penetrating through the roar of the rushing water, often given by bird flying past along watercourse. Song, often heard even in depths of the coldest winter, a slowly delivered, rather soft series of alternating hard strained, harsh, squeaky and throaty notes.

(Bohemian) **Waxwing** *Bombycilla garrulus* **W**5(4)
L 18–21 cm. Breeds in northern parts of the coniferous belt, often in remote, lichen-rich, mature forest in damp, mossy terrain. Nest high up on branch, often in pine. In some years large flocks move south in winter, reaching W Europe, when often seen eating rowan berries in gardens and suburban roads. Nevertheless, remains alert and rather nervous.

IDENTIFICATION Starling-sized, compact in build with thick neck. *Large crest on crown* combined with *reddish-buff* colour eliminates all other species. Narrow black eye-mask and *black bib*, *yellow tail-tip* plus *yellow and white pattern on wing*. Flight straight with long undulations; flocks keep tight formation. – Adult ♂: Tips of primaries edged yellow on outer web and white-edged on inner web (forming *V-angles*); broad yellow terminal tail-band; many long red waxy appendages on secondaries; all-black bib with well-demarcated lower edge. – Adult ♀: Like adult ♂ but sometimes incomplete white angles on primary tips; thinner yellow tail-band; often fewer and shorter waxy appendages; blurred lower edge to bib. – 1st-year: Lacks white tips to *inner* webs of primaries, has just white tips to outer webs (no angles).

VOICE Contact-call a pleasant ringing 'sirrrrr' as from a small bell, often in pealing chorus from flock before rising. Song slow and halting, a series of call notes mixed with hard, raucous sounds, 'sirr sirrrrr chark-chark chi-chark sirrrr sirrrr...' etc.

Common Bulbul *Pycnonotus barbatus* —
L 19–21 cm. Breeds in gardens, around cultivations, by watercourses in mountains and at oases, so long as vegetation present. Does not shun proximity of man, and before long is noticed: noisy, flies about a lot, often seen in small groups, often perches openly. Resident.

IDENTIFICATION A barely thrush-sized, rather *long-tailed*, *dark grey* and dirty greyish-white bird. *Head is sooty-grey* (lores almost black), upperparts almost equally dark grey, and underparts slightly paler brown-grey with *whitish vent*. Tail black, wings dark grey. Sexes and ages alike. *Flight straight and a little unsteady, wings rounded*. Often opens and closes tail in flight.

VOICE Very loud and noisy. Flocks often utter a repeated, hoarse, slightly casual 'chahr chahr chahr...'. When uneasy, bulbuls give sharper but similar 'tshirr' in persistent series. Song powerful with characteristic jerky, uneven rhythm, varies in length and detail, e.g. 'chick chille**wi**, chu**wü**', delivered most frequently at dawn and dusk.

Spectacled Bulbul *Pycnonotus xanthopygos* —
L 19–21 cm. Breeding habitat and habits very like those of Common Bulbul, to which it is closely related (ranges of the two species meet at Suez Canal). Lives in palm groves, wadis with some vegetation, gardens etc. Resident.

IDENTIFICATION Like Common Bulbul, but differs in having *lemon-yellow vent*, darker, almost *black head* with *narrow white eye-ring*, proportionately slightly longer but thinner bill and slightly more square-cut tail.

VOICE Appears to be very like Common Bulbul's.

Wren

Dipper

Waxwing

Common Bulbul

Spectacled Bulbul

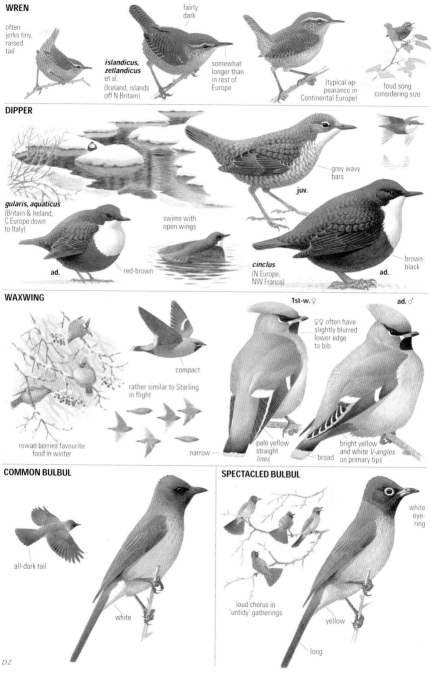

WREN

often jerks tiny, raised tail

fairly dark

islandicus, zetlandicus et al. (Iceland, islands off N Britain)

somewhat longer than in rest of Europe

(typical appearance in Continental Europe)

loud song considering size

DIPPER

grey wavy bars

juv.

gularis, aquaticus (Britain & Ireland, C Europe down to Italy)

swims with open wings

red-brown

ad.

cinclus (N Europe, NW France)

brown-black

ad.

WAXWING

1st-w. ♀

ad. ♂

compact

rather similar to Starling in flight

♀♀ often have slightly blurred lower edge to bib

rowan berries favourite food in winter

narrow

pale yellow straight *lines*

broad

bright yellow and white *V-angles* on primary tips

COMMON BULBUL

all-dark tail

white

SPECTACLED BULBUL

white eye-ring

loud chorus in 'untidy' gatherings

yellow

long

DZ

ACCENTORS Prunellidae

Five small passerines with features of sparrows as well as warblers and small thrushes, spending much time on ground or in shrub layer. Bill rather thin and pointed (but has rather deep base), plumage mostly brown, buff, grey and black. Wings rather short and rounded. Sexes and ages very similar. Forage mostly on ground, hopping in crouched posture.

Dunnock Prunella modularis   rB1 / W

L 13–14½ cm. Breeds in parks, gardens, open woodland, heaths and commons with gorse or scrub, areas with hedges and thick shrubbery, also young conifer stands; but in N Europe mainly in dense spruce plantations, also in juniper country and upland forest. Resident; migratory in N. Rather shy and retiring in summer. Food mostly insects. Nests in thick bush or low down in conifer.

IDENTIFICATION Robin-sized, with warbler-like *thin bill*. Rather House Sparrow-like *brown and streaked upperparts*. Characteristic *blue-grey head* (ear-coverts and crown tinged grey-brown) *and breast*. Legs red-brown. Lacks white in tail. Greater coverts have fine pale spots at tips, at times appearing as thin wing-bar. Overall impression, however, is of a *uniformly coloured and rather dark* bird. Flight jerky, light and springing. Often perches in view when singing, but otherwise mostly keeps hidden, and is rather difficult to catch sight of, dives down into cover at slightest disturbance. – Juv.: Browner, *more boldly streaked*, and has pale chin. – Variation: Birds in Ireland and NW Scotland (ssp. *hebridium*) are darker, especially above and on breast. Birds in rest of Britain (*occidentalis*) something between those and birds of Continental Europe (*modularis*).

VOICE Alarm-call (also at times as contact) a rather strong, uninflected pipe with discordant tone, 'tiih'. Call on migration, when often heard at first light or in late evening, uttered especially in flight, a ringing or shivering, very thin 'tihihihi'. Song, usually given from top of bush or medium-sized conifer, clear and quite loud, an irresolute shuttling or patchwork of sounds *c.*2 sec. long at quite even pitch, 'tütellititelletitütellütotelitelleti' or similar.

Alpine Accentor Prunella collaris   V***

L 15–17½ cm. Breeds in high alpine country, usually at 1800–3000 m. Found mostly in barren areas with boulders and low-growing plants. Rather sociable, and small groups can be seen even during breeding season. Largely resident. Food mostly insects and seeds. Nests in rock crevice.

IDENTIFICATION When walking in the right terrain and one or more Skylark-sized, compact and rather dark birds fly up, the alternatives are few: Alpine Accentor, Horned Lark, Water Pipit or some bunting. Of these, Alpine Accentor is the strongest flyer, fast and in shallow dips almost like a small thrush. If seen perched, it shows *light yellow patch at bill-base*, a *dark panel across wing* formed by the greater coverts and, in good light, *heavy red-brown flank streaking*. At really close range, some pale spotting is visible on throat-centre and fine white tips on wing-coverts. – Variation: Birds in Turkey (ssp. *montana*) are somewhat more pale brown and less heavily streaked above.

VOICE On rising, gives muffled lark-like rolling calls, e.g. 'drrü drrü, drrip', 'tschirr'. May also utter stifled click like

a chat. Song a drawn-out, creaking and trilling phrase with no clear structure: some bubbling notes recall Crested Tit, others are squeaky. Generally delivered from perch, occasionally in fluttering song-flight.

Siberian Accentor Prunella montanella   —

L 13–14½ cm. Breeds in N Siberia and on both sides of N Urals in willows and birch forest bordering bogs, tundra and rivers, also in open, impoverished conifer forest. Migratory, winters in SE Asia. Rare vagrant in W Europe. Shy, keeps mostly in cover.

IDENTIFICATION Roughly the size of Dunnock. Characterized by *broad and long buff supercilium* (widest behind eye) accentuated by *brownish-black crown* (darkest at sides) and *dark cheeks. Entire underside yellowish rusty-buff* (some with intimation of dark feather centres on breast). Above, varies somewhat in colour: *usually distinctly reddish-brown* with darker red-brown streaks, but sometimes more cold dark brown with mere hint of red-brown tinge and heavily black-spotted (then more like Black-throated Accentor).

VOICE Call a fine 'ti-ti-ti'. Song a rather monotonous Dunnock-like verse, high-pitched and with quite *hard r-sound*; minimal range on scale.

Radde's Accentor Prunella ocularis   —

L 13–14 cm. Breeds in high alpine habitats at 2000–3000 m, in boulder and shrub terrain only just below treeline. Resident or short-distance migrant. Lively and restless, scampers on ground, flicks wings, flies between low bushes, rarely stays in one spot for long.

IDENTIFICATION As Dunnock in size. Seen briefly, plumage most like Siberian Accentor, thus with *broad, pale supercilium, dark crown* and dark cheeks, and warm buff underparts. Differs from Siberian Accentor in that supercilium is dirty white or creamy (not saturated yellow-buff), and buff colour below is *tinged orange and concentrated on breast*, with some contrast against whiter belly (as on Black-throated Accentor) and throat. At close range, throat-sides show fine dark spots.

VOICE Call Dunnock-like, a fine 'ti-ti-ti'. Song *crystal-clear* in tone, a fast verse in which some notes are repeated several times and short *high trills* interwoven.

Black-throated Accentor Prunella atrogularis   —

L 13–14½ cm. Breeds in spruce thickets and bushy country, also in deciduous forest, often on upper slopes (Urals). (In C Asia, also found in tall conifer forest in mountain valleys.) Very rare vagrant in W Europe, mainly in autumn.

IDENTIFICATION Like Siberian and Radde's Accentors, with *brown-black crown* and *broad buff supercilium*. Distinguished by *black throat*, easy to see in breeding plumage but harder with autumn immatures, when broad pale fringes conceal some (rarely, on 1st-winter ♀, almost all) of the dark colour. Note that *back is dull dark brown* (not strongly tinged reddish-brown) with dark spotting, also that *warm orange-buff breast contrasts with whiter belly*. Breast has some dark feather centres.

VOICE Call like that of other smaller accentors, a fine 'ti-ti-ti'. Song Dunnock-like and shuttling with little change in pitch, though verses somewhat shorter and volume a bit weaker; contains fewer clear notes than Dunnock's.

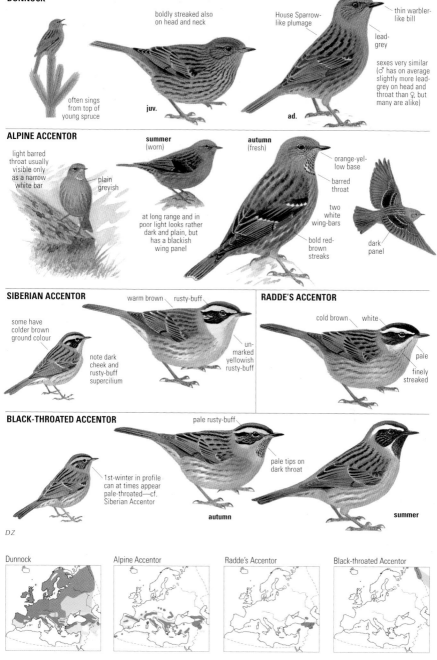

DUNNOCK

often sings from top of young spruce

boldly streaked also on head and neck

juv.

House Sparrow-like plumage

thin warbler-like bill

lead-grey

sexes very similar (♂ has on average slightly more lead-grey on head and throat than ♀, but many are alike)

ad.

ALPINE ACCENTOR

light barred throat usually visible only as a narrow white bar

plain greyish

summer (worn)

at long range and in poor light looks rather dark and plain, but has a blackish wing panel

autumn (fresh)

orange-yellow base

barred throat

two white wing-bars

bold red-brown streaks

dark panel

SIBERIAN ACCENTOR

some have colder brown ground colour

note dark cheek and rusty-buff supercilium

warm brown   rusty-buff

un-marked yellowish rusty-buff

RADDE'S ACCENTOR

cold brown   white

pale

finely streaked

BLACK-THROATED ACCENTOR

1st-winter in profile can at times appear pale-throated—cf. Siberian Accentor

pale rusty-buff

pale tips on dark throat

autumn

summer

DZ

Dunnock

Alpine Accentor

Radde's Accentor

Black-throated Accentor

THRUSHES *Turdidae*

Large family of small to medium-sized passerines with well-developed songs. Juvenile plumage in most cases spotted. The true thrushes (pp. 274–279) are bigger, with strong legs and bill; 16 species. The smaller thrushes (chats) comprise rather dissimilar, often brightly coloured species, such as nightingales, redstarts, wheatears, rock thrushes; 31 species.

(European) **Robin** *Erithacus rubecula* r**B**1 / **W**

L 12½–14 cm. Breeds in woodland, gardens, parks, forest edge, generally with some dense vegetation and open areas; in N Europe prefers spruce forest with some deciduous element (e.g. birch), also mixed forest. Migratory in N Europe. Wary but by no means shy. Food insects, snails, worms. Nests in hollow stump, bank, crevice etc.

IDENTIFICATION Small and brownish with *rusty-red 'bib'* (covers entire breast and face). *Narrow yellow wing-bar* (most obvious on juveniles). Often looks rather big-headed. Has *thin and rather long legs*. At times ruffles up feathers so that it looks rounded and compact, but more often looks rather slim. Droops wings, hops rapidly on ground with feet together, curtseys and cocks short tail. Perches motionless, makes a sudden movement, stands still again and so on. – Juvenile: Whole plumage finely spotted. Lacks red bib.

VOICE Call a short, hard 'tick'. When nervous, not least at roosting time and 'reveille', the ticking calls are protracted into long rapid series, 'tick-ick-ick-ick-...', sounding like a watch being wound up. Alarm an extremely thin and sharp, ventriloquial 'tsiiih'. On nocturnal migration a thin, hoarse 'tsi'. Song often begins with a few high, drawn-out, thin notes, then the verse drops in pitch and speeds up with fast runs of trembling and excited clear squeaky notes; tempo and volume vary, no two verses are the same.

(Common) **Nightingale** *Luscinia megarhynchos* m**B**4

L 15–16½ cm. This is the 'real' nightingale, with the more beautiful song, which has found a place in literature and in the minds of everyday people. Breeds in woods and groves with rich undergrowth, often by water but also in drier habitats with dense shrubbery; at times in gardens and orchards. Summer visitor (mainly Apr–Sep), winters in S Africa.

IDENTIFICATION More often heard than seen, and when seen its appearance is, for many, surprisingly plain: *brown above* with *rusty-red tail and rump*, grey-buff below with diffusely paler throat. The *rather big black eye* is set off by an *indistinct whitish eye-ring*. Very like Thrush Nightingale, and sometimes inseparable in field, but at close range a shade redder on uppertail and *lacks obvious grey vermiculation on lower throat/breast* (but can have light grey shading). – Variation: Birds in Central Asia (*hafizi*) are

paler, longer-tailed and have a hint of a pale supercilium.

VOICE Has no conspicuous calls. Alarm a whistled, slightly upslurred 'üihp', as well as a creaking 'errrr'. Song powerful and melodic, varied throughout, phrases rather short (2–4 sec.) with often equal-length pauses in between, consisting of trilling sounds, fluted whistles and rippling or gurgling notes; the song is best recognized by recurring whistles in crescendo, 'lu lu lü lü li li'.

Thrush Nightingale *Luscinia luscinia* **V**∗∗

L 15–17 cm. The nightingale of N and E Europe, where a less vocally pleasing substitute for the 'real' nightingale of W and S Europe. Breeds in thick, damp, shady deciduous forest, often in hazel stands, shrubbery and waterside scrub; also in thickly wooded parks, gardens. Summer visitor, winters in Africa. Vagrant in Britain (Apr–Jun, Aug–Oct).

IDENTIFICATION Confusingly like Nightingale. On average *somewhat less reddish-brown on tail and rump*, a shade greyer brown on back, and as a rule has rather distinct *grey vermiculation on lower throat/breast* (but none of these features is absolute or easy to judge in field).

VOICE Lacks conspicuous calls. Alarm a piercing, ventriloquial, straight whistle, 'ihp' (like alarm of Collared Flycatcher), also a creaking hard 'errrr'. Song more loud than beautiful (still remarkable!), series of tongue-clicking and gurgling notes, the verses often introduced by a few pensive sharp whistles. Audible for kilometres on still nights.

Rufous Bush Robin *Cercotrichas galactotes* **V**∗∗∗

L 15–17 cm. Breeds in dry, rather open country with dense shrubbery, hedges, fruit orchards; fond of tamarisk, prickly-pear cactus, pistachio trees; often near human habitation. Summer visitor (mid May–Sep), winters S of Sahara.

IDENTIFICATION Brownish above and dirty white below, with *long red-brown tail with black and white tips* to outer feathers. Bold head markings, with *white supercilium* and *narrow dark eye-stripe* plus often *dark lateral crown-stripe*. Spends much time on ground. Often spreads tail and jerks it upwards, then closes and slowly lowers it. Also flicks and opens wings. Sexes and ages alike. – Variation: In Spain, NW Africa, Egypt and Israel (ssp. *galactotes*) the back is warm brown and contrasts little with tail, and breast is buff, whereas birds in Greece and Turkey (*syriacus*) have slightly more grey-brown back, have grey tone to breast and flanks and have more contrasted head markings.

VOICE Call a hard tongue-clicking and a soft straight whistle, 'üh'; also a peculiar, insect-like buzzing sound, 'bzzzzz'. Song thrush-like and clear with rather melancholy tone, may be likened to lethargic song of Song Thrush (short phrases, short pauses), but higher and more chirping.

Robin

Nightingale

Thrush Nightingale

Rufous Bush Robin

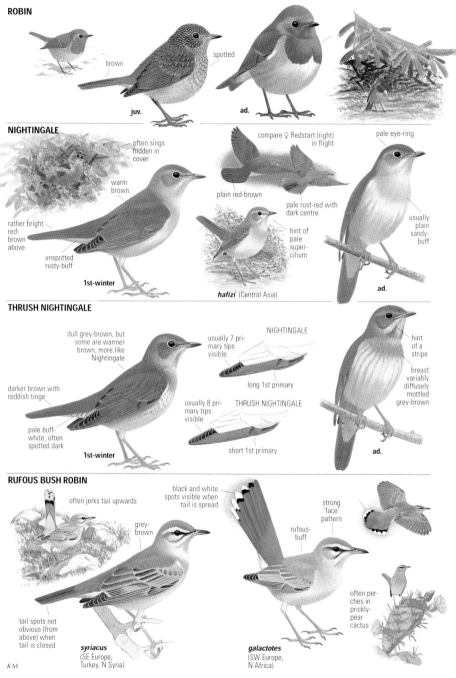

ROBIN

brown

spotted

juv.

ad.

NIGHTINGALE

often sings hidden in cover

warm brown

compare ♀ Redstart (right) in flight

plain red-brown

pale rust-red with dark centre

pale eye-ring

rather bright red-brown above

unspotted rusty-buff

1st-winter

hint of pale supercilium

hafizi (Central Asia)

usually plain sandy-buff

ad.

THRUSH NIGHTINGALE

dull grey-brown, but some are warmer brown, more like Nightingale

usually 7 primary tips visible

NIGHTINGALE

long 1st primary

darker brown with reddish tinge

pale buff-white, often spotted dark

1st-winter

usually 8 primary tips visible

THRUSH NIGHTINGALE

short 1st primary

hint of a stripe

breast variably diffusely mottled grey-brown

ad.

RUFOUS BUSH ROBIN

often jerks tail upwards

black and white spots visible when tail is spread

grey-brown

strong 'face' pattern

rufous-buff

tail spots not obvious (from above) when tail is closed

syriacus (SE Europe, Turkey, N Syria)

galactotes (SW Europe, N Africa)

often perches in prickly-pear cactus

KM

Bluethroat *Luscinia svecica* **P**4

L 13–14 cm. Breeds in N Europe among willows and soggy upland birch forest, in rest of Europe in swampland by fens and rivers overgrown with bushes, reeds, alder etc. Summer visitor, winters mainly from NE Africa to W India. Passage migrant in Britain (Mar–May, Aug–Oct). Food insects. Nests in tussock or low in dense willow bush.

IDENTIFICATION A rather small and slim bird with long thin legs, in all plumages told by *obvious whitish supercilium* and *rusty-red patch on sides of tail-base* (often seen in flight, or when perched bird flicks tail up). – ♂: Bright blue bib, bordered below by a narrow black and white band and a broader rusty-red one. Inlaid in centre of the blue, birds in chiefly N Europe (ssp. *svecica*) have a *rusty throat patch*, those in rest of Europe, E Turkey and Caucasus (incl. *cyanecula*, *magna*) a *small white patch* or none at all. In autumn, some of the bright throat colours are replaced by yellowish-white areas. – ♀: Variable throat markings; usually just an arc of black spots on creamy-white ground, older birds occasionally with some blue, plus black and rusty border across breast (those with most blue can look quite ♂-like). – Juvenile: Finely spotted like juvenile Robin, but note tail markings.

VOICE Commonest call a dry, throaty clicking 'track' (like flag halyard flapping in the wind). When agitated, also a wheatear-like whistled 'hiit' (and at times a Redstart imitation, '**hui**t'). In autumn a hoarse, cracked 'bzrü' may also be heard. Song powerful and clear, often starts with a long-repeated, loud, metallic 'zrü', or a polysyllabic 'zri-zri-**zrütt**' or the like, which slowly speeds up and suddenly turns into a cascade of melodious or hard and squeaky notes, often mixed with good imitations of other species (even reindeer bells may be mimicked!).

Red-flanked Bluetail *Tarsiger cyanurus* **V***

L 13–14 cm. Breeds in taiga, mainly in rolling, upland terrain in undisturbed, damp, mossy spruce forest with some birch. Rare breeder in E Finland (arrives from late May). Long-distance migrant, winters in SE Asia. Rare vagrant in W Europe. Rather shy. Food insects. Nests in hollow trunk or stump, in bank among roots etc.

IDENTIFICATION Seen well in good light, adult ♂ is a beautiful bird with *dull blue upperparts* (only rump, tail-base, wing-bend and crown-side are brighter blue), *orange flanks* and white underparts. Wing blue or (usually) olive-tinged grey-brown. ♀, 1st-summer ♂ and autumn immatures more modest in olive-grey and off-white and can easily be overlooked, are blue only on uppertail, but this normally looks just dark in field. Instead note *orange patch on flanks*, dusky breast and *grey cheeks* framing *narrow white bib*, also *whitish eye-ring*. Often flicks wings and tail.

VOICE Alarm-calls somewhat recall Black Redstart's: an often repeated, whistling, straight 'viht', and a muffled, hard, slightly throaty 'track'. Song, often delivered from treetop at very first light, a rather constant, fast, short, clear, melancholy verse, not unlike Redstart's but deeper and clearer, 'itrü-**chürr**-tre-tre-tru-trurr'.

White-throated Robin *Irania gutturalis* **V***

L 16½–18 cm. Breeds on dry, rocky slopes, often above 1000 m, with dense bushes and scattered trees. Summer visitor (mostly end Apr–Aug), winters in E Africa. Very rare vagrant in N Europe. Rather shy, but sings from open perch, and occasionally in gliding song-flight. Food mostly insects. Nests in bush or low down in thick-foliaged tree.

IDENTIFICATION Rather big with slimness of a thrush, with long neck, long legs and *long, heavy bill*, and *long black* (♂) or *dark grey* (♀) *tail* which is often raised. – Adult ♂: Unmistakable, with *orange breast*, *black head-sides* framing *narrow white bib*, with *white supercilium* and *lead-grey upperparts*. – ♀/1st-winter ♂: Grey-sullied buff-white below (breast weakly vermiculated grey) with *pale orange flanks*. Pale eye-ring and forehead. Brownish-grey above.

VOICE Call disyllabic, 'chi-**litt**', not that unlike Pied Wagtail. When agitated, a clicking 'check'. Alarm also a creaking 'churrr'. Song *very fast and twittering*, full of sharp whistles and hard, creaky calls, often given at such high speed that the notes seem to stick in the throat; can recall an ecstatically singing *Sylvia* warbler or shrike.

Siberian Rubythroat *Luscinia calliope* **V***

L 14½–16 cm. Breeds in mixed coniferous forest with rich element of birch, willow and undergrowth, often in damp spots; at times also in well-wooded parks. Summer visitor (mainly late Apr–early Sep), winters in SE Asia. Shy, tends to keep well concealed. Nests low in bush or in tussock.

IDENTIFICATION Like a cross between Bluethroat and Nightingale, long-legged but rather short-tailed. In all plumages *dark lores* and *pale supercilium*. – Adult ♂: *Red bib* narrowly edged black; *submoustachial stripe white*; *lores black*. – ♀/1st-winter ♂: More diffuse head markings (*grey lores*; *smudgy submoustachial stripe*) and either partly light red bib (older ♀) or off-white chin without black frame.

VOICE When nervous, a whistling, disyllabic '**ii**-lü' and a tongue-clicking 'chack' (as Fieldfare but weaker); sometimes also a muffled creaking 'arrr'. Song rippling, *chatty and calm*, like a Garden Warbler if anything, but recognized by sprinkling of harder, lower and more strained notes (voice like Finsch's Wheatear) as well as higher whistles (thus rather wide amplitude); some individuals interweave skilful imitations of a wide range of species.

Bluethroat   Red-flanked Bluetail   White-throated Robin   Siberian Rubythroat

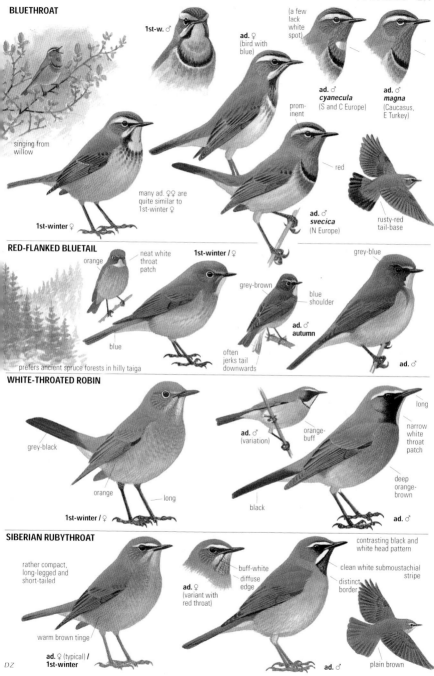

BLUETHROAT

1st-w. ♂

ad. ♀
(bird with
blue)

(a few
lack
white
spot)

ad. ♂
cyanecula
(S and C Europe)

ad. ♂
magna
(Caucasus,
E Turkey)

singing from
willow

prom-
inent

red

many ad. ♀♀ are
quite similar to
1st-winter ♀

1st-winter ♀

ad. ♂
svecica
(N Europe)

rusty-red
tail-base

RED-FLANKED BLUETAIL

orange

neat white
throat
patch

1st-winter / ♀

grey-blue

grey-brown

blue
shoulder

ad. ♂
autumn

blue

often
jerks tail
downwards

ad. ♂

prefers ancient spruce forests in hilly taiga

WHITE-THROATED ROBIN

grey-black

ad. ♂
(variation)

orange-
buff

long

narrow
white
throat
patch

deep
orange-
brown

orange

long

black

1st-winter / ♀

ad. ♂

SIBERIAN RUBYTHROAT

contrasting black and
white head pattern

rather compact,
long-legged and
short-tailed

ad. ♀
(variant with
red throat)

buff-white
diffuse
edge

clean white submoustachial
stripe

distinct
border

warm brown tinge

ad. ♀ (typical) /
1st-winter

plain brown

ad. ♂

DZ

(Common) **Redstart** *Phoenicurus phoenicurus* m**B**3 / **P**2
L 13–14½ cm. Breeds in woodland, often old deciduous and mixed, in gardens and parks, but in N (incl. Scotland) also in older, derelict pine forest. Passage migrants in coastal scrub. Summer visitor (Apr–Sep), winters in Africa. Rather unobtrusive. Keeps mainly to trees and bushes, with mostly only fleeting visits to ground. Nests in tree hole or nestbox.

IDENTIFICATION Rather slim. Usually perches fairly erect and *vibrates tail* so that the *rusty-red colour* is exposed. – Adult ♂: *Black throat, orange-red breast, white forehead, ash-grey crown and back*. In autumn the bright colours are partially concealed by buff fringes. – 1st-winter ♂: Rather ♀-like, but has greyish-black elements on throat, orange-mottled breast and sometimes a little white showing on forehead. – ♀: Grey-brown above and buff-white below. Like ♀ Black Redstart, but is *paler* and *less grey in tone*, and has distinctly *paler throat, lower breast and central belly*. Rarely more ♂-like with orangey breast. – Variation: ♂ in E Turkey, Caucasus and Middle East (ssp. *samamisicus*) is darker above, with white wing patch (variable in size), and ♀, too, often has hint of paleness on secondaries.

VOICE Call a soft whistled, upslurred 'huit' (in *samamisicus* a straight 'ih' like Collared Flycatcher), often followed by clicking 'tick-tick-tick'. Song from very first light, a short, soft, melancholy verse at high pitch, often with standard beginning but with different ending in terms of details, e.g. 'sih **trüi-trüi-trüi** si-si pli si**veuy** si'.

Black Redstart *Phoenicurus ochruros*   m**B**5 / **P**4 / **W**5
L 13–14½ cm. Breeds both in uplands, on slopes with boulders, cliffs and scattered bushes, and at lower levels in towns, docklands and industrial areas, where the natural mountains are substituted by church towers, chimneys and factory buildings. Very local in Britain, in lowlands, also passage / winter visitors on coasts. Nests in recess or hole in building.

IDENTIFICATION Size and shape as Redstart, and has similar behaviour: perches upright, constantly vibrates its *rusty-red tail*, is rather shy and nervous, often flits about. – Adult ♂ (Europe): *Greyish-black with bold white wing patch*. – 1st-summer ♂: Lacks white wing patch (some have at most hint of narrow stripe). Colour of body varies, many as grey-brown as ♀, some grey-black like adult ♂. – ♀/1st-winter: *Sooty brown-grey* on head and body, clearly darker than ♀ Redstart (dark also on throat, lower breast and belly, where Redstart obviously paler). – Variation: ♂ in greater part of Europe (ssp. *gibraltariensis*) has grey upperparts, but in Iberia (*aterrimus*) these are often blacker; ♂ in Turkey and Caucasus (*ochruros*) usually has some rusty-red on belly; ♂ in Middle East (*semirufus*) is quite distinct, has entire belly and lower breast rust-red with sharply demarcated

black bib, has black back and lacks white wing patch.

VOICE Call a straight, slightly sharp whistle, 'vist', often repeated impatiently. When highly agitated, a discreet clicking is added, 'vist, tk-tk-tk'. Song loud, frequently given at first light from high perch, usually consists of four parts: starts with a few whistles and a rattling repetition of same note, followed by a pause *c.* 2 sec. long, then a peculiar crackling sound (not very far-carrying), after which the verse terminates with some brief whistled notes, e.g. 'si-srü **till-ill-ill-ill-ill**.......(krschkrschkrsch) **srü**svisvi'; the sequence of the four components may sometimes be switched around.

Moussier's Redstart *Phoenicurus moussieri*   [**V*****]
L 12–13 cm. Breeds in open country with bushes, scattered trees and small woods, often on mountain slopes; also in open, bushy coastal forest, in cultivations and gardens. Predominantly resident. Rather bold. Nests in hole or recess.

IDENTIFICATION Small and compact, *tail and wings fairly short*. Constantly vibrates *rusty-red tail*, flicks wings, often perches in open. – Adult ♂: Unmistakable, with *entirely rusty-red underparts* and rump, rest of *upperparts black* with *large white wing patch* and *white forehead-band that runs back over eye and well down neck-side*. In autumn plumage, black areas have brown fringes. – ♀: Like a short-tailed ♀ Redstart with *more saturated orange below* and with *a faint pale panel on wing* (where ♂ has white wing patch). – 1st-winter ♂: Like adult ♂, but black areas are brown-grey (broadly fringed pale) and remiges are browner.

VOICE Call a thin whistle, 'hit', and a soft 'chirrrr'. Song a thin twitter, shuttling and slightly irregular in composition, roughly like Dunnock, squeaky notes with occasional short 'chirr' notes inserted; verses 2–5 sec. long.

Güldenstädt's Redstart *Phoenicurus erythrogaster* —
L 15–16½ cm. Breeds in high alpine terrain on bare, rocky slopes with scant vegetation right up to the summer snowline, from 2200 m (more often above 3000 m) to *c.* 5000 m. Winters in valleys down to 1500 m (at times 900 m).

IDENTIFICATION *Quite big* (but size not always easy to determine at distance in alpine habitat!), sturdy and broad-chested with large head. Often perches openly on jutting rock. Restless, often changes perch. Flight strong, almost thrush-like. – Adult ♂: Unmistakable: *white crown / nape* (in fresh plumage tinged greyish-yellow), *very big white wing patch, dark rust-red underparts*, and *black bib*. (Note that local race of Redstart has white wing patch, but that Black Redstart lacks this.) – ♀: Like an oversized, pale ♀ Black Redstart but with *hint of small pale wing patch* at bases of flight-feathers.

VOICE Call 'tsi' or 'tsi tek-tek'. Song a brief, clear Rock Thrush-like verse with hard sounds interwoven.

Redstart

Black Redstart

Moussier's Redstart   Güldenstädt's Redstart

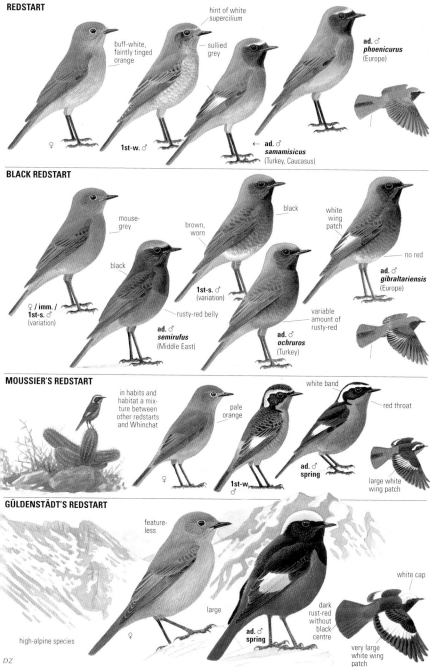

REDSTART

buff-white, faintly tinged orange

hint of white supercilium

sullied grey

♀

1st-w. ♂

ad. ♂
phoenicurus
(Europe)

← **ad. ♂**
samamisicus
(Turkey, Caucasus)

BLACK REDSTART

mouse-grey

black

black

brown, worn

black

white wing patch

no red

♀ / imm. /
1st-s. ♂
(variation)

1st-s. ♂
(variation)

rusty-red belly

ad. ♂
semirufus
(Middle East)

variable amount of rusty-red

ad. ♂
ochruros
(Turkey)

ad. ♂
gibraltariensis
(Europe)

MOUSSIER'S REDSTART

in habits and habitat a mixture between other redstarts and Whinchat

pale orange

white band

red throat

♀

**1st-w.
♂**

ad. ♂
spring

large white wing patch

GÜLDENSTÄDT'S REDSTART

feature-less

white cap

large

dark rust-red without black centre

high-alpine species

♀

ad. ♂
spring

very large white wing patch

DZ

(Northern) **Wheatear** *Oenanthe oenanthe* mB2 / P2

L 14–16½ cm. Breeds in open, stony country with meadowland, often on moorland, coastal grassland, pasture and farmland with stone walls, downland, locally coastal shingle. In S Europe mostly high up in alpine country. Summer visitor to Britain & Ireland (mainly Mar–Oct), winters in Africa; Greenland and Canadian breeders (ssp. *leucorhoa*) also winter in Africa, are thus among the world's real long-distance migrants (moreover cross wide oceans non-stop). Food insects. Nests in hole in rock crevice, cairn, stone wall, rabbit burrow etc.

IDENTIFICATION *Tail black and white* in all plumages (black *T-pattern* at tip, white base). *Upperparts grey or grey-brown.* White or *pale buff supercilium*. – Adult ♂ spring–summer: *Ash-grey crown and upperparts*, white supercilium, black eye-mask, black wings, and yellowish-buff colour on throat and breast (can fade to almost white in late summer). – ♀/ autumn: Grey-brown above and buff below with darker wings and ear-coverts, lighter buff supercilium. ♂ in autumn identified by black wings (with narrow pale fringes), black lores and some black on ear-coverts. ♀ and 1st-winter similar, have dark brown wings, lack black on head; paler birds confusable with Isabelline Wheatear (see latter). – Variation: In e.g. Greenland and Iceland (*leucorhoa*) larger, somewhat darker birds breed. In NW Africa (*seebohmi*) ♂ has black bib and ♀ grey-black or mottled grey bib.

VOICE Call a straight whistle, like indrawn 'hiit', as well as a tongue-clicking 'chack'. Song, often delivered from elevated perch (top of a rock, wire or the like) but sometimes in short song-flight, an explosive, fast, hard chirpy and crackling verse with interwoven whistling 'hiit', varying in details and hard to transcribe; sometimes contains one or two imitations of other birds. Often sings at first light and just before, but also during day.

Isabelline Wheatear *Oenanthe isabellina* V***

L 15–16½ cm. Breeds on short-grass plains or slopes in warm, dry climates, e.g. at border between natural steppe and semi-desert, often with scattered boulders. Migratory. Nest usually in ground hole (e.g. rodent burrow).

IDENTIFICATION Like autumn-plumaged Wheatear, but differs in: somewhat *bigger* size, longer tarsi and more *upright posture; broader black terminal tail-band* (intermediate between Wheatear and Desert Wheatear); *paler wings* with broader buff fringes, so *wing-coverts appear closer in tone to upperparts* than to dark brown primaries, and in flight against dark background wing looks paler; *supercilium whitest before eye, buff and narrower behind* (whitest and broadest behind eye on Wheatear). Sexes similar, but ♂ has on average blacker lores.

VOICE Call a fairly sharp 'chip', sometimes with hint of downslur, 'chiü'; also a stifled clicking 'chack'. Song distinctive, drawn out (verses often 10–15 sec., pauses brief), 'chatty', and including diagnostic 'Harpo Marx whistles' (fast, short wolf-whistles), 'vi-vi-vi-vü-vü-vü-vuy-vuy-...', hard, crunchy sounds and also more or less good imitations.

Desert Wheatear *Oenanthe deserti* V**

L 14½–15½ cm. Breeds on dry, sandy steppe-like heath or in semi-desert with scattered bushes, low vegetation and rocks (but shuns pure sand desert). Short-distance migrant. Food insects. Nests in hole in ground or in rock crevice.

IDENTIFICATION *Tail almost all black*, white only at very base of sides. Rump buffy-white, conspicuous in flight. Remiges in flight rather light grey-brown. – ♂: Invariably *black bib*. Resembles black-throated morph of Black-eared Wheatear, but differs in black tail and in having *whitish scapulars*, not black, so that folded wing shows narrower area of black. In autumn, black areas have pale fringes. 1st-summers have browner wings than adults. – ♀: Note, besides tail pattern, quite *pale and grey-brown* colours; breast buff-brown (not orange-tinged); upperparts light yellow-tinged grey-buff; *scapulars at least as pale as mantle*; reddish-brown ear-coverts and dirty yellow-white supercilium. Occasionally has darkish throat.

VOICE Call a squeaky, drawn-out 'viieh', a hard clicking 'tsack' and a thin, muffled rattle, 'tk-tk-tk'. Song characteristic, a rather constantly repeated, always *short*, clear fluting and tremulous verse *dropping* in pitch and sounding desperately *mournful* in tone, 'trüü-trururu'.

Blackstart *Cercomela melanura* —

L 14–16 cm. Breeds in rocky desert, in wadis and on boulder-strewn mountain slopes with scattered shrubbery and acacias. Resident. Bold, will approach very close without showing any fear. Spends much time on ground. Often perches low in acacias. Food insects. Nests in rock crevice.

IDENTIFICATION *All-grey* plumage (lighter below) with *all-black tail*. Black alula contrasts with lighter grey wing-coverts. Often fans tail and wings and closes them again, especially on landing or when changing perch. Also pumps tail downwards. Sexes and ages alike.

VOICE Single phrases of song (see below) seem to be used as call. Alarm a whistled 'vih'. When agitated, a crackly or frizzling 'bshreh', somewhat recalling e.g. Pied Wheatear. Song consists of 2–3 quite deep, clear fluting syllables with accent on the first, repeated at 4–5-sec. intervals, 'chürre-lu...... trrü-troo...... chürrlü...... chürrchur......'; tone is desolate and melancholy, and volume is often amplified by the bare rock faces.

Wheatear   Isabelline Wheatear   Desert Wheatear   Blackstart

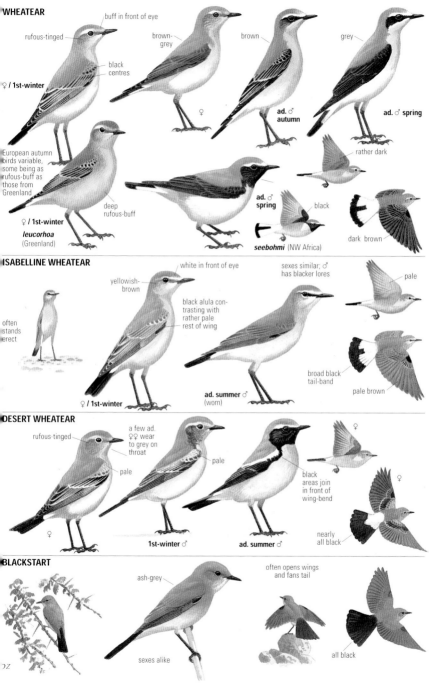

WHEATEAR

buff in front of eye

rufous-tinged

black centres

♀ / 1st-winter

brown-grey

♀

brown

grey

ad. ♂ autumn

ad. ♂ spring

European autumn birds variable, some being as rufous-buff as those from Greenland

deep rufous-buff

♀ / 1st-winter
leucorhoa (Greenland)

ad. ♂ spring

seebohmi (NW Africa)

rather dark

black

dark brown

ISABELLINE WHEATEAR

white in front of eye

yellowish-brown

black alula contrasting with rather pale rest of wing

sexes similar; ♂ has blacker lores

pale

often stands erect

♀ / 1st-winter

ad. summer ♂ (worn)

broad black tail-band

pale brown

DESERT WHEATEAR

rufous-tinged

a few ad. ♀♀ wear to grey on throat

pale

pale

1st-winter ♂

♀

ad. summer ♂

black areas join in front of wing-bend

♀

nearly all black

BLACKSTART

ash-grey

often opens wings and fans tail

sexes alike

all black

ɔZ

Black-eared Wheatear *Oenanthe hispanica* V**

L 13½–15½ cm. Breeds in open country with scattered bushes, trees and rocks, usually below 600 m but locally higher; often in barren pastureland, along streamsides, on stony slopes. Migrant, winters S of Sahara. Food insects. Nests under boulder or in ground hole or thick tussock.

IDENTIFICATION Rather small, slim and long-tailed. Often adopts crouched posture. As Pied Wheatear (but unlike Northern, Isabelline, Finsch's, Mourning and others), does not have uniform-width terminal tail-band but has *more black along outer edges of tail* and *less black in centre of each half of tail* (on some, black terminal band is fully broken by white). Two morphs in both sexes, one white-throated (commonest in W) and one black-throated (dominates in E). – ♂: *Mantle/back white*, tinged yellow-ochre in fresh plumage. Black of head/throat does not meet black of wing (cf. Finsch's Wheatear). – ♀: Like ♀ Pied Wheatear, but is *warmer yellowish grey-brown above* and *more uniformly yellow-orange on breast*. – Variation: Western race (*hispanica*) ♂ has less extensive eye-mask or bib, also ♂♀ in fresh plumage are more yellow-ochre on mantle and breast; rather short primary projection. Eastern, from S Italy and Balkans eastward (*melanoleuca*), has more extensive black on head of ♂, which is more black and white in summer, and ♀ is more a dull greyish yellow-brown above (and thus more like ♀ Pied); long primary projection (± as Pied).

VOICE Call usually a broken, almost hissing 'brsche', sometimes also a more Wheatear-like clicking 'tshack'. Alarm a descending whistle, 'viü'. Song a short, chirping and dry, rather explosive verse (can recall song of Short-toed Lark, or speeded-up Whitethroat), e.g. 'chuchürrche-chuchirr-tri'. Often a few syllables or entire verse replaced by good mimicry of e.g. Barn Swallow or Red-rumped Swallow, Linnet or Goldfinch. Song is rather variable, and doubtful whether it can be safely distinguished from that of Pied. Also has a chattering subsong with harsh and hoarse sounds mixed with chirpy and clearer whistled notes and mimicry.

Pied Wheatear *Oenanthe pleschanka* V**

L 14–16½ cm. Breeds on barren mountain slopes with low vegetation, high plateaux with boulder-strewn grassland, at times adjoining grazed or cultivated but bare areas; generally ascends higher and selects more precipitous habitats than Black-eared Wheatear. Migrant, winters mostly in E Africa; main passage thought to pass E and S of Jordan. Food insects. Nests in rock crevice, ground hole, under boulder.

IDENTIFICATION Like Black-eared Wheatear in size, shape and tail pattern (i.e. *black terminal band* not uniform in width, but *broader along tail-sides and narrower in centre of each half of tail*), and some ♀ and autumn plumages can be

extremely difficult to separate. – ♂ summer: *Black mantle patch, meets black throat at sides. Wings dark in flight* (light on Mourning Wheatear). *Breast buff in fresh plumage, undertail-coverts light yellowish-white* (Mourning always pure white on breast, rusty on undertail-coverts). Adult has blacker wings, 1st-summer browner; in addition, 1st-summer is not so perfectly black and white, retains traces of winter plumage. (A white-throated morph, 'vittata', occurs very rarely.) – ♂ winter: Since black mantle has broad grey brown fringes, broader on 1st-winter than on adult, similarity to eastern Black-eared Wheatear arises. Is, however, *colder brown-grey above* with *more distinct pale feather tips* (scaly). – ♀: Very like eastern Black-eared Wheatear but *darker and colder earth-brown above*, in fresh plumage *pale scaled*, and is *pinkish rusty-brown or pinkish-grey on breast* often with *irregular lower border* against pale belly and with tendency towards *diffuse mottling* (♀ Black-eared more evenly yellow-orange on breast with more regular lower border and no mottling). *Throat* in spring variably *dark*, most showing hint of this also in autumn (but some then look rather pale-throated); dark of throat extends a bit further towards breast than on Black-eared Wheatear (but when head sunk between shoulders this becomes hard to judge).

VOICE Strongly reminiscent of Black-eared Wheatear's and the two species seem not easy to distinguish by voice. Main call a cracked, frizzling 'brsche', at times also throaty clicking 'tshak' notes. Alarm a whistling 'vih(e)'. Song verses are often somewhat shorter, and intervening pauses longer, than Black-eared's, but song is similarly explosive twittering and dry, e.g. 'surtru-**shirr**-echu'; some variation in intonation, can at times resemble Whinchat's song. Verses occasionally protracted and some mimicry included.

Cyprus Wheatear *Oenanthe cypriaca* –

L 14–15 cm. Formerly considered an isolated race of Pied Wheatear, now usually regarded as a full species. Breeds only in Cyprus, where common mid Mar–early Oct in barren grassy and rocky areas at all levels, often in and around villages; often perches in treetops, especially when singing. Winters in S Sudan and Ethiopia, stops off on passage in e.g. Israel and Egypt.

IDENTIFICATION Like Pied Wheatear, but differs in: *slightly shorter wings* (shorter primary projection) *and tail*, looks compact and large-headed; *broader black terminal tail-band, less white on nape*, not continuing onto mantle (does on Pied); *smaller white patch on tail-base* above; *underparts more saturated yellow-ochre* in autumn, and breast never fades to fully whitish in summer. Sexes similar, i.e. ♂ always has *dark* (grey-black or dark brown-grey) *throat and back* and has *some white on nape; crown* in autumn *sooty-grey or* ♀ and 1st-winter ♂, but some white usually visible on crown-sides (can create white supercilium), wearing to more white in summer. 1st-summer ♂ has contrast between brown-grey remiges and black back/rest of wing.

VOICE Calls a frizzling 'brzü', a hoarse, hard 'tschick', an upslurred whistle, 'jüi' (occasionally downslurred 'jiü'). Song totally diagnostic among the wheatears, a series of similar cracked, hoarse notes, 'bizz-bizz-bizz-bizz-bizz...' completely lacking dry twittering and varied character of its relatives; verses usually 3–10 sec. long.

Black-eared Wheatear   Pied Wheatear

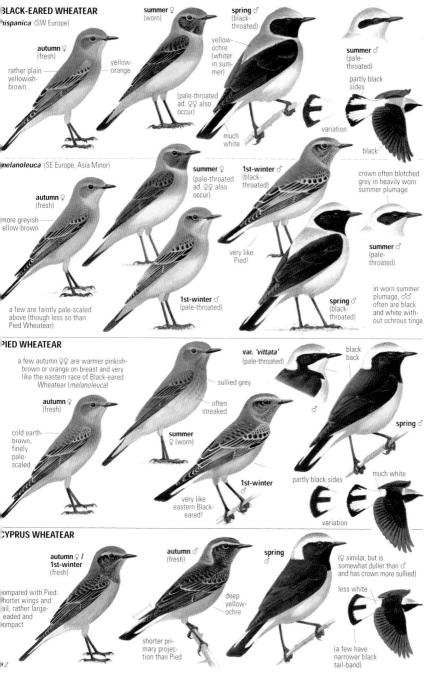

BLACK-EARED WHEATEAR
hispanica (SW Europe)

summer ♀
(worn)

spring ♂
(black-throated)

autumn ♀
(fresh)

rather plain
yellowish-brown

yellow-orange

yellow-ochre
(whiter in summer)

(pale-throated ad. ♀♀ also occur)

summer ♂
(pale-throated)

partly black sides

much white

variation

black

---

melanoleuca (SE Europe, Asia Minor)

summer ♀
(pale-throated ad. ♀♀ also occur)

1st-winter ♂
(black-throated)

crown often blotched grey in heavily worn summer plumage

autumn ♀
(fresh)

more greyish
ellow-brown

very like
Pied!

summer ♂
(pale-throated)

1st-winter ♂
(pale-throated)

spring ♂
(black-throated)

a few are faintly pale-scaled above (though less so than Pied Wheatear)

in worn summer plumage, ♂♂ often are black and white without ochrous tinge

PIED WHEATEAR

a few autumn ♀♀ are warmer pinkish-brown or orange on breast and very like the eastern race of Black-eared Wheatear (*melanoleuca*)

var. 'vittata'
(pale-throated)

black back

autumn ♀
(fresh)

sullied grey

often streaked

♂

spring ♂

cold earth-brown, finely pale-scaled

summer
♀ (worn)

1st-winter
♂

partly black sides

much white

very like
eastern Black-eared!

variation

CYPRUS WHEATEAR

autumn ♀ /
1st-winter
(fresh)

autumn ♂
(fresh)

spring
♂

(♀ similar, but is somewhat duller than ♂ and has crown more sullied)

ompared with Pied:
horter wings and
ail, rather large-
eaded and
ompact

deep
yellow-ochre

less white

shorter pri-mary projec-tion than Pied

(a few have narrower black tail-band)

Z

Finsch's Wheatear *Oenanthe finschii* —

L 15–16 cm. Breeds on barren mountainsides and rocky plateaus with low vegetation. Short-distance migrant. Winters and makes stopovers at higher and cooler altitudes than most of its relatives. Defends territory aggressively and successfully against other wheatears. Restless and fidgety. Shy, flies far away, watches intently. Food mostly insects, but also some plant material. Nests usually in hollow in rock or in crevice.

IDENTIFICATION A trifle bigger than Black-eared Wheatear, and has proportionately *somewhat bigger head and thicker legs and bill*. Tail has *uniformly wide dark terminal band* (like Mourning Wheatear, unlike Black-eared and Pied). In flight, has rather pale remiges. – Adult ♂: Black shoulders and wings but *white back* (rather narrow area, can be hard to see in side view, but is obvious on bird flying away). Much *black on throat*, extends well down and *joins at sides with black of wings*. Remiges finely tipped white. White of crown and mantle/back tinged *buffy-pink* in fresh plumage, crown whiter with *dusky grey centre* when worn. Breast white (negligible buff tinge), undertail-coverts with hint of pinkish-buff. – 1st-year ♂: As adult ♂, but remiges and, especially, *primary coverts browner*, the latter *with pale tips*. – ♀: Predominantly *brown-grey and dirty white* (lacks warmer buff-brown tone on breast shown by Black-eared and Pied) with rather *contrastless greater-coverts*; distinct pale tips to primary coverts. Ear-coverts usually reddish-brown. Off-white supercilium. Throat colour variable, majority are *dusky grey* (in worn plumage some almost as dark as ♂), often darkest at sides and lower edge, others apparently all pale. Note tail pattern.

VOICE Call a short 'tsit', often repeated; also has a pebble-clinking 'tsheck-tsheck' and a rasping 'bsheh'. Song varied throughout, short, clear and loud verses at slow tempo with 'bent whistles' and occasional interwoven scraping, creaky, almost 'electrical' notes (voice thereby very different from Black-eared Wheatear's), e.g. 'tk-tk suiiih-va chi-chi trrüü-u........ chu-chu kretrü-chiiih-a...' etc. Mimicry rare in song. Performs song-flight.

Mourning Wheatear *Oenanthe lugens* —

L 14½–16½ cm. Breeds in barren mountain tracts, on steep slopes and ravines or poorly vegetated wadis, sometimes in flatter, boulder-strewn or rocky terrain with meagre vegetation. Short-distance migrant or resident. Food mostly insects. Nests in rock crevice, under rock or in ground hole.

IDENTIFICATION Like Pied Wheatear, but differences include: *uniformly broad dark terminal tail-band* (cf. Pied); in flight *pale bases to flight-feathers* clearly contrasting with narrowly darker tips and with darker wing-coverts (striking

contrast in Middle East, ssp. *lugens*, less contrast in NW Africa, *halophila*; Pied has more uniformly dark wings in flight); slightly heavier bill and legs. – ♂ *halophila / ♂ lugens*: Like a Pied Wheatear, but differs in above-mentioned general characters, also in: *smaller black bib, covers only throat* and does not reach onto upper breast; always *pure white breast* but distinct *rusty-buff colour on undertail coverts* (most obvious in *lugens*); *white of nape less extensive does not reach onto upper mantle*; 1st-year has *white tips to primary coverts* and often some outer greater coverts, forming small white patch (not seen on Pied). In S Syria/N Jordan a rare morph occurs with all-black body and head (but still with pale remex bases). – ♀ *halophila* (♀ *lugens* has ♂ colours!): *Light buff-grey above* with whitish background colour, paler than Finsch's Wheatear. Off-white supercilium. Throat pale or, more often, dusky grey, fairly dark in worn plumage (greyish-black and sharply demarcated). Note tail pattern, and paler flight-feather bases in flight.

VOICE Calls are a straight whistled 'hiit' and a clicking 'tschack'; sometimes also an almost crossbill-like clipped 'chüp-chüp'. When disturbed, often gives a cracked 'bzrü' on rising. Song short verses, well spaced, with clear and melancholy ring, jingling and rolling (closest to *Blue Rock Thrush* voice), e.g. 'tritra-**chürr**-tru'; often a 'tschack' as prelude or interwoven, and mimicry may also be inserted at times. Relatively little variation; the song is sometimes protracted into longer verses. Performs song-flight.

Hooded Wheatear *Oenanthe monacha* —

L 15½–17 cm. Breeds in unvegetated mountain deserts, in steep rocky ravines and wadis, often with boulders. Usually resident. Often takes larger flying insects in characteristic manner after long chases high up in air. Often perches rather unobtrusively on a rock, only to disappear the next moment down into a ravine. Nests in rock crevice.

IDENTIFICATION *Rather big* with *large head* and *long bill*, long wings and long tail but *rather short legs*. Often adopts crouched posture. – ♂: Tail has *much white* and lacks proper black terminal band, has *black only on central feathers and minimally at corners*, which reinforces long-tailed impression. (Same tail pattern is seen only on White-crowned Wheatear, but this has black breast and belly, black nape, smaller bill and longer legs.) *Black* mantle, throat and *upper breast*, black even on upper flanks (the black unites with wing-edge). The white of crown narrows on nape. – ♀: Same tail pattern as ♂, but the white is replaced by *light rusty-brown*. Entire plumage *pale grey-brown* with somewhat paler underparts and *rusty rump*. Wings with darker centres and sandy fringes. Note *long bill*.

VOICE Less well known. Calls a straight whistled 'vit', a clicking 'tschack' and a rolling, thick 'prrü'. Song *chatty and composed*, the verses often rather long, consisting mostly of crackling calls and hard, knocking sounds but also occasional clearer and softer notes, also with plenty of mimicry of other birds.

Finsch's Wheatear

Mourning Wheatear

Hooded Wheatear

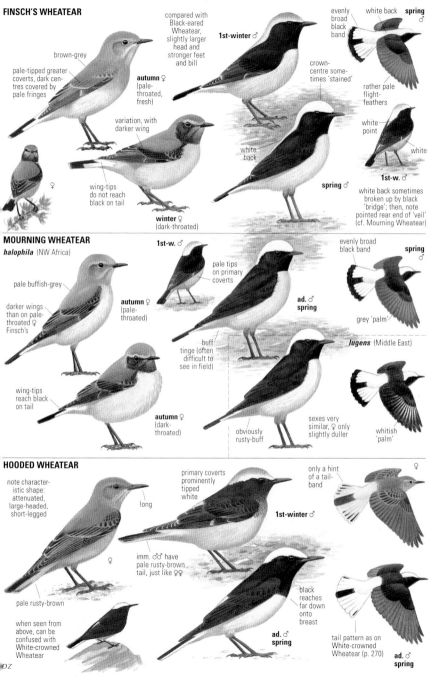

FINSCH'S WHEATEAR

brown-grey

pale-tipped greater coverts, dark centres covered by pale fringes

♀

compared with Black-eared Wheatear, slightly larger head and stronger feet and bill

autumn ♀
(pale-throated, fresh)

variation, with darker wing

wing-tips do not reach black on tail

winter ♀
(dark-throated)

1st-winter ♂

crown-centre sometimes 'stained'

white back

spring ♂

evenly broad black band

white back

rather pale flight-feathers

white point

white

1st-w. ♂

white back sometimes broken up by black 'bridge'; then, note pointed rear end of 'veil' (cf. Mourning Wheatear)

spring ♂

MOURNING WHEATEAR

halophila (NW Africa)

pale buffish-grey

darker wings than on pale-throated ♀ Finsch's

wing-tips reach black on tail

1st-w. ♂

autumn ♀
(pale-throated)

pale tips on primary coverts

ad. ♂ spring

buff tinge (often difficult to see in field)

autumn ♀
(dark-throated)

obviously rusty-buff

evenly broad black band

spring ♂

grey 'palm'

lugens (Middle East)

sexes very similar, ♀ only slightly duller

whitish 'palm'

HOODED WHEATEAR

note characteristic shape: attenuated, large-headed, short-legged

long

♀

pale rusty-brown

when seen from above, can be confused with White-crowned Wheatear

primary coverts prominently tipped white

1st-winter ♂

imm. ♂♂ have pale rusty-brown tail, just like ♀♀

black reaches far down onto breast

ad. ♂ spring

only a hint of a tail-band

♀

tail pattern as on White-crowned Wheatear (p. 270)

ad. ♂ spring

DZ

White-crowned Wheatear *Oenanthe leucopyga* [**V**∗∗∗]

L 17–18½ cm. Breeds in desolate mountain deserts, on barren stony plains, in ravines, wadis and at fault-line precipices; also on or next to houses at oases. Is a true desert bird, thriving in terrain totally devoid of vegetation. Boulder country seems also to attract it. Resident. Often shy (locally more bold). Food insects. Nests in rock crevice or hole.

IDENTIFICATION About as *large* as Black Wheatear, but is *slimmer* and has longer wings and tail and narrower bill. Flight fast and strong. *All-black* plumage with *white crown*, but the white 'coronet' is not acquired until one year of age; occasional younger birds have scattered white feathers in otherwise black crown. *Tail has much white* with black central line and only small black markings on outer corners (same tail pattern as ♂ Hooded Wheatear). In flight, shows *all-dark wings*. Sexes alike.

VOICE Rich and varied repertoire. Powerful voice, good mimic ('the Hill Myna' of the desert'). Calls a shrill whistled 'hiit', a high cracked 'bizz' and a hoarse, throaty 'tschreh'. Song often loud with many clear whistled sounds; for long periods repeats short verses with e.g. a few *descending whistle notes* as major component, 'si-sü-so-trui-trü'; surprisingly *expert imitations* are often inserted as parts of the song. A chatty, more soft subsong also occurs. Sometimes performs song-flight with fluttering wings and fanned tail.

Black Wheatear *Oenanthe leucura*   —

L 16–18 cm. Breeds on steep dry slopes with rock outcrops, landslip precipices, bare areas, bushes and scattered trees, from sea-level to 3000 m (mostly below 2000 m). Avoids flatter terrain, denser woodland and usually proximity of man. Resident. Shy, flushes early, usually flies uphill. Food mostly insects. Nests in rock crevice or other hollow.

IDENTIFICATION Big and *hefty*, with rather *big head* and *heavy bill*. Pumps tail upwards, then slowly lowers it. Flight strong, wings broadly rounded. *All dark* (♂ black, ♀ sooty-brown) with white tail-base, and the typical wheatear tail markings of black T-pattern on white background. *Terminal tail-band strongly developed and uniformly broad*, roughly as on Wheatear. Flight-feathers dark (but against the light they contrast somewhat paler against dark wing-coverts). Sole confusion risk is younger White-crowned Wheatear, but that is slimmer and has incomplete tail-band.

VOICE Calls a descending, whistled 'piüp', often repeated in series, and a slightly thick clicking 'chett-chett'; sometimes a rolling 'cherrr'. Song of 'coarsely twittering' verses, a bit lower-pitched than other wheatears in same region, somewhat thrush-like (but without e.g. Blue Rock Thrush's melancholy ring and clear, rolling voice). Has undulating song-flight.

Persian Wheatear *Oenanthe xanthoprymna*   —

L 14–15 cm. Breeds on barren mountain slopes with low, meagre vegetation, often quite high up (1200–4000 m). Largely migratory; also seen on passage and in winter at lower levels. Rather bold. Usually perches on low bushes and rocks, does not pump tail much. Food mostly insects.

IDENTIFICATION Much as Wheatear in size and shape. With Red-rumped Wheatear shares characteristic of having *rusty tail-base*. – ♂: *Black bib*, dirty white breast, white supercilium, grey crown and mantle/back*, some pale fringes on wing-feathers so that these look somewhat variegated. Differs from Red-rumped Wheatear e.g. in *narrower pale fringes to wing-coverts* (wings hence rather dark in spring), *greyer mantle/back* and slightly smaller size and slimmer shape. Older ♂♂ seem always to have *pure white at base of tail-sides*, while 1st-year have rusty-buff – ♀: Like ♂, but throat dusky grey (variably dark, some almost black as ♂), supercilium indistinct, crown to back a browner grey. Base of tail-sides often white but sometimes rusty-buff (age-related or two morphs?). – Variation: In Caucasus (ssp., or full species [?], *chrysopygia*) different in appearance: entirely grey, brown and buff with rusty tail-base, lacks dark bib, sexes alike.

VOICE Calls a whistle on descending scale, 'chiüp', as well as a thick-voiced clicking 'tschack'; the latter may be repeated in fast rattling series, 'chr'r'r'r'. Song rather constant, a short, twittering verse with some deep and clear notes but also hoarse and scratchy sounds, usually without any mimicry; occasionally longer verses.

Red-rumped Wheatear *Oenanthe moesta*   —

L 14½–16 cm. Breeds mostly at lower levels on flat, dry, sandy or clayey heaths or in more barren, stony semi-desert, at times among tamarisk bushes and scanty low vegetation; avoids pure sand desert. Spends much time on ground. Resident. Food insects. Nests in ground hole.

IDENTIFICATION Resembles Persian Wheatear (see that species), but note: slightly *larger size, longer bill and legs, all-dark tail* (with hint of rusty-red base, mostly on ♀), *white edges to greater coverts form pale panel*, mostly on ♂; *pale wing-bar* along medial coverts; ♂'s *mantle/back and scapulars black* in worn plumage; on ♀ *rusty-buff colour on crown/nape/head-sides, also light buffish-white panel on wing*. Pumps tail upwards and slowly lowers it.

VOICE When agitated, a repeated short 'prrit', almost like Little Bustard. Song unusual, is rather soft and protracted, consists largely of long series of strained, rolling, drawn-out, slightly disyllabic notes which rise (occasionally fall) in semi-tones, e.g. 'churrurr chorrorr chürrür, chirrirr...'. Shorter, simpler verses also uttered.

White-crowned Wheatear

Black Wheatear

Persian Wheatear

Red-rumped Wheatear

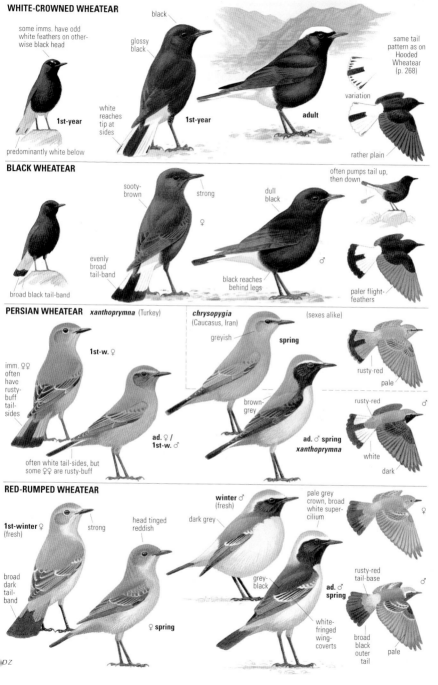

WHITE-CROWNED WHEATEAR

some imms. have odd white feathers on otherwise black head

1st-year

predominantly white below

black

glossy black

white reaches tip at sides

1st-year

adult

same tail pattern as on Hooded Wheatear (p. 268)

variation

rather plain

BLACK WHEATEAR

sooty-brown

strong

♀

dull black

black reaches behind legs

♂

often pumps tail up, then down

evenly broad tail-band

broad black tail-band

paler flight-feathers

PERSIAN WHEATEAR   *xanthoprymna* (Turkey)

chrysopygia (Caucasus, Iran)

greyish

spring

(sexes alike)

1st-w. ♀

imm. ♀♀ often have rusty-buff tail-sides

often white tail-sides, but some ♀♀ are rusty-buff

ad. ♀ / 1st-w. ♂

brown-grey

ad. ♂ spring *xanthoprymna*

rusty-red

pale

rusty-red

♂

white

dark

RED-RUMPED WHEATEAR

1st-winter ♀ (fresh)

strong

broad dark tail-band

head tinged reddish

dark grey

♀ **spring**

winter ♂ (fresh)

pale grey crown, broad white super-cilium

grey-black

ad. ♂ spring

white-fringed wing-coverts

♀

rusty-red tail-base

♂

broad black outer tail

pale

DZ

Whinchat *Saxicola rubetra* mB3 / P3

L 12–14 cm. Breeds in uncultivated, usually damp areas, e.g. rough pastureland, commons, tussocky grassland, water meadows, also bracken-covered slopes. Summer visitor (Apr–Oct), winters in Africa. Food insects. Nests in tussock.

IDENTIFICATION *Short-tailed* and plump. Perches upright, twitches or vibrates tail, flies off low. *Rump dark-spotted yellow-brown.* A little white on tail-base, glimpsed in flight. – Adult ♂: Brownish-black head-side *framed by white stripes. Throat / breast orange-buff.* One or two *white wing patches.* – ♀/1st-winter: Buffish-white supercilium, light brown head-side, normally no white wing patch.

VOICE When agitated, a soft, short whistle and a clicking call, 'yu tek, yu tek-tek'…'. Song (often at night) a varied, loud, fast, short verse with mix of hoarse rasping sounds, clear deep notes and mimicry; verse begins a little haltingly, accelerates and is abruptly cut short; a recurrent variant resembles compressed version of Corn Bunting song.

Fuerteventura Stonechat *Saxicola dacotiae* —

L 11–12½ cm. Breeds only on Fuerteventura (Canary Islands; prob. max. total 1000 pairs) on barren slopes and in ravines with bushes and odd trees. Resident. Food insects.

IDENTIFICATION Adult ♂: *Head brown-black* with *narrow white throat* (continues at lower edge onto neck-side) and *short white supercilium;* breast orange-buff. Small white wing patch. *Rump dark.* – 1st-winter ♂: Duller than adult. Usually no white wing patch (a hint at most). In fresh plumage a *pale panel along secondaries* and a faint pale wing-bar along greater coverts. – ♀: Paler and greyer than ♂, head brown-grey, faintly spotted; supercilium diffuse.

VOICE Quiet. Voice like Stonechat.

(Common) Stonechat *Saxicola torquata* rB3 / P

L 11½–13 cm. Breeds in open areas with poor or low vegetation, often heather and gorse. Found both at low level near sea and on higher moorland (incl. above treeline). Two rather distinct groups of races, one in W, C and S Europe (mainly ssp. *rubicola*; resident except in N), other in easternmost Europe and around Caspian Sea (*maura* and others; migratory). Nests low in gorse or tussock.

IDENTIFICATION Adult ♂: Entire *head* (incl. chin) *black* (in autumn plumage partly concealed by pale fringes); large *white patch on neck-side* (reaches farther towards nape in *maura*). *Breast orange* (extends to flanks in *rubicola*, more restricted orange patch in *maura*). *Rump* brown and *dark-mottled* (*rubicola*; bleached in summer, can then show small white patch) or *unspotted rusty-buff* (*maura*; bleaches to *large white square*). Birds from steppes W of Caspian Sea (*variegata*) have much white on tail with black T-pattern of

wheatear type. – ♀: Throat dusky brown (*rubicola*; may be almost entirely concealed by pale fringes in autumn) or at all times pale (*maura*). Eastern birds have hint of *buff-white supercilium* and paler ground colour.

VOICE Alarm rather like Black Redstart's, a shrill, sharp whistle and a throaty clicking, 'vist trak-trak, vist…'. Song a short, high-voiced, twittering or squeaky verse that recalls both Horned Lark and Dunnock; song rather monotonous, lacks Whinchat's variation and wider tonal range.

Blue Rock Thrush *Monticola solitarius* — [V***]

L 21–23 cm. Breeds in rocky, precipitous habitats on coasts, in mountain ravines and on mountainsides with boulders and rock outcrops, locally also in stone quarries, on ruins, churches and even inhabited buildings in flat terrain; thus, unlike Rock Thrush, also inhabits lower levels. Mainly resident. Wary, often takes cover. Food insects, plant matter, small lizards. Nests in cavity or recess in cliff or wall.

IDENTIFICATION *Large* and *slim* with *long bill*. (Against the light and at distance beware similarly long-billed Mistle Thrush, which also breeds in the S European mountains!) ♂ dull *blue-grey* with dark wings (1st-winter even duller blue and vermiculated dark, primary coverts tipped pale). ♀ dark brown, vermiculated below, with *dark brown tail*.

VOICE Call a disyllabic squeaky pipe, 'üh-vih'; also a deep clicking 'chook'. Song varies somewhat, often like Rock Thrush's (genuine confusion risk!), is loud but not that soft, has clear and rolling or tremulous tone (r-sound), strongly melancholy ring, often shuttling back and forth.

(Rufous-tailed) Rock Thrush *Monticola saxatilis* V***

L 17–20 cm. Breeds on steep, dry, rocky mountain slopes or higher-lying alpine meadows. Found above 1500 m (odd exceptions), and thus usually chooses higher sites than Blue Rock Thrush. Summer visitor (mostly Mar / Apr–Sep), winters S of Sahara. Shy. Food insects, plant matter, small lizards. Nests in rock cavity, under boulder or in ground.

IDENTIFICATION ♂ in spring unmistakable (but garish colours remarkably camouflaged in strong mountain light). ♂ winter plus ♀ and immatures all similar, more anonymous, brownish and *densely vermiculated dark*, told by *short rusty-red tail*, stocky build and rather long bill; ♂♂ often revealed by intimation of *pure white spotting on back* (♀ at the most buffish-white) and touch of blue-grey on crown and throat.

VOICE Call a short, squeaky 'viht'; also a clicking 'chak'. Song, sometimes in undulating song-flight with terminal glide, a *soft*, clear and melodic verse (with melancholy basic tone) which often drops in pitch; at distance can recall both Redwing and Blackbird; like Blue Rock Thrush's, but is softer and not quite so melancholy in tone.

Whinchat   Stonechat   Blue Rock Thrush   Rock Thrush

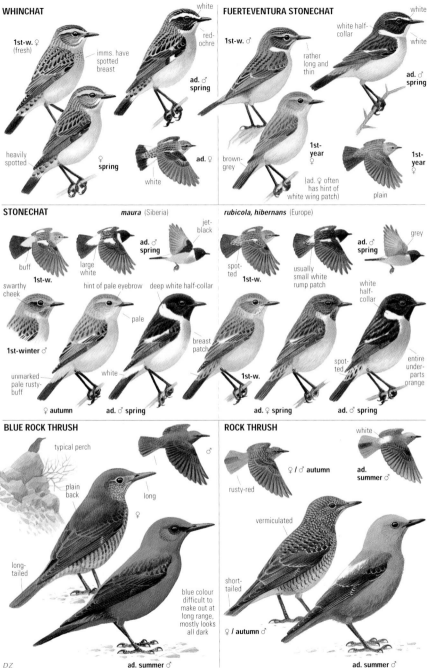

WHINCHAT

1st-w. ♀ (fresh)

imms. have spotted breast

white

red-ochre

ad. ♂

heavily spotted

♀ spring

white

ad. ♀

FUERTEVENTURA STONECHAT

1st-w. ♂

rather long and thin

white half-collar

white

white

ad. ♂ spring

brown-grey

1st-year ♀

(ad. ♀ often has hint of white wing patch)

1st-year ♀

plain

STONECHAT

maura (Siberia)

jet-black

ad. ♂ spring

buff

large white

1st-w.

swarthy cheek

hint of pale eyebrow

pale

deep white half-collar

breast patch

1st-winter ♂

unmarked pale rusty-buff

white

♀ autumn

ad. ♂ spring

rubicola, hibernans (Europe)

spotted

1st-w.

usually small white rump patch

grey

ad. ♂ spring

white half-collar

1st-w.

spotted

entire under-parts orange

ad. ♀ spring

ad. ♂ spring

BLUE ROCK THRUSH

typical perch

plain back

long

♀

long-tailed

blue colour difficult to make out at long range, mostly looks all dark

ad. summer ♂

ROCK THRUSH

white

♀ / ♂ autumn

ad. summer ♂

rusty-red

vermiculated

short-tailed

♀ / autumn ♂

ad. summer ♂

DZ

Song Thrush *Turdus philomelos* r(m)**B**2 / **P+W**

L 20–22 cm. Breeds in lush woodland, parks and well-vegetated gardens. N populations migratory, winter in W and S Europe. Often rather tame. Food snails, insects, worms. Nest, often well concealed in e.g. ivy, hedge, on bank, a moss-clad bowl with smooth grey interior (of clay and decayed wood).

IDENTIFICATION Small and rather compact, *fairly short-tailed*. Fast, slightly jerky flight. Brown above, and yellowish-white or *white below, densely sprinkled with black spots* (cf. Mistle Thrush). *Underwing rusty-buff*, sometimes perceptible in flight. Often has *slightly warmer ochre tone on flanks* next to wing-edge (and on breast), but never rusty-red like Redwing, and lacks latter's white head-stripes. Sexes alike.

VOICE Call a rather discreet, fine, sharp 'zit' (not so hard and clicking as Robin's, and a little softer than Rustic Bunting's). Alarm an excited series of 'electrical' scolding sounds, 'tix-ix-ix-ix-ix-...' (sharper, higher-pitched than Blackbird's). Song *loud and proclaiming*, sounds 'cocksure' and 'dogmatic'; strongly varied, often squeaky and shrill cascades of notes, pauses few and very brief; characteristic is recurring repetitions 2–4 times of same group of notes, e.g. 'kück**li**vi kück**li**vi, tixi tixi tixi, **pii**-eh, trrü-trrü-trrü tixi**fix**, chü-chü-chü, ko-ku-ki**klix** ko-ku-ki**klix**,...'.

Redwing *Turdus iliacus* m**B**5 / **W**1

L 19–23 cm. A characteristic bird of N Europe's conifer forests, extending into upland birch forest, even into willow zone; 'at southern limits also mixed woodland, regenerating scrub, often near water. In Britain & Ireland very rare breeder (mostly Scotland), but abundant winter visitor to fields, woodland edge, parks etc. Rather shy.

IDENTIFICATION *Small* (Song Thrush size), rather short-tailed and compact, with fairly big head. Note *whitish stripes above eye and beneath cheek*, also *rusty-red flanks* when perched, and *rusty-red underwing* in flight (redder colour than on Song Thrush). Sexes alike.

VOICE Call on migration a protracted, indrawn 'stüüüf' (hint of hoarseness); often heard on October nights, even over towns and cities. Also has a nasal 'gack'. Alarm a hoarse, rattling scold, 'tret-tret-tret-tret-...'. Song highly variable among individuals but constant within each one, recognized by general tone and structure: rather short verses, with 3–6-sec. intervals, consisting of a loud, easily transcribed section immediately followed by a soft squeaky twitter; among common introductory themes e.g. descending 'chirre chürre chorre', rising 'tru-tra-tro-trü-tri', soft Common Rosefinch-like 'vi**dje**-vi**djü**', short and mournful 'trüi trai', clear ringing 'tüllüllüllüllüllüll...' etc. Flocks at migration stopovers sometimes give noisy chorus of squeaks.

Mistle Thrush *Turdus viscivorus* r**B**2 / **W**2

L 26–29 cm. Breeds in open woodland, parks, orchards, large gardens, scrub, groups of conifers. In S Europe often found on mountain slopes in treeline zone, and forages on alpine meadows and bare mountain. In Britain & Ireland mostly resident, with immigrants from N Europe Sep–Apr; in winter also on fields. Wary and rather shy in much of range, less so in W Europe. Nest grass-lined, in tree.

IDENTIFICATION Big, and patterned basically as Song Thrush, but normally easily told by calls, *larger size*, more *elongated* and *long-tailed* shape, *more powerful flight with longer undulations* (not jerky and hopping), also *white underwings*. At times, *white tips to outer tail-feathers* can be made out. Perched bird seen in gap in foliage can be more difficult to distinguish from Song Thrush. Note: *paler brown-grey head-side and neck-side*; tendency towards *bigger black patch on breast-side* and irregular *dark markings on neck-side*; *more rounded black spots* on breast and belly; *greyer wing-feathers with paler edges*.

VOICE Call a characteristic drawn-out, wooden dry rattle, 'zer'r'r'r'r'. Alarm a hard rattling call resembling Fieldfare's but slightly drier. Song most like Blackbird's: short, varied verses with clear and loud voice; differs in more desolate and slightly harder tone, faster tempo and shorter pauses, smaller tonal range (i.e. sounds a little more monotonous), no (or fewer) squeaky notes at end of each verse, 'tru**i**trüvu... chu**ri**chu**ru**... chü**vu**tru... churuvü**tru**...'.

Fieldfare *Turdus pilaris* m**B**5 / **W**1

L 22–27 cm. Breeds in various types of woodland and bush scrub, also in parks, avenues of trees and gardens. Food in summer worms and insects. In Britain & Ireland, very rare local breeder; abundant passage and winter visitor, large flocks on open fields and other grassy areas, also taking rowan berries, fallen fruit etc. Often nests in small colonies (for extra protection against corvids, which are actively pursued in flight and sometimes bombarded with excrement); twig nest rather high up in treetops, often in a main fork.

IDENTIFICATION Big, *long-tailed*, stocky thrush. In flight, apart from tail length, identified by *light grey rump* (shows well from behind), *white underwings* (shown otherwise only by Mistle Thrush) and rather *flapping, less undulating flight. Red-brown back* and grey crown/nape. Heavily spotted below, and breast has rusty-yellow tinge. Sexes similar. – Juvenile: Identified by pale spots on wing-coverts.

VOICE Migrants utter a squeaky 'gih' and also chattering 'schack-schack-schack'. When pursuing crows, gives furious chatter. Song simple, a few chattering notes with no clear structure, short pause, more chatter and so on. In song-flight, gives ecstatically chattering, drawn-out, faster song.

Song Thrush

Redwing

Mistle Thrush

Fieldfare

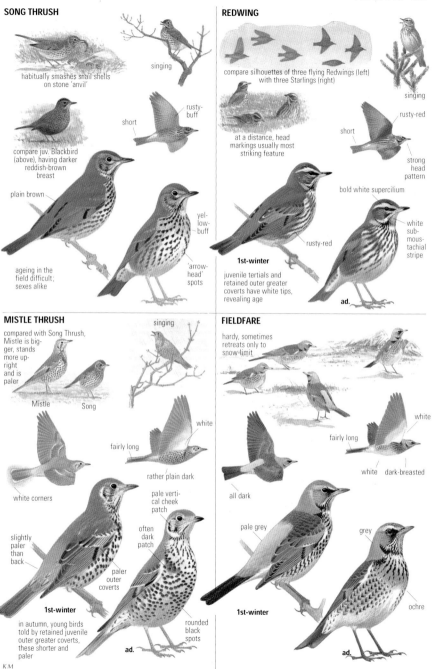

SONG THRUSH

singing

habitually smashes snail shells on stone 'anvil'

compare juv. Blackbird (above), having darker reddish-brown breast

short

rusty-buff

plain brown

yel-low-buff

ageing in the field difficult; sexes alike

'arrow-head' spots

REDWING

compare silhouettes of three flying Redwings (left) with three Starlings (right)

at a distance, head markings usually most striking feature

singing

rusty-red

short

strong head pattern

bold white supercilium

rusty-red

1st-winter

white sub-mous-tachial stripe

juvenile tertials and retained outer greater coverts have white tips, revealing age

ad.

MISTLE THRUSH

compared with Song Thrush, Mistle is big-ger, stands more up-right and is paler

singing

Mistle   Song

white

fairly long

rather plain dark

white corners

pale verti-cal cheek patch

slightly paler than back

often dark patch

paler outer coverts

1st-winter

in autumn, young birds told by retained juvenile outer greater coverts, these shorter and paler

rounded black spots

ad.

FIELDFARE

hardy, sometimes retreats only to snow-limit

white

fairly long

white   dark-breasted

all dark

pale grey

grey

1st-winter

ochre

ad.

KM

(Common) Blackbird *Turdus merula*   r(m)**B**1 / **P**+**W**1

L 23½–29 cm. Breeds commonly in woodland, parks and gardens, also in juniper country. N populations migratory, winter mainly in W Europe Sep/Oct–Mar/Apr. Confiding. Often sings from rooftop or TV aerial, but also from treetop in wood. Food earthworms, insects, berries. Nests in bush, on trellis, behind logs etc. (Map on p. 278.)

IDENTIFICATION ♂: *All black*, in spring and summer with *yellow bill* and *narrow yellow eye-ring*, making it unmistakable to any birdwatcher. But the beginner seeing a black bird with yellow bill on the lawn must eliminate the Starling: the Blackbird is *not a flocking bird*, has *long tail* (which is often jerked upwards and slowly lowered), often makes quick *two-footed bounds* or walks a few steps before *standing dead-still* for a few seconds (looking out for worms), takes a few more steps, etc. Also, plumage lacks pale spots. – ♀: Sooty-brown with slightly *lighter brownish-white throat* and *diffuse mottling on breast*. Bill dark. – Juvenile: Like ♀, but with small pale spots on upperparts.

VOICE Rich repertoire. Noisy. Common calls: a deep 'pok'; on migration, a quiet, fine rolling 'srrri' (more jingling and 'looser' than Treecreeper's). When agitated: a very fine, Robin-like, straight 'tsiih'; hard clacking 'chack-ack-ack-ack-...'. Alarm: at the sight of a cat or owl, or prior to going to roost, series of metallic, high 'pli-pli-pli-pli-pli-...', which (often on take-off) turn into a crescendo. Song well known for its melodic, mellow tone, a clear and loud fluting (almost in the major key) at slow tempo and on wide, often sliding scale, with soft twitter appended; verses rather short, repeated at 3–5-sec. intervals. Some have desolate tone, sound quite like Mistle Thrush (see that species, p. 274).

Ring Ouzel *Turdus torquatus*   m**B**3 / **P**

L 24–27 cm. Breeds in uplands in gulleys or on steep boulder-strewn slopes, on bare mountainside or, in Continental Europe, in upland forest. Migratory in much of range; in Britain & Ireland, moorland breeders arrive Apr and leave Sep, with migrants from Fenno-Scandia Mar–May and Sep– Nov. Shy. Food insects, worms, berries. Nests in rock crevice, hollow stump, hole in wall etc. (Map on p. 278.)

IDENTIFICATION Size and shape roughly as Blackbird. – Adult: Predominantly *black* or sooty brownish-black with *white half-moon across breast* (on ♀♀, but also some ♂♂, the white has narrow brown feather fringes, most obvious in fresh plumage) and *yellow bill* with dark tip. Wing-feathers have pale edges, and in flight *wings appear much paler* than Blackbird's. Sexes similar, but ♂ on average blacker with whiter half-moon. – 1st-winter: ♂ resembles adult ♀, has hint of pale half-moon. ♀ usually completely lacks pale half-moon, can be confused with Blackbird but has somewhat paler wings than latter (though by no means as pale as adult Ring Ouzel!). – Variation: Birds in S and C Europe (ssp. *alpestris*) have pale-scaled underparts and paler wings.

VOICE Call a stony clicking 'tück', harder and somewhat higher-pitched than Blackbird's call. Also a Fieldfare-like squeak. Song loud and desolate-sounding, a few repeated notes or motifs at slow tempo; several types included, e.g. 'trrü trrü trrü trrü.... si-**vütt** si-**vütt** si-**vütt**.... chuv**üü** chuv**üü** chuv**üü** chuv**üü**....' etc.

Swainson's Thrush *Catharus ustulatus*   **V*****

L 16–18 cm. N American species, rare vagrant in Europe, mainly in autumn. Quite vigilant.

IDENTIFICATION Fairly small, and basically like Song Thrush in pattern, but *dark spots on underparts smaller* and *restricted to throat and breast* (Song Thrush heavily spotted down to belly and flanks) and in flight has typical *Catharus* (and *Zoothera*) *underwing markings of broad white and dark bands*. Narrow dark malar stripe. Flanks greyish. Resembles Grey-cheeked Thrush, but has *buff-tinged and more distinct eye-ring* (not greyish-white and narrow), as well as *weak buff tinge to cheeks* and *clear buff-white streak above lores*. Olive-tinged grey-brown above (but note that more rusty-toned birds breed in NW America).

VOICE Flight-call, often at night, a high, soft, upslurred 'kvüüi'. When nervous, a sharp, resonant 'chipp'.

Grey-cheeked Thrush *Catharus minimus*   **V*****

L 15–17 cm. N American species, rare vagrant in Europe, mainly in autumn. Shy, preferring to remain in cover.

IDENTIFICATION Small. As on other *Catharus* thrushes, *underwing* has *white–dark–white pattern*. Resembles Swainson's Thrush (finely spotted dark on lower throat and breast, narrow dark malar stripe, greyish flanks, uniformly grey-brown above) but differs in *more greyish-white ground colour on head-side and throat*, usually *narrower and less prominent grey-white eye-ring* (can be slightly stronger on 1st-winter), and *lack of distinct pale supraloral stripe*. – Variation: Race *bicknelli* (considered separate species by some) is small, with *faint* rusty tone to tail, and half of lower mandible yellow.

VOICE On migration, often at night, gives a shrill piping, drawn-out 'tsii(ü)' (hint of drop in pitch).

Hermit Thrush *Catharus guttatus*   **V*****

L 15–17 cm. N American species, very rare vagrant in Europe. Shy, almost always remaining concealed.

IDENTIFICATION Small. As on other *Catharus* thrushes, *underwing* has *white–dark–white pattern*. *Breast* only *sparsely and sparingly spotted*, but *spots are large*. Flanks usually entirely unspotted. Grey-brown above, with *rusty-red tone to rump and tail* (like Nightingale, but is slightly bigger, more compact and shorter-tailed than that species, besides other plumage differences). *White eye-ring*. Often jerks tail upwards and slowly lowers it.

VOICE Call a Blackbird-like though higher and more stifled 'chück', repeated in series. Also has a strained, nasal, tit-like 'veeüh' (faintly upslurred).

Veery *Catharus fuscescens*   **V*****

L 16–18 cm. N American species, very rare vagrant in Europe (a few autumn records). Shy, prefers to stay in cover.

IDENTIFICATION Small. As on other *Catharus* thrushes, *underwing* has *white–dark–white pattern*. Very similar to Grey-cheeked and Swainson's Thrushes, but *throat/breast spotting is less distinct* and less extensive. In addition, *upperparts* are *entirely rusty-toned* (only rump and tail red-brown on Hermit Thrush; but note that western race of Grey-cheeked is similarly reddish-brown above). Eye-ring always narrow and indistinct.

VOICE Call a whistled, hoarse 'pyiu' (downslurred).

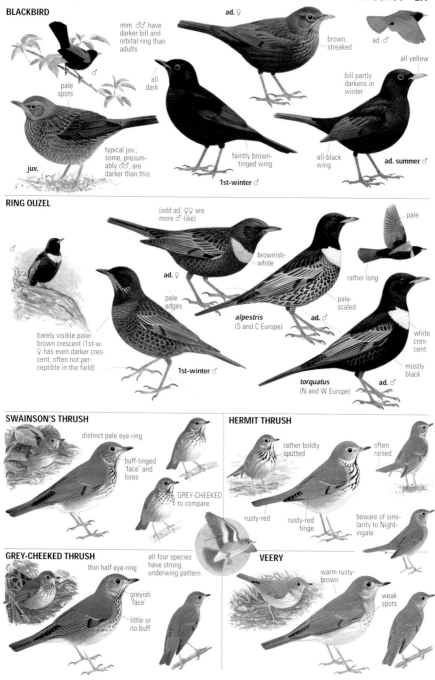

BLACKBIRD

imm. ♂♂ have darker bill and orbital ring than adults

ad. ♀

brown, streaked

ad. ♂

all yellow

bill partly darkens in winter

pale spots

all dark

all-black wing

faintly brown-tinged wing

ad. summer ♂

typical juv.; some, presumably ♂♂, are darker than this

juv.

1st-winter ♂

♂

RING OUZEL

(odd ad. ♀♀ are more ♂-like)

pale

brownish-white

rather long

ad. ♀

pale edges

pale-scaled

alpestris (S and C Europe)

ad. ♂

white crescent

barely visible paler brown crescent (1st-w. ♀ has even darker crescent, often not perceptible in the field)

1st-winter ♂

mostly black

torquatus (N and W Europe)

ad. ♂

SWAINSON'S THRUSH

distinct pale eye-ring

buff-tinged 'face' and lores

GREY-CHEEKED to compare

HERMIT THRUSH

rather boldly spotted

often raised

rusty-red

rusty-red tinge

beware of similarity to Nightingale

GREY-CHEEKED THRUSH

thin half eye-ring

greyish 'face'

little or no buff

all four species have strong underwing pattern

VEERY

warm rusty-brown

weak spots

White's Thrush   *Zoothera dauma*   V***

L 27–31 cm. Breeds locally just W of Ural mountains, but main distribution in Siberian taiga and in E Asia. Territories often in dense, wet taiga dominated by conifers. Summer visitor, winters in SE Asia, returning to breeding sites at end of May. Rare vagrant in W Europe. Usually forages on ground, for insects, molluscs, worms, berries. Very shy; when spotted, flies up into dense tree crown and perches motionless, or deftly takes cover in undergrowth.

IDENTIFICATION   *Large* and elongated (but tail not that long), with *heavy head and bill*. In powerful flight, gently undulating over longer distances, *broadly white-framed black band on underwing* may sometimes be glimpsed. Plumage otherwise mostly just olive-tinged grey-brown at distance, but at close range handsomely *black-scaled, including on entire upperparts*. Black scaly markings sometimes coalesce on breast, which can then appear rather dark. *Wings fairly variegated* (incl. dark-tipped buffish-yellow primary coverts, bicoloured remiges). Sexes alike.

VOICE   Silent except for its song, which is striking: monotonous, drawn-out, ventriloquial, almost mechanical second-long whistles with pauses of 5–10 sec. between, 'tüüü..... tüüü..... tüüü...'; audible at 1 km. Sometimes two alternating pitches, apparently by pair duetting.

Siberian Thrush   *Zoothera sibirica*   V***

L 20–21½ cm. Siberian taiga species, very rare vagrant in Europe, mainly in autumn and winter. Very shy.

IDENTIFICATION   Size of Song Thrush. In all plumages, broad white-bordered dark (black on ♂) band on underwing and white-tipped tail-feathers. Sexes differ. – Adult ♂: Mostly *dark lead-grey* (looks black in field) with *white supercilium*. Belly and flanks show much white. – 1st-year ♂: Like adult ♂, but has *some white on throat and head-sides*, supercilium is not pure white, and has *browner wing-feathers and primary coverts*. Many also have some distinct white streaks and dark vermiculations on breast and flanks. – ♀: *Olive-brown above* and on flanks. Narrow yellowish-white wing-bar on greater coverts. Supercilium buff. Breast yellowish-white with *dark crescent-shaped spots*.

VOICE   Call a fine, discordant 'tsii' or a short 'zit'.

American Robin   *Turdus migratorius*   V***

L 22–25 cm. N American species (emigrants' red-breasted substitute for the European Robin), rare vagrant in Europe, mainly in autumn and winter. Confiding (often a garden bird in America).

IDENTIFICATION   Rather heavily built, with shape and behaviour roughly as Fieldfare, thus long-winged and a good flyer. *Entire breast, flanks and upper belly rusty-red* (buff-

white tips in fresh plumage, narrowest on ad. ♂). *Dark grey above* (faint brown tinge on ♀ and 1st-winter), *head almost black* (duller on ♀ and 1st-winter) with white 'eyelid spots' above and below eye. Throat white, with coarse, dense black spotting. Adult has almost *all-yellow bill* in spring, but darker in winter months; 1st-winter has all-dark bill.

VOICE   Blackbird-like, including deep chacking 'chok-chok-chok' and more excited 'kli-kli-kli-...'.

Dark-throated Thrush   *Turdus ruficollis*   V***

L 23–26 cm. Two distinct races, of which the black-throated (*atrogularis*) breeds in Siberian taiga, westward to the W slopes of Urals; occasionally strays to W Europe, especially in late autumn and winter. The red-throated (*ruficollis*) breeds farther S and E, is a very rare vagrant in Europe.

IDENTIFICATION   Fieldfare-shaped. Both races: *rusty-buff underwing*; contrast between dark (black or red-brown) on throat/breast and *relatively unmarked belly/undertail-coverts* (the latter always whitish); *plain brownish-grey upperparts. Flanks* only *diffusely spotted grey*. Adult ♂ has uniformly dark bib, finely pale-fringed in autumn. Adult ♀ and 1st-winter ♂ similar, heavily dark-spotted and -streaked on breast (markings partly merging) and throat-sides (♂ finely streaked on entire throat, ♀ usually not). 1st-winter ♀ has sparser dark streaking on breast and throat-sides. *Tail* of black-throated grey-brown, of red-throated *rusty-red*.

VOICE   Call a Fieldfare-like whining 'gvih gvih'. When uneasy, a Redwing-like 'gyack' and hard Ring Ouzel-like 'tack tack'. Song little known; apparently short fluting phrases, at good intervals, with few squeaky sounds, e.g. 'chür̈re-chu..... chuvü-chuvü-strix..... chuli, chill̈vita...'.

Eyebrowed Thrush   *Turdus obscurus*   V***

L 21–23 cm. Autumn vagrant in Europe from Siberian taiga.

IDENTIFICATION   Size of Song Thrush, slim, small head, short bill. *Flanks orange-buff.* Prominent *white supercilium, dark lore* and beneath this a *white stripe under eye.* Underwing greyish-white. Adult ♂ is almost uniformly grey on throat, cheeks and neck, whereas other plumages have off-white throat with black spots and white-spotted dark cheeks.

VOICE   Migration call a Redwing-like, fine 'ts(r)iih'.

Dusky Thrush   *Turdus naumanni*   V***

L 20–23 cm. Two very different races (plus intermediates locally), of which the black-spotted (*eunomus*) breeds in C Siberian taiga N to tundra border, and the red-spotted (*naumanni*) farther south. Both are only rare vagrants in Europe.

IDENTIFICATION   Shape of Song Thrush. Both races have ± *reddish-brown underwing, pale supercilium* (whitish or rusty-tinged) and *dark-spotted flanks.* Otherwise marked differences. – Black-spotted: variably *extensive bright rusty-brown on upperwing*; dark, black-spotted back; whitish underparts with *heavy brownish-black spots on flanks* and a sometimes complete *black band across breast*; supercilium whitish. Sexes similar, ♂ more neat. – Red-spotted ('Naumann's Thrush'): much *rusty-red on tail*; upperwing/mantle grey-brown, mantle nearly *unmarked*; *underparts heavily spotted red-brown*; *pale supercilium* ± *rusty-tinged* (buff-white on 1st-winter).

VOICE   When flushed, a plaintive 'kvi-vih' (nasal, hard, almost francolin-like!). Also clacking 'chack-chack'.

Blackbird   (See p. 276.)   Ring Ouzel   (See p. 276.)

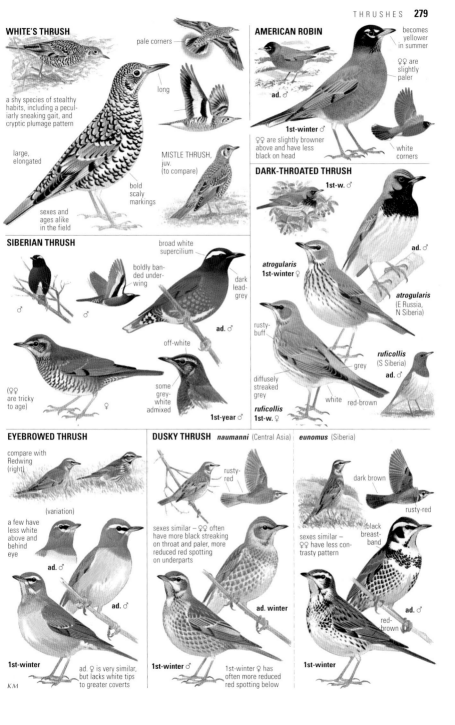

WHITE'S THRUSH

pale corners

long

a shy species of stealthy habits, including a peculiarly sneaking gait, and cryptic plumage pattern

large, elongated

MISTLE THRUSH, juv. (to compare)

bold scaly markings

sexes and ages alike in the field

SIBERIAN THRUSH

broad white supercilium

boldly banded under-wing

dark lead-grey

ad. ♂

♂

♂

off-white

(♀♀ are tricky to age)

some grey-white admixed

♀

1st-year ♂

EYEBROWED THRUSH

compare with Redwing (right)

(variation)

a few have less white above and behind eye

ad. ♂

ad. ♂

1st-winter

ad. ♀ is very similar, but lacks white tips to greater coverts

AMERICAN ROBIN

becomes yellower in summer

♀♀ are slightly paler

ad. ♂

1st-winter ♂

♀♀ are slightly browner above and have less black on head

white corners

DARK-THROATED THRUSH

1st-w. ♂

ad. ♂

atrogularis
1st-winter ♀

atrogularis
(E Russia, N Siberia)

rusty-buff

ruficollis
(S Siberia)
ad. ♂

grey

diffusely streaked grey

white   red-brown

ruficollis
1st-w. ♀

DUSKY THRUSH   *naumanni* (Central Asia)

rusty-red

sexes similar – ♀♀ often have more black streaking on throat and paler, more reduced red spotting on underparts

ad. winter

1st-winter ♂

1st-winter ♀ has often more reduced red spotting below

eunomus (Siberia)

dark brown

rusty-red

sexes similar – ♀♀ have less contrasty pattern

black breast-band

ad. ♂

red-brown

1st-winter

K M

WARBLERS *Sylviidae*

are a large family of small or roughly sparrow-sized insect-eaters. 56 species are treated here, of which 14 breed in Britain & Ireland. They have attractive songs, or at least marked vocal powers. All species inhabit woodland, shrubbery or tall vegetation, and most are, because of their diet, pronounced migrants.

The warblers are lively and nimble in their movements. They constantly hop or fly from one perch to another, and often nervously twitch or flick their wings or tail. They spend long periods concealed in the vegetation, and contacts with them are usually no more than brief glimpses. Fortunately, most species have characteristic calls.

A general overview of this great variety of small and elusive birds may more easily be gained by learning the five main genera. These are presented below.

NB: The species in the genera *Acrocephalus* and *Locustella* have been combined and grouped according to streaked or unstreaked plumage. Further, the largest genus, *Sylvia*, has been placed at the beginning of the warbler section. These departures from the usual systematics have been made with the purpose of helping beginners more easily to locate in the book a warbler that they have seen in the field.

Sylvia
(17 species.) Often live in dense, thorny thickets, or else in woodland. Sturdily built, with rather heavy bill and strong feet. The tail is narrow and square-ended. Their plumage col-

Whitethroat

ours are brown or grey above and white or buff below, males sometimes with rusty-red or pinkish on throat and breast and black on head (the only warbler genus in which the sexes are often somewhat dissimilar). The song of most is fast, uneven and twittering, and usually a great deal of experience is required to distinguish the species by calls. Males of several species have a short song-flight.

Acrocephalus
(10 species.) Live mostly in open swampland (reeds, bushes etc.). Slim, with long, pointed bill and flat forehead. Quite broad and bluntly rounded tail. Agile and active, they hop up reed stems, climb nimbly, sometimes with pointed tail

Reed Warbler

downwards, then dive back down into the vegetation. Plumage brown above, buff-white below, some having pale supercilium. No white on tail. Sexes alike. Song varied, often diagnostic, verses long and often containing excited sounds which are repeated several times, in some species also masterly mimicry. Often heard at night.

Locustella
(5 species.) Resemble *Acrocephalus*, but have more rounded and broader tail and more streaked plumage which is often darker, keep more to the ground and low vegetation,

and often scamper away unseen on the ground rather than flying off. Typically nocturnal singers. Four species have a monotonous, mechanical, insect-like song.

Grasshopper Warbler

Hippolais
(6 species.) Live in woods or in bushes with trees nearby. Closely related to *Acrocephalus*, differing in more square-ended tail and broader bill-base. Plumage brownish-grey or grey-green above, dirty white or yellowish-white below (those with green and yellow elements can recall *Phylloscopus*, see below). Sometimes the secondaries have pale edges. Sexes alike. Song loud, drawn out, excitable or chattering, in a couple of species including mimicry.

Icterine Warbler

Phylloscopus
(11 species.) Breed mostly in woodland, spending much time in treetops (but nest placed on ground). Most species are small, with slender bill and legs. Tail rather narrow and short, and square-ended (or even slightly forked). Tirelessly on the go and nimble, flutter and move about in the foliage, the smallest even hovering. Plumage usually grey-green above and white or yellowish-white below. Some species have one or two narrow pale wing-bars, and most have a pale (yellow or white) supercilium. Song loud and usually clear and pleasing, varying greatly among species.

Willow Warbler

JUDGING COLOUR IN VARYING LIGHT

Warbler identification involves assessing colours correctly. Backlighting or strong direct light impart entirely different effects to the same colour, and birds living in the aquarium-green light of the canopy foliage easily become 'miscoloured'. Here, try to watch the bird for as long as possible and from several different angles against the light, to see it both in shadow and in sunlight.

Below:
Blyth's Reed Warbler against the light: upperpart colour becomes dark and hard to judge, contrasts in head markings increase. Note also the flat forehead!

Above:
Singing Blyth's Reed Warbler in strong direct light: upperparts look pale and brown. Note also the peaked crown!

Above:
Blyth's Reed Warbler in sunlit foliage: green tones in plumage intensified. Head markings become indistinct.

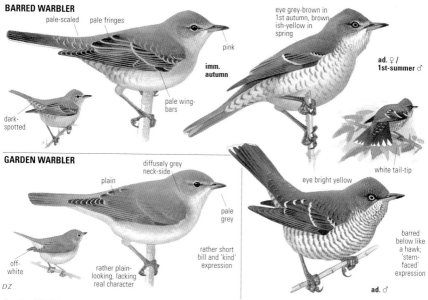

BARRED WARBLER

pale-scaled
pale fringes
pink
imm. autumn
pale wing-bars
dark-spotted

eye grey-brown in 1st autumn, brownish-yellow in spring

ad. ♀ / 1st-summer ♂

white tail-tip

GARDEN WARBLER

diffusely grey neck-side
plain
pale grey
rather short bill and 'kind' expression

eye bright yellow

barred below like a hawk; 'stern-faced' expression

off-white
rather plain-looking, lacking real character

DZ

ad. ♂

Garden Warbler *Sylvia borin*   m**B**2 / **P**2

L 13–14½ cm. Breeds in woods with clearings, in groves, overgrown parks and larger gardens with tall trees (not content with just shrubbery and solitary trees) with rich undergrowth. Summer visitor (in Britain & Ireland mainly mid Apr–Sep, passage migrants to Oct), winters in tropical Africa. Discreet in habits, difficult to see other than briefly. Nests low down in bush or dense herbage.

IDENTIFICATION 'Anonymous'appearance, an olive brown-grey and rather plump warbler with no obvious features. *Bill rather thick and stubby*, bluish grey-buff with slightly darker tip. Legs light greyish, rather strong. Diffuse paler eye-ring (around dark eye) and even less prominent pale, short supercilium. *Often an inkling of a purer grey tinge on neck-side.* Sexes and ages similar, but 1st-autumn birds have fresher wings with paler tips to tertials and remiges.

VOICE Call (heard from foliage, usually without bird being seen) a cackling series of slightly nasal,'thick'clicks, 'chek, chek, chek, chek,...'; tempo quickens with increasing unease. (Blackcap's anxiety-call a harder and more distinct clicking.) Song beautiful, 3–8 sec.-long verses of rapid, rather deep notes, one moment thrush-like and the next harsher, not forming any clear melody but *shuttling*

irresolutely up and down: it sounds like a *rippling brook*. Lacks Blackcap's flute-like final notes. Some are harder-voiced, can easily be confused with Barred Warbler.

Barred Warbler *Sylvia nisoria*   **P**4

L 15½–17 cm. Breeds in tall bushes with scattered trees in open country, but also in bushy glades in open forest; shares habitat, and often territory, with Red-backed Shrike. Summer visitor, migration as Garden Warbler; passage migrant in Britain, mainly on E coast (Aug–mid Oct, rare in spring). Skulking, but occasionally seen flying between bushes, and in spring in near-level song-flight.

IDENTIFICATION A large, heavily built *Sylvia*; *long-tailed*. Wing-coverts and tertials ± pale-edged. Some white at tips of tail-feathers. – Adult ♂: *Iris bright yellow. Upperparts lead-grey*, darkest on head, with *distinct white fringes to wing-coverts and tertials.* Entire *underparts closely and heavily vermiculated* dark grey. – Adult ♀/1st-year ♂: Like adult ♂, but iris often slightly duller yellow, upperparts more brown-grey and barring below not so obvious and complete. (1st-year ♀ minimally barred, has browner tone above and yellow-brown iris.) – 1st-autumn: Grey-brown above, buffish-grey and unbarred below. Iris dark. Identified by *light buffish-grey tertial and covert fringes.*

VOICE Call characteristic, a loud rattle, dying towards end, 'trrrrr't't-t', somewhat recalling scolding House Sparrow; sometimes also added to song; tempo varies, is occasionally slower. Alarm a hoarse, muffled 'chaihr'. Song like Garden Warbler's (at times confusingly so!), but almost always audibly *harder and more rasping* and with slightly *higher pitch*. Even more similar is the ecstatic song of some Whitethroats, and at times the rattling call must be heard or the bird seen before certain identification is made.

Garden Warbler

Barred Warbler

Blackcap *Sylvia atricapilla*   m**B**2 / **P**2 / **W**4

L 13½–15 cm. Breeds in shady woodland with dense under-storey, and in parks and gardens with rank undergrowth. In Britain & Ireland common in deciduous and mixed wood-land. A characteristic bird over large parts of C and S Europe, where it can be very common. Migratory in N and E, short-distance migrant or resident in W and S. Easier to see than e.g. Garden Warbler. Nests low down in bush.

IDENTIFICATION Rather stocky build, roughly as Garden Warbler. Dirty grey above and light olive-grey below, ♂ with *small black cap* (reaches only to upper part of eye on the moderately large head; cf. the small-bodied and big-headed tits, p. 318, which have larger black cap as well as black bib), ♀ and juvenile with *red-brown cap*. 1st-winter ♂ has cap brown, black or a mixture of both colours. Tail lacks white in all plumages. Bill and legs grey.

VOICE Call a tongue-clicking 'teck' (harder and louder than Lesser Whitethroat's 'tett'), when uneasy repeated in long series, 'teck-teck-teck-...', occasionally with drawn-out, hoarse 'schreh' notes interposed. Song one of the finest; begins like Garden Warbler's with an irresolute chattering (can be shortened or omitted altogether, often so during heat of midday and in S Europe), *turning into clear, slightly melancholy flute-like notes at end*. As other *Sylvia* warblers, the Blackcap can occasionally produce a drawn-out sub-song of mimicry and squeaky, rasping sounds.

Orphean Warbler *Sylvia hortensis*   V***

L 15–16 cm. Breeds in deciduous woods (e.g. in oak forest, olive groves or luxuriant riverine vegetation), in tall scrub with some trees, often on rocky, sunny mountain slopes, also locally in pine forest. Migratory, winters S of Sahara. Rather shy and elusive at breeding site, keeps mostly in treetops. Nest often at breast height, in bush or low tree.

IDENTIFICATION Large, somewhat bigger than Blackcap, and has *longer bill* and slightly *bigger head*. Greyish above, dirty white below. Tail square-ended, with sides white-edged. – Adult ♂: *Greyish-black on ear-coverts, lores and forehead,* sometimes dark also on crown (but always indistinct border with grey hindcrown/nape, unlike Sardinian Warbler). *Iris pale* (esp. in W Europe). – Adult ♀: Head less black than ♂'s (often only ear-coverts and lores are darker grey, giving impression of outsized Lesser Whitethroat), and upperparts are tinged brown. Iris variable, often with narrow pale ring, sometimes (esp. in Turkey and Middle East) rather dark. – 1st-winter: Like adult ♀, but *head lacks any black,* iris grey (♂) or brown-tinged grey (♀), and *iris always dark*.

VOICE Call a tongue-clicking 'teck', barely distinguish-able from Blackcap's. Also has a buzzing rattle when agi-tated, 'trrrrr', somewhat recalling Rüppell's Warbler, and

a Barred Warbler-like hoarse 'chaih'. Song in SW Europe (ssp. *hortensis*) a simple composition of clear motifs re-peated a few times in Ring Ouzel fashion, e.g. 'türu türu türu türu..... liru liru liru trü...'; in SE (*crassirostris*) the verses are longer and more varied, can recall Nightingale, e.g. '**trü trü trü** shivü shivü, yu-yu-yu-brü-**trüh**'.

Arabian Warbler *Sylvia leucomelaena*   —

L 14½–16 cm. Breeds in acacia stands in semi-desert. Resi-dent. Relatively shy; restless and mobile, often disappears without a trace, despite openness of breeding terrain.

IDENTIFICATION Most like Orphean Warbler, but has *longer and round-tipped tail* with *white tips to outer feathers* (not white sides as on Orphean), also always *dark eye* with *trace of white eye-ring, shorter bill* and *blacker cap*. Brilliant white throat. Often perches quite upright, but also hops about in crouched posture in dense acacia crowns. *Con-stantly flicks tail downwards.* Total impression in fact not at all unlike that of a bulbul (which often found in same ter-ritory). Sexes similar. Immature has brown-grey crown.

VOICE Call a rather 'thick' clicking 't(r)ack', often repeat-ed. Song short verses at slow pace with clear, attractive voice and wide tonal range, can recall Blackcap, eastern Orphean Warbler, Rustic Bunting or, at distance, even Blackbird.

Lesser Whitethroat *Sylvia curruca*   m**B**3 / **P**2

L 11½–13½ cm. Breeds in farmland and parkland with mature hedgerows, in young conifers, gardens with hedges and berry bushes, even pure thorn scrub (but not so often as Whitethroat, and prefers some trees). Summer visitor, winters in NE Africa. Very numerous in E Mediterranean on passage (esp. early Apr). Unobtrusive at breeding site, its presence revealed mainly by its voice. Nests in dense bush.

IDENTIFICATION *Small* but *compact* and rather short-tailed *Sylvia*. Within the region, always *grey-brown above* with greyer crown and tail. Best feature is *darker grey ear-coverts*, darker than crown, combined with small size and *dark grey legs*. Some have suggestion of greyish-white supercilium. *Iris dark* (grey or brown). *Bill shortish, dark* with paler blue-grey base. – Variation: To the east, both small paler and browner populations, ssp. *minula* and others, and large dark ones, ssp. *althaea*, occur. No definite records of these exist from Europe, and field identification tricky.

VOICE Call a quiet, dry, clicking 'tett'. On migration, e.g. in Middle East, also a chattering, scolding 'che-che-che-che' (superficially like Blue Tit). Song in Europe a *rattling, loud series*, 'tell-tell-tell-tell-tell', preceded by a short scratchy warble. In Turkey, Caucasus and Siberia, emphasis usually on the scratchy warble, while the rattle sequence is shortened or omitted. Intermediate versions also occur.

Blackcap   Orphean Warbler   Arabian Warbler   Lesser Whitethroat

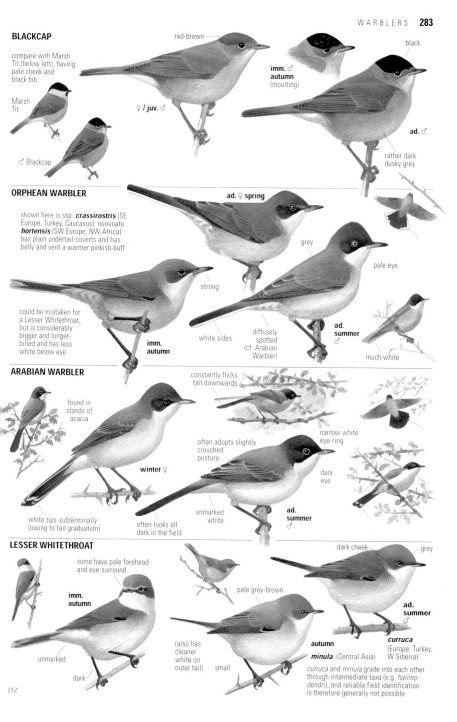

BLACKCAP

compare with Marsh Tit (below left), having pale cheek and black bib

red-brown

black

imm. ♂ autumn (moulting)

Marsh Tit

♀ / juv. ♂

♂ Blackcap

ad. ♂

rather dark dusky grey

ORPHEAN WARBLER

shown here is ssp. **crassirostris** (SE Europe, Turkey, Caucasus); nominate **hortensis** (SW Europe, NW Africa) has plain undertail-coverts and has belly and vent a warmer pinkish-buff

ad. ♀ spring

grey

pale eye

could be mistaken for a Lesser Whitethroat, but is considerably bigger and longer-billed and has less white below eye

strong

imm. autumn

white sides

diffusely spotted (cf. Arabian Warbler)

ad. summer ♂

much white

ARABIAN WARBLER

found in stands of acacia

constantly flicks tail downwards

narrow white eye-ring

often adopts slightly crouched posture

dark eye

winter ♀

white tips *subterminally* (owing to tail graduation)

unmarked white

often looks all dark in the field

ad. summer ♂

LESSER WHITETHROAT

some have pale forehead and eye-surround

dark cheek

grey

imm. autumn

pale grey-brown

ad. summer ♂

curruca (Europe, Turkey, W Siberia)

unmarked

dark

(also has cleaner white on outer tail)

small

autumn

minula (Central Asia)

curruca and *minula* grade into each other through intermediate taxa (e.g. *halimodendri*), and reliable field identification is therefore generally not possible

DZ

Sardinian Warbler *Sylvia melanocephala*   V**

L 13–14 cm. Breeds in tall bushes and open woodland with dense thickets, locally also in mere waist-high vegetation; sometimes in gardens or tree clumps close to habitation. Primarily resident. Active and restless, is not shy, often reveals itself. Nests in bush, usually rather low down.

IDENTIFICATION About size of Lesser Whitethroat, *compact* and rather large-headed. Flicks wings and tail, often adopts crouched posture with head lowered. In all plumages: *white throat* but *rather dark flanks*; *red-brown eye-ring* (reddest on ♂, duller on ♀) outside red orbital ring; rounded, *rather long tail*; on adult, dark tail-feathers with white tail-corners. Iris ochre (adult) or grey-brown (imm.). – ♂ (from Aug): *Black cap* with usually diffuse border against *dark grey mantle*; mid-grey flanks. – ♀: Grey head (may have some greyish-black on forecrown and ear-coverts), *brown back*, greyish-brown flanks. – Variation: E Mediterranean birds (ssp. *momus*) slightly smaller and paler.

VOICE Call a loud, very hard 'tseck'. More characteristic is the 'rattle-call', a series of mono- or disyllabic rattling notes at rapid speed, 'trr-trr-trr-trr-trr' or 'tü-**trru** tü-**trru** tü-**trru** tü-**trru**', or with first note deviating, 'tu**rett** trett-trett-trett-trett'. Song a *Sylvia* chatter very familiar in S Europe, usually short (2–5 sec.), harsh, rattling verses at high speed with very brief whistled notes inserted; includes a great deal of the 'trr-trr' rattling sound. Observers should learn this species' song to enable easier comparisons.

Ménétries's Warbler *Sylvia mystacea*   —

L 12–13 cm. Breeds in bushes, often tamarisk, or in open wood with undergrowth (maquis), in drier, open and high-lying terrain, but also along watercourses, on fringes of palm groves etc. Migrant, winters around Red Sea.

IDENTIFICATION Very like Sardinian Warbler, especially of ssp. *momus*, but neater and has slightly shorter tail. – ♂ told by *dark cap* not being velvety black but more *dull greyish-black* and *less extensive* at rear; also, *flanks are not so grey* but *whitish*; majority in Turkey have white throat and breast-centre, but some (and most of those in Caucasus and Central Asia) have *pinky or light brick-red tone to throat / breast*. – ♀ told from Sardinian (*momus*) by: *paler* and *more uniform sandy-brown upperparts* (without contrastingly greyer head); more uniform buff-washed grey-white underparts; usually *white eye-ring*; more uniform grey-brown tertials (darker with more distinct pale edges on Sardinian); paler bill with light grey or pinkish base (blue-grey on Sardinian).

VOICE A tongue-clicking 'tseck' like Sardinian Warbler's, also a sparrow-like chattering 'cher'r'r'r' quite unlike Sardinian's rattle-call, more like Rüppell's Warbler (but shorter and more feeble). Song like Sardinian's, with 'simmer-

ing', chattering notes interspersed with clear whistles, but tempo somewhat slower and rhythm a little more jerky.

Cyprus Warbler *Sylvia melanothorax*   —

L 12½–13½ cm. Breeds in dense shrubbery in open terrain (maquis) in Cyprus, where fairly common. Summer visitor (Mar–Oct), winters in Israel, Jordan and Sinai; holds winter territories in barren wadis. Shy. Nests low down in bush.

IDENTIFICATION Looks like a Sardinian Warbler with *dark-spotted underparts* and *narrow white eye-ring* (outside indistinct brick-brown orbital ring). In all plumages, greyish upperparts and *contrasting pale edges to tertials, secondaries and greater coverts* (as Rüppell's Warbler); *undertail-coverts* have *dark centres*; flanks greyish(-buff); bill-base pinkish. – Adult ♂ has black cap and is heavily dark-spotted below; 1st-winter ♀ has few or almost no spots visible below; adult ♀ and 1st-year ♂ are intermediate between those two, have some greyish-black on forecrown and cheeks.

VOICE Call a throaty clicking 'zreck'. When agitated, gives hoarse drawn-out 'tschreh tschreh...'. Alarm a rattling, high-pitched 'ze-ze-ze-ze-ze-...'; sometimes Sardinian-like 'tri-tr'tr'tr'tr'tr...' (though faster). Song a dry, rugged warble, rather monotonous, virtually lacking clear whistled notes. Tempo slow and slightly jerky and uneven.

Rüppell's Warbler *Sylvia rueppelli*   V***

L 12½–13½ cm. Breeds in dense, often thorny or prickly shrubbery with some low trees on arid, rocky mountain slopes, sometimes in open oak forest with shrub layer (tall maquis). Summer visitor, winters S of Sahara. Rather shy at breeding site, but ♂ often seen in song-flight in spring (at times 'butterfly-flight'). Nests low down in dense bush.

IDENTIFICATION Size of Sardinian Warbler, but slimmer and with slightly smaller head and more obvious neck. Characteristic of all plumages is *grey upperparts* with *contrasting pale edges to dark tertials, secondaries and often greater coverts*; alula often strikingly black. Bill narrow and longish, on some (not all) with clearly decurved tip. – ♂ (from Jan): *Black* crown, *head-sides and throat* (unique), distinct white moustachial stripe. Orbital ring and legs dull brick-brown. – ♀ / juvenile ♂: Crown and mantle greyish (faintly tinged brown). Orbital ring rather weak, brownish-white. Some spring ♀♀ have dark grey on throat. Told from immature ♀ Cyprus Warbler by *unmarked greyish-white undertail-coverts, light greyish-white flanks* and *pale blue-grey bill-base*.

VOICE Call a distinct clicking 'zack', most like Blackcap's, also a dry rattling 'zrrr' and intermediates. Alarm a sparrow-like rattling series, often more drawn out, faster and feebler-voiced than Barred Warbler's, 'zerrrrrrrrr'r'r...'. Occasionally a 'bubbling' nasal scold, 'zett-ett-ett-ett-...'. Song resembles Sardinian's most, but has slightly *slower tempo, lower pitch* and more 'bouncing', *shuttling* character between lower, 'chatting' warbled notes and high, clear whistled notes; the warble is also more pleasing and sonorous than Sardinian's.

Sardinian Warbler   Ménétries's Warbler   Rüppell's Warbler

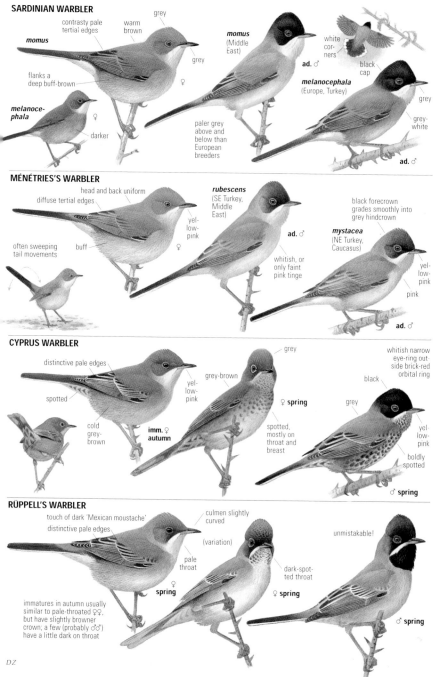

SARDINIAN WARBLER

momus
contrasty pale tertial edges
warm brown
grey
grey
♀

momus (Middle East)
white corners
black cap
ad. ♂

flanks a deep buff-brown

melanocephala
♀

melanocephala (Europe, Turkey)
grey
grey-white

darker

paler grey above and below than European breeders

ad. ♂

MÉNÉTRIES'S WARBLER

head and back uniform
diffuse tertial edges

rubescens (SE Turkey, Middle East)
yellow-pink
♀

ad. ♂

often sweeping tail movements
buff

whitish, or only faint pink tinge

black forecrown grades smoothly into grey hindcrown

mystacea (NE Turkey, Caucasus)
yellow-pink
pink

ad. ♂

CYPRUS WARBLER

grey
distinctive pale edges

spotted

grey-brown

♀ spring

whitish narrow eye-ring outside brick-red orbital ring

black

grey
yellow-pink

cold grey-brown

imm. ♀ autumn

yellow-pink

spotted, mostly on throat and breast

boldly spotted

♂ spring

RÜPPELL'S WARBLER

touch of dark 'Mexican moustache'
distinctive pale edges

culmen slightly curved

(variation)

unmistakable!

pale throat

dark-spotted throat

♀ spring

immatures in autumn usually similar to pale-throated ♀♀, but have slightly browner crown; a few (probably ♂♂) have a little dark on throat

♀ spring

♂ spring

DZ

(Common) Whitethroat *Sylvia communis*   m**B**2 / **P**1

L 13–15 cm. Breeds in scrubby areas, in farmland with hedgerows, woodland edge and open deciduous woodland with scrub. Summer visitor (in Britain & Ireland May–Aug, passage migrants to Oct), winters S of Sahara. Often sings from bushtop, wire or in short ascending song-flight.

IDENTIFICATION Rather big, *sturdy* and *long-tailed*, somewhat heavy and slow in movements compared with its smaller congeners. *Bill strong* with diffusely paler base. *Legs* rather strong, *yellow-brown*. Distinguished in all plumages by *broad rusty-brown edges to tertials and greater coverts* (a feature shared only with Spectacled and Tristram's Warblers), which contrast with grey-brown back. White tailsides. – Adult ♂: Grey head, *white eye-ring* and throat, pink-tinged breast. Iris reddish-ochre. – Other plumages: Grey-brown head, diffuse eye-ring, off-white throat, buffy-white breast, iris grey-brown or yellow-brown.

VOICE Call a hoarse 'vaihd vaihd vaihd' with slightly lilting, nasal tone. Alarm a drawn-out, hoarse 'chaihr', recalling Dartford Warbler's. Song from perched bird normally very characteristic, a short, fast verse with *scratchy, hoarse, gruff voice*, delivered in *jerky* and *jolting rhythm*, roughly 'Take it to**day**, take it too?'. In song-flight, and at times in other circumstances, verses are drawn out and voice becomes more like other *Sylvia* species, at times confusingly like Barred Warbler's! Sings frequently.

Spectacled Warbler *Sylvia conspicillata*   **V**∗∗∗

L 12–13 cm. Breeds in low bushes and scrub (garrigue) on mountain slopes, in brush and herbaceous vegetation on dry heaths or saltflats. Short-distance migrant or resident. Rather shy, yet often seen in the open. Nests low in bush.

IDENTIFICATION Like a *small* and *slim* Whitethroat (with rusty-brown wing-panel and white eye-ring), but has *shorter primary projection*, proportionally smaller body/*bigger head*, and *narrower bill* with paler inner part of lower mandible; also consistently *quicker* and 'more nervous' in movements. – Adult ♂: Differs from Whitethroat in: *greyish-black lores* and forecheeks; *darker brownish-pink breast* and touch of grey on lower throat. – ♀/1st-winter: Resembles both Whitethroat and Subalpine Warbler. Told from former by smaller size, short wing, slimmer bill, broader rusty-brown wing-covert fringes (so that hardly any grey-black centres visible); from latter by shorter primary projection, brighter rusty colour on wing and *paler yellow-pink legs*.

VOICE Call a high, dry buzzing 'drr', often strung together in long series with short syllables inserted, 'drrrrrr-dr-dr-dr-drrrrrrr...' ('rattlesnake rattle'). Song a usually high, fast warble which is often introduced by several clear whistled notes (which can sound a bit like Crested Lark).

Subalpine Warbler *Sylvia cantillans*   **V**∗∗

L 12–13 cm. Breeds in various habitats, often in bushes on dry slopes or sandy heaths, also in open woodland (often holm oak) or in lush shrubbery beside watercourses etc. Summer visitor (mostly Apr–Sep), winters S of Sahara. Discreet habits, but has short song-flight. Nests in thick bush.

IDENTIFICATION Size as Lesser Whitethroat, but *more slender* in build; fairly short-tailed. – Adult ♂: Easily identified by *lead-grey head* and grey mantle, and by having *brick-red on throat*, bordered by *white moustaches*, and on breast. Eye-ring and orbital ring brick-red. Legs brownish-pink. – Adult ♀: As ♂, but throat/breast usually only lightly washed brownish-pink (cf. ♂ Ménétries's Warbler); more *brownish above* and not lead-grey on head; faintly brick-coloured or *whitish eye-ring* (outside indistinct red-brown orbital ring). Legs greyish brown-pink. – 1st-winter: As ♀, but browner above, buff-white below, and initially with greyish yellow-brown iris (adult more reddish).

VOICE Call a Lesser Whitethroat-like dry clicking 'tett', often rapidly repeated in long series (unlike e.g. Sardinian Warbler); some variation: on W Mediterranean islands 'trrrrt', in SE Europe and Turkey 'trek' (often doubled). At times gives muffled, creaky 'ehd' like Trumpeter Finch, and when agitated a hoarse 'tscheh tscheh tscheh...'. Song *higher-pitched* than Sardinian's, and verses on average a bit longer; almost Linnet-like in 'rippling' and *bouncing* nature, a rambling mix of harsh twitters and short, high squeaky notes.

Desert Warbler *Sylvia nana*   **V**∗∗

L 11½–12½ cm. Breeds in semi-desert (sandy or stony) or on dry steppe. W race in N Africa (*deserti*) is mainly resident, while E race in Asia (*nana*) is migratory. Active and restless, often runs on ground. Not hard to see owing to openness of habitat. Nests low in bush.

IDENTIFICATION *Small. Light sandy-coloured upperparts*, gives immediate pointer to species, but in brief glimpse other pale brown species are possible contenders. *Ochre fringes to tertials and greater coverts* and *broad off-white eye-ring* can recall Spectacled Warbler. Bear in mind that: *eye is yellow* (never dark); *legs light yellow-brown* (not pinkish-brown); *uppertail bright rusty-brown*, central feathers with black small streaks. *Bill slender, dull yellow with just dark tip* and culmen. – Variation: Race *deserti* (see above) is pale yellow-buff above; *nana* is grey-brown like a pale ♀ Whitethroat.

VOICE Call a chattering high 'cherr r̄ r̄ r̄' (can recall both sparrow and Blue Tit). Song rather distinctive, a clear jingling, slightly jerky verse (almost Whitethroat-like in rhythm); best recognized by *high, clear voice* and by fact that it contains so few harsh notes. The chattering alarm is sometimes annexed to the song.

Whitethroat   Spectacled Warbler   Subalpine Warbler   Desert Warbler

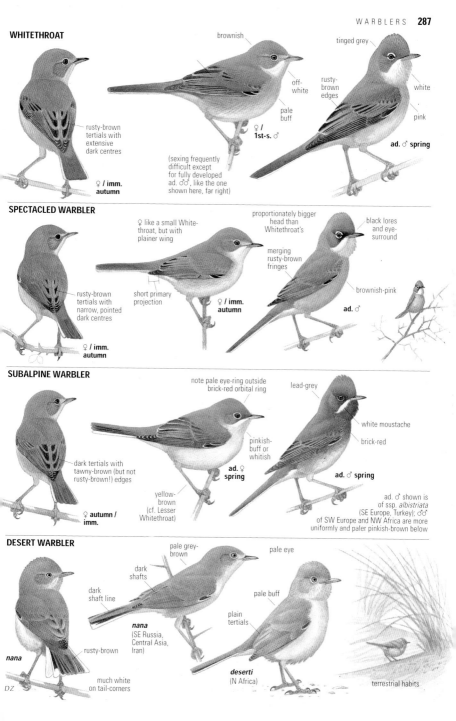

WHITETHROAT

rusty-brown tertials with extensive dark centres

♀ / imm. autumn

brownish

off-white

pale buff

♀ / 1st-s. ♂

(sexing frequently difficult except for fully developed ad. ♂♂, like the one shown here, far right)

tinged grey

rusty-brown edges

white

pink

ad. ♂ spring

SPECTACLED WARBLER

rusty-brown tertials with narrow, pointed dark centres

♀ / imm. autumn

♀ like a small White-throat, but with plainer wing

short primary projection

♀ / imm. autumn

proportionately bigger head than Whitethroat's

merging rusty-brown fringes

black lores and eye-surround

brownish-pink

ad. ♂

SUBALPINE WARBLER

dark tertials with tawny-brown (but not rusty-brown!) edges

♀ autumn / imm.

note pale eye-ring outside brick-red orbital ring

pinkish-buff or whitish

ad. ♀ spring

yellow-brown (cf. Lesser Whitethroat)

lead-grey

white moustache

brick-red

ad. ♂ spring

ad. ♂ shown is of ssp. *albistriata* (SE Europe, Turkey); ♂♂ of SW Europe and NW Africa are more uniformly and paler pinkish-brown below

DESERT WARBLER

nana

rusty-brown

much white on tail-corners

pale grey-brown

dark shafts

dark shaft line

nana (SE Russia, Central Asia, Iran)

pale eye

pale buff

plain tertials

deserti (N Africa)

terrestrial habits

DZ

Dartford Warbler *Sylvia undata* **r**B4

L 13–14 cm. Breeds on bushy coastal heaths or in higher sites (low maquis, garrigue), sometimes also in open pine or oak wood with whin and heather. In Britain mostly on heaths with gorse and heather. Mostly resident. Rather inquisitive and fearless, often reveals itself. Nests low in bush.

IDENTIFICATION *Small*, smaller even than Spectacled Warbler, but has *longer tail* which is often *cocked*. Flight fluttering and jerky, bobbing tail. *Dark grey* or grey-brown above, *dull wine-red below* (often appears all dark at distance and in poor light; cf. Marmora's Warbler) with fine off-white spots on throat (close-range views) and dirty white belly-centre. Iris red-brown, *orbital ring red*. Sexes similar, but ♀ browner above and not so saturated wine-red below. – Juvenile: Lacks red orbital ring, has dark iris, and is even browner than ♀; very like juvenile Marmora's (which see).

VOICE Call distinctive, a *drawn-out, harsh*, 'chaihhrr' (sometimes with extra note, 'chaihhrr-chr'). Alarm a chattering 'trrü-tr'r'r'r'r', rather like Sardinian Warbler but higher in pitch. Song short *high-speed* bursts of a rattling warble with occasional whistled notes inserted; has *faster tempo, weaker voice* and *lower pitch* than Sardinian's.

Marmora's Warbler *Sylvia sarda* **V*****

L 13–14 cm. Breeds on hillsides in low maquis and garrigue (up to c. 1000 m altitude) and in rocky coastal scrub (heather, cistus etc.); avoids woodland. Resident, or winters in N Africa. Nests low down in bush.

IDENTIFICATION Size/shape as Dartford Warbler (though on average not quite so long-tailed), as is behaviour. Distinguished from that species by *grey underparts* and *lack of distinct, pale spots on throat* (ad. ♂ can show hint, ♀ and juv. have entire throat paler grey-white). Sexes similar, but adult ♂ often has darker (grey-black) forehead and lores. – Juvenile: Very like juvenile Dartford Warbler, but has whiter throat, breast-centre and belly (not so warm grey-buff), and flanks are more greyish-buff (less warm brown).

VOICE Alarm a throaty, generally muffled 'chreck' or 'tscheck'. Song like those of Sardinian and Dartford Warblers, but pitch a little higher and general impression not so hard and 'rattling'; verses usually end with a rather *clear trill* or a *clear shuttling warble*.

Tristram's Warbler *Sylvia deserticola* —

L 11½–12½ cm. Breeds on bare mountain slopes or heaths with bushy vegetation (low maquis, garrigue); scattered holm oaks and cedars tolerated. Mostly resident, but some move short distance south in winter, and often found at slightly lower level and on flatter ground, e.g. in semi-desert or dry steppe with low, dry bushes. Nests in bush.

IDENTIFICATION Small and rather long-tailed (tail somewhat shorter than Dartford Warbler's), plumage intermediate between Spectacled (*rusty-brown on wing, white eye-ring*) and Subalpine (*brick-red on throat, breast and flanks*, at least *hint of white moustachial stripe*). Note: entire throat red-brown, finely scaled white when fresh; grey on head and back. Autumn birds, however, browner above and throat appears pale in similar plumage to Spectacled.

VOICE Call 'check'. Alarm a sparrow-like chatter, 'chett-ett-ett-ett-ett-ett-...', with slight nasal tone. Song fast and twittering with a few short whistles inserted, thus like several other *Sylvia* warblers; somewhat softer and more pleasing, not quite so rapid and 'rattling' as Sardinian's.

Scrub Warbler *Scotocerca inquieta* —

L 10–11 cm. Breeds in semi-desert and on dry, sandy or stony steppe with low bushes or grass (wadis, garrigue), sometimes in same habitat as Spectacled Warbler but more often alongside Desert Lark and Mourning Wheatear. Resident. Bold, lively, restless. Nests low down in vegetation.

IDENTIFICATION A small *pale sandy-coloured* ball of feathers with *long, narrow, dark tail* which is often held raised. *Head relatively big*, with characteristic *broad, pale supercilium* set off by *narrow dark eye-stripe* and dark-streaked crown. Legs long and appear to be set far back.

VOICE Calls variable. When agitated, a metallic, dry descending trill, 'prrrrrrr'. Highly characteristic is a disyllabic whistle with second note lower, 'wii-wew'; a four-syllable variant with notes successively falling seems to have mainly a song function, 'sii-sü-su-so' (at distance almost like Common Sandpiper call). True song often introduced by differing first syllable, e.g. 'tsris rü-sii-sü-su' or 'trsirr-vuy-vuy-vuy'.

Graceful Prinia *Prinia gracilis* —

L 10–11 cm. Breeds in S Turkey and in Middle East in shrubbery and tall grass in both wet and drier habitats, often along ditches, riversides and pools, on sandy ground, in agricultural areas and near buildings, wherever there is dense undergrowth, tamarisk bushes, reeds, rushes etc. Resident. Bold, active. Nests low in vegetation.

IDENTIFICATION Recalls Scrub Warbler, but note: *head smaller, more rounded* and *more uniform in colour* (lacks both pale supercilium and dark eye-stripe); more *dark-streaked above*; long *tail is strongly graduated* and each feather has *black-and-white tip*. Breeding ♂ has *black bill*.

VOICE Call an explosive 'tlipp!' or a metallic rattling trill, 'srrrrrrrt', often repeated and with somewhat 'swaying' rhythm. Alarm a sharp 'tsiit', not unlike that of Tree and Red-throated Pipits, but harder. Song a frenzied grinding 'srr**lip** srr**lip** srr**lip** srr**lip**...'.

Dartford Warbler

Marmora's Warbler

Tristram's Warbler

Scrub Warbler

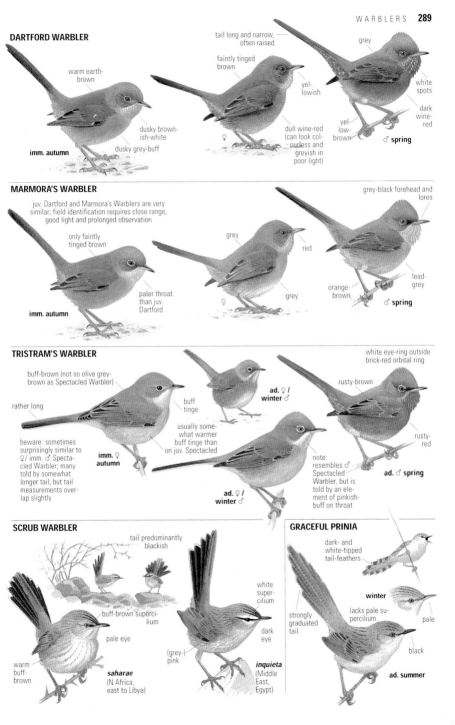

DARTFORD WARBLER

warm earth-brown

dusky brownish-white

dusky grey-buff

imm. autumn

tail long and narrow, often raised

faintly tinged brown

♀

yellowish

dull wine-red (can look colourless and greyish in poor light)

grey

white spots

dark wine-red

yellow-brown

♂ **spring**

MARMORA'S WARBLER

juv. Dartford and Marmora's Warblers are very similar; field identification requires close range, good light and prolonged observation

only faintly tinged brown

paler throat than juv. Dartford

imm. autumn

grey

grey

♀

red

grey-black forehead and lores

lead-grey

orange-brown

♂ **spring**

TRISTRAM'S WARBLER

buff-brown (not so olive grey-brown as Spectacled Warbler)

rather long

beware: sometimes surprisingly similar to ♀/ imm. ♂ Spectacled Warbler; many told by somewhat longer tail, but tail measurements overlap slightly

buff tinge

imm. ♀ autumn

usually somewhat warmer buff tinge than on juv. Spectacled

ad. ♀ / winter ♂

note: resembles ♂ Spectacled Warbler, but is told by an element of pinkish-buff on throat

white eye-ring outside brick-red orbital ring

rusty-brown

rusty-red

ad. ♂ spring

SCRUB WARBLER

tail predominantly blackish

buff-brown supercilium

pale eye

warm buff-brown

saharae (N Africa, east to Libya)

white supercilium

dark eye

(grey-)pink

inquieta (Middle East, Egypt)

GRACEFUL PRINIA

dark- and white-tipped tail-feathers

winter

pale

lacks pale supercilium

strongly graduated tail

black

ad. summer

Sedge Warbler *Acrocephalus schoenobaenus* m**B**2 / **P**

L 11½–13 cm. Breeds in dense vegetation in marshy areas: in reeds (preferably with some bushes and herbage), in tall rushes, in riverside willows, in swampy bushland or along ditches and canals with lush herbage, grass, reeds, etc.; locally also drier habitats. Summer visitor (in Britain & Ireland mid Apr–Sep/Oct), winters S of Sahara. Mobile, bold, often in open. Nests low in dense vegetation.

IDENTIFICATION A buff-and-brown warbler with pointed head and a *distinct and quite long off-white or buff-white supercilium* which contrasts with *rather dark, diffusely streaked crown* and cheeks. Mantle/back diffusely dark-streaked, but in the field often appear almost uniform brown. In flight, from behind, shows *warmer yellow-brown rump*. Crown darker at sides, creating slightly lighter brown broad central band, on some juveniles so distinct that confusion can arise with Aquatic Warbler (which see). Cf. also Moustached Warbler and Pallas's Grasshopper Warbler. – Juvenile: As a rule, distinct dark spots on breast and fresher wing than adult.

VOICE Anxiety-call a muffled, dry rolling 'errrrr'. Alarm a sharp 'tsek!'. Song, often in brief song-flight, loud, long sequences of not very varied *excited notes* now and then relieved by *rapid cascades of trills and whistles* and occasional interwoven mimicry (e.g. of Coot, Wood Sandpiper, Yellow Wagtail), e.g.'zrüzrü-trett zrüzrüzrü-trett zrüzrüzrü psit trutrutru-pürrrrrrrrrrrurrrrrr **vi-vi-vi** lülülü ze**tre** ze**tre**...'.

Aquatic Warbler *Acrocephalus paludicola* **V**(**P**)∗∗

L 11½–13 cm. Breeds only in open, waterlogged sedge meadows and prefers just foot-high vegetation, so now rare (after so much draining); main known stronghold in E Poland. Summer visitor, winters in W Africa, passes through Holland and Morocco; regular autumn vagrant in Britain. Rather shy and retiring. Nests in sedge tussock.

IDENTIFICATION Like Sedge Warbler in shape and general appearance; differs as follows: *narrow, distinct yellow median crown-stripe* (much more prominent and narrower than on any juvenile Sedge); two clear *yellow-buff bands along mantle-sides*, and *heavier black streaking on upperparts*; normally *paler and more yellowish-white overall impression* (but at distance and in evening light nevertheless surprisingly dark and Sedge Warbler-like); *pale lores*, so supercilium looks broad at front (juveniles and some adults; other adults have slightly darker loral stripe). Silhouette when singing distinctive: tail pointing down, *neck extended* to the limit with each verse. – Sexes alike. Adult almost always has breast and flanks finely streaked, whereas juvenile does not.

VOICE Call a clicking 'chack'. When anxious, a Sedge Warbler-like 'errrr'. Alarm short, hoarse 'tscht' notes (like a grasshopper!). Song (mostly in evening, up to dusk; mainly perched, only seldom in short song-flight) like a sleepy Sedge Warbler; almost all verses start with a churring 'trrrrr' (like anxiety-call), immediately followed by a series of whistles, 'jüjüjüjü' or 'dididdidi (a bit like Wood Sandpiper, but shriller and 'looser'); for long periods, utters nothing but churr and whistle... pause... churr and whistle... etc.; at times more complex verses with 4–5 motifs.

Moustached Warbler *Acrocephalus melanopogon* **V**∗∗∗

L 12–13½ cm. Breeds, mostly locally and sparingly, in reedbeds, often adjoining small open patches and mixed with bulrush stands. Fond of dense areas of fallen reed, where it often hops along low down. Mainly resident in W, migratory in E (present at Austrian breeding sites mostly Mar–Sep). Does not perform song-flight. Nests low down in reeds.

IDENTIFICATION Quite similar to Sedge Warbler, yet distinctive when seen well. Is marginally larger and more compact. Often hops on ground or near water, frequently flicks tail and raises it slightly. Differs from Sedge Warbler in: *short primary projection* (at most a third of tertials, two-thirds on Sedge); *whiter supercilium, which is squarer-ended and broader at rear, more uniformly dark crown* (can appear unstreaked brownish-black in field) and cheeks, lower edge of cheeks with *hint of narrow black moustachial stripe; reddish-brown tone in fresh plumage* (spring), especially on rump, nape, neck- and breast-sides; whiter underparts (not buffy yellow-white). – Variation: In E Turkey, Caucasus and Middle East (ssp. *mimicus*) more like Sedge Warbler, with greyer-brown, less rusty plumage and paler, more streaked crown.

VOICE Call a muffled, 'throaty' clicking 'treck' (thus *thicker voice* than Sedge Warbler, rather like Stonechat). Variations include shorter 'trk', which in excitement turns into fast clicking series, 'tk-tk-tk-tk-...'; also rolling 'trrrt'. Song like Reed Warbler's but more animated, a little faster, softer and more varied, and best recognized by recurring *series of Nightingale-like rising whistled notes*.

Zitting Cisticola *Cisticola juncidis* **V**∗∗∗

(Alternative name: FAN-TAILED WARBLER.) L 10–11 cm. Breeds in open flat country in warm climates in tall grass or in fields; prefers drier terrain and avoids trees. Resident. Nests low in vegetation. (Map on p. 292.)

IDENTIFICATION *Small*, podgy and *short-tailed*, sandybrown and *dark-streaked*. *Undulating song-flight* can at times reveal that *tail is strongly rounded* and below is dark and *broadly tipped white*, also that *wings are short and rounded*. On perched bird, the short tail eliminates confusion with Graceful Prinia (which it otherwise most resembles). In breeding season, sexes separable: ♂ has black bill and paler head-sides, ♀ light brown bill and more uniformly dark head.

VOICE Call a loud 'chipp!'. Song a monotonous repetition of one short, sharp note, uttered for long periods (usually in wide circling song-flight) with regular and barely second-long pauses, 'dzip... dzip... dzip... dzip... dzip...'.

Sedge Warbler

Aquatic Warbler

Moustached Warbler

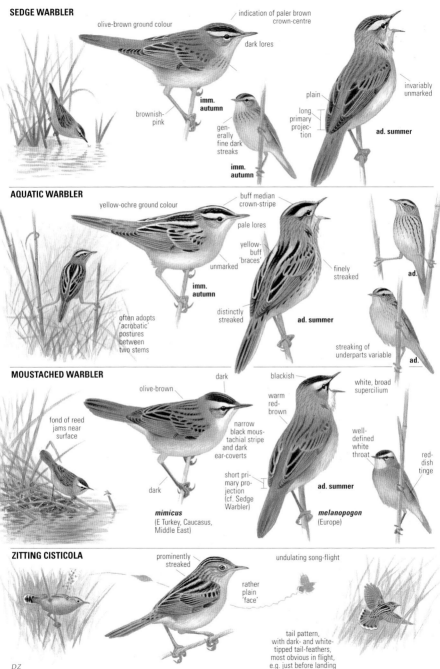

SEDGE WARBLER

olive-brown ground colour

indication of paler brown crown-centre

dark lores

imm. autumn

brownish-pink

generally fine dark streaks

imm. autumn

plain

long primary projection

invariably unmarked

ad. summer

AQUATIC WARBLER

yellow-ochre ground colour

buff median crown-stripe

pale lores

yellow-buff 'braces'

unmarked

imm. autumn

finely streaked

ad.

often adopts 'acrobatic' postures between two stems

distinctly streaked

ad. summer

streaking of underparts variable

ad.

MOUSTACHED WARBLER

dark

olive-brown

blackish

warm red-brown

white, broad supercilium

fond of reed jams near surface

narrow black moustachial stripe and dark ear-coverts

well-defined white throat

reddish tinge

dark

short primary projection (cf. Sedge Warbler)

mimicus (E Turkey, Caucasus, Middle East)

ad. summer

melanopogon (Europe)

ZITTING CISTICOLA

prominently streaked

undulating song-flight

rather plain 'face'

tail pattern, with dark- and white-tipped tail-feathers, most obvious in flight, e.g. just before landing

DZ

(Common) Grasshopper Warbler *Locustella naevia* m**B**3
L 12½–13½ cm. Breeds in habitats with low, thick vegetation, often in tussocky marshland beside lakes (where tussocks tallest), in young conifer plantations or clear-felled areas, among tall grass and herbage with scattered bushes, often along riversides. Summer visitor (in Britain & Ireland May–Jul), winters so far as known in tropical Africa. Except when singing, very hard to see; keeps well concealed and creeps in grass like a mouse. Nests low in dense vegetation.

IDENTIFICATION A Sedge Warbler-sized, grey-brown bird with no striking plumage features. *Dark-spotted above on olive-tinged grey-brown* ground; off-white or sometimes warmer buffy yellow-white below, *unspotted* or with variable amount of *small dark spots on throat* and upper breast (many have a few spots only; rarely, showing dense heavy spotting, and in addition some diffuse streaking on flanks, producing similarity to Lanceolated Warbler; cf. latter). Distinguished from Sedge Warbler by: *lack of prominent, whitish supercilium* (has just faint suggestion); *off-white*, diffusely *streaked undertail-coverts*; olive-tinged grey-brown and weakly dark-spotted *rump not contrasting appreciably with back*; evenly fine-streaked crown without darker sides. Legs pinkish, bill rather dark. Tertials dark, with bases broadly and diffusely edged brown. Sexes alike. In autumn, juveniles often yellowish below while adults are off-white.

VOICE Call a sharp, piercing 'psvitt'. Song peculiar, an insect-like, *mechanical, dry ringing or whirring* reel, 'sir'r'r'r'r'r'r'r'r'...', heard mostly from late dusk and at night, and which continues for a minute or more. The sound may be likened to an alarm clock with muffled clapper; volume varies somewhat depending on how bird turns its head. (Three congeners have similar song: Lanceolated, Savi's and River Warblers. See those for differences.)

Lanceolated Warbler *Locustella lanceolata* **V**∗∗
L 11½–12½ cm. Breeds in swampy pine forest with rank undergrowth, among willows and herbage in waterlogged clearings in the taiga, also in more open habitats such as extensive marshes with rushes and scattered bushes. Habits as Grasshopper Warbler, but winters in SE Asia and does not arrive at breeding sites until end of May/Jun.

IDENTIFICATION *Small and compact*, looks *shorter-necked* and *shorter-tailed* than Grasshopper and Pallas's Grasshopper Warblers, at times also a mite bigger-headed. Coloration much as Grasshopper Warbler, i.e. usually has grey tone to the *dull brown* plumage, but is always *more heavily black-streaked*, both above and below. In typical plumage, *throat, breast and flanks distinctly and narrowly streaked black* (least obvious on throat); occasional heavily streaked Grasshopper Warblers have *dense spotting on* central/lower throat and upper breast (almost forming bib) and have some *smudgy long streaks* on flanks. Other Lanceolated (often juvs.) have only sparse streaking on throat/breast and can be unstreaked on flanks, much resemble Grasshopper Warblers; identified by markings being in form of *sparse, distinct streaks* (not more diffuse, rounded spots) and these being *more evenly distributed both on throat and on breast*. Note, for all Lanceolated: *tertials are almost black with narrow, sharply defined and complete brownish-white fringes* (on a few, outer web has slightly broader fringe, but this always sharply defined, not diffuse as on Grasshopper Warbler); *undertail-coverts rusty yellow-buff* or buffish-white, appearing unstreaked or with distinct black shaft spots.

VOICE Call a clicking 'chick'. Song like Grasshopper Warbler's but differs in: slightly higher pitch; slightly faster tempo; on average shorter verses (rarely over 1 min.; Grasshopper often 5–10 min.); *sharper, more piercing* sound; *hint of River Warbler-like shuttling*, 'zizizizizizi...', unlike Grasshopper's more uniform and dry reeling. (Although, rarely, aberrant Grasshopper Warblers with vocal defect occur which can sound very similar!)

Pallas's Grasshopper Warbler *Locustella certhiola* **V**∗∗∗
L 13–14 cm. Breeds in Siberia, parts of Central Asia, Mongolia and farther eastwards, in soggy grassland with dense shrubbery or in thick riverside vegetation (reeds, rushes, willows), in damp forest clearings or bog margins etc. Very rare autumn vagrant in Europe. Mostly remains concealed low down in vegetation, difficult to see.

IDENTIFICATION Can be described as something between Grasshopper Warbler and Sedge Warbler. Has *pale supercilium* which is a touch more prominent than Grasshopper's, but nothing like Sedge's long and well-marked one. Ground colour of *upperparts* usually a shade more *reddish-brown*, not so olive-grey as Grasshopper's, and dark spotting on crown, back and uppertail-coverts averages heavier (though some similar), while rump is often contrastingly reddish-brown and unstreaked (quite like Sedge Warbler). Most important features: *tail-feathers have white tips* (can be worn off, or be slightly more diffuse on some juveniles) with dark subterminal marks; tertials dark brown with sharply defined light brown edge to outer web and (almost without exception) a *white spot near tip of inner web*; *undertail-coverts* entirely (or almost so) *unstreaked, rusty-buff* (with whiter tips). Underparts plain off-white with only faint yellow-buff wash to breast and flanks (adult), or distinctly yellow-buff with warmer tone to throat, breast and flanks and with breast spotted.

VOICE Several different calls, including clicking 'chick', shorter ticking 'pt', dry rolling 'trrrrrt'. Song not monotonously mechanical and insect-like as with most congeners, but a verse made up, as with an *Acrocephalus*, of fast repetitions of different motifs, e.g. 'tri-tri prt-prt chiv-chiv-chiv srrrrrt **sivih-sivih-sivih**; song rather soft, but the final 'sivih' notes are quite loud and carry far.

Grasshopper Warbler

Lanceolated Warbler

Pallas's Grasshopper Warbler

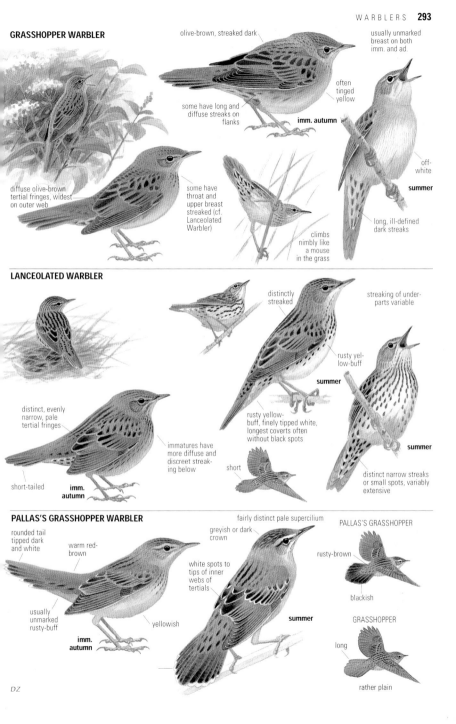

GRASSHOPPER WARBLER

olive-brown, streaked dark

usually unmarked breast on both imm. and ad.

often tinged yellow

imm. autumn

some have long and diffuse streaks on flanks

diffuse olive-brown tertial fringes, widest on outer web

some have throat and upper breast streaked (cf. Lanceolated Warbler)

off-white

summer

climbs nimbly like a mouse in the grass

long, ill-defined dark streaks

LANCEOLATED WARBLER

distinctly streaked

streaking of under-parts variable

rusty yellow-buff

summer

distinct, evenly narrow, pale tertial fringes

rusty yellow-buff, finely tipped white, longest coverts often without black spots

immatures have more diffuse and discreet streaking below

short-tailed

imm. autumn

short

summer

distinct narrow streaks or small spots, variably extensive

PALLAS'S GRASSHOPPER WARBLER

fairly distinct pale supercilium

greyish or dark crown

PALLAS'S GRASSHOPPER

rounded tail tipped dark and white

warm red-brown

rusty-brown

white spots to tips of inner webs of tertials

blackish

usually unmarked rusty-buff

yellowish

summer

imm. autumn

GRASSHOPPER

long

rather plain

DZ

River Warbler *Locustella fluviatilis*   **V*****

L 14½–16 cm. Breeds in soggy young deciduous growth along rivers and at swamp edges; can thrive in small stands of dense and shady swamp forest (birch, willow, alder), but not in low shrubland. Summer visitor (mostly mid May–Aug), winters in E Africa. Shy and elusive (except when singing). Nests near ground in dense vegetation.

IDENTIFICATION A rather large, dark, elongate warbler with broad, rounded tail. *Upperparts are uniform dark grey-brown*, sometimes with slight olive-green tone. Underparts dirty white with olive-tinged brown-grey flanks. The only salient features are a *short and indistinct, off-white supercilium* and a contiguous pale eye-ring, *diffuse grey mottling* (of varying strength; some are poorly marked) *on upper breast* (sometimes lower throat, too), and *olive-brown undertail-coverts with broad whitish tips* (produce spotted impression). At close range, outer web of outermost long primary off-white, edge of wing curved, and undertail-coverts cover almost entire length of tail (features common to all *Locustella* species). Bill rather dark, legs pink. Sexes and ages usually inseparable in the field.

VOICE Calls not very distinctive, a 'zrr' and a throaty 'tschick'. Song, fortunately, much more characteristic, a remarkable machine-like shuttling which carries on with only short breaks from dusk to morning hours, 'zre-zre-zre-zre-zre-...' or 'dze-dze-dze-dze-dze-...'; some variation in tempo (usually rather sluggish) and pitch. The sound can be likened to that of a 'giant wartbider' (i.e. a bush cricket) or a powerful sewing-machine; at close range, a metallic overtone is audible.

Savi's Warbler *Locustella luscinioides*   **m**B5 / **V****

L 13½–15 cm. Breeds in extensive, tall reedbeds, less often in bulrushes or rushes or other dense waterside vegetation. Summer visitor (mid Apr–Aug/Sep), winters S of Sahara; very rare breeder in Britain & Ireland, only handful of localities. Moves about discreetly in cover, but not really shy. Nests low down in dense vegetation.

IDENTIFICATION Bearing in mind habitat (dense, tall reeds) and its uniform brown and off-white plumage, can be confused with Reed Warbler; like that species, it is red-brown above and has short, indistinct, pale supercilium. Differs in: *long pale reddish-brown undertail-coverts with diffusely paler tips* (usually look almost uniformly coloured in field, but some have pale tips distinct enough to create similarity to River Warbler; cf. latter); *curved wing-edge* (wing straighter on *Acrocephalus*) with *whitish outer web to outermost long primary*; *more uniform and slightly darker reddish-brown upperparts* (lacks Reed's usually contrasting warmer red-brown rump); brown-grey wash on

breast and tinge of reddish brown-grey on flanks (lacks Reed's buffy-yellow tones); broader tail with fine dark bars on upperside (requires good light and close view). Legs brownish grey-pink. – Variation: E populations (especially from Caspian Sea eastwards, ssp. *fusca*) have olive-grey cast above and are generally less red-brown, often have slightly stronger greyish tinge to breast and usually have more distinct pale tips to undertail-coverts, thus in several respects are closer to River Warbler.

VOICE Call a sharp, metallic 'pvitt!'. Song most like Grasshopper Warbler's, i.e. consists of an endless reeling, insect-like sound, given mainly at night. Differs, however (apart from fact that singer perches out in tall, dense reeds!), in *higher frequency, lower pitch* and in the noise, 'surrrrrrrrr...', sounding more of a *hard and noteless buzzing* than a high whirr. A possible confusion risk at distance and at night in S and C Europe is the mole-cricket. Song verses begin with an accelerating series of clicks which turn into the reel, 'pt... pt pt-ptptptsurrrrrr...'.

Cetti's Warbler *Cettia cetti*   **r**B4

L 13–14 cm. Breeds in dense, rather tall and often well-delimited vegetation, preferably near but not in water, e.g. in drier tall reeds with scattered bushes, stands of papyrus, willow, bamboo, various thick bushes etc.; sometimes breeds near human habitation, in thickly wooded parkland, beside reservoirs and canals etc. Mainly resident, but migratory in E. Generally keeps concealed in vegetation, often hops on ground or low down in shrubbery. Nests low down in dense vegetation.

IDENTIFICATION A medium-sized, rather compact warbler, *short-necked* and *broad-tailed*, with *short, strongly rounded wings*. Bill pointed. Plumage *uniform red-brown above*, dusky greyish-white below with rusty tinge on flanks and belly. Head pattern roughly as on Reed and Savi's Warblers, the two species which it superficially most resembles, i.e. has a *narrow and not particularly distinct pale supercilium* which is set off by dark lores and dark eye-stripe. Best identified by: body shape and *short primary projection*; *longer supercilium* than Reed and Savi's; faint *grey tone on ear-coverts and neck- and breast-sides* but slightly warmer (greyish) *red-brown, rather dark tone on lower flanks and belly*; *dark brown undertail-coverts* with narrow pale fringes; relatively *short undertail-coverts* reaching only halfway along tail. Lively and active, flicks wings and tail, often cocks tail. Sexes and ages alike.

VOICE Call an explosive, metallic 'plitt!' which may be repeated in series and turn into rattling 'plir'r'r'r'. Song consists of a *sudden and loud outburst* of metallic, clanging notes; rhythm characteristic: first 1–4 slightly tentative notes, usually with final one stressed, then a *half-stop* followed by a rapid series of groups of similar notes, at times dying at end, e.g. 'plitt, plitt-**plütt**!.. ti**chutt**-ti**chutt**-ti**chutt** chütt, chutt!' (or, why not: 'Listen!.... What's my name?...Cetti-Cetti-Cetti—that's it!').

River Warbler   Savi's Warbler   Cetti's Warbler

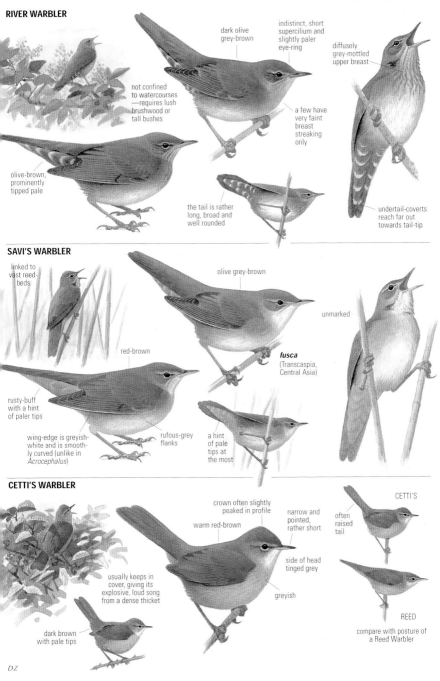

RIVER WARBLER

dark olive grey-brown

indistinct, short supercilium and slightly paler eye-ring

diffusely grey-mottled upper breast

not confined to watercourses —requires lush brushwood or tall bushes

a few have very faint breast streaking only

olive-brown, prominently tipped pale

the tail is rather long, broad and well rounded

undertail-coverts reach far out towards tail-tip

SAVI'S WARBLER

linked to vast reed-beds

olive grey-brown

unmarked

red-brown

fusca (Transcaspia, Central Asia)

rusty-buff with a hint of paler tips

wing-edge is greyish-white and is smoothly curved (unlike in *Acrocephalus*)

rufous-grey flanks

a hint of pale tips at the most

CETTI'S WARBLER

crown often slightly peaked in profile

warm red-brown

narrow and pointed, rather short

CETTI'S

often raised tail

side of head tinged grey

usually keeps in cover, giving its explosive, loud song from a dense thicket

greyish

dark brown with pale tips

REED

compare with posture of a Reed Warbler

DZ

(European) Reed Warbler *Acrocephalus scirpaceus* m**B**2

L 12½–14 cm. Breeds in reedbeds, especially dense and tall ones growing in a certain depth of water (but which need not be large); locally, e.g. Britain, extends into willowherb, rape fields, migrants also in scrub etc. Summer visitor (in Britain mostly mid Apr–Sep/Oct), winters in tropical Africa. Rather bold, inquisitive and mobile, easy to see. Nest basket-shaped, woven around a few reed stems at medium height.

IDENTIFICATION A typical *Acrocephalus*: pointed head with *flat forehead* and *long, slender bill*. Climbs nimbly on reed stems, and colours in fact match favoured habitat of previous year's reeds, i.e. *uniform brown above* and *buff-white below* with warmest tone on flanks and undertail-coverts. Has a short and rather indistinct pale *supercilium*, which normally *does not extend past eye*; lores dark. Brown colour of crown and mantle/back usually has slight olive-grey tinge, while *rump is somewhat lighter and warmer rusty-brown*. Sexes alike. In late summer, adult is somewhat worn and more grey-brown above and whitish below, juvenile warm rusty-brown above and saturated buff on flanks. (Cf. very similar Marsh and Blyth's Reed Warblers.) – Variation: Eastern birds (esp. E of Black Sea, ssp. *fuscus*) are slightly darker and greyer above and paler below, i.e. are more like Marsh, Blyth's Reed, Olivaceous and Savi's Warblers.

VOICE Call a short, unobtrusive 'che', sometimes slightly harder, almost clicking 'chk'. When agitated, drawn-out hoarse 'chreeh', thick rolling 'chrrrre' and disyllabic 'trr-rr'. Song, heard most at dusk and dawn, is 'chatty' and slow-paced, consists mostly of jittery notes which are repeated 2–3 times, interrupted by occasional mimicry or whistles, e.g. 'trett trett trett **ti**rri **ti**rri trü trü **ti**e tre tre vi-vü-vu tre tre trü trü **ti**rri **ti**rri...'. Now and then tempo is raised, but Reed Warbler never achieves the real crescendo of Sedge Warbler.

Marsh Warbler *Acrocephalus palustris* m**B**4–5 / **P**4

L 13–15 cm. Breeds in rank herbaceous vegetation, often in damp stands of meadowsweet, nettle, cow parsley etc., often beside ditches or soggy wasteland, sometimes on fringe of reedbed if growing on slightly drier ground and mixed with herbage. Summer visitor (in Britain rare and local, mid Apr–Sep), winters in tropical Africa. Unobtrusive habits.

IDENTIFICATION Very like Reed Warbler. Told by: *song*; breeding habitat (few exceptions); slightly *shorter bill* and *more rounded head shape*, gives 'kinder' appearance; often even less distinct pale supercilium, but slightly more prominent pale eye-ring; in spring, crown and mantle rather light grey-brown with faint *green cast*; somewhat more *yellowish below*; on average somewhat longer primary projection and more distinct white tips to each primary (but quite a few Marsh and Reed Warblers similar in this

respect). – Juvenile: Warmer brown above with rusty-yellow rump, thus *extremely like Reed Warbler*; legs light yellowish-pink (light brown-grey on juv. Reed).

VOICE Calls similar to Reed Warbler's. Song, heard most from nightfall to dawn, a stream, broken by only brief pauses, of whirring, excitable and whistling notes with for the most part *high voice* and *furious tempo*, which on closer study proves to consist almost exclusively of *expert mimicry* (often e.g. Blue Tit, Blackbird, Chaffinch, Magpie, Barn Swallow, Linnet, Common Gull, Quail, Bee-eater, Jackdaw). Now and then longer passages of fast, dry trills occur, 'prri-prri-prrü-prri-...', and hoarse 'ti-**zaih**, ti-**zaih**'. Tempo varies, slower passages of listless repetitions can at times recall Blyth's Reed Warbler, but speed soon picks up again.

Blyth's Reed Warbler *Acrocephalus dumetorum* V***

L 12½–14 cm. Breeds in scrub on open ground, in overgrown clearings in deciduous forest, in bushes along riversides etc. Not attracted to reeds or waterlogged ground. Summer visitor (in Finland mostly late May–Aug), winters in India. Habits as Marsh Warbler. (Map on p. 298.)

IDENTIFICATION Resembles Reed and Marsh Warblers. Told by: *song*; habitat (few borderline cases); songpost in bush or lower tree (not in reeds or herbage; few exceptions); somewhat *more obvious and longer pale supercilium, extends just beyond eye*; rather *short primary projection; legs rather dark*, brown-grey (never light pinkish); *long bill* and *flat forehead* as Reed Warbler; *greyish-brown upperparts*, and flanks more olive-grey than buff. Some have markedly uniform brown wing, without contrasting dark centres to tertials, alula and greater coverts. – Juvenile: Rusty-toned above (like Reed).

VOICE Call a somewhat variable clicking 'zeck', often repeated 2–3 times, as well as a rolling 'zrrrrt'. Song characteristic (safest indication in field identification), given mostly at night, varied groups of notes, often with masterful mimicry inserted, which are *repeated at slow pace 3–5* times, sometimes even up to 10 times; often *the clicking call is stuck in between each repetition*. Neat scale exercises such as 'loh-lü-**lii**-a' (steps up the scale) recur regularly.

Paddyfield Warbler *Acrocephalus agricola* V***

L 12–13½ cm. Breeds in reeds (sometimes also bulrush and other plants), seemingly having broadly the same habitat requirements as Reed Warbler. Summer visitor (mostly May–Aug), winters in India. Nests low in reeds. (Map on p. 298.)

IDENTIFICATION *Smaller* than Reed Warbler, with somewhat *shorter bill* and *longer tail*. Colour varies but is usually *paler* brown than Reed, rusty-coloured in fresh plumage, more grey-brown when worn. Facial expression different owing to short bill which has *black distal area on straw-yellow lower mandible*, also to *uniformly broad, long pale supercilium*, sometimes accentuated by hint of dark crown-side edge. Most have warm *rusty yellow-brown rump* (worn birds can be grey-brown; cf. Booted Warbler) and *short primary projection*.

VOICE Call variable, 'check', 'chre', 'zack', somewhat feebler than e.g. Reed Warbler. When nervous, a weak rolling 'cherrr'. Song most like Marsh's, a fast stream consisting mostly of mimicry; voice, however, weaker, tempo constantly high, and the song more 'bouncing', and lacking hoarse drawn-out sounds and dry trilling runs.

Reed Warbler   Marsh Warbler

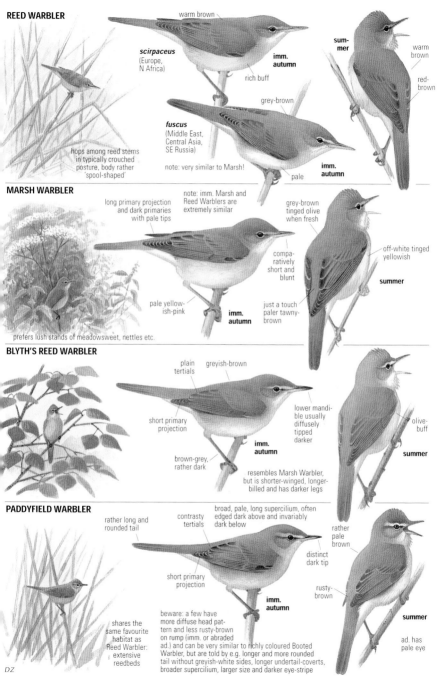

REED WARBLER

warm brown

scirpaceus
(Europe,
N Africa)

**imm.
autumn**

rich buff

sum-
mer

warm
brown

red-
brown

grey-brown

fuscus
(Middle East,
Central Asia,
SE Russia)

note: very similar to Marsh!

pale

**imm.
autumn**

hops among reed stems
in typically crouched
posture, body rather
'spool-shaped'

MARSH WARBLER

note: imm. Marsh and
Reed Warblers are
extremely similar

long primary projection
and dark primaries
with pale tips

grey-brown
tinged olive
when fresh

off-white tinged
yellowish

compa-
ratively
short and
blunt

summer

pale yellow-
ish-pink

**imm.
autumn**

just a touch
paler tawny-
brown

prefers lush stands of meadowsweet, nettles etc.

BLYTH'S REED WARBLER

plain
tertials

greyish-brown

short primary
projection

lower mandi-
ble usually
diffusely
tipped
darker

olive-
buff

**imm.
autumn**

summer

brown-grey,
rather dark

resembles Marsh Warbler,
but is shorter-winged, longer-
billed and has darker legs

PADDYFIELD WARBLER

rather long and
rounded tail

contrasty
tertials

broad, pale, long supercilium, often
edged dark above and invariably
dark below

rather
pale
brown

distinct
dark tip

short primary
projection

rusty-
brown

**imm.
autumn**

summer

shares the
same favourite
habitat as
Reed Warbler:
extensive
reedbeds

beware: a few have
more diffuse head pat-
tern and less rusty-brown
on rump (imm. or abraded
ad.) and can be very similar to richly coloured Booted
Warbler, but are told by e.g. longer and more rounded
tail without greyish-white sides, longer undertail-coverts,
broader supercilium, larger size and darker eye-stripe

ad. has
pale eye

DZ

Great Reed Warbler *Acrocephalus arundinaceus* **V**＊＊

L 16–20 cm. Breeds in tall, dense and preferably extensive reedbeds, often on edge by gaps or open water; if necessary makes do with smaller reedbeds, e.g. along canals and dykes. Summer visitor (mostly May–Aug in N of range), winters in tropical Africa. Basket-shaped nest woven around several strong reed stems at medium height above water.

IDENTIFICATION In many respects a *larger version of Reed Warbler*, similar in colour (brown above, buff-white below) and with same habitat and same type of song. Apart from size and gruffer voice, differs in: proportionately somewhat *larger head and bill* (thick and long like thrush's); almost always *dark spot at tip of lower mandible* (never shown by Reed); slightly longer tail; somewhat longer primary projection (with clear white tips to primaries); often slightly more distinct, *broader pale supercilium* and on average *darker lores and eye-stripe*; often a trifle paler and more greybrown nape/hindneck. At closest range, a few fine grey streaks sometimes visible on lower throat/upper breast. Legs pinky-brown or brown-grey. Sexes alike. – Adult late summer: Usually somewhat worn, with lighter brown-grey cast above and whiter below. Primaries worn, brownish-grey. – Juvenile: Plumage uniformly fresh, warm rusty-brown above and buffish below. Primaries fresh, dark with pale tips.

VOICE Call less often heard, a coarse clicking with slightly 'thick' voice, 'kshack', or with more audible r-sound, 'krrack'. In anxiety, utters hard rolling 'krrrrr'. Song roughly as Reed's in composition, with various repeated hoarse notes, but is very loud, far-carrying, recognized by gruff, croaking voice and by recurring series of repeated shrill falsetto sounds, e.g. 'trr trr karra-karra-karra **krie-krie-krie** trr-trr-**kie-kie**'.

Clamorous Reed Warbler *Acrocephalus stentoreus* —

L 16–18 cm. Breeds in dense stands of papyrus, secondarily also in reedbeds, bulrushes, maize and other dense vegetation tall enough to hide a man, in association with water or at least marshland. Within the region mostly resident. Nest similar to Great Reed Warbler's.

IDENTIFICATION Resembles Great Reed Warbler in size, song and habitat (although, unlike Great Reed, prefers papyrus if offered a choice), but differs in several ways in terms of shape and plumage details. Clamorous Reed gives a quite different impression owing to its *shorter, rounded wings* (*short primary projection* when perched) and its *longer and more rounded tail* and *somewhat longer and*, especially, *narrower bill*. Differences in proportions are visible not least in flight, when it looks *shorter-bodied*. Brown above, roughly similar to Great Reed, but generally darker below. In addition, a less common dark (melanis-

tic) morph occurs in Middle East, as well as intermediates. Usually *upperparts are rather dark red-brown* and *underparts shabby brownish-buff with just slightly paler throat* (colours can recall Savi's Warbler rather than Great Reed). The buff-white *supercilium* is sometimes shorter and in particular narrower and thereby less prominent than on Great Reed, and *lores and eye-stripe are not so dark*. Dark individuals often lack supercilium altogether, also have darker bill (almost like young Starlings). Legs greyish.

VOICE Similar to Great Reed's, especially calls, a slightly 'thick' 'track' and, when agitated, a hard rolling 'trrrrr'. Song gruff-voiced like Great Reed's, but verses *more tentative* in composition and have *more uncertain pattern* ('chacking' like Fieldfares before dawn!), and *shrill falsetto notes are mostly given singly*, not in fast series as in Great Reed; a typical verse might go 'track, track, track karra-**kru**-kih karra-**kru**-kih chivi **trü** chivi **chih**'.

Thick-billed Warbler *Acrocephalus aedon* **V**＊＊＊

L 16–17½ cm. Breeds in S Siberia in dense vegetation of willows, young birch etc. beside taiga bogs, also in young growth in clear-fell with rank shrubbery. Winters in India. Extremely rare autumn vagrant in Europe.

IDENTIFICATION Like a cross between Great Reed and Garden Warblers, i.e. an *Acrocephalus* not quite the size of Great Reed, with *short, stubby bill* and no particular plumage features. *Head appears rather big and round in shape*, and tail-base is fairly narrow but *tail long and rounded at tip*. The heavy bill has distinctly downcurved culmen at tip. Plumage is greyish-brown above with slightly *warmer red-brown rump and tail-base* (in flight can recall Nightingale or Thrush Nightingale, since tail is not only rusty but also long and rounded), and is dirty white below with buff tinge to breast, flanks and undertail-coverts. Lacks prominent supercilium, has just *light grey lores* and diffuse buffy grey-white eye-ring. Crown is slightly warmer brown, on many creating *suggestion of brown cap*. Primary projection medium-long. Legs brownish-grey or blue-grey. Rather sluggish in actions, often hops in forward-crouched posture with tail lowered (can bring to mind a babbler).

VOICE Call a clicking 'tshack' or 'chack', often given in series, varying in volume, sometimes powerful. Occasionally a hoarse Red-backed Shrike-like 'veht' in alarm (mimicry?). Song a *fast, loud stream of mimicry* of other species supplemented with twittering and excitable sounds, many calls repeated 2–3 times; most like Marsh and Icterine Warblers owing to tempo, mimicry and powerful voice; lacks Marsh's harsh, repeated 'ti-**zaih**' and very fastest runs of dry whirring trills, and is often *harder-voiced*; lacks Icterine's whining nasal notes.

Great Reed Warbler   Clamorous Reed Warbler   Blyth's Reed Warbler(See p. 296.)   Paddyfield Warbler (See p. 296.)

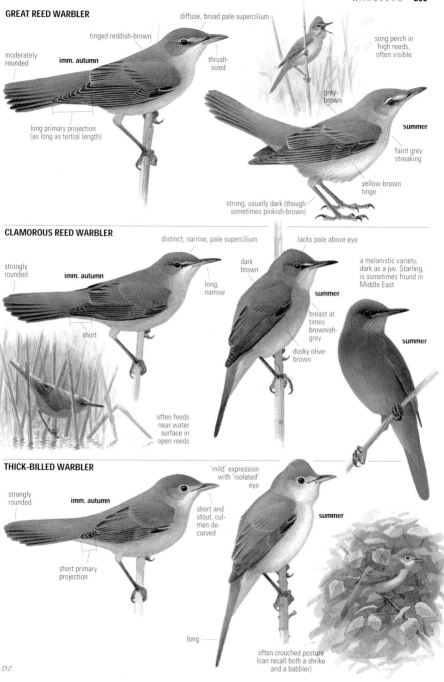

GREAT REED WARBLER

diffuse, broad pale supercilium

tinged reddish-brown

song perch in high reeds, often visible

moderately rounded

imm. autumn

thrush-sized

grey-brown

summer

faint grey streaking

long primary projection (as long as tertial length)

yellow-brown tinge

strong, usually dark (though sometimes pinkish-brown)

CLAMOROUS REED WARBLER

distinct, narrow, pale supercilium

lacks pale above eye

strongly rounded

imm. autumn

dark brown

a melanistic variety, dark as a juv. Starling, is sometimes found in Middle East

long, narrow

summer

breast at times brownish-grey

short

dusky olive-brown

summer

often feeds near water surface in open reeds

THICK-BILLED WARBLER

'mild' expression with 'isolated' eye

strongly rounded

imm. autumn

short and stout, culmen de-curved

summer

short primary projection

long

often crouched posture (can recall both a shrike and a babbler)

DZ

Icterine Warbler *Hippolais icterina* **P**4

L 12–13½ cm. Breeds in woodland, both in damp but open deciduous forest with undergrowth and clearings and in patches of pine forest in cultivated tracts (but then needs some deciduous trees in territory); also found in birch clumps in pastureland, in parks and well-wooded gardens. Summer visitor, winters in tropical Africa; passage migrant in Britain & Ireland, mostly E and S coasts (Aug–Oct, few in spring). Keeps high in treetops, hard to see. Nest suspended in branch fork, usually 1–4 m up.

IDENTIFICATION A typical *Hippolais* warbler in shape, with *broad-based, rather heavy bill*, quite large head (often with crown-feathers raised), long wings (*primary projection about equal to tertial length*, and emarginations on outer webs level with tertial tip or *just outside* this; cf. Melodious Warbler), and fairly short, *square-ended tail*. *Greyish-green above*, a shade paler than Willow Warbler, *uniform light yellow below* (most obvious in spring, more washed out in late summer). Characteristic are: *pale lores* and contiguous with these rather indistinct yellow-white supercilium, pale eye-ring and fairly *pale, yellowish-pink bill-side*; pale edges to tertials and secondaries create *pale panel on folded wing*, most obvious in spring, often almost entirely worn off on autumn adult. *Primaries dark grey with clear pale tips*. *Legs* greyish, often *blue-grey*. Sexes alike. – Juvenile: Upperparts have faint brown tinge, are not quite so green as on adult, and pale wing-panel is more buffy-yellow (and therefore not quite so prominent). Underparts are usually paler yellow (can appear whitish in field).

VOICE Call at breeding site a cheerful, melodic trisyllabic 'teh-teh-lüüit'. Silent on passage, but occasionally a clicking 'teck'. In anxiety, 'teck' or 'te te te...' in short series. Song *loud, fast*, drawn out, varied, spiced with imitations of other species. Best recognized by recurrent *nasal, shrill note*s, e.g. 'gie gie...'. Also recognized by the typical call being interwoven into the verse. Repetitions (often 2–4) are more common than in Marsh Warbler, and tempo slower.

Melodious Warbler *Hippolais polyglotta* **P**4

L 12–13 cm. Replaces Icterine Warbler in SW Europe and breeds in similar habitats (often found in stands of willow, white poplar, acacia and oak), but also in lower vegetation such as shrubbery (bramble, raspberry, tree heath, tamarisk, holm oak) with scattered trees. Summer visitor, winters in W Africa; passage migrant in Britain & Ireland, mostly S and W coasts (Aug–Oct, few in spring). Nest as Icterine's.

IDENTIFICATION Like Icterine Warbler, and solitary birds on passage require close study. In shape a trifle more plump and 'more kindly-looking', with *subtly shorter bill* and clearly shorter and less pointed wing (*primary projection*

between half and two-thirds of tertial length*, and emarginations on outer webs situated *just inside* tertial tip; cf. Icterine). Plumage similar, but upperparts a shade more brownish-green, not so greyish, and underparts are often pale yellow with a faint buff-brown suffusion. In the field, it nevertheless often looks *pale buffy yellow-white below* (and can even be confused with e.g. Marsh Warbler). Has *pale lores*, eye-ring and bill-side and indistinct supercilium, exactly as Icterine. However, the *wing is more uniform in colour*, and pale edges to tertials and secondaries are usually almost entirely (at times fully) abraded. *Primaries often slightly worn and brown-grey*, almost invariably lack distinct pale tips. *Legs* greyish, *often somewhat brownish* but occasionally almost blue-grey as on Icterine. Sexes alike. – Juvenile: Pale wing-panel brownish-yellow and moderately contrasting. Primaries fresh and slightly darker brown-grey.

VOICE At breeding site gives various short clicking calls, e.g. 'tett', 'tre-te-te-tü', drawn-out series of 'te-te-te-te-te-...' and faster sparrow-like chattering 'tr'r'r'r'r'rt'. Rather silent on passage. Song *babbling*, drawn-out verses at high speed, at times lightning-fast and with fragments of mimicry (then Marsh Warbler-like), sometimes not quite so fast and with somewhat shrill tone (when Icterine-like), sometimes simpler in structure, more shuttling, excitable and nasal (then like Olivaceous Warbler; real confusion risk).

Olive-tree Warbler *Hippolais olivetorum* —

L 16–18 cm. Breeds in open forest with scrubby clearings, in tall maquis (holm oak, cork oak) or olive or almond groves etc., often on slopes. Summer visitor (mostly early May–Aug), winters in tropical Africa. Keeps well hidden, hard to catch sight of. Nests in dense bush or low tree.

IDENTIFICATION *Very big* (Great Reed Warbler size) and elongated, with *long, powerful bill* and *sloping forehead* (unless crown-feathers raised). *Wings long* (primary projection = tertial length, thus much longer than on Upcher's Warbler), with *dark greyish-black primaries*. Plumage resembles Olivaceous and Upcher's, i.e. is *grey above* (sometimes with negligible green tinge to rump) and *off-white below* (often dusky grey on breast and flanks), but told by: more distinct *pale wing-panel* formed by whitish edges to longest tertial and inner secondaries (the white concentrated at middle of feathers), and *almost complete lack of pale supercilium* (has merely a whitish spot above lores and a diffuse pale eye-ring). Legs strong, (blue-)grey. Sexes alike.

VOICE Call a short, deep tongue-clicke, 'chack' (varies, can sound feebler). Alarm a throaty, slightly nasal chattering 'kerrekekekek', like a giant Blue Tit. Song gruff-voiced and raucous, the verses rather primitive in structure with cyclical repetition, can sound almost like an amplified Olivaceous Warbler at slow speed, e.g. 'chak chü chi-chak chira chuk chi-chi chak-era chak chü chi-chak...'; with tentative start to a verse, or during heat of midday, it can sound almost like a coarse-voiced Reed Warbler or a sleepy Great Reed Warbler.

Icterine Warbler

Melodious Warbler

Olive-tree Warbler

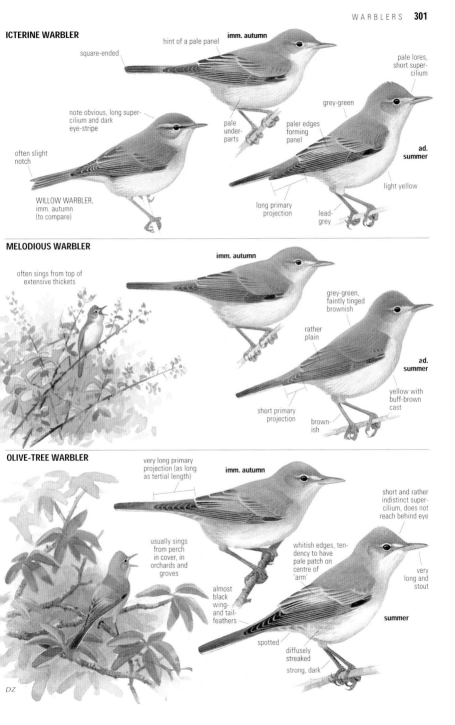

ICTERINE WARBLER

imm. autumn

hint of a pale panel

square-ended

pale lores,
short super-
cilium

grey-green

note obvious, long super-
cilium and dark
eye-stripe

pale
under-
parts

paler edges
forming
panel

often slight
notch

**ad.
summer**

WILLOW WARBLER,
imm. autumn
(to compare)

long primary
projection

lead-
grey

light yellow

MELODIOUS WARBLER

imm. autumn

often sings from top of
extensive thickets

grey-green,
faintly tinged
brownish

rather
plain

**ad.
summer**

short primary
projection

brown-
ish

yellow with
buff-brown
cast

OLIVE-TREE WARBLER

very long primary
projection (as long
as tertial length)

imm. autumn

short and rather
indistinct super-
cilium, does not
reach behind eye

usually sings
from perch
in cover, in
orchards and
groves

whitish edges, ten-
dency to have
pale patch on
centre of
'arm'

very
long and
stout

almost
black
wing-
and tail-
feathers

summer

spotted

diffusely
streaked

strong, dark

DZ

Upcher's Warbler *Hippolais languida* —

L 14–15 cm. Breeds in bushy areas (maquis with alder buckthorn, tamarisk, pistachio etc.) and cultivations in dry, barren terrain, often on slopes in river valleys or at higher levels. Summer visitor (May–Aug/Sep), winters in E Africa.

IDENTIFICATION Very like Olivaceous Warbler but a trifle *bigger*, with *somewhat longer bill, legs and tail*. Often *head shape a little more rounded*, with steeper forehead. Tail looks a little broader, too. Plumage is similarly grey above and off-white below, but differs in having upperparts purer grey and *tail-feathers and wing-tips somewhat darker greyish-black* (though paler brown when worn), in longest tertial and inner secondaries having paler greyish-white edges which create *suggestion of pale wing-panel*, also in lores being on average a shade paler and more smudgy grey. Has habit of *swinging tail*, including *sideways*, and *fanning it a little*. Often glides the final stage before landing on new perch. Olive-tree Warbler is bigger and lacks supercilium (see that species).

VOICE Call a hard clicking 'zack'. In anxiety, a fast, dry simmering 'trrrt'. Alarm a long series of 'soggy', slightly impure clicking calls, 'scheck scheck scheck…'; tempo varies. Song a *Hippolais*-type warble, delivered energetically and with nasal keynote, regularly repeated cycles of twitters mixed with high scraping whistles and isolated pieces of mimicry; pitch swings up and down, and tempo fluctuates. Repeats certain phrases several times (like Blyth's Reed Warbler); often sticks on high, 'bent' whistle, interspersed with rattle, '…vieh vieh vieh trrrt vieh vieh vieh chechecheche vieh…'.

Olivaceous Warbler *Hippolais pallida* V***

L 12–14 cm. Breeds in drier bushy country (holm oak, cistus, bramble) and in scrub forest in uncultivable areas (e.g. black poplar), as well as in moister strips along watercourses (osiers) and in gardens and cultivations. Summer visitor to region (mostly May–Aug), winters S of Sahara. Nests relatively low in dense bush or shortish tree.

IDENTIFICATION More like a washed-out Reed Warbler than like the congeneric Icterine Warbler; same size as Reed Warbler and has same pointed head with *flat forehead* and *long, narrow bill*, and virtually the same 'facial expression' with *dark lores, short pale supercilium* ending at rear edge of eye and *pale eye-ring*. Told from Reed Warbler (incl. from worn, greyish individuals of eastern race *fuscus*) by: habit of regularly *flicking tail downwards* when hopping among vegetation; grey or *grey-tinged brownish-green rump* (*never rusty yellow-brown* colour); practically *square-ended tail* with narrow *grey-white outer edges and white tips* to outer feathers; always *greyish upperparts* (olive-brown tone subordinate; Reed Warbler normally browner, but *fuscus* can be similarly grey) and *whiter underparts* (Reed yellowish-buff on flanks

and vent); *broader bill-base* seen head-on; usually somewhat shorter primary projection (a good half of tertial length against Reed's two-thirds, but many are similar); often better-defined and narrower pale line over lores (Reed's more blurred, but many the same); lower mandible yellowish (not pink as on Reed, though some similar); iris dark brown or grey-brown; legs grey-brown. Very like Booted Warbler of southern race *rama*, but differs in tail movements, longer primary projection and tendency towards paler edges and white tips to secondaries. – Variation: Birds in Iberia and NW Africa (ssp. *opaca*) are bigger, have more brown tone to the grey upperparts and have heavier bill; those in SE Europe and Middle East (*elaeica*) smaller, in fresh plumage more green-tinged above, and have narrower bill.

VOICE Call a clicking 'tsack' or 'chack', slightly 'thick' and a bit nasal in quality, like a cross between Blackcap and Garden Warbler. Rapid series of tongue-clicks (with nasal undertone) also heard, 'zet-zet-zet-zet-…', and a sparrow-like, muffled rattle, 'chr'r'r'r'r' and quiet 'chrrre'. (Several calls thus recall Melodious Warbler.) Song a *babbling*, somewhat *hoarse* warble with *nasal* undertone which continues quite *monotonously* in a *cyclical pattern*, rising and falling in pitch; tempo mostly slow, though rhythm slightly uneven. Does not mimic other species.

Booted Warbler *Hippolais caligata* V**

L 11–12½ cm. Breeds in low, thick vegetation (low bushes, often spiraea, woody herbage, sometimes in lower, denser trees) in natural steppe or in other open terrain, sometimes in damp meadows. Summer visitor, winters in India.

IDENTIFICATION *Smallest* of its genus. Russian and N Kazakhstan breeders (ssp. *caligata*) are small, with *short, rather dark bill*, have *fairly dark lores* and rather distinct but *short, pale supercilium*, can recall a *Phylloscopus* rather than *Hippolais*. In fresh plumage buffish-brown above, more greyish-brown when worn. Flanks often buffish. Told by: *pale-edged outer tail-feathers*; often a *dark shade on sides of forecrown* above supercilium; *broad bill-base* visible seen head-on; bill heavier than Chiffchaff's and with paler brownish-pink sides. Legs brownish-pink with darker toes. Occasionally bobs tail, but does not flick it downwards like Olivaceous Warbler. Can be confused with Paddyfield Warbler (see p. 296). – Variation: Birds breeding E of Caspian Sea and in Central Asia (*rama*; rarely seen in W Europe) very like Olivaceous (of race *elaeica*) in that they have somewhat longer bill and paler underparts. Note, however, *tail actions, short primary projection, long tail* and *lighter* (greyish-)*pink legs*.

VOICE Call a dry tongue-clicking 'zett', like two pebbles knocked together, somewhat less hard than that of Lesser Whitethroat. In anxiety, a dry rolling, muffled 'zerrrr'. Song a *fast, 'simmering'* verse of *c.* 2–6 sec. which 'boils over' with energy, a chirping and nasal, chattering *very rapid stream* of short, almost bouncing and 'trembling' notes. Does not contain mimicry. (Song of *rama* very similar, but has on average a slightly harder voice.)

Upcher's Warbler   Olivaceous Warbler   Booted Warbler

UPCHER'S WARBLER

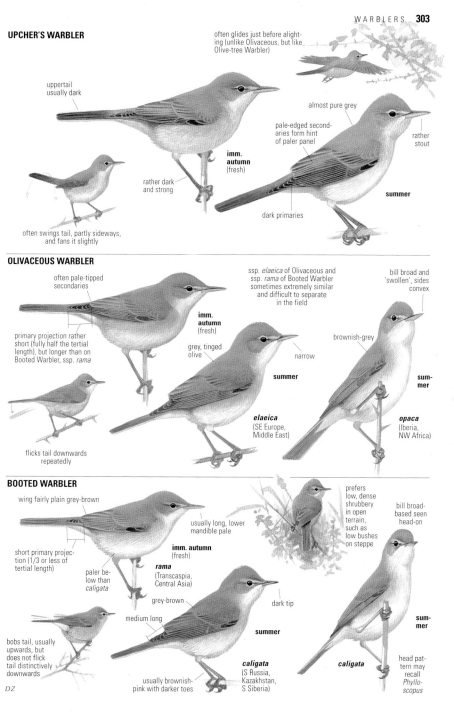

often glides just before alighting (unlike Olivaceous, but like Olive-tree Warbler)

uppertail usually dark

imm. autumn (fresh)

rather dark and strong

often swings tail, partly sideways, and fans it slightly

almost pure grey

pale-edged secondaries form hint of paler panel

rather stout

summer

dark primaries

OLIVACEOUS WARBLER

often pale-tipped secondaries

ssp. *elaeica* of Olivaceous and ssp. *rama* of Booted Warbler sometimes extremely similar and difficult to separate in the field

bill broad and 'swollen', sides convex

imm. autumn (fresh)

primary projection rather short (fully half the tertial length), but longer than on Booted Warbler, ssp. *rama*

grey, tinged olive

narrow

brownish-grey

summer

sum-mer

flicks tail downwards repeatedly

elaeica (SE Europe, Middle East)

opaca (Iberia, NW Africa)

BOOTED WARBLER

wing fairly plain grey-brown

prefers low, dense shrubbery in open terrain, such as low bushes on steppe

bill broad-based seen head-on

usually long, lower mandible pale

imm. autumn (fresh)

short primary projection (1/3 or less of tertial length)

rama (Transcaspia, Central Asia)

paler below than *caligata*

grey-brown

dark tip

medium long

summer

sum-mer

bobs tail, usually upwards, but does not flick tail distinctively downwards

caligata (S Russia, Kazakhstan, S Siberia)

usually brownish-pink with darker toes

caligata

head pattern may recall *Phylloscopus*

DZ

Willow Warbler *Phylloscopus trochilus*   m**B**1 / **P**

L 11–12½ cm. Breeds commonly wherever a few trees or taller bushes exist, is one of N Europe's commonest birds, with over 3 million in Britain & Ireland (despite this, it is rather unknown to non-birdwatchers); found in upland birch and willow zone, in all types of woodland and in copses and more wooded parks and gardens. Summer visitor (in Britain & Ireland Apr–Sep), winters in tropical Africa. Not shy. Domed nest on ground, lined with feathers.

IDENTIFICATION Small and neat in build, with thin legs and pointed bill. Lively and restless, flits about in tree crowns and bushes in search of insects. Most distinctive feature a *whitish supercilium. Greyish brown-green above* (green tone obvious in W Europe, birds in N Fenno-Scandia often being grey-brown), sometimes a shade paler and brighter green on rump. *Yellowish-white on throat and breast*, whiter on belly. *Legs* usually *brownish-pink* (occasionally dark brown-grey!). Lacks wing-bars and prominent pale edges to tertials (but odd few have such pale edges to secondaries as to create faint hint of pale wing-panel). Commonest confusion risk is Chiffchaff, but note, in addition to *voice*: normally brownish-pink or *light brown legs* (Chiffchaff's black or dark brown-grey); on average *longer and bolder pale supercilium* and *darker lores and eye-stripe*, giving more patterned 'face'; *ear-coverts* olive-grey but usually rather *pale just below eye* (Chiffchaff's more uniformly dark, so white lower eye-crescent stands out); on average somewhat *longer and heavier bill* with more obvious *yellow-pink at side/base*; somewhat more elongated shape, not so compact and chubby; longer primary projection (often *c.* three-quarters of tertial length; Chiffchaff half to two-thirds, but often difficult to judge reliably in field). – Juvenile/1st-winter: More *saturated pale yellow below* and on supercilium. Sometimes faint buff tinge to breast-side.

VOICE Call a soft whistle, disyllabic and upslurred, '**hu**itt'; varies a little (and some are more like Chiffchaff's faster and differently stressed 'hü**itt**'); very like Redstart's call, but a bit weaker. Song a frequently repeated soft whistling, somewhat descending verse *c.* 3 sec. long, e.g. 'sisisi-**vüy-vüy-vüy** svi-svi-vi tuuy tuuy tuuy si-si-**sviiy**-sü'; recognized by delightfully sweet voice with softly inflected notes, by fast, sharp opening notes and lower, often slightly stifled terminal notes.

Wood Warbler *Phylloscopus sibilatrix*   m**B**3

L 11–12½ cm. Breeds mainly in closed, very shady yet still rather open woods, often on slightly sloping ground. Favoured habitats are beech wood with at least sprinkling of younger trees, also oak forest, generally with minimal undergrowth (in N Europe, also mixed spruce and deciduous forest). Summer visitor (in Britain mostly mid Apr–Aug; rare Ireland), winters in tropical Africa. Rather

unobtrusive in habits, but not shy. Nest in ground vegetation like Willow Warbler's, but *without feather lining*.

IDENTIFICATION Size of Willow Warbler and similarly *elongated* in shape, but has *even longer and more pointed wings* (primary projection ≥ tertial length), which makes it look *shorter-tailed*. Told by saturated *dark moss-green upperparts* (at times tinged grey) with *contrasting pale tertial edges, yellow-green edges to remiges* and greater coverts, very *long and prominent yellow supercilium*, and *well-marked grey-green eye-stripe* from lores backwards. *Throat, ear-coverts and upper breast pale lemon-yellow* usually *abruptly demarcated from silky-white rest of underparts*. (Rare individuals occur with absence of yellow, sometimes also of green pigments, look brown and white; need to be identified by voice, size, shape and distinct head markings.) Cf. also Bonelli's Warbler.

VOICE Call a sharp 'zip'. When agitated, a muffled fluty note with slightly melancholy quality, 'tüh'. Song highly distinctive, an accelerating series of sharp, metallic, call-like notes ending in an almost pulsating trill, 'zip... zip... zip, zip, zip zip zip zip-zip-zip-zipzipzipzvürrrrürrrr' (often likened to a spinning coin on a marble slab). An alternative song is interposed now and again between the reeling song verses, a series of melancholy, initially intensified, soft notes, 'tüh tüh tüh-tüh-tüh-tüh' (vaguely like Willow Tit, but sequence is faster and the notes straighter).

Bonelli's Warbler *Phylloscopus bonelli*   **V**∗∗∗

L 10½–12 cm. Breeds in various types of woodland and at various altitudes, in N usually at lower levels in more open forest with some understorey, in S more often on mountain slopes in pine or oak forest. Summer visitor (mostly end Apr–Aug), winters in tropical Africa.

IDENTIFICATION Not quite size of Willow Warbler. Typical plumage features: *yellowish rump* which contrasts with duller back; *whitish underparts*, without obvious yellow or buff on throat, breast or belly; *primaries and tail-feathers edged light yellowish-green; tertials dark with contrasting whitish edges*; pale-edged secondaries produce *pale panel on folded wing; unbroken pale eye-ring; pale lores* and *light grey ear-coverts*, giving pale 'face' (but note that in field some show rather dark lores and distinct supercilium); darkish, brown-grey legs. – Variation: Birds from C Europe westward (ssp. *bonelli*) have slight brown cast to the green on crown and mantle/back. In E (*orientalis*), upperparts slightly more (greenish-)grey, and pale unmoulted greater coverts often form pale wing-bar. See also voice.

VOICE Usual call a distinctly disyllabic, whistled 'hü-**if**' (*bonelli*); or a monosyllabic, flat 'chipp' (*orientalis*), almost like House Sparrow fledgling (more muffled on passage, 'iss[t]'). Both races seem to use the disyllabic 'hü-**if**' in agitation. Song a simple repetition of one high note, e.g. 'svi-svi-svi-svi-svi-svi-svi-svi'; voice 'silvery' and laughing, a bit like Wood Warbler's. Some verses run in higher gear, almost like a trill from Blue Tit song, 'viviviviviviivi', commoner in E Europe (*orientalis*).

Willow Warbler   Wood Warbler   Bonelli's Warbler

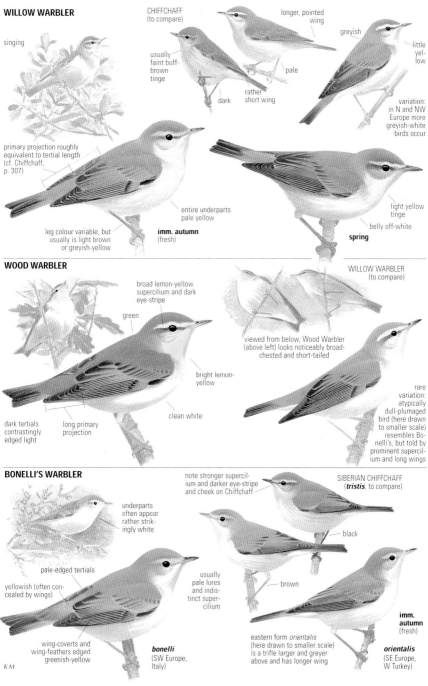

WILLOW WARBLER

singing

CHIFFCHAFF
(to compare)

longer, pointed wing

usually faint buff-brown tinge

dark

rather short wing

pale

greyish

little yellow

variation: in N and NW Europe more greyish-white birds occur

primary projection roughly equivalent to tertial length (cf. Chiffchaff, p. 307)

imm. autumn
(fresh)

entire underparts pale yellow

leg colour variable, but usually is light brown or greyish-yellow

light yellow tinge

belly off-white

spring

WOOD WARBLER

broad lemon-yellow supercilium and dark eye-stripe

green

bright lemon-yellow

clean white

dark tertials contrastingly edged light

long primary projection

WILLOW WARBLER
(to compare)

viewed from below, Wood Warbler (above left) looks noticeably broad-chested and short-tailed

rare variation: atypically dull-plumaged bird (here drawn to smaller scale) resembles Bonelli's, but told by prominent supercilium and long wings

BONELLI'S WARBLER

note stronger supercilium and darker eye-stripe and cheek on Chiffchaff

underparts often appear rather strikingly white

pale-edged tertials

yellowish (often concealed by wings)

wing-coverts and wing-feathers edged greenish-yellow

bonelli
(SW Europe, Italy)

usually pale lores and indistinct supercilium

SIBERIAN CHIFFCHAFF
(**tristis**, to compare)

black

brown

imm. autumn
(fresh)

eastern form orientalis (here drawn to smaller scale) is a trifle larger and greyer above and has longer wing

orientalis
(SE Europe, W Turkey)

KM

Chiffchaff *Phylloscopus collybita* m(r)**B**2 / **P**1 / **W**4

L 10–12 cm. Breeds in woodland, normally open and with tall deciduous trees and moderate shrub layer (locally also in conifer forest with some deciduous). Mainly summer visitor to Britain & Ireland (mid Mar–Oct), winters around Mediterranean and partly S of Sahara; scarce in winter, when also in scrub, reeds, gardens etc. Active, confident.

IDENTIFICATION *Very like Willow Warbler.* Grey-tinged brownish-green above (rump sometimes slightly brighter green), off-white below with variable yellow and buff tinge on throat and breast. Often more distinct element of *buffy-brown on breast-side*, especially in autumn, than shown by Willow Warbler. Distinguished by: *dark legs; fine, often rather dark bill;* usually *rather short and indistinct pale supercilium;* moderately *dark eye-stripe* which *divides whitish eye-ring at front and rear;* rather uniformly dark below eye and on ear-coverts, so that *white lower eye-crescent* shows well; short primary projection (but can look rather long when primaries drooped). At times *flicks tail downwards* (not seen from Willow Warbler). – Variation (see also under Voice): Birds in the greater part of Europe (ssp. *collybita*) and in N Fenno-Scandia (*abietinus*) are very similar, but *abietinus* averages a shade paler; in the extreme NE, green and yellow elements in the plumage gradually decrease.

VOICE Call a soft whistled 'hüitt', faintly upslurred and with emphasis at end, varying somewhat (and, exceptionally, like Willow Warbler's call). Alarm at nest a straight 'fiit'. In late summer–autumn, juveniles occasionally emit straight calls, 'hiip' (which can then be confused with Siberian Chiffchaff; see latter). Song a *slow and measured* series of well-spaced clear, forceful, *monosyllabic* (exceptionally disyllabic) notes on *two or three pitches,* 'silt silt silt sult silt silt sult sült sült silt...'. Birds newly arrived at breeding site add a muffled 'perre perre' between verses. – W Iberian birds (ssp. *ibericus*) have downslurred call, 'fiü', and song which starts normally but contains variable faltering passages and soft whistles ('svüi-svüi-svüi-...'). In Canary Islands (*canariensis*; proposed as full species), song is explosive like Cetti's Warbler's.

Caucasian Chiffchaff *Phylloscopus collybita lorenzii* —

L 10–11½ cm. Best regarded as a (distinct) race of Chiffchaff (though treated as full species by some). Breeds on mountain slopes, usually at 1700–2500 m, in willow or other bushes or in more open spruce forest near treeline.

IDENTIFICATION Very like Siberian Chiffchaff, greyish-brown above and dirty white below, but differs in *lacking all trace of green, including on wings and back/rump.* Is also somewhat *darker* and warmer brown above. Buff-white *supercilium often broad and long* but sometimes less distinct.

VOICE Call a slightly melancholy pipe, faintly downslurred,

'tüü(u)', rather like Siberian Chiffchaff. Song not unlike N European Chiffchaff's, 'pyit pyüt pyet pyüt pyet pyit pyet pyüt...'; tempo a bit faster, verses shorter and tone slightly more squeaky. Sometimes stifled 'te-ti' between verses.

Siberian Chiffchaff *Phylloscopus collybita tristis* **V**∗

L 11–12½ cm. An eastern race of Chiffchaff. Breeds in coniferous taiga forest from the Ural region eastwards. Migratory, winters mainly in India; odd birds stray to Europe annually in autumn (end Sep–Oct).

IDENTIFICATION Differs from European Chiffchaffs in being *grey-brown on crown, nape and mantle* (no trace of green), and *light rusty-buff on supercilium, ear-coverts and neck- and breast-sides* (no trace of yellow). Back/rump, however, show weak olive-green tone, and remiges and rectrices are narrowly edged green. On some, a small yellowish patch is visible on wing-bend. *Bill and legs always black.* In fresh autumn plumage, quite a few immatures have light grey-brown tips to greater coverts enough to create suggestion of pale wing-bar. (It should be stressed that certain N European birds of race *abietinus* can be similarly grey-brown, also that it is usually very difficult *in the field* to confirm for certain that all trace of yellow is lacking on head and breast.)

VOICE Call a mournful, piping, straight (or negligibly downslurred) 'vii(e)p'. Song clearly *faster* and more *varied* than European Chiffchaff's, the notes run together, *pitch is higher* and more notes are *multisyllabic* than monosyllabic. (Can at distance be taken for Greenish Warbler.)

Dusky Warbler *Phylloscopus fuscatus* **V**∗∗

L 10½–12 cm. Breeds in Siberia in willows and other shrubbery on taiga bogs or on wet meadows. Migratory, winters in SE Asia; very rare autumn vagrant in W Europe.

IDENTIFICATION Chiffchaff-like in shape, closest to a Caucasian Chiffchaff in coloration, with *rusty-tinged dark grey-brown upperparts* and off-white underparts. Identified by: *thin red-brown legs; narrow bill* with a little red-brown at base; *long, distinct, pale supercilium, well defined, white and usually narrow before eye* and usually broader and sometimes *tinged rusty-buff behind eye; broad dark eye-stripe.* Breast-sides, flanks and undertail-coverts light rusty.

VOICE Call a hard clicking 'teck', like Lesser Whitethroat.

Radde's Warbler *Phylloscopus schwarzi* **V**∗∗

L 11½–12½ cm. Breeds in Siberia in the taiga; requires glades beside watercourses with rank undergrowth. Migratory, winters in SE Asia; rare autumn vagrant in Europe.

IDENTIFICATION Willow Warbler size but sturdier, with slightly *larger head* (often with steeper forehead in profile), *stronger bill and legs. Rather dark brown with olive-grey cast* above, off-white below with *warm yellow-buff* (or more olive-brown) *tone* on breast, flanks and, especially, *vent and undertail-coverts. Strong pale supercilium* and *dark eye-stripe.* Told from Dusky Warbler by: *thicker bill; thicker and* on average *paler pinky-brown legs;* in front of eye *supercilium more diffusely defined, broad and in fresh plumage yellow-buff,* behind eye usually whitish. A bit *more sluggish* in movements than Dusky, not so active and restless.

VOICE Call a soft, slightly nasal, 'thick' clicking 'chrep' or 'chett', sometimes in simmering series.

Chiffchaff   Caucasian Chiffchaff

CHIFFCHAFF

usually rather indistinct pale supercilium

variation: birds in N and E paler on average, sometimes with more prominent pale supercilium

primary projection only a good half of tertial length

a certain variation in e.g. amount of yellow on underparts even in W and C Europe, usually making subspecific identification impossible

leg colour variable, but usually is dark brown or greyish-black (rarely paler brown)

collybita (W and C Europe)

autumn (fresh)

abietinus (N and NE Europe)

spring

SIBERIAN CHIFF-CHAFF

lacks green tinge on crown/mantle and yellow on supercilium/breast, often has a hint of a short, pale wing-bar

CAUCASIAN CHIFFCHAFF

all brown

DUSKY WARBLER

supercilium buff-brown at rear, whitest at front

fore-part of supercilium well defined

fine, pointed

usually washed dull grey-brown

legs usually not strikingly pale or thick-looking

usually buff-brown, rather concolorous with flanks and breast

a certain variation in head pattern; all-white supercilium occurs rarely

RADDE'S WARBLER

supercilium whitest at rear, warm buff at front

supercilium diffusely defined at front

short, stout, blunt-tipped

buff-brown, often with yellowish-olive cast

legs often more strikingly pale and thick-looking than on Dusky

often noticeably tinged apricot-buff

autumn birds with prominent yellow tinge below are probably invariably young

note how the shape of the supercilium behind eye changes with head posture

KM

Arctic Warbler *Phylloscopus borealis* **V**∗∗

L 11½–13 cm. Breeds in northernmost forest belt, in Fenno-Scandia usually in pure upland birch forest and often on sloping ground near a brook, farther E also in coniferous forest with plenty of birch and willow. Summer visitor (in Sweden end Jun–Aug), winters in SE Asia (incl. S Thailand, Burma, Indonesia) and thus has an almost record-long migration route. Active, spends much time in tree crowns, but is not really shy. Nest on ground, *no feather lining*.

IDENTIFICATION Just larger than Willow Warbler. Most like Greenish Warbler owing to *greenish-grey upperparts*, *off-white underparts*, very *distinct and long supercilium*, *long and broad dark eye-stripe* and a *short, narrow whitish wing-bar*, but distinguished by: bigger size; rather plump body but proportionately *not so big head*; *thicker and more wedge-shaped bill* (heavy base, pointed tip), with *dark tip to lower mandible* (lacking on Greenish); tendency towards *olive-grey tinge* (at times in form of diffuse spotting) *on breast and flanks*; *dark lores extend to bill-base*, but *pale supercilium ends short of forehead*. Primary projection fairly long. Tertials uniformly greyish-green. Primaries often have brownish edges (just as on Radde's, by the way). Ear-coverts are usually mottled dark. Exceptionally, wing-bar is worn off on one wing or even on both; occasionally shows hint of a second, shorter wing-bar on median coverts. Legs brownish-pink, sometimes darker brown-grey. Often looks 'snub-nosed', with flat forehead and slightly peaked hindcrown.

VOICE Call a short, sharp, scratchy 'dzri' (a bit like Dipper, easily penetrates through noise of rushing brook), quite unlike other *Phylloscopus* species. Song a fast, rather hard whirring trill at low pitch, 'sresresresresresresre...'; recalls Cirl Bunting song; now and then pitch drops ('vowel change') or tempo changes halfway through song.

Greenish Warbler *Phylloscopus trochiloides* **V**∗

L 9½–10½ cm. Breeds in Europe (ssp. *viridanus*) in lowland deciduous or mixed forest (oak, elm, lime), often in tall groves and parks, also in small dense copses (alder, birch, rowan, oak) along coasts or in spruce forest mixed with deciduous. Summer visitor (broadly May–Sep, varies with latitude), winters in India; a few reach Britain annually (mostly Jun–Jul, often sing). Nest usually on ground.

IDENTIFICATION Small (as Chiffchaff), with proportionately *rather large head* and *rounded crown*. *Greenish-grey above, off-white below* with faint hint of yellow on throat and breast. Distinguished by *long, distinct, whitish supercilium* (which often extends onto forehead, past nostril; cf. Arctic Warbler) and a *short, narrow, slightly diffuse whitish wing-bar*. Always lacks second (median-covert) wing-bar (cf. Two-barred Greenish and Green Warblers), but in fresh plumage

sometimes has a few slightly paler grey-green covert tips, which can look like a wing-bar in the field. Dark eye-stripe normally not quite so well marked as on Arctic; lores usually with only a *dark spot in front of eye and not reaching bill-base* (few exceptions). *Lower mandible pale.*

VOICE Call a frothy, faintly disyllabic 't'sli', or more clearly disyllabic (almost White Wagtail-like) 'tisli'. Song, which has sharp, high call-like quality, is a short, vaguely shuttling verse, often with slightly jerky rhythm and a half-stop inserted, e.g. 'ti**sli**-zizi-ti**sli**-züt-**sit**zlie-**zi**, t'**sli**-zit-**sli**-sli'; sometimes the verse ends with a trill (can be strikingly Wren-like), sometimes it sounds more like Coal Tit.

Two-barred Greenish Warbler
Phylloscopus trochiloides plumbeitarsus **V**∗∗∗

L 10–11 cm. An eastern race of Greenish Warbler. Breeds in C and E Siberian taiga; very rare autumn vagrant in Europe.

IDENTIFICATION Very like European Greenish Warbler. Safest features are that *wing-bar* on tips of greater coverts is *longer* (extends to scapulars), *broader* (rule of thumb: broader than tarsus) and *better demarcated*, also that a *short, narrow second wing-bar* is usually present on median-covert tips. Other differences are only averages and insignificant: a shade greener, less grey above; rather purer white below; slightly stronger yellow tinge on eyebrow and head-/neck-side; slightly heavier (but not longer) bill; somewhat darker eye-stripe behind eye. Told from Yellow-browed by more *uniformly coloured tertials, all-pale lower mandible* and *size*.

VOICE Very like that of European Greenish, and often impossible to separate with certainty. Call usually slightly fuller and more clearly disyllabic, 'tsi-z'li' (but essentially the same). Song on average lower in pitch, with longer verses and softer voice (but often sounds the same in field).

Green Warbler *Phylloscopus (trochiloides) nitidus* — (?)

L 10–11 cm. A rather well-marked race of Greenish Warbler, close to being a full species. Breeds on mountain slopes in NE Turkey, Caucasus and N Iran in lush deciduous and mixed forest, locally also in conifer-dominated forest, at times close to treeline among birch, alder, beech, juniper, willow and lower growth. Summer visitor (early May–Aug/Sep), winters in S India. Habits otherwise as Greenish.

IDENTIFICATION Resembles Greenish Warbler (ssp. *viridanus*), but differs in *Wood Warbler-green upperparts* and *distinct light yellow tone to supercilium, cheeks, neck-sides, throat and upper breast*. (Though note that yellow and green tints easily disappear among sunlit foliage, so similarity to *viridanus* often amplified in field.) *Yellow-white wing-bar* obvious, and at times short trace of a second one visible. The yellow supercilium ends short of bill-base, does not reach forehead as on most Greenish.

VOICE Very like Two-barred Greenish, i.e. call full, and song on average slightly longer, lower and softer (subtle and not a constant difference).

Arctic Warbler

Greenish Warbler

Green Warbler

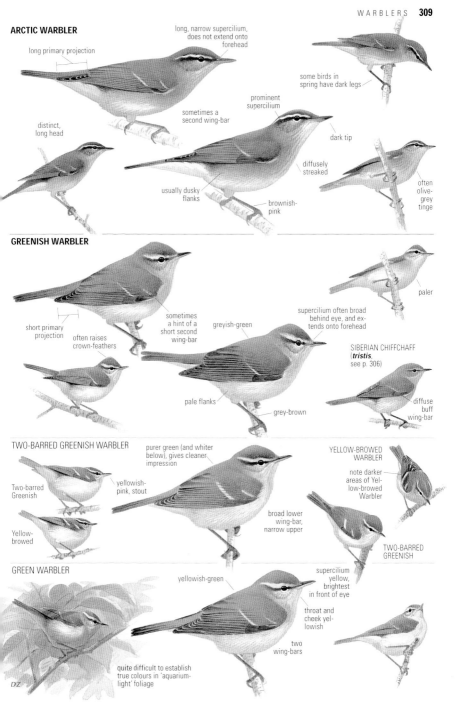

ARCTIC WARBLER

long primary projection

distinct, long head

long, narrow supercilium, does not extend onto forehead

sometimes a second wing-bar

usually dusky flanks

prominent supercilium

dark tip

diffusely streaked

brownish-pink

some birds in spring have dark legs

often olive-grey tinge

GREENISH WARBLER

short primary projection

often raises crown-feathers

sometimes a hint of a short second wing-bar

greyish-green

pale flanks

grey-brown

supercilium often broad behind eye, and extends onto forehead

paler

SIBERIAN CHIFFCHAFF (*tristis*, see p. 306)

diffuse buff wing-bar

TWO-BARRED GREENISH WARBLER

Two-barred Greenish

Yellow-browed

purer green (and whiter below), gives cleaner impression

yellowish-pink, stout

broad lower wing-bar, narrow upper

YELLOW-BROWED WARBLER

note darker areas of Yellow-browed Warbler

TWO-BARRED GREENISH

GREEN WARBLER

yellowish-green

quite difficult to establish true colours in 'aquarium-light' foliage

supercilium yellow, brightest in front of eye

throat and cheek yellowish

two wing-bars

DZ

Yellow-browed Warbler *Phylloscopus inornatus* **V**∗

L 9–10½ cm. Rare visitor from Siberian taiga; most records in late Sep–Oct in trees and scrub along coasts. Agile and restless, frequently flicks its wings. Often associates with other *Phylloscopus* warblers and Goldcrests.

IDENTIFICATION Often first attracts attention by its call. Smaller than Chiffchaff, with *quicker action*. Greyish-green above, off-white below, legs medium brown. *Long and very prominent supercilium* pale yellow above dark eye-stripe. *Broad yellowish-white wing-bar* on tips of greater coverts, and a shorter, less conspicuous second bar on tips of median coverts. *Tertials* (esp. shorter two) *edged yellowish-white*, which eliminates Greenish Warbler. Sides of crown can be a shade darker grey-green, often giving a hint of a pale crown-stripe, esp. on hindcrown. (Cf. Hume's Leaf Warbler.)

VOICE Vocal. Commonest call a loud, penetrating, high-pitched 'sweest' or 'tso**eest**', the quality of the call often recalling Coal Tit, though higher-pitched and more clearly rising. Song a few hesitant, very fine notes, 'tsewee, sese-wee…sewees' (somewhat recalling Hazel Grouse).

Hume's Leaf Warbler *Phylloscopus humei* **V**∗∗∗

L 9–10 cm. Very rare autumn or winter visitor from Central Asian mountain forests. Closely related to Yellow-browed Warbler (regarded by some as conspecific).

IDENTIFICATION Very similar to Yellow-browed Warbler, and at times inseparable on plumage. In fresh autumn plumage, slightly more dull and greyish-green above; supercilium (fore-part), cheeks and breast-sides faintly buff-tinged; flight-feathers and wing-coverts not quite so dark grey; light tips to median coverts rather dusky, not so distinct and pale; bill and legs often somewhat darker. In worn spring plumage usually inseparable from Yellow-browed Warbler.

VOICE *Best told from Yellow-browed by voice*. Call outside breeding a forceful whistling 'dsweet', or disyllabic, slightly descending 'ds**ee**wo' (rather similar to alternative song; cf. below). Song a drawn-out, at end slightly falling, buzzing note, 'bzzzzzzzzeeo' (like a drawn-out call of Redwing). Alternative song is a downcurled and rather low-pitched 'v**ee**slo', frequently doubled or repeated several times.

Pallas's Warbler *Phylloscopus proregulus* **V**∗

L 9–9½ cm. Rare autumn visitor (mostly Oct–Nov) from Asia. Actions often rather Goldcrest-like, constantly fluttering and hovering among bushes or in tree canopy, and may even hang upside-down in tit fashion.

IDENTIFICATION *Very small*, hardly larger than Goldcrest. Differs from Yellow-browed in striking *pale yellow* (or whitish) *rump patch*, obvious when hovering or when feeding on the ground, but otherwise may be difficult to see. *Crown very*

dark olive-green, divided by *clear-cut pale yellow central crown-stripe*. Often looks large-headed. Seen from below, note *long dark eye-stripe* and *vividly yellow supercilium*.

VOICE Less vocal than Yellow-browed. Commonest a call a quiet, slightly rising 'chuee', rather modest, soft and nasal. Also, a finer, straighter 'pih'. Song surprisingly loud and trilling in Wren-like fashion ('Canary of the taiga').

Goldcrest *Regulus regulus* **rB1 / P+W1**

L 8½–9½ cm. Breeds in coniferous or mixed woods, preferring spruces or firs; on Continent often at higher elevations. Partly resident, partly migratory. Associates with tits in winter. In woods, keeps high in canopy, restlessly moving and hovering among branches. Confiding, easy to approach.

IDENTIFICATION Attention usually attracted by thin, high-pitched calls. *Minute size* (smallest bird in Europe) and combination of being pale green above and off-white below eliminates all but a few. Short neck and proportionately large head give compact, rounded impression. Dark 'pepper-corn' *eye looking large* in otherwise pale, bland face. *Crown-stripe yellow, bordered black* at sides. – Adult ♂: *Much orange admixed in yellow crown-stripe*, generally hidden on relaxed bird but shown in display or when feathers are fluffed up. – Adult ♀: Usually *no orange on crown*, but a few have a very little (normally not seen in the field) in centre. – Juvenile: Crown plainer than adult, bill conspicuously pale. Acquires adult-like 1st-winter plumage by end of summer. – Variation: On outer Canary Islands (Tenerife, La Palma, La Gomera, Hierro) obvious *black band across forecrown*, and tertials less pale-tipped (ssp. *teneriffae*; or separate species?).

VOICE Vocal. Commonest call a thin, high-pitched, reedy 'zree-zree-zree' (3–4 syllables). Song a *cyclic* repetition (4–6 times) of a high-pitched, rhythmic 'pit**ee**tilü', ending with a little trill or Treecreeper-like flourish, 'zezesuz**ree**o'. Difficult to hear for many elderly people.

Firecrest *Regulus ignicapillus* **rB4 / P3**

L 9–10 cm. Breeds in deciduous and mixed woods, but will also be found in conifers (incl. pines, cedars). Short-range migrant. Behaviour as Goldcrest. Nests in conifers.

IDENTIFICATION Like Goldcrest, best located and identified by its calls. *Minute size* and general coloration narrow possibilities down to a few. Unlike Goldcrest, has *prominent white supercilium* and *black eye-stripe*. Also, *side of neck bright greenish-yellow*, tinged ochrous, not plain grey-green as on Goldcrest. Crown as Goldcrest, but black lateral crown-stripes join across forehead. – Adult ♂: *Much orange on crown*, usually visible also when relaxed. – Adult ♀: *No or very little orange* visible on centre of crown, those with most being difficult to sex in the field. – Juvenile: Lacks distinct crown pattern until autumn moult, but has striped face pattern reminiscent of adult but duller. – Variation: On Madeira (ssp. *madeirensis*) shorter supercilium and longer bill.

VOICE Contact-call similar to that of Goldcrest but slightly lower-pitched, usually opens with a longer and more stressed note followed by 2–3 shorter and slightly accelerating and rising notes, 'züü zü-zi-zi'. Song a *repetition of the same fine, high-pitched note*, slightly rising in pitch initially and in strength, and ending in a brief trill; it lacks the cyclic rhythm of Goldcrest's song.

Goldcrest

Firecrest

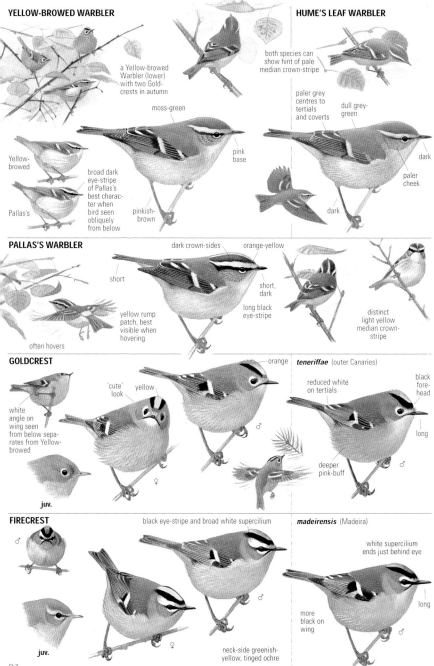

YELLOW-BROWED WARBLER

HUME'S LEAF WARBLER

a Yellow-browed Warbler (lower) with two Goldcrests in autumn

both species can show hint of pale median crown-stripe

moss-green

paler grey centres to tertials and coverts

dull grey-green

pink base

dark

Yellow-browed

paler cheek

broad dark eye-stripe of Pallas's best character when bird seen obliquely from below

pinkish-brown

Pallas's

dark

dark

PALLAS'S WARBLER

dark crown-sides

orange-yellow

short

short, dark

yellow rump patch, best visible when hovering

long black eye-stripe

distinct light yellow median crown-stripe

often hovers

GOLDCREST

orange

teneriffae (outer Canaries)

'cute' look

yellow

reduced white on tertials

black fore-head

white angle on wing seen from below separates from Yellow-browed

♂

long

deeper pink-buff

♂

♀

juv.

FIRECREST

black eye-stripe and broad white supercilium

madeirensis (Madeira)

white supercilium ends just behind eye

♂

long

more black on wing

♂

juv.

♀

neck-side greenish-yellow, tinged ochre

DZ

FLYCATCHERS *Muscicapidae*

Small passerines, five native species within region. Characteristic habit of choosing prominent perches, where they remain quite still, often upright, between frequent dashing forays to catch insects in the air, on the ground or in foliage. Short legs, delicate feet and broad but pointed bill (gape wide). Often flick tail or wings. Juvenile plumages spotted.

Spotted Flycatcher *Muscicapa striata* mB2

L 13½–15 cm. Breeds in gardens, parks and in forests, often appearing to prefer spots with small glades and openings among tall deciduous trees. Summer visitor, wintering in Africa. Nests in recess on tree trunk or building, often against a wall on branch of climbing shrub.

IDENTIFICATION Medium-small, greyish-brown, rather slim passerine, lacking obvious features. Head rather large, with rounded crown in profile; bill dark, fairly long and strong. *Tail and wings long*, lower body rather slim. Black *legs short*. Dull *grey-brown upperparts* and *off-white underparts* unmarked except for *dark streaking of breast, sides of throat, forehead* and *forecrown* (best seen head-on; ground colour of forecrown slightly paler grey-brown than rest of upperparts). 'Peppercorn' eye dark, with indistinct, narrow palish eye-ring. In fresh plumage, secondaries diffusely edged pale and may form indistinct lighter panel on folded wing, but this still very different from wing patch of ♀ Pied Flycatcher. Sexes alike, ages similar and generally not separable in the field. – Sits rather upright, often quite exposed, flicking its tail and watching for flying insects, then makes quick sally to snap prey, alighting on same or new perch. Flight fast and agile. When hunting, often darts sideways from perch to catch insect, sometimes rises quickly several metres and hovers, at other times may glide for a few seconds during long, sweeping dives.

VOICE Vocal, but repertoire unobtrusive and primitive, and often overlooked. Call a short, shrill 'zee', not unlike what can be heard from other species such as Chaffinch, Hawfinch and Robin. Alarm more characteristic, a call-like note immediately followed by one or two short, dry, clicking ones, 'eez-tk(-tk)'. Song a series of simple, *quiet*, high-pitched, squeaky or scratchy notes, often mixed with a few soft trills, rhythm a little uneven with *notes well spaced*.

Red-breasted Flycatcher *Ficedula parva* V∗ / (P4–5)

L 11–12 cm. Breeds in forests in a variety of habitats, mostly in lush, dense patches with rich undergrowth and a brook or other water, preferring deciduous woods but not shunning mixed. Summer visitor (mainly May–Sep), wintering in W Asia. Food insects. Nests in tree-hole or recess on trunk.

IDENTIFICATION Small like a Chiffchaff, and frequently

with similar quick movements, restlessly dashing around in canopy (different from other flycatchers). However, now and then sits still on perch watching for insects, revealing its flycatcher identity by flicking its wings and cocking its rather long tail, sometimes quite high up over back, occasionally spread enough to show the characteristic Wheatear-like pattern of the *tail in black and white*. Upperparts mainly brown, underparts whitish. Narrow eye-ring whitish, eye dark. Rather small bill dark, with pinkish-brown base to lower mandible. – Adult ♂: *Orange-red throat patch* (size somewhat variable, possibly partly age-related) with rather diffuse lower border against buffish off-white breast, but sharply defined laterally by *lead-grey sides to neck*; lead-grey colour also invades head and nape. Uppertail-coverts jet-black. – Subadult ♂: Like adult, but orange-red colour restricted to small patch on chin and upper throat only, and lead-grey fainter and more restricted. – 1st-summer ♂/♀♀: No orange-red on throat, and no lead-grey on head and neck. Uppertail-coverts brown, not black. Underparts tinged creamy-buff. – 1st-winter: Like 1st-summer ♂/♀♀, but underparts rich buff, and wing-coverts tipped buff and forming wing-bar on greater coverts; tertials edged buff. – Variation: ♂♂ from Ural and eastwards have red throat patch completely encircled by lead-grey, a different song, and ♀♀ and young have colder, less buff, underparts, darker base of bill, and jet-black uppertail-coverts (possibly a separate species, 'Taiga Flycatcher' *Ficedula albicilla*?).

VOICE Vocal. Common call on migration a slurred rattle, 'serrrt', like a soft Wren. Other calls: anxiety and alarm a short, soft disyllabic whistle, 'dilü' (sometimes 'düli'); a short, shrill 'zree' (like opening notes to song); dry clicking 'tek' notes. Song opens with a few high-pitched, sharp notes followed by rhythmical notes in Pied Flycatcher fashion (but voice a little clearer and pace a fraction slower) and ends with typical descending series of clear notes: 'zri...zri...zri, chee chee dee-**cha** dee-**cha** dee-**cha** chü chü chü, tü tü tu tu too taa' (common comparison with Willow Warbler far-fetched!).

Brown Flycatcher *Muscicapa dauurica* [V∗∗∗]

L 12–13 cm. Vagrant from Siberia, where it breeds in taiga. Behaviour and habitat much as for Spotted Flycatcher.

IDENTIFICATION Brown-grey above and off-white below, much like a small Spotted Flycatcher, differing in having *unstreaked forecrown* and usually a *uniform pale brown-grey wash across breast* only (a few have some diffuse blotches on breast but never distinct, narrow streaks); prominent *whitish eye-ring* (around rather large dark eye) and *whitish lores*. Bill strong, long and flat in profile, broad-based with slightly convex sides seen from below, and with pinkish or *straw-coloured base to lower mandible*, visible from the side. In fresh plumage, secondaries and longest tertials are edged slightly paler brown, forming an indistinct palish wing patch, but much fainter than on Pied Flycatcher. – Note that Sooty Flycatcher *M. sibirica* (not treated) is similar, but has more blotchy and dark markings on breast, less white on lores, and darker sides of lower mandible; also has undertail-coverts blotched dark (unmarked whitish on Brown).

VOICE Call similar to Spotted's, a high-pitched, piercing 'tzi'. Song thin, high-pitched, squeaky notes in rapid succession mixed with a few imitations and softer trills.

Spotted Flycatcher Red-breasted Flycatcher

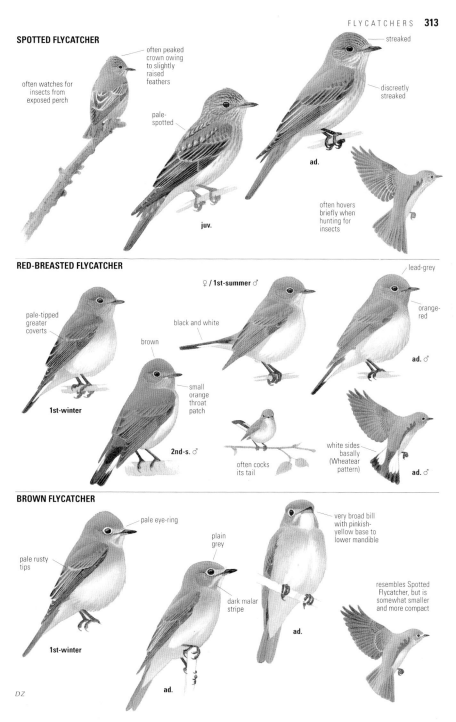

SPOTTED FLYCATCHER

often watches for insects from exposed perch

often peaked crown owing to slightly raised feathers

pale-spotted

streaked

discreetly streaked

ad.

often hovers briefly when hunting for insects

juv.

RED-BREASTED FLYCATCHER

pale-tipped greater coverts

1st-winter

♀ / 1st-summer ♂

black and white

brown

small orange throat patch

2nd-s. ♂

often cocks its tail

lead-grey

orange-red

ad. ♂

white sides basally (Wheatear pattern)

ad. ♂

BROWN FLYCATCHER

pale eye-ring

pale rusty tips

1st-winter

plain grey

dark malar stripe

ad.

very broad bill with pinkish-yellow base to lower mandible

resembles Spotted Flycatcher, but is somewhat smaller and more compact

ad.

DZ

(European) Pied Flycatcher *Ficedula hypoleuca* mB3

L 12–13½ cm. Breeds in gardens, parks, mixed and deciduous open forests, even in remote taiga habitats. Summer visitor, wintering in W Africa. Particularly attracted to mature oak trees providing airy surroundings and rich insect life. Active and restless. Nests in tree-hole or box.

IDENTIFICATION Rather compact flycatcher, sexes dissimilar, most spring ♂♂ basically black and white, other plumages brown and off-white. Sits rather horizontally, *often cocking tail* nervously and *flicking one wing upwards*. All have *white or buff-white wing patch* on otherwise dark wing, narrow white sides to tail (few exceptions), and whitish underparts. Important to note amount of *white visible on primary bases* on folded wing: usually *none* or *only indistinct and off-white narrow wedge*, barely extending beyond tips of primary coverts; when white more extensive and pure, still only a narrow patch extending to tips of primary coverts. – Adult summer ♂: *Upperparts blackish* or dark brown-grey with usually *small white patch on forehead* (often divided in two, one spot on each side; rarely larger—see below). Primaries and some wing-coverts rather dark and fresh, still a little browner than rest of wing and blackest parts of body. Coloration variable, some being blacker above, others looking patchy; others again are brown-grey (more frequent in E Europe) and very similar to ♀♀ but usually distinguished by white on forehead, *extensive white on outer webs of tertials*, and *blacker uppertail*, though sexes exceptionally can look alike in brown variety of plumage. A few have paler grey rump. – 1st-summer ♂: Similar to adult ♂, but in close view primaries and some wing-coverts are more abraded and browner. On average, upperparts less black, more grey-brown. – Adult ♀: Upperparts brown. No white patch on forehead (very little indistinct buff-white at most). White on tertials virtually never covering whole outer web, only outer margin distally; whole tips to tertials narrowly and evenly edged white. – Adult autumn ♂: Like adult ♀, but sometimes recognized by *blacker uppertail* and rather blackish wing-coverts. – 1st-winter: Like ♀, but has a 'step' between broad white edge on outer web and narrow one on inner web on tips of tertials. – Variation: Adult summer ♂ in SW (NW Africa, C Spain) looks like a ♂ Collared Flycatcher without white collar, is very black with large white patch on forehead, much white in wing, and has all-black tail; some are even semi-collared.

VOICE Vocal. Alarm a persistently repeated short, metallic 'pik, pik, pik, ...'. Call a quiet clicking 'tec'. Song loud, rhythmic, delivered frequently, a 2-sec.-long phrase typically with repetitive elements and sudden changes of pitch, 'zi **vree**zi **vree**zi **vree**zi tsu tsu chu-**vee** chu-**vee** zi zi zi' and variations; at times inserts a pleasing, melodious figure.

Collared Flycatcher *Ficedula albicollis* V***

L 12–13½ cm. Breeds in deciduous woods with glades and undergrowth, and in lush gardens and parks. Summer visitor (May–Aug), wintering in Africa. Behaviour and nesting much as for Pied Flycatcher, with which it can hybridize.

IDENTIFICATION Adult summer ♂ instantly recognized by *broad white collar* around neck. Otherwise shares all characteristics with NW African Pied Flycatcher (ssp. *speculigera*): large white patch on forehead, very black upperparts incl. primaries, large white patch on base of primaries, and all-black tail. Rump often pale grey or even white. – 1st-summer ♂ has browner primaries, smaller white areas, but has the white collar. – ♀ and 1st-winter very similar to Pied, but spring ♀ slightly paler and tinged more greyish above, and on all a *small pure white club-shaped or rectangular patch present on base of primaries*, inside primary coverts, being more extensive and reaching closer to outer edge of wing than on any Pied. – Adult autumn ♂: Brown above like autumn ♀♀ and 1st-winter, but recognized by *blackish wing with large white primary patch.* – For differences from Semi-collared Flycatcher, see that species.

VOICE Contact/alarm a *drawn-out, straight, thin whistle*, almost as if 'inhaling', 'eehp' (like a note from the song; recalling Thrush Nightingale alarm). Also a quiet clicking 'tec'. Song completely different from that of Pied, a series of rather slowly delivered drawn-out, harsh or strained whistling notes, often with marked changes in pitch.

Semi-collared Flycatcher *Ficedula semitorquata* —

L 12–13½ cm. Breeds in deciduous or mixed woods in mountains at lower and middle levels, often in copses along rivers. Summer visitor, wintering in Africa.

IDENTIFICATION Intermediate between Pied and Collared, but with certain distinctions. On summer ♂, white on side of neck usually reaches farther back than on Pied (but a few are confusingly similar); look for prominent *white tips to median wing-coverts* (may merge with large white wing patch, though); more *white on primary bases* than on Pied (about as much as on 1st-summer ♂ Collared), and *extensive white on outer tail-feathers* (sometimes visible from below on perched bird). Adult ♀ very similar to ♀ Collared, and often inseparable in the field; typically has *white-tipped median coverts*, but these may rarely be absent (and rarely there is a hint of such pale tips on Collared, too); white on primary bases somewhat less extensive on average (but some overlap).

VOICE Contact/alarm-call a clear, straight piping note, 'tüüp', lower-pitched than in Collared, almost like Siberian Chiffchaff (ssp. *tristis*) at a distance. Sometimes a thinner, slightly shrill and rising 'tüihp'. Contact-call also a quiet clicking 'tec'. Song intermediate between Collared and Pied Flycatchers. Slower than Pied, more like Collared, but some rhythmic repetition of combination of notes as in Pied; has thin, shrill voice with many rolling notes, and keeps more even pitch than Collared, e.g. 'sree sü-sü, sru-ti sru-ti sru-ti srrih si-vi sri'.

Pied Flycatcher

Collared Flycatcher

Semi-collared Flycatcher

PIED FLYCATCHER

1st-winter

brown

usually brown

ad. ♀

insignificant pale mark, never reaches close to wing-edge

ad. s. ♂

small patch

ad. s. ♂

white patch

predominantly grey-brown

black tail-base

ad. summer ♂
(grey-brown variant)

often dark hind-neck, but a few acquire almost complete white collar

speculigera (NW Africa)

iberiae (C Spain)

large patch

large patch

all black

ad. s. ♂

large patch

ad. summer ♂

black 'bridge' on hindneck

Pied Fly-catcher × Collared Flycatcher

hybrid, ad. summer ♂

COLLARED FLYCATCHER

1st-winter

sometimes a second wing-bar

pale grey-ish-brown

basally broad white edges to dark tertials, merge to form white patch (cf. Semi-collared Flycatcher)

ad. ♀

a few have a little grey on hindneck

brown

1st-s. ♂

variable, but often rather large patch

small white patch

large white patch, extends nearly to wing-edge

ad. s. ♂

usually all black

ad. s. ♂

white neck-collar

often much white

large patch

large white patch

black

ad. summer ♂

SEMI-COLLARED FLYCATCHER

pale grey-ish-brown

commonly thin white edges to rather pale brown tertials (cf. Collared Fly-catcher)

rather pale

DZ

ad. ♀

ad. s. ♂

white second wing-bar

variation

tail-base white seen from below

much white on tail-sides

ad. s. ♂

semi-collar

small patch

white-tipped median coverts

much white

ad. summer ♂

TITS *Paridae* and others

Small, lively, rather plump passerines with short bill. Nine species of the genus *Parus* are woodland-dwellers, nest in cavities and in winter gather in mixed flocks (roving tit bands). Mainly residents. The three species on p. 320 belong to other familiese and differ to an extent in habits.

Great Tit *Parus major*   rB1 / W4

L 13½–15 cm. Breeds in all kinds of woodland (incl. in desolate taiga in far N) and in immediate proximity of man in parks and gardens. Frequent visitor to birdtables and seed-dispensers, thus well known. Bold, at times plain audacious, may take seed from outstretched hand. Food insects and seeds, suet, beech nuts etc. Nests in roomy nestbox, tree-hole (e.g. decayed fruit tree), air duct and even letterbox.

IDENTIFICATION Largest tit, easily identified by *yellow underparts* with black central band, glossy *blue-black head* with *big white cheek patches*, moss-green back and narrow white wing-bar on blue-grey wing (cf. Blue and Coal Tits). Bill and legs sturdy. Sexes similar, but ♂ usually has stronger yellow colour below with *broader black median band* (forms all-black patch in centre of belly), while ♀ is often somewhat paler yellow and has narrower and often broken black line. – Juvenile: Resembles adult, but has yellowish cheek patch without complete black border along lower edge.

VOICE Rich repertoire. Main calls cheerful, include a somewhat Chaffinch-like 'ping ping', a cheery 'si **yu**tti **yu**tti' and a chatty 'ti **tuu**i'. A kind of inquiring, more timid 'ti ti tüh' is often heard in autumn. Scolds with harsh 'che-che-che-che-che-...' (Magpie fashion). Fledged young fill the summer wood with insistent, shrill 'tet**e**te tet**e**te...'. Song, heard as early as late winter, a simple, seesawing ditty with slightly mechanical intonation, e.g. '**ti**-ta **ti**-ta **ti**-ta...' or trisyllabic and with different stress, 'ti-ti-**ta** ti-ti-**ta** ti-ti-**ta**...'.

Coal Tit *Parus ater*   rB2 / W4

L 10–11½ cm. Breeds mainly in conifer woods, often with some taller spruces; locally also in pine or mixed forest. Resident, but along with Blue Tit is the most mobile tit in autumn, N populations in some years moving south in large numbers. Forages (for seeds, insects, spiders) much in tops of trees and in outer branches. Nests in hole, sometimes in rootpile or rock crevice.

IDENTIFICATION Looks like a small and almost colourless cousin of the Great Tit, with similarly *black head with large white cheek patches* and *narrow white wing-bar*. Proportions are different, however, with bigger head and *fuller nape* which merges more into mantle. *Underparts* are not bright yellow but *dusky greyish-buff* and in addition lack black central band. Views from behind reveal best fea-

ture, an oval *white patch on nape*. When a trifle agitated, it may raise a small crest like a tiny 'spike' on hindcrown. Back blue-grey. Besides white wing-bar on tips of greater coverts, it also has a second bar in the form of a shorter 'string of beads' along median coverts. – Variation: Birds in Britain and in Iberia are more olive-toned, not so blue on back, and flanks are tinged reddish-brown. In Ireland, underparts and cheeks are faintly yellowish as well.

VOICE Call is various fine, clear, almost straight notes, singly or a few together, with melancholy ring, e.g. 'tüüh', 'tih tüh-e'. Song, often delivered from top of tallest tree in territory, like Great Tit's though 'played at too fast a speed', a high-voiced, very *fast* scraping series with call-like tone, 'sit**chu**-sit**chu**-sit**chu**-sit**chu**-...'.

Blue Tit *Parus caeruleus*   rB1 / W3

L 10½–12 cm. Breeds in woodland, preferring deciduous or mixed woods, and in parks and gardens. Resident, but N populations move SW in some autumns, sometimes in huge numbers. Often seen at birdtables in winter. Readily hangs upside-down on nut-holders and at tips of birch twigs. Nests in hole or nestbox.

IDENTIFICATION A smallish tit with a *small but rounded head* compressed into shoulders (often looks neckless). Shape combined with its lively disposition and strong head pattern, with *black eye-stripe* and small *blue skull-cap* on otherwise white head, give an attractive and captivating appearance. *Underparts yellow* with narrow greyish-black central stripe on belly. *Wings bluish*, with bright blue on greater coverts and wing-bend. Sexes similar (♀ usually a bit duller).

VOICE Rich repertoire of mostly fine, clear calls. Main call a fast, high 'sisisüdu' with final note lower, sometimes just 'sisisi' (can sound almost as sharp as Grey Wagtail). Alarm a scolding series with ending stressed and somewhat halting, 'ker'r'r'r'rek-ek-**ek**'. Song a couple of drawn-out, sharp notes followed by a silvery trill on lower pitch, 'siiih siiih, si-sürrrrr'; sometimes song consists of two rapidly repeated short verses, 'si-si-sürr, si-si-sürr' (Treecreeper-like voice).

Azure Tit *Parus cyanus*   —

L 12–13 cm. Breeds in woods, often in riverside willows and in scrub bordering wetlands. Rare vagrant in W Europe.

IDENTIFICATION Unmistakable, with *white and blue plumage*. Sole confusion risks are albinistic Blue Tit or hybrid with Blue Tit (*'pleskii'*). Note *white crown* (without blue cap), *long tail* with *white corners*, *very broad white wing-bars*, and *much white on tertials and tips of flight-feathers*.

VOICE Calls most similar to Blue Tit's, e.g. 'tsi-tsi-tserrr de-de-de'. Song like a mixture of Blue and Crested Tit, 'tsi-tsi-tsruih tsi-tsi-tsruih tsi-tsi-tsruih...'.

Great Tit   Coal Tit   Blue Tit   Azure Tit

GREAT TIT

black

yellowish cheek

narrow un-even band

wide black belly patch

white sides

juv.

ad. ♂

COAL TIT

olive-grey, tinged buff

small, with big head

white nape patch

blue-grey

can erect small tuft; sings from top of spruce in N Europe

cypriotes (Cyprus)

deep rufous-buff

olive tinge

brownish-white

two wing-bars

britannicus (Britain, Iberia)

ledouci (Algeria, Tunisia)

yellowish

BLUE TIT

yellowish

blue 'beret'

often hangs upside-down

juv.

no white

blue-black

blue

wide blue 'collar'

deep blue

teneriffae (C Canaries)

dark; lacks wing-bars (ad.); narrow white supercilium

ultramarinus (NW Africa)

little white

ad. ♂

hybrid Blue Tit × Azure Tit (*'pleskii'*)

AZURE TIT

all-white crown

broad white wing-bars and tertial tips

extensive white corners

DZ

Crested Tit *Parus cristatus* ⌐**B**4

L 10½–12 cm. Breeds in coniferous forest, often in older moss- and lichen-rich spruce (in Britain confined to Caledonian pine forest of Scotland), locally in S Europe in deciduous woodland. Resident. In N Europe joins winter tit bands. Often forages on ground or low branches. Not exactly shy, though usually difficult to approach. Does not visit birdtables. Nest excavated in rotten trunk or stump.

IDENTIFICATION Rather small, with brownish upperparts and dirty white underparts. *Head* neatly *patterned in black and white* and furnished with a *pointed, triangular crest* which is always visible (but which may be raised to varying extents). Sexes and ages alike in field. – Variation: Minimal. In W and S Europe upperparts warmer brown, headsides have faint buff tone and flanks tinged reddish-brown.

VOICE Advertising-call a characteristic 'bubbling', cheery trill, 'burrur**ret**', often repeated, quite different from calls of other tits (but a bit like Snow Bunting's). Also short sharp conversational 'zit' notes. Song a series of calls and sharp notes, delivered alternately at rapid pace, 'zi-zi-**züt** burrurre zi-zi-**züt** burrurre zi-zi-**züt** burrurre...' and so on.

Willow Tit *Parus montanus* ⌐**B**3

L 12–13 cm. Breeds in coniferous forest, often at higher elevation, and in upland birch forest, as well as (mainly in W and C Europe) at lower levels in deciduous and mixed woods with birch, alder and willow, along rivers, in scrub in overgrown marshland etc. Resident. Not seen at birdtables in winter. Nest excavated in rotten, usually narrow trunk.

IDENTIFICATION Rather big head, full nape. Plumage *grey-brown and off-white* with *black cap* and *black bib*. Confusingly like Marsh Tit; best told by voice, also by *pale panel on secondaries* (on summer adults occasionally lost through abrasion, and a few newly moulted autumn Marsh Tits can have suggestion of pale secondary edges) contrasting with the otherwise brown-grey folded wing. Further differences exist (but are difficult to see in field, or are not absolute): black crown is always *dull* (glossy on adult Marsh); bib is on average larger, and cap extends farther down nape; head-sides average whiter. Sexes and ages alike. – Variation: Fenno-Scandian, Russian and E European birds (ssp. *borealis*) are whitish on head-sides and below and brown-grey above, while British birds (*kleinschmidti*) are darker, distinctly brownish above, more soiled on cheeks and buff on flanks. Continental Europe harbours at least a couple of races of intermediate appearance.

VOICE Call 1–2 short notes followed by 2–4 lower, hoarse, harsh, drawn-out notes, 'zi-zi **taah taah taah**', quite unlike Marsh Tit's (but very like that of Siberian, which see). Also fine conversational 'zi' notes. Song of two main types: a series of pensive, melancholy, Wood Warbler-like notes, 'tiu tiu tiu tiu tiu tiu' (in Alps and parts of E Europe dialectal difference with straighter note, 'düü düü düü...'), and a rather variable high-pitched short warble ending in a trill.

Marsh Tit *Parus palustris* ⌐**B**3

L 11½–13 cm. Breeds in unthinned, often damp deciduous woods with plenty of dead and dying trees; also in larger gardens and parks with older fruit trees and understorey. Resident. May be seen at birdtables in winter. Fearless. Dominant over Willow Tit where ranges overlap. Nests in cavity (tree-hole made by Willow Tit, nestbox, natural hole etc.).

IDENTIFICATION Very like Willow Tit (which see), and best told by voice. Has proportionately somewhat smaller head (but difference not striking). Most important plumage difference is *lack of obvious pale panel on secondaries* on folded wing (fresh autumn birds can show suspicion of a diffuse pale area). More subtle differences are that *black cap is glossy* (though duller on immatures), cheeks are on average less clean white and black bib somewhat smaller (though large overlap). Marsh Tit in N Europe is a shade browner above and not so whitish below as Willow, but in W and C Europe the two species are similar in basic colour.

VOICE Call an explosive, spirited 'pi**chay**', sometimes slightly longer 'zizi**chay**', or with (vaguely) Blue Tit-like scold appended, 'pi**chay**-de-de-de-de-de-de-**det**'. Several types of song occur, and same bird can vary; recognized by vocal tone. Common song type is a repetition of a single loud note, 'chüpp chüpp chüpp chüpp...' (fast variants become Greenfinch-like, 'chipchipchipchip...'); another type more like Coal Tit, 'wita-wita-wita-wita-...', or is a mixture of the two, 'ti-chüpp ti-**chüpp** ti-**chüpp**...'.

Siberian Tit *Parus cinctus* —

L 12½–14 cm. Breeds in old undisturbed conifer forest in N, mostly lichen-rich ancient pine forest, but also in lower upland birch forest. Resident; rare S of breeding area.

IDENTIFICATION Resembles Willow Tit (which is found in same habitat), but has fluffier feathering, appears to have somewhat bigger head, and has much *bigger dark bib* (often with broken lower edge), *rusty-buff colour on flanks* and *dull dark brown cap* (not black). Back is darker and browner than northern Willow Tit's.

VOICE Call confusingly similar to Willow Tit's, 'zi-zi **tah tah tah**', but the harsh notes are not so drawn out and as a rule not so firmly stressed. Contact-call a fine 'tsih'. Song a grinding, buzzing series, 'chi-**ürr** chi-**ürr** chi-**ürr**...', as well as a more Marsh Tit-like simple verse, 'che-che-che-che-...'. Function of a more melodic brief warble, 'zi-zi-jütvuy', which may be repeated, is more uncertain.

Sombre Tit *Parus lugubris* —

L 13–14 cm. Breeds in open deciduous forest on mountain slopes or lower down in rocky terrain with trees and bushes; often in fruit orchards. Resident. Unobtrusive in behaviour.

IDENTIFICATION Proportions and size roughly as Great Tit. Much as Willow Tit in coloration, but with (brown-tinged) *greyish-black cap* drawn farther down onto head-sides and with *much bigger dark bib*, with result that the *off-white colour of cheeks* becomes a *typically narrow wedge*. Bill heavy.

VOICE Calls Blue Tit-like 'si-si-si' and scolding, sparrow-like 'kerr'r'r'r', often combined; or more grating, 'zri-zri-zri', and scold more like Great Tit's, 'checheche-che...'. Song a fast, unsophisticated series in Marsh Tit style, with impure, grating voice, 'chriv-chriv-chriv-...'.

Crested Tit

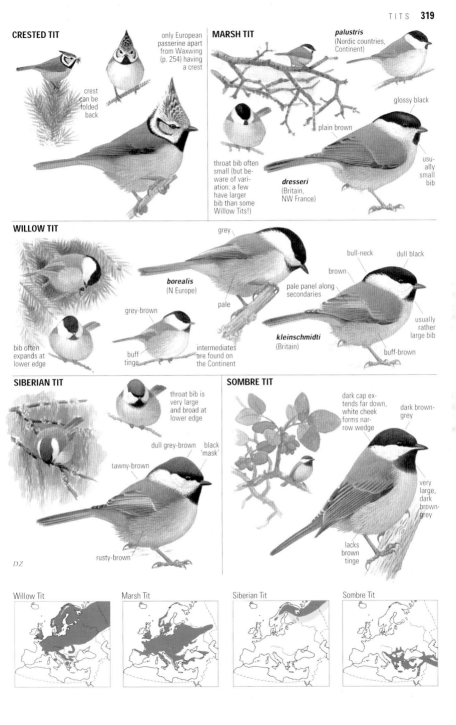

CRESTED TIT

only European passerine apart from Waxwing (p. 254) having a crest

crest can be folded back

MARSH TIT

palustris (Nordic countries, Continent)

glossy black

plain brown

throat bib often small (but beware of variation: a few have larger bib than some Willow Tits!)

dresseri (Britain, NW France)

usually small bib

WILLOW TIT

grey

borealis (N Europe)

pale

grey-brown

bib often expands at lower edge

buff tinge

intermediates are found on the Continent

bull-neck

dull black

brown

pale panel along secondaries

kleinschmidti (Britain)

usually rather large bib

buff-brown

SIBERIAN TIT

throat bib is very large and broad at lower edge

dull grey-brown

black 'mask'

tawny-brown

rusty-brown

SOMBRE TIT

dark cap extends far down, white cheek forms narrow wedge

dark brown-grey

very large, dark brown-grey

lacks brown tinge

DZ

Willow Tit

Marsh Tit

Siberian Tit

Sombre Tit

Long-tailed Tit *Aegithalos caudatus*   ʳ**B**2

L 13–15 cm (of which tail 7–9). Rather closely related to the true tits (pp. 316–319), but placed in a separate family. Breeds in deciduous and mixed woods with rich undergrowth (often hazel and goat willow) and some dead/dying trees, also bushy places. Mainly resident. In flocks for most of year, usually seen in small family parties which move quickly through woods and gardens. Confiding but restless, normally allows only brief views. Builds a closed, oval nest of moss in branch fork, held together with spiders' webs and cleverly camouflaged with birch bark and lichen.

IDENTIFICATION A very *small and rotund tit with long tail*; in flight, looks like a tiny pale ball with a tail. Flight is skipping and with short undulations. Clings acrobatically to thin twigs, can hang upside-down. *Head and underparts whitish*, with (Britain & Ireland, race *rosaceus*) broad *black band from side of forehead back along crown-side*, finely dark-streaked ear-coverts, light *reddish-brown flanks and belly*, and often gorget of dark spots across breast. *Back black, with wine-red or reddish-brown colour* on scapulars. Narrow tail is black with white edges. In close view, short bill and black peppercorn eye with orange orbital ring. Sexes alike. – Juvenile: Has *forehead and entire side of head dark*. Moults into adult plumage Jul–early Oct. – Variation: In N Europe (*caudatus*), adult has all-white head (no dark bands) and is whiter below, with pink flanks. Continental birds (mostly *europaeus*) as British & Irish, but head-side either cleaner or more soiled (in S Spain, Italy and Turkey even grey-striped). A zone of intermediate forms exists between birds with all-white head and those with dark band on crown-side. Turkish birds (*tephronotus*) have dark throat patch, grey back and shorter tail than European ones.

VOICE Restlessly moving parties utter loud trisyllabic, sharp 'srih-srih-srih' and slightly explosive rippling calls, 'zerrrr'. Also has chatty clicking calls, 'pt' (or 'zepp'). Drawn-out, high trills sometimes heard, e.g. when nervous and excited. Song rather soft, twittering, seldom heard.

Bearded Reedling *Panurus biarmicus*   ʳ**B**4

L 14–15½ cm. Sole European representative of the babbler family, but with numerous relatives in Africa and Asia. Breeds colonially in large reedbeds at lowland lakes and swamp margins. Very local in Britain, almost entire population confined to E and S coasts of England. Mainly resident, but dispersive, undertakes sporadic eruptions in autumn (signalled by high 'towering flights' over breeding lake in dense, highly excited flocks), some at least reaching more southerly winter grounds. Numbers may be severely reduced by cold winters. Feeds on insects and reed seeds. Nest of reed stems low in reeds.

IDENTIFICATION A small, *light yellowish-brown* bird with *long pale yellow-brown tail* glimpsed among the dense jungle of reeds should always be a Bearded Tit. Flight a little unsteady, with irregular, shallow undulations and whirring wingbeats, almost as if billowing forwards. Climbs reed stems nimbly. Often twitches tail or raises and fans it. Occasionally spreads tail in flight, too. – Adult ♂: *Head light blue-grey* with *long, black drooping moustache* (in other words, despite name, does not have beard!). Throat white. *Undertail-coverts black.* – Adult ♀: Head buffish-brown without black moustache. Throat off-white. Undertail-coverts buff. – Juvenile: Like adult ♀, but has *black back* and *black areas on tail*, and plumage is a bit more yellowish-buff. ♂ separated from ♀ by all-black lores and orange-yellow bill (♀: greyish or brown lores and grey-brown to greyish-black bill). Moults to adult appearance Jul–Oct.

VOICE Usually reveals its presence by flight- and flock-call, a lively, sort of twanging and slightly impure 'psching', which is repeated and echoes in chorus from the reedbeds when a flock decamps and flies a short distance. Also has a rolling 'chirrr' and softer, clicking 'pett'. Song 3–4 discordant, squeaky notes, e.g. 'pshin-dshick-tschreeh'.

(Eurasian) Penduline Tit *Remiz pendulinus*   **V****

L 10–11½ cm. Placed in a separate family, one reason being its aberrant breeding biology. Breeds in deciduous trees bordering rivers and lakeshores, in young regrowth beside overgrown swamps etc. Requires access to suitable nesting trees with thin, hanging branches (birch, willow, alder). Migratory in N, resident in S. Has spread towards NW in recent decades. Food mostly insects and spiders. Polygamous breeding habits. Several nests may be sited close to each other, but is not a true colonial nester; the same ♂ can start more than one nest. Nest unusual, fixed skilfully at end of a thin hanging branch, is pouch-shaped and furnished with entrance tunnel; exterior is pale and downy owing to interwoven seed-hairs of willow, aspen and bulrush.

IDENTIFICATION *Very small*, with *conical and sharply pointed bill*. Adult almost like a ♂ Red-backed Shrike in coloration, with *black mask through eye, light grey crown/nape* and *reddish-brown mantle/back*. ♂ has broader eye-mask than ♀ and darker red-brown back, which is noticeable when pair seen together. ♂ also has stronger sprinkling of diffuse red-brown spots on breast than ♀. Flight is light and a little springy. Climbs nimbly on thinnest branches, freely hangs upside-down. – Juvenile: Duller. Eye-mask grey-brown and poorly indicated (never black), back drab yellowish grey-brown, crown greyish-buff with slightly paler forehead.

VOICE Call a fine, whistled 'tsiiiü', faintly downslurred; sounds tender and almost 'dreamy' in tone (more drawn out than Reed Bunting's 'siu', softer and more downslurred than Robin's 'tsiiih'). Song a simple ditty with the call (or fragments of it) interwoven and with high trills, well spaced, e.g. 'tsiiü... sirrrr... tvitvitvi... tsiiü... zver'r'r'... tsiiü...' (like a soft, high-voiced Greenfinch).

Long-tailed Tit   Bearded Reedling   Penduline Tit

LONG-TAILED TIT

mostly seen in small parties, a bird of social habits

dark head-sides

all white

juv.

caudatus
(N Europe)

ad.

head-sides streaked black

black bib

short

grey

black band

red-brown

tephronotus
(Turkey)

dusky head-sides

irbii
(S and C Iberia)

europaeus
(C Europe)

ad.

(birds in W Europe—ssp. *rosaceus*—are similar, but have dark-spotted breast)

BEARDED REEDLING

flight with whirring wing-beats

♀ variation

♀

juv. ♀

climbs nimbly in reed-stem 'jungle'

black

♂

juv. ♂

black sides

PENDULINE TIT

pouch-shaped nest in birch tree

fine, pointed

juv.

narrow 'mask'

brown

broad 'mask'

deep rufous

♀

red-brown

♂

DZ

NUTHATCHES *Sittidae*

Six small to medium-sized, compact passerines with big head and strong feet, specialized in climbing on sloping surfaces, including head-first downwards or upside-down on underside of branches. Long, awl-shaped bill and short tail. Food insects, seeds, nuts; store food reserves. Nest in hole or crevice, sometimes wholly or partly walled with mud.

(Eurasian) **Nuthatch** *Sitta europaea* ⌐**B**3

L 12–14½ cm. Breeds in mixed and deciduous woods with some older trees and in larger parks and gardens. Resident. Commonest nuthatch, and widespread. Food insects, seeds and nuts. In winter often visits birdtables in worst Rambo style, chases off others, scatters seeds in all directions. Nests in tree-hole; if entrance is too big, it may be plastered with mud until size suitable. Nest chamber of pine-bark flakes.

IDENTIFICATION Silhouette distinctive: *neckless*, with *big head* and *long pointed bill*. Quick and active, makes sudden movements, climbs jerkily but nimbly on branches and trunks. Ability to *climb downwards head-first* eliminates treecreepers. Flight on short, rounded wings is straight over shorter distances, in short undulations over longer stretches. *Blue-grey above* and paler below, with *black eye-stripe*. Sexes similar, but ♂ has more intense *red-brown colour on flanks* (near leg). – Variation: Continental and British birds (ssp. *caesia* and others) have warm rusty-buff tone below. Those in Fenno-Scandia (*europaea*) are whitish on breast and belly-centre and lack white on forehead. In E Russia and Siberia (*asiatica*) small, paler blue-grey birds with white on forehead occur; occasionally seen in winter in Finland.

VOICE Rich repertoire of loud calls, used frequently; is therefore usually first located by voice. When foraging, commonly utters sharp conversational 'zit' and associated more drawn-out 'ziit'; sharper than similar tit calls. When excited and as warning, uses a forceful and very loud 'twett' (or slightly upslurred 'chuitt'), which is often repeated in short groups with brief pause in between. Several song types, all loud; delivered from high perch. Often heard is a slightly slower series of single whistling notes which are bent either up or down, 'vuih, vuih, vuih, vuih...' or 'viiu, viiu, viiu, viiu...'; other song variants are a fast, almost trilling 'vivivivivi...' with clear tone, also a slower and more rhythmically grouped 'jujuju jujuju...'.

Corsican **Nuthatch** *Sitta whiteheadi* —

L 11–12 cm. Breeds in tall pine woods in Corsica (endemic, total only *c.* 2000 pairs), especially at 1000–1500 m altitude, mostly in steep-sided valleys; in winter sometimes at lower levels. Food pine seeds, insects. Nests in hole in pine.

IDENTIFICATION *Small*, with *small head* and *short bill*.

White supercilium contrasts with ♂'s *black crown* (blue-grey on ♀) and *black eye-stripe* (grey on ♀). Underparts greyish-buff, throat whiter. Lacks reddish-brown in plumage. Forages high up in pines, mostly at ends of branches like a tit.

VOICE When nervous or agitated, hoarse drawn-out 'pschehr', slowly repeated, somewhat reminiscent of anxious Starling. Song a clear and loud, fast trilling 'dididi-dididi...', almost like Alpine Swift (but not dropping in pitch and slowing down like latter); tempo varies a bit. Similar trills can be used as contact-call.

Krüper's **Nuthatch** *Sitta krueperi* —

L 11½–12½ cm. Breeds in forest at variable level, mostly in coniferous at higher altitude. Prefers pine forest on Lesbos and in Turkey, but evidently spruce in other places. Mainly resident. Food seeds and insects. Nests in tree-hole.

IDENTIFICATION *Small*, with *small head* and *relatively short bill*. Blue-grey upperparts and dirty greyish-white underparts as other nuthatches, but identified by combination of *reddish-brown breast patch*, *white supercilium* and *black forecrown*. Sexes similar, but on ♂ black crown patch is bigger and more sharply defined at rear, lores and eye-stripe blacker, flanks more blue-grey (tinged brownish on ♀).

VOICE When nervous or agitated, hoarse, harsh 'eehch', sometimes in almost Great Spotted Cuckoo-like fast scolding series, 'zreh-zreh-zreh-zreh...'. Call Greenfinch-like, gently upslurred, 'dvui'. Song a fast shuttling series in shrill, nasal tone and alternate high and low notes, sounds like an old-fashioned ball-horn on a bicycle or like a toy trumpet, 'tutitutitutituti...'; speed varies: in highest gear, it sounds like a trill, in lowest, the series is spelt out. Monosyllabic 'ti-ti-ti-ti-...' series are also heard occasionally.

Algerian **Nuthatch** *Sitta ledanti*

L 11½–12½ cm. Breeds locally in N Algeria (not discovered until 1975; *c.* 100–200 pairs known) in oak forest (350–1120 m) or mixed forest of e.g. oak, maple, poplar and conifers (2000 m). Resident. Nests in tree-hole.

IDENTIFICATION Very like Corsican Nuthatch (*small*, *white supercilium*, *dark eye-stripe*, *greyish-buff underparts* with whiter throat), but ♂ has (as Krüper's) just *black forecrown* (♀ greyish-black or dark grey) sharply demarcated from *blue-grey hindcrown/nape* and back (border diffuse on ♀), and *underparts are paler and more warm pinky-buff.*

VOICE When nervous or agitated, a harsh 'scherh', repeated a few times. Song a slowly repeated, nasal whistling or fluting call on rising pitch and with a short coda, 'vuü-di vuü-di vuü-di...'; occasionally rapid disyllabic trills, 'di-du-di-du-di-du...'.

Nuthatch

Corsican Nuthatch

Krüper's Nuthatch

Algerian Nuthatch

NUTHATCH

reduced amount of red-brown

all nuthatches can climb head-first downwards

asiatica
(E Russia, Siberia)

small, pale subspecies

white supercilium, often white forehead

♂

europaea
(Fenno-Scandia, W Russia)

dark red-brown

♂

caesia
(Britain, Continental Europe)

♂

♂♂ invariably told by dark red-brown vent

breast and belly rusty-buff

♀

europaea

rusty-buff vent

CORSICAN NUTHATCH

♀

diffuse grey centres

grey

♂

whole crown black

pale greyish-buff

KRÜPER'S NUTHATCH

singing ♂

less extensive black on crown, rear edge ill-defined

♀

buffish grey-white

red-brown

blue-grey

♂

black cap on forecrown, rear edge well marked

large rusty-red patch

ALGERIAN NUTHATCH

extremely small relict population in Algerian ancient montane forests

♀

sometimes dark grey forecrown

pale

♂

black fore-crown

pale greyish-buff

DZ

(Western) Rock Nuthatch *Sitta neumayer* —

L 14–15½ cm. Breeds in rocky terrain (often limestone) with scattered bushes and trees at variable level (sometimes coastal cliffs, more often 1000–2500 m). Nest, in rock crevice, made of mud, closed and with entrance tunnel.

IDENTIFICATION A trifle bigger than Nuthatch (marginal, barely noticeable in field), but has *slightly longer bill, paler blue-grey colour above* and *lacks red-brown on flanks* and undertail-coverts. (Has faint tinge of reddish-buff on flanks/belly, roughly as local S European Nuthatches, but is *whiter on breast*.) Tail is uniformly grey without white and black markings, but this more difficult to see in the field. Pale upperparts, long bill and *habitat* often best features for species. Resembles Eastern Rock Nuthatch. Active, restless.

VOICE Often heard, loud. Song (by both sexes, at times in duet) drawn-out series of clear whistles; the series speed up often and drop in pitch, at distance can momentarily be taken for Woodlark song (but is much more cutting, not so soft), e.g. 'vi-**yu** vi-**yu** vi-**yu**... tui-tui-tui-tui-... vivivivivi... trrrrtititi-ti-ti-ti-tü tü tü tu... **ti**-vü **ti**-vü **ti**-va, **ti**-vü...'.

Eastern Rock Nuthatch *Sitta tephronota* —

L 16–18 cm. Breeds in similar habitats to Rock Nuthatch, but normally not below 1000 m, and does not shun forest. Often perches in trees, and found in oak forest with some rocks and boulders. Mud-plastered nest on rock or in tree.

IDENTIFICATION *Distinctly bigger* than Rock Nuthatch, and appears to have proportionately even *bigger head and heavier bill*. Plumage differs in that the *black eye-stripe expands behind eye into a broad band* and *runs farther down neck-side*; both *black bands clearly visible from behind* on nape of perched bird (can only just be made out on Western Rock). Often perches upright.

VOICE Resembles Rock Nuthatch's, but voice somewhat more powerful and has a *clearly deeper pitch*, and *tempo* is on average *slower*. Song e.g. '**tu**-ti **tu**-ti **tu**-ti... vitt-vitt-vitt-vitt-vitt-... choo-choo-choo-choo-... **tvui tvui tvui tvui**...'.

WALLCREEPER *Tichodromadidae*

Only one species in this family, which is very closely related to the nuthatches and often treated as a subfamily of those.

Wallcreeper *Tichodroma muraria* **V***∗∗∗

L 15½–17 cm. Breeds in rocky terrain, on sheer cliff faces with some vegetation and nearby water, at 1000–3000 m altitude. Lives in inaccessible sites, is hard to see. Found at lower levels in winter, sometimes on buildings and in quarries; then not too shy. Food insects. Nests in cliff crevice.

IDENTIFICATION The Hoopoe of the rock face! When creeping over a cliff wall it can, with its grey and black colours

(blood-red of wing only glimpsed), elude observation, but when shifting position the *broad, rounded wings* are spread, gaudily *marked with red, black and white* above. Flight fluttering and jerky, with brief glides. – ♂ summer: Throat and breast all black. Much red on wing. – ♀ summer: Throat greyish-white with smaller grey-black central patch. Less red on wing. – Winter: Throat / breast pale greyish-white.

VOICE Rather silent. Song drawn-out, kind of strained whistles with glissando and with typical pattern in which one note rises, then one falls, 'tu... rruuüh... ziiüu...'

TREECREEPERS *Certhiidae*

Small brown-spotted and white birds with pointed, slightly decurved bill and stiff tail-feathers. Two similar species. Quiet and unobtrusive, creep jerkily up trunks and thicker branches (like mouse), then fly down to base of next tree and so on. Food insects. Nest under bark flake on trunk.

(Eurasian) Treecreeper *Certhia familiaris* r**B**2

L 12½–14 cm. Breeds in woods, often with coniferous element. Prefers denser patches. Mostly resident, but populations in N and E periodically wander southward.

IDENTIFICATION Has on average *somewhat shorter bill* than Short-toed Treecreeper, and at least birds in N Europe are *whiter below*, have *whiter supercilium* and *whiter, more contrasting pale spots on crown /mantle*. (Continental birds of both species are, however, very similarly coloured.) Fine differences exist in wing pattern (see plate) but require photograph or extremely close view. Voice is best clue!

VOICE Call repeated, fine, 'buzzing' whistles, 'srri' (softer and more unobtrusive than Blackbird call). Sometimes also thin, 'pure' notes (without r-sound), 'tiih', loosely repeated. Song a high 2–3-sec.-long verse (Blue Tit voice) on *falling pitch* and with a slight flourish or *trill at end*. (Beware: some can imitate Short-toed Treecreeper song!)

Short-toed Treecreeper *Certhia brachydactyla* **V***∗∗∗

L 12–13½ cm. Breeds in woods. Habits and habitat choice as Treecreeper, but is more a bird of lowland and deciduous woodland. Also found in parks and gardens in towns.

IDENTIFICATION Confusingly similar to Treecreeper. *Lower flanks are on average more brownish* and *bill a touch longer*, but individual variation and minor differences render this of little help in the field. Voice, however, is important!

VOICE Call a strong, Coal Tit-like 'tüüt' with clear and penetrating quality, often repeated several times at slightly increasing trotting pace, '**tüüt**, tüüt, tüüt tüüt...'. A more Treecreeper-like 'srri' heard rarely. Song a *short verse* with *jolting rhythm, even pitch* and call-like voice, '**tüüt** e-to e-ti**titt**'. (Beware: some can imitate Treecreeper song!)

Rock Nuthatch   Eastern Rock Nuthatch   Wallcreeper   Treecreeper

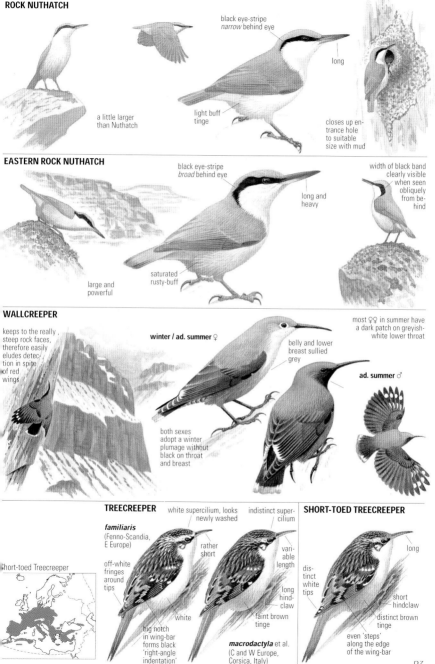

ROCK NUTHATCH

a little larger
than Nuthatch

black eye-stripe
narrow behind eye

long

light buff
tinge

closes up en-
trance hole
to suitable
size with mud

EASTERN ROCK NUTHATCH

black eye-stripe
broad behind eye

long and
heavy

width of black band
clearly visible
when seen
obliquely
from be-
hind

large and
powerful

saturated
rusty-buff

WALLCREEPER

keeps to the really
steep rock faces,
therefore easily
eludes detec-
tion in spite
of red
wings

winter / ad. summer ♀

belly and lower
breast sullied
grey

most ♀♀ in summer have
a dark patch on greyish-
white lower throat

ad. summer ♂

both sexes
adopt a winter
plumage without
black on throat
and breast

TREECREEPER

white supercilium, looks
newly washed

indistinct super-
cilium

SHORT-TOED TREECREEPER

familiaris
(Fenno-Scandia,
E Europe)

rather
short

variable
length

long

off-white
fringes
around
tips

long
hind-
claw

dis-
tinct
white
tips

short
hindclaw

white

big notch
in wing-bar
forms black
'right-angle
indentation'

faint brown
tinge

macrodactyla et al.
(C and W Europe,
Corsica, Italy)

distinct brown
tinge

even 'steps'
along the edge
of the wing-bar

Short-toed Treecreeper

DZ

SHRIKES *Laniidae*

Seven medium-sized passerines with long tail, strong bill with hooked tip, strong feet, sharp claws and generally a broad dark band through or behind eye. Spend long periods perched motionless at top of bush or in tree on lookout for prey (insects, lizards, small rodents, small birds). Majority are long-distance migrants. Nest in branch fork in bushes.

Red-backed Shrike *Lanius collurio*   **P**5

L 16–18 cm. Breeds in open cultivated country, often heaths and pastures with hawthorn, sloe and dog-rose, also on juniper slopes. Sun-loving summer visitor which winters in tropical Africa and returns in May. Insect specialist. Some set up food stores by spearing surplus on bush thorns.

IDENTIFICATION Often perches upright, when nervous jerks tail sideways. – Adult ♂: Breast and belly light brownish-pink; *no vermiculation* on flanks. Throat white. *Crown light ash-grey, mantle reddish-brown.* Broad *black eye-stripe* ('bandit's mask'), often with narrow white border above and on forehead. *Tail black, with white sides at base* (wheatear pattern). Sometimes small white patch at base of primaries. – Adult ♀: Dirty yellow-white below with *coarse vermiculations*. Crown brown or brownish-grey, nape greyer, mantle duller brown than ♂; variably vermiculated above. *Eye-stripe brown*; lores often pale. *Tail dark brown with narrow white edges.* Rarely more like ♂. – Juvenile/1st-winter: Like ♀, but usually *more heavily vermiculated above*. A few with warmer brown uppertail confusingly like immature Isabelline Shrike (which see).

VOICE Alarm a nasal, hoarse 'vehv', loosely repeated. When highly agitated, series of tongue-clicking 'tschek'. Song quiet (can be construed as subsong), rather seldom heard; harsh and squeaky sounds mixed with expert mimicry of other birds; can be very much like Marsh Warbler song!

Isabelline Shrike *Lanius isabellinus*   **V**∗∗∗

L 16–18 cm. Rare vagrant from S Siberian and Central Asian steppe (ssp. *phoenicuroides*) or W China tablelands (*isabellinus*). Seen mostly in autumn, in same habitat as the European Red-backed Shrike.

IDENTIFICATION Adult is sandy grey-brown above and buffish-white below, with rust-red uppertail. Usually black eye-mask and small white primary-base patch. Sexes similar; ♂ has blacker mask, ♀ is often faintly vermiculated on breast and sides. In race *phoenicuroides*, crown/nape usually rusty-brown. In Europe mostly immatures seen (in autumn). These are partially vermiculated dark above and can strongly resemble young Red-backed. Note: somewhat *paler and greyer ground colour above* with less or *no vermiculation on mantle and nape; paler and brighter rusty-red colour on*

uppertail (but a few are similar in this respect!); shorter primary projection. (Cf. also Brown Shrike, p. 384.)

Woodchat Shrike *Lanius senator*   **V**∗

L 17–19 cm. Breeds in open wooded areas with glades interspersed cultivations and scattered trees, preferably in association with fruit orchards. Usually requires some sandy or bare ground in territory. Tropical migrant (Africa).

IDENTIFICATION Adult ♂: Easily identified by *red-brown crown and nape, black eye-mask, forehead and mantle.* Wings black above, usually with white *primary-base patch.* Large *white scapular patch* and uppertail-coverts add further to 'showy' appearance, especially in flight. – Adult ♀: As ♂ but duller, with *dark brown-grey mantle*, and often *some buffy-white mixed with black of forehead and eye-mask.* Some are borderline cases, impossible to sex in the field. – Juvenile/1st-winter: *Grey-vermiculated* above, on breast and on flanks. Basic colour grey, with variable elements of brown; almost always distinctly *reddish-brown on neck side, greater coverts and tertials.* Note *suggestion of pale scapular patch* and *pale rump*; pale primary patch diffusely defined and tinged rusty. – Variation: On W Mediterranean islands (ssp. *badius*) white primary patch lacking, and forehead has less black. In C Turkey and eastward (*niloticus*) breeders have extra big primary patch (pure white on juv. too), white tail-base and much black on forehead; often incipient adult features as early as 1st autumn.

VOICE Alarm a series of short, hoarse calls, 've-ve-ve-...' or faster, like a hoarse trill, 'dsherrrrr'. Song rather loud, sometimes fast stream of squeaky and clicking notes, sometimes slower with expert mimicry; phrases sometimes repeated several times, but as a rule a bit varied in detail.

Masked Shrike *Lanius nubicus*   —

L 17–18½ cm. Breeds in open woodland with bushes and glades, usually associated with smallish cultivations, often on hillsides with stone pines, oak and thorn bushes. Often uses less exposed perches than its relatives, takes cover in treetops or larger shrubberies. Winters in Africa.

IDENTIFICATION *Smallest* shrike. Slimmer than Red-backed and has *longer, narrower tail.* Black (♂) or grey (♀) above with *white forehead* and *white scapular patches. Large white primary-base patches* striking in flight. *Flanks orange* (more saturated on ♂). – Juvenile: Grey, white and black, heavily vermiculated and with hint of *pale scapular patch* and large white primary patch, like eastern juvenile Woodchat; told from latter by smaller size, *lack of reddish-brown on wing and nape*, by *dark uppertail-coverts, narrow tail, small bill* and more uniformly dark tertials and greater coverts.

VOICE When nervous, a snipe-like 'chaihr'; alarm a dry rattle. Song (surprisingly enough) superficially like both Olive-tree and Olivaceous Warblers, a rather flat verse with cyclic repetition and harsh voice; more rugged and jolting in structure with slower tempo than Olivaceous, not quite so grating, and low as Olive-tree.

Red-backed Shrike

Woodchat Shrike

Masked Shrike

RED-BACKED SHRIKE

♂

often grey tinge

invariably boldly barred

black with white sides basally

grey

ash-grey

1st-winter

dark brown

reddish-brown

watches from top of bush

dark brown

pale base

vermiculated

pink

juv.

ad. ♀

ad. ♂

ad. ♂

ISABELLINE SHRIKE

RED-BACKED, 1st-w. (to compare)

1st-w.

often greyish

1st-winter

pale

1st-winter

ad. ♂

small white patch

usually red-brown

faintly barred

strongly barred

light rusty-red

rusty-red

grey-brown

a few young Red-backed Shrikes have warmer red-brown uppertail (above right) and can be confusingly similar to young Isabelline Shrike

← variation →

phoenicuroides
(Central Asia)

ad. ♂

WOODCHAT SHRIKE

senator
(Europe except W Mediterranean islands)

badius
(W Mediterranean islands)

stout

often paler red-brown than ♂

ad. ♂

old from juv. Red-backed e.g. by pale scapulars

pale

pale scapulars

dark grey

white

black

grey-brown, compact

lacks pale patch

sometimes vermiculated

small buffish patch

1st-winter

1st-winter

ad. ♀

ad. ♂

MASKED SHRIKE

trace of barring

ad. ♂

smaller, slimmer and purer grey than juv. Woodchat Shrike

small

long, narrow

black

watching for insects from shadowed perch acacia

dark

dark grey

black

long, narrow, black and white

large clean white patch, distinctly set off

juv.

1st-winter

ad. ♀

deep orange

ad. ♂

Great Grey Shrike *Lanius excubitor*   **P+W**4–5

L 22–26 cm. Wide distribution, with habitat and habits different in S and N. N European birds (ssp. *excubitor*) breed in upland birch forest, thinly pine-clad bogs, in clearings; short-range migrant. Southern populations (several races) live in the more open, often dry country provided lookout posts (e.g. wires, trees) and nest sites (thick bushes) exist; resident.

IDENTIFICATION A *big, light grey and white* shrike with large head, *black eye-mask*, black, rather short and *blunt wings* with *relatively large white primary-base patch*, and *long, rounded tail*, black with white sides. Scans from exposed perch, jerks tail sideways, *flies in deep undulations* when moving longer distances; can hover. Sexes similar.
– Juvenile: Dirty grey above, virtually wholly unvermiculated, but off-white below with close grey vermiculations.
– Variation: In S France and Iberia (ssp. *meridionalis*): darker and brown-tinged above, pink-grey below; narrow, distinct white supercilium and forehead; small wing patch (on 'hand' only). In N Africa: both a coastal similarly dark form but with grey breast and no white supercilium (*algeriensis*), and a paler desert form with much white on wing and tail (*elegans*). In S Middle East (*aucheri*): a little black on forehead (but much less than Lesser Grey Shrike). In N Central Asia (*pallidirostris*): large wing patch (on 'hand' only), buff tinge below, rather short, narrow tail.

VOICE Call usually a drawn-out trill, 'prrrih'. In anxiety, a hoarse 'vaihk vaihk vaihk'. Song quiet, a simple phrase, e.g. a metallic or squeaky double note, or various short notes followed by hoarse trill, repeated rhythmically once per 1–3 sec.; also has a soft subsong with mimicry.

Lesser Grey Shrike *Lanius minor*   **V**∗∗∗

L 19–21 cm. Breeds in open terrain with cultivations, fruit orchards, avenues of poplars and scattered trees and groves (but not in woodland). Warmth-loving, is most at home in lowland. Often seen scanning from roadside telephone wires.

IDENTIFICATION Size between Great Grey and Red-backed Shrikes. Large rounded head, stout bill. Like Great Grey (similar colours and *white primary-patch*), but adult differs in *black forehead and forecrown* (solid black and more extensive on ♂, smaller and mottled grey on ♀), *longer primary projection* and proportionately slightly *shorter and less strongly rounded tail*. Breast and belly pale salmon-pink.
– Juvenile: Lacks black on forehead. Vermiculated on crown and mantle, but not below (reverse of juv. Great Grey).

VOICE Rather silent. Call a Magpie-like chacking, 'tsche-tsche'. Song a hard and screaming parakeet-like 'tschilip!', given at intervals from treetop or doubled in display-flight. A rasping, drawn-out song full of mimicry is also heard, apparently mostly from unpaired ♂♂.

Black-crowned Tchagra *Tchagra senegala*   –

L 21–24 cm. Breeds in NW Africa in low-lying, dry, ope bushy country. Resident. Frequently hops on ground, oft perches low down in bushes. Rather shy and elusive, b loud calls reveal its presence. Food insects, small lizards et

IDENTIFICATION Strongly patterned head, with *bla crown, broad, long creamy-white supercilium* and *black ey stripe*. Heavy black bill. *Wing bright rusty-brown. Ta long*, black and broadly tipped white. Sexes and ages alik

VOICE Song remarkably loud, powerful glissando whis tles, rising or falling; sound like human wolf-whistle ♀ has rattling trill, 'trrrrrr...', sometimes in duet with ♂.

SUNBIRDS *Nectariniidae*

Tiny, dapper birds which, with their thin pointed bill, oft lustrous plumage colours and habit of feeding on flow nectar, can be said to be the hummingbirds of the Old Worl Hover only rarely (and not with rapid insect-like win beats), but perch to inspect flowers. Nest in tree crowns.

Palestine Sunbird *Nectarinia osea*   –

L 11–12 cm. Breeds especially in dry, savanna-like acac terrain but also alongside cultivations, in parks, gardens a such places where nectar-producing flowers exist. Resider or makes just local movements. Food nectar and insects.

IDENTIFICATION Full of life, *fast-moving and agile*. Oft flicks tail nervously. *Flight fast and jerky*. Bill black, slend *pointed and downcurved.* – ♂ breeding (c. Dec–Jul): All bla with, at close range and in correct light, metallic blue a lilac sheen. – ♀: Grey-brown above, grey-white below. – eclipse: Like ♀, at times with a few scattered black feathers.

VOICE Rich repertoire of loud calls. Whistled 'viyu', li something between Nuthatch and Hume's Leaf Warbler (also a rising 'tvüit' with cheerful merry tone; also has 'ele tric' tongue-clicking 'züt-züt-züt züt züt...'. Song a fe whistled notes followed by a rattling trill, 'tvui tvui tv tirrrrrr', at distance a bit like song of Black Redstart.

Nile Valley Sunbird *Anthreptes metallicus*   –

L 9–10 cm (plus tail projection of ♂ 4½–6½). Within t region breeds only near Cairo. Habitat as Palestine Su bird. May perform minor migratory movements.

IDENTIFICATION Tiny. Nervous actions, flicks wings a fans tail. *Bill slightly decurved, quite short.* ♂ unmistakab in breeding plumage (c. Dec–Jul), with *green-glossed uppe parts*, *black breast*, *yellow belly* and *thin tail projectio* Other plumages grey-brown above, with off-white thro and *yellowish-white belly*; eclipse somewhat stronger yello and can have a few glossy coverts and some dark on throa

VOICE Rather similar to Palestine Sunbird's.

Great Grey Shrike   Lesser Grey Shrike   Black-crowned Tchagra   Palestine Sunbird

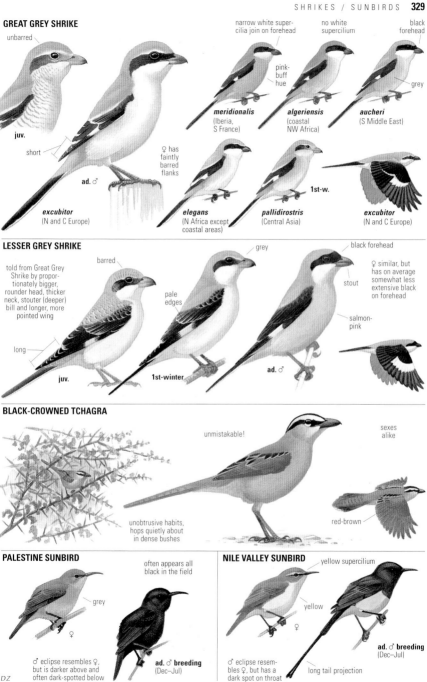

GREAT GREY SHRIKE

unbarred

juv.

short

ad. ♂

excubitor
(N and C Europe)

narrow white super-
cilia join on forehead

no white
supercilium

black
forehead

pink-
buff
hue

grey

meridionalis
(Iberia,
S France)

algeriensis
(coastal
NW Africa)

aucheri
(S Middle East)

♀ has
faintly
barred flanks

elegans
(N Africa except
coastal areas)

pallidirostris
(Central Asia)

1st-w.

excubitor
(N and C Europe)

LESSER GREY SHRIKE

told from Great Grey
Shrike by propor-
tionately bigger,
rounder head, thicker
neck, stouter (deeper)
bill and longer, more
pointed wing

long

barred

pale
edges

grey

black forehead

stout

♀ similar, but
has on average
somewhat less
extensive black
on forehead

salmon-
pink

juv.

1st-winter

ad. ♂

BLACK-CROWNED TCHAGRA

unmistakable!

sexes
alike

unobtrusive habits,
hops quietly about
in dense bushes

red-brown

PALESTINE SUNBIRD

grey

♀

often appears all
black in the field

ad. ♂ breeding
(Dec–Jul)

♂ eclipse resembles ♀,
but is darker above and
often dark-spotted below

NILE VALLEY SUNBIRD

yellow supercilium

yellow

♀

ad. ♂ breeding
(Dec–Jul)

♂ eclipse resem-
bles ♀, but has a
dark spot on throat

long tail projection

DZ

Fulvous Babbler *Turdoides fulvus* —

L 23–25 cm. Resident breeder in arid bush country, in semi-desert with scattered trees and bushes, in palm groves with undergrowth, by oases etc. Lives in flocks. Nest often in thick thorny bush, sometimes in palm.

IDENTIFICATION Barely thrush-sized, *long-tailed*. Rather *uniformly pale reddish sandy-brown* (warmer in colour than Arabian Babbler) with poorly defined dark feather centres on crown, nape and mantle. Throat whitish. *Bill strong*, slightly decurved, usually *greyish-black* (touch of yellow at gape on ♂), but straw-yellow with dark tip in NE Africa (ssp. *acaciae*). Iris usually *dark*. Legs thick, light brown.

VOICE Repertoire rather varied; noisy. Call short 'chitt' notes and various drawn-out trills, e.g. a rather hard rolling sound with metallic tone (like a giant Temminck's Stint), often on higher note, 'priür'r'r'r'r'r'r'...'. Song a series of piping diphthongs, 'piü piü-piü-piü piiay'.

Arabian Babbler *Turdoides squamiceps* —

L 25–29 cm. Resident breeder in arid bush country, in semi-desert with some acacia and tamarisk, near cultivations and gardens. Lives in flocks. Nest usually in thick bush.

IDENTIFICATION A thrush-sized, *light grey-brown* bird with *long tail*. Head and neck somewhat greyer than body, and *crown and nape finely spotted dark* (dark feather centres). *Bill strong and slightly decurved*, greyish-black (all younger birds, older ♂♂) or straw-yellow with diffuse darker tip (older ♀♀). Iris pale yellow (♂), ochre (♀) or grey-brown (juv.). Flight fluttering and direct; glides on extended wings. Hops two-footed, and jerks its usually cocked tail.

VOICE Utters chatty whistles with piping tone, e.g. 'pyü pyuvü pii **pyü**vu pvie...' and so on; more characteristic is a *high, piercing trill*, 'zvir'r'r'r'r'r'r'...'. Alarm a trill and hoarse 'ksherh' notes, like a small Jay. Song a series of piping whistles, '**pi**ay **pi**ay **pi**ay **pi**ay **pi**ay...'. Also has a soft, harsh subsong.

CROWS *Corvidae*

Medium-sized to large, heavily built passerines. Legs sturdy, bill strong. Highly evolved, alert, quick to learn. Social, often seen in flocks. Some species, such as Jackdaw and Raven, are skilled flyers, indeed nothing short of aerial acrobats, while others, e.g. the magpies and jays, have short and broad wings and fluttering flight. Most are residents, but many of those breeding in the far N and NE migrate short-ish distances to SW. Plumages mostly black, grey, white, brown and buff. Sexes alike. Omnivores; food comprises insects, seeds, nuts, berries, refuse, offal, eggs and young of other birds, etc. Usually build stick nest in tree crown.

Azure-winged Magpie *Cyanopica cyanus* —

L 31–35 cm (of which tail 16–20). Resident breeder in Iberia in woods mainly of stone pine but also deciduous trees. Odd gap in distribution all the way to Far East. Outside breeding season, roams about in family parties or larger groups. Alert and rather shy. Dashes around nimbly in dense treetops when foraging. Food mostly insects and berries. Nest often at edge of crown of holm oak.

IDENTIFICATION Medium-large, rather slim and *long-tailed*. In shadow of treetops, often seen only as a grey-brown bird with strong contrast between *black cap* and *whitish throat*. But better light reveals the beautiful *light blue colour on wings and tail* and the brownish-pink tone to back and buff tone to breast and belly. Primaries edged white. Flight fluttering like Magpie's, but lighter and more elastic.

VOICE Several calls; most commonly heard (e.g. frequently repeated from moving flocks) is a high, grinding, slightly nasal, gently upslurred 'vrrüiih'; sometimes high 'kui' and whining 'vih-e' heard. Alarm a drawn-out, high-frequency, hard rolling or rattling 'krrrrrrr...'. Song seldom heard and poorly known, a soft, squeaky twitter.

(Common) Magpie *Pica pica* ┌**B**2 (1?)

L 40–51 cm (of which tail 20–30). Breeds commonly around farms and villages wherever there are a few trees, often also patches of short-cropped grass or bare ground; also common in urban areas. Thus associated with proximity of man, which gives advantage of ready supply of food and reasonable protection against predators. Resident. At times gathers in noisy flocks of 5–25 birds, known as magpie parliaments, and in winter may roost in even larger flocks. Sounds the alarm against cats. Vigilant but not timid, swoops down and patrols lawns and flower beds in centre of noisy cities in search of worms, insects or food remains. Has false reputation of being a silver thief. Builds roofed stick nest in tree crown (looks like large witch's broom).

IDENTIFICATION Unmistakable—probably the bird which most people recognize. *Black and white*, with *very long*, green-glossed *tail*. In flight, short, rounded *wings show large white panels on 'hand'*. Flight fluttering, on straight course, with occasional sweeping glides, sometimes from high rooftop right down to ground. Walks confidently and slightly jerkily with tail often raised, and also makes strong bounds.

VOICE Most calls are hoarse and unmusical. Perhaps best known is the alarm-call against cat or owl, long-drawn-out, fast, very hoarse staccato series, 'tsche-tsche-tsche-tsche-tsche-...'. Other calls rather varied, usually hard, hoarse and whining sounds mixed together; disyllabic, clicking 'cha-ka!', 'chi**ah**-cha' etc. in conversation. Song more rarely heard, a quiet, harsh twittering 'subsong'.

Fulvous Babbler

Arabian Babbler

Azure-winged Magpie

Magpie

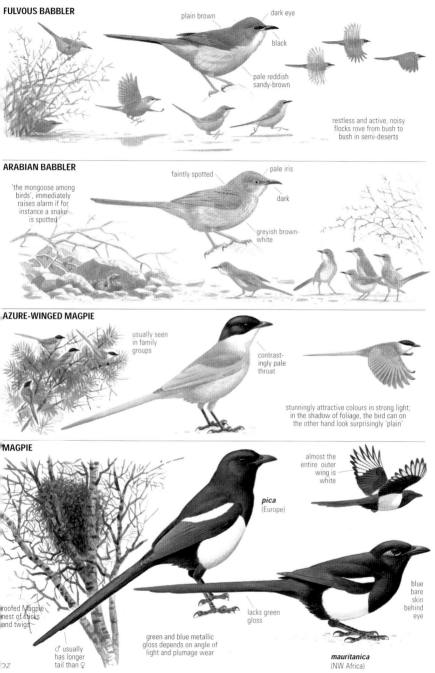

FULVOUS BABBLER

plain brown

dark eye

black

pale reddish sandy-brown

restless and active, noisy flocks rove from bush to bush in semi-deserts

ARABIAN BABBLER

'the mongoose among birds', immediately raises alarm if for instance a snake is spotted

faintly spotted

pale iris

dark

greyish brown-white

AZURE-WINGED MAGPIE

usually seen in family groups

contrast-ingly pale throat

stunningly attractive colours in strong light; in the shadow of foliage, the bird can on the other hand look surprisingly 'plain'

MAGPIE

almost the entire outer wing is white

pica (Europe)

blue bare skin behind eye

roofed Magpie nest of sticks and twigs

lacks green gloss

♂ usually has longer tail than ♀

green and blue metallic gloss depends on angle of light and plumage wear

mauritanica (NW Africa)

(Eurasian) **Jay** *Garrulus glandarius* ⌐**B**2 / (**W**)

L 32–35 cm, WS 54–58 cm. Breeds in various types of woodland, both coniferous and deciduous, and in larger wooded parks. Prefers areas with acorns (secondarily beech nuts, hornbeam seeds), which are cached in autumn as winter food; shipments high up with crop full of acorns can extend over several kilometres. Mostly resident, but N populations migrate S and SW in some autumns. Vigilant and shy, difficult to approach. Omnivore; summer diet includes a good many eggs and young of small birds. Nests usually in tree.

IDENTIFICATION Plumage striking, yet a bird which few city-dwellers are acquainted with. Mainly *pinkish grey-brown* with whitish throat and vent. *Above, on wing-bend, a light blue panel*, finely vermiculated black. Head has a *broad black moustachial stripe* at throat-side, also black-spotted whitish crown (in Europe; race *glandarius*). Crown-feathers can be raised, creating pointed head shape. In flight, conspicuous *large white rump patch* and broad white wing-band on 'arm'. Flight fluttering and a little uneven, on straight course. Told at long range from similarly flapping Nutcracker by *rather long tail* and *short bill*. – Variation: British & Irish birds (*rufitergum, hibernicus*) are darker red-brown. In Caucasus (*krynicki*), Middle East (*atricapillus*) and central N Africa (*cervicalis*), crown is all black and bill thicker. In NE Russia (*brandtii*) head is reddish-brown.

VOICE Most often heard is the characteristic, loud and intense, hoarse scream, 'kschaach!', which normally functions as warning but is sometimes used also as advertising-call; often repeated a couple of times in quick succession; when a flock of Jays catches sight of an owl, Goshawk or marten, a real uproar can break out in the wood! Sometimes gives a descending mew, 'piyeh', very like Buzzard's, but confusion seldom arises since the Buzzard calls almost invariably from the skies whereas the Jay is always heard from dense woods. Mimicry of its arch-enemy the Goshawk's cackle is often practised, too, 'kya-kya-kya-...'. Song is heard at times during late winter, a rather odd mixture of clucking, knocking, mewing and raucous sounds; quiet, does not carry far.

Siberian Jay *Perisoreus infaustus* —

L 26–29 cm. Breeds in the northern coniferous forests, with some preference for denser, older forest with element of beard lichen. Resident. Caches insects, seeds and berries for winter requirements, hides the food in trees (in bark crevices, among needles etc.). Omnivore, forages partly at camp fires and at elk-slaughtering sites, and in summer robs some small birds' nests. Often goes about its business quietly and confidently even when forest walkers intrude quite closely upon it.

IDENTIFICATION Roughly thrush-sized, fairly *long-tailed*, *dark* and *uniform*. Plumage is grey-brown with element of

brownish-pink, and with *darker brown crown* and somewhat paler brownish-white throat. Bushy nostril feathering forms a *small buff patch on forehead*. In flight, which is noiseless, smooth and fast with glides and sharp turns among the spruce branches, shows *rusty-brown panel near wing-bend above* and *rusty-brown tail-base and tail-sides*. Sexes and ages alike.

VOICE For the most part rather silent. Occasionally gives short mewing 'geay' notes, upslurred 'kui' and thinner 'kiiy'. In momentary excitement, Siberian Jays may erupt into louder outburst with Jay-like screams (though feebler), 'kreh', and longer mewing 'geeaih'. Song seldom heard, a low 'subsong' (audible at only *c.* 20 m) of twittering, whistling and mewing sounds.

(Spotted) **Nutcracker** *Nucifraga caryocatactes* **V*****

L 32–35 cm, WS 49–53 cm. Breeds almost exclusively in areas with easy access to spruce forests for nesting and rich supply of either hazel or arolla pine for winter food stores. Nuts and seeds are cached in the ground layer during late summer–autumn, and nut depots are memorized in detail and can be re-found in winter with great accuracy, even beneath thick snow cover. European breeders (ssp. *caryocatactes*), which are vigilant and shy, are mainly residents. In some years, when the arolla pine's seed crop is poor in the far NE, large flocks of the slender-billed race (*macrorhynchos*), however, migrate in late summer and early autumn from NE Russia and Siberia all the way to C Europe, where they are relatively tame in behaviour; no concentrated return passage of Siberian birds noted. Omnivorous in summer. Nests in thick spruce (occasionally pine), usually against trunk. Early breeder.

IDENTIFICATION Size of a Jay but with quite different proportions: *tail is short* (best feature in flight) and *bill long and powerful*. Head is more elongate than Jay's and lacks hint of crest. *Plumage is dark brown* and *sprinkled with small white spots*; crown and greater part of wings are, by contrast, unspotted brownish-black. Wings broad and rounded. Flight direct, often high up, with fluttering, slightly hesitant wingbeats recalling Jay. From below, shows contrasting *white vent* and *white tail-tip*. Sexes alike and ages similar. – Variation: In Europe, bill is heavier (thicker base) and tail has narrower white tip. In Siberian race macrorhynchos, bill is more uniformly narrow and averages a trifle longer, and tail has broader white tip.

VOICE A rather silent bird on the whole. Does, however, have a characteristic call heard recurrently, at least seasonally (early spring, summer), a drawn-out, hard rolling sound with an almost machine-like quality, 'krrrrreh', which is often repeated a few times in rapid succession; it is longer, feebler and at higher frequency than Hooded Crow's usual call, and the pitch is more even and mechanical. Soft Jackdaw-like calls, 'yaik' and 'kya', sometimes given. Song seldom heard, a quiet 'subsong' of squeaky, harsh and twittering sounds, of same type as Magpie's.

Jay

Siberian Jay

Nutcracker

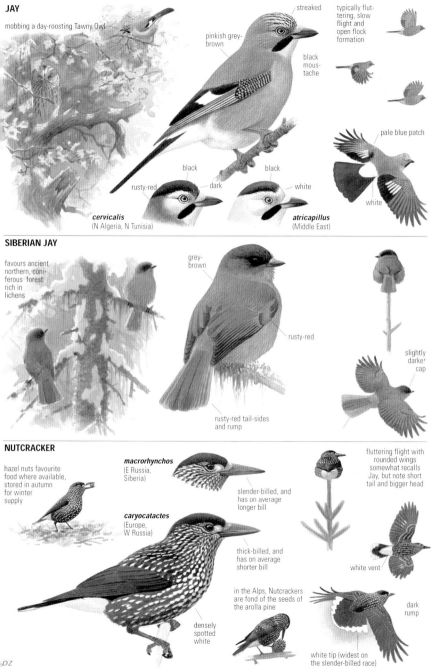

JAY

mobbing a day-roosting Tawny Owl

streaked

pinkish grey-brown

black moustache

typically fluttering, slow flight and open flock formation

pale blue patch

white

black

rusty-red

dark

cervicalis
(N Algeria, N Tunisia)

black

white

atricapillus
(Middle East)

SIBERIAN JAY

favours ancient northern, coniferous forest rich in lichens

grey-brown

rusty-red

slightly darker cap

rusty-red tail-sides and rump

NUTCRACKER

hazel nuts favourite food where available, stored in autumn for winter supply

macrorhynchos
(E Russia, Siberia)

slender-billed, and has on average longer bill

caryocatactes
(Europe, W Russia)

thick-billed, and has on average shorter bill

in the Alps, Nutcrackers are fond of the seeds of the arolla pine

densely spotted white

fluttering flight with rounded wings somewhat recalls Jay, but note short tail and bigger head

white vent

dark rump

white tip (widest on the slender-billed race)

DZ

(Western) **Jackdaw** *Corvus monedula* rB2 / W
L 30–34 cm, WS 64–73 cm. Breeds both in immediate vicinity of man, i.e. in cavities in houses and other buildings, and in mature parks and deciduous woods with hollow trees; also locally in mountains and on sea-cliffs. Short-range migrant in N, otherwise resident. Pairs for life, and pair-members almost always seen together, often perch close together, look 'amorous'. Also very social, forages in flocks and, especially in autumn, gathers at dusk in large throngs to roost in favoured copses or town parks. Can become quite tame where not persecuted. Omnivore. Nests in chimney, air shaft, tree-hole, duck nestbox, cave, rock crevice etc.

IDENTIFICATION At distance *all dark*, and often included in the term 'crow' by the layman. At closer range, however, *dark grey*, not black, and has *lighter grey neck-side and nape*. Eye, moreover, is *greyish-white*, and bill is much more slender than on Hooded / Carrion Crow and Rook. On ground, struts around quickly with upright posture. In flight, told from Hooded / Carrion Crow by *faster and slightly deeper beats* of the proportionately somewhat longer and narrower wings, also by broad but short neck, and by short bill that gives bird a somewhat 'docked' appearance at front. As a rule also flies in *denser flocks* than crows (almost as pigeons), but flock formation can be similar. Sexes and ages alike. – Variation: Birds from NE Europe (ssp. *soemmerringii*) have paler neck-side, especially in fresh autumn plumage, producing greyish-white patch on lower neck; intergrades into nominate race in Fenno-Scandia, so racial determination risky. Jackdaws in S and W Europe (*spermologus*) are darker.

VOICE Voluble. Conversational- and advertising-calls rather short and cutting and quite pleasing, some also hoarse and harsh. Often utters jolting 'kya', readily repeated in energetic series, harder 'kyack!', drawn-out 'kyaar' and slightly harsher 'tschreh', but details and volume vary with mood; often the birds chatter quietly together, when perched on a chimney and billing and cooing. Alarm-call is a furious, hoarse, drawn-out 'chaiihr'. A cackling noise is heard from large roosting flocks, before they settle for the night.

(Red-billed) **Chough** *Pyrrhocorax pyrrhocorax* rB4
L 37–41 cm, WS 68–80 cm. Breeds in mountains (at 1200–3000 m, locally even higher) with steep precipices and ravines, as well as along steep rocky coasts (thus around sea-level) with caves and deep clefts. Resident. Often fearless and approachable. Social in habits except when breeding, but colonies may occur, sometimes mixed with Alpine Choughs, when suitable nest sites are few. Forages on ground, for insects and other small invertebrates and berries. Nests on cliff-ledge or in cave, in crevice, at times also on or in cavity in building.

IDENTIFICATION A *glossy metallic black*, fully Jackdaw-sized bird with distinctive proportions: *wings are rather long* and *uniformly broad right up to body*, has *blunt wing-tips* which are *deeply 'fingered'*, has *rather short tail* (equals wing width) which is *straight-ended*, and the *red bill* is long, pointed and decurved. The red legs are rather long. On perched bird, wing-tips reach tail-tip (tail protrudes clearly beyond wing-tips on Alpine Chough). Acrobatic flyer—the Chough may be likened to an air-show pilot in an old biplane: despite the broad and 'frayed' wings, the bird rolls and turns over with the greatest of ease, and it plunges in tail-chases on *folded wings* (only carpals stick out) with a whizzing sound, only immediately to shoot skywards again. Sexes alike. – Juvenile: Bill is dull orange-yellow and shorter than adult's, plumage duller sooty-black. Legs are often duller red.

VOICE The most typical call, often uttered as advertising-call in flight, is a cutting, almost whizzing, slightly descending 'chiach', akin to some calls of Jackdaw but more piercing, higher-pitched and with thicker-voiced ending. The call varies in details, so that a whole spectrum of related calls occurs, 'chiaa', 'chrai', '**chi**-ah', 'tschraah' etc.

Alpine Chough *Pyrrhocorax graculus* —
L 36–39 cm, WS 65–74 cm. Breeds only in mountains (at 1500–3900 m) with steep, inaccessible precipices. Resident. Gregarious, and may be seen all year in large flocks (several hundred). Often visits top station restaurants at ski resorts in search of food remains, and can then be quite fearless. Restless, and before long moves on again over the mountain peaks. Feeds largely on insects in summer, on berries, seeds and food scraps in winter. Nests on cliff-ledge or in cavity.

IDENTIFICATION Resembles its relative the Chough in being *all black* and in having red legs, 'fingered' primaries and *contrastingly jet-black underwing-coverts*, also in acrobatic flight with headlong plunges and playful tail-chases. Differs, however, even at long range, in: *longer tail* (longer than wing width) *with narrower base and rounded tip*; somewhat shorter wings with *bulging rear edge of 'arm'* and slightly *narrower wing-base*, and *more rounded wing-tip with fewer and not such long 'fingers'*. At closer range, the diagnostic short and *bright yellow bill* is visible. At distance can also be confused with roughly same-sized Jackdaw, but that has shorter tail (barely equal to wing width), broader tail-base, broader head/neck and uniformly grey underwing. – Juvenile: Sooty-black, somewhat duller than adult, also dark legs and often dark tip to yellow bill.

VOICE At least 90% of repertoire is characteristic and cannot be confused with Chough's. Commonest call from wandering flocks, e.g. around top stations at ski resorts, is a high, rolling 'zirrrrr' with an almost electric quality, also a piercing, whizzing 'ziieh' and something between the two, e.g. 'zrrrieh'. Anxiety-call a slightly deeper and fuller 'krrrrü'. Occasional calls are more like Chough's.

Jackdaw

Chough

Alpine Chough

JACKDAW

'chimney-sweep bird', fond of chimneys

often seen in pairs

grey nape

dark

uniformly grey under-wing

CHOUGH

ferocious dives with wings folded back

broad outer wing, deeply 'fingered'

darker coverts

short

tail-base broad

brownish-yellow

short

juv.

ad.

long, red

ALPINE CHOUGH

rounded wing-tip with fairly short 'fingers'

darker coverts

tail length longer than wing width

tail-base narrow

yellow

feeding on mountain slope

gregarious, roves in dense flocks, restless and constantly on the move, one moment high in the sky, the next sweeping low over the ground

long

short-legged

DZ

Rook *Corvus frugilegus* r**B**1 / **W**
L 41–49 cm, WS 81–94 cm. Breeds in colonies (rookeries) in agricultural areas. Builds loose stick nests close together in crowns of tree clumps near farms and in villages; in spring, before trees in leaf, nests look like large witches' brooms. Forages in flocks on ploughed fields, on pasture and along ditchsides, often accompanied by Jackdaws. Relatively bold where not persecuted. Omnivore, but takes mostly insects and earthworms. Migratory in far NE.

IDENTIFICATION Size of Hooded/Carrion Crow (and often misconstrued as one), with *all-black plumage* which from certain angles shows reddish-lilac gloss. Adult told by *bare greyish-white skin around bill-base* and lack of nostril feathering, but usually also has a different profile from Carrion Crow, with *flat forehead, peaked crown* and *'short nape'*, *flattened breast* and *ample belly* (ruffled, drooping belly-feathers). Bare bill-base develops Feb–May of 2nd calendar-year; up to then immatures are very like Carrion Crow, but at close range told by somewhat different bill shape with *straighter culmen and more pointed tip*, also usually by calls. Experienced observers may be able to tell that Rook is *slightly more flexible*, faster and deeper *wingbeats*, plus *more rounded*, almost wedge-shaped *tail-tip* and on average somewhat longer 'hand' and narrower wing-tip (subtle!).

VOICE Hoarse, nasal, noisy croaks without open rolling r-sound of Carrion Crows, more grinding and irascible 'geaah', 'geeeh', 'gra gra grah...' and the like. Noise from a rookery at nest-building and mating time can be deafening.

Hooded Crow *Corvus corone cornix* r**B**2 / (**W**)
L 44–51 cm, WS 84–100 cm. Breeds in open woodland, on moors and wooded shores, in tree clumps in farming areas and in larger town parks. Resident in large parts of Europe, but many Finnish and Russian crows migrate in winter to Sweden and the North Sea countries. Hybridizes with Carrion Crow (see below), another race of same species. Vigilant and shy with good reasons, for is an outlaw in most countries. Omnivore, robs other birds' nests, takes refuse and carrion, insects and other invertebrates on fields and seashores (incl. small fish, mussels etc.), berries, seeds etc. Builds open stick nest in tree crown, usually well concealed.

IDENTIFICATION Size of Rook and similar in shape, but recognized immediately by *bicoloured plumage* with dirty *light grey body* and black wings and tail along with *black head and straggly black bib down to breast* (cf. House Crow, p. 338). Flight is rather apathetic, almost sloppy, the wingbeats a little hesitant and without any bite (unlike Jackdaw's somewhat deeper and more resolute beats). Often flies high up. Flock formation generally loose.

VOICE Noisy. Calls are mostly hoarse, hard and croaking.

Commonest call, also functioning as song, is a hard rolling croak repeated 3–4 times, 'krra krra kraa' (with individual variation; at times Rook-like without rolling 'r', 'gaah...'). Birds bicker among themselves, or mob Sparrowhawk and owls, with stifled but stubborn grating 'krrrr krrrr...'; but, when it comes to the dreaded Goshawk, it gives full vent to loud, hard and indignant 'krrah' notes.

Carrion Crow *Corvus corone corone* r**B**2 / (**W**)
L 44–51 cm, WS 84–100 cm. A geographical race of same species as Hooded Crow (above), which it replaces in W and SW Europe. Habitats and habits as for Hooded race.

IDENTIFICATION Shape and size exactly as for Hooded Crow, but differs in having *entire plumage black* (with faint metallic green and bluish-lilac gloss when fresh). Told from Raven by considerably smaller size, by broader, shorter wings, by *more listless flight* with shallower wingbeats, and by fact that *rear edge of tail is rounded*, not wedge-shaped. Harder to separate from immature Rook, but at close range shows *thicker bill* which is *blunter, with more curved culmen* at tip; flight is somewhat lazier, and wings a little shorter and broader (though differences minute!).

VOICE Very like Hooded Crow's, but often sounds a bit harder and more 'malevolent' in tone, not so rolling and open. Difference of doubtful use in field, however, bearing in mind individual variation in, especially, Hooded Crow.

(Common) Raven *Corvus corax* r**B**3–4
L 54–67 cm, WS 115–130 cm. Breeds in deserted woods, in uplands and on coastal cliffs. Has large territory, roams widely. Pairs for life. Resident. Very shy and wary. Omnivore. In winter, frequent visitor at carrion. Builds stick nest on inaccessible cliff-ledge, in tree or occasionally on power pylon. Breeds early in spring.

IDENTIFICATION Largest passerine, *bigger than a Buzzard*. Plumage *all black* with metallic sheen (green, bluish-lilac). *Bill very thick*, this often visible in flight, as is heavy, sometimes *shaggy throat feathering*. Typical flight silhouette, with *long and proportionately narrow wings* with 'fingered' but *rather long and narrow 'hand'*, also *well projecting neck area* and *wedge-shaped tail-tip*. Flight distinctive, too, often rather high up with *slow but deep and driving, elastic wing-beats* with slightly *backswept 'hand'*, speed fast. Often occurs in pairs. Often soars, when wings held flat or even slightly lowered, not raised as with a buzzard or Golden Eagle.

VOICE Loud, clanging, jarring with rolled r-sound. Call a deep 'korrp', sometimes repeated 3–4 times. Alarm a faster, hard 'krack-krack-krack'. Shows spring feelings with various rather odd calls, knocking and clucking sounds and a resounding 'klong'.

Rook   Hooded Crow   Carrion Crow   Raven

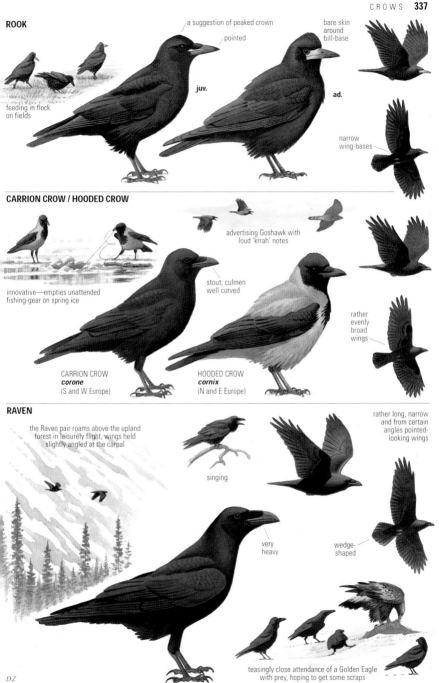

ROOK

a suggestion of peaked crown

pointed

bare skin around bill-base

juv.

ad.

feeding in flock on fields

narrow wing-bases

CARRION CROW / HOODED CROW

advertising Goshawk with loud 'krrah' notes

innovative—empties unattended fishing-gear on spring ice

stout; culmen well curved

rather evenly broad wings

CARRION CROW
corone
(S and W Europe)

HOODED CROW
cornix
(N and E Europe)

RAVEN

the Raven pair roams above the upland forest in leisurely flight, wings held slightly angled at the carpal

rather long, narrow and from certain angles pointed-looking wings

singing

very heavy

wedge-shaped

teasingly close attendance of a Golden Eagle with prey, hoping to get some scraps

DZ

Brown-necked Raven *Corvus ruficollis* —

L 48–56 cm, WS 103–120 cm. Breeds in desert and dry steppe, and at times seen patrolling mountain deserts and rocky wadis but is not a mountain bird. Resident. Wary and shy, often rather difficult to approach. Nests in tree crown, on power pole or cliff-ledge, exceptionally on ground.

IDENTIFICATION Very like Raven, and not easily separable in field. Calls often the best clue (see below). Is *a trifle smaller* than Raven, but difficult to assess without direct comparison. Shape and flight resemble Raven's, but has proportionately *somewhat smaller* (thinner) *bill*, somewhat less bushy throat feathering and *slightly narrower 'hand'* (one 'finger' fewer at wing-tip). Quite often flies with bill pointing downward, and not uncommonly has less obvious wedge-shape to tail-tip (can show slightly projecting central rectrices as on Red-footed Falcon), but these features do not always hold, or are hard to make out. At closest range may show *bronze-brown colour on nape* (Raven can show indication). Toes often yellowish (at least in Middle East).

VOICE Calls include a surprisingly *crow-like* croaking 'krii-eh', a bit hoarse and high-pitched, not deep and resounding or with rolling 'r' as Raven's. Another call, again more like Hooded Crow than Raven, is a strained, grumbling 'grreu grreu grreu', perhaps with territorial function.

Fan-tailed Raven *Corvus rhipidurus* —

L 45–52 cm, WS 103–110 cm. Breeds in mountain desert and locally lower down in rocky, barren tracts. Resident. Social, often seen in flocks. Frequently soars, and performs aerobatics. Omnivore; visits refuse tips, cultivations, oases etc. Nests on cliff, on ledge or in cave.

IDENTIFICATION Size of Brown-necked Raven, smaller than Raven. Has very short tail; on ground, wing-tips extend far beyond tail-tip (wings and tail equal in length on Brown-necked). Bill rather short and thick but head fairly small (can give vulture impression). Often seen walking around on ground with half-open bill. In flight, immediately recognized by most peculiar silhouette with very broad wings, broadest next to body, and docked tail.

VOICE Call a Raven-like, 'loosely' rolling and gentle-sounding 'korr korr'. In irritation, e.g. when mobbing a raptor, utters a high, rolling 'trrrü trrrü...' with dry wooden ring.

House Crow *Corvus splendens* —

L 37–42 cm, WS 68–80 cm. Indian species which has relatively recently found its way to the region via ships (or introduced?). Breeds colonially in vicinity of man, close to ports and towns with ready access to trees and food in form of refuse (fish offal, edible items at rubbish tips etc.).

Omnivore. Social, almost always in flocks. Builds stick nest high in tree.

IDENTIFICATION A real character; between Jackdaw and Hooded Crow in size, but slimmer and more elegant in shape than either. On ground, is *rather slim and lanky*, with *strikingly long legs* and long wings, *small head*, but proportionately *large bill* which is often emphasized by steep forehead. The plumage recalls Hooded × Carrion Crow hybrids, i.e. *head with bib attached and back, wings and tail are black* while *rest is dark grey* (nape, neck and upper breast a shade paler, medium grey). Close views reveal that the *black on head ends just behind eye* and is thus less extensive than on Hooded Crow. In flight, contrast between black and grey often difficult to see at range, when the bird just looks all dark. *Wings are slim like Rook's and slightly angled* at carpal, and so, with its rather long, heavy bill and *long tail*, it looks at distance like a miniature Raven.

VOICE Quiet. Has a muffled, somewhat Hooded Crow-like croak, 'kraar'. Mobs raptors with harder 'krao-krao'.

STARLINGS *Sturnidae*

Four mid-sized passerines, compact, with short, strong feet and pointed bill. Often seen in large, dense flocks. Spend much time walking on ground, gait rapid. Varied diet. Nest in hole. One Asiatic species is treated below, while the three European species are described on the next spread.

Tristram's Starling *Onychognathus tristramii* —

L 24–27 cm. Breeds in barren mountain tracts, especially in or near ravines, wadis and valleys with some vegetation. Resident. Gregarious, often seen in smallish parties (flocks of 10–50 not unusual) except when breeding. Food insects, fruits and berries. At times visits lower-lying cultivations to feed. Nests in cavity in rock face.

IDENTIFICATION Size approximately as Starling, but somewhat *longer-tailed* and *slimmer in build*. Plumage broadly all *black*, at certain angles with bluish-lilac lustre. Main feature a *big, bright orange* (copper-coloured) *wing-panel* on 'hand', conspicuous on flying birds but otherwise visible only as narrow band along edge of folded wing. Eye (brownish-)red. Sexes separable by ♀ having greyish head and neck with diffuse darker streaking or spotting.

VOICE Noisy and *loud*. Voice, moreover, very characteristic: flocks moving along mountainsides emit loud glissando calls, sounding like *wolf-whistles* or like tuning in an old radio and getting distorted tones at full amplification, '**viyvuviy**' or '**vooviiyuu**'. Alarm a hoarse scream, 'veeech', recalling Golden Oriole but with more malevolent tone. Supposed song a soft series of squeaky and rasping notes.

Brown-necked Raven Fan-tailed Raven House Crow Tristram's Starling

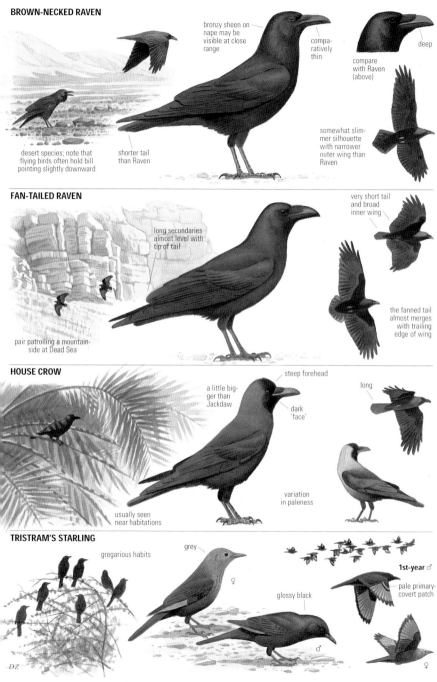

BROWN-NECKED RAVEN

bronzy sheen on nape may be visible at close range

comparatively thin

deep

compare with Raven (above)

somewhat slimmer silhouette with narrower outer wing than Raven

desert species; note that flying birds often hold bill pointing slightly downward

shorter tail than Raven

FAN-TAILED RAVEN

very short tail and broad inner wing

long secondaries almost level with tip of tail

the fanned tail almost merges with trailing edge of wing

pair patrolling a mountainside at Dead Sea

HOUSE CROW

steep forehead

a little bigger than Jackdaw

long

dark 'face'

variation in paleness

usually seen near habitations

TRISTRAM'S STARLING

gregarious habits

grey

♀

glossy black

1st-year ♂

pale primary-covert patch

♂

♀

DZ

(Common) Starling *Sturnus vulgaris* rB1 / W+P1

L 19–22 cm. Familiar breeder in farmland and suburban areas, and in woodland (esp. with oak). Post-breeding flocks, sometimes of enormous size, forage on fields, in gardens, on cherry trees, on shoreline seaweed etc. In Britain & Ireland largely resident, but massive influx from N and NE Europe *c.* Aug–Mar, some roosting in urban sites.

IDENTIFICATION When a *black* bird with *yellow bill* lands on the lawn, beginners have to decide between Starling and Blackbird. On closer inspection the differences are considerable: Starling has some *yellowish-white spots* in the plumage, the feathers have a *metallic green and violet sheen*, the *tail is short* and the *bill rather long and pointed*, it does not make two-footed hops but *walks with jerky, energetic movements* and so on. Flight fast and slightly undulating, silhouette distinctive with *rather pointed wings* and *short tail*. Legs brownish-pink. Sexes similar (♂ in spring has wholly unspotted breast and blue-grey at base of lower mandible, ♀ retains some pale spots below and has yellowish-white lower-mandible base). – Winter: Bill dark. Entire plumage densely sprinkled with yellowish-white spots. Chin whitish. – Juvenile: All *dull dirty brown*. Adult-like 1st-winter plumage acquired end Jul–Sep; immatures with pale-spotted body but retaining dull brown head are easily recognized.

VOICE Rich repertoire. On take-off and in flight, often a short buzzing 'chürrr'. Alarm at nest a hoarse, drawn-out 'steeh' and on sight of hawk a sharp 'kyett!'. Young beg with rippling, hoarse buzz, which from fledged young can at times become almost a metallic rattle. Song in vicinity of proposed nest site in spring, but also occasionally on warm sunny days in autumn and winter, consists of loud glissando whistles and rather soft, knocking sounds, squeaks and fine imitations of other birds, e.g. often Lapwing, Curlew, Coot, House Sparrow, Magpie and Hooded/Carrion Crow.

Spotless Starling *Sturnus unicolor* —

L 19–22 cm. Resident breeder around habitations and farmyards, sometimes in olive groves or on cliffs with cavities available. Habits otherwise as Starling's. Besides Iberia, found also in Corsica, Sardinia, Sicily and NW Africa.

IDENTIFICATION Very like Starling, but in spring and summer is *entirely unspotted black* (♀ and 1st-year ♂ can still have some fine spots on undertail-coverts) with more uniformly purple gloss (green from certain angles) than Starling. In winter plumage, ♀ and immatures have pale spots on back, belly and undertail-coverts. *Crown* usually *unspotted*, unlike normal winter-plumaged Starlings. *Legs light pink*.

VOICE Very like Starling's, but whistles of song sharper in tone, as well as clearer and louder and often also upward-bent, and trills are often stronger and more rolling.

Rose-coloured Starling *Sturnus roseus* V**

L 19–22 cm. Breeds colonially in agricultural country or on steppe, occurrence erratic, adapts opportunistically to mass emergences of grasshoppers and other insects. A few stray to NW Europe, mostly in summer.

IDENTIFICATION *Body pink*, head, wings and tail black, on adult ♂ with metallic lilac sheen on head and green sheen on wings; *long drooping crest on nape*. ♀ somewhat duller, with shorter crest and brown-toned back. Immatures have pink of back and belly soiled grey-brown and generally lack metallic sheen and nuchal crest. Juvenile like a washed-out young Starling, but has *shorter and blunter, yellowish bill*, some contrast between darker wings and paler body and, in particular, *pale rump* in flight (beware aberrantly pale young Starlings, though these always have dark, pointed bill).

VOICE Calls short, harsh. Song, often given with trembling 'penguin wings', a jingling, noisy chorus of knocking, squeaky and silvery sounds, like older immature Starlings.

ORIOLES Oriolidae

Medium-sized passerines with quite elongate, thrush-like shape. Mostly hide in tree crowns. Only one species in region.

(Eurasian) Golden Oriole *Oriolus oriolus* mB5 / P5

L 22–25 cm. Breeds in lofty deciduous forest (few conifers admixed not a hindrance), in agricultural areas with deciduous copses, often near rivers or lakes, in larger parks etc. In Britain rare, in commercial poplars. Summer visitor (May–Aug), winters in tropical Africa. Shy, restless, mobile. Difficult to catch sight of on breeding grounds, keeps concealed high up in foliage (even yellow ♂ blends into the sun-dappled leaves and escapes detection!). Food insects, berries. Nest suspended in branch fork (Walt Disney style) high in canopy.

IDENTIFICATION Flight fast and sweeping through foliage, over longer stretches thrush-like, in long, shallow undulations. – Adult ♂: Unmistakable, *bright yellow with black wings and black tail* and reddish bill. Lores and tertials black. – ♀/1st-summer ♂/juvenile: *Green above, off-white with fine streaking below*. Variable amount of yellowish-green or yellow on flanks and belly. (Note that occasional ad. ♀♀ can be very yellow and unstreaked below, and hard to separate from ad. ♂ in field, but have dark grey lores and partially olive tertials and central tail-feathers.)

VOICE Often emits a screaming, hoarse 'veeaahk', somewhat reminiscent of Jay but with more nasal and more strained voice. Also has a falcon-like, fast 'gigigigigi'. Song a beautiful, loud, fluting whistle, confusable only (at distance) with Blackbird song, e.g. 'foh-flüo-**fih**-fioo' or shorter 'fo **flüh**-füo' or just 'fiooh', the details varied.

Starling   Spotless Starling   Rose-coloured Starling   Golden Oriole

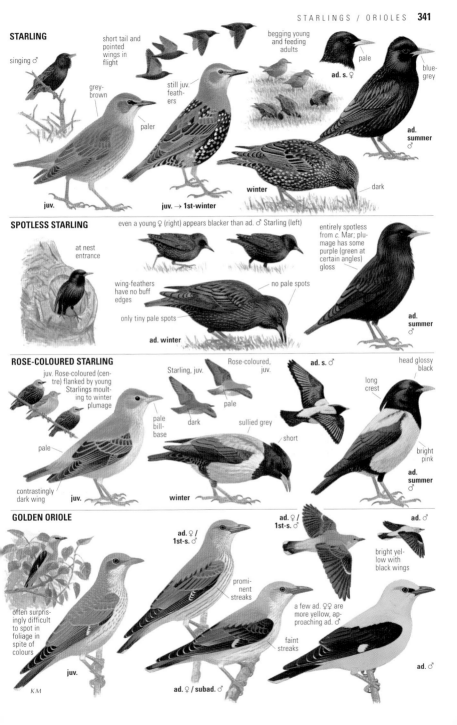

STARLING

singing ♂

short tail and pointed wings in flight

begging young and feeding adults

pale

ad. s. ♀

blue-grey

grey-brown

paler

still juv. feathers

ad. summer ♂

juv.

juv. → 1st-winter

winter

dark

SPOTLESS STARLING

even a young ♀ (right) appears blacker than ad. ♂ Starling (left)

at nest entrance

entirely spotless from c. Mar; plumage has some purple (green at certain angles) gloss

ad. summer ♂

wing-feathers have no buff edges

no pale spots

only tiny pale spots

ad. winter

ROSE-COLOURED STARLING

juv. Rose-coloured (centre) flanked by young Starlings moulting to winter plumage

Rose-coloured, juv.

Starling, juv.

pale

ad. s. ♂

head glossy black

long crest

pale bill-base

dark

sullied grey

short

pale

bright pink

contrastingly dark wing

juv.

winter

ad. summer ♂

GOLDEN ORIOLE

ad. ♀ / 1st-s. ♂

ad. ♂

bright yellow with black wings

prominent streaks

often surprisingly difficult to spot in foliage in spite of colours

a few ad. ♀♀ are more yellow, approaching ad. ♂

faint streaks

ad. ♂

juv.

ad. ♀ / subad. ♂

KM

SPARROWS *Passeridae*

Sturdily built passerines with conical bill suited for consuming seeds. Closely related to the weavers *Ploceidae*, which occur mainly in Africa, but also to the finches (pp. 346–361). Differ from latter in e.g. having more primitive vocal repertoire, often building bulkier and more 'twiggy' nest and having complete moult from juvenile to 1st-winter plumage in summer. Food seeds, also some insects.

House Sparrow *Passer domesticus* r**B**1

L 14–16 cm. Breeds in proximity of man both in rural and in urban areas. Is therefore well known, and often thought of as the most numerous bird, which is far from the case (commonest in Britain are Wren and Chaffinch). Resident. Social, even when breeding, and usually occurs in dense flocks. Nests under roof tiles, in air duct, recess, sometimes in tree. Hybridizes with Spanish Sparrow (which see).

IDENTIFICATION Robust, with broad body and fairly big head with *stout bill*. Plumage rather bushy and 'loose', and often looks matted and unkempt. Main features are *heavily black-streaked brownish back*, *squat posture* with legs drawn in when perched, and laborious and clumsy, 'drilling' flight with *continuously whirring wingbeats*. Sexes differ. – ♂: *Black bib*, lores and eye region. *Grey crown* with chestnut-brown sides. Throat-sides whitish, but *cheeks usually dusky grey*. *Broad white wing-bar*. Bill predominantly black when breeding. – ♀/juvenile: Dusky brownish grey-white below, and dirty brown above with black-streaked back. Often a distinct light dirty buff supercilium. Juvenile ♂ moults in the first black throat-feathers in Aug–Sep.

VOICE A great variety of simple chirping or chattering sounds, varied in details according to situation and mood. During courtship, long series of well-spaced monosyllabic chirps slightly varied throughout, e.g. 'chilp chev chilp chelp chürp...'. In irritation, typical rattling 'cher'r'r'r'r'.

Spanish Sparrow *Passer hispaniolensis* **V**∗∗∗

L 14–16 cm. Breeds locally near man in cavities in buildings, as House Sparrow, but more often found in tall shrubbery or in clumps of trees, usually beside rivers or marshes and often in large colonies. Closed nests of straw and twigs. Also builds in stick nest of larger birds (e.g. White Stork). Resident or short-range migrant in W, mainly migratory in E; in E Mediterranean in spring and autumn, seen *migrating by day in typically dense flocks*, which move in purposeful, billowing low flight and at surprisingly high speed. Often hybridizes with House Sparrow, and intermediates can be seen where the two species meet, mainly in N Africa. Rather stable hybrid forms occur in southernmost Switzerland, N and C Italy and Corsica (× *italiae*) and in Malta (× *maltae*).

IDENTIFICATION Like House Sparrow. 'Pure' ♂ usually easily recognized by combination of: *wholly chestnut-brown crown*; *big, broad black bib* which *meets black shoulders*; *coarsely black-spotted flanks*; *whitish cheeks*; *narrow white supercilium* (sometimes broken just above eye); in spring and summer largely *black on mantle and shoulders*. – ♂ of hybrid form ×*italiae* (see above) lacks (or has greatly restricted) black spotting on flanks, has less black on mantle and shoulders, and has narrower and clearly broken white supercilium. – ♀: Normally impossible to separate in field from House Sparrow (has on average slightly bigger bill, paler belly and sometimes hint of grey streaking on flanks, but differences as a rule too vague for safe identification).

VOICE Like House Sparrow's, but a bit *higher* and more *metallic* in tone. *Fast, monotonous* series, e.g. 'chili-chili-chili-...', often heard. The hum from larger colonies has a typically musical ring, is audible at several hundred metres.

(Eurasian) Tree Sparrow *Passer montanus* r**B**2–3

L 12½–14 cm. Breeds in open woodland, usually near cultivated land or human habitation, locally around houses and in gardens like House Sparrow. Resident. Nests in natural tree-hole, in nestbox or in cavity in building.

IDENTIFICATION Smaller and neater than House Sparrow, with ♂ of which it is still often confused by the layman. Like that species, has black-streaked brown back, distinct white wing-bar, black bib, lores and bill, and underparts dusky, but told by: *wholly vinaceous red-brown crown*; *pure white head-side* with *big black cheek patch*; *smaller black bib* which does not expand into large patch on breast; *narrow white neck-collar* (broken only on nape). Sexes and ages alike.

VOICE Rather like House Sparrow's. Distinctive, however, is a 'tsu**witt**', slightly nasal and disyllabic, with cheery tone. In flight, often a dry 'tett-ett-ett-ett'. Song a fast series of 'tsvit' and variants, like House's chatter but a bit higher-pitched.

Dead Sea Sparrow *Passer moabiticus* —

L 12–13 cm. Breeds in dry lowland areas with tamarisk or other bushes and access to open water; not tied to man. Resident and nomadic. Rather shy.

IDENTIFICATION Small. ♂ has *dark grey crown, nape and cheeks* (tinged brown in fresh autumn plumage), small black bib, *pale supercilium becoming buff at rear*, and characteristic *light yellow neck-side*. ♀ like a *small* but *pale* House Sparrow; a few have trace of yellow on neck-side.

VOICE Recalls both Spanish and House Sparrow's, but a little feebler than both. Flight-call repeated high, disyllabic 'chi-vit'. Song consists of fast, rolling 'trirp-trirp-trirp-trirp' or slower series of sonorous but more varied chirps, 'chilp chrilp chrirp chilp...'.

House Sparrow

Spanish Sparrow

Tree Sparrow

Dead Sea Sparrow

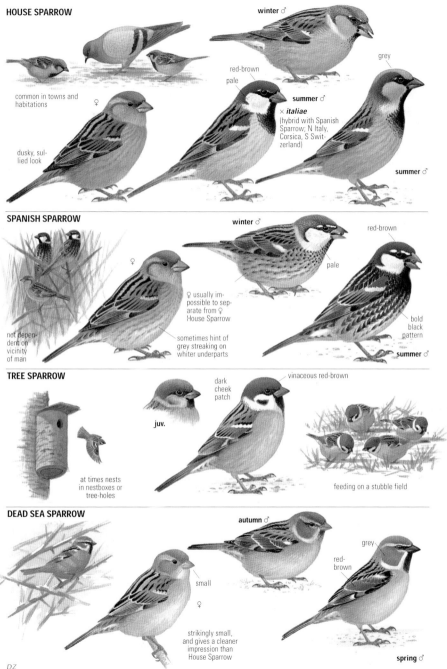

HOUSE SPARROW

winter ♂

common in towns and habitations

♀

dusky, sullied look

red-brown

pale

summer ♂

× *italiae*
(hybrid with Spanish Sparrow; N Italy, Corsica, S Switzerland)

grey

summer ♂

SPANISH SPARROW

winter ♂

♀

not dependent on vicinity of man

♀ usually impossible to separate from ♀ House Sparrow

sometimes hint of grey streaking on whiter underparts

red-brown

pale

bold black pattern

summer ♂

TREE SPARROW

dark cheek patch

juv.

vinaceous red-brown

at times nests in nestboxes or tree-holes

feeding on a stubble field

DEAD SEA SPARROW

autumn ♂

small

♀

strikingly small, and gives a cleaner impression than House Sparrow

grey

red-brown

spring ♂

DZ

Rock Sparrow *Petronia petronia* —

L 15–17 cm. Breeds in various habitats with bare surfaces: rock faces in alps, ravines, wadis, quarries, rocky desert tracts, open terrain with walls, ruins and even occupied buildings, locally also alpine meadows with boulders, cultivations. Resident. Social, can be seen in large flocks in non-breeding season. Nests in cavity in rocks or in crevice.

IDENTIFICATION Rather big and *very stocky*, with broad head and *hefty bill*. Markings typically heavy and stripy, with patterned wing and *broad pale supercilium* between *dark crown-side* and dark eye-stripe. Greater part of *whitish underparts heavily and openly streaked brownish-grey* (look rather dark at distance). *A yellow spot where throat meets breast* (though often hard to see when bird perched in hunched-up posture). Tail dark with *large white terminal patches on outer feathers*, seen best in flight. *Undertail-coverts dark with broad pale fringes.* Sexes alike.

VOICE Voluble. Call a short nasal 'vüi'. In anxiety, a hard trilling 'tii-tür'r'r'r'. Most typical is a loud, drawn-out call in glissando, repeated and varied as song, 'sle-veeit' or 'tveyu**i**t'; sounds slightly nasal, creaky and 'seductive' in tone; occasionally shorter 'tvü**i**t' heard.

Hill Sparrow *Carpospiza brachydactyla* —

(Altern. name: PALE ROCK SPARROW.) L 14½–15½ cm. Breeds in arid and hilly areas on barren slopes with scattered bushes and some ground vegetation. Migratory.

IDENTIFICATION Rather slim, with small head, and *large, short and podgy bill* swollen at very base. Plumage rather *light grey-buff* with no obvious features (back lacks heavy streaking). On closer inspection, shows a poorly indicated, short, pale supercilium and a diffusely paler eye-ring, as well as two very indistinct pale wing-bars. *Bill* when breeding is rather *dark grey* with slightly paler base to lower mandible, during winter months somewhat lighter grey-buff. In flight, shows *small white spots on tail-tip*.

VOICE Call a Greenfinch-like 'dvui', also a short, low-pitched trill, 'trrü' (can recall distant Bee-eater). Song a plain, full-second-long throaty buzz, 'bzrüüüüiz', like an insect or electric motor, sometimes prefaced by a few short grace-notes, 'bz-bz-bz-bzrüüüüiz' (Corn Bunting-like).

Chestnut-shouldered Sparrow *Gymornis xanthocollis* —

L 13–14½ cm. Breeds within the region only at a few places in SE Turkey in groves and cultivations, e.g. of almond, olive and date palm, or in dry scrub with scattered trees. Migratory, winters in India; returns in May.

IDENTIFICATION A rather small and *slim* sparrow with small head but *long and strong, conical, pointed bill*, the size of which is accentuated by flat forehead/crown (though may

erect crown-feathers). Plumage brown-grey with somewhat paler belly and *double wing-bar*. ♂ told from ♀ by *reddish-brown lesser coverts, yellow throat patch, dark lores* and, in breeding season, *black bill*. Tail square-ended. Legs grey.

VOICE Resembles House Sparrow's. Simple chirping song, but tempo characteristically fast and tone full and ringing. Call a piercing 'chi**ah**'(like miniature Chough).

Desert Sparrow *Passer simplex* —

L 13–14½ cm. Breeds in sand deserts at oases, near settlements or cultivations. Resident and nomadic. Nests in cavity.

IDENTIFICATION Like a washed-out, small House Sparrow. Plumage *very pale buff*, like sunlit desert sand. Sexes very different once juvenile plumage exchanged for adult type in summer. – ♂: *Black bib, lores and eye region*; when breeding, *black bill*; brownish-black primary coverts, alula, outer greater coverts, primary tips and tertial centres; *grey tinge to crown and mantle.* – ♀: Almost uniformly pale buffy-white, with warmer *ochre tone on crown/mantle* and ochre tinge to breast; lacks black bib, and dark wing-markings are brownish-grey, not brownish-black as on ♂. Bill always pale. – Juvenile: As ♀, but wing markings even more lacking in contrast (seen best on tertials in rear view).

VOICE Like House Sparrow's but more metallic, and mixed with White Wagtail-like high 'chi-vi chi-vi'. Often gives Greenfinch-like 'chüpp-chüpp-chüpp' in flight.

(White-winged) Snowfinch *Montifringilla nivalis* —

L 16½–19 cm. Breeds on bare mountains, often at 1900–3100 m. Resident, and remains at rather high altitude even in winter (exceptionally down to 1000 m). Often seen foraging at ski-resort restaurants; restless but often quite fearless.

IDENTIFICATION A fairly *big and elongate*, long-winged bird with conspicuous white panels on tail and wings. Hopping on ground, a rather dull grey-brown bird showing one narrow but long white wing-panel. When it takes off, the white is dominant: greater part of *inner wing is white*, and *tail is white with narrow black central band* (and thin black terminal band). At close range, shows dull earth-brown mantle/back, greyish head, and dirty white underparts with a small and often diffuse black bib. Bill black when breeding, ivory-yellow during winter. Flight fast and powerful, undulating over longer stretches. Sexes similar.

VOICE Rich repertoire. Calls include a hoarse 'zyiiih', a creaky mewing 'myaih', short 'ti ti zü' and, often when nervous, a Crested Tit-like rolling 'tir'r'r'r'. Also has a clattering 'chett-chett-chett-chett'. Song, delivered from perch on boulder or in circling gliding flight, has sparrow quality, is variable, halting and jolting with recurrent dry, strained trills. Also has a soft, twittering subsong.

Rock Sparrow   Hill Sparrow   Desert Sparrow   Snowfinch

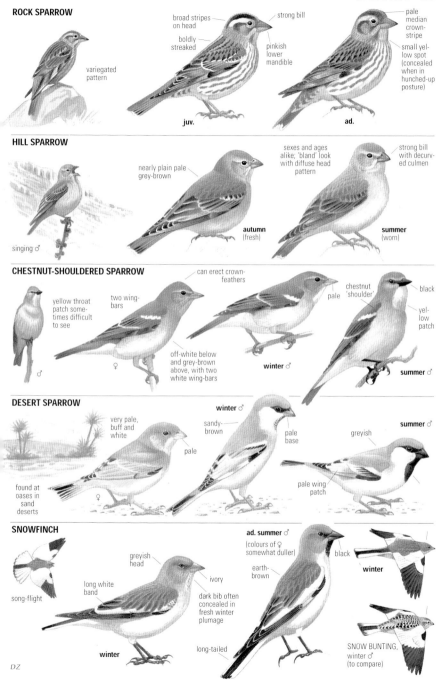

ROCK SPARROW

variegated pattern

broad stripes on head

strong bill

boldly streaked

pinkish lower mandible

juv.

pale median crown-stripe

small yellow spot (concealed when in hunched-up posture)

ad.

HILL SPARROW

singing ♂

nearly plain pale grey-brown

sexes and ages alike; 'bland' look with diffuse head pattern

strong bill with decurved culmen

autumn (fresh)

summer (worn)

CHESTNUT-SHOULDERED SPARROW

yellow throat patch sometimes difficult to see

♂

two wing-bars

can erect crown-feathers

off-white below and grey-brown above, with two white wing-bars

♀

pale

winter ♂

chestnut 'shoulder'

black

yellow patch

summer ♂

DESERT SPARROW

found at oases in sand deserts

very pale, buff and white

pale

♀

winter ♂

sandy-brown

pale base

pale wing patch

summer ♂

greyish

SNOWFINCH

song-flight

long white band

greyish head

ivory

dark bib often concealed in fresh winter plumage

winter

long-tailed

ad. summer ♂ (colours of ♀ somewhat duller)

earth-brown

black

winter

SNOW BUNTING, winter ♂ (to compare)

DZ

FINCHES *Fringillidae*

A large and varied group of relatively small passerines with large, conical bill. Tail of most narrow, with indented tip. Flight powerful, undulating. Most species are accomplished and frequent singers. Often social in habits outside breeding season; migrate and forage in flocks. Most important food is seeds, which are split or husked with the heavy bill; in summer also take some insects. Build open, basket-shaped nests which are usually placed in thick bushes or trees.

(Common) Chaffinch *Fringilla coelebs*   rB1 / W+P1

L 14–16 cm. Breeds commonly in all types of woodland and in parks and gardens, and is Britain's second commonest bird after Wren (estimated *c.* 5.4 million pairs). Prefers rather more open woods to dense ones, and often forages on ground. Resident British & Irish population augmented by large autumn/winter influx from N and NE Europe. Builds neat nest in tree fork, camouflaged on outside with lichens and moss.

IDENTIFICATION Size of House Sparrow, but slimmer and has longer tail. Usually easily recognized by *double white wing-bar, white tail-sides* and *grey-green rump*. – ♂ (once in plumage moulted Jul–Sep): *Head-side and breast rusty-red; crown and nape blue-grey* (tinged brown in fresh autumn plumage); mantle reddish-brown. – ♀/juvenile: Grey-green above with faint brown tinge, greyish-white below; narrower wing-bars than ♂. – Flight strong and undulating. On migration forms fairly loose flocks (a bit looser than Brambling, but mixed flocks common). Often alights with a few fluttering sweeping turns, showing white patterns.

VOICE Powerful voice and frequent singing make this one of the birds most heard in woodland and parks. Several calls characteristic once learned. Perched bird gives a spirited, sharp 'fink!' (only Great Tit's 'ping' is confusable), while in flight it has a more unobtrusive 'yupp' (softer than Brambling's 'yeck', weaker than Greenfinch's 'jüpp!'), which is repeated frequently by migrating flocks overhead. Also heard often in N Europe is a forceful, upcurled whistle, 'hüitt', often persistently repeated, which in S Scandinavia, England and Continental Europe is commonly replaced by a rolling, straight, discordant whistle, 'rrhü' (and many local variants; in S Europe also a Thrush Nightingale-like uninflected 'hiit'); function varies between advertising, warning and territory maintenance, and the call is often termed the 'rain-song'. When highly agitated, a sharp, fine piping note, 'ziih'. Fledged young beg with a loud 'chripp'. Song highly characteristic, rather constant in delivery and tirelessly repeated, a bright, loud, almost rattling verse introduced by 3–4 rapidly repeated sharp notes which turn into a similar series of lower notes, the whole terminating

in a lively flourish, 'zitt-zitt-zitt-zitt-sett-sett-sett-chatt-chiter**ii**dia'; some Chaffinches add an almost out-of-place, Great Spotted Woodpecker-like 'kick' at the very end.

Brambling *Fringilla montifringilla*   W+P1–3 / (m**B**5)

L 14–16 cm. Common breeder in upland birch forest of Fenno-Scandia; absent from dense, tall forest, prefers more open woodlands with some deciduous growth. Summer visitor to breeding sites (mostly mid Apr–Oct), winters in C and S Europe, but in mild winters many remain in S Scandinavia. Rather shy. Food mainly seeds, in summer also insects and in winter often beech nuts. In some winters when beech mast plentiful, enormous flocks gather around beech trees. Builds nest in tree fork, generally in birch, also in spruce.

IDENTIFICATION Same size and shape as Chaffinch, but in all plumages recognized by *white rump* (tinged yellow on juvenile) and little or *no white on sides of tail*. Like Chaffinch, has pale wing markings, but these are partially rusty-yellow as well as narrower and less conspicuous. Flight as Chaffinch's, but single-species passage flocks are often somewhat more compact. – ♂ summer: *Head, nape, shoulders and mantle glossy blue-black*. Throat, breast and lesser wing-coverts unspotted rusty-yellow. Some dark spots on lower flanks. Bill black. – ♀: Crown, mantle/back and nape-sides rather dark grey-brown, head-sides and central nape paler buffy grey-white, *breast buffish*. – ♂ winter: Black areas of summer plumage partly concealed by fairly broad rusty-buff fringes, giving somewhat piebald appearance. Bill straw-yellow with dark tip. Most reliably told from ♀ by *black showing through on entire head-side*. Younger ♂♂ have black-spotted lesser coverts and broader pale fringes to upperparts.

VOICE Has characteristic call, a loud, croaking or hard, nasal 'te-**ehp**', uttered both in flight and when perched. Migrating flocks give hard, short, slightly nasal 'yeck' calls (cf. Chaffinch), oft repeated. In anxiety, utters repeated, fine, silver-clear notes, 'slitt, slitt, slitt,...'. Song very distinctive and with desolate ring, a slowly repeated, straight, barely second-long, crude buzzing note, 'rrrrrhüh', which can recall a distant wood-cutting crosscut saw.

Blue Chaffinch *Fringilla teydea*   —

L 16–18 cm. Breeds in pine forest at 1200–1800 m altitude in Tenerife (relatively numerous) and Gran Canaria (scarce). Resident. Normally forages in pine woods but sometimes in bushy areas on mountainsides, and exceptionally (in severe weather) can be seen in cultivations down to *c.* 500 m. Generally seen singly or in small flocks (<10). Food mainly seeds of Canary pine. Late breeder, end May–Jul (Aug).

IDENTIFICATION Noticeably *bigger* than Chaffinch and more front-heavy, with *heavier breast, head and bill*. Both sexes have *poorly indicated, narrow greyish-white wing-bars* and *lack white on tail*. The stout, conical bill is rather pale grey. – ♂: *Dark grey-blue on head and mantle, paler lead-grey on throat, breast and flanks*; undertail-coverts white. – ♀: Brown-grey above, greyish-white below.

VOICE Call a disyllabic 'chrooit', with cracked and slightly squeaky voice. Song shorter than Chaffinch's and not so forceful, has decelerating ending of a few repeated, rather harsh, descending notes, the last of which is drawn out, e.g. 'sitt-sitt-sitt rüha-rüha, rrüü**aah**'.

Chaffinch   Brambling

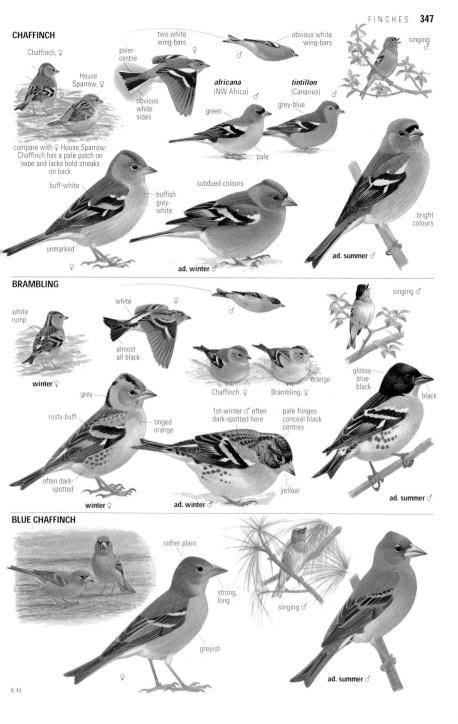

CHAFFINCH

Chaffinch, ♀

House Sparrow, ♀

compare with ♀ House Sparrow: Chaffinch has a pale patch on nape and lacks bold streaks on back

buff-white

unmarked

♀

paler centre

two white wing-bars ♀

obvious white sides

obvious white wing-bars

♂

singing ♂

africana (NW Africa) ♂

green

pale

tintillon (Canaries) ♂

grey-blue

buffish grey-white

subdued colours

bright colours

ad. winter ♂

ad. summer ♂

BRAMBLING

white rump

winter ♀

white

almost all black

♀

♂

grey

rusty-buff

tinged orange

often dark-spotted

winter ♀

Chaffinch, ♀

Brambling, ♀

orange

1st-winter ♂ often dark-spotted here

pale fringes conceal black centres

yellow

ad. winter ♂

singing ♂

glossy blue-black

black

ad. summer ♂

BLUE CHAFFINCH

rather plain

strong, long

greyish

♀

singing ♂

ad. summer ♂

KM

(Common) Linnet *Carduelis cannabina*   r+m**B**2 / **P**+**W**

L 12½–14 cm. Breeds in areas with thick bushes, in gardens and especially on coastal heaths with gorse, locally also in orchards. Restless and active, often rises in hopping flight only soon to drop down again. Pair-members stay close together throughout summer.

IDENTIFICATION *Slim* and rather long-tailed, with *short grey bill*. In all plumages, *brown mantle and back* and buffy-white throat with indistinct dark spotting in centre. *Side of head typically marked* with pale above and beneath eye and dusky cheeks with pale spot in centre. *Primaries edged white.* – Adult ♂: *Red on forehead and breast* (in autumn brownish-red and partly concealed by pale fringes). Uniform grey nape. – ♀/juvenile: No red in plumage; brown-grey nape and lightly streaked breast, and streaked crown. Juvenile somewhat more streaked and duller brown above than adult ♀.

VOICE Flight-call a dry but still slightly nasal, bouncing 'tigg-**itt**' or 'tett-ett-**ett**'; uttered with particular intensity on rising. Song a mixture of short, rattling syllables akin to call plus musical whistling notes. Sometimes gives drawn-out verses delivered at rather fast tempo, but more often the song is 'on low heat', and the verses are short and well spaced. Common elements in the song, besides the call, are e.g. 'p**iuu**', 'trrrüh' and 'tu-ki-**yüü**'.

Twite *Carduelis flavirostris*   r(m)**B**3 / **W**3–4

L 12½–14 cm. Breeds on treeless moors and bare coastal heaths (incl. crofting lands in Scotland and Ireland), many moving in Oct–Nov mainly to coasts of North Sea / S Baltic, returning in Mar–Apr. Often forages at refuse tips and on tilled fields, may then be seen in large, dense flocks of hundreds of birds. Restless and mobile, but not shy.

IDENTIFICATION Resembles a Linnet in size and shape, but on average has a trifle *longer and more deeply cleft tail*, smaller head and slightly bushier, 'looser' feathering. Told from 1st-winter Linnet by: *more heavily dark-streaked*, usually distinctly *buff-tinged plumage*; *lack of dark brown* (cinnamon) *above*; *no dark spotting on throat-centre*; *bolder pale wing-bar* (buff-white tips to greater coverts); ♂ in addition has *pink on rump*, most obvious in spring but usually visible also in fresh autumn plumage (absent on ♀). *Bill yellow* (with dark tip) in winter, brown-grey when breeding.

VOICE Call a rather short and hard 'yett', somewhere between flight-calls of Brambling, Redpoll and Linnet, and which can be rather hard to pick out in mixed finch flocks, as well as a characteristic *drawn-out and slightly rising, bleating* 'tveeiht' (hence 'Twite'!). Song more like Citril Finch's than Linnet's, fast trills, buzzing sounds and sequences of twitters, recognized by interwoven low rattling 'trrrrrrr' notes; traces of the bleating call often heard also in the song.

(Common) Redpoll *Carduelis flammea*   m(r)**B**2 / **W**2

L 11½–14 cm. Breeds in birch forest, young conifers, less often in willows on bare mountains, as well as in small thick deciduous copses in open terrain, e.g. meadows, dunes and heaths; in the Alps often in larch-dominated conifer forest above 1400 m. In Britain & Ireland partial migrant and winter visitor, very numerous in some years (invasions), often in alders in winter. Mobile and restless, dense winter flocks seldom stay in one spot for long, and even during breeding the birds roam widely, often high up. Clings nimbly, even upside-down, to tips of birch twigs. Nests in branch fork.

IDENTIFICATION Greyish and dark-streaked, with small *yellowish finch-type bill with dark culmen, pale wing-bars, black bib, black loral region* and dark forehead plus *red forecrown*. In good view, only confusion risk is Arctic Redpoll (which see). *Rump streaked*, but note that some (esp. ad. ♂) have white (or light red) ground colour with very faint streaks and in field can be confused with Arctic. Only adult ♂ has much bright red on breast, otherwise sexes and ages are difficult to separate in field. – Variation: Birds in British Isles, C Europe and SW Scandinavia (ssp. *cabaret*) are smaller and darker brownish than those in Fenno-Scandia (*flammea*).

VOICE Call, given often in flight, an almost echoing, hard and metallic, repeated 'chett-chett-chett'. When nervous, a somewhat Greenfinch-like but feebler and usually hoarser 'jüih' (used also as advertising-call). Song consists of the metallic call interspersed with dry, reeling 'serrrrrrr'; delivered mostly in undulating, wide-ranging song-flight.

Arctic Redpoll *Carduelis hornemanni*   **V**∗∗

L 12–14 cm. Breeds as a rule in willows and in low, open birch forest on or near tundra or upland heath, rarely also in tall, closed upland birch forest. Migratory habits unclear; some move southward with Redpoll flocks in winter months. Nests in willow bush or in birch fork.

IDENTIFICATION Very like Redpoll, and in certain plumages impossible to separate reliably. *Bill small* and pointed, with *straight culmen*. Rather fluffy, 'loose' plumage. – Adult ♂: Large *unmarked white* (or faintly pink) *rump*. Only *few and narrow dark streaks on flanks*, contributing to pale overall impression. *Ground colour of mantle/back pale*. Forehead usually pale. *Breast light pink* (never bright red). – ♀: Lacks pink on breast and rump. Many have a small unspotted white rump patch, but some (probably imms.) have faintly streaked grey-white rump and are deceptively like Redpolls. Flank streaking varies, some being heavily streaked.

VOICE Very like Redpoll's and difficult to distinguish from latter's. The reeling trill is on average a little softer and has more cracked and almost 'lisping' quality, and the 'chett-chett-chett' call is also softer and higher in tone.

Linnet   Twite   Redpoll   Arctic Redpoll

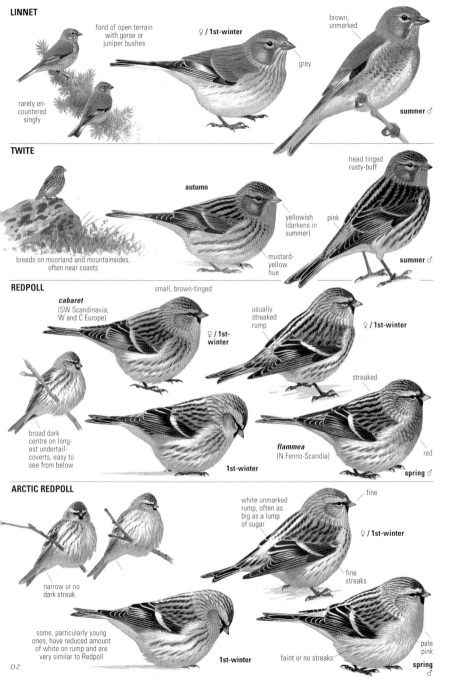

LINNET

fond of open terrain with gorse or juniper bushes

brown, unmarked

♀ / **1st-winter**

grey

rarely encountered singly

summer ♂

TWITE

head tinged rusty-buff

autumn

yellowish (darkens in summer)

pink

mustard-yellow hue

breeds on moorland and mountainsides, often near coasts

summer ♂

REDPOLL

small, brown-tinged

cabaret (SW Scandinavia, W and C Europe)

usually streaked rump

♀ / **1st-winter**

♀ / **1st-winter**

streaked

broad dark centre on longest undertail-coverts, easy to see from below

flammea (N Fenno-Scandia)

red

1st-winter

spring ♂

ARCTIC REDPOLL

fine

white unmarked rump, often as big as a lump of sugar

♀ / **1st-winter**

fine streaks

narrow or no dark streak

some, particularly young ones, have reduced amount of white on rump and are very similar to Redpoll

pale pink

1st-winter

faint or no streaks

spring ♂

DZ

(European) **Goldfinch** *Carduelis carduelis*   m(r)**B**2 / **P**

L 12–13½ cm. Breeds in low-lying deciduous and mixed woodland, in plantations and in orchards and gardens. Mainly summer visitor (mostly Apr–early Nov), majority winter in S and W Europe. Often seen in flocks after breeding. Frequently forages on seeding thistles, burdocks etc. Nests in tree crown, often among thinner outer branches.

IDENTIFICATION Unmistakable with its *red 'face'*, its otherwise *black and white head*, the *jet-black wing with broad yellow wing-bar* (visible also on perched bird) and prominent *white rump* and *black tail with white spots*. Sexes in practice alike in the field. Bill very long and pointed, ivory-white. – Juvenile (up to Aug– Oct): Head grey-brown and diffusely streaked, without adult's red, white and black pattern.

VOICE Call very characteristic, a trisyllabic, skipping and cheery 'ticke**litt**'; conversational monosyllabic 'litt' or disyllabic 'te**litt**' sometimes heard from foraging flocks. Flocks also give rasping 'tschrre' notes. Song rather quiet, akin to Siskin's and consists of rapid trills, mewing notes and twittering sequences but *always recognized by interwoven call note* or long series of 'te**litt**-te**litt**-te**litt**'.

(European) **Greenfinch** *Carduelis chloris*   r(m)**B**2 / **W**

L 14–16 cm. Breeds at woodland edge, in wooded pasture and copses, in bushy areas and in parks and gardens. Common also in villages and towns. Hardy, and many overwinter in N, but some migrate to W and SW Europe. Always wary, at times shy. Nests in tree, bush or trellis.

IDENTIFICATION Compared with its relatives, is a heavier bird with *stouter body, head and bill*. Bill rather pale pink or ivory-coloured. Perched bird recognized by *yellow edges to primaries* which form a yellow panel, by *greenish tone to underparts* in all plumages and, in flight (besides the yellow on primaries), by *yellow at base of tail-sides*. – ♂: *Yellowish-green breast*, grey-green upperparts, greyish head-side and *light grey wing-panel*. Much yellow on primaries and tail. – ♀: Duller and drabber grey colours, mantle / back tinged brown, less yellow on wings and tail. – Juvenile: Diffusely streaked.

VOICE Call a short, forceful 'jüpp', usually repeated in fast series and becoming short trills, 'jüp-üp-üp'. Another call is a loud, upcurled 'ju**it**'. Song of two totally different types, one an unmusical, frizzling or wheezy 'dschrüüüüuh' which is repeated with long pauses, the other a pleasing and drawn-out Canary-type song consisting of trills and fast runs of whistles and twitters, a bit like Tree Pipit's song, e.g. 'jüpp-jüpp-jüpp jürrrrrrrrrr tuy-tuy-tuy-tuy-tuy ju**it** chipp-chipp-chipp-chipp-chipp dürdürdürdür jürrrrrrrrr...'; sometimes the wheezing song type is woven into the musical song.

(Eurasian) **Siskin** *Carduelis spinus*   r(m)**B**2 / **P**+**W**2

L 11–12½ cm. Breeds in coniferous and mixed forest, mainly in spruce; prefers alder and birch nearby for food. In Britain & Ireland, winter influxes from N and E Europe, sometimes on huge scale. Often large flocks in winter, when also visits garden nut-baskets. Mobile, roams far and wide, even when breeding. Not that shy. Nests high up in spruce.

IDENTIFICATION Small and neat, with rather small head and short tail. Told by *dark wing with contrasting yellow or yellowish-white markings* and by *yellow bases to tail-sides* (Greenfinch style); in addition has *heavily streaked lower flanks*. – ♂ (from Sep): *Crown and bib black* (partly concealed by light grey fringes when fresh); eyebrow, *breast and rump unstreaked greenish-yellow*. – ♀: Crown grey-green, breast and rump white with yellow-green tinge and diffusely streaked. – Juvenile: Brownish mantle / back; head palish, streaked dark.

VOICE Two similar disyllabic whistled calls with characteristic ring, one descending and the other rising, 'ti**lu**' and 'tlu**ih**'; the two are freely mixed together by overhead parties. Occasional calls sound straighter and cracked in tone. A stifled, rattling call, 'tetete', is also heard, both from flying and from feeding birds. Song a flowing series of twittering and trilling notes with traces of mimicry (some are masterly mimics), now and then broken by a *drawn-out choking or wheezing note*.

Citril Finch *Serinus citrinella*   —

L 11½–12½ cm. Breeds in mountain forests at *c.* 700 m and up to treeline, usually in spruce stands adjoining alpine meadows and clearings. In Corsica also in low-growing tree-heath above treeline (to 1650 m). Mostly arboreal, but often forages on ground. Primarily resident.

IDENTIFICATION Placed in genus *Serinus* but more like a redpoll or Siskin in appearance, with rather *long and pointed bill*. *Two yellowish-green wing-bars*, but otherwise no pale markings on wings and tail in flight. – ♂: 'Face', *underparts and rump yellowish-green*; *hindcrown/nape ashgrey*; *mantle and back unstreaked olive-grey*. – ♀: Duller and greyer; less yellow-green in plumage, especially on 'face'; mantle and back lightly streaked. – Variation: In Corsica and Sardinia (ssp. *corsicana*), mantle and back are brown and dark-streaked and underparts brighter yellow.

VOICE Calls with *cracked or lilting tone* (like Red-fronted and Syrian Serins), monosyllabic short 'teh', e.g. loosely repeated in flight, or fast, bouncing 'te-te-te', or with more emphatic first syllable and almost trembling ending, 'pi-re're're'. Begging- and anxiety-calls sharp 'ziit' and piping 'tüht'. Song recalls both Siskin's and Linnet's, contains short wheezy notes (much shorter than Siskin's), a lot of Redpoll-like *buzzing trills* and almost Chaffinch-like passages.

Goldfinch   Greenfinch   Siskin   Citril Finch

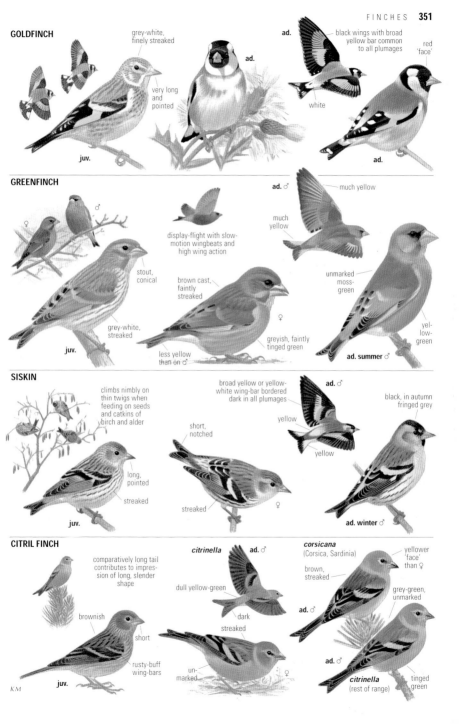

GOLDFINCH

grey-white, finely streaked

ad.

black wings with broad yellow bar common to all plumages

red 'face'

ad.

very long and pointed

white

juv.

ad.

GREENFINCH

♂

♀

much yellow

much yellow

ad. ♂

display-flight with slow-motion wingbeats and high wing action

stout, conical

brown cast, faintly streaked

♀

unmarked moss-green

yel-low-green

grey-white, streaked

greyish, faintly tinged green

juv.

less yellow than on ♂

ad. summer ♂

SISKIN

climbs nimbly on thin twigs when feeding on seeds and catkins of birch and alder

broad yellow or yellow-white wing-bar bordered dark in all plumages

ad. ♂

black, in autumn fringed grey

short, notched

yellow

yellow

long, pointed

streaked

streaked

♀

juv.

ad. winter ♂

CITRIL FINCH

comparatively long tail contributes to impression of long, slender shape

citrinella   ad. ♂

corsicana (Corsica, Sardinia)

yellower 'face' than ♀

dull yellow-green

brown, streaked

ad. ♂

grey-green, unmarked

brownish

dark

streaked

short

rusty-buff wing-bars

un-marked

♀

ad. ♂

citrinella (rest of range)

tinged green

KM   juv.

(European) Serin *Serinus serinus* P5 / (mB)

L 11–12 cm. Breeds in tree clumps and woodland edge, also in gardens, parks, churchyards, orchards etc., preferably with some conifers (often silver fir, thuja, cypress etc.). Rare on passage in Britain (mostly May, Sep–Oct), a few breeding (irregularly) in S. Bold. Makes frequent aerial excursions. Nests rather high in thick conifer or in citrus grove.

IDENTIFICATION Small, with proportionately *large head* and *tiny little bill*. Important features are its small size and its *energetic, skipping flight* and often *restless* behaviour. Mantle and back, belly and *flanks* always heavily *streaked*. On side of head *long pale supercilium* extends down onto *pale neck-side*, framing darker *cheek with pale central spot* (Linnet style). *Rump pale*, bright yellow and contrasting on ♂, duller greenish-yellow (sometimes not very obvious) on ♀. ♂ has *forehead, facial markings, neck-side and breast bright lemon-yellow*, these areas being paler yellowish-white on ♀. – Juvenile: All areas which are yellow on adult are buffish-white.

VOICE Call is a buzzing or bouncing trill, 'zir'r'r'rl', with typically high and silvery, clear voice. Alarm an upcurled 'tü-ih', much as Redpoll's but more clearly disyllabic. Song a *frantically fast* and almost strained stream of squeaky, sharp and jingling notes (often likened to crushing glass, and call-note voice recognizable) at *even pitch*, delivered from treetop or in song-flight with stiff 'slow-motion' wingbeats.

(Atlantic) Canary *Serinus canaria* —

L 12½–13½ cm. Original form of the domestic Canary. Breeds in Madeira and Canary Islands (though not on Fuerteventura and Lanzarote) in orchards, copses, shrubbery, hedges etc. from sea-level to *c.* 1500 m. Resident. Social habits. Mobile, flies a lot. Nests in bush or thick tree.

IDENTIFICATION Compared with Serin, is a *bigger*, more *elongate* bird with *longer bill and tail* and shorter wing (only moderate primary projection). Has some grey and pale brown in the plumage and has *more diffuse, more washed-out pattern* than Serin, and lacks latter's distinctly contrasting dark crown against pale forehead. – ♂: Greenish-yellow facial markings, nape and neck markings, throat, breast-centre and rump; head-side and crown diffusely grey; lower flanks light yellow, streaked. – ♀: Duller, less yellow; pale rump indistinct. – Juvenile: Lacks yellow.

VOICE A rather characteristic call is a slightly descending, tremulous 'ti-ti-türr' with cracked, 'lilting' tone. Also an upslurred, Greenfinch-like 'juit', a somewhat Siskin-like falling 'tiüh', and a silvery 'tvi-vi-vi-vi' rather like Serin's. Song is most like that of Goldfinch and has same tempo; contains nasal, discordant notes, rapid twitters, muffled trills and many high notes.

Syrian Serin *Serinus syriacus* —

L 12–13 cm. Breeds on lower mountain slopes and in hilly high-lying terrain with scattered trees and bushes, sometimes also in orchards. Some remain in breeding area but often move to lower levels, while others migrate to S Israel and Sinai. Rather shy. Nests in tree.

IDENTIFICATION Only a trifle bigger than Serin, but is a bit *more elongate and long-tailed*, with proportionately slightly smaller head. *Bill small and short*, as Serin's. Plumage somewhat reminiscent of Citril Finch, is rather *uniform and pale* with lightly streaked olive-grey mantle, *unstreaked yellowish-green rump* and pale yellow-tinged grey-white underparts with *no or just minimal streaking*. *Wings* distinctly *greenish* in both sexes. – ♂: Bright yellow forehead, eye-surround and throat; grey-toned crown, nape and cheeks; *lacks Serin's dark crown and yellow supercilium and neck-side framing darker cheek*. – ♀: Duller, is less yellow, somewhat more olive-grey and streaked. – Juvenile: All areas which are grey on adult are buffish-white.

VOICE Call a dry still slightly nasal, and rolling or tremulous 'pe-re-ret' or 'pü-tü', closest to Citril Finch's but lower in pitch. An almost Greenfinch-like, forceful 'chüpp', at times repeated, and a higher, faster variant, 'chip-ip-ip-ip', are often given, too; both these are heard in the song as well. Song most like Red-fronted Serin's and Citril Finch's, squeaky and twittering notes at fast pace, sometimes with strained buzzing sounds admixed. Verses usually fairly short but delivered in rapid succession with only brief pauses.

Red-fronted Serin *Serinus pusillus* —

L 11½–12½ cm. Breeds in mountain areas near or just below treeline in coniferous and mixed forest, often along watercourses in high-lying valleys with sparse, low vegetation or by alpine meadows, with some juniper and rhododendron. Moves to somewhat lower levels in winter. Social. Generally not shy. Nests in low bush or dense tree.

IDENTIFICATION *Small* as Serin (but marginally longer tail), and makes similar *restless* aerial excursions in *bounding flight*. Unmistakable in adult plumage, having *black head* with dazzling *red patch on forecrown*. Plumage otherwise is *densely and heavily black-streaked*, and overall appearance is dark. *Rump orange-yellow*, diffusely streaked. Sexes often alike, but some ♀♀ have black on head less solid and extensive (are dark-streaked sooty-grey on hindcrown, behind eye and on breast), and red crown patch is often slightly smaller. – Juvenile (up to Oct/Nov, occasionally still in Mar): Head largely uniform cinnamon-brown.

VOICE Call a simmering, twittering trill, 'tvir'r'r', cheery and 'sweet' in tone and resembling both Citril Finch's and Syrian Serin's; the trill (which is invariably long like Serin's, not short like that of Citril Finch's, which often also has monosyllabic calls) drops very slightly at end. Song a long, twittering and frenzied series, like a fast Goldfinch song, and also like Citril Finch's: trills and rapid whistles mixed with short wheezing sounds.

Serin

Syrian Serin

Red-fronted Serin

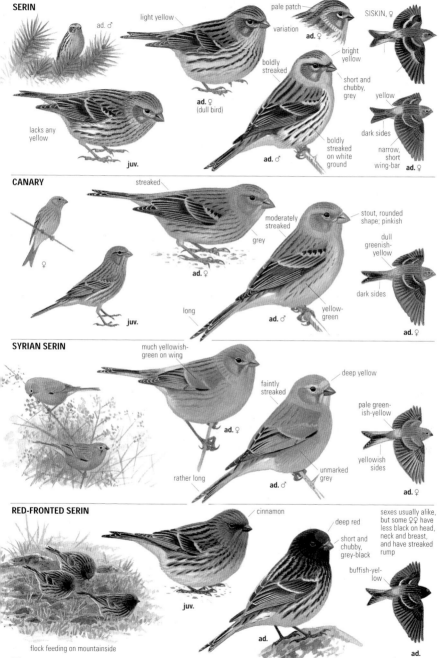

SERIN

ad. ♂

light yellow

pale patch

variation

ad. ♀

SISKIN, ♀

bright yellow

short and chubby, grey

boldly streaked

ad. ♀
(dull bird)

yellow

dark sides

narrow, short wing-bar **ad. ♀**

lacks any yellow

juv.

boldly streaked on white ground

ad. ♂

CANARY

streaked

moderately streaked

grey

stout, rounded shape; pinkish

dull greenish-yellow

♀

dark sides

juv.

long

yellow-green

ad. ♀

ad. ♂

ad. ♀

SYRIAN SERIN

much yellowish-green on wing

faintly streaked

deep yellow

pale greenish-yellow

ad. ♀

yellowish sides

rather long

unmarked grey

ad. ♂

ad. ♀

RED-FRONTED SERIN

cinnamon

deep red

short and chubby, grey-black

sexes usually alike, but some ♀♀ have less black on head, neck and breast, and have streaked rump

buffish-yellow

juv.

flock feeding on mountainside

ad.

ad.

DZ

(Eurasian) **Bullfinch** *Pyrrhula pyrrhula*   r**B**2

L 15½–17½ cm. Breeds in mixed woods, in parks and larger gardens, in churchyards etc. with some conifers, sometimes (esp. in Fenno-Scandia) also in coniferous forest. Mostly resident, but some N European breeders migrate (mainly end Oct) to S Scandinavia and C Europe. Not really shy, but unobtrusive and easily overlooked in summer. Quiet, almost sluggish in behaviour. Often seen in pairs or in small, rather loose flocks. Food various kinds of seeds and shoots of fruit trees; also some insects in summer. Nests in bush or tree, often on sheltered branch.

IDENTIFICATION A rather big and very *compact* finch which looks bull-necked or *neckless*, has *plump body*, quite big head, and short but deep, *'podgy' bill*. Bearing in mind its fairly sedentary lifestyle, has surprisingly long wings and long tail, and flight is fast and in long undulations; at range, still recognized by plump body and broad neck. In rear view, identified in flight by *white rump patch* contrasting with *black tail* and *grey back*. Also has a *broad, off-white wing-bar*. Adult has black crown and 'face', and sexes best separated by underpart colour, ♂ *bright red*, ♀ greyish-buff. ♂ also has pure ash-grey mantle and back, whereas ♀ has the grey tinged brownish. – Juvenile (up to Sep–Oct): Head entirely grey-brown, and sexes are alike (being ♀-coloured below).

VOICE Call a short whistle or fluted note, low-pitched, discreet and almost inhaled, usually with melancholy ring, 'phü', or with hint of drop at end, 'phew'; locally in Europe with distinctly falling pitch, 'phü-ew'. Conversational call, sometimes when flushed, a stifled, repeated 'bütt'. Song soft, slowly recited, halting and tentative, a mixture of call-like, low-pitched fluted notes and choking squeaky and scraping notes; often double-noted 'phü-phü' inserted, or the fluted notes are drawn out into melancholy descending notes, 'pyüüuh'. Some notes are so muffled that they are audible only at very closest range, making the song sound even more discontinuous and hesitant at distance.

Pine Grosbeak *Pinicola enucleator*   V***

L 19–22 cm. Breeds in taiga, usually in mature, undisturbed coniferous forest with some birch and berry-bearing shrubs. Probably mainly resident, but in some autumns mass southward eruptions occur (usually end Oct and in Nov). Unobtrusive and retiring during breeding, but in winter quite fearless (old Swedish colloquial name 'silly fool'), and flocks may then readily feed on rowan berries in gardens and roadside trees in town centres. Food seeds, buds and shoots of e.g. spruce and birch, also berries of rowan, bilberry, cowberry etc. In dense forest sometimes forages quietly down in shrub layer. Nests against trunk, usually of spruce.

IDENTIFICATION *Thrush-sized*, hefty body and thickset, neckless silhouette; *long-tailed*. Bill short and deep with curved culmen. In all plumages, *double white wing-bar* (greater and median coverts have white tips and narrow white outer edges) and *white outer edges to tertials* contrasting with otherwise greyish-black wings. Flight powerful and fast, in deep undulations. – Adult ♂: Greater part of plumage *raspberry-red* (with touch of light grey); mantle/ back and uppertail-coverts spotted dark. – ♀/1st-year ♂: Red colour of adult ♂ replaced by *greyish yellow-orange*.

VOICE Call in flight clear, loud, fluting 'plüit' and 'ju-jü', or, especially when alert before fusing, multisyllabic 'plüi-jih, püllidijüh' and the like. Flocks converse with low, fast 'bütt-bütt-bütt...'. Song very pleasing, with desolate ring well tuned to the deserted breeding forests, a very fast, rapidly repeated, high and silver-clear short verse (2–3 sec.) which yodels or shuttles irresolutely on a couple of notes; the verse is often a shade more stressed in middle than at start and end, may perhaps recall Wood Sandpiper display; can sound like 'pilidü-pilüdi-pilidü-pilidipü-pilüpipi' or similar.

Hawfinch *Coccothraustes coccothraustes*   r**B**4

L 16½–18 cm. Breeds in deciduous and mixed woods, preferring mature lofty deciduous with plenty of oak, hornbeam, beech, ash and elm. Also attracted to fruit trees, especially cherries, kernels of which it cracks with its powerful bill (can generate over 50 kg force!). Diet also includes insects. Very wary and shy and difficult to observe, spends most time up in canopy or seen flying fast high up between woodland-edge trees. Usually nests well up in deciduous tree, against trunk or in fork, in fairly exposed site.

IDENTIFICATION A rather big finch with totally distinctive proportions: has *very powerful, triangular bill*, *big head* and thick neck, but *short tail*. (Size of head due to powerful jaw muscles; the Hawfinch is a flying pair of nut-crackers!). Dominant colours are *rusty-brown and buff* with black, white and grey embellishments. Bill in summer greyish-black with blue-grey base, in winter ivory-white or pale yellow-brown. Wings glossy blue-black, inner primaries with club-shaped extensions. Sexes similar, but separable by ♂ having all-black remiges, while ♀ has an ash-grey panel on secondaries. In flight, shows conspicuous *broad white wing-bar on 'hand'*, and the short *tail is white-tipped*. – Juvenile: Breast greyish-yellow, belly coarsely spotted dark.

VOICE Has a very hard and sharp clicking 'pix!' with an almost electric quality, or like the sound made by jabbing a spike into solid granite; with a bit of practice easy to recognize and distinguish from e.g. Robin's ticking 'tic'; often repeated at slow pace in undulating flight (one 'pix!' on each rise). Besides this call, has more anonymous 'zrri' and 'zih' which are easily drowned in the varied sounds from the woodland's Chaffinches, Spotted Flycatchers, thrushes and others. Song a rather quiet, stumbling series of 'zih' and 'zrri' notes, rather hard to make out.

Bullfinch

Pine Grosbeak

Hawfinch

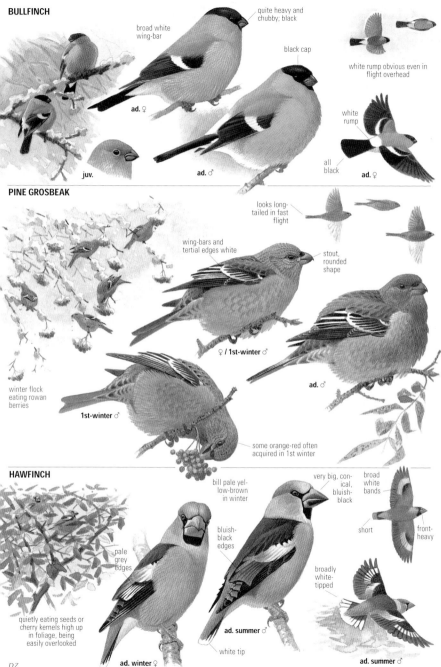

BULLFINCH

broad white wing-bar

quite heavy and chubby; black

black cap

white rump obvious even in flight overhead

ad. ♀

white rump

all black

ad. ♂

juv.

ad. ♀

PINE GROSBEAK

looks long-tailed in fast flight

wing-bars and tertial edges white

stout, rounded shape

♀ / 1st-winter ♂

winter flock eating rowan berries

1st-winter ♂

ad. ♂

some orange-red often acquired in 1st winter

HAWFINCH

bill pale yel-low-brown in winter

very big, con-ical, bluish-black

broad white bands

short

front-heavy

bluish-black edges

broadly white-tipped

pale grey edges

quietly eating seeds or cherry kernels high up in foliage, being easily overlooked

ad. winter ♀

white tip

ad. summer ♂

ad. summer ♂

DZ

CROSSBILLS *Loxia*

Chunky finches with large head and bull-neck, long wings and deeply cleft tail, plus heavy bill with crossed tips, an adaptation for prising open cones and extracting seeds. Often breed early in year (Feb–Mar), but breeding season protracted. Generally resident in northern coniferous forests, but periodic food shortages trigger mass eruptions towards S and W. Often silent when feeding (easily overlooked; watch for falling cones and seed wings discarded by the birds), when they clamber about nimbly like small parrots. High-flying family parties attract attention to their repeated loud, metallic calls. Flight undulating.

Parrot Crossbill *Loxia pytyopsittacus*   **V**∗∗/ (m**B**5)

L 16–18 cm. Breeds in N and E Europe in pine forests or in conifer woods with plenty of pines; seen also in spruce during irruptions. Not so common as Common Crossbill, but quite numerous in some invasion years; exact status poorly known. Has bred in Britain. Nests high up in pine.

IDENTIFICATION A shade bigger than Common Crossbill and with proportionately somewhat bigger head and bill and thicker neck (more bull-necked in profile). Best identified by *larger, thicker bill*, roughly *as deep as it is long* and with *lower mandible almost as deep as upper*; culmen more strongly curved, so bill-tip looks blunter; lower mandible has *lower edge S-shaped, with parrot-like bulge in middle*. Tip of lower mandible normally not visible beyond culmen in profile (often is on Common). – Post-juvenile ♂: Head, underparts and rump brick-red, on some with variable amount of yellow-orange and greyish-green (not strictly age-related). – Post-juvenile ♀: Grey-green or dull yellowish-green, unstreaked below, rump often palest and most yellow. Back and head-sides brownish, wings and tail dark brown-grey. – Juvenile: Grey, with boldly streaked underparts. Some streaked feathers can remain through 1st winter.

VOICE Calls frequently. Call very like Common Crossbill's, but on average *deeper and harder*, more echoing, often less 'clipping' (cf. Common Crossbill) and with harder initial consonant, 'tüpp-tüpp-tüpp-...'. Difference can be detected by the trained ear, and is easiest way (outside Britain) to identify the species despite some individual variation in voice. Song a mix of strained trills and soft twitters with call-like notes (latter distinguishing it); some notes are repeated rapidly a few times.

Scottish Crossbill *Loxia scotica*   r**B**4

L 15½–17 cm. Breeds in N Scotland in ancient pine forest. Resident; any movements poorly known. Nests in pine.

IDENTIFICATION Plumage as Common and Parrot Crossbills; size, structure, bill size and voice intermediate between

those two. Best identified by distribution and often discernibly heavier bill than Common Crossbill (though some overlap). Within this species' range in Scotland, Parrot Crossbill probably not safely distinguishable in the field.

VOICE Call intermediate between those of Common Crossbill and Parrot Crossbill.

Common Crossbill *Loxia curvirostra*   r**B**(3–)4 / (**W**)

L 15–17 cm. Breeds in conifers, including smallish clumps, prefers spruce. Commonest and most widely distributed crossbill, but numbers fluctuate regionally. Nests high up.

IDENTIFICATION Plumages as Parrot Crossbill (which see), but is a trifle smaller, with proportionately somewhat *smaller head, slimmer neck* and *smaller bill*. Note that *bill is longer than it is deep*, with culmen only moderately curved. *Lower mandible less deep than upper and lower edge lacks obvious S-shape with bulging centre*. (For rare variant with narrow pale wing-bars, see under Two-barred Crossbill.)

VOICE Calls frequently. Call a loud, metallic, fairly high 'glipp', usually repeated in series, 'glipp-glipp-glipp-...'; generally sounds 'clipping', as if an 'l' is inserted after rather soft initial consonant. A certain variation in pitch and volume occurs, dependent on age, individual or mood, but pitch is always higher (vowel *i*) than in Parrot Crossbill (vowel *ü*). Song resembles Parrot Crossbill's, but is recognized by interwoven call-notes.

Two-barred Crossbill *Loxia leucoptera*   **V**∗∗∗

L 14½–16 cm. Probably breeds regularly only in Russia; in some years nests in Finland and Sweden. Prefers larch cones; often takes rowan berries in winter.

IDENTIFICATION Plumages similar to those of other crossbills, but adult ♂ often brighter, raspberry-red, and scapulars and tail-coverts have darker centres. A bit smaller than Common Crossbill (though some overlap), and bill not as heavy. Best identified by voice and by *broad white wing-bars and clear-cut broad white tips to tertials*. – Adult: Very broad white wing-bars and tertial tips make it unmistakable. – Juvenile: Underparts streaked; wing-bars and tertial tips considerably narrower than on adult. (Some Common Crossbills have pale/white wing-bars and tertial tips, but usually one or both wing-bars are incomplete, and tertials generally have just narrow pale fringes at tip, not broad, clear-cut and white tips.) – 1st-year: Some are identifiable by retained juvenile wing-coverts and tertials with little white.

VOICE Call weaker and higher than Common Crossbill's and not so metallic and echoing, 'chipp-chipp-chipp-...'. Also has a diagnostic nasal, slightly discordant piping as if from a muted toy trumpet, 'tviiht' (contact-, alarm- and, less often, flight-call). Song fast, varied and twittering, Siskin-like.

Parrot Crossbill   Scottish Crossbill   Common Crossbill   Two-barred Crossbill

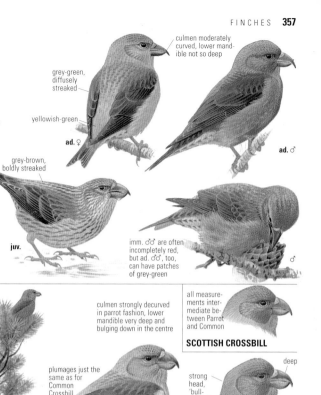

COMMON CROSSBILL

spruce-cone specialist

culmen moderately curved, lower mandible not so deep

grey-green, diffusely streaked

yellowish-green

ad. ♀

ad. ♂

grey-brown, boldly streaked

juv.

imm. ♂♂ are often incompletely red, but ad. ♂♂, too, can have patches of grey-green

♂

PARROT CROSSBILL

pine-cone specialist

culmen strongly decurved in parrot fashion, lower mandible very deep and bulging down in the centre

all measurements intermediate between Parrot and Common

SCOTTISH CROSSBILL

plumages just the same as for Common Crossbill

deep

strong head, 'bull-necked'

ad. ♀

ad. ♂

TWO-BARRED CROSSBILL

Common Crossbills very rarely have white wing-bars, too, but these bars are narrower, and tertial tips are evenly fringed white, do not have more white at sides

larch-cone specialist

wing of wing-barred ♀ Common Crossbill to compare

boldly spotted black

broad white wing-bars, the lower widest towards back

ad. ♀

juv.

ad. ♂

more bright red than brick-red

DZ

Common Rosefinch *Carpodacus erythrinus* **V**∗/(m**B**5)

L 13½–15 cm. Breeds in deciduous scrub and lush bushy areas, often on soggy overgrown lakeshores, in hazel stands, parks and smaller copses, along watercourses and field margins, and also bushy clearings in deciduous woods. Summer visitor (mostly end May–Aug), winters in India. A comparatively recent colonist from E. Has bred in Britain. Relatively bold, ♂ often sings from exposed perch; species is otherwise mainly quiet and retiring, easily eludes detection. Food mostly seeds, shoots and buds, some insects. Nests low down in bush or thicker small tree.

IDENTIFICATION Barely Bullfinch-sized, somewhat front-heavy finch with rather heavy breast and head/neck, but slim rear end and long tail. *Bill hefty*. Full adult ♂ distinctive with its red colour and its song, but ♀ and majority of younger ♂♂ are more nondescript and harder to identify (and in fleeting view can be confused with Corn Bunting, ♀ House Sparrow, pale young ♀ Yellowhammer etc.). Note: bill shape; '*colourless*' *brown-grey* plumage with little contrast between upperparts and underparts; rather *uniform brown-grey head*; diffuse dark mottling on crown, back and underparts; *two narrow and rather indistinct pale wing-bars*; pale tertial edges. No white on tail. – Adult ♂: *Red* on breast, crown, cheeks and rump; pale wing-bars often pinkish. – 1st-summer ♂: Majority are ♀-like, brownish-grey with no trace of red (and normally inseparable from ♀♀). Some acquire red feathers, however, and a few are adult-like; usually still identifiable by greyish-white wing-bars, scattered brown-grey feathers among the red, and sometimes by some worn wing- and tail-feathers. – ♀: All brownish-grey; wing-bars narrow and greyish-white. – Juvenile: Like ♀, but has fresher plumage with slightly warmer olive-brown tone and heavier dark spotting, and has buffish wing-bars.

VOICE Call an upslurred whistle, 'vüih', at times a bit hoarse and rather Greenfinch-like but otherwise with slightly softer voice (cf. song); sometimes heard also from overhead migrants. Song a typically soft whistling consisting of a few rhythmic notes in glissando, e.g. 'vidye-vüy-viidya' or 'vidye-vüdya-vüy'. Birds can be called up by high wolf-whistles. When excited, e.g. when courting ♀, ♂ also gives quiet, ecstatically chattering, twittering notes between the loud song verses.

Sinai Rosefinch *Carpodacus synoicus* —

L 13–14½ cm. Breeds in mountain deserts in wadis and ravines, locally on ruins. Requires water within reasonable flying distance, otherwise lives in very barren, rocky surroundings. Resident. Mobile, and rather difficult to get close to (but locally less shy). Visits drinking spots in morning (c. 09.00 hrs) and afternoon, but on hot days also several times during midday. Sometimes seen in small flocks (often family parties). Food mostly seeds. Nests in rock crevice, often high on cliff face, occasionally near ground.

IDENTIFICATION Size and shape much as Common Rosefinch, but *bill is somewhat smaller* and *culmen slightly less curved*. In all plumages, *pale* and without prominent markings, *almost totally lacks dark streaking above* and has *no pale wing-bars*. – Adult ♂: *Red 'face'*, paler *pink underparts, head-side and rump*; brown hindcrown, nape and mantle have tinge of pink, too. *Forecrown and crown-side have silvery-white feather tips*, with slightly fainter silvery-white also on rear cheeks. – ♀/1st-summer ♂: Almost uniform light grey-brown, like dry mud, the head marginally browner; wing-covert fringes a shade lighter than rest of wing. (Can be taken for a lark, bearing in mind colour and pale, heavy bill.) Occasional younger ♂♂ (maybe adult ♀♀, too) can have a little pink on 'face' and on underparts.

VOICE Flight-call on rising a surprisingly sparrow-like 'chip... chip...' (or 'chiepp'), with hard ending. Voice is thick (i.e. the sound has overtones), making the call at times, e.g. in an echoing wadi, reminiscent of Bearded Tit's. Perched birds give a rather rattling, piping, somewhat House Sparrow-like chatter, 'tviht, cheht tvüt, tviht–tviht...'. Song (imperfectly known?) is sometimes stated to be short, clear and melodic, but according to other sources it consists of a simple verse of rather sparrow-like, chirping notes (cf. above!).

Great Rosefinch *Carpodacus rubicilla* —

L 19–20½ cm. Alpine species breeding on bare mountains at above 2500 m (usually above 3000 m), generally on sunny, boulder-strewn slopes with grass, herbage and scattered low birches and rhododendron patches. Resident, but in winter descends to c. 2000 m or lower depending on snow situation; then seen in small flocks, and rather mobile. As a rule shy, difficult to approach. Late nester, often not incubating until end Jul. Nests in rock crevice or under boulder.

IDENTIFICATION *Big* as Pine Grosbeak, and similarly stocky. *Bill heavy*. Wings and tail rather long. Flight deeply undulating over longer stretches. Plumage quite *dark*, which together with size and manner of flight can at distance give thrush-like impression. – Adult ♂: *Dark raspberry-red sprinkled with fine white spots* on crown and underparts. Rather *swarthy on lores and around eye*, giving 'stern' facial expression. Rear cheeks have pinkish-white lustre. *Bill rather pale, yellowish-grey*. – ♀/1st-summer ♂: Entirely brownish-grey (no red) and heavily streaked dark; lores, eye region and forecheeks fairly dark. Bill grey-brown.

VOICE Call a high, cheerful 'tvui', often uttered in undulating flight. Alarm a discordant, thick, sparrow-like 'chick'. Song is a plain, clear-voiced verse at slow pace and on somewhat descending pitch, e.g. 'chüih, chü-chü-chü tvutvutvu-tsü'; some verses are longer, and the delivery varies a bit.

Common Rosefinch

Sinai Rosefinch

Great Rosefinch

COMMON ROSEFINCH

ad. ♂

♀-type plumage is non-descript—still, chubby bill and dark beady eye typical

two buff-white wing-bars obvious

short and stout, rounded shape

red head and breast

red

juv. is somewhat richer olive-brown than ad. ♀

juv.

♀ / 1st-summer ♂

ad. ♂

SINAI ROSEFINCH

one ♂ (closest at right) and two ♀♀ (far right) in typical desert habitat

slightly browner head

pale grey-brown, lacking features

silvery-white crown

ad. ♂

ad. ♀ / 1st-summer ♂

at certain angles the red looks more pink

ad. ♂

GREAT ROSEFINCH

rather distinctly streaked

big and long-tailed, flight deeply undulating

heavy, pale

Pine Grosbeak size

raspberry-red, finely spotted white

high-alpine species

ad. ♀

long

ad. ♂

DZ

Trumpeter Finch *Bucanetes githagineus*   **V***

L 11½–13 cm. Breeds in rocky and stony desert and semi-desert at lower or moderately high levels; also thrives in barren, unvegetated terrain so long as water exists within flying distance. Rather common in Canary Islands. Resident, but mobile. Rather bold. Social in habits, but flocks usually quite small. Nests on ground in crevice or under vegetation.

IDENTIFICATION *Small*, long-winged finch with rather big head and *short but very thick and stout bill. Narrow pale eye-ring.* Contrastingly *dark* (almost black) *primary tips and tail-feathers* with *narrow pale edges.* – ♂ summer: Distinctive *pale red bill* and *pinkish legs,* vivid *pink tail-sides* at base, pink-tinged rump, belly and lower flanks, *pink edges to flight-feathers and greater coverts* and unstreaked warm brown mantle and back, otherwise plumage is *uniformly light grey* (partly suffused pink). – ♀/♂ winter: Bill pale greyish yellow-brown, often with faint pink tinge; legs light ochraceous-pink. Plumage colours somewhat more subdued, with less pink and pure grey, more buff and brownish-grey tones. – Juvenile: Lacks pink.

VOICE Call short, jolting, nasal 'ahp' notes with lilting or discordant tone (as in the song, though lower-pitched), often repeated; volume and pitch vary somewhat. Song consists mainly of a peculiar nasal and drawn-out buzzing note, a loud hoarse buzz with even and mechanical tone, 'aaaaaahp', like the sound from a small toy trumpet; sometimes two pitches audible. Often the song begins or ends with a few short, clear notes, e.g. 'chu chu zi aaaaaahp'.

Mongolian Finch *Bucanetes mongolicus*   —

L 11½–13 cm. Breeds in barren, rocky mountain tracts at over 2000 m. Resident, or makes only short movements down to lower levels after breeding. Seen on ground or in flight, often in small parties. Not shy. Nests on ground.

IDENTIFICATION Size of Trumpeter Finch, and very like that species, but has slightly *smaller bill* (esp. less deep base) which is always *yellowish-brown* or light grey-brown, never pink or light red. Further, *head is light brown like mantle* (never contrastingly grey), *crown to back* in all plumages *lightly but distinctly dark-streaked* (as good as uniform on Trumpeter), and wing pattern is different, this especially noticeable on adult ♂ (but harder to see on some ♀♀). Thus, in flight, shows a *short, broad, white bar on secondaries* and a *hint of second wing-bar at base of greater coverts.* Secondaries are also more broadly tipped white than on Trumpeter. Usually shows *narrow white patch on 'arm'* on folded wing.

VOICE In flight, often utters a rising note immediately preceded by a short grace-note, 'tu-vüiit', sometimes also shorter 'tvüi' or 'tui'. Song a pleasing, melodic, short verse, e.g. 'viit-vüah...vreyah', repeated at slow pace.

Crimson-winged Finch *Rhodopechys sanguinea*   —

L 13–15 cm. Alpine species which breeds in bare mountain tracts at 1700–3300 m (locally 1100 m), but in winter often found lower down. Often inhabits steep precipices, ravines and boulder-strewn slopes practically devoid of vegetation. Social habits, small parties may be seen throughout year. Mobile, often forages and drinks far from nest site. Rather shy for the most part. Food mainly seeds. Nests in rock crevice or cavity, occasionally in low bush.

IDENTIFICATION *Big head, thick neck* and *heavy, triangular bill, shortish tail* but *long wings.* Best plumage features are: *pinkish-white bases to secondaries and primary coverts* forming pale wing-panel, visible also on folded wing; *black crown* (in fresh plumage partly concealed by light brown fringes); brown on head-sides, breast-sides, flanks and mantle/back, the last unstreaked; uniform dirty buff throat, nape and crown- and neck-sides. Sexes similar, but ♀ duller.

VOICE Has a variety of calls, often di- or multisyllabic: sonorous 'chiv**li**' and 'chu-che**lütt**' (at distance recalls Woodlark), slightly shrill, somewhat House Sparrow-like 'ju**vü**-ju**vü**', and higher 'picha'. Song, often delivered from a rock pinnacle but at times in deeply undulating song-flight, a rapid, quite short, rhythmic verse repeated fairly constantly throughout and recognizable by its rhythm and its sonorous, musical tone; sometimes a drawn-out and stressed note is heard towards the end of the verse, e.g. 'chodlü-chodlü-udle-fri**iiih**-chodlü'. A shorter verse occasionally given in flight.

Desert Finch *Rhodospiza obsoleta*   —

L 13–14 cm. Breeds in open, dry, usually flat country with scattered trees and bushes, often by irrigated cultivations, in gardens, at oases etc. (thus, despite name, not a real desert bird!). Largely resident, making short dispersive movements outside breeding season. Often appears in flocks. Unlike Trumpeter Finch, readily perches in trees, but food, seeds, is taken mostly on ground. Nests in fork of bush or tree.

IDENTIFICATION A *sandy-coloured* or grey-buff finch with characteristic wing and tail markings: *black, finely white-edged primary tips,* and on closed wing a *large white and pink panel* broken only by black alula and black primary-covert tips. – ♂: *Tertials black,* narrowly edged white. *Bill black. Lores black* on adult, pale on 1st-winter. – ♀: Tertial centres, bill and lores grey-brown.

VOICE Three often heard calls: commonest a simmering 'drrr'r' falling at end, also a bent 'tvoi' (or 'tvio') sounding like something between Common Rosefinch and Tree Sparrow, and finally a lilting 'dveüüt' recalling both Twite and Rock Sparrow. Song a soft, halting series of short, uneven notes, sometimes with interwoven drawn-out buzzing notes almost like those of Trumpeter Finch.

Trumpeter Finch   Mongolian Finch   Crimson-winged Finch   Desert Finch

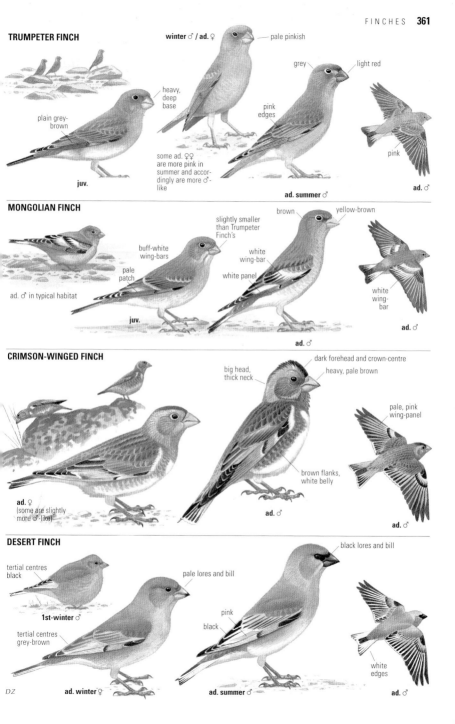

TRUMPETER FINCH

winter ♂ / ad. ♀ — pale pinkish

grey — light red

heavy, deep base

plain grey-brown

pink edges

pink

juv.

some ad. ♀♀ are more pink in summer and accordingly are more ♂-like

ad. summer ♂

ad. ♂

MONGOLIAN FINCH

slightly smaller than Trumpeter Finch's

brown — yellow-brown

buff-white wing-bars

white wing-bar

pale patch

white panel

white wing-bar

ad. ♂ in typical habitat

juv.

ad. ♂

ad. ♂

CRIMSON-WINGED FINCH

dark forehead and crown-centre

big head, thick neck

heavy, pale brown

pale, pink wing-panel

brown flanks, white belly

ad. ♀
(some are slightly more ♂-like)

ad. ♂

ad. ♂

DESERT FINCH

black lores and bill

tertial centres black

pale lores and bill

pink

black

1st-winter ♂

tertial centres grey-brown

white edges

DZ   **ad. winter ♀**   **ad. summer ♂**   **ad. ♂**

NORTH AMERICAN PASSERINES

Every year a number of North American passerines become disoriented and a few are recorded in Europe, primarily in Britain, Ireland and Iceland. Although the feat by small landbirds of surviving a flight over the Atlantic is impressive, they are assisted by prevailing westerly winds, and a strong tail-wind is probably a prerequisite for a successful crossing. At times the birds may also rest on ships for shorter or longer periods. Two spreads show those species which have been recorded about ten times or more within the treated region, i.e. those which have now become reasonably regular visitors to Europe. See also pp. 276–279, where a few American thrushes are treated.

VIREOS *Vireonidae*

The vireos constitute a large family of American passerines resembling both warblers and flycatchers but with no real counterpart in Europe. They are generally placed near the New World wood-warblers, but according to recent findings could be more closely related to the corvids. Most are fairly small and similarly coloured, grey and green above and off-white below. They have a stout, flycatcher-like bill.

Red-eyed Vireo *Vireo olivaceus* V*

L 13–14 cm. Annual vagrant in autumn to British Isles (usually 1–3, up to 14 in 1985), mostly end Sep–mid Oct. Also recorded Iceland, Netherlands, Belgium, Germany, France and Spain. Arboreal; vagrants in Europe often seek mature gardens, but in windswept coastal areas may be found in hedgerows, willows, etc. Frequently keeps well hidden or quiet, will 'disappear' for long spells.
IDENTIFICATION The size of an Icterine Warbler, and somewhat recalls one, having rather *large head* and *heavy bill*, *fairly short and straight-ended tail*, olive-green upperparts and lead-grey legs. Recognized by striking head markings: *long, well-marked, whitish supercilium bordered dark above* (distinctly) *and below* (shorter), and *blue-grey crown*. The *red* (or red-brown) *iris* sometimes discernible. Rather sluggish and slow when not moving far, more like a Garden Warbler than a Willow Warbler, but can certainly make dashing sallies now and then. Call is a slightly squeaky, nasal 'chway'.

WOOD-WARBLERS *Parulidae*

The American wood-warblers are a large family of small arboreal insect-eating birds. Although they have a thin, pointed bill and warbler-like habits, they are most closely related to the buntings (pp. 366–377). Often distinctly patterned in bright colours. Most have *large white patches on the tail*, visible from below or when the tail is spread.

Black-and-white Warbler *Mniotilta varia* V**

L 11½–13 cm. Very rare vagrant in autumn to e.g. Iceland, Faroes, and the British Isles.
IDENTIFICATION Has a peculiar habit of *creeping along tree trunks* and thicker branches, at times with head down almost like a nuthatch. Characteristically *broadly striped plumage in black and white*, with a *white median crown-stripe* and a *white supercilium*. Bill *very long and narrow*. Sexes similar; adult ♂ has some black on throat and breast. 1st-winter ♂ *boldly*

streaked blackish on flanks and undertail-coverts; 1st-winter ♀ much *less distinctly streaked* on underparts and has *buffier-tinged ear-coverts and flanks* than ♂. Call a Robin-like click-ing 'tic' or a thin 'ziit'.

Northern Parula *Parula americana* V**

L 10½–11½ cm. Rare autumn vagrant to Iceland, British Isles and France, mostly end Sep–mid Oct. Behaviour rather like that of a Goldcrest, moves restlessly, will hover at times or hang upside-down.
IDENTIFICATION *Small*. Fairly dark *bluish grey-green above* (head and edges of wing-feathers more bluish, esp. on adult, mantle always green), with *two* narrow, distinct *white wing-bars*. Thin white eye-ring, broken in front and behind. *Throat and breast yellow, belly white*. ♂ has hint of a dark breast-band, missing on ♀. In Europe usually silent.

Blackpoll Warbler *Dendroica striata* V**

L 12–13 cm. Rare autumn vagrant to British Isles, mostly end Sep–Oct. Also recorded in Iceland and France.
IDENTIFICATION The vernacular name refers to the ♂ summer plumage, but this is not seen in Europe. Autumn birds are *yellow-tinged on cheek, eye-surround, throat and breast*. Belly and *undertail-coverts are white*. Crown, back and indistinct eye-stripe dull olive-green, *back rather thinly streaked dark*. Wing dark with *two well-marked but rather thin white wing-bars* and *white edges to tertials*. Breast and flanks finely streaked on most. *Feet yellowish-brown* or brown-grey, soles orange-yellow. Call a hard but liquid 'chip'.

Yellow-rumped Warbler *Dendroica coronata* V***

L 12½–13½ cm. Rare autumn vagrant to British Isles, mostly in Oct. Also recorded in Norway and Iceland. Vagrants may spend much time foraging in short grass, often joining flocks of pipits.
IDENTIFICATION In all plumages recognized by *yellow rump patch* and *whitish throat* (lower throat sometimes tinged buff), being the only wood-warbler with this combination (Magnolia Warbler, *D. magnolia*, has pale yellow throat). Autumn birds are *brown above, moderately streaked dark*, and have *two light wing-bars*, white underparts with dark streaks on breast and flanks, and a small *yellow patch on breast-side* near wing-bend (can be missing on 1st-winter ♀). Sometimes a *small yellow patch on centre of crown* (often concealed by brown fringes, or missing, esp. on 1st-winter ♀). Ear-coverts and lores fairly dark grey-brown, indistinct supercilium, usually rather prominent whitish eye-ring. Uppertail-coverts and tail-feathers edged blue-grey. Vagrants often vocal, call a hard, liquid 'chick', often uttered in flight.

American Redstart *Setophaga ruticilla* V***

L 13–14 cm. Very rare autumn vagrant to British Isles, mostly in Oct. Also recorded in Iceland and France. Has very active, darting movements.
IDENTIFICATION Long-tailed. Often raises and spreads tail and droops wings. ♀/1st-winter ♂ have head grey, back and wing olive-grey, underparts off-white, and have *large yellow patches on tail, a small yellow wing patch* and a *yellow* (♀) or *orange-yellow* (1st-winter ♂) *diffuse patch on side of breast at* wing-bend. Call a clicking 'chik' and a thin 'tsiit'.

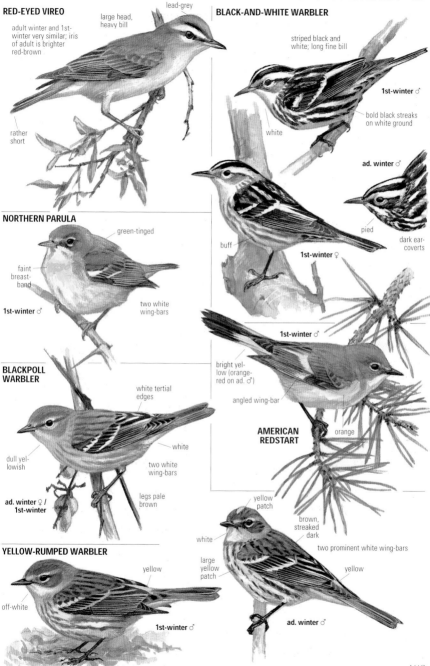

RED-EYED VIREO

adult winter and 1st-winter very similar; iris of adult is brighter red-brown

lead-grey

large head, heavy bill

rather short

BLACK-AND-WHITE WARBLER

striped black and white; long fine bill

1st-winter ♂

bold black streaks on white ground

white

ad. winter ♂

pied

dark ear-coverts

buff

1st-winter ♀

NORTHERN PARULA

green-tinged

faint breast-band

1st-winter ♂

two white wing-bars

1st-winter ♂

bright yel-low (orange-red on ad. ♂)

angled wing-bar

AMERICAN REDSTART

orange

BLACKPOLL WARBLER

white tertial edges

white

dull yel-lowish

two white wing-bars

ad. winter ♀ /
1st-winter

legs pale brown

YELLOW-RUMPED WARBLER

yellow

off-white

1st-winter ♂

yellow patch

white

large yellow patch

brown, streaked dark

two prominent white wing-bars

yellow

ad. winter ♂

LMQ

Rose-breasted Grosbeak *Pheucticus ludovicianus* V***

L 17½–20 cm. An American bunting placed in the sub-family *Cardinalinae* (cardinals, New World grosbeaks and others, more like European finches than buntings in appearance). Rare autumn vagrant in Europe, almost exclusively in Oct and most often in British Isles.

IDENTIFICATION *Big* and stocky, with *heavy head and bill* almost of Hawfinch proportions. *Bill* predominantly *pale*, often with obvious *pink* tone. Adult ♂ summer is handsome (white belly, black upperparts with white rump and white wing markings and a large red breast patch), but has not yet been recorded in Europe. All records here have involved birds in 1st-winter plumage. These resemble adult ♀ and, besides stout, conical, pink bill, are identified by: very *broad and distinct whitish supercilium* and *whitish neck-side* almost completely framing brown ear-coverts; dark brown, finely dark-streaked crown with narrow *whitish median crown-stripe*; a *white patch below eye* and a diffuse pale spot on rearmost ear-coverts; *two white wing-bars* and *white spots at tips of tertials*. Above, brown and dark-streaked; below, off-white with buff tinge, or occasionally more obvious buffy-yellow tone, and with dark streaking on throat-side, breast and flanks. 1st-winter ♂ can often be told from ♀ by much *broader white wing-bar on median coverts, bigger white patch on primary bases* and *light red tinge on breast*, or by fact that a bit of red from axillaries is just visible. Call a hard 'chick'.

Dark-eyed Junco *Junco hyemalis* V**

L 13½–14½ cm. An American bunting which, like White-throated Sparrow (below), is part of the subfamily *Emberizinae*. Rare vagrant in Europe, chiefly in spring but occasionally at other seasons, too. Forages almost invariably by hopping on ground. Jerks tail. Takes cover in trees and bushes.

IDENTIFICATION *Pink finch-type bill, sooty-grey upperparts, head and breast* and *white belly* give unmistakable appearance. Tail long with *white outer edges*, obvious in flight. Legs reddish-brown, toes darker. Sexes rather similar, but ♀ lighter grey with brown tinge above, and with belly not pure white. Call a clicking 'tick', which may be repeated in fast series, and a frothy tongue-clicking 'check'.

White-throated Sparrow *Zonotrichia albicollis* V***

L 15–17 cm. An American bunting (see p. 366), included in the subfamily *Emberizinae*. Rare vagrant in Europe, chiefly in spring but occasionally at other seasons. Forages mostly by hopping on ground. Often takes cover in bushes.

IDENTIFICATION Recognized by *white throat* (can be finely edged black at lower edge), *grey breast, broad pale supercilium*, and *broad dark lateral crown-stripes* sandwiching a *pale median crown-stripe*. Also has black eye-stripe and *uniform grey cheeks*. Head markings usually black and white, typically with *yellow tone to supercilium in front of eye*. Some, including most 1st-winters, have the pale head markings tinged light brown. 1st-winter also has slightly less clear-cut, off-white throat (instead of pure white and sharply defined as on adult). Call a sharp, fine,'ziit' and a hard 'chink'. – Can be confused with White-crowned Sparrow *Z. leucophrys*, recorded a few times in Europe, but that has light grey throat (tinged buff-white on 1st-winter), light grey head- and neck-sides, is grey around nape, and has broad white crown-band.

Indigo Bunting *Passerina cyanea* [V***]?

L 11½–13 cm. An American bunting (subfamily *Cardinalinae*). Rare vagrant in Europe, including in British Isles, Nordic countries and Netherlands. Recorded at all seasons, with some preponderance for summer. That some records involve escaped cagebirds cannot be ruled out: species is often kept in captivity.

IDENTIFICATION Adult ♂ summer is an elegant bird, *all blue* with *dark lores* and *light blue-grey lower mandible*. (Can be confused only with Blue Grosbeak *Guiraca caerulea* [not treated here], but that is bigger and has red-brown wing-bars.) At distance just looks 'dark'. In winter plumage the blue is largely concealed by brown fringes. – ♀/1st-winter: More nondescript, being *reddish grey-brown above* with faint dark streaking, and yellowish grey-brown below with grey breast spotting. *Tail-feathers, uppertail-coverts* and at times primaries *edged blue-green* (often absent on 1st-winter ♀) 1st-winter has slightly more distinct light brown wing-bar and heavier breast spotting than adult ♀. Call a sharp 'tsick'.

TROUPIALS, COWBIRDS et al. *Icteridae*

A family occurring only in America. Most species show features of both starlings and finches. Plumage often black, sometimes with some bright colours, and have either powerful finch-like bill or long, narrow and pointed bill and sturdy, rather long legs. Tail often long, with rounded tip.

Northern Oriole *Icterus galbula* V***

L 17–19 cm. Rare autumn vagrant in British Isles; odd records elsewhere in Europe; most in Sep–Oct; occasional winter and spring records.

IDENTIFICATION Large and *long-tailed*, with *long, pointed bill*. Adult ♂ summer unmistakable. ♀ and winter plumages recognized by: *two white wing-bars*, broadest and most obvious on median coverts; *underparts vivid yellow* strongest on throat, breast and undertail-coverts; *greyish-yellow tail and rump*. Mantle and back somewhat variable olive-brown with heavy dark spotting (indicative of ♂) or more uniformly grey (indicates ♀). Adult ♀ and 1st-winter ♂ can show some black on head and throat. Call a disyllabic, clear and full whistle,'pyoo-li'; also has a nasal chatter.

Bobolink *Dolichonyx oryzivorus* V**

L 16–18 cm. Rare autumn vagrant in British Isles; occasional records elsewhere in Europe; all records Sep–Nov but for one in spring. Habits in part lark-like, inhabits low crops and stubble fields. Also perches in bushes and reeds.

IDENTIFICATION Adult ♂ summer unmistakable. ♀ and winter plumages not unlike ♀ House Sparrow but *yellower in tone*; are brown and dark-streaked above and yellowish-white below, with buff supercilium, *dark lateral crown stripe* and *buff median crown-stripe, pale lores* but *distinct dark eye-stripe* above *pale, buff cheek*. *Two pale bands on mantle* (roughly as on Aquatic Warbler). Surprisingly similar to ♀ Yellow-breasted Bunting (p. 374), but is much bigger and *lacks dark lower border to cheek*. Often stands upright on ground and extends neck, when head looks quite small. *Tail-feathers* narrow and *pointed. Flightpath straight*, not undulating. Call in flight a sharp 'pink'.

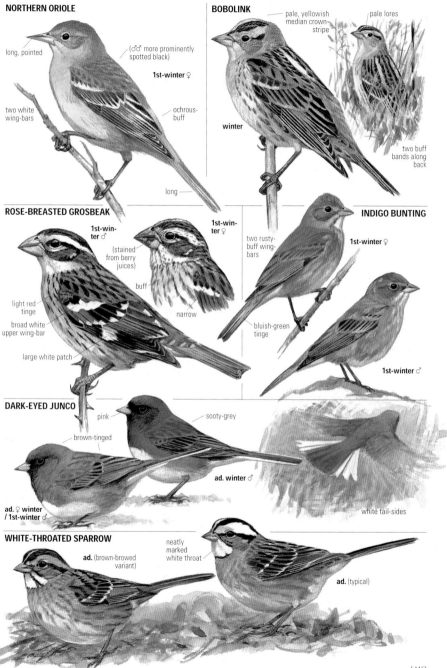

NORTHERN ORIOLE

long, pointed

two white wing-bars

(♂♂ more prominently spotted black)

1st-winter ♀

ochrous-buff

long

BOBOLINK

pale, yellowish median crown-stripe

pale lores

winter

two buff bands along back

ROSE-BREASTED GROSBEAK

1st-winter ♂

1st-winter ♀

(stained from berry juices)

buff

narrow

light red tinge

broad white upper wing-bar

large white patch

INDIGO BUNTING

two rusty-buff wing-bars

1st-winter ♀

bluish-green tinge

1st-winter ♂

DARK-EYED JUNCO

pink

sooty-grey

brown-tinged

ad. winter ♂

white tail-sides

ad. ♀ winter / 1st-winter ♂

WHITE-THROATED SPARROW

neatly marked white throat

ad. (brown-browed variant)

ad. (typical)

LMQ

BUNTINGS *Emberizidae*
More terrestrial than the closely related finches. Majority of species belong to genus *Emberiza*, have triangular bill and characteristic plumage colours and pattern. Song loud, often short and species-specific. Most species are migratory. Favoured food grass seeds. Nest in tussock or low in bush.

(Common) Reed Bunting *Emberiza schoeniclus* rB2/W2
L 13½–15½ cm. Breeds in reedbeds, tall rushes and shrubbery on wet ground or at lake margins, also in drier sites (young conifer plantations, rape fields etc.). In Britain & Ireland resident, with immigrants from N and E Continent late Sep–Apr/May. ♂ easy to see in breeding season, sings from reed stem or bushtop, but species otherwise rather unobtrusive; flies off in springing, slightly uneven and jerky flight, quickly taking cover in vegetation.

IDENTIFICATION Mid-sized bunting. *Bill small* (except in SE Europe and areas around Black and Caspian Seas, where bill is strong and sturdy) and *dark*. *Plumage mostly brown and buffy-white* with *dark streaking and white tail-sides*. – ♂ summer: Easily identified by *black head and throat* with *pure white neck band* and *narrow white moustachial stripe*. – Other plumages: Buffish supercilium and grey-brown crown and cheeks. ♂♂ usually told by dusky or irregularly black-spotted throat, while ♀♀ have unspotted buffish-white throat-centre with distinct black malar stripes. *Lesser wing-coverts reddish-brown*. Cheeks always slightly swarthy (never uniform red-brown as on Little Bunting). Legs red-brown or black (darker than Little's).

VOICE Calls include a high, softly downslurred 'siü' and a slightly impure, ringing 'bzü', heard mostly from autumn migrants. On territory, sometimes short, sharp 'zi zi...'. Song a brief, simple verse, usually at *slow tempo*, a few sharp rolling notes spelt out and ending with a couple of faster notes or a short trill, e.g. 'sripp, sripp, sria, srisrisirr'; varies in detail, and occasionally faster, but species nevertheless recognized by voice.

Pallas's Reed Bunting *Emberiza pallasi* V***
L 12–13½ cm. Breeds in similar habitat to N populations of Reed Bunting, i.e. on tundra along watercourses in lower vegetation (herbage, brush, dwarf birch, low shrubs), but also in e.g. open larch forest bordering tundra. Migrant, winters in SE Asia, returns to European breeding grounds late, in mid Jun. Behaviour rather like Reed Bunting's.

IDENTIFICATION A small version of Reed Bunting, with similar habits. Identified by: *small* size (no bigger than Little Bunting); *narrower and weaker bill* with, in ♀-type plumages, *pinkish base to lower mandible* (Reed Bunting has somewhat heavier and darker bill); *ash-grey* (♂) or *dull brown* (♀) *lesser*

coverts; in ♀-type plumages *almost no streaks on breast and flanks*, so dark malar stripes stand out as only obvious markings on underparts; *two buff-white wing-bars* (more prominent than on Reed); *more uniformly brown crown and cheeks* (Reed: dark border to cheeks and sometimes crownsides); usually discernibly *paler, more buffy-yellow ground colour* (but some eastern Reed are similarly pale). Sexing as for Reed Bunting. Adult ♂ has contrastingly *greyish-white rump* (but shown also by some Reed in SE Russia).

VOICE Call a rather full, sparrow-like, somewhat downslurred 'tschialp' and a slightly rasping 'tschirp'. Said also to have a more Reed Bunting-like fine 'dsiu'. Song very *plain and flat*, consists of a short series of monotonous, rasping notes, 'srih-srih-srih-srih'; little variation.

Little Bunting *Emberiza pusilla* V*
L 12–13½ cm. Breeds in NE Europe in taiga, often in glades and open coniferous forest with scattering of birch and willow, but also in upland birch forest with some spruce; most territories beside watercourses. Rare but regular vagrant in Britain, mostly in autumn (Sep–Oct) but with increasing frequency of overwintering. Spends much time on ground.

IDENTIFICATION *Small*. In summer plumage, has *red-brown head* with *black lateral crown-stripes* and *white eye-ring*. In autumn, most likely to be confused with ♀ Reed Bunting, but told by: *call*; bolder *white eye-ring*; *uniform red-brown* or orangey yellow-brown *cheeks* with narrow dark border at rear (but without dark edge bordering entire throatside); *rather light red-brown lores and fore-supercilium*; a *distinct pale* (reddish-brown) *median crown-stripe* between dark crown-sides; often a *small light buff spot on rearmost cheek*; proportionately somewhat *longer bill* with *straight culmen*; more prominent buff-white wing-bars; greybrown lesser coverts; invariably pinkish legs. Sexes alike (individual variation greater than slight tendency for adult ♂ to have more distinct head markings than ♀).

VOICE Call a sharp, short clicking 'zick'; volume varies with mood. Song pleasing and melodic, is quite short and high-pitched and contains both clear notes and more rasping, hard, rolling sounds, e.g. 'trütrütrütrü srrri tüüy sivisivi chu si' or 'si**trü**-si**trü**-si**trü** srisrisri svi-svi-sürrr'.

Yellow-browed Bunting *Emberiza chrysophrys* V***
L 13–14 cm. An extremely rare autumn vagrant from E Siberia; recorded a few times end Sep–Oct.

IDENTIFICATION Barely as large as Rustic Bunting. Rather *big head* and stout bill. *Straight culmen, pink lower mandible*. In summer unmistakable: *bright yellow eyebrow*, (brownish-) *black crown* with *narrow white median crown-stripe*. In autumn more like Little and Rustic Buntings, but retains a *tinge of yellow in eyebrow* and *trace of the white crown-stripe*. *Flanks and breast narrowly and distinctly streaked black*.

VOICE Call a sharp, piercing click, 'zick!' (like Little Bunting's). Song short, has a *slow tempo*, often starts with a *drawn-out soft note*, ends more rapidly.

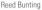
Reed Bunting

Pallas's Reed Bunting

Little Bunting

REED BUNTING

more greyish-tinged on average than 1st-w. ♀ (but many are intermediate)

broad white collar

all black

hint of dark bib

winter ♂

singing

1st-winter ♂

paler brown crown-centre

dark streak to base of bill

red-brown

grey

very heavy

ad. summer ♂

ad. s. ♂

brown

(a few acquire more ♂-like head pattern)

reiseri, caspia (SE Europe, Turkey)

red-brown or grey-brown

1st-winter ♀

brown

ad. summer ♀

PALLAS'S REED BUNTING

fine

buff

rather plain brown

pink

prominent buff band along back

dull brown

pale

grey

practically unmarked

unmarked

pale wing-bars

ad. ♀ / 1st-winter

ad. winter ♂

ad. summer ♂

LITTLE BUNTING

prominent, narrow, pale eye-ring

straight culmen

red-brown

ad. summer / 1st-winter

grey

grey-brown

whitish wing-bar

white

red-brown centre of mantle

ad. ♀ / 1st-w. ♂

distinct, narrow streaks

invariably pink

distinct red-brown median crown-stripe

those with obvious red-brown throat and jet-black lateral crown-stripes are nearly always ad. ♂♂

DZ   **ad. summer**

YELLOW-BROWED BUNTING

brown-black

pink

narrow white

black

fore-part of supercilium yellow

red-brown tinge

short, distinct streaks

ad. summer ♂

Snow Bunting *Plectrophenax nivalis* mB5 / P+W3–4

L 15½–18 cm. Breeds in high-alpine habitat in boulder zone of high mountains, but also along northern rocky coasts and on open, treeless high moors and tundra. Predominantly passage and winter visitor in Britain & Ireland (mostly mid Sep–Apr), mainly from Scandinavia and Greenland, but small numbers breed in Scotland. In winter, often seen in large, dense flocks, mostly along seashores, some on moors and open coastal pasture. Quite confiding, but restless and mobile, continually on the move.

IDENTIFICATION *Large white panels on inner wing* and white at tail-base, flash in flight. Can be confused only with Snowfinch of S Europe (p. 344), but that species stays in its breeding mountains and does not descend to the lowlands where Snow Bunting winters (records of Snow Finch below 500 m exceptional), is bigger, has more white on tail etc. – ♂ summer: Unmistakable, with *all-white head and breast and all-black back*. – ♀ summer: Diffusely spotted grey on crown, cheeks and breast-sides; back is not solid black. – Juvenile: Very different: *grey head*, and breast diffusely soiled grey. (This plumage not seen away from breeding sites.) – Autumn: All plumages similar, with *rusty yellow-brown tone* on breast-side, cheek, crown/nape and shoulders; back yellow-brown and streaked black. *Bill yellowish with black tip*. ♂ has *more white on wing and on primary coverts* (latter often white with black tips, forming isolated black spot on white wing-edge) and blacker wing-tip than ♀. – Variation: Compared with Fenno-Scandian birds (ssp. *nivalis*), Icelandic birds (*insulae*), of which some resident in Iceland and some winter in British Isles and Netherlands, have slightly darker plumage with darker primary coverts (often brown on ♂, too).

VOICE Calls, which often reveal birds overhead, are a rippling, Crested Tit-like 'per'r'r'rit', and a soft but emphatic whistle, 'pyüu', much as Little Ringed Plover; the whistle is given mostly by lone birds. When irritated (e.g. overcrowding in larger flocks, territorial disputes), gives a hoarse 'bersch'. Song a brief twitter with clear voice (almost like Rustic Bunting, but somewhat harder) and desolate ring (as Lapland Longspur), e.g. '**swi**to-sü**vee**-vi**tü**ta-sü**veh**'.

Lapland Longspur *Calcarius lapponicus* P+W4 / (mB5)

(Alternative name: LAPLAND BUNTING.) L 14–15½ cm. Breeds in upland wet willows and on bare mountains and moors (also tundra) and open bogs with dwarf birch, creeping willow and scrub. Scarce passage and winter visitor in Britain & Ireland (Aug/Sep–May), often singly or in small parties, on coastal fields and meadowland; has bred in Scotland. Most winter on cultivated steppe in SE Europe. Rather wary, creeps away on ground or freezes, then rises quite high when flushed, flight powerful.

IDENTIFICATION A rather *heavily built* medium-sized bunting with quite *thick but short bill* and *long, straight hindclaw*. *Bill straw-yellow* (slightly darker and greyer on juvenile) *with dark tip*. Legs rather dark brown. – In summer plumage ♂ is unmistakable (black head/throat, yellowish-white band behind eye and down across neck-side to breast-side, red-brown nape, white belly), and ♀, too, identified by *red-brown nape* and by diffuse *greyish-white patch on breast* and *pale bill*. – In fresh autumn plumage more like Reed Bunting, but told by: *broad red-brown edges to tertials and greater coverts*, the latter forming on closed wing a reddish-brown panel framed by *narrow pale wing-bars*; bill; *paler grey-brown median crown-stripe* (paler and more distinct than on Reed); *grey-brown heavily streaked rump*; sometimes *reddish-brown nape*. Sexes and ages very similar in autumn, but adult ♂ sometimes distinguishable by intimation of red-brown nape and by dense black breast spotting (thus not sparse streaks).

VOICE Rather vocal. A couple of calls correspond to those of Snow Bunting: on migration (often when flushed) a dry rattling 'pr'r'r'rt', a bit harder and drier than Snow Bunting's, and a short whistled 'chu' (rarely very Snow Bunting-like 'pyu'); also a slightly hoarse or more voiced 'chüp', often from high-flying birds (incl. nocturnal migrants). At nest site, nervous disyllabic 'tihü' also heard. Song a short, rather constant jingling verse with desolate ring, e.g. 'kretle-**krlii**-trr kritle-kretle-trü'; somewhat recalls that of Horned Lark (partly same habitat!) but lacks latter's hesitant introduction. Performs occasional high song-flight with fanned tail and intermittent hovering, when verses protracted.

Rustic Bunting *Emberiza rustica* V**

L 13–14½ cm. Breeds in swampy spruce or pine forest with birch, willow and other deciduous trees or in dense, water-logged deciduous forest. Summer visitor (May–Sep), winters in SE Asia; autumn vagrant in Britain. Unobtrusive. On passage, stops off in swampy bushland, easily escapes detection; often singly or in quite small parties on passage, but large flocks occur on coasts of Gulf of Bothnia.

IDENTIFICATION Same size as Reed Bunting. Told by *white belly, plain reddish-brown rump, red-brown spots on flanks*, pinky-brown legs, *longish bill* with *straight culmen* and *pink lower mandible*. – ♂ summer: *Red-brown band on breast and nape. Black head* with *white supercilium and small white spot on nape*. – ♀ summer: Crown and cheeks spotted brown, supercilium off-white, the red-brown on nape narrow. Some are very like ♂. – Autumn: Black and red-brown areas partly concealed by buff-brown fringes; sexing and ageing in field doubtful. Like Little Bunting, often has a dark-edged *buff-white spot on rear cheek* and *distinct pale eyebrow*.

VOICE Call and alarm a short piercing 'zit', sharper than Song Thrush's call, more cutting than Robin's 'tick'. Song, often heard during light night-time hours, unmistakable through its soft, rather gloomy, melodic quality, its lack of hard or sharp sounds, and the jaunty rhythm; a verse may go '**duu**-dele-**düü**do-de**luu**-delü'.

Snow Bunting

Lapland Longspur

Rustic Bunting

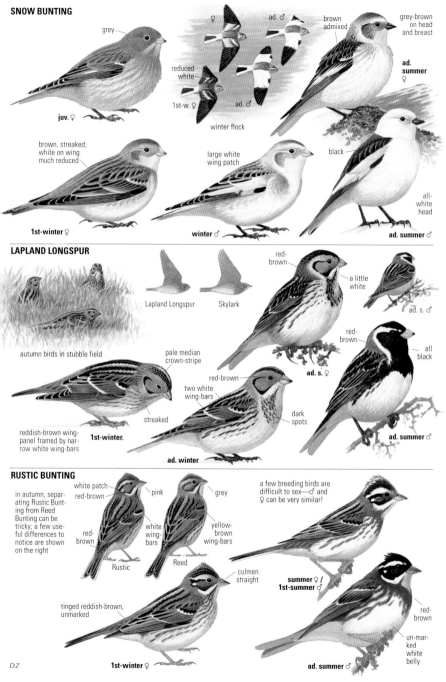

SNOW BUNTING

grey

♀
ad. ♂

brown
admixed

grey-brown
on head
and breast

reduced
white

1st-w. ♀
ad. ♂

**ad.
summer**
♀

winter flock

juv. ♀

brown, streaked;
white on wing
much reduced

large white
wing patch

black

all-
white
head

1st-winter ♀

winter ♂

ad. summer ♂

LAPLAND LONGSPUR

autumn birds in stubble field

Lapland Longspur   Skylark

red-
brown

a little
white

ad. s. ♂

red-
brown

all
black

pale median
crown-stripe

red-brown

two white
wing-bars

ad. s. ♀

reddish-brown wing-
panel framed by nar-
row white wing-bars

streaked

dark
spots

1st-winter.

ad. summer ♂

ad. winter

RUSTIC BUNTING

in autumn, separating Rustic Bunting from Reed
Bunting can be
tricky; a few use-
ful differences to
notice are shown
on the right

white patch
red-brown

pink

grey

a few breeding birds are
difficult to sex—♂ and
♀ can be very similar!

red-
brown

white
wing-
bars

yellow-
brown
wing-bars

Rustic   Reed

culmen
straight

summer ♀ /
1st-summer ♂

tinged reddish-brown,
unmarked

red-
brown

un-
marked
white belly

1st-winter ♀

ad. summer ♂

DZ

Ortolan Bunting *Emberiza hortulana* **P**5

L 15–16½ cm. Breeds at lower levels in agricultural country with some patches of trees and deciduous copses, in open wooded pasture and in clearings, and in S Europe, Turkey and Caucasus in mountain regions, usually in glades or at forest edge, often above 1500 m. Summer visitor (mainly Apr–Sep), winters in tropical Africa. Nocturnal migrant. Forages mostly on ground, often on dry, short-grazed grassy areas. Rather shy and wary, quick to take cover.

IDENTIFICATION Medium-sized, slim bunting. *Bill rather long. Legs and bill* buffish-pink, culmen a shade darker and with straight profile. *Yellowish-white eye-ring* in all plumages, as well as *heavily dark-streaked grey-brown mantle* and *dark malar stripe on light yellow ground* (though juv. lacks yellow up to Jul/Aug). *Flanks and belly* have variably distinct *orange-brown tone* (except juv.), and *head and nape* are usually *olive-toned*. *Rump grey-brown and streaked.* – ♂ summer: Head, broad breast-band and narrow malar stripes *plain olive-grey;* belly and flanks *saturated orange-brown.* – ♀ summer/adult autumn: Crown, breast and malar stripe *finely dark-spotted.* Olive-grey breast-band narrow or indistinct; orange colour below sometimes weaker. Some ♂♂ = ♂ summer, i.e. have unspotted olive-grey breast-band. – 1st-winter: Head brown-grey (without green tinge) and boldly streaked; malar stripe, breast and upper flanks heavily streaked. Eye-ring buffish-white. Throat faint buffy-yellow.

VOICE Call a metallic, almost disyllabic 'sli-e', also a short and slightly jolting, at distance almost clicking 'chu'; these two are given alternately at *c.* 2-sec. intervals, e.g. on nocturnal passage. Also has a flatter clicking 'plett', e.g. when flushed. Song a plain verse with typically *ringing tone* and with repeated theme changed a good halfway through; can sound *like an echo*, 'srü-srü-srü-srü-dru-dru-dru' or 'sia sia sia drü drü'; the 'echoing' notes are often lower. Mountain-dwelling Ortolans of S Europe have the ringing tone in the first stage but generally cut short the second part to a single, slightly bent, drawn-out final note, 'srü-srü-srü-srü-chuuüy' (so confusion risk with Cretzschmar's can arise: see latter).

Cretzschmar's Bunting *Emberiza caesia* **V**∗∗∗

L 14–15½ cm. Breeds on sunny and dry, bare mountain slopes with mixture of rock outcrops, grass and thorn bushes. In regions where Ortolan Bunting occurs in vicinity, Cretzschmar's often (but not always) breeds at lower levels, usually below 1350 m. Mainly coastal. Summer visitor (in Greece mostly mid Apr–Aug), winters S of Red Sea. Night migrant. Perches on ground or low rocks, but also uses low bushes as songpost. Not shy. Migrant flocks, at times quite large, often seen at stopovers in S Israel in Mar.

IDENTIFICATION Somewhat smaller than Ortolan Bunt-

ing, which it otherwise resembles in shape. Legs and bill as on Ortolan, but *bill a trifle shorter.* Bold *eye-ring is white* (not yellowish). *Rump red-brown*, saturated and unstreaked on adult ♂, duller red-brown on adult ♀, only tinged red-brown and also streaked on 1st-winter. Plumages much as Ortolan, but latter's green tone on head, breast and malar stripe are replaced by *lead-grey*, and Ortolan's light yellow throat by *rusty-red* or white. Adult ♂ has *very dark orange-brown colour on underparts:* seen head-on at distance, breast and throat look distinctly paler than the dark belly, an impression never given by Ortolan. 1st-winter is very like Ortolan, but has whiter throat and eye-ring and faint red-brown tinge on rump.

VOICE Calls of Ortolan type, and because of some dialectal variation very similar at times; as a rule, however, recognized both by sharp, rasping note ('tsrip') and by melancholy ring and quite low-pitched, full whistle with faint downslur ('chüu'). Also has drier 'plett', very like Ortolan's. Song rather like S European Ortolan's, having same structure with (2–)3 repeated short notes and a drawn-out terminal one, 'ji ji ji **jüüü**' or slightly faster 'si si-si-**siüüh**', but can be told by fact that it *always lacks the pleasant ringing tone* in the first part; some singers alternate this with hoarse (at times really asthmatic!) song variants, 'cha-cha-cha-**cheeeh**'.

Grey-necked Bunting *Emberiza buchanani* —

L 14–15½ cm. Breeds on bare mountain slopes or high plateaux, mostly above 2000 m, with rock outcrops, scant vegetation and scattered low bushes. Has similar habitat requirements to Rock Bunting and southern populations of Ortolan Bunting. Summer visitor (in E Turkey mainly Apr/May–Aug/Sep), winters in India. Quite placid, not shy.

IDENTIFICATION Like Cretzschmar's Buntings, but *somewhat longer-tailed.* Bill long and narrow, all pink (lacks dark culmen). *Eye-ring white. Mantle/back* invariably *discreetly spotted*, looks rather *uniform brown-grey* in fresh plumage. *Rump plain brown-grey*, or just faintly streaked. – Adult ♂: Greyish head (dirty grey, sometimes ash-grey); minute off-white throat patch and off-white (longer) submoustachial stripe; *cold red-brown breast* (with fine whitish fringes when fresh), looks vermiculated); *brownish-white belly* and *red-brown shoulders.* – Adult ♀: Like ♂, but *duller* and has *finely streaked breast* and streaked crown. – 1st-winter: Rump dull brown without rusty tone, mantle/back only moderately spotted. Note narrow, pointed bill and white eye-ring.

VOICE Calls similar to those of Cretzschmar's and Cinereous Buntings, a forceful 'chüpp' and a higher and sharper 'zrip'; these are alternated and vary in detail. Song, too, is like those of its congeners, perhaps most like that of Cinereous: plain, short, with slightly scratchy voice (usually not so nice a ringing sound as Ortolan's), 'srü-srüsrü **srih**-srusru' or 'sri-srisri-sus**riih**-sria'; slightly wider scale range also occurs, 'tru-trü-**tri** tre-tra'; often *third syllable from end most stressed.*

Ortolan Bunting

Cretzschmar's Bunting

Grey-necked Bunting

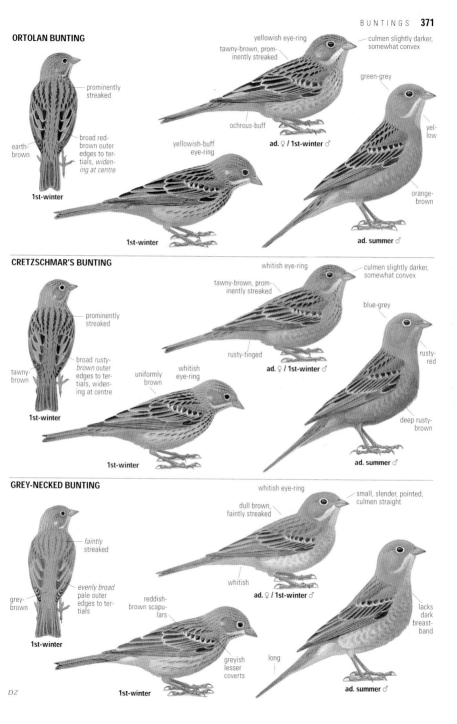

ORTOLAN BUNTING

prominently streaked

earth-brown

broad red-brown outer edges to tertials, *widening at centre*

1st-winter

yellowish eye-ring

tawny-brown, prominently streaked

ochrous-buff

yellowish-buff eye-ring

1st-winter

culmen slightly darker, somewhat convex

green-grey

ad. ♀ / 1st-winter ♂

yellow

orange-brown

ad. summer ♂

CRETZSCHMAR'S BUNTING

prominently streaked

tawny-brown

broad *rusty-brown* outer edges to tertials, widening at centre

1st-winter

whitish eye-ring

tawny-brown, prominently streaked

rusty-tinged

whitish eye-ring

uniformly brown

1st-winter

culmen slightly darker, somewhat convex

blue-grey

ad. ♀ / 1st-winter ♂

rusty-red

deep rusty-brown

ad. summer ♂

GREY-NECKED BUNTING

faintly streaked

grey-brown

evenly broad pale outer edges to tertials

1st-winter

whitish eye-ring

dull brown, faintly streaked

whitish

ad. ♀ / 1st-winter ♂

small, slender, pointed, culmen straight

reddish-brown scapulars

greyish lesser coverts

long

1st-winter

lacks dark breast-band

ad. summer ♂

DZ

Yellowhammer *Emberiza citrinella* r**B**1 (2?)

L 15½–17 cm. Breeds commonly in farmland, in bushy areas, woodland edge and wooded pasture, in glades and clearings, on heaths and coastal meadows. Predominantly resident, but many Scandinavian birds migrate Oct–mid Nov to North Sea countries, returning Mar/Apr. Wary without being really shy, usually flushes early; often gains height, perches high in tree or drops into thick bushes.

IDENTIFICATION Fairly big and *long-tailed* with *unmarked red-brown rump* and *elements of yellow* in plumage. Mantle/ back olive-brown, heavily streaked black. Bill rather small, lower mandible light blue-grey. *Much white on tail-corners*, often seen in flight, when looks longer-tailed than e.g. Reed Bunting. Flight in *long undulations* and slightly jerky. – ♂ summer: Unmistakable, having *almost entirely yellow head* with just a few dark markings on crown- and head-sides. *Saturated yellow below*, with much *olive-green and red-brown on breast* and with *flanks streaked red-brown*. – ♀ summer: Greyish-green, streaked crown, at times with a small yellow spot, grey-green head-side with no yellow. Underparts *paler yellow, with greyish-black streaking on breast and flanks*. – Autumn: ♂ often told by intimation of deep yellow on head and underparts, and by *olive-green and red-brown colour on breast*. ♀ rather like ♂ summer. 1st-winter ♀ often has almost wholly brown and streaked head and buff-white underparts with only faint yellow tinge; note: yellow on underparts can be hard to see in field—cf. Pine Bunting!

VOICE Call a discordant 'stüff'. Also has variety of more stifled, short, clicking calls, 'pt...pt, pt, pitti**litt**...'; also sharp 'tsit' and fine, drawn-out 'tsiih'. Song well known, a run of 5–8 rapidly repeated short notes and a different ending, e.g. 'si-si-si-si-si-si-**süüü**'; the penultimate note is often higher and the last lower, 'sre-sre-sre-sre-sre-sre **siii-**suuu' ('little bit of bread and NO cheese!'); voice occasionally more River Warbler-like, 'dzre-dzre-dzre-...'.

Pine Bunting *Emberiza leucocephalos* **V*****

L16–17½ cm. Breeds in Siberia (apparently not W of Urals) in similar habitats to closely related Yellowhammer, but more associated with forest than latter. Hybridizes to some extent with Yellowhammer in W Siberia. Migratory, winters in Central Asia and locally W to Middle East and S Europe. Rare vagrant in W Europe, mostly in autumn and winter.

IDENTIFICATION A sibling species of Yellowhammer in which all yellow pigment is replaced by white. Adult ♂ (sometimes ♀, too) in addition has *reddish-brown throat and supercilium*. Autumn birds, especially 1st-winter ♀, often hard to separate from pale young ♀ of Yellowhammer. Note: *ground colour of underparts whitish with no suggestion of yellow*; *mantle/back* rather *pale, greyish*-brown *without green*

tone; *shoulder* often with *red-brown tone*; light brown-tinged off-white *supercilium without yellow*; narrow pale *edges to primaries white*, not yellow; *flanks streaked* predominantly *red-brown*, not greyish-black as on tricky Yellowhammers.

VOICE Most calls are just like Yellowhammer's, at least to the human ear. Besides the usual 'stüff' call, occasionally gives a slightly different 'tsick' and a faintly downslurred 'chüeh'. Song sounds exactly like Yellowhammer's.

Cirl Bunting *Emberiza cirlus* r**B**4

L 15–16½ cm. Breeds at woodland edge, in glades, in larger parks etc.; prefers slightly hilly terrain with some tallish trees and thick bushes and hedges, often found on dry sunny slopes (south- and east-facing), e.g. with vineyards, but avoids open plains. In far SW often on mountain slopes to c.1500 m. Resident. Huge decline in N of range, in Britain now confined to handful of coastal sites in SW England.

IDENTIFICATION Like Yellowhammer but a bit smaller, with proportionately *slightly bigger bill* and shorter tail. ♂ unmistakable, with *black throat and eye-stripe* and *broad olive-green breast-band*. ♀ and 1st-winter are very like Yellowhammer, but distinguished by: *olive-tinged grey-brown* and *streaked rump* (not virtually unstreaked red-brown); *greater contrast on head-side* between dark markings and pale ground colour; *reddish-brown shoulders, plainer* brown-grey *greater coverts*; *wholly greenish grey-brown, streaked crown* (no hint of paler crown-centre); tendency towards more two-toned bill.

VOICE Call a fine, sharp clicking 'zitt'. Also has somewhat Reed Bunting-like, downslurred 'siiü' and, e.g. in pursuit-chase, fast sharp trills, 'zir'r'r' (can recall Long-tailed Tit). The song is a fully second-long, flat, dry trill, 'sre'sre'sre'sre'sre'sre'sre'sre', rather rattling and metallic; sometimes shifts between two pitches; at distance can to some extent recall song of Arctic Warbler.

Cinereous Bunting *Emberiza cineracea* —

L 16–17 cm. Breeds locally and often sparingly on dry, stony slopes with low vegetation, maquis and scattered trees. Summer visitor, winters around Red Sea.

IDENTIFICATION Rather big and *slim* and *long-tailed*. With its *pale and almost unstreaked* plumage, its *narrow pale eye-ring* and *rather heavy, pale bill*, most resembles a ♀ Black-headed Bunting, but differences include *white tail-corners*. – ♂: *Yellowish throat; plain yellowish-grey head; grey breast; greyish mantle/back* with discreet dark spotting. – ♀/1st-winter: Buffy-white throat; mantle and head brownish; crown finely streaked; breast grey-brown, finely streaked.

VOICE Calls quite like those of Cretzschmar's and Grey-necked Buntings, a sharp, rasping 'tschrip' as well as a full 'chülp' (or shorter 'chü') which are often uttered alternately and varied in detail. Song like Grey-necked's, a plain, rapidly delivered verse with slightly hoarse voice and uneven pace, e.g. 'zre, zrü-zrü-zrü **zrih**-zra'; often ends with a high and a low note in rapid succession.

Yellowhammer

Cirl Bunting

Cinereous Bunting

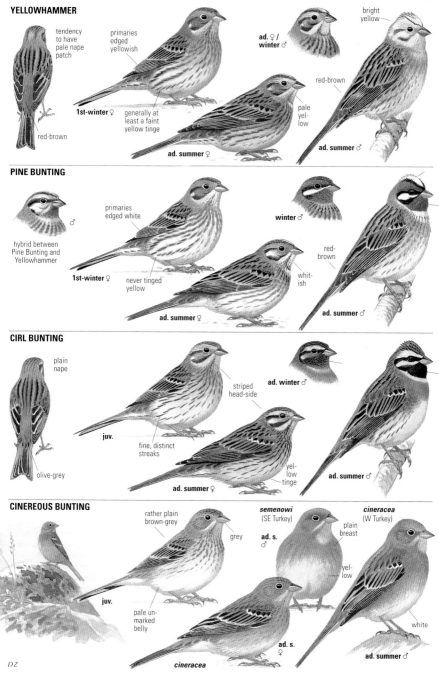

YELLOWHAMMER

tendency to have pale nape patch

primaries edged yellowish

1st-winter ♀

generally at least a faint yellow tinge

red-brown

ad. summer ♀

ad. ♀ / winter ♂

bright yellow

red-brown

pale yellow

ad. summer ♂

PINE BUNTING

♂

hybrid between Pine Bunting and Yellowhammer

primaries edged white

1st-winter ♀

never tinged yellow

ad. summer ♀

winter ♂

whitish

red-brown

ad. summer ♂

CIRL BUNTING

plain nape

juv.

olive-grey

striped head-side

fine, distinct streaks

ad. summer ♀

ad. winter ♂

yellow tinge

ad. summer ♂

CINEREOUS BUNTING

juv.

rather plain brown-grey

grey

pale un-marked belly

cineracea

semenowi (SE Turkey)

ad. s. ♂

ad. s. ♀

cineracea (W Turkey)

plain breast

yellow

white

ad. summer ♂

DZ

Red-headed Bunting *Emberiza bruniceps* [V∗∗∗]

L 15–16½ cm. Very closely related to Black-headed Bunting, and hybridizes with latter where the two meet (SE Caspian Sea). Breeds on steppe (cultivated or not) with some bushes or scattered trees, in semi-desert, on open mountain slopes or high-lying plains. Summer visitor (by Volga mostly early Jun–early Aug), winters in India. Not that shy. Rare records in W Europe, but all these are generally regarded as involving escaped cagebirds; a few, however, probably refer to genuine vagrants.

IDENTIFICATION *Fairly big* and rather long-tailed. *No white on tail*. – ♂: Unmistakable. Besides *red-brown mask*, note *yellowish rump* and *yellowish-green, streaked mantle*. – ♀: Rather nondescript and hard to identify. Note: *long, heavy, light grey bill; narrow buffy-white eye-ring*; dull light brown mantle/back and head/nape with only *modest, fine streaking* on mantle and forecrown; usually lightly streaked yellow-green or *yellowish rump*; wholly *unstreaked dirty yellowish-white underparts* and *bright yellow undertail-coverts*. – 1st-winter: Like ♀, but has *buffish-white breast* (sometimes with fine streaks), *more heavily streaked grey-brown mantle/back* and rump without yellow-green tone. Very like Black-headed Bunting, and often inseparable from that species.

VOICE Has many calls, most recalling those of congeners, including rather Ortolan-like 'chüpp' and Cretzschmar's-like 'zrit', also quite Yellowhammer-like 'chüh', sharp 'tsit' and fast series of clicks, 'ptr'r'r'. Song is to human ear identical to Black-headed Bunting's, a slightly accelerating verse with low pitch, jerky rhythm and very rolling r-sound, 'zrit...zrit...srütt, srütt-srütt sütter**i**-sütt sütter**reh**'; the pitch drops a little during the verse.

Black-headed Bunting *Emberiza melanocephala* **V**∗∗∗

L 15½–17½ cm. Very close relative of Red-headed Bunting, and the two hybridize locally. Breeds in open, dry country with bushes, often in farmland with scattered tree clumps, in vineyards and orchards, in riverine woodland, at forest edge and in glades, as well as on drier mountain slopes with thorn bushes and isolated trees. Summer visitor (in Greece mainly early May–end Jul), winters in India. Not shy.

IDENTIFICATION *Fairly large*, a trifle bigger than Red-headed, and similarly long-tailed. *Lacks white on tail*. – ♂: Unmistakable. Apart from *black hood*, note *unstreaked red-brown upperparts*. – ♀: Very like Red-headed and often difficult to separate in field. Has *slightly longer bill* and sometimes *faint red-brown tone* to the dull grey-brown mantle/back. *Rump dull brown* or tinged yellow-brown (never has green tinge of some Red-headed). In addition, *crown* is sometimes *more distinctly dark-streaked* and ear-coverts a little darker. – 1st-winter: Very like Red-headed

(which see) and often not safely separable in the field.

VOICE Most calls are very like those of the closely related Red-headed Bunting, and because of some variation in articulation (in both species) safe field separation based on voice alone is impossible. Song as Red-headed's (above).

Yellow-breasted Bunting *Emberiza aureola* **V**∗∗

L 14–15½ cm. Breeds in NE Europe and large parts of Siberia (where very common) in bushy areas, deciduous scrub and copses, often along watercourses, lakesides and at edge of wetlands. Summer visitor (in Finland mostly mid Jun–end Jul), winters in SE Asia. Rather confiding.

IDENTIFICATION Roughly size of Reed Bunting; has *longer bill* than latter, with *straighter culmen* and *pink* (not greyish-black) *lower mandible*. In all plumages, *element of yellow or buffy-yellow below* and *sparse, narrow streaks on flanks*. – ♂ summer: *Black 'face'*, unmarked *dark red-brown upperparts*, *red-brown breast-band*, saturated yellow underparts, *large white wing patch*. 1st-year has *small and dark-spotted white wing patch*, a *sprinkling of brown and white on black 'face'*, narrow or broken breast-band; some are paler yellow below. – ♀/1st-winter: *Buffy yellow-white supercilium*; dark rear eye-stripe and a *dark lower border to light yellow-brown cheek*; *dark crown-sides* frame narrow, paler grey-brown median crown-stripe; *white on tail-sides* (unlike ♀ Chestnut Bunting, which has all-dark tail). *Rump grey-brown* (with faint red-brown tinge), *heavily streaked*. Undertail-coverts whitish.

VOICE Call/alarm a sharp clicking 'tsick'. Song easily recognized by dominant element of clear loud notes repeated in pairs and wide tonal range, often in steps up the scale (but verses commonly seesaw up and down in pitch at end), 'tru-tru trüa-trüa **tri-tri** cha' (last note falling) or 'trü-trü, tra, tro-tro **triih**' (lowest pitch in middle). Wide individual variation.

Chestnut Bunting *Emberiza rutila* [V∗∗∗]

L 12½–13½ cm. Breeds in E Siberian taiga. Migratory, winters in SE Asia. Very rare autumn vagrant in W Europe, incl. in Norway, Netherlands and Malta. (Some spring records of adult ♂♂ deemed likely to have involved escapes.)

IDENTIFICATION Small. *Rump unmarked red-brown*. *Underparts light yellow*. Bill longish, with pink at base of lower mandible. ♂ unmistakable. ♀/1st-winter is rather like Yellow-breasted Bunting, differs in: *smaller* size; *unspotted red-brown rump*; *more strongly indicated malar stripe*; *white throat* but *yellowish undertail-coverts*; *all-dark tail*.

VOICE Call a short, hard, sharp clicking 'zit', sometimes rapidly repeated. Song a brief, loud, rather fast verse which may be likened to a snippet of Pallas's Warbler or Olive-backed Pipit song; quite often each phrase starts with three slow, pure notes or double notes, followed by a characteristic *scratchy, trilling* section (lacking in rather similar song of Yellow-browed Bunting) and a softer, Yellow-start-like ending (as Yellow-browed), e.g. 'tvia tvia tvia sre-sre-sre sisicha'. Cf. also Little Bunting.

Red-headed Bunting

Black-headed Bunting

Yellow-breasted Bunting

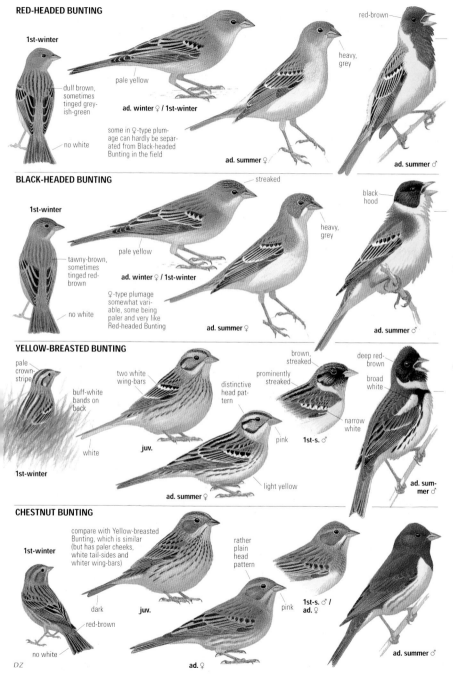

RED-HEADED BUNTING

1st-winter

dull brown, sometimes tinged grey-ish-green

pale yellow

no white

ad. winter ♀ / 1st-winter

some in ♀-type plumage can hardly be separated from Black-headed Bunting in the field

ad. summer ♀

heavy, grey

red-brown

ad. summer ♂

BLACK-HEADED BUNTING

1st-winter

tawny-brown, sometimes tinged red-brown

pale yellow

no white

ad. winter ♀ / 1st-winter

streaked

♀-type plumage somewhat variable, some being paler and very like Red-headed Bunting

ad. summer ♀

heavy, grey

black hood

ad. summer ♂

YELLOW-BREASTED BUNTING

pale crown-stripe

buff-white bands on back

white

1st-winter

two white wing-bars

juv.

distinctive head pattern

pink

light yellow

ad. summer ♀

brown, streaked

prominently streaked

narrow white

1st-s. ♂

deep red-brown

broad white

ad. summer ♂

CHESTNUT BUNTING

1st-winter

compare with Yellow-breasted Bunting, which is similar (but has paler cheeks, white tail-sides and whiter wing-bars)

dark

red-brown

no white

juv.

rather plain head pattern

pink

1st-s. ♂ / ad. ♀

ad. ♀

ad. summer ♂

DZ

Corn Bunting *Miliaria calandra*   r**B**3

L 16–19 cm. In greater part of its European range breeds in extensive, open farmland, mostly where cereals, fodder plants and leguminous plants are cultivated on a large scale. Requires elevated songpost, but isolated trees and bushes or telephone wires, or even just fence posts, will suffice. In S of range, breeds also on dry mountain slopes with low thorn bushes. Huge decline in NW Europe since 1960s. Mostly resident. Social, often seen in small loose flocks. Complex breeding habits; locally 2–3 ♀♀ per ♂. Not very shy.

IDENTIFICATION Big, with quite *heavy body* and *stout bill*. Often looks rather *large-headed*. Plumage not unlike that of a lark, dark-streaked grey-brown above and buffy-white below with dark streaks on throat-side, breast and (more narrowly) flanks. *Tail lacks white.* Head-side shows no striking pattern, is somewhat irregularly streaked on buff-white ground, with *darker malar stripe* and *lower edge of cheek*, and has a *dark spot on rearmost ear-coverts*. In worn plumage (summer), breast streaks often coalesce to form irregular dark patterns. *Legs and bill-side yellowish-pink.* Sexes alike. Moves short distances often with fairly *ponderous flight and dangling legs* (can give lark-like impression); over longer stretches flies in deep undulations.

VOICE Call a discordant, metallic 'tsritt', also a short clicking 'bitt' or 'bt', often rapidly repeated in 'electrified' series, 'bt'bt'bt'bt…'. Song is characteristic (but can be skilfully imitated by some Whinchats), a brief, little-varied and oft repeated verse with *halting start, accelerating* to a *squeaky, jingling ending*, 'tück tück-zick-zik-zkzkzkzrississss'.

Rock Bunting *Emberiza cia*   **V****

L 15–16½ cm. Breeds on steep, often boulder-strewn or rocky, open mountain slopes immediately above treeline (often below 1500 m in Europe) with grass and herbage along with thorn bushes and scattered trees, sometimes in glades and alpine meadows just below treeline; locally in coastal regions down to sea-level. Chiefly resident, but in winter usually descends to lower levels. Not really shy, but unobtrusive and is easily overlooked when ♂ not singing.

IDENTIFICATION Fairly big, short-winged but *long-tailed*. Identified in all plumages by contrasty head markings, with *dark stripes along crown-side, through eye and framing cheek*, combined with *ash-grey throat* and *ash-grey breast* (mostly on ♂), *rusty-brown* (or on young ♀ orange-buff) *belly, white outer tail-corners*, and *grey lesser wing-coverts*. Lower mandible pale lead-grey. *Rump unstreaked red-brown*. Sexes similar. – Adult ♂: Black head markings, whitish supercilium, unspotted pale lead-grey on throat and breast, and unstreaked flanks. – ♀: Occasionally inseparable from ♂ in field, but many can be told by less

extensive grey on breast, light streaking on lower throat, breast and flanks, and more diffuse head pattern.

VOICE Call a short, sharp 'tsi', also a drawn-out 'tsiii', at times faintly downslurred and then rather Reed Bunting-like, 'tsiü'; when nervous, fine twittering series, 'tir'r'r' (like begging young White Wagtails). Song *high-pitched* and *clear*, a melodic verse with distinct scale changes and often typically *tentative introduction* and uneven rhythm, e.g. 'sütt, titt-itt, svi cha-cha-sivi-süasüa, sitt sivisürrr si'.

House Bunting *Emberiza striolata*   —

L 13–14 cm. Two discrete populations. In NW Africa (ssp. *sahari*), resident breeder in proximity of man by settlements, on mountain slopes with small cultivations and scattered bushes and trees, at times also in village gardens, where it is anything but shy (even flies unconcernedly into houses; cf. name) and nests in cavities, on ledges or in recesses in houses; sometimes also in rock crevices and the like. In Middle East (*striolata*), lives in uninhabited, barren mountain regions with scant vegetation, where it is shy and rather difficult to observe and breeds only in rock crevices; resident, but in winter occasionally moves to cultivated fields and plains at lower levels. – (Bearing in mind that the two populations differ quite clearly in appearance, voice and to some extent habits and ecology, a split into two species might be expected in the future.)

IDENTIFICATION A *fairly small* bunting with *much rusty-brown on wing*, with *dark spots or shading on throat/ breast*, *straw-yellow lower mandible* and *no white on tail*. Can recall Rock Bunting as head is often greyish-white with dark stripes, but differs in: smaller size; tail lacking pure white (Rock Bunting has white outer corners); yellowish lower mandible (Rock Bunting: light grey); dark-mottled throat and breast (Rock: unspotted light grey); *rusty-brown lesser coverts* (Rock: grey); *no white wing-bars* (Rock: two narrow ones). ♀ is more brownish than grey on head, neck and breast, and head markings are less distinct. – Variation: Race *sahari* (see above) has much *richer rusty-brown colour on belly and wings* and is as good as *unspotted on rusty-brown mantle* (has only fine shaft streaks), whereas *striolata* is *paler below* and *heavily dark-spotted on brown-grey upper-parts*. In addition, ♂ *striolata* has on average more contrasty greyish-white and black head markings, while head of ♂ *sahari* is more swarthy and diffusely patterned.

VOICE Race *sahari*: Calls whining, mewing and drawn-out, slightly Rock Sparrow-like 'che-**veeh**-e', 'che**vay** che**vaay**' and similar, also rather Tree Sparrow-like 'tsuvitt' and somewhat Greenfinch-like 'chüpp'; song like a mix of sleepy Chaffinch, Common Rosefinch and Goldfinch, a chirping verse often rising a bit at very end,'tve-tvi tve **vitt**ya-**trrü**oo-tvetvittyü'. – Race *striolata*: Seems rather different; calls include a nasal, whining 'chueht', a shorter 'tvett' and hoarse, House Sparrow-like 'chriff'; song a plain, stumbling, halting, rather flat series of House Sparrow-like syllables,'chi-vi chirp-chüvi chüv-chie-chirp' and similar.

Corn Bunting

Rock Bunting

House Bunting

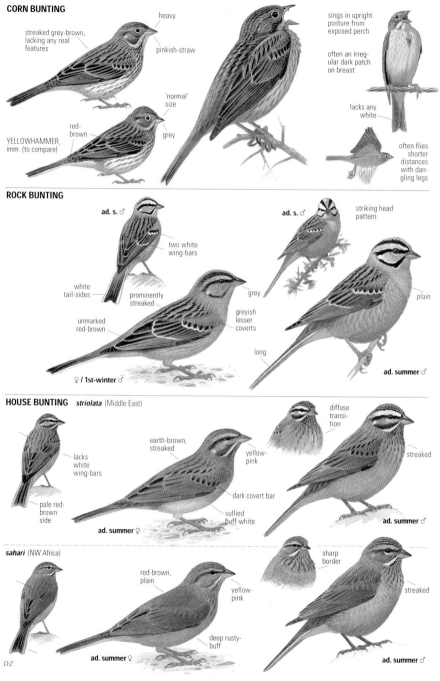

CORN BUNTING

streaked grey-brown, lacking any real features

heavy

pinkish-straw

'normal' size

red-brown

grey

YELLOWHAMMER, imm. (to compare)

sings in upright posture from exposed perch

often an irregular dark patch on breast

lacks any white

often flies shorter distances with dangling legs

ROCK BUNTING

ad. s. ♂

two white wing-bars

white tail-sides

prominently streaked

unmarked red-brown

♀ / 1st-winter ♂

grey

greyish lesser coverts

long

ad. s. ♂

striking head pattern

plain

ad. summer ♂

HOUSE BUNTING *striolata* (Middle East)

lacks white wing-bars

pale red-brown side

earth-brown, streaked

yellow-pink

dark covert bar

sullied buff-white

ad. summer ♀

diffuse transition

streaked

ad. summer ♂

sahari (NW Africa)

red-brown, plain

yellow-pink

deep rusty-buff

ad. summer ♀

sharp border

streaked

ad. summer ♂

DZ

Vagrants

Those species which have been recorded only a few times within the region treated, which largely corresponds to the West Palearctic (see definition p. 6), are briefly described below. As a rule, this means 3–9 records in total during the 1900s (but strict consistency over numbers has not been sought, and new records of rarities continue to be reported). Those seeking fuller descriptions for the majority of these species are referred to Alström, Colston & Lewington (1992), *Rare Birds of Britain and Europe*, and to the larger handbooks and the regional field guides (see literature list on p. 392). Accidentals (generally 1–2 records in all) are simply listed on pp. 386–388.

Red-billed Tropicbird *Phaethon aethereus* V***

L 45–50 cm (plus tail projection on ad. *c.* 45), WS 100–115 cm. Breeds in Cape Verdes and in S Atlantic, Red Sea and Persian Gulf. Observed also in Portugal, Canary Islands, Madeira and Israel. (A record in Netherlands not accepted as definitely genuine vagrant.) – A rather large and pale bird, *white* with *black outer primaries*, black spots above on innermost 'arm', a *black eye-stripe* and greyish-black vermiculation on mantle/back and lesser upperwing-coverts. Adult has *bright red bill* and *very long, thin tail-streamers*. Juvenile lacks streamers, and has yellowish-brown bill with dark tip and black terminal tail-band. Often flies high up with mechanical wingbeats, much as a Sandwich Tern. Often hovers before plunging, and makes brief glides in searching flight.

Magnificent Frigatebird *Fregata magnificens* V***

L 90–110 cm, WS 215–245 cm. Breeds in Cape Verdes and in C and S America. A few definite records in Europe (incl. in Britain, Denmark and France), plus several records of indeterminate frigatebirds. – *Very big*, with *long, narrow, pointed wings, long, deeply forked tail* (normally held closed in flight and then appears very long and narrow) and retracted head with long, powerful, cormorant-like bill. Often flies with slow, intermittent wingbeats with slightly *backward-angled hand* (pointed carpal!), frequently glides and makes deft manoeuvres. ♂ is *all black* with light grey bill (red throat-sac is rarely shown away from breeding sites), ♀ has *white area on crop* between breast and lower belly, while immature has in addition a *whitish head*.

Snowy Egret *Egretta thula* V***

L 55–65 cm, WS 90–105 cm. American species which has been recorded in Iceland. – Very like closely related Little Egret and, like that, has *dark tarsi with yellow toes*, but told by: almost invariably distinctly *yellowish rear to lower tarsus*, sometimes so extensive that on much of tarsus only front is dark (Little: all-dark tarsus); *more saturated yellow toes* incuding soles (Little: duller yellow toes with greenish-tinged soles); *bright yellow lores* outside courtship period (blue-grey or greenish-grey on European Littles); on adult summer *bushier and shorter white nape plume*; slightly smaller, and has shorter neck and legs.

Goliath Heron *Ardea goliath* —

L 135–150 cm, WS 210–230 cm. Breeds in tropical Africa and in E Iraq. Occasional records within treated region, including in Israel (spring and autumn) and Syria (end 1800s). – *Very big* heron, as Grey Heron with *blue-grey upperwing* and white foreneck with black stripes, but with *red-brown crown and hindneck*, dark *red-brown underbody*, *powerful black bill* and black legs. Adult has a *red-brown crest on hindcrown*. Juvenile lacks crest and is somewhat paler.

Yellow-billed Stork *Mycteria ibis* —

L 95–105 cm, WS 150–165 cm. Breeds in tropical Africa. Seen occasionally in Israel, Turkey and elsewhere. – Recalls a White Stork, but has *red facial mask* (can be partly orange) and *yellowish bill* (with slightly darker yellowish-orange tip). Plumage white, *wing-coverts, shoulders and mantle/back tinged pink*. Legs red. In flight very like White Stork; best told, even at long range, by *black tail*. Immature is sullied grey-brown, has grey-green legs and pinkish-yellow mask.

Red-billed Tropicbird
ad.

Magnificent
Frigatebird

ad. ♀

ad. ♂

Snowy
Egret

Goliath Heron

juv.

DZ   Yellow-billed Stork

Lesser Scaup *Aythya affinis* V**

L 38–45 cm. N American species found occasionally in Europe, including Britain, Ireland (one ♂ seen seven winters in a row), Sweden, Netherlands, Belgium, France and Spain. One Swiss record considered not genuine vagrant. – Like a *small* (barely Tufted Duck size) Scaup, but told by: *peaked hindcrown* giving angular head profile as on ♀ Tufted (Scaup: always rounded rear head); *wing-bar* white on 'arm' but *brownish-grey on 'hand'* (all white on Scaup); adult ♂ having *coarser dark vermiculation on mantle/back* and *more violet* than green *gloss* on head. – ♀ Scaup-like in pattern, told by size, head profile and wing-bar.

Lesser Scaup
ad. ♂

Spectacled Eider *Somateria fischeri*

L 50–58 cm. Breeds in Alaska and NE Siberia. A few winter records from N Norway. – Size of Velvet Scoter, thus *clearly smaller than Eider*. Recalls Eider, but ♂ has *black breast*, large, *rounded 'white spectacles'* on predominantly *green head*, and *orange bill* partly concealed by velvety-textured, green and white feathering; ♀ has *light buff 'spectacles'* on somewhat darker grey-brown head.

Spectacled Eider
ad. ♂

Pallas's Fish Eagle *Haliaeetus leucoryphus* —

L 73–84 cm, WS 185–210 cm. Breeds on lakes and rivers in Central Asia and eastward in S Asia. Declining; formerly bred at N Caspian Sea. Vagrants recorded in e.g. Finland, Norway, Poland and Israel. A few recent records in Germany and Netherlands thought likely not to be genuine vagrants. – Adult easily identified by *white*, evenly rounded, medium-long *tail with broad black terminal band* (as young Golden Eagle), dark brown body and *all-dark wings*, and contrastingly *buffy-white head*. Rather long, bare, light grey tarsi. Immature pale cinnamon-brown on head and body, with dark brown band through and behind eye; in flight, told by *broad white bands along centre of underwing* ending in *white 'armpits'*, *large white patch on inner 'palm'*, and *all-dark tail*.

Pallas's Fish Eagle
juv.

Rüppell's Vulture *Gyps rueppellii* —

L 90–105 cm, WS 220–255 cm. Breeds in Africa. Rarely strays to N Egypt. – Somewhat smaller than Griffon Vulture. Adult distinctive, with *dark plumage densely sprinkled with broad buffy-white feather tips* (variegated impression in close view, mostly dark at long range). *Bill orange-yellow*, set off by *dark cere*. Long *neck* bare (only sparse white 'fluff'), *light purplish* or reddish. Ruff white. Immature *lightly streaked buffy-brown*, with *black bill* and *light red neck*.

Rüppell's
Vulture

Bateleur *Terathopius ecaudatus* —

L 50–60 cm, WS 170–180 cm. Breeds in Africa. Vagrants recorded in N Egypt and in Israel. – Unmistakable owing to its long, peculiarly shaped wings with *bulging rear edge to 'arm'* and *constricted inner 'hand'*, so that wing-tip is narrow but still deeply 'fingered'. In addition, *tail is 'docked'*, on adult so short that *feet clearly stick out behind* in flight. Flight often fast with elastic wingbeats, holds wings raised in V-shape when gliding, performs flight-rolls etc.

Bateleur

ad.

juv.

American Kestrel *Falco sparverius* V***

L 23–27 cm. American species, recorded as a vagrant in Britain, Denmark and Malta. – Looks much like a *small* Kestrel with longish narrow-based tail; often hovers with fanned tail, which is *reddish-brown with broader black terminal band* (broader on ♂). Irrespective of plumage, identified by very contrasty head pattern with *pointed black moustachial stripe* and *two black marks on cheek and nape-side*. Both sexes have *blue-grey crown with reddish-brown centre* and black-barred red-brown mantle/back, but ♂ has *blue-grey wings*, ♀ red-brown.

American
Kestrel
juv. ♀

Allen's Gallinule *Porphyrula alleni* V***

L 22–25 cm. Breeds in tropical Africa. Vagrants recorded in several countries, incl. Morocco, Spain, Canary Islands, Israel, Germany, France and Finland (and pre-1950s in Britain). Frequents dense, wet swamps, difficult to see. – *Small*, no bigger than a Water Rail. *Short all-red bill* and *dark blue and green* plumage. Like American Purple Gallinule (below), but clearly smaller, has *red legs* and *dark central undertail-coverts* (as on Moorhen), so that white at stern is divided in middle. Juvenile looks like cross between young Ruff and ♀ Little Crake (!).

Allen's Gallinule

DZ

American Purple Gallinule

American Coot

ad.

Sandhill Crane

Arabian Bustard

Crab Plover

Egyptian Plover

Oriental Pratincole

juv.

Great Knot

DZ

American Purple Gallinule *Porphyrula martinica*   V***
L 29–33 cm. Breeds in N America. Vagrant in Canary Islands, Iceland, Britain, Norway and Switzerland. – Somewhat Moorhen-like, but has *no white line along flanks*, legs are a bit longer, and *underparts are deep ultramarine-blue* with *upperparts greenish*. Bill red with yellow tip, but *frontal shield blue-grey*. Like Allen's Gallinule but *bigger*, with *all-white undertail-coverts* and *yellow legs*.

American Coot *Fulica americana*   V***
L 31–37 cm. Breeds in N America. Recorded in, among others, Britain, Ireland, Iceland and Portugal. – Like European Coot, but differs in *dark band across outer bill* (which is tinged bluish), *white sides to undertail-coverts* and a small *dark* (reddish) *spot on uppermost frontal shield*. Is also somewhat slimmer, has *straighter back profile* and has *paler grey body plumage* than European Coot.

Sandhill Crane *Grus canadensis*   V***
L 80–95 cm, WS 155–180 cm. Breeds in N America and NE Siberia and winters in southern N America and Mexico. Vagrant in Britain, Faroes and Netherlands. – Nominate race, the one which has been recorded in Europe, is *smaller than Crane*. Plumage is *grey* with diffuse spotting; breeding birds acquire rusty tone above, as Crane. Adult has *white throat and side of head* and *red forehead/forecrown*. Juvenile harder to separate from juvenile Crane, but is *more distinctly rusty-brown above* on back and wing-coverts and on head.

Arabian Bustard *Ardeotis arabs*   —
L 70–90 cm. Breeds in Africa S of Sahara. Formerly bred in Morocco, where still found occasionally. – *Grey-brown* and *big*, with *finely vermiculated neck feathering* (thick and bushy on adult ♂). Nape shows a *short crest*, enhanced by a black stripe along crown-side; crest mostly held flat, not very obvious except during display. Has *less white on wing* (seen in flight) than other bustards.

Crab Plover *Dromas ardeola*   —
L 38–41 cm. Breeds in Persian Gulf, Oman and Gulf of Aden. Vagrant in Turkey, Syria, Israel and Egypt. – *Large, black and white*. Resembles if anything an Avocet whose thin upcurved *bill* has been replaced by a *straight, thick, dagger-shaped* one. Often stands erect like a Cream-coloured Courser, but can crouch like a plover, too. Actions plover-like: runs, stops and watches, runs and so on. Flight-call somewhat Gull-billed Tern-like, 'wedde-**vek**, wedde-**vek**,...'.

Egyptian Plover *Pluvianus aegyptius*   —
L 19–21 cm. Breeds in tropical Africa. Recorded in Libya and Egypt. – A rather small and *compact* wader with *broad wings* and shortish legs. Plumage unmistakable, with *broad black and white stripes on wings*, black-and-white head pattern and *orange underparts* with *black breast-band*. Almost always seen by rivers.

Oriental Pratincole *Glareola maldivarum*   V***
L 23–27 cm. Breeds in S Asia from India eastward. Vagrant in e.g. Britain and Cyprus. – *Underwing reddish-brown* (as on Collared Pratincole), but *upperwing dark* and *without clear white trailing edge to 'arm'* (as on Black-winged Pratincole). Note: *tail-streamers short*, terminate 2–3 cm *short of wing-tips* on standing bird, give stub-tailed appearance in flight; *warmer orange-buff tone to bib and upper belly* (below brown-grey breast patch); somewhat thicker, blunter bill; often a short black gape-line; on average *broader black-and-white frame to bib* and *blacker lores* than on Collared.

Great Knot *Calidris tenuirostris*   V***
L 24–27 cm. Breeds in NE Siberia. Vagrant in several W European countries (incl. Britain) and in Morocco and Israel. – Marginally bigger than a Knot, and with different proportions: longer neck, *smaller head*, *longer and slightly decurved bill with thick base but thinner tip*, long wings giving *attenuated, protracted rear end*. In summer plumage distinctive, with *coarse dark breast spotting, arrowheads on flanks, contrasty upperparts* with broadly white-fringed dark feathers, and *rusty-brown on shoulders*. In winter plumage resembles Knot, but more distinctly streaked above and spotted on breast.

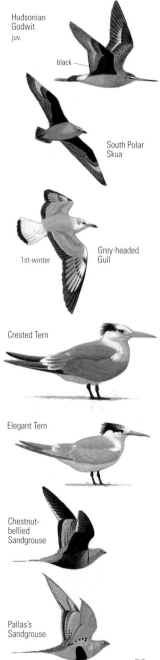

Hudsonian
Godwit
juv.

black

South Polar
Skua

Grey-headed
Gull

1st-winter

Crested Tern

Elegant Tern

Chestnut-
bellied
Sandgrouse

Pallas's
Sandgrouse

Hudsonian Godwit *Limosa haemastica* **V***
L 37–42 cm. N American species, recorded a few times in Britain and in Denmark. – Not unlike Bar-tailed Godwit in size and shape (but has even *more obviously upturned bill* and is somewhat more *long-legged*), but closer to Black-tailed in plumage, having *white wing-bar, white rump* and *all-black tail*. In flight, shows Grey Plover-like *black 'armpits'*; underwing-coverts very dark, too.

South Polar Skua *Stercorarius maccormicki* —
L 48–56 cm, WS 130–140 cm. Breeds on islands in S Atlantic. Vagrants observed in Faroes, Israel and Egypt; some additional unconfirmed reports from N Atlantic. – Very like Great Skua, but is marginally smaller and has slightly smaller head and narrower wings. Wide variation in colours but in all plumages *lacks reddish-brown tones*, is more cold grey-brown. Light and intermediate birds have *light brown and fairly uniformly coloured underbody and head, which contrast with very dark underwing-coverts* and with the dark and fairly uniform upperparts. The darkest birds are extremely similar to dark juvenile Great Skuas.

Grey-headed Gull *Larus cirrocephalus* —
L 39–43 cm. Breeds in tropical Africa and in S America. Recorded in e.g. Israel, Jordan, Tunisia, Morocco and Spain. – A bit *bigger than Black-headed Gull*, with *more black on wing-tip*, and in addition has *two white spots in the black* near tip. *Underwing dark*. Adult summer has *light grey hood*. *Wings broader* and somewhat *blunter* than on Black-headed. Bill rather long, and *feathering of forehead at bill-base drawn out and shallowly sloping* as on Slender-billed Gull.

(Greater) Crested Tern *Sterna bergii* —
L 50–54 cm (incl. tail-streamers 7–10). Breeds from S Africa to Pacific Ocean, incl. Red Sea and Persian Gulf. Vagrant up to Suez and at Eilat in Israel. – Very *big*, long-winged. *White forehead* even in breeding plumage (though narrow right at front). Black crown with *bristly, loose crest. Bill very long and fairly narrow* with slightly decurved culmen, usually *pale greenish-yellow* (a bit brighter yellow during courtship). In Middle East (ssp. *velox*), mantle, *rump and upperwing rather dark grey* (esp. seen in overcast weather) without light blue tinge of e.g. Lesser Crested Tern (p. 188). Commonest call a deep croaking 'karrack'.

Elegant Tern *Sterna elegans* **V***
L 39–43 cm. Breeds in west C America. Remarkably, one took up residence during 1974–85 in a Sandwich Tern colony in France, where it paired with a Sandwich and produced young; also seen in 1987, and two different individuals in 1984. Vagrants recorded also in Ireland, Belgium and Spain. – Very like Lesser Crested Tern (p. 188), but has *somewhat longer and more decurved bill* which is often *slightly brighter orange* with tip sometimes a bit yellower. *Shaggier crest* than Lesser Crested. In winter plumage, white forehead but with *black neatly around eye* and backwards. Also confusable with Royal Tern (p. 188), but differences include longer, narrower bill.

Chestnut-bellied Sandgrouse *Pterocles exustus* —
L 28–32 cm. Breeds in Africa. In 1800s bred at Suez, and occurred sparingly there as late as 1929; now extinct in N Egypt. Vagrant in Hungary. – *Brownish-black belly*. Told from Black-bellied Sandgrouse by *all-dark underwing* and *narrow tail projections*, from Spotted Sandgrouse by e.g. *dark primaries above*. In flight, utters Willow Grouse-like grating 'vitt-karr-arr'.

Pallas's Sandgrouse *Syrrhaptes paradoxus* **V***
L 27–32 cm (tail projections of ad. 4–11). Breeds on Asian steppes. Rare and irregular vagrant in W Europe (in Britain most recently 1990), at times in minor invasions which can lead to breeding (e.g. 1888–89). – *Black belly patch*, rather *pale wings above and below*. ♂ told from similar Spotted Sandgrouse by having *mantle to rump heavily barred black* while *upperwing-coverts are uniform* in colour. Diagnostic needle-like pointed outer primaries rarely seen in the field. ♀ has more black spots on crown, nape and wing-coverts than ♂.

DZ

African Collared Dove

White-throated Needletail

Chimney Swift

Pacific Swift

Belted Kingfisher

Northern Flicker

♂

♂

Yellow-bellied Sapsucker

African Collared Dove *Streptopelia roseogrisea*   —

L 28–30 cm. Breeds in sub-Saharan Africa and Arabian peninsula. Occasional or rare winter vagrant in S Israel. See also Barbary Dove (p. 390). – Very like Collared Dove, but *a bit smaller* and has slightly *shorter tail*. Plumage is a shade *paler* than Collared's, with *whiter belly*, but *flight-feathers* and *uppertail* on the other hand are *darker*, giving slightly greater contrast. The multisyllabic song is recognized by the first syllable being higher and drawn out, followed by hint of a pause and then a falling section with *rolling r-sound*, 'kaaw, kurroo-ooh'.

White-throated Needletail *Hirundapus caudacutus*   **V∗∗∗**

L 19–21 cm, WS 50–54 cm. Breeds in S Siberia and Central Asia. Vagrant in e.g. Britain, Ireland, Sweden, Norway and Finland. – *Big*, with *heavy, compact body*, neckless, stub-tailed (shape something between fat cigar and 'flying barrel'). *Flight impressively fast*, the bird seems to draw easily away from other swifts (though these are still fast flyers!). Identified otherwise by *white vent* (which extends a bit onto flanks) and *brownish-white back*.

Chimney Swift *Chaetura pelagica*   **V∗∗∗**

L 12–13 cm. Breeds in N America. Autumn vagrant in Britain. – *Small*, with *thickset body* and *broad wings*. Plumage rather *uniform grey-brown*, just *a bit paler on throat and upper breast*. Fine tail-spines seen only at close range. Flight is one moment fast on backswept wings, the next slower with fast, shallow wingbeats relieved by glides. Call a rapid twitter.

Pacific Swift *Apus pacificus*   **V∗∗∗**

L 18–19 cm. Breeds in Asia, from C Siberia eastwards. Vagrant in Britain and Norway. – Like a Common Swift with white rump patch. To eliminate possibility of a partially albinistic Swift, look for: slightly *deeper tail-fork*; longer wings; slightly *more projecting, heavier head*, which can give impression of *slimmer body*; often *somewhat larger white chin patch*; pale-scaled underbody; coarser and *harsher call clearly dropping at end*, 'vriiüh' (can recall Pallid Swift).

Belted Kingfisher *Ceryle alcyon*   **V∗∗∗**

(Illustrated also on p. 221.) L 31–34 cm. Breeds in N America. Vagrant in Britain, Ireland, Iceland and Netherlands. – Big and hefty. *Lead-grey above* with a *white neck band*, white below, ♂ with a *lead-grey breast-band*, ♀ with a similar grey breast-band and an additional narrower *reddish-brown band* just below this. Elongated crown- and nape-feathers can be erected, form *straggly crest*. Small white loral spot.

Northern Flicker *Colaptes auratus*   **[V∗∗∗]**

L 27–30 cm. N American species, recorded in Britain (as corpse), Ireland and Denmark (both presumed ship-assisted). – As *big* as Grey-headed Woodpecker, *densely spotted black* on body and wings but head and neck almost uniform. White rump patch (indistinct on some). *Head-side and throat reddish-buff*, crown and nape grey. *Large black horizontal patch on breast*. A *small red patch on nape*. ♂ has strong black moustachial stripe, lacking on ♀. Undertail light yellow.

Yellow-bellied Sapsucker *Sphyrapicus varius*   **V∗∗∗**

L 18–21 cm. N American species. Migratory. Somewhat recalls Three-toed Woodpecker, e.g. in habit of drinking sap. Vagrant in Britain, Ireland and Iceland. – *Black and white*, adult with *red crown*, and ♂ also with *red throat* (white on ♀). *Side of head broadly striped black and white*. Throat framed by black band, which *on breast* widens into *broad black patch* (lacking on 1st-winter). There is a *white oblong patch on wing*. Mantle/back finely mottled black and white. Underparts tinged yellowish (sometimes most strongly on breast-side).

DZ

Cliff Swallow

(American) Cliff Swallow *Hirundo pyrrhonota*   **V*****
L 13–14 cm. Breeds in N America. Vagrants recorded in autumn in Britain and Iceland. – Most closely related to House Martin and similar in shape (but with *square-ended tail* and *broader wings*). Distinctively coloured head, with *cheeks, throat and neck-sides reddish-brown, nape pale* so that blue-black crown forms isolated skull-cap, and has *creamy-white forehead. Rump orange.* At distance, confusion with Red-rumped Swallow conceivable, but *lacks tail-streamers* and *back has diffuse white streaking.* Greyish-black patch between throat and breast. Call a nasal, sparrow-like 'chiev'.

White-eared Bulbul

White-eared Bulbul *Pycnonotus leucotis*   —
L 18–20 cm. Closest breeders in Iraq and around Persian Gulf. Vagrant in Israel and Jordan. – Like White-spectacled Bulbul (p. 254), brown-grey above, with sooty-black head and *yellow undertail-coverts*, but immediately told by large, Great Tit-like *white patch on side of head.* Greyish-black tail-feathers have white tips.

(Grey) Hypocolius *Hypocolius ampelinus*   —
L 22–25 cm. Most closely related to Waxwing. Breeds in Iraq, Iran and Pakistan. Occasional in Turkey, Israel and Egypt. – Somewhat recalls a shrike with its *light grey colour* and *long tail*, but differs in that *wing, too, is mostly light grey and plain* (not black with white markings). Adult ♂ has a *black patch on side of head* which continues into a *narrow nape band* (♀ has uniformly light grey head) and *black primaries with broad white tips* (♀ greyish with small black tips).

Hypocolius ♂

Northern Mockingbird *Mimus polyglottos*   **V*****
L 25–28 cm. N American species. Vagrant in Britain and Netherlands. – Thrush-sized, *long-tailed* and rather short-winged. Bill strong, dark. Rather *light grey above*, with *black wings* and *two white wing-bars*, and narrow greyish-white edges to tertials and secondaries. In flight, shows a *large white patch on 'palm'. Tail black with white sides.* Uniform buffish- or greyish-white below.

Northern Mockingbird

(Grey) Catbird *Dumetella carolinensis*   **V*****
L 19–22 cm. Relative of Northern Mockingbird. Breeds in N America. Vagrant in Channel Islands, Ireland and Germany. – Like a small thrush with long tail. Adult is *uniform ash-grey*, with *black crown* and *dark reddish-brown vent.* Hops on ground or keeps to low vegetation.

Catbird

Black Bush Robin *Cercotrichas podobe*   —
L 20–23 cm. Breeds in Africa in savanna belt S of Sahara, and in Arabia. First recorded in Israel in 1981, and bred at Eilat in 1994. – *Entirely sooty-black*, with *long tail* which is often *held straight up* and quickly spread or flicked. *Tail-feathers broadly tipped white*, undertail-coverts narrowly tipped white. Long-legged. Perches mostly on ground or in low bushes. Sings from bushtop; song rather like that of Rufous Bush Robin, often accompanied by tail-raising.

Black Bush Robin

Pied Bushchat *Saxicola caprata*   —
L 13–14½ cm. Breeds in Central Asia and S Asia. Vagrant in Cyprus and Israel. – Somewhat bigger than Stonechat. Adult ♂ is *all black, with white rump*, white belly and small *white shoulder patch.* ♀ and immature ♂ are brownish-grey like ♀ Black Redstart, but differ from latter in *shorter all-dark tail* with only rump rusty-coloured; told from dark ♀ Stonechat of race *rubicola* by *all-dark wing* (just hint of pale patch on some) and *paler throat.*

ad. ♂   Pied Bushchat

Gray's Grasshopper Warbler *Locustella fasciolata*   —
L 16½–17½ cm. Breeds in Asia, from C Siberia eastward. Vagrant in France and Denmark, both at end Sep. – A large *Locustella* with rather big head and *heavy, long bill.* Uniformly *dark olive-tinged grey-brown above*, sometimes with some *rusty tone.* Underparts somewhat paler olivey greyish-white, with diffuse dusky area or faint spotting on breast. *Short, poorly indicated paler supercilium. Undertail-coverts uniform rusty-buff* (cf. River Warbler, p. 294). Song loud and bulbul-like, with jolting rhythm. Call a discordant stifled click.

Gray's Grasshopper Warbler

DZ

Basra Reed Warbler

Brown Shrike

ad.

Long-tailed Shrike

ad.

Daurian Jackdaw

ad.

Evening Grosbeak

ad. ♂

Tennessee Warbler

winter

Yellow Warbler

1st-winter ♂

Blackburnian Warbler

♂ winter

DZ

Basra Reed Warbler *Acrocephalus griseldis* —

L 15½–17 cm. Endemic breeder in E Iraq in extensive beds of papyrus and reed. Winters in E Africa. Recorded a few times in Israel on passage. – Rather like Great Reed Warbler but a bit smaller, has more *olive-toned brown* (not so rusty) *upperparts, whiter underparts* (esp. belly and undertail-coverts) and distinctly *narrower and* proportionately somewhat *longer and more pointed bill*. Narrow, clear-cut supercilium above lore. Long primary projection but *shortish tail*. Legs rather short, greyish. Call a gruff 'chaarr', deeper than Reed Warbler's.

Brown Shrike *Lanius cristatus* V***

L 17–19 cm. Breeds in Siberia and E Asia. Vagrant in Britain, Denmark. – Very like Isabelline Shrike (p. 326), but has *darker red-brown uppertail* (not so orange-brown), *narrower, faintly barred tail-feathers* and *more rounded tail-tip*; bill slightly heavier. *Underparts saturated yellowish-buff* (Isabelline more buff-white), and mantle/back brown with faint olive tinge. Normally *no white primary-base patch*. Short primary projection distinguishes it from Red-backed Shrike.

Long-tailed Shrike *Lanius schach* —

L 21½–24 cm. Breeds in Asia. Vagrant in Hungary, Israel and Turkey. – Rather big and *long-tailed*, tail strongly rounded. Black facial mask and forehead (smaller than on ♂ Lesser Grey Shrike), light grey on crown and mantle. *Rump, back and scapulars are rusty yellow-brown*, and vent, too, is rusty-yellow. Small white primary-base patch on adult. Deep bill.

Daurian Jackdaw *Corvus dauuricus* —

L 30–34 cm. Breeds in SE Siberia, Mongolia and NE China. Vagrant in Finland, Sweden, Denmark, Germany and Netherlands. – Same size and shape as Jackdaw, but differs in all plumages in having *dark eye* (ad. Jackdaw has whitish iris, juv. grey) and in adult plumage *pale grey-white nape, neck-ring and belly* (not unlike a well-marked, dwarf Hooded Crow). Silvery-white feather tips at rear of head-side. 1st-year plumage either similar (light morph; less common) or dark grey like Jackdaw (dark morph; seems to be the commoner), with only hint of paler, slate-grey belly; dark morph lacks Jackdaw's paler grey nape.

Evening Grosbeak *Hesperiphona vespertina* V***

L 18–20 cm. N American specis. Vagrant in Britain and Norway. All records in spring, several involving ♂♂. – Starling-sized. *Big, triangular, light greenish-yellow bill*. ♂ is *yellow and olive-brown* with black tail and *black wings with white tertials*; forehead and crown-sides yellow, crown-centre black. ♀ more reminiscent of Hawfinch, buffy greyish-white and grey-brown with white patches on wings and tail; *usually has yellow tinge on neck-side*. Yellow axillaries.

Tennessee Warbler *Vermivora peregrina* V***

L 10½–12 cm. Breeds in N America. Autumn vagrants recorded in Britain, Faroes and Iceland. (New World wood-warblers are actually thin-billed buntings which fill corresponding niche to that occupied by warblers in Europe.) – In autumn plumage can be taken for a *Phylloscopus* warbler owing to its *green upperparts, yellowish underparts* and *yellow supercilium*. Legs dark grey, pointed *bill rather long and light grey with dark culmen*. Call a sharp 'tsiit'.

Yellow Warbler *Dendroica petechia* V***

L 11½–13 cm. Breeds in N America. Autumn vagrant in Britain. – In autumn plumage, a *yellowish bird* with slightly darker *grey-green upperparts* and *hint of yellow wing-bar*. Adult ♂ has strong yellow colour on head and underparts and *reddish-brown streaks below*. ♀ and immatures are duller, with greener crown/nape and only faint or non-existent red-brown streaks below. Spread tail shows *yellow panels on inner webs*. Call a distinct 'tsipp'.

Blackburnian Warbler *Dendroica fusca* V***

L 11½–13 cm. Breeds in N America. Autumn vagrants recorded in Britain and Iceland. – Identified in autumn plumage by *double broad white wing-bars, streaked flanks* and *yellow tone to supercilium, neck-side, throat, breast and upper flanks*. Shows *indication of narrow yellow median stripe on forecrown*.

Ovenbird *Seiurus aurocapillus* **V***

L 13½–15 cm. N American species. A *ground-dwelling*, forest bird. Autumn vagrants recorded in Britain and Ireland. – *Uniform greenish-brown above*, pale below with *bold black spots* and narrow black malar stripes. *Pale eye-ring on otherwise uniform brown side of head. Reddish-brown median crown-stripe bordered by narrow black stripes*. Trips along on ground like a pipit.

Northern Waterthrush *Seiurus noveboracensis* **V***

L 13–14½ cm. N American species. Habits as those of congeneric Ovenbird, but associated more with water. Vagrants recorded in Britain, Ireland, Channel Islands and France. – Not unlike a pipit, but has *longer and more prominent supercilium, heavier head and bill*, shorter tail, and habit of often *bobbing rear end*. Bill dark but legs pale pink.

(Common) Yellowthroat *Geothlypis trichas* **V***

L 12–13 cm. N American species, recorded a few times in Britain. – Told by *unmarked* plumage, olive-green above and off-white below with *yellow throat* and *yellowish undertail-coverts*; flanks brownish-white. Adult ♂ has a *black mask* extending over forehead, bordered at rear by light grey. 1st-winter ♂ has dusky ear-coverts and a little dark colour on forehead. ♀ has olive-brown head.

Scarlet Tanager *Piranga olivacea* **V***

L 15½–17 cm. N American species; belongs to family *Thraupidae*, found only in New World. Vagrants recorded in Britain, Ireland and Iceland, nearly all in Oct. – *Bill heavy, rather long* and pointed. In autumn plumage, *head and body greyish yellow-green*, palest below. Adult ♂ has brightest yellow colour below, yellow tone to crown and greener mantle/back. *Wings darker than back*, grey on ♀, *black* on adult ♂ and grey with some blacker coverts and tertials on 1st-winter. (Not illustrated.)

Fox Sparrow *Passerella iliaca* **V***

L 16½–17½ cm. N American species, related to buntings of Europe. Vagrant in Ireland, Iceland, Germany and Italy. – *Big, long-tailed*. Distinguished by *reddish-brown uppertail, some reddish-brown on wing, ear-coverts* and often on breast-side. *Crown-side and neck-side dark ash-grey*. Underparts white with bold triangular dark spots (red-brown on breast). No white on tail.

Song Sparrow *Melospiza melodia* **V***

L 13–15 cm. N American species. A few spring and summer records in Britain and Norway. – Medium-sized, *long-tailed*. Short, rounded wings. Bill size variable, often rather narrow and pointed. *Brown lateral crown-stripes* and a grey, *paler median stripe*, also *grey head-side* with *brown stripes backwards from eye, along lower edge of ear-coverts and on throat-side*. Distinct dark streaks below, *on upper breast* usually coalescing to form *a small dark patch*.

White-crowned Sparrow *Zonotrichia leucophrys* **V***

L 15–16 cm. N American species. Vagrant in Britain, Iceland, Netherlands and France. – Close relative of White-throated Sparrow (p. 364), but differs as follows: lacks clearly defined white throat; has *very broad white median crown-stripe* with *bold black border*; white supercilium *never yellow in front of eye*; cheeks and neck-sides plain ash-grey, form *broad pale neck-collar*; upperparts grey, not brown. 1st-winter has brown and buffish-white head markings.

Black-faced Bunting *Emberiza spodocephala* **V***

L 14–15½ cm. Breeds in Siberia in waterlogged forest or on overgrown bogs. Vagrant in Britain, Denmark, Finland, Netherlands and Germany. – A streaked bunting with slightly *soiled yellowish-white, grey* and *brown* plumage. Adult ♂ has *olive-grey head/breast* and *swarthy 'face'*. Autumn birds are more nondescript; note *uniform* (or only diffusely spotted) *brownish-grey rump, olive-grey tone to cheek and neck-side, dirty and rather indistinct paler supercilium, yellow tinge to underparts*, straight culmen and partially pink lower mandible. Call a sharp 'zit', similar to that of Song Thrush.

Ovenbird

Northern Waterthrush

Yellow-throat

1st-winter ♂

Fox Sparrow

Song Sparrow

White-crowned Sparrow

ad. ♂

Black-faced Bunting

DZ

Accidentals

The species listed below have been recorded only once or twice (in a few cases more) within the region treated in this book (roughly corresponding to the Western Palearctic; see definition on p. 6). Apart from English and scientific names, the origin of each species is given (main or closest breeding range) and where and when they have been recorded. Records which in all likelihood refer only to escapes from captivity, or the authenticity of which may be questionable, have been excluded from the list. Published records have been covered until the end of June 1998.

SPECIES		ORIGIN	RECORDED
Ostrich	*Struthio camelus*	Africa	Israel (occasional up to 1920s), Egypt (old records in Sinai), Jordan (1930s?)
Yellow-nosed Albatross	*Diomedea chlororhynchos*	South Atlantic	Norway (Apr 1994)
Shy Albatross	*Diomedea cauta*	South Atlantic, Indian Ocean	Israel (Feb–Mar 1981)
Wandering Albatross	*Diomedea exulans*	South Atlantic, Indian Ocean	France (1830), Belgium (Sep 1833), Italy (Oct 1957), Portugal (Oct 1963)
Soft-plumaged Petrel	*Pterodroma mollis*	South Atlantic	Israel (Mar 1997)
Atlantic Petrel	*Pterodroma incerta*	South Atlantic	Israel (May 1982; Apr 1989)
Black-capped Petrel	*Pterodroma hasitata*	West Indies	Great Britain (spring 1850; Dec 1984)
Streaked Shearwater	*Calonectris leucomelas*	Pacific & Indian Oceans	Israel (Jun–Sep 1992; May–Jul 1993)
Flesh-footed Shearwater	*Puffinus carneipes*	Indian & Pacific Oceans	Israel (Aug 1980)
Wedge-tailed Shearwater	*Puffinus pacificus*	Indian & Pacific Oceans	Egypt (Mar 1989)
Audubon's Shearwater	*Puffinus lherminieri*	Indian & Pacific Oceans, West Indies	Israel (Jan–Feb 1985; Dec 1989), Egypt (Sep 1991)
Masked Booby	*Sula dactylatra*	West Indies, South Atlantic, Indian Ocean	Spain (Oct and Dec 1985; Jan 1986; presumably same bird)
Cape Gannet	*Morus capensis*	South Atlantic	Spain (Jan 1985)
Double-crested Cormorant	*Phalacrocorax auritus*	North America	Great Britain (Jan–Apr 1989), Ireland (Nov 1995–Jan 1996)
African Darter	*Anhinga rufa*	Africa	Turkey (bred 1933–*c.* 1950), Israel (occasional 1950s), Morocco (Aug 1985)
Lesser Frigatebird	*Fregata ariel*	Tropical Oceans	Israel (Dec 1997)
Least Bittern	*Ixobrychus exilis*	America	Iceland (Sep 1970), Morocco (Mar 1988)
Schrenck's Bittern	*Ixobrychus eurhythmus*	East Asia	Italy (Nov 1912)
Dwarf Bittern	*Ixobrychus sturmii*	Africa	Canary Islands (1889 or 1890)
Black Heron	*Egretta ardesiaca*	Africa	Israel (Oct 1982)
Intermediate Egret	*Egretta intermedia*	Asia	Jordan (Apr 1963), Egypt (Dec 1981)
Black-headed Heron	*Ardea melanocephala*	Africa	France (*c.* 1845; Nov 1971), Israel (Oct–Dec 1987)
Marabou Stork	*Leptoptilos crumeniferus*	Africa	Israel (May 1951; Apr–May 1957) (Records in Spain and Germany probably not genuine.)
Sacred Ibis	*Threskiornis aethiopicus*	Africa, Iraq	Azerbaijan (1944), Egypt (1889; 1891), Canary Islands (Mar 1991). – (See also p. 389.)
White-faced Whistling Duck	*Dendrocygna viduata*	Africa, South America	Canary Islands (*c.* 1968)
Lesser Whistling Duck	*Dendrocygna javanica*	South Asia	Israel (Nov 1966–Mar 1967)
Spur-winged Goose	*Plectropterus gambensis*	Africa	Morocco (Jun 1984)
Cotton Pygmy-goose	*Nettapus coromandelianus*	South Asia, Australia	Jordan (Apr 1997)
Cape Teal	*Anas capensis*	Africa	Israel (Jun–Oct 1978; May 1982; Jul 1984)
Red-billed Teal	*Anas erythrorhyncha*	Africa	Israel (Jun–Jul 1958)

SPECIES		ORIGIN	RECORDED
Cape Shoveler	*Anas smithii*	Africa	Morocco (Apr 1978)
Southern Pochard	*Netta erythrophthalma*	Africa, South America	Israel (Apr–May 1998)
Canvasback	*Aythya valisineria*	North America	Iceland (Apr 1977), Great Britain (Nov 1997–Mar 1998)
Redhead	*Aythya americana*	North America	Great Britain (Mar 1996)
Crested Honey Buzzard	*Pernis ptilorhyncus*	Siberia, Central Asia	Israel (May 1994), Turkey (Sep 1996)
American Swallow-tailed Kite	*Elanoides forficatus*	America	Canary Islands (Mar 1998)
Bald Eagle	*Haliaeetus leucocephalus*	North America	Ireland (Jan 1973; Nov 1987), Great Britain (Oct 1978)
Shikra	*Accipiter badius*	Asia, Africa	Azerbaijan (Jun 1933; bred), Israel (Apr 1987)
Swainson's Buzzard (Hawk)	*Buteo swainsoni*	North America	Norway (May 1986)
Amur Falcon	*Falco amurensis*	East Asia	Italy (May 1995; May 1997; May 1998)
Striped Crake	*Porzana marginalis*	Africa	Algeria (Jan 1867), Libya (Feb 1970), Morocco (Nov 1989)
Hooded Crane	*Grus monacha*	Asia	Russia (date?)
Three-banded Plover	*Charadrius tricollaris*	Africa	Egypt (Mar 1993)
Black-headed Lapwing	*Vanellus tectus*	Africa	Israel (1869; 1995), Jordan (1995)
Swinhoe's Snipe	*Gallinago megala*	Siberia	Israel (Feb–Mar 1998)
Eskimo Curlew	*Numenius borealis*	North America	Great Britain (5 autumn records 19th cent.), Ireland (Oct 1870)
Willet	*Catoptrophorus semipalmatus*	North America	Finland (Sep 1983), Norway (Oct 1992–Jan 1993).
Grey-tailed Tattler	*Heteroscelus brevipes*	Siberia	Great Britain (Oct–Nov 1981; Nov–Dec 1994)
Brown-headed Gull	*Larus brunnicephalus*	Central Asia	Israel (May 1985)
Glaucous-winged Gull	*Larus glaucescens*	West North America, North Pacific Ocean	Canary Islands ? (Feb 1992), Morocco (Jan 1996)
Aleutian Tern	*Sterna aleutica*	Bering Sea	Great Britain (May 1979), Norway (Sep 1997)
American Little Tern	*Sterna antillarum*	America	Great Britain (summers 1983–92; same bird)
Brown Noddy	*Anous stolidus*	West Indies, South Red Sea, Persian Gulf	Germany (Oct 1912)
African Skimmer	*Rynchops flavirostris*	Africa	Israel (*c.* 1934), Morocco (Jan 1987)
Ancient Murrelet	*Synthliboramphus antiquus*	Pacific Ocean	Great Britain (springs 1990, 1991 and 1992; prob. same bird)
Crested Auklet	*Aethia cristatella*	Bering Sea	Iceland (Aug 1912)
Parakeet Auklet	*Cyclorrhynchus psittacula*	Bering Sea	Sweden (Dec 1860)
Tufted Puffin	*Lunda cirrhata*	Pacific Ocean	Sweden (Jun 1994)
Yellow-eyed Dove	*Columba eversmanni*	Asia	Russia (date?)
(American) Mourning Dove	*Zenaida macroura*	North & Central America	Great Britain (Oct–Nov 1989)
Didric Cuckoo	*Chrysococcyx caprius*	Africa	Cyprus (Jun 1982), Israel (Mar 1994)
Indian Roller	*Coracias benghalensis*	Iraq, South Asia	Syria (date?)
Eastern Phoebe	*Sayornis phoebe*	North America	Great Britain (Apr 1987)
Acadian Flycatcher	*Empidonax virescens*	North America	Iceland (Nov 1967)
Chestnut-headed Sparrow-lark	*Eremopterix signata*	East Africa	Israel (May 1983)
Hume's Short-toed Lark	*Calandrella acutirostris*	East Central Asia, Himalayas	Israel (Feb 1986)

SPECIES	ORIGIN	RECORDED
Tree Swallow	*Tachycineta bicolor*	North America	Great Britain (Jun 1990)
Ethiopian Swallow	*Hirundo aethiopica*	Africa	Israel (Mar 1991)
Wire-tailed Swallow	*Hirundo smithii*	Africa, South Asia	Egypt (Mar 1995)
Cedar Waxwing	*Bombycilla cedrorum*	North America	Great Britain (Jun 1985; Feb 1996), Iceland (Apr–Jul 1989)
Brown Thrasher	*Toxostoma rufum*	North America	Great Britain (Nov 1966–Feb 1967)
Siberian Blue Robin	*Luscinia cyane*	Siberia	Channel Islands (Oct 1975)
Eversmann's Redstart	*Phoenicurus erythronotus*	Central Asia, NW Mongolia	Russia (Oct 1881; Oct 1888), Turkey (according to Cramp *et al.*)
Varied Thrush	*Zoothera naevia*	North America	Great Britain (Nov 1982)
Wood Thrush	*Hylocichla mustelina*	North America	Iceland (Oct 1967), Great Britain (Oct 1987)
Tickell's Thrush	*Turdus unicolor*	West Himalayas	Germany (Oct 1932)
Eastern Crowned Leaf Warbler	*Phylloscopus coronatus*	East Asia	Germany (Oct 1843)
Plain Leaf Warbler	*Phylloscopus neglectus*	Central Asia	Jordan (Apr 1963), Sweden (Oct 1991)
Ruby-crowned Kinglet	*Regulus calendula*	North America	Iceland (Nov 1987)
Red-breasted Nuthatch	*Sitta canadensis*	North America	Iceland (Jan 1970), Great Britain (Oct 1989–May 1990)
Yellow-throated Vireo	*Vireo flavifrons*	North America	Great Britain (Sep 1990)
Philadelphia Vireo	*Vireo philadelphicus*	North America	Ireland (Oct 1985), Great Britain (Oct 1987)
Long-tailed Rosefinch	*Uragus sibiricus*	Siberia	W Kazakhstan, Russia (Records in W Europe are probably all escapes.)
Golden-winged Warbler	*Vermivora chrysoptera*	North America	Great Britain (Jan–Apr 1989)
Chestnut-sided Warbler	*Dendroica pensylvanica*	North America	Great Britain (Sep 1985; Oct 1995)
Cerulean Warbler	*Dendroica cerulea*	North America	Iceland (Oct 1997)
Black-throated Blue Warbler	*Dendroica caerulescens*	North America	Iceland (Sep 1988)
Black-throated Green Warbler	*Dendroica virens*	North America	Germany (Nov 1858) (A record in Iceland probably an escape)
Cape May Warbler	*Dendroica tigrina*	North America	Great Britain (Jun 1977)
Magnolia Warbler	*Dendroica magnolia*	North America	Great Britain (Sep 1981), Iceland (Sep–Dec 1995; Oct 1995)
Palm Warbler	*Dendroica palmarum*	North America	Iceland (Oct 1997)
Bay-breasted Warbler	*Dendroica castanea*	North America	Great Britain (Oct 1995)
Hooded Warbler	*Wilsonia citrina*	North America	Great Britain (Sep 1970; Sep 1992)
Wilson's Warbler	*Wilsonia pusilla*	North America	Great Britain (Oct 1985)
Canada Warbler	*Wilsonia canadensis*	North America	Iceland (Sep 1973)
Summer Tanager	*Piranga rubra*	North America	Great Britain (Sep 1957)
Rufous-sided Towhee	*Pipilo erythrophthalmus*	North America	Great Britain (Jun 1966)
Lark Sparrow	*Chondestes grammacus*	North America	Great Britain (Jun–Jul 1981; May 1991)
Savannah Sparrow	*Passerculus sandwichensis*	North America	Great Britain (Apr 1982; Sep–Oct 1987)
Cinnamon-breasted Bunting	*Emberiza tahapisi*	Africa	Egypt (Apr 1984)
Brown-headed Cowbird	*Molothrus ater*	North America	Norway (Jun 1987), Great Britain (Apr 1988)
Yellow-headed Blackbird	*Xanthocephalus xanthocephalus*	North America	Iceland (Jul 1983) (Records in Sweden, Norway and Great Britain probably not genuine.)

Introduced breeding species and species recorded only as escapes

A number of species which are not part of the region's natural fauna but which have been introduced by man or become established with human assistance and now breed locally in the wild without continued dependency on man are described briefly below.

Also incorporated here are some non-breeding species which have been seen in the region on several occasions, but which in all cases most likely originate from captivity and thus are not genuine wild birds occurring naturally.

Some introduced species are so well known that they have been included in the main section of the book, or have been placed there to facilitate comparison with similar species:

Canada Goose (p. 44), Egyptian and Bar-headed Goose, Mandarin and Wood Duck (46), Ruddy Duck (68), Pheasant, Golden Pheasant and Lady Amherst's Pheasant (112), Ring-necked Parakeet (222) and Indigo Bunting (364).

It should be pointed out that a large number of wildfowl from various parts of the world are kept in bird collections. These are sometimes free-flying and can therefore appear at traditional birdwatching sites; not all such species can be included here. There is also a heavy trade in cagebirds, and species from e.g. Asia, Australia and Africa are imported into Europe on a large scale; some of these escape and appear in the wild.

Pink-backed Pelican *Pelecanus rufescens* —

L 125–135 cm, WS 225–260 cm. Breeds in Africa. Recorded occasionally in Israel, Egypt, Sweden, Denmark, Poland, Netherlands, France, Austria, Germany, Switzerland, Spain and Morocco. The Israeli and Egyptian records may possibly refer to genuine vagrants, while the rest certainly involve free-flying escapes. – Looks like a subadult White Pelican, is not clean white but *dirty greyish-pink*. Is somewhat *smaller* and has slightly *shorter bill*; in addition, *lacks dark on culmen and gape*. In spring, a *dark patch by eye*.

Pink-backed Pelican

African Spoonbill *Platalea alba* —

L 85–95 cm. Breeds in Africa. Recorded several times in France, a couple of times in Spain and once each in Denmark and Austria. All records probably involve escapes from bird collections. – Same size as Eurasian Spoonbill. *White plumage* and *pinkish-red legs* and *pinkish-red bill* (with blue-grey at centre).

African Spoonbill

Sacred Ibis *Threskiornis aethiopicus* —

L 60–85 cm, WS 110–125 cm. Breeds in Africa. Introduced in France in 1976, where a free-flying population still breeds. Occasionally seen elsewhere, e.g. Denmark. – White, with black downcurved bill, head, neck, and with *plume-like tertials*.

Lesser Flamingo *Phoenicopterus minor* —

L 80–90 cm, WS 90–100 cm. Breeds in C and E Africa. Several records in Morocco and a few in Spain. In 1994 a pair attempted to breed in Camargue, France. A number of records also in N Europe, but these most likely refer to escapes from collections. – *Small*. Plumage *pink* with red stripes on back and shoulders. *Legs entirely red, bill deep red with small black tip*.

Sacred Ibis

Black Swan *Cygnus atratus* [r**B**5]

L 110–140 cm. Australian species. Introduced self-sustaining populations exist in Britain, Iceland, Poland and Netherlands. – *All black* with *red bill*.

Ross's Goose *Anser rossii* [**V**∗∗∗]

L 53–66 cm. Breeds in Canada. Seen in winter in Netherlands in several years (origins much debated). Records in Britain, Germany and Sweden regarded as escapes. – Like white morph of Snow Goose, but is *smaller* and has *shorter neck and bill. Bill-base greenish-blue*. Grey morph exists, but very rare.

Lesser Flamingo

Falcated Duck *Anas falcata* [**V**∗∗∗]

L 46–54 cm. Breeds in E Asia. Has been encountered in a great many European countries, e.g. Britain, France, Spain, Netherlands, Belgium, Germany, Denmark, Sweden and Finland. Records as a rule thought to involve escapes; species is common in bird collections. – ♂ unmistakable, with *all-green head* with *gently sloping forehead* and *full nape*. ♀ can recall a *small, broad-winged* Pintail, has *narrow, dark bill* and vermiculated head-side. In flight, shows *dark speculum*.

Falcated Duck ♂

DZ

Cinnamon Teal *Anas cyanoptera* [**V**∗∗∗]

L 38–48 cm. Breeds in western N America and S America. Very rarely seen free-flying in Europe, and then most likely involving escapes only. – Both sexes have *green speculum* and *bright blue upperwing-covert patch*. ♂ is uniformly red-brown with dark crown and back. ♀ like Blue-winged Teal (see plate p. 53), but is more reddish and has *less contrasting head pattern*.

Bufflehead *Bucephala albeola* **V**∗∗∗[?]

L 32–39 cm. Breeds in N America. Annual records in Iceland 1988–93 and several in Britain (where some could be genuine vagrants). Records in Portugal, Spain, Finland, Denmark, Netherlands and France, but these generally considered not spontaneous. – Barely the size of Tufted Duck, ♂ having black back and *black head* with a *large white patch on head-side* (behind and above eye). ♀ has a small white patch on cheek. *Eye dark*, bill light grey.

Bufflehead ♂

Hooded Merganser *Lophodytes cucullatus* **V**∗∗∗[?]

L 42–50 cm. Breeds in N America. Records in Iceland and Britain could involve some genuine vagrants, but observations in Sweden, Denmark, Finland, Norway, Germany, Netherlands and France usually considered escapes from captivity. – ♂ has black head with a *white comb-shaped nape-crest with black border*, which can be fanned. *Flanks reddish-brown*. ♀ has a small brown crest and *yellow bill*.

♂

Hooded Merganser

California Quail *Callipepla californica* —

L 24–27 cm. Breeds in N America. Introduced in Europe, and feral stocks exist locally in e.g. Denmark, Germany, Italy and Corsica. – *Uniform blue-grey above and on breast*, coarsely spotted white on belly. Both sexes have a *black plume* on forecrown (bigger on ♂). ♂ also has *white-bordered black throat* and *white supercilium*. ♀ has finely spotted head. Display-call 'ka-**kah**-ko'.

Northern Bobwhite *Colinus virginianus* —

L 24–26 cm. Breeds in N America. Introduced in Europe, breeds in e.g. C France. – Mainly *reddish-brown* with white and black spots and streaks. ♂ has *black head* with *white supercilium and throat*, while ♀ has head patterned dark brown and light rusty-brown. Display-call a clear whistling 'tüh tve**iit**'.

California
Quail

Daurian Partridge *Perdix dauurica* —

L 26–30 cm. Breeds in S Siberia and Central Asia. Local feral populations exist in Italy, Russia and Ukraine. – Like Grey Partridge, but slightly smaller; has *yellow-brown tinge on breast* and *black* (not reddish-brown) *belly patch*.

Reeves's Pheasant *Syrmaticus reevesii* —

L ♂ 140–190 cm, ♀ 60–85 cm. Chinese species introduced in Europe and now breeding in wild in e.g. France and Czech Republic. Forest-dweller. – Large. Mottled brown like Pheasant, but told by ♂'s *extremely long tail* (100–150 cm!), *white head with black band* from bill back to nape, and *white spot beneath eye*.

Barbary Dove

Wild Turkey *Meleagris gallopavo* —

L 90–125 cm. Introduced from N America as long ago as 1500s and reared in captivity ever since. A feral population breeds in wild in Germany. – *Greyish-black* with metallic gloss. *Head bare, red and light blue* with *peculiar flaps of skin*, some drooping over bill. Tail can be raised Capercaillie-like. Long-legged.

Barbary Dove *Streptopelia roseogrisea* var. 'risoria' —

L 27–29 cm. A long-domesticated form of African Collared Dove (p. 382). A few pairs breed in Tenerife in Canary Islands, originating from escaped cagebirds. – Very like Collared Dove but *smaller*, has slightly *shorter tail*, *paler* buffy grey-white plumage, and is almost white on belly (Collared Dove light grey). Black neck-side marking is often broader, more rounded, not a narrow cross-bar. Is also a touch smaller and paler than the wild ancestral form.

Monk
Parakeet

Monk Parakeet *Myiopsitta monachus* —

L 28–31 cm. S American species. Breeds locally in small colonies in Canary Islands, Italy and Slovakia; the birds originate from escaped cagebirds.

DZ

– Predominantly bright green, with lighter green belly and bluer wings. Long, pointed, green tail. Forehead, throat and *breast light grey.* (Cf. also Rose-ringed Parakeet, p. 222.)

Common Myna *Acridotheres tristis* —

L 22–25 cm. Indian starling which is spreading N and W. Breeds in e.g. Russia, Arabia and Tenerife (since 1993), in all cases originating from escaped cagebirds. – About size of Starling, brown with sooty-black head, *yellow bill* and *bare yellow skin behind eye*, also *yellow legs. Large white patches on 'hand'* striking in flight. Fearless, lives near human habitation. Very loud and noisy.

Streaked Weaver *Ploceus manyar* —

L 12–13 cm. African species. Escaped cagebirds have established colonies in reedbeds in the Nile delta, Egypt. – *Big head* and *sturdy bill.* Tail short and square-cut, legs rather short. ♂ has *yellow crown, dark head-side* and heavily streaked buffy brownish-white underparts, and during breeding *black bill.* ♀ has *yellow supercilium, yellow neck-side patch* and dark cheeks and crown. Bill ivory-yellow.

Red-billed Firefinch *Lagonosticta senegala* —

L 9½–11 cm. African species. Introduced at El Golea, Algeria. – *Small.* Tiny pale spots on breast-side. ♂ is *red* (incl. bill), with browner wings and black tail. ♀ is grey-brown, with *red lores, bill and rump.*

Common Waxbill *Estrilda astrild* —

L 11–12 cm. African species, introduced in Iberian peninsula, where it now breeds locally, mainly in Portugal. Sedentary. Breeds in reeds, bulrushes, rushes, spiraea etc., season protracted (Feb–Nov). – *Small,* grey-brown, finely vermiculated, with *red eye-mask,* a *red patch on belly-centre* and *black* (or dark brown) *vent.* Bill *red* on adult, brownish-black on juvenile. Song a three-syllable, simple verse, two harsh notes followed by a rising, somewhat rolling note, 'chre-chre-srri'.

Red Avadavat *Amandava amandava* —

L 9½–10½ cm. Indian species. Introduced in e.g. Spain, Po delta and Nile delta. Breeds in autumn (spring in Nile delta) in lush waterside vegetation, but also in cultivated crops. – *Very small.* In all plumages, grey-brown upperparts with fine *white spots on wing-coverts and tertials, red uppertail-coverts* and dark tail. Adult ♂ May–Dec has greater part of *head and underparts saturated red, underparts sprinkled with white spots.* ♀ and ♂ winter–spring are off-white below, with buffish-grey on breast and *yellow tone on belly.* Dark lores. ♂ has more red on uppertail-coverts with more distinct white spots, and has *tinge of red on belly.* Flight-call short, muffled 'chick-chick'; when foraging, sharp 'zsi' notes. Song a series of falling, clear, soft notes, often terminating in brief trill.

Indian Silverbill *Lonchura malabarica* —

L 11–12 cm. Indian species. Since 1988 has also bred in Israel, and from 1990 in Jordan; likely origin is escaped cagebirds. Social habits, even when breeding. Fearless. – *Small. Stout silvery-grey bill. Uniform light brown upperparts,* whitish underparts with brown-tinged flanks, black primaries and *long, tapering black tail. Uppertail-coverts white.* Sexes alike. Juvenile has shorter, blunter tail, and brownish 'face' and brownish rump.

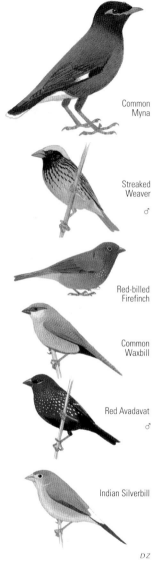

Common Myna

Streaked Weaver

♂

Red-billed Firefinch

Common Waxbill

Red Avadavat

♂

Indian Silverbill

DZ

References

The references listed below have been consulted during the work with this book, many of them repeatedly. Without them our work had been much more difficult and the end result less good. They can all be recommended.

For the preparation of the distribution maps all know national checklists and atlas surveys referring to the treate range have been used. Owing to lack of space they have bee omitted from the list below.

Ali, S. & Ripley, S. D. (1987) *Compact Handbook of the Birds of India and Pakistan.* 2nd ed. Oxford Univ. Press, Oxford.

Alström, P., Colston, P. & Lewington, I. (1991) *A Field Guide to the Rare Breeding Birds of Britain and Europe.* Domino, Jersey.

Alula. Ornithological magazine (4 issues/yr). Helsinki.

Andersson, B., Svensson, L. & Zetterström, D. (1990) *Fågelsång i Sverige.* Mono Music, Stockholm. (CD and booklet.)

Beaman, M. (1994) *Palearctic Birds.* Harrier, Stonyhurst.

Bergmann, H.-H. & Helb, H.-W. (1982) *Stimmen der Vögel Europas.* BLV, Munich.

Birding World. Ornithological magazine (12 issues/yr).

Breife, B., Holmström, N. & Blomqvist, L. (1993) *Sjöfågelboken.* ('Seabirds.') SOF, Lund. (In Swedish).

British Birds. Ornithological magazine (12 issues/yr).

Brown, L. H., Urban, E. K., Newman, K., Fry, C. H. & Keith, G. S. (ed.) (1982–97) *The Birds of Africa.* Vol. 1–5. Academic Press.

Byers, C., Olsson, U. & Curson, J. (1995) *Buntings and Sparrows.* Pica.

Campbell, B. & Lack, E. (ed.) (1985) *A Dictionary of Birds.* Poyser.

Chappuis, C. (1987) *Migrateurs et hivernants.* 2 sound cassettes. Grande Couronne, France.

Clement, P., Harris, A. & Davis, J. (1993) *Finches & Sparrows.* Helm.

Cramp, S., Simmons, K. E. L. & Perrins, C. M. (ed.) (1977–94) *The Birds of the Western Palearctic.* Vol. 1–9. Oxford Univ. Press.

Curry-Lindahl, K. (ed.) et al. (1959–62). *Våra fåglar i Norden.* Vol. 1–4. 2nd ed. Natur och Kultur, Stockholm. (In Swedish.)

Curson, J., Quinn, D. & Beadle, D. (1994) *New World Warblers.* Helm.

Delin, H. & Svensson, L. (1988) *Photographic Guide to the Birds of Britain & Europe.* Hamlyn.

Dutch Birding. Ornithological magazine (6 issues/yr).

Farrand Jr, J. (ed.) et al. (1983) *The Audubon Society Master Guide to Birding.* Vol. 1–3. Knopf, New York.

Ferguson-Lees, J. et al. (1983) *The Shell Guide to the Birds of Britain and Ireland.* Michael Joseph, London.

Forsman, D. (1984) *Rovfågelsguiden.* Lintutieto, Helsingfors.

Glutz, U. N. (publ.), Bauer, K., Bezzel, E. et al. (1966–97) *Handbuch der Vögel Mitteleuropas.* Vol. 1–14. Aula-Verlag, Wiesbaden.

Gooders, J. (ed.) (1969–71) *Birds of the World.* Vol. 1–5. IPC Magazines Ltd, London.

Grant, P. J. (1986) *Gulls: a guide to identification.* 2nd ed. Poyser.

Gulledge, J. (prod.) et al. (1983) *A field guide to bird songs of Eastern and Central North America.* 2nd ed. 2 sound cassettes. Cornell.

Hagemeijer, W. J. M. & Blair, M. J. (ed.) (1997) *The EBCC Atlas of European Breeding Birds.* Poyser.

Hancock, J. & Kushlan, J. (1984) *The Herons Handbook.* Harper & Row, New York.

Harrap, S. & Quinn, D. (1996) *Tits, Nuthatches & Treecreepers.* Helm.

Harrison, P. (1989) *Seabirds of the World.* Helm.

Hayman, P., Marchant, J. & Prater, T. (1986) *Shorebirds.* Croom Helm.

Hollom, P. A. D., Porter, R. F., Christensen, S. & Willis, I. (1988) *Birds of the Middle East and North Africa.* Poyser.

del Hoyo, J., Elliott, A. & Sargatal, J. (ed.) (1992–97) *Handbook of t. Birds of the World.* Vol. 1–4. Lynx, Barcelona.

Jonsson, L. (1993) *Birds of Europe with North Africa and the Mid East.* Helm.

Kaufman, K. (1990) *Advanced Birding.* Houghton Mifflin, Boston.

Lefranc, N. & Worfolk, T. (1997) *Shrikes.* Pica.

Limicola. Ornithological magazine (6 issues/yr). Einbeck-Drübe

Madge, S. & Burn, H. (1988) *Wildfowl.* Helm.

Madge, S. & Burn, H. (1991) *Crows and Jays.* Helm.

Malling Olsen, K. (1995) *Terns of Europe and North America.* Hel

McAdams, D. G. (1994) *Complete Photographic Index to Prem Birding Periodicals and Books.* 2nd ed. Flensburg.

Mild, K. (1987) *Soviet Bird Songs.* 2 sound cassettes. Stockholm.

Mild, K. (1990) *Bird Songs of Israel and the Middle East.* 2 sou cassettes. Stockholm.

Palmer, R. S. (ed.) (1962–88) *Handbook of North American Bird* Vol. 1–5. Yale Univ. Press, New Haven.

Palmér, S. & Boswall, J. (1981) *A Field Guide to the Bird Songs Britain and Europe.* 16 sound cassettes. Swedish Radio.

Pyle, P., Howell. S. N. G., Yunick, R. P. & DeSante, D. F. (198 *Identification Guide to North American Passerines.* Slate Cre Press, Bolinas, California.

Roché, J. C. (1990) *All the bird songs of Britain and Europe.* 4 C Sittelle, Mens, France.

Rogasjeva, H. (1992) *The Birds of Central Siberia.* Husum.

Rosenberg, E. (1953) *Fåglar i Sverige.* Svensk Natur, Stockholm. (Swedish.)

Schubert, M. (1981) *Stimmen der Vögel Zentralasiens.* 2 LP record Eterna.

Schubert, M. (1984) *Stimmen der Vögel. VII. Vogelstimmen Sü osteuropas* (2). 1 LP-record. Eterna.

Shirihai, H., Christie, D. & Harris, A. (1996) *Birder's Guide European and Middle Eastern birds.* MacMillan.

Stresemann, E., Portenko, L. A., Dahthe, H., Neufeldt, I. A. et a (1960–88) *Atlas der Verbreitung palaearktischer Vögel.* Vol. 1–1 Akademie-Verlag, Berlin.

Svensson, L. (1984) *Soviet Birds.* 1 sound cassette. Stockholm.

Svensson, L. (1992) *Identification Guide to European Passerines.* 4 ed. Stockholm.

Ticehurst, C. B. (1938) *A Systematic Review of the Genus Phyllosc pus.* British Museum, London.

Vaurie, C. (1959, 1965) *The Birds of the Palearctic Fauna.* Vol. 1– Witherby.

Veprintsev, B. N. (1982–86) 'Birds of the Soviet Union: A Sou Guide.' 7 LP-records. Melodia, Moscow.

Vinicombe, K., Harris, A. & Tucker, L. (1989) *Bird Identificatio* MacMillan.

Voous, K. H. (1977) *List of Recent Holarctic Bird Species.* BO London.

Vår Fågelvärld. Ornithological magazine (8 issues/yr), published Ornithological Society of Sweden (SOF), Stockholm.

Zink, G. (1973–85) *Der Zug europäischer Singvögel.* Vol. 1– Vogelzug-Verlag, Möggingen.

ndex